ALWAYS ON THE SAME PATH

Always on the Same Path

Essays on Foreign Law and Comparative Methodology
Volume II

BASIL S. MARKESINIS

FOREWORD
By
Prof. Dr. Iuta Limbach
President of the German Constitutional Court
and
The Rt. Hon. the Lord Wilberforce PC

HART PUBLISHING
OXFORD AND PORTLAND, OREGON
2001

Hart Publishing
Oxford and Portland, Oregon

Published in North America (US and Canada) by
Hart Publishing
c/o International Specialized Book Services
5804 NE Hassalo Street
Portland, Oregon
97213–3644
USA

Distributed in Netherlands, Belgium and Luxembourg by
Intersentia, Churchillaan 108
B2900 Schoten
Antwerpen
Belgium

Hart Publishing is a specialist legal publisher based in Oxford, England. To order further copies of this book or to request a list of other publications please write to:

Hart Publishing, Salters Boatyard, Folly Bridge, Abingdon Rd, Oxford, OX1 4LB
Telephone: +44 (0)1865 245533 Fax: +44 (0) 1865 794882
email: mail@hartpub.co.uk
WEBSITE: http//:www.hartpub.co.uk

British Library Cataloguing in Publication Data
Data Available

ISBN 1 84113–069–9 (Hardback)

Typeset in 10/12 pt Sabon
by Best-set Typesetter Ltd., Hong Kong

Printed and bound in Great Britain by
Biddles Ltd, www.biddles.co.uk

To Eugenie, Julietta, and Spyros George
who give so much and ask for so little

Preface

This second volume of essays on foreign and comparative law marks thirty years as a full-time law teacher in England. These years were rich in experiences, largely because I was fortunate enough to spend them in five major law faculties—Cambridge, Queen Mary and Westfield, University College London, Oxford and, again, University College London. But they have also been immensely rewarding because of the friendships I made with learned members of the judicial, practising and teaching professions. The first volume attempted to give a list of names of those who had influenced my work and helped me in my career. Four years later, the list needs up dating though I again repeat two names that figured prominently on my earlier list—that of Jack Hamson and of Sir Roy Goode since both are with me always though, alas, the former only in a mental manner.

Lords Bingham, Goff and Woolf top the judicial list for taking so much interest and giving me so much help in my European endeavours. More precisely, my five years with Lord Goff, during which he and I worked to get the Oxford Institute of European and Comparative Law on the road, were among the most instructive in my entire life. They also made me reflect time and again on how wise the ancient Greek were in believing that the best way to learn and be educated was by being attached to a more senior and learned man. I was; and I owe him more than I can ever repay.

The following colleagues have also helped me in my work in more ways than one and I am sorry that for reasons of space I can only list names in alphabetical order and abstain for amplifying on the reasons for my intellectual debts. They are: David Anderson (of the UT Law School), Michael Coester and Dagmar Coester Waltjen (of the Munich Law Faculty) Cindy Estlund (of the Columbia Law School), Michael Gergen (of the UT Law School), Joe Jamail (of Houston), Gibson Gayle (formerly of Fulbright and Jabowski, Houston), Douglas Laycock (of the UT Law School) Brian Leiter (of the UT Law School), Noelle Lenoir (of the French Conseil Constitutionnel), Iuta Limbach (President of the German Constitutional Court), George Mitsopoulos (President of the Academy of Athens), Etien Picard (of the Sorbonne), David Robertson (of the UT Law School), Walter Odersky (Emeritus President of the Bundesgerichtshof), Bill Powers (Dean of the UT Law School), Michael Sharlot (formerly Dean of the UT Law School), Peter Schlechtriem (of the Freiburg Law Faculty) and my mentor and friend, the late Charles Alan Wright (of the UT Law School).

Different in kind but just as deep is my debt to Keith Clark, Chris Perrin,

Simon Davies and Chris Bright of Clifford Chance. I was for five years the Clifford Chance Professor of Comparative Law at the University of Oxford and everything I managed to achieve there for that great law faculty was due not just to their firm's support but also to their friendship and constant encouragement given whenever needed. It is my great good fortune that all these colleagues and their firm, with whom I share its global mentality and aspirations, have agreed to continue our association even after my move to London meant giving up their eponymous chair.

Books are written in libraries and my good fortune was to work at the Tarlton Law Library which is so imaginatively directed by the indefatigable Professor Roy Mersky and is staffed by such able librarians as Jonathan Prater, Keith Ann Stivenson, and Mike Widener (among others) To them as well as to my two secretaries, Pamela Harries and Consuelo Akin I also express my deepest appreciation and gratitude.

But the greatest debt of all goes to my mother who instilled in me her undying love for England and things English to such a deep extent that over the years I have even felt able to criticise what I felt was mine but thought could be improved from foreign observation. From birth, and thanks to her, I was thus able to partake of Two Worlds—her English one and my father's Greek/Venetian—so different and yet so similar.

28 August 2000 *Basil Markesinis*

Contents

Foreword

Being asked to provide a Foreword to this second volume of Basil Markesinis' articles on foreign law and comparative methodology was not only an honour; carrying out this undertaking also proved a source of great pleasure. For it offered me a welcome pretext to read and recall to my mind the content of these essays. As expected, this proved to be a very inspiring exercise. I have had for a long time had the privilege of knowing the author not only as an erudite scholar, but also as a congenial host of scientific gatherings of lawyers from Europe and all around the globe. At least one of the qualities which, to my mind, has predestined him for the rewarding task he has undertaken in his life is reflected in the writings collected here. This is his distinguished curiosity in and open-mindedness towards different cultures and legal systems. Mine is not the task to comment on the diverse topics gathered in this volume. However, as I am working with German constitutional law on a daily basis, I feel I ought to add a few remarks on the essays dealing with this topic.

In chapter seven and eight of this volume, Basil Markesinis gives a highly knowledgeable outline of the so-called "horizontal" or "radiating" effect that basic or human rights have on German private law. During the now almost fifty years of its existence, the Federal Constitutional Court has designed its own way of how the basic rights—which were originally designed to protect the individual from intrusions by the state—may also influence the legal relationships between individuals governed by private law. The author of this book renders the development of German case law in this area clearly and accurately, beginning with the early decision of the Federal Labour Court and then citing some of the Constitutional Court's own key passages, starting with the famous "Lüth" decision of 1958. This survey of five decades of German jurisdiction does not only offer a close look at the crucial judicial questions raised in these disputes; it also has the interesting side-effect of presenting a kaleidoscope of controversial issues in recent German history, such as the disputes about nuclear power plants, abortion law, or governmental reaction to terrorists' blackmail. Far from being merely descriptive, by comparing the German concepts to similar Common law ideas and notions, Basil Markesinis draws conclusions as to how the German ideas might prove fruitful to the future application of the Human Rights Act in English law. I firmly believe that the ideas set out in this book can and will inspire common and continental lawyers alike. As Basil Markesinis rightly puts it himself: Comparative law is not a one way street, but a constant process of give and take.

At the threshold of the 21st century, all of us—as European lawyers—are facing a unique situation: we are witnessing a process of globalisation which is marked by the emergence of broad international markets and an easy flow of funds from one country to the other. European integration has created a vast common market; and the economic options presented by the worldwide web are only just beginning to surface. All these developments are posing challenges that must be met by all, not least by our legal professionals. But it is not only economic co-operation that is on the increase; so is the international exchange of legal ideas. A truly fine example of academic collaboration of this kind can be found in chapter nine of this volume, which was co-authored by Basil Markesinis with three eminent scholars from France, Germany, and Cambridge, England.

It is my hope that, in the interest of promoting further fruitful collaboration of Europe's different judicial systems, this book will reach as many readers as possible.

Karlsruhe, 28 August 2000

Professor Dr. Iuta Limbach,
President of the Federal Constitutional Court,
Germany.

Foreword

This book will be welcomed by readers of Professor Markesinis' seminal "Foreign Law and Comparative Methodology" which is happily being contemporaneously reprinted. Together, these works embody Professor Markesinis' strategy, over 30 years of academic life, to persuade academics, practitioners in the law, judges, and legislators, not only of the intellectual stimulus of comparative law, but of the practical benefit in their vocations which they can gain from a systematic study and use of the material provided by the law of other systems and countries.

This strategy has made significant progress in the last ten years and the present (AD 2000) is, for many reasons, opportune for spreading it further and more strongly. First, there is a far greater consciousness of the direct relevance for our understanding of our own law, of its defects and merits, of its relation to, not only the law of the Commonwealth and other English-speaking systems (which has been accepted for at least 50 years), but systems of the civil law, which were generally, before Markesinis, put on one side as, no doubt interesting and civilising, but, if not of a "lesser breed", at least unhelpful for the solution of our problems. These essays show, in various ways, how many of the doctrines, thought to be specifically English, have been derived in the times when judges and academics were well read in the great French and German writers and in the laws based upon them. I recall the "frisson" which went through the audience of the Clifford Chance Millennium Lectures when Professor Markesinis demonstrated that so English a creature as the law in *Hadley* v. *Baxendale* (1854, damages) was solidly based on civil law doctrines reaching back to Justinian and beyond. Similarly, if English law had made itself familiar with the civil law development of a *jus quaesitum tertio* it would not have taken so long for Parliament (in default of judicial initiative) to have passed the Contracts (Rights of Third Parties) Act 1999.

Secondly, there is the question of accessibility. Judges cannot be expected to make use of foreign law unless it can be presented to them in a usable manner. Now there is a change. If Lord Goff's ground-breaking speech in *White* v. *Jones* (1995) did nothing else, it certainly demonstrated that German law, in intricate detail, can be used to bring light to an area unexplored by ours. And two developments will surely help in this: the introduction, on a permanent basis, of legal assistants to the Lords of Appeal (due to start this year) and the accessibility of websites on which French and German law, at least, can be accessed. The argument of non-availability no longer holds.

Thirdly, these are easily seen areas in which controlled and intelligent access to European law will become not just useful, but essential. Professor Markesinis gives two examples:

a) *Devolution issues, arising from the recent constitutional reforms.* Hitherto, the tendency has been to look at models in the USA, Canada, Australia, New Zealand, not beyond. But Professor Markesinis shows convincingly that valuable insights may be drawn from the German model, under the Federal Republic's present constitution.
b) *Privacy.* To my mind the most valuable part of the book lies in the presentation of German Cases on privacy, translated in full. I have no doubt that, in Britain, the most important series of cases, under the Human Rights Act 1998, will be those in which the courts, probably the House of Lords, will have to work out, from the European Convention on Human Rights, a law on privacy, on which Parliament has so signally failed to act. Putting it very briefly, the German approach shows us the way, avoiding the brutal simplicity of the First Amendment, to work out a balance between the right of free speech and the right of privacy—it being noted, as Markesinis shows, that German courts have, in some contexts, affirmed the privacy of speech as strongly as it has been done in the USA. I believe that these cases and the insights they offer will be of help to our judges in their (quasi-legislative) task.

Professor Markesinis will, no doubt, continue in London the work which he has so successfully pioneered in Oxford, to the enlightenment of us all. These essays represent an ongoing contribution to our law, its study and practice.

Richard Wilberforce
August 2000

Acknowledgments

The pieces reproduced in this volume first appeared in the following form. Thanks are extended to the original publishers and (where appropriate) to my co-authors.

"Judicial Style and Judicial Reasoning in England and Germany" in [2000] *CLJ*; "Our Debt to Europe" in *The Coming Together of the Common Law and the Civil Law: The Clifford Chance Millennium Lectures*, Hart Publishing (2000) (pp. 37–66); "The Familiarity of the Unknown" in *The Search for Principle. Essays in Honour of Lord Goff of Chieveley* (eds William Swadling and G. Jones), OUP (1999) (pp. 59–77); "Reading Through a Foreign Judgment" in *The Law of Obligations, Essays in Celebration of John Flemming* (eds P. Cane and Jane Stapleton) (1998) (pp. 261–283); "Foreign Law and Foreign Ideas in the English Courts: The Contemporary English Contribution to the Use of Foreign Law and Comparative Methodology" in *Academia Analecta* (1998), Royal Netherlands Academy for Arts and Sciences (19 pp.); "Why a Code is not the Best Way to Advance the Cause of European Legal Unity" in *European Review of Private Law* Autumn, 1997 issue (pp. 519–524); "Der wachsende Einfluß der Menschenrechte auf das englische Deliktsrecht" in *Festschrift für Hans Stoll zum 75 Geburtstag*, Mohr, Tübingen (2001); "Privacy, Freedom of Expression and the Horizontal Effect of the Human Rights Bill: Lessons from Germany", The Wilberforce Lecture 115 (1999) *LQR* (pp. 47–88); "The Applicability of Human Rights as between Individuals under German Constitutional Law" (co-authored with Dr Stefan Enchelamier) in *Protecting Privacy, The Clifford Chance Lectures*, vol. IV (1998) (ed. B.S. Markesinis) (xii + 248 pp.); *Tortious Liability of Statutory Bodies* (co-authored with Jean Bernard Auby, Simon Deakin, and Dagmar Coester-Waltjen), Hart Publishing (1999).

Table of Cases

GERMANY

Bundesverfassungsgericht (Federal Constitutional Court)

Reichsgericht

Bundesgerichtshof (Federal Court)

Bundesarbeitsgericht (Federal Labour Court)

Instanzgerichte

FRANCE

Conseil d'Etat

ITALY

SWITZERLAND

Introduction

THE ESSAYS REPRODUCED in this book are meant to provide a companion volume to the one published by Hart Publishing in 1997 entitled *Foreign Law and Comparative Methodology: A Subject and a Thesis*. Turning the first part of that title into the subtitle of this book and supplementing it with the words "Always on the Same Path" is meant to stress my continued conviction that the path I embarked upon exactly thirty years ago, when I landed my first academic post in this country, remains one worth pursuing further. My aims as a teacher and as a scholar were set out in the introduction to the earlier volume and need not be repeated, especially since the first volume is being reissued with this one. Suffice it to say that I remain interested in the development of a method that can make foreign material and, above all ideas, accessible to our judges. This is because, as I have been arguing for a long time, it is they and not my academic colleagues who can stimulate a revival in comparative studies in this country.

My disappointment with those of my academic colleagues who profess an interest in foreign law and cultures, notwithstanding my growing admiration for many of the younger scholars who have entered this arena in the last decade or so, is due mainly to one fact. Simply stated it is that few if any of them have seen fit to push their respective institutions into developing a wider and *corporate* vision about the utility—practical and theoretical—of the study of foreign law. The paper-filling Erasmus and Socrates programmes have thus been the main if not sole institutional examples of university European foreign policy in action.[1] Thus, for many of my colleagues their time has been devoted to the cultivation of their scholarship in the cloisters of their University, ignoring or avoiding the wider political[2] appeal that the study of foreign law holds for individuals, academic institutions, and our country as a whole. These wider aims, particularly relevant in the context of the role this country can play in the emerging Europe of the twenty-first century, have been crucial to my work. They have

[1] The two most notable exceptions are, in my view, the initiative of the University of Birmingham in the direction of German studies and the still pioneering double degree course in English and French law instituted by the late Professors Chloros and Tunc nearly thirty years ago linking Paris I and King's College, London.

[2] I am, of course, not using political in any *party-political* sense.

thus been the lodestar that has dominated my mind and guided my efforts in Oxford where I founded and directed for five years its new Institute of European and Comparative Law. Since they form an inextricable part of my purely academic work, and have been publicly endorsed by Lord Goff, arguably the most senior and most comparatively minded judge of the post-War period, I refer the interested reader to my last Annual Report as Director of the Oxford Institute which was published in the Spring of 2000.[3] For this Report also contains some ideas on what the tasks of the modern professor of foreign and comparative law should be. I need hardly add the admission that my vision is still incomplete and needs refining. But I have used every conceivable opportunity to publish my thoughts on the future of my subject and how it can be used in pursuit of wider objectives, since I remain anxious to stimulate new thinking. I also feel that having entered the last phase of my own university career, what concerns me most now is not what will happen to me next but whether my subject can be brought out of the darkness into which it sank between roughly the year 1975 and the 1990s. My conviction that what I am trying to achieve for British comparatists is useful to them and to our country remains firm, especially as I never cease to marvel at the excellence of the work that comes from the pens of such foreign colleagues as Christian von Bar, Dagmar Coester-Waltjen, Peter Grimm, Werner Ebke, Johannes Köndgen, Hein Kötz, Peter Schlechtriem, Reiner Schulze, Jürgen Schwarze, Reinhard Zimmerman—to mention just a few German colleagues who are currently active in the field of comparative law. I marvel, but also feel frustrated that we can no longer boast abroad that we can match such talent by showing off a Harold Gutteridge, a Jack Hamson, a Harry Lawson, a Tony Honoré or, if I may borrow one colleague from the USA, a Jack Dawson.

If one wishes to be honest one must thus admit that scholarship such as that produced by my German comparative colleagues simply no longer exists in my country. Yet I remain convinced that if it emerged, it would be used by our judges. This belief is grounded not only in the fact that in over thirty years in my profession I have had many an occasion to meet and speak to some of our senior judges who remain as intellectually curious as the best of academics. It is also strengthened by the fact that the number of decisions that have referred to foreign law has increased in a marked way during recent years. I discussed this topic in my inaugural lecture as a Fellow of the Royal Netherlands Academy;[4] and the number of judicial instances in which this has happened since that lecture was given four years

[3] The sentence which, in my view, most captures these wider aims of my work is the following: "Professor Markesinis is, I believe, fully justified in his claim that the Institute is serving not only Oxford University and the cause of education but also . . . the broader national interest . . .". Institute of European and Comparative Law, *Annual Report for the year 1999–2000*, p. 2.

[4] See chap. 2, below.

ago has grown even further.[5] The view that foreign law, if suitably presented to our judges, can be used by them in their daily work, is gaining ground. The study of foreign law can no longer have only a cultural mission—a *mission civilisatrice* as our French colleagues, in their usual felicitous manner, call it. And the instances I have in mind, though not numerous in any objective sense, support my conviction and are particularly important. For they do not involve the use of foreign law in the context of a foreign treaty or in a conflict of laws situation—when such a use would be normal and expected—but evince our judges' willingness to derive inspiration from whatever quarter an interesting idea originates. In the same vein, I should add that in my view just as important is the fact that our senior judges are increasingly willing to write speculative pieces about the law and in them make use of foreign, especially continental European, material. When one ponders over this statement for a minute and realises that this list of "writing judges" has included in very recent times such judicial luminaries as—in alphabetical order—Dame Mary Arden, Lord Bingham, Lord Cooke, Lord Goff, Lord Hoffmann, Lord Hope, Lord Irvine of Lairg, LC, Sir John Laws, Lord Mustill, Lord Roger, Lord Scarman, Sir Stephen Sedley, Lord Slynn, Lord Stein, Lord Woolf, one can only reach one conclusion. Such an interest in the fermentation of legal ideas in Europe has not been evidenced in judicial writings in the Common law since the days of Holmes and Cardozo in the United States and, somewhat earlier, in the work of some of our own great 19th-century jurists such as Austin, Blackburn, Jessel, Anson, Pollock, Maitland and Lord Macmillan. I discuss this phenomenon in the first of the essays reproduced in this book,[6] and explore—in an admittedly tentative manner—some of the reasons which have led many of my contemporaries[7] to underplay this intellectual debt to French and German law and, arguably overstate, the insular features of the English Common law. Once again, however, the breadth of my research makes me feel conscious of the fact that I have only begun scratching the surface of the problem.

I may, perhaps, be over-stressing the above-mentioned internationalist trends that have merged in the most recent past[8] but I do not think I am

[5] Thus, see chap. 2, below.

[6] See chap. 1, below.

[7] But not all. Thus note Professor Bryan Simpson's "Innovation in the Nineteenth Century Contract Law" 91 *LQR* (1975) 247*ff*. Cynics might, of course, note that the fact this erudite scholar had to find his recognition as a University teacher in the USA and not in England is proof enough that the internationalist spirit is not easily rewarded in England. In these isles, another pioneering Europeanist was the late Professor Mitchell; but being based in the University of Edinburgh seems to have been reason enough for his English colleagues to ignore the European work he did for his University.

[8] For the purposes of illustration, I glean some extracts, which, in my view, would have been unthinkable even thirty years ago. The senior judicial posts occupied by their makers also suggests that more of this thinking will find its way in judgments and, via the courts, into our law curriculum. Thus note the Lord Chancellor's remarks in "The Influence of Europe on Public Law in the United Kingdom" in *The Clifford Chance Millennium Lectures, The Coming*

off the mark when I say that they will be reinforced. Reinforced and, perhaps, reoriented in the direction of public law, especially as our human rights and devolution legislation[9] forces us to look more and more at other models, including the European ones and—not yet noticed let alone discussed—force us to compare civilian solutions to commonwealth solutions on issues involving human rights. Here, again, I thus feel tempted to preach heterodoxy and argue that the predominance of the American material will slowly be challenged as the greatest if not unique source of intellectual inspiration. This unthinkable intellectual re-orientation will be facilitated by the fact that more and more of our judges speak foreign languages, continue to display academic predilections, and will continue to be supplied with foreign materials suitably prepared for them by practitioners. In this context I welcome the latest decision of the House of Lords in *Panatown* for in it we find not only evidence that some of the judges took judicial cognisance of the foreign material placed before them but also evidence that counsel made a very deliberate attempt to master and present the foreign material in a judge-friendly manner.[10] The reaction of surprise or even partially-concealed hostility that thus met the publication of Lord Goff's judgment in *White* v. *Jones* is thus giving way to a new realisation that if foreign law can be presented to our judges in a usable manner, they will take advantage of it. My prediction is that we have now reached a stage that our top judges do not have to clothe civilian thinking in common law terms, as apparently the great Lord Atkin did in *Donoghue* v. *Stevenson*[11]

Together of the Common Law and the Civil Law, (ed. BS Markesinis) (Hart, Oxford, 2000) at p. 11: "In order for the United Kingdom to play [an active role], European law must influence and—to some extent—infiltrate our national legal order. In this sense "European law in Britain" is a necessary and inevitable concomitant of "Britain in Europe"." From the same collection of essays note also Lord Bingham's remarks that "The things that unite us [with European law] are greater than the things which divide us." *Op. cit.*, p. 35.

[9] I have not yet found the time to enter the devolution/federalism debate but, again, I feel that our lawyers would do well to start realising that the German model offers an interesting alternative to the ones better known such as the American, Canadian or Australian. One topic which thus merits closer study is the doctrine of Federal Committee—*Bundestreue*—not least because it is a creation not of statute but of judicial inventiveness on the part of the judges of the German Constitutional Court. That this principle could, for instance, be invoked both by the Scottish and English sides to support their respective political positions is, in my view, a sign of the richness of the doctrine.

[10] Mr Hannes Unberath, a candidate for the D.Phil in Oxford and currently working under the supervision of Professor Francis Reynolds, was thus hired by the respondents' solicitors in *Alfred McAlpine Construction Ltd.* v. *Panatown Ltd.* (1998) 58 *Con. L. R.* 46, to advise on German law. Mr Unberath's participation is noteworthy not only because his stimulating piece "Third Party Losses and Black Holes: Another View", 115 *LQR* (1999) 535 was, despite his youthful age, cited by the court. More importantly from my point of view is the preparatory work that he did in this case to assist English counsel to understand and then present in a judge-friendly manner the rich but complicated German material. I am grateful to Mr Unberath for filling me in with some of these background details which form an important part of my thesis.

[11] On which see Professor Robin Evans-Jones' interesting article "Roman Law in Scotland and England and the Development of one Law for Britain", 115 *LQR* (1999), 605.

to make them more acceptable. The stage of open cross-fertilisation is *ante portas* if it has not already arrived. My further prediction is that foreign, especially French and German law, will supplant Roman law in the curriculum of our Universities as well as becoming a source of inspiration for our courts. Not everyone will welcome this change, of course; but Julian the Apostate provides a famous example where history shows us what happens to those who harp back to a dead past instead of espousing the living future. The Pythoness of Delphi said as much in her last oracle even though it meant that it brought about the end of her business.[12]

A sustained effort to make this modern European material available in English, especially through the growing number of websites that reproduce it, will also encourage our judges to reflect whether some of the basic European ideas are, in fact, closer to our views than those found in America. One that is prominent in my mind and which I think our new Human Rights Act will, eventually, reveal is the continental European belief that speech rights and personality rights must be balanced the one against the other, our Continental legal history having nothing equivalent to the American First Amendment. For this reason, I have included in chapter eleven translations of thirteen leading German decisions on privacy—six made available to an English audience for the first time—in order to show how balanced, casuistic and transplantable to our soil German law is. But, as I also noted in my Wilberforce Lecture,[13] this German desire to balance competing values has not led the German courts to afford inadequate protection to speech rights. On the contrary, in some cases they have gone far beyond our positions and protected speech which in England would have been damned by our law of defamation. This, too, is thus an important point; and only the focused use of foreign law can make it. And it is important, since our press has not hesitated to mischaracterise the foreign laws on human privacy in its continued battle to prevent an enhanced protection of human privacy at home. I hope that the fourth volume of the Clifford Chance Lectures,[14] which I edited nearly two years ago, has now provided some information about the privacy laws of such countries as France, Italy, and Germany. That is why the last chapter of this book aims to make more accessible some of the leading German cases on this subject. The debates that will be conducted in the future should therefore be, if not wiser, at least better informed.

The past never changes; history that records it often does. Nearly one hundred years after Dicey held centre stage, he is arguably remembered as

[12] "Tell the King [Julian], the fairwrought hall has fallen to the ground. No longer has Phoebus a hut, nor a prophetic laurel, nor a spring that speaks. The water of speech even is quenched" HW Parke and DEW Wormell, *The Delphic Oracle* (Basil Blackwell, Oxford, 1956), vol. I, 290; vol. II, 194.

[13] Reproduced in this volume in chap. 7.

[14] *Protecting Privacy,* OUP (1999). The essay reproduced in chapter 8, below, comes from this work.

much for his early destructive appraisal of French administrative law as he is for his selection of the themes which he thought dominated the English constitution. French administrative law no longer needs any defenders. The inspiring work of the late Professor Hamson, and the more modern and meticulous comparative accounts found in the work of Professors Neville Brown and John Bell, have ensured a wider English interest in the subject. More importantly, they have also brought comparative law and methodology to the field of public law. Our real debt to the work of all these colleagues is in no way diminished if one says that it has failed only in so far as it has neglected to give equal prominence to German public law. This huge corpus of legal knowledge is thus still largely unknown in this country. Many of the essays[15] in this volume have thus deliberately been devoted to this legal system as a conscious effort to contribute to a new trend[16] to make the rudiments of German public law more widely available to our legal audiences. No one more than this author is conscious of the fact that in this effort he has only succeeded in scratching the surface. But if anyone still doubts the validity of such an exercise he would do well to consult Professor Jürgen Schwarze's magisterial work on the subject of comparative administrative law or look at some of the works published in English by Professor Dieter Grimm, currently Professor at the Humboldt University of Berlin and until recently a Justice at the German Constitutional Court.

In a little-known piece published in the first year of the twentieth century F. W. Maitland rightly described the 19th as the century of the new civil codes.[17] I venture the thought that the great historian, who in so many of his works forcefully stressed his admiration for the German legal mind, would have characterised the end of the 20th as the epoch which saw the emergence of public law as at least the equal of private law both in the legal curriculum and the work of our courts. In this change, judges and academics have played an equal part; for what we have today is, in my view, as much the work of Lords Reid, Denning, Wilberforce and Woolf as it is of Sir William Wade, Paul Craig, Carol Harlow, Jeffrey Jowell, or the late Stanley de Smith. And all have an eye for the foreign and European.

In my own attempts to deal with issues of public law I have, once again, applied my preferred method of focusing on narrow factual configurations

[15] Notably the essays reproduced in chaps. 7, 8 and 9.

[16] The trend is at its strongest in the USA where one finds in the works of Professors Donald Kommers, David Currie and Peter Quint thought-provoking presentations of our neighbour's public law. A glance at the footnote references will also reveal the long history behind some of these German ideas—including that of proportionality which so many treat and fear as a creation of the Court of the European Communities.

[17] "A Survey of the Century", *The Twentieth Century*, Jan. 1901, reprinted in *The Collected Papers of Frederick William Maitland*, ed. by HAL Fisher vol. III (1911), pp. 432*ff*.

and then teasing out of them more ideas as well as more information about the (foreign) system as a whole. The long essay written with three colleagues—one from Germany, one from France and one from Cambridge—proves, I hope that the method tested and found workable in the area of private law, can also be of use in the domain of public law. But as this particular work shows such surveys can only attain their full potential if they branch out into different sections of the law in order to seek explanations that cannot exist in the legal compartment where the research commenced. Such forays incidentally also show two other things, which I hope I will elaborate further in some future essay.

First, they raise the question of whether differences in substantive rules can be explained by differences in procedure or damage awards or, as I would rather put it, differences in the law in action. Here, beyond raising the idea, I pause to stress the need for more comparative work to be done in the area of procedural law. The second point they raise is to what extent one can really remain in the domain of public law without also crossing the boundary of private law. Many of the issues raised by *Stovin* v. *Wise*, *X* v. *Bedfordshire*, and *Barrett*, confirm this point as well as the need to revert one day to the question how watertight this division between private and public law really is. All these cases, of course, also show how strong the European influence is becoming on our law.

My delight that this is so will come as no surprise to those—on both sides of the Channel—who know my European credentials. But my belief in Europe and in particular in a more integrated legal education has not blurred my judgment to the point of convincing me to join the European Code movement. One essay reproduced here[18] thus expresses my doubts about this effort. And, once again, I am happy to see them shared by our most internationalist of judges—Lord Goff.[19] I see the many current efforts to draft a European Code as being, at best, a utopian dream and at worst an ingenious way of raising funds for academic "get-togethers" (which, of course, is not a bad thing for those involved in them). On this issue, again, I thus remain on the path that I have long chosen as the more appropriate one for promoting knowledge and understanding of European law—one also travelled by such eminent foreign colleagues (and good friends) as Professors Hein Kötz and Reinhard Zimmermann. I do, however, make one exception to these (private) codification exercises and that is the one which Professor Olé Lando has led for over twenty years, demonstrating tenacity, a clearly defined academic purpose as well as an admirable ability to hold together a team of eminent prima donnas. As a set of rules that can be freely adopted by willing and interesting parties, I think his exercise has much to commend it.

[18] See chap. 5, below.

[19] "Coming Together—The Future", *The Clifford Chance Millennium Lectures, The Coming Together of the Common Law and the Civil Law* (ed. by BS Markesinis) (Hart Publishing, Oxford, 2000), 239.

A preface, like an overture of an opera, can only sketch out what is to follow; it cannot and must not replace or duplicate the parts that follow. But the last theme I wish to touch on here is the *Osman* theme since this, too, like most European themes, has raised many eyebrows. To Lord Hoffmann goes the "credit" for expressing in the strongest possible terms his fears about the creeping Europeanisation of our law.[20] But not all our judges have expressed themselves in such strong terms. Thus, more measured were the reactions of Lord Browne-Wilkinson expressed, as they were, in the form of doubts as to whether article 6 of the Convention could be used to "create" new rights. My own view was (and is) that the main significance of *Osman* lay not so much in the correct or debatable use of article 6 of the Convention—a use which is likely to bring its demise. The thrust of *Osman* lies in its dislike of the extended use of the notion of duty of care to create wide, *de facto* immunities for an ever-growing group of statutory bodies. The state of our law before *Osman* was (and is) not to everyone's satisfaction. But presenting the *Osman* of the European Court as an impermissible meddling with the allocation of local authority resources was a somewhat exaggerated reaction by those who like the (old?) status quo. The Strasbourg court is not a stranger to controversy. In the very recent past, it has created much concern not only in England but also in France and Germany. The way to react to such judgments seems to me to encourage further dialogue and improve mutual understanding—not to "bash" Europe. In fact, our courts seem to have closed their ears to all extreme voices and adopted a more restrained attitude towards striking out orders. Devices other than that of duty of care and the new mechanisms now available to our judges under the Woolf reforms are, in my view, likely to reduce the tension in the long run and make all talk about *Osman* redundant. I hope they will also achieve a more sensible balance between blanket immunities and frivolous claims that waste judicial time. The comparative examination of the whole topic, attempted in the ninth chapter of this book, may have helped show to those who did not come to the subject with closed minds that blanket immunity for statutory bodies may not be the only option. At the same time it may have helped them realise that a liability rule can be controlled by other means; and it should not be used as an excuse to award crippling damages. Those who, having read chapter nine, are left with this impression may well be those who understand best the main lesson of comparative law: give and take. That is also one of the main messages of this book.

[20] Most notably in his lecture delivered to the Common Law Bar Association on 25 November 1998 and subsequently published (in slightly toned down tones) in 62 *MLR* (1999), pp. 159*ff*.

NOTE: After the text of the introduction was completed and while it was being edited by the publishers, the House of Lords handed down its judgment in *Phelps* v. *Hillingdon* (and a further three similar cases) [2000] 3 WLR 776. While not tackling, let alone confronting *Osman*, their Lordships have again (indirectly) taken cognisance of its dislike of strike out actions through the use of the blunt notion of duty of care. Thus, as in *Barrett* and *Essex* before it, *Phelps* overruled the Court of Appeal's strike out orders and, more significantly, its pernicious attempt (in *Phelps*) to subvert Lord Browne-Wilkinson opinion, that local authorities, though not primarily liable might be held accountable under the rules of vicarious liability. It is submitted that this change is as welcome to deserving plaintiffs as it will be to scholars complaining about the overkill effect inherent in the notion of duty of care. But for those who wrote the piece that appears in this book as chapter nine, the judgments in *Phelps* represent an almost wholehearted (though unacknowledged) adoption of their arguments advanced in order to question the policy views that allegedly justified the results reached in *Hill*, *Stovin* and *Elguzouli*. The following extracts from the opinions of Lords Nicholls and Clyde thus deserve to be read in juxtaposition with chapter nine. Just as importantly, they may provide the academic writer the comfort that he need not always be a *vox clamantis in deserto*. So, even on this front—academic/judicial co-operation—one can report another favourable change in the English legal landscape which, thirty years ago, would have been unimaginable, even by those who might have deemed it highly desirable. Thus, Lord Nicholls of Birkenhead said (at p. 804):

"I can see no escape from the conclusion that teachers do, indeed, owe such duties. The principle objection raised to this conclusion is the spectre of a rash of "gold-digging" actions brought on behalf of under-achieving children by discontented parents, perhaps many years after the events complained of. If teachers are liable, education authorities will be vicariously liable, since the negligent acts or omissions were committed in the course of the teachers; employment. So, it is said, the limited resources of education authorities and the time of teaching staff will be diverted away from teaching and into defending unmeritorious legal claims . . . I am not persuaded by these fears. I do not think they provide sufficient reason for treating work in the classroom as territory, which the courts must never enter. "Never" is an unattractive absolute in this context. This would bar a claim, however obvious it was that something had gone badly wrong, and however serious the consequences for the particular child. If a teacher carelessly teaches the wrong syllabus for an external examination, and provable financial loss follows, why should there be no liability? Denial of the existence of a cause of action is seldom, if ever, the appropriate response to fear of its abuse. Rather, the courts, with their enhanced powers of case-management, must seek to evolve means of weeding out obviously hopeless claims as expeditiously as is consistent with the court having a sufficiently full factual picture of all the circumstances of the case."

Lord Clyde completed the onslaught on the arguments of the timorous when he said (at p. 809):

"In the present case I am not persuaded that there are sufficient grounds to exclude these claims even on grounds of public policy alone. It does not seem to me that there is any wider interest of the law which would require that no remedy in damages be available. I am not persuaded that the recognition of a liability upon employees of the education authority for damages for negligence in education would lead to a flood of claims, or even vexatious claims, which would overwhelm the school authorities, nor that it would add burdens and distractions to the already intensive life of teachers. Nor that it should inspire some peculiarity defensive attitude in the performance of their professional responsibilities. On the contrary, it may have the healthy effect of securing that high standards are sought and secured. If it is thought that there would only be a few claims and for that reason the duty should not be recognised, the answer must be that if the are only a few only claims there is less reason to refuse to allow them to be entertained. As regards the need for this remedy, even if there are alternative procedures by which some form of redress might be obtained, such as resort to judicial review or to an ombudsman or the adoption of such statutory procedures as are open to parents, which might achieve some correction of the situation for the future, it may only be through a claim for damages at common law that compensation for the damage done to the child may be secured for the past as well as the future."

1

Our Debt to Europe:[1] *Past, Present and Future*

1. INTRODUCTORY REMARKS

On the 4th of February 1998 I attended a lecture given at the Travellers' Club by the Lord Chief Justice. Europe was the theme; and the effect that it was having on our law. The Chief Justice spoke forcefully, diplomatically, and with his usual clarity. I recall all this as clearly as I do the sceptical tone of the questions that were put to him when he finished. It was disturbing to note that the scepticism was prompted by the usual degree of misinformation. We were all, for instance, reminded of the (alleged) bad habit of our French neighbours to treat people as guilty until proven innocent! Such misinformation is permissible, though no less unattractive, if the audience, though educated, is not one specialised in legal matters (which was the case with most in the audience that night). Unfortunately, however, we also encounter it in the writings of some of our most learned judges and jurists. One, for instance, and names are really irrelevant for our purposes, told us many years ago that the advantage of having our contract law put in the form of a Code was that we would then be able to find all the relevant law very easily. Another, some years later, repeated the commonly held belief about the (apparently) errant ways of French criminal law. More recently, a very learned colleague referred to Germany being subject to the Napoleonic Code. The examples could, alas, be multiplied but this would

[1] I am, of course, using the term here in the typically British way to refer to the Continent of Europe. The impact that Continental—mainly German law—had on the development of the law in the USA is much better documented. From the considerable literature see: Herbst, *The German Historical School in American Scholarship: A Study in the Transfer of Culture* (1965); Clark, "Tracing the Roots of American Legal Education—A Nineteenth-Century German Connection" 51 *RabelsZ* (1987), 313 *ff.*; Herget and Wallace "The German Free Law Movement as the Source of American Legal Realism" 73 *Va. L. Rev.* 399 (1987); Herman, "Llewellyn, the Civilian, Speculations on the Contribution of Continental Experience to the Uniform Commercial Code" 56 *Tul. L. Rev.* 125, 1161 (1982); Hoeflich, *Roman Law and Civil Law and the Development of Anglo-American Jurisprudence in the Nineteenth Century* (1997); Reimann (ed. and contr.) *The Reception of Continental Ideas in the Common Law World 1820–1920* (1993); Riesenfeld, "The Influence of German Legal Theory on American Law: The Heritage of Savigny and His Disciples" 37 *Am. J. Comp. L* (1989).

serve no purpose. For my aim here is not to criticise the commission of errors for, as the saying goes, to err is human but to forgive divine. What I wish to attack is the arrogance and prejudice, which I think, lies behind critical statements about European law, especially when they form part—consciously or unconsciously—of the campaign about our position in Europe over the next hundred years and more. My own view as a scholar is that we have in law, as in so many other areas, more that unites us with Europe than separates us. I also share the views of colleagues such as Professor Reinhard Zimmermann (and others present here today) that we owe many intellectual debts to Europe. The wider realisation of these debts should, I think, help dispel persisting fears about the effects of growing integration with Europe and thus help us assume the kind of leading role that I think we deserve to play in the shaping of the next thousand years.

This aim I hope to achieve by presenting some thoughts under four headings. Firstly, I would like to substantiate my claim about the existence of the intellectual debt. Because of lack of space I shall begin by focusing on our law of contract. Though this forms only one part of the law of obligations and an even smaller part of private law as a whole, it should, I think, be sufficient for my purposes. For in our contract law we were always taught that we find some of the clearest signs of the genius of the Common law. My own view, partly based on the learning of others who have looked at this topic before me, is that matters are not that clear cut and that greater modesty on our part might be called for. Then I would like to mention briefly a few reasons why the debt is there in the first place and speculate as to why it is nowadays so unacknowledged. I shall, next, return to a favourite theme of mine in order to show how this interaction between legal cultures can and should continue in the future. At this stage, however, I shall shift the emphasis from contract law to public law for I think that much of the future of comparative law lies in this branch of the law. In the final part of the paper I shall conclude with some very general thoughts about how we, in England, can contribute to this melting pot of ideas. Though standing on its own, the paper should thus be seen as part of my wider effort to contribute to the creation of a workable methodology of comparative law.[2]

[2] My ideas on this can be found in a collection of essays recently published under the title *Foreign Law and Comparative Methodology: A Subject and a Thesis* (1997).

2. CONTRACT LAW: OUR DEBT TO EUROPEAN JURISTIC REASONING

In his Francis Mann Lecture[3] Lord Bingham reminded us that in the 19th century the authority of Pothier[4] was, for a judge asked to decide a given legal issue, the next best thing to an English decision to the point.[5] But appropriately, it was an eminent legal historian—Professor Brian Simpson[6]—and an equally learned German émigré—Professor Stefan Riesenfeld of the University of California at Berkeley School of Law[7]—who have reminded us of the even greater debt to a long line of German and Dutch jurists, ranging from Pufendorf, Grotius, Savigny and the other Pandectists of the 19th century. We thus see that the doctrine of offer and acceptance was, in the 19th century, superimposed on the earlier doctrine of consideration. And we now see it performing, in part at least, some of the requirements of consideration but also new functions generated by the emerging contracts concluded by correspondence. But that is not all. For the importation of the continental doctrine clarified in English minds the distinction—hitherto not always clear—between *promissio* and *pollititatio*, which however, in Continental doctrine was clearly perceived since at least the drafting of the Digest Title on *De Pollicitationibus*.[8] Sir Frederick Pollock, in the first edition of his *Principles of Contract*[9], thus kindly obliges us by admitting freely that his use of the word "proposal"[10] corresponds to the German expression *Antrag*. His notion of "acceptance", required *inter alia* to turn the promise into a contract, is the counterpart of the German *Annahme*.

We can, for present purposes, ignore the doctrine of consideration largely because its comparative examination requires a chapter if not a book of its own. But we cannot ignore the fact that a strong case has been made that it be seen as a local version of the civilian *causa promissionis*. But we should note that the doctrine's subsequent accretions—such as that found in the

[3] "There is a World Elsewhere: The Changing Perspectives of English Law", (1992) 41 *ICLQ*, 513 at p. 528.

[4] Whose *Treatise on the Law of Obligations*, translated by William David Evans, appeared in 1806, four years after the first American edition saw the light of day. The original (French) edition first appeared between 1761 and 1764.

[5] *Cox* v. *Troy* (1822) 5 B & All. 474, 480; 106 E.R. 1264 (per Best J.)

[6] "Innovation in Nineteenth Century Contract Law" 91 *LQR* (1975) 247*ff*.

[7] "The Impact of Roman Law on the Common Law System", (1985) 2, *Lesotho Law Journal*, 267*ff*. Reinhard Zimmermann, "Belohnungsversprechen: 'pollicitatio', 'promise' oder 'offer'"? *ZfRV* 1998, 133*ff*.

[8] "Pactum est duorum consensus atque conventio, pollitatio vero offerentis solus promissium". D. 50.12.3.

[9] (1876), at pp. 1, 4 and 5 and n. 1.

[10] In later editions replaced by the term "offer".

infamous decision of *Foakes* v. *Beer*[11]—not only depart from the civilian tradition but are, in contemporary scholarship, also increasingly seen as creating troublesome anomalies requiring new devices and techniques to mitigate their unfair results.

But one of the by-products of consideration—the rigid adherence to the doctrine of privity—calls for a few brief comments. For here, again, we see English law departing from the civilian model which emerged from the Middle Ages onwards and, by the 19th century, both in Europe and the USA,[12] had come to recognise an ever-increasing number of exceptions allowing third parties to sue directly the promissor. Of course, English law progressively developed *ad hoc* solutions, statutory or judicial, to mitigate the rigours of the old doctrine. But despite growing calls for reform, it has remained attached to the doctrine. Traditional common lawyers, one suspects instinctively suspicious of civilian ideas, have comforted themselves that by hook or by crook the English practice avoided in the end injustice that English doctrine had the tendency to cause.[13] But by the 1990s a series of papers from the Law Commission,[14] came to advocate with increasing eloquence and resolution the need to abandon the doctrine. The fact that, more often than not, it seemed to pay more attention to Commonwealth innovations can only be expected. For the informed reader cannot fail to see that the move towards the (chronologically older) civilian—Germanic rather than French—doctrine is also notable. Some references in these Reports make it clear that this was, indeed, brought to the attention of the Commissioners; but a full extent of the acknowledgement of the debt has yet to come.

Professor Simpson's magnificent article makes clear to anyone who reads it that the debt to civilian doctrine extends to the areas of mistake, intention to create legal transactions, frustration, and much more. What, since the early part of this century we have come to call frustration, is in fact an interesting topic. For in Lord Blackburn's famous judgment in *Taylor* v. *Caldwell*[15] we find a blend of a common law idea—the notion of an implied condition which very nearly prevailed in the interesting case of *Hall* v. *Wright*[16] decided only five years before *Taylor*—but also the civilian doctrine which dictates that an *obligatio de certo corpore* is discharged if the object has perished.[17] Blackburn the judge was, in fact, able to use the research of Blackburn the writer who, twenty years earlier, had written his

[11] (1884) 9 App. Cas. 605.
[12] Thus, see, *Lawrence* v. *Fox* 20 NY 268 (1859).
[13] Thus, see Professor Reynolds' remarks in "Privity of Contract" 113 (1997) *LQR*, 53.
[14] The one containing its definitive proposals being *Privity of Contract: Contracts for the benefit of Third Parties*, No 242, 1996.
[15] (1863) 32 L.J.Q.B. 164.
[16] (1858) El. Bl. & El. 746, 765.
[17] D. 45. 1.

Treatise on the Effect of the Contract of Sale on the Legal Rights of Property and Possession of Goods, Wares and Merchandises.[18] In his elegant Hamlyn Lectures[19] the late C. H. S. Fifoot described this work as "an early essay in comparative law". For in his book Blackburn had made extensive use of Pothier's *Treatise on the Contract of Sale* as well as using Roman law. In fact, references to both systems appear in the *Taylor* judgment. And, ironically, they give the French writer the dubious and unusual distinction to have influenced (in part) the development of English law but having failed to impress his own law. For it is well known that French civil law[20] failed to adopt any notion akin to our doctrine of frustration.

Let me complete this brief *tour d'horizon* by adding one more example to show our debt to Continental legal thought. I derive some of my information from an unpublished piece written by Professor Bernard Rudden of my own University. It refers to what is often seen to be, especially by contemporary American authors, a very "English rule": the rule (or rules) in *Hadley* v. *Baxendale.*[21] For many modern legal economists like to see in this litigation a typical example of law made at the time of nascent industrialisation. In this respect, the interpretation of Professor Richard Danzig of the Stanford Law School, takes the biscuit for, writing in 1975 an avowedly historical article,[22] he maintained that: "*Hadley* v. *Baxendale* can usefully be analysed as a judicial invention in an age of industrial invention.... Arising squarely in the middle of the industrial revolution and directly in the midst of the 'Great Boom' of 1820–74, *Hadley* v. *Baxendale* was a product of those times. The case was shaped by the increasing sophistication of the economy and the law ..." The truth could hardly be more different. For we know that Counsel in that case had been citing Sedgwick *On Damages*[23] and Sedgwick was mainly relying on the *Code Civil*—arts 1149–51—which are based on the writings of Pothier who, in turn, derived most of his ideas from Domat's work on the *Coûtumes de Paris.*[24] Professor Rudden then makes a plausible case that these views can be traced back to Dumoulin's *Tractatus de Quod Interest,*[25] Cino da Pistoia's *Lectura super*

[18] Published in London in 1845. See, also, Reinhard Zimmermann, "Heard melodies are sweet, but those unheard are sweeter ..." Condicio tacita, implied condition und die Fortbildung des europäischen Vertragsrechts, *AcP* 193 (1993), 212*ff.*

[19] *Judge and Jurist in the Reign of Victoria* (1959), at p. 16. In his *History of English Law*, vol. XV (1965), 506, informs us that Sir James Shaw Willes, another of the great mid-Victorian judges, had a sound knowledge of foreign law.

[20] The doctrine of *improvison* is known only in public law.

[21] (1854) 9 Ex. 341.

[22] "*Hadley* v. *Baxendale*: A Study in the Industrialisation of the Law", IV *JLS* (1975) 249, 250 259. See, also, Judge Posner's remarks in *Economic Analysis of Law*, 3rd ed. (1986) #4.9: "[B]y the famous case of *Hadley* v. *Baxendale* ... incentives are created to allocate the risks in the most efficient manner."

[23] *A Treatise on the Measure of Damages*, 1st ed. 1847.

[24] *Les lois civiles dans leur ordre naturel*, Book 1, tit. II, sale.

[25] Written in 1546.

Codicem: *ad* C. 7 47,[26] and from there back to a number of Justinianic texts.

The debt to civilian thought is thus, once again, there to be seen. Yet why have contemporary British contract lawyers, and some notable legal historians, so persistently refused to acknowledge their huge intellectual debt to continental legal thought? Professor John Baker, for instance, talks in his excellent text book of English law "flourish[ing] in *noble isolation* [sic] from Europe";[27] and that most learned of our contemporary contract lawyers, Sir Guenther Treitel, concealed his vast knowledge of Continental law until mid-life when he started writing monographs on comparative contract law,[28] and then kept it rigorously apart from his Common law work. Indeed, at times we find more than this tendency to present English law as having an autonomous existence of its own. For we can even find eminent contract lawyers castigating those of their brothers who "with [a] penchant for self flagellation" over-criticise the Common law by presenting it as being inferior to the modern civilian systems.[29] One is, therefore, inclined to agree with Professor Simpson's conclusion that "It has become the aim of a number of modern English legal writers to avoid incursions into both history and other legal traditions; English law is to be presented as capable of standing alone. But in this they conceal the historical origins of much of what they transmit as homespun law, just as they conceal, too, the historical source of the literary tradition in which they stand."[30] But when scholars take such introverted positions they not only distort history; they are also, one hopes inadvertently, providing ammunition to a political argument that is attempting to depict Europe as a divisive and, even, dangerous issue. The attitudes that Professor Simpson (and I along with him) regret, thus not only call for condemnation: they raise the question of what lies behind them.

3. THE REASONS FOR THE DEBT AND WHY WE ARE, NOWADAYS, TRYING TO CONCEAL IT

Such insularity was not, as already shown, always fashionable; and it was certainly not a position advocated by our intellectual élites. From about the second half of the eighteenth century judges were, if anything, unashamedly

[26] Written, probably, during the early part of the 14th century.

[27] *An Introduction to English Legal History*, 3rd ed. (1990), 35.

[28] And still keeps it totally out of his classic textbook.

[29] The truncated quotation comes from Professor Reynolds' comments in "Privity of Contract" 113 (1997) *LQR*, 53 where the learned author, while welcoming the proposals of the Law Commission to reform the doctrine for privity, argues that authors (presumably such as myself) underestimated the extent to which the common law mitigated its harshness in practice.

[30] *Op.cit.*, note 6, above at pp. 256–7.

internationalist in spirit, learning, and, sometimes, background. Sir William Jones, whose *Essay on the Law of Bailments* published in 1781 may well be regarded as the first modern monograph on English contract law, was a classical scholar who drew openly on many systems including the Roman and the Hindu. Blackstone, as well, had had some civilian training; and it may be partly because of this that Lord Mansfield (unsuccessfully) proposed him for the Regius Chair at Oxford. Leone Levi was an Italian Jew; and we all know how much he did to reform commercial law through his overtly comparative works.[31] Benjamin was another Jew who, during the first half of his remarkable life, had benefited from an American civilian background. All this shows in his work on the *Sale of Goods*. William Markby's *Elements of Law Considered with Reference to Principles of General Jurisprudence*,[32] may now be forgotten. Yet, not only did it adopt Pandectist models; it was also very influential in its time. Maitland adored Germany, hardly lost an opportunity to express his admiration for its 19th-century intellectual achievements, and by all accounts his idol—Gierke—reciprocated the admiration by describing him as a "genius".[33] Dicey, Pollock and Anson—to whom we shall return later on—were, as the late Professor Lawson put it so felicitously, "members of the very remarkable Victorian intellectual aristocracy[34] and, as such, able to look at English law with some detachment from outside".[35] Indeed, it was political developments abroad, namely the creation of the Empire that gave a great stimulus to such outward-looking habits. Thus, the Victorian pre-occupation with India *forced* many of the jurists of that era to re-examine English law from without as well as from within as part of their effort to determine what could be used in their attempts to draw up legislation for that sub-continent.

The Second World War proved an unfortunate turning point. As I shall state further down, the inward trend can be traced back to the various scars that it left on the collective psyche. But before this trend became established, our country benefited from one last wave of émigrés. Thus the exodus from Germany, that gained momentum in the 1930s, ensured that the (mainly) central European and Jewish influence continued after the War thanks to the presence of (forced) émigrés like Martin Wolf, Sir Otto Kahn Freund,

[31] In his *International Commercial Law*, published in 1887 he thus had the courage (audacity) to consider the law of, among others, Austria, Belgium, England, Germany, Greece, Italy, the Netherlands, Portugal, Russia, Spain and Sweden. In his earlier *Manual of Mercantile Law of Great Britain and Ireland* (1854) his approach was, once again, comparative in style.

[32] Published in 1871 (and since 1986 available in microfiche).

[33] According to the distinguished émigré Professor Martin Wolff. The story is recounted by the late Professor Lawson in his "Doctrinal Writing: A Foreign Element in English Law" in *Ius Privatum Gentium—Festschrift für Max Rheinstein* (1969), vol. I, pp. 191*ff.*, n. 44.

[34] On which see Lord Annan's "The Victorian Intellectual Aristocracy" in *Studies in Social History: A Tribute to GM Trevelyan* (ed. JH Plumb) chap. 8 (1995).

[35] Lawson, "Doctrinal Writing: A Foreign Element in English Law" in *Ius Privatum Gentium—Festschrift für Max Rheinstein* (1969), vol. I, 191 at p. 210.

Kurt Lipstein, Francis Mann, Clive Schmithoff, or E. J. Cohn.[36] To this group we must add another, namely a brilliant group of Jewish students—like Zamir and Rubinstein—whose London Ph.D. theses[37] gave a great impetus to the development of our administrative law. So why, despite this, did we progressively lapse into the state of insularity which I, for one, deplore? Before considering some possible explanations I would like to exclude one: a strange and sudden kind of collective amnesia that has led us to forget how inclined towards Europe were our intellectual élites of the 19th century.

I discard what I have called collective amnesia as a cause of the prevailing tendency to underplay our intellectual debt to Europe not because I have any particular faith in the broad reading of the current generation of lawyers: I do not. I exclude it, however, because I know that the European work of these past masters is well known, as it well ought to be, to our contemporary textbook writers. Thus, the material that has led distinguished legal historians such as Professors Simpson and, before him, Maitland,[38] Fifoot[39] and Lawson,[40] (from England), Berman[41] and Helmholz[42] (from the USA) and Wieacker[43] and Zimmermann[44] (from Germany), forms some of the most elegant writings of contemporary legal history. But this material is not just elegantly presented; it is unequivocal

[36] I am not including here earlier émigrés such as Sir Hersch Lauterpacht, Professor Felix Jolowicz or Lassa Oppenheimer, who possessed all the manifold talents of the central European Jewish émigrés. The Germanic background of Sir Guenther Treitel must also be noted.

[37] *The Declaratory Judgment* (1962) by I Zamir and *Jurisdiction and Illegality* by A Rubinstein (1965). The influence that the Jewish-German émigrés had on American law is well documented. Thus, see, EC Stiefel and F Mecklenburg, *Deutsche Juristen im amerikanischen Exil (1933–1955)* (1991) and, more recently, Lutter, Stiefel and Hoeflich (eds.) *Der Einfluss deutscher Emigranten auf die Rechtsentwicklung in den USA und in Deutschland. Vorträge und Referate des Bonner Symposium im September 1991* (1994). The role of the Jewish immigrants in England is not so well documented though, in addition to Professor Goodhart's book mentioned above see, also, Professor Lipstein's contribution in Carlebach, Hirschfeld, Newman, Paucker and Pulzer (eds.) *Second Chance. Two Centuries of German-Speaking Jews in the United Kingdom* (1991) pp. 221*ff.*

[38] His Introduction to Gierke's *Political Theories of the Middle Ages* is a sustained tribute to Savigny the Romanist and historian. Ironically, of course, Gierke was, in later life to be a severe critic of the Pandectists for over-emphasising Roman law and ignoring the Germanic elements in the law. But that is another matter!

[39] Who, for instance, in the first chapter of his masterly Hamlyn Lectures, *op.cit.*, note 19, above, at pp. 7–8: "The influence of Germany was not confined to history. It flowed through every branch of English culture . . . English law was not insulated from these currents of thought and opinion."

[40] "Doctrinal Writing: A Foreign Element in English Law", *Ius Privatum Gentium—Festschrift für Max Rheinstein* (1969) vol. I, pp. 191*ff.*

[41] *The Formation of Western Legal Tradition* (1983), 39.

[42] *Canon Law and the Law of England* (1987); "Continental Law and Common Law: Historical Strangers or Companions?" (1990) *Duke Law Journal*, 1207.

[43] "Foundations of European Legal Culture" 38 *Am. J. Comp. L.*, 1 (1990) and, more extensively, in his masterly *Privatrechtsgeschichte der Neuzeit* (1967) *passim.*

[44] "Savigny's Legacy. Legal History, Comparative Law, and the Emergence of a European Legal Science" 112 (1996) *LQR*, 576, esp. 587*ff.*

in emphasising the strong influence that European legal and philosophical ideas had on modern, English law. In his Hamlyn Lectures,[45] for instance, the late C. H. S. Fifoot made much of the fact that in his *Principles of Contract* Sir Frederick Pollock "sought . . . to examine the inter-play of law and equity, and [to] set the results not only against Roman, Continental and American models, but also against the Indian Contract Act." "Anson", he tells us further down, "was even more fervently than Pollock, the disciple of Savigny, and it was through the superior vision of the master that he hoped to irradiate the concepts of obligation and agreement and to correct the English astigmatism."[46] Indeed, one could go further and suggest that so pervasive was the influence of German philosophy and law on the intelligentsia of the 19th century that even those authors[47] who chose to attack German conceptualism—which reached its peak at about this period—were, themselves, greatly influenced by Germanic ideas.[48]

So "ignorance" of these past debts is certainly not the reason for our current cultivation of insularity. The question that thus arises is this. If these

[45] *Op.cit.* note 19, above, at p. 28.

[46] Yet, the 27th edition of his classic text book, so skilfully updated by Professor Beatson, not only ignores the European influence but starts its account with the following statement: "The principles of the *English* law of contract are almost entirely the creation of *English* courts . . ." The statement is correct if read together with the phrase that follows it: "and the legislature has, until recently, played a relatively small part in their development". Yet I have italicised the words "English" since, to an uninitiated reader they certainly conceal the European debt, which Anson, among others, regarded as so great. But even the growing (and more recent) European influence is only grudgingly mentioned in one short paragraph on page 18 of the text. The above, in my view, lend further credence to the complaints made by Professor Simpson, *op.cit.*, note 6 above; but they do not give any clues as to what reasons may lie behind such attitudes.

[47] Such as Oliver Wendell Holmes in his celebrated monograph *The Common Law*. More recently, however, authors such as Professor Mathias Reimann have suggested that Holmes's real target was not the German Pandectists but his Harvard colleague, Christopher Columbus Langdell. For the latter believed, in a matter which reminds one of contemporary German legal doctrine, that abstract principles can be used to build a coherent and consistent legal system. See, "Holmes Common Law and German Legal Science" in *The Legacy of Oliver Wendell Holmes Jr.* (ed. by Robert W Gordon) (1992), pp. 72*ff.* Writing in 1887—in vol. 3 of the *Law Quarterly Review*, 118, esp. 123*ff.*—Langdell, himself, stressed his eagerness to move the law curriculum of the Harvard Law School away from the English world and closer to the European model. Of course, both Langdell, and the even more influential President of Harvard University Charles Eliot, had acquired a first-hand knowledge of the European, mainly German, scene by spending time in Europe.

[48] Holmes exemplifies this phenomenon since his debt to Savigny and, even, to that most Germanic of German philosophers Immanuel Kant, (in so far as both wish to banish moral ideas from the jurist's mind) is considerable. Yet Holmes rarely fully acknowledges these intellectual debts. Understandably, therefore, one specialist commentator observes that Holmes was "notorious for not giving credit to his intellectual forebears and for being petty in his insistence on the primacy of his own contributions". See, Touster, "Holmes a Hundred Years Ago: The Common Law and Legal Theory", *Hofstra L. Rev.* 10 (1982), 673 at 687. Jhering's attack on the tendencies of the early Pandectists to abstract and generalise to excess is forcefully stated in some of his later works such as *Scherz und Ernst in der Jurisprudenz* (1885, 4th ed. 1892), 341, 2 and *Besitzwille: Zugleich eine Kritik der herrschenden juristischen Methode* (1889) 283, 4. Many other examples can be given which suggest that Holmes was deliberately ignoring such comments in mounting his own attack against his real target.

debts are known, why are they being "hushed up" or, at the very least, seriously minimised? Could Professor Simpson be suggesting[49] some kind of deliberate historical revisionism? And if so, what may be the reasons behind it? Though it may be rather too drastic to read such a strong assertion in Professor Simpson's cautiously phrased sentences, the idea that he might at least be hinting at something like this does not strike me as being so preposterous. In exploring this idea further, one might well be advised to consider how the autochthonous lawyers may have (unintentionally) combined with the wave of post-World War Two (forced) émigrés to produce this result.

One explanation why some members of the latter group may have succumbed to this tendency seems fairly obvious. The temptation to present themselves as being more English than the English must have been considerable. After all, being a refugee in England is very different from being a refugee in the melting pot culture of the Americas; and that is why I think we find this "rejection of the past" more in the former country than in the latter. I am, myself, personally aware of examples—and names need not be mentioned here—that make such a thesis plausible. Having met and talked to many of these colleagues, and being an émigré albeit a voluntary one myself, I am beginning to see why playing down the intellectual strengths of their Germanic origins seemed a small price to pay in exchange for joining the "spiritual ancestry"[50] of the host nation and thus achieving "recognition" in the country of choice.[51] We are, of course, here in the precarious domain of subjective interpretations of the personalities and characters of judges and jurists. Yet, whatever the dangers, the task of studying more carefully the backgrounds, philosophies, and temperaments of those included in the more recent waves of immigration must, one day, be undertaken more systematically than it has hitherto been done. For, as the late C. H. S. Fifoot observed:[52] "Law . . . is made by men. Whatever the pitfalls, it is less misleading to adopt or adapt Carlyle's[53] creed and approach legal

[49] See text and note 30, above.

[50] See Baade, "Time and Meaning. Notes on the Intertemporal Law of the Statutory Construction and Constitutional Interpretation" 43 *Am. J. Comp. L.* 319, at p. 341 (1995).

[51] One of them who, somehow, came to think that I might be asked to have a hand in the drafting of his *Times* obituary asked me "to play down the fact that he was both German and Jewish". When I enquired, half in jest "what is then left?" he just smiled!

[52] *Op.cit.*, note 19, above, at p. 12. It is both intriguing and gratifying to note that such advice was, essentially, given also by the late Professor Max Rheinstein in one of his most famous essays "Die Rechtshonoratioren und ihr Einfluss auf Charakter und Funktionen der Rechtsordnungen" (1970) 34 *RabelsZ*, 1*ff*. In. our treatise *The [German] Law of Contracts and Restitution* (1998), Professor Lorenz, Dr Dannemann and I have, on several occasions, (e.g. chaps. 1 and 6) given instances of how the understanding (or, sometimes, misunderstanding) of the law by one influential jurist has deeply affected subsequent developments. Mommsen's "Die Unmöglichkeit der Leistung in ihrem Einfluss auf obligatorische Verhältnisse' in *Beiträge zum Obligationenrecht*, I (1853) is one such example.

[53] His celebrated (but nowadays out of fashion) lectures on *On Heroes, Hero-Worship, and the Heroic in History* were delivered in May 1840 and were published in London a year later.

history through biography. English lawyers, of all men, should believe in the power of the great judge.[54] Incidentally, one need not fear that adopting an 'heroic' approach to law would lead us into the kind of controversies which arose—erroneously it seems to me—from Carlyle's famous aphorism that, at bottom, all history is the 'Biography of great men'. For, as the most recent scholarship on his work shows, 'The Carlylean hero does not create history out of titanic will, but rather responds to the monitions and the forces alive in his world.'"[55]

But what about the autochthonous jurists? Why did they, too, choose to under-play the common European ancestry? Once again, one can only advance some very tentative suggestions. I offer four for consideration.

First, it is widely said that the inhabitants of modern England have lost their self-confidence. Nothing is these days shielded from criticism: the Monarchy, Parliament, and the Courts. The tendency for self-flagellation, to borrow Professor Reynolds' expression, came mainly after the Second World War when, in the famous words of Dean Acheson, "Britain lost an Empire and went in search of a role". I find this a very revealing phrase. For not only many refused to give up what they had lost—remember, for instance, that the so-called "east of Suez" policy found strong advocates even among the most thoughtful in the Conservative Party. The country, its leaders, and its lawyers became over-dependent on the so-called special relationship with the USA (or the Commonwealth) neglecting Europe's inexorable pull both on the economic and political field. But what I say is, I believe, true not only of politics and the world of finance. I think it applies with even greater force to law, legal education, and legal thinking. The community of language with the USA provides, in my view, only a partial reason

Numerous inconclusive debates have taken place about the reasons why he excluded from his list certain "professions" or individuals (for instance, his beloved Goethe). It would thus be idle to speculate why he never included a chapter on "The Hero as Judge". Perhaps, one reason for such an omission is the fact that the giants of the Victorian era had still to come. From an earlier era, Lord Mansfield could, of course, have supplied a perfect model. But then one must remember that at the time when the lectures were being delivered, the courts were undoing the last remnants of the Mansfield revolution. Thus, see: *Eastwood* v. *Kenyon* (1840) 11 A & E 438, at p. 450. One must, therefore, hope that the omission will be made good by some other future writer.

[54] And, on the basis of what has already been said, one should add the great jurist.

[55] Thomas Carlyle *On Heroes, Hero-Worship, and the Heroic in History*, University of California Press (1993), introduction by Michael K. Goldberg at p. lix. On the previous page, Professor Goldberg states that the "superior insights [of heroes], and their actions based on them, crystallise what is merely latent". To me, this comes very close to Professor Simpson's observations on page 252 of his already-cited article, where he states: "The point is not that the common law of contract was simply a jungle of unrelated instances, though it is certainly not always easy to identify and formulate the doctrine that is latent in the sources . . . It is rather that there existed no literary tradition of expounding the law of contract in a form which invites the reader to proceed to the solution of problems by applying general principles of substantive law . . ." This, the great 19th-century judges and jurists did; and, arguably, this represents their major contribution to the development of our contemporary law.

for this Americano-mania which we find in many contemporary debates in our law.[56]

Loss of confidence and loss of a sense of direction usually leads to confusion; and such feelings, it seems to me, push people inwards.[57] The confidence of the Victorians, when we find the height of the pro-Europe intellectual movement is exemplified by the famous laconic phrase attributed to Sir George Jessel.[58] Lord Annan, in his elegant study of the Victorian "aristocracy of intellect", discusses and explains this phenomenon. He thus shows how its members "judged people by an exterior standard of . . . intellectual merit". "Because their own proud standards were assured they tolerated a wide variety of belief."[59] Going beyond England, I think a strong case can be made for the proposition that the more confident the civilisation the more willing it is to graft new shoots on its trunks to encourage richer and differentiated growth. Such confidence, apart from brief intervals, has been conspicuously absent for the better part of the second half of the twentieth century. And this lack of confidence is, I believe, one reason for England—and I am deliberately excluding Scotland from this exercise—being unwilling to open up to what we have nowadays convinced ourselves to be different if not alien. It is tempting to suggest that those living in the past are fighting to cling to *die Welt von gestern*, to borrow the title of Zweig's last (and tragic) work. Security, it would seem, comes for them by re-asserting their distinctiveness; and in this case it means putting as much "blue water"—literally and metaphorically—between themselves and "Europe". This attitude has been a key feature of internal party politics for the last ten years or more; and I do not think it is that improbable to argue that we can also find traces of the phenomenon in the work of the academic community. Indeed, some have allowed themselves such flights of (academic) fancy that have led them to discover parallels between the collapsed regimes of Eastern Europe and the emerging European Union![60]

Secondly, I think we have progressively moved away from encouraging a wider culture. I made this the topic of my inaugural lecture in Oxford.

[56] For instance in calls that we introduce some kind of *New York Times* v. *Sullivan* (376 US 254 (1964)) rule in our law of defamation instead of attempting to understand the more balanced German model.

[57] Re-reading Lord Bingham's Mann Lecture, *op.cit.*, note 3, above, especially at p. 514, I find traces of the same idea.

[58] "I may be wrong, and often am, but I never doubt." In later times Jessel, apparently, disclaimed that he could have ever used the words "often wrong". But otherwise, he accepted the authenticity of the attribution. See, Goodhart, *Five Jewish Lawyers of the Common Law* (1949), 70, note 23.

[59] Note 34, above, at p. 250.

[60] "[As] the twentieth century . . . meanders to its end, we see the leaders of Western Europe adamant to create an insanely bureaucratic and multilingual ideological empire such as the nations of Eastern Europe have just broken loose from . . ." Weir, "The Staggering March of Negligence", *Essays in Honour of John Fleming* (eds. P Cane and J Stapleton) (1998).

So I need not come back to it again here.[61] The emphasis on the functional curriculum, that my colleague Professor Peter Birks has attacked so eloquently but alas, without success, is thus taking its toll. The "conversion courses" will not produce Pollock's and Maitland's whatever else they do. This, I think, is so obvious a point I need not labour it further.[62] Yet the neo-conservative theories that dominated our country in the 1980s have pushed both academic law and the system of administration of justice into thinking in terms of "returns", "market solutions", "cost-benefit analyses" which Lord Mustill, among others, has caustically—and rightly—condemned in a little-noticed lecture.[63]

Thirdly, the sovereignty issue, which has been allowed to inhibit our relations with Europe to such an extent, has also taken its toll on the education system. For here, as in the rest of Europe, the triumph of the sovereign state in the 19th century made legal education inward looking. Rudolf von Jhering noted this phenomenon at its height when he remarked that "... legal science has been brought down to the plane of territorial jurisprudence" as "the scientific boundaries in law have been made coterminous to the political".[64] Thus, whereas the teaching of scientific subjects remained international and, nowadays have increasingly become more so, law has, with few exceptions and until at least the seventies, retained its local character. The tendency of our current textbooks to proclaim the "Englishness" of their subject matter fits well into this climate. Yet Jhering, though writing almost a century and a half ago was, once again, right in maintaining that "Nations do not lead an isolated existence but, like humans, have a common existence.... [they] live in a world of constant contact and reciprocal influence, of give and take, of borrowing and giving: in a sentence a complex system of exchanges that embrace every side of human existence."[65] Every banker and economist has come to recognise the validity of this statement. Why are some lawyers still dragging their feet?

A final reason may be the following. When English lawyers turned to Roman law they already had a corpus of their own law but lacked the superior jurisprudential techniques and categories offered by the Roman law as developed by generations of Continental European jurists. In that sense, French and German law could be described as being not only older but also more developed than contemporary English law. One hundred and fifty years later the situation has changed. English law has grown in stature and

[61] Author, "The Comparatist (or a Plea for a Broader Legal Education)", reprinted in *Foreign Law and Comparative Methodology: A Subject and a Thesis* (Oxford 1997) pp. 15*ff*.

[62] Though Annan, again, note 34 above at pp. 250–1, may prompt some sad comparisons with the decline of educational standards at home.

[63] "What do Judges Do?" *Särtryck Ur Juridisk Tidskrift* 1995–96 Nr 3 611, esp. 614*ff*.

[64] Von Jhering, *Geist des römischen Rechts*, 3rd ed. (1873), vol. I, pp. 11 and 15.

[65] *Ibid*., at pp. 5 and 6.

sophistication; and the acquisition of an academic component to the law, especially during the last one hundred years, has made up for the need to borrow from elsewhere.

Such arguments in my opinion confirm, unwillingly perhaps, the view that serious intellectual debts have *already* been incurred; but they do not undermine the thesis advanced here. For, at best, they only suggest that future borrowings are not likely to take the form they took in the 19th century. This approach, however, cannot deny the undeniable fact that a new form of Europeanisation is currently taking place thanks to a growing number of Directives, International Conventions, and the spreading influence of the case law of the two European courts in Luxembourg and in Strasbourg. Thus, it cannot be used as a reason for saying that no further borrowings are likely to happen. The give and take in law and other academic subjects never comes to an end. If anything, because people and ideas travel better than they used to, the trend will increase. Further down, I shall be arguing that in my view there remain some important areas, mainly of public law, where the European models still have much that is inspiring.

The problem of explaining the current, insular mode thus remains unanswered if one remains at a legal or purely rational level. To avoid such an intellectual impasse one has to go into politics to find an answer. But European politics provide not only part of the explanation for what has been happening thus far. European politics also provide strong clues as to what will happen in the future. Thus in "Europe" I find at least a partial palliative to the problems and objections that I have mentioned. But since trying to explain why this is so would turn this paper into a sociological rather than a legal essay I would like, instead, to concentrate my arguments on two specific points. The first will be a technical one: how best can we re-ignite the interest of our judges in foreign law in general and European law in particular? I shall discuss this in section 4 of this paper while retaining for section 5 my views about future borrowings and where and how they are likely to occur.

4. HOW CAN WE INCREASE INTELLECTUAL INTERACTION AND BORROWINGS?

The mental blocks towards foreign models are caused by understandable reaction towards events in Germany in the 1930s and 1940s, chauvinism, prejudice, scepticism about the utility of foreign ideas, and concern about (lack of) time and space to make proper use of them. These are all, undoubtedly, major stumbling blocks; but in a shrinking world of increased economic inter-dependence they will all have to be overcome. In such a new and challenging environment, how does one proceed to make the best of other people's *ideas*? The italicised word is crucial; for my thesis has always been that it is the basic idea that should be studied and, if found attractive, transplanted. By contrast, the conceptual apparel in which it is clothed can be discarded or, at any rate, studied only when a mere technical command of the law is required. I can think of at least two ways of attempting this task. First, you get the interested parties to talk to one another in a *focused* context; then you present the ideas of one side to the other in a way that makes sense to the receiver of the "new" information. Dr. Dannemann and I once called this the need, first to "deconstruct" and then "reconstruct" German law.[66] It is something which comparative lawyers have not done enough up to now.

The Goff/von Bar Anglo-German judicial conferences of recent times have developed an attractive (but not exclusive) format for achieving the first aim. In fact, two judicial conferences have been held thus far; and a third one is being planned.[67] In my view, the second of these conferences scored more highly than the first. The reason is because the organisers chose to ask their high-powered participants to talk about a set of problems confronted in a number of carefully pre-selected decisions taken from both systems—the English and the German—and arising in similar factual contexts. The variety of issues raised in one of these cases I have, myself, discussed in a comparative piece dedicated to the memory of the late John Fleming.[68] Even a quick perusal of the material I have reproduced in that essay will convince the reader that this way of approaching foreign law rapidly reveals the actual differences and similarities that exist between the legal systems that are being compared. But it does more than that since the study of focused problems also provides a convenient springboard for broader examination of the foreign system. Thus, to give but one example from this particular topic, the greater generosity shown by the American decisions towards the child's wrongful birth claim can quickly be explained by reference to the German system's willingness to continue the parental obligation to maintain the child beyond the age of majority. This not only reveals a difference in the family law provisions of the two systems; it also shows how the answer to tort problems may, sometimes, be determined by the position adopted by a particular system in other parts of its law such as family or inheritance law. The comparison thus progresses from the obvious to the less obvious, from the particular to the more general, providing, *en passant*, the novice observer with broader and interesting information about the system that he is trying to understand. And all this is achieved quite painlessly by staying mostly on a factual plane and

[66] "The Legacy of History on German Contract Law" *Essays for Roy Goode* (ed. Ross Cranston) (1997) pp. 1–28.

[67] The first of which was reported in *RabelsZ* 58 (1994) 421*ff*.

[68] "Reading Through a Foreign Judgement" *The Law of Obligations: A Celebration of John Fleming* (eds. Peter Cane and Jane Stapleton) (1998), chap. 10.

avoiding the confusion that comes with all efforts to explain each other's legal jargon. Incidentally, this moving from one part of the Code to another or, even, a different branch of the law, is an undeniable feature of German law, which can reach great sophistication in that system. This is especially true in restitution kind of problems where the method of "paragraph chains" (*Paragraphenketten*) can reach great complexity and prove off-putting to an impatient English lawyer.

The above observations naturally lead to my second point, already hinted at in the previous paragraph. One still has to show one's "native" colleagues that the *idea* found in a foreign system is worth copying; and discovering what the idea is and whether it works in practice may not always be easy given the differences in structure, concepts, and techniques that exist between different legal systems. It takes a special kind of training to disentangle the two; and that is where comparative lawyers can make their major contribution to the study of law. To make my point, I thus move from generalities to specifics. But since the ideas are complex and the material that supports them voluminous, I propose to sub-divide the remainder of this section into four sub-sections. Thus, in the first I shall state the theoretical point I wish to discuss in this paper stressing, of course, that others can be subjected to a similar kind of analysis. In the second and third sub-sections I shall sketch the German and US approaches to my problem, placing most of the emphasis on the difficulties that obscure the substantive similarities. In the final sub-section I shall try to draw this material together in the form of some specific conclusions. In attempting the above, I am not unaware of the price one has to pay for compressing[69] such complex material into a small space. But, I believe this is a price worth paying if the exercise can lead to the development of a theory of comparative methodology that will be judge- and practitioner-friendly.

(a) The problem. As English courts come to grapple with the new Human Rights legislation I believe they will, sooner rather than later, be forced to realise that the traditional public/private law divide, until recently unknown in our system, is in fact breaking down in most systems. Thus, in Germany, where the public/private law divide has been an almost axiomatic feature of its law, this change has been noticed for at least fifty years now though, admittedly, there is considerable disagreement as to how German lawyers should cope with its consequences. In Germany, when it comes to human rights, this debate has come to be expressed by the short-hand phrase *mittelbare Drittwirkung der Grundrechte* (though often the

[69] In attempting this I have had the benefit of the advice of a number of American colleagues namely (in alphabetical order) Professors Hans Baade, Donald Kommers, and Douglas Laycock. All are gratefully thanked and, at the same time, absolved from the errors of my ways.

protection in the private domain is achieved by other, not strictly speaking constitutional, means). Rendering the German notion into English as "the third party (*indirect*) effect of constitutional rights" makes the underlying idea marginally more intelligible but, at the same time, even less acceptable to a traditional Common lawyer. For we all know (and until recent times unquestionably accepted) that Human Rights were developed to protect individuals against intrusions by the state and that, therefore, they were designed to work in a "vertical" manner. Giving them a "horizontal" effect, so as to enable them to regulate the relations between private entities as well, runs the risk of undermining private autonomy on which our private law—especially the Common law—has for so long been based. "Privatising Human Rights"[70] thus poses serious philosophical problems, especially for those who believe that the state should be interfering with individual autonomy as little as possible. Though this worry is, if anything, more forcefully reflected in the American legal literature, it is also found in the writings of many German jurists.[71] Yet, despite its significance, this philosophical point need not be laboured in this paper. For it is obvious that in its jurisprudential form this debate is unlikely to produce a conclusive answer to our problem since the legal answer, ultimately, will always be coloured by the observer's political views. More significantly, if we go down this path we are unlikely to discover whether the notion exists and works in countries other than Germany.

I thus start from the premise that a need for some kind of *Drittwirkung* approach will prove necessary even to our own system. For, as our doyen of public lawyers put it so eloquently, "it would, indeed, be a poor sort of 'incorporation' which exempted private individuals and bodies from respecting the fundamental rights of their fellow-citizens and drove them back to Strasbourg . . . the very evil which 'incorporation' is supposed to remedy."[72] So the horizontality issue will arise and, in my view, it will be one of the more thorny ones that will confront our judges once the new legislation is in force. If I am right in this prediction, and I think time will prove me right, we must at least make the effort to understand German law, since it has accumulated much experience on this matter—an experi-

[70] The expression belongs to Andrew Clapham who is one of the few British lawyers to address the problem of horizontality with much originality—most recently in "The Privatisation of Human Rights" (1996) 1 *EHRLR*, 20.

[71] Dürig in Maunz/Dürig, *Grundgesetz Kommentar*, Art. 1, Abs. III, Rdnr. 129–30. Criticism has thus been voiced at the increasing "constitutionalisation of such areas of private law as landlord and tenant, surety, and employment law. See: Zöllner, "Regelungsspielräume im Schuldvertagsrecht", *AcP* 196 (1996), 1; Oeter, "'Drittwirkung' der Grundrechte und die Autonomie des Privatrechts", *AöR* 119 (1994), 529. Roellecke, "Das Mietrecht des BVerfG", *NJW* 1992, 1649; Medicus, "Der Grundsatz der Verhältnismäßigkeit im Privatrecht" *AcP* 192 (1992), 35.

[72] Sir William Wade, "Human Rights and the Judiciary", Judicial Studies Board *Annual Lecture 1998*, 5.

ence which, at present, we in England, simply do not have.[73] But even if we surmount the hurdle of understanding the German material, the adoption of some kind of *Drittwirkung* doctrine will still be hampered by the philosophical objections levelled against the doctrine. That is why I believe progress on this matter will be facilitated only if we present to our audiences factual situations that have been litigated *both* in Germany and the USA that show that the notion, *in substance if not in form*, also exists and works in both systems. I thus propose to offer examples from two broad areas of human rights law—sex and race discrimination, and speech rights—in both instances emphasising the degree of protection offered to individuals in private, not state, contexts.

(b) Sex (and race) discrimination. Once again, my main concern is the applicability of human rights law in the private workplace.

During the last thirty years or so United States law has taken great strides towards protecting the human rights of individuals in the private workplace and against powerful private actors.[74] This is obvious from the civil rights legislation that came into being in the mid-1960s and the way in which this has been progressively applied by the courts.[75] To be sure, the picture that emerges seems more complex than the one that one encounters in Germany. Thus, in the USA the source of the rules can be attributed both to statutory material[76] and judicial activism.[77] The available remedies also vary enormously depending upon the rule that is being used.[78] The method of

[73] But which the Germans do. Thus, see: "Privacy, Freedom of Speech and the Horizontality of the Human Rights Bill" *1998 Wilberforce Lecture*, 115 (1999) *LQR*, 47*ff*. See, also, "The Applicability of Human Rights as between Individuals under German Constitutional Law (with Dr. Stefan Enchelmaier) in *Protecting Privacy* (ed. BS Markesinis) (1998), chap. 8.

[74] The (main) equality clause of the German Constitution of 1949 can be found in Art. 3 paragraph 3 of which declares that "No one may be prejudiced or favoured because of sex, ancestry, race, language, homeland and origin, faith or religious or political opinions. Persons may not be discriminated against because of their disability."

[75] Starting with Title VII of the Civil Rights Act of 1964, now codified as 42 USC § 2000. This declares it to be an "unlawful employment practice to fail or refuse to hire or to discharge any individual, or otherwise to discriminate against any individual . . . because of such individual's race, colour, religion, sex or national origin".

[76] For instance, see: The Age Discrimination in Employment Act, 29 USCA §§ 621*ff*. The "Equal Pay" amendment to the Fair Labour Standards Act, 29 USCA § 206 (d). The Fair Housing Act, 42 USCA § 2000e-5. The National Labour Relations Act, s. 7 (which applies to almost all private sector employees), and multiple enactments in every state.

[77] E.g. by important decisions such as the (controversial) *Jones* v. *Alfred E. Mayer Co.*, 392 US 409 (1968) where the dissenters, essentially, objected with the court's interference with Congress's work in the Fair Housing Act. See, also, *Runyon* v. *McCrary* 427 US 160 (1976) where the court held that the reach of USC § 1981 extends to private relationships as well as those that involved the state. In its original version § 1981 proclaimed that "All persons within the jurisdiction of the US shall have the same right . . . to make and enforce contracts, . . . and to full and equal protection of all laws . . ."

[78] Thus under the original version of Title VII complaints should go through the Equal Employment Opportunity Commission whereas with the passing of the Civil Right Act of 1991 judges and juries were authorised to award compensatory and punitive damages to victims of intentional sex and race discrimination. For more details see, *inter alia*, Livingston, "The Civil Rights Act 1991 and EEOC Enforcement" 23 *Stetson L. Rev.* 53 (1993).

adjudicating about complaints is anything but uniform. The resulting complexity is so great that even experts in the field may not be aware that a remedy may be available.[79] As if all this were not enough, the entire debate is strongly coloured by a clash between right and left. In this clash the left typically argues that discrimination is still rampant and the courts making it hard to prove, while the right maintains with equal passion that discrimination is not in the employers' interest and that false claims are more common than real discrimination. To the above one must, finally, add the debates about the respective merits of regulation versus deregulation and about the proper limits of the powers of a non-elected judiciary. The American judicial debate thus appears to be more overtly politicised than the German.

For a foreign observer, be he English or German, such complexity is particularly daunting. Yet if we are to deal with foreign systems, as we increasingly will be called upon to do, we must at least attempt to find ways to de-mystify them and make them accessible to outside observers. This is not, as some academics have argued from their red brick towers,[80] a question of intellectual arrogance but of practical necessities. Transactions will be facilitated and, even, ideas will begin to travel more easily if and only if lawyers learn to look for the "corpus" of foreign law and are not put off by its differing apparel. We thus need urgently a methodology that can (a) help us set aside (without too much distortion) the differences in appearances and, when that is done, (b) help us show the strengths and weaknesses of the foreign system as well as the similarities it bears with our own. In our shrinking world, this will be needed even more in the future than it has been in the past.

A comparative study on how United States and German law have approached these problems leaves one in no doubt that both are striving for the same final goal. My belief is that both in the United States and Germany the dividing line between discriminatory private action and discriminatory state action has become blurred. On the whole, the consensus is that they are also reaching the overall goals with similar effect[81] though one could argue that American *statutory* protection goes further than the typical *constitutional* protection in at least two ways. First, the Constitution protects only against deliberate discrimination whereas Title VII (and many other statutory rules that have flowed from this key law) requires justification of apparently neutral rules that disproportionately exclude minorities, such as testing programmes. Secondly, statutory protection goes further in so far as the non-discrimination regime in the US

[79] See the comments of Professor Estlund in "Free Speech and Due Process in the Workplace", 71 *Ind. L. J.* 101, 108 and n. 68 (1995).

[80] For instance Professor Legrand "Are civilians educable?" 18 No. 2 *Legal Studies*, 216 at 227 n. 62 (1998).

[81] See the compact and, on the whole, politically neutral presentation by Professor Currie in his excellent *The Constitution of the Federal Republic of Germany* (1994), pp. 322*ff*.

has been largely generalised to cover such varied topics as age, pregnancy, handicap and sexual orientation,[82] some of which have yet to make an appearance on the German scene.[83]

The above broad community of aims and results must not be allowed to obscure differences of interpretative techniques since, methodologically speaking, German jurists seem to prefer a more holistic interpretation of their Constitution than their American counterparts do. In the German case law we thus find equality notions influencing the results of other disputes even though they allegedly bear a closer connection with different constitutional provisions.[84] Nor, secondly, should one fail to note that the United States has extended such protection in the domain of private relationships though it has done so (mainly) through specific federal[85] or state statutes that have proliferated after the Equal Rights legislation of the mid-1960s. Many of these "rights" go well beyond the normal ambit of constitutional protection though, admittedly, and for the reasons already alluded to, the improved protection has come about in a very Hegelian manner.[86] Thirdly,

[82] Thus see: CT ST s. 46a–81c; NJ ST 10; 2–1; 10; 5–12; 5–33; RI ST s. 28-5-7; VT ST 21 s. 495; WA ST T. 49. 60; WI ST 16.765; 111.31; (all including "sexual orientation" as a prohibited heading of discrimination). Some states have gone even further and, under the pressure of the smokers lobby, have prohibited discrimination for lawful activities "off the [employers'] premises". Thus, see, CO ST s. 24 34–205.5. In the light of such provisions one must entertain some doubts as to how convincing Professor Currie's claim is that "the list of suspect classifications is significantly longer in Germany than it is in the United States." *Op.cit.*, 324.

[83] Disability (*Behinderung*) was added to Art. 3(3) of the Constitution in 1994. But the German legislator has thus far refused to include in Art. 3 of the *Federal* Constitution—though see Art. 12.(2) of the Constitution of the State of Brandenburg of 1992—the notion of sexuelle *Identität* ("sexual orientation"). In its judgment of 17 February 1998, Case C-249/96, the Court of the European Communities, took the same view. It thus held that it was legal for an (English) employer to refuse to extend travel concessions to the homosexual cohabitee of one of his workers, such travel concessions being available to the spouses or heterosexual partners of his workforce. The Court, however, conceded that after the Treaty of Amsterdam has come into force the Council may, under certain conditions, take appropriate action to eliminate discrimination based on sexual orientation. If (or when) Community law changes in this respect, German municipal law will then be forced to follow suit. The notion of equality, once again, will then have been extended not because of the wording of the national Constitution (or the decision of the national legislator) but because of developments on the international legal scene. See, in this context, the observation made in the following paragraph of the text, above.

[84] For illustrations see Professor Kommers' excellent *The Constitutional Jurisprudence of the Federal Republic of Germany*, 2nd ed. (1997) esp. pp. 289*ff.*

[85] Mainly, it seems to me, by "exploiting" the "commerce clause", which enables Congress to prohibit all forms of discrimination having a substantial effect on interstate commerce. Since the Supreme Court more or less seems to leave it to Congress to decide what interstate commerce is and how substantial the effect of discrimination is, the latter has the ability to reach nearly all forms of private discrimination. But Congress is *empowered* but *not constitutionally required* to pass such legislation; and here there may be a difference with German Constitutional law. Congress, of course, also has broad power under section 5 of the 14th Amendment to enact remedial legislation for discriminatory *state* activity. (I am grateful to Professor Kommers for reminding me of these points.)

[86] *Patterson* v. *McLean Credit Union* 41 US 164 (1988) offers a good illustration of this for in that case a much more conservative court, adopting a hypertechnical interpretation of

in Germany the catalyst for such protection seems to have been not *internal* political "unrest" (as is the case in the USA) but *external* influences, mainly[87] in the form of various European Community Directives that were then incorporated into domestic German law. Moreover, it is interesting to note that this *enlarged* (and European-inspired) protection against sex discrimination first appeared in the domain of private law relations and was only later extended by statute to cover public service employees.[88] To this interesting list of differences one must, however, add a notable similarity. Thus, in this area of human rights' law—race equality in particular[89]—neither system felt the need for a *Drittwirkung* type of doctrine even though both have reached the same conclusion: that protection against sex

§ 1981 took the view that this provision, prohibiting discrimination and harassment, did not apply to post-formation discrimination. One suspects, however, that the real reason why they adopted such a narrow interpretation of the text was the court's (sincere) belief that the earlier decisions of *Jones* and *Runyon* were wrong. Be that as it may, the (still) Democrat-controlled Congress then swung into action and, by passing the Civil Rights Act 1991, overruled *Patterson* by clarifying the words "make and enforce contracts" to include performance, modification, and termination.

[87] But not exclusively, as the seminal *Nocturnal Employment* case (BVerfGE 85, 191) of 1992 shows. For in that case the Constitutional Court declared unconstitutional a statute that forbade the employment of women as blue-collar workers during the night allegedly on the grounds of protecting health and safety. As Professor Kommers rightly points out "The old GDR [East Germany] had no such statute, and in the face of mass unemployment among East German women after reunification, it would have seemed callous to saddle these women with the added burden of a ban on nocturnal work." *Op.cit.*, note 84, above. The European influence is, however, also obvious in the judgment since the Constitutional Court took note of a 1991 decision of the European Court of Justice invalidating a similar French prohibition. See: *The Republic* [France] v. *Alfred Stoeckel*, Case C-345/89.

[88] See, for instance, the *Arbeitsrechtliches EG-Anpassungsgesetz*, BGBl (1980), 1308 (Fair Employment Act) extended in 1994 by the *Gesetz zur Durchsetzung der Gleichberechtigung von Frauen und Männern*, Art. 1, s. a BGBl I (1994), 1406. The (initial) limitation to private contracts was never very convincing. The "Female Fitter" decision of the Constitutional court—BverfGE 89, 276—decided on 16 November 1993 (and before the 1994 law altered § 613 (a) BGB) illustrates this point. There, a University Institute—in principle a public employer—wished to hire a fitter for a project, which was financed by private funds. The method of financing and implementation of the project apparently brought the employment relationship within the domain of private law. The court found that the plaintiff—a female fitter—had been discriminated against. For first, she had been told that the post was physically too demanding for a woman and then, later, the employer had added the reason that the male fitter actually employed had superior experience to the woman candidate. The court was wary of arguments added ex post facto; and also expressed doubts about the validity of concerns connected with experience in jobs that were traditionally male dominated. This last type of criterion was bound to place women at a disadvantage. (See observations at p. 290*ff.*) The applicants' complaint was thus successful.

[89] German law has, in contrast to that of the United States law, little case law to show in the domain of race inequality. Characteristically, however, in his *magnum opus*—Maunz/Dürig, *op.cit.* Note 71, above, Art. 1 Abs. III, Rdnr 133—Professor Dürig offers a *Drittwirkung* example of race discrimination: a contract not to let an apartment to a Jew would be contrary to good morals and thus void. Cf. Cass. 3ème civ, 6 mars 1996, *JCP* 1996, ed. G, IV, 973 and *JCP* 1997, 22764 where the French court of cassation held that Art. 8.1 of the European Convention on Human Rights could be used to set aside a clause in a private lease, which prevented a tenant from allowing his close relatives to reside in the leased premises.

harassment should not depend upon the public or private status of the employer.[90]

But more than what has just been asserted emerges from this rich material. For the comparatively minded teacher can, if so inclined, draw even wider conclusions from these texts—rich, varied, and contradictory though they sometimes are. Thus, to return to my earlier point, starting from fairly narrow factual situations, he can show not only how two different systems have attempted to solve the problems they present. He can go further than that and also use the material to tell his students something about the interaction of the political and judicial process. Not content with describing this, he might even ask the more inquisitive of the students to consider how this political interaction is manifested in systems such as the English and the German where the judicial debates are more prone to concealing the political forces that influence these battles. This, incidentally, is the best place to bring into the discussion the debate about the continuing force of the theory of autonomy of the will and move the debate from the practical to the theoretical field. Finally, in advocating to English lawyers the possibility of giving a horizontal effect to their new Human Rights legislation, the comparatist can claim that the idea that human rights need to be protected against powerful entities (public or private) is neither as alien nor as dangerous as it may sound. For, if this brief survey demonstrates anything, it is surely that in substance if not in form many of these concerns, voiced in Germany since the Second World War, have come to be shared by both courts and academics in the most market-oriented economy of the world: the USA.

(c) Constitutional protection of speech in the workplace. In the previous sub-paragraph we noted that in the field of sex equality German and American law are not that different, at any rate in their results if not in their theories. The need to protect individual rights against private actors, especially employers, is strong in both systems. And, in a broad sort of way, it has taken the same kind of form—statutory interventions of different kinds supplemented by bold case law. But when we move to protection of speech rights in the private workplace we find in the United States a picture that is not only complex but also different. Yet we also encounter some case law developments, which, though rejected (or qualified) by most State jurisdictions, show that methodologically the German solution is perfectly transplantable to the US. Indeed, a foreign observer would be justified in arguing that where American courts have used these techniques they have produced fairer results for the plaintiffs in question than the leading German case. So, once again, let us turn to specifics, for here comparative methodology

[90] This view is advanced by Hartwin Bungert, "Gleichberechtigung von Mann und Frau im amerikanischen und deutschen Verfassungsrecht" 89 *Zeitschrift für Vergleichende Rechtswissenschaft*, 441, 463*ff.* (1990).

can be even more instructive in revealing how similar the two (apparently different) systems can be.

Thus, in both systems we find speech disputes that arose in a private employment relationship. In both instances, the plaintiffs/employees indulged in a political activity, which did not meet with the approval of their (private) employers. Finally, in both the employers' attempt to dismiss the employees was countered by the argument that such an action would, in the final analysis, conflict with basic Human Rights enshrined in the Constitutions of the two countries. It was precisely this kind of factual setting that in Germany launched the expression *unmittelbare Dittwirkung* (*direct* third party effect)[91] in the sense that the Human Rights articles of the Constitution *directly* governed such disputes. Four years later, however, the Constitutional Court[92] adopted a more subtle variant propounding the view that Constitutional provisions had a "radiating effect" (*Ausstrahlungswirkung*) on private law, "influencing" rather than "directly governing" its relationships. Much ink has flowed in America[93] to show that—rightly or wrongly, this is not the point here—the parallel American doctrine of "state action", extended to its furthest reach in *Shelley* v. *Kraemer*,[94] is not as wide as the German doctrine of *Drittwirkung*.[95] Yet whatever may be the right answer, the fact remains that a few American courts have, in the context of the factual situation here examined, had little difficulty in adopting a *basic* stance which is very similar to the one found in Germany. What is interesting about this case law is that it allowed the constitutional law to penetrate the private law dispute not through the "state action" doctrine but through another amorphous notion, that of "public policy".

Novosel v. *Nationwide Insurance Company*[96] gives us the perfect illustration. In this case, the Court of Appeals of the Third Circuit took the view

[91] BArbGE 1, 185 (1954). The judgment of the Court, presided over by Judge Hans-Carl Nipperdey, draws heavily on his earlier writings as an academic, notably his seminal "Gleicher Lohn der Frau für gleiche Leistung. Ein Beitrag zur Auslegung der Grundrechte" in *Recht der Arbeit* 1950, 121*ff*. As is explained in what follows in the text the theory that now prevails allows the constitutional rules to have an indirect, over-arching effect on private law relations but denies to them any direct applicability.

[92] BVerfGE 7, 195 (1958).

[93] Professor Peter Quint has collected the references in his excellent "Free Speech and Private Law in German Constitutional Theory" 48 *Maryland L. Rev*. 247 (1989).

[94] 334 US, 1 (1948).

[95] But see, *Sullivan* v. *Barnett*, 139 F. 3d 158 (3rd Cir. 998), petition for cert. Pending No 97–2000. That the problem is not going away can be seen in the discussion of Siegel, "The Constitution and Private Government: Toward the Recognition of Constitutional Rights in Private Residential Communities Fifty Years After *Marsh* v. *Alabama*" 6 *William and Mary Bill of Rights Law Journal*, 461 (1998).

[96] 721 F. 2d 894 (1983). The (predictably adverse) reactions to *Novosel* are discussed by Professor Perritt "The Future of Wrongful Dismissal Claims: Where does Employer Self-Interest Lie?" in 58 *U. Cin. L. Rev*. 397, esp. pp. 402*ff*. (1989) where the author describes the *Novosel* doctrine as "an important model for possible future expansion of the public policy tort into *a constitutionalization of private employment*". (Emphasis added.)

that the concern for rights of political expression, which animated First Amendment *public*[97] employee cases, was also applicable to *private* employees under Pennsylvania law.[98] The Court was thus able to state in distinctly Nipperdeian terms that "The protection of important political freedoms . . . goes well beyond the question whether the threat comes from state or private bodies."[99]

Other cases, which have followed this line of argument, could be quoted.[100] Yet it will suffice to mention but two since they relate to the right of privacy which is likely to cause most of the headaches when our new Human Rights legislation comes into force. Thus, in the Californian case of *Semore* v. *Pool*[101] the Court of Appeal of the Fourth District held that the right of privacy in the California Constitution prohibits a private employer from conducting arbitrary drug testing and that the dismissal of the employee for failing to submit to the proposed test violated the public policy of the state. The position was re-affirmed four years later by the (state) Supreme Court in *Hill* v. *National Collegiate Athletic Assn.*[102] where the court held that the privacy clause of Article 1, section 2, of the State Constitution, "creates a right of action against private as well as government agencies".[103] Accordingly, when a private employee's contract is

[97] Thus, to stick with the same State, see *Hunter* v. *Port Authority of Allegheny County* 419 A 2d. 631 (1980): Employer's right to dismiss employee of an "at-will employment" is circumscribed by requirements of public policy which may be derived directly from First Amendment of the US Constitution and s. 7 of the Pennsylvania Constitution.

[98] In *Borse* v. *Piece Goods Shop, Inc.* 963 F. 2d 611 (1992) the court refused to extend the *Novosel* ruling to a dismissal of an employee who refused to submit herself to urinalysis screening for drug use. Significantly, however, it refused to hold ". . . that a constitutional provision may never serve as a source of public policy in . . . wrongful discharge actions [taking place in a private workplace]". It is precisely this last point, which brings the two systems closer together than they are commonly believed to be.

[99] *Ibid.* at p. 900.

[100] For instance: *Devlin* v. *North Shore Door Co.* 1995 WL 277, 110 (Ohio App. 8 Dist.): "Clear 'public policy' sufficient to justify an exception to the employment-at-will doctrine . . . may be discerned by the Ohio judiciary based on sources such as the Constitution of Ohio and the United States . . ."

[101] 217 Cal. App. 3rd 1087, 266 Cal. Rptr. 280 (1990).

[102] 7 Cal. 4th 1, 26 Cal. Rptr. 2d 834, 865 P. 2d 633 (1994). This has been followed in different contexts. See, for instance, *Pettus* v. *Cole* 49 Cal. App. 4th 402, 57 Cal. Rptr. 2d 46. (Employee made prima facie showing that disclosure to employer of detailed medical information by psychiatrists in connection with request for disability leave violated his constitutional right to privacy as he had legally cognizable interest in preserving privacy of his medical history and psychological profile.)

[103] Once again, the generality of this statement is of especial significance for the wider comparative point that I am trying to make. One must, however, also note two further points. First, in n. 20 (p. 869) of the *Hill* judgment referred to above, the court expressed doubts as to the continued validity of the *Semore* ruling. Secondly, courts, as we already noted when mentioning the *Borse* judgment in note 81, above, are reluctant to apply these principles in drug-testing cases. Thus, in *Jennings* v. *Minco Technology Labs Inc.* 765 SW 2d 497 (1989), a Texas court not only held that employers can require drug testing (and dismiss employees of "at will" contracts if they refuse to comply); it also slapped the employee with attorneys' fees for even raising the issue.

terminated on the grounds that he refused to take a random drug test, the employee may invoke the public policy exception to the "at-will termination" doctrine to assert a violation of his constitutional right of privacy.

The above discussion and the case law given in the notes reveals, once again, the lack of a solution that is uniformly acceptable to the fifty American jurisdictions. It also reveals that the wider *Novosel* doctrine—that the Constitutional texts can help shape the public policy exceptions to the doctrine that "at will contracts" can be terminated by the employer for any reason or no reason—has had a mixed reception. In particular, the drug testing cases, which seem to have shown the greater reluctance to use this technique, may in part be explicable by the general desire to fight the drug war with all means available setting aside what are seen as legalistic niceties. A more general explanation for rejecting the *Novosel* approach may be linked to the wider debate alluded to in the previous sub-section, concerning the desirability of taking such powers away from the legislator and giving them to the judiciary. But, in my view, the validity of my thesis remains unaffected by these attempts to keep the judicially created exceptions to the employment "at will" doctrine to a minimum. For what the *Novosel* case law shows is that that the *Drittwirkung* technique is not entirely inconceivable even in the United States in the sense that constitutional ideas can and do enter into the domain of a private law dispute. To be sure, in Germany this "revolution" came about through the use of some of the quasi-metaphysical concepts relied upon by the court in *Lüth* such as *Drittwirkung, Wechselwirkung, Ausstrahlungswirkung*, in combination with some of the most amorphous paragraphs found in the Civil Code. That in America the same result came about through the equally amorphous concept of public policy is, I submit, a matter of relative detail. What does, however, matter is the realisation that human rights are, nowadays, seriously threatened from powerful private entities as much as they are by the State. A theory of horizontality of some kind is thus called for. How, precisely, we implement it must, however, be left to the techniques used by and the philosophies prevalent to each system that has to face this problem.

Finally, one must not bring this discussion to an end without noting that *Novosel* in the USA achieved what eluded the *Bundesarbeitsgericht* in Germany. For at the end of the day the latter court, despite its grandiloquent declarations, failed to come to the assistance of the employee who was dismissed simply because his political views differed from those of his employer. But then, perhaps we can come back to the point we made at the beginning of this section: the German case involved a communist sympathiser. This may give us as intriguing a clue as the drug-testing cases do in their own way in the USA. For one must not forget that the German case was litigated in the early 1950s. It is thus arguably right to suggest that the legal decision must be seen against the political realities that prevailed at that time. The final conclusion of the German court, that limiting the speech rights of the dismissed employee is admissible if it serves to protect some other competing legal value (*Rechtsgut*), can thus be seen as a sham. A sham that clothes in legalistic language a decision of political expediency that the climate of the times made almost unavoidable. That such a (harsh) interpretation is not entirely fanciful can be seen from the fact that the court found no constitutional text to peg such an approach but, instead, chose to trump constitutional protected speech rights by relying on previous court practice and academic writings.[104]

(d) Some tentative conclusions. Three, I believe, are in order.

First, the treasures of German law have to be mined at great personal effort. The effort lies in discovering the basic idea behind complex theorising. This makes the German legal model, despite its undoubted intellectual virtues, a difficult one to follow. To put it differently, it makes it a model worth studying for the sake of tapping its undoubted intellectual originality but not ideal for the purposes of literal transplantation. As I put it elsewhere, German law must first be "deconstructed" and then "reconstructed" before English lawyers can use it.[105]

Secondly, American law is far too varied, too complex and, on the whole, too rooted in private market philosophies to lend itself to facile comparisons. Searching for factual equivalents of the *Drittwirkung* phenomenon may be, if not impossible, certainly too perilous an exercise to be undertaken with any conviction of reliability. Yet, workable models for comparing legal systems in a meaningful way are needed, so the effort to devise them should, at least, be made; and in my submission the attempt made above can serve as a working model.

Finally, and at a most technical level, the German case law may suggest an interesting phenomenon. For given the fact that at the end of the day the "dissenting" American employee was protected whereas his German counterpart was not, I am left with the impression that the German courts often seem to be establishing a distinction between horizontal application and the substance of the obligation. This means that while on the one hand they seem to be drawing individuals into the sphere of obligations created by the relevant provisions of their Constitution, on the other they are also

[104] BArbGE 1, 185, 194–5 (1954). A second constitutional challenge in that case was based on the idea that the dismissal violated Art. 3(3) of the Constitution, which prohibits discrimination on grounds of political opinion. Though the Court held that this constitutional provision as well had a horizontal effect it, again, held that it had not been violated in this instance. Subsequent case law has, however, shown greater sensitivity to the employee's political views, especially if the facts of the case suggested that the employer had, by dismissing the employee, over-reacted to the latter's stance. Thus, see: BArbGE 47, 363 (1984).

[105] Markesinis and Dannemann, "The Legacy of History on German Contract Law", in *Essays for Roy Goode* Cranston ed. (OUP, 1997), pp. 1–28.

diluting the substance of the obligation for a variety of reasons which are often not obvious from the judgments. This is not the place to consider whether this is the result of being influenced by wider and not always, strictly speaking, legal considerations. But it is appropriate to make the point, even in a passing manner, since I think we may, once again, be finding echoes of this phenomenon in recent English and American decisions.

5. FUTURE DEBTS AND WAYS OF PAYING THEM OFF

I would now like to bring these brief observations to a close by means of seven propositions.

First, I believe there is a tendency, deeply rooted in human nature, to look around and borrow, where possible, good and tested ideas. The doctrine of binding precedent is, after all, in part based on this belief. Increased travel, common education programmes and the pursuit of a growing number of common economic aims will, in my view, broaden this natural habit so as to include foreign experiences and ideas. To be sure, the coming together and borrowing will decreasingly be the product of an inspired decision of a few widely educated judges and jurists and become a by-product of contemporary cosmopolitanism and enhanced, trans-border interaction. Though I am no particular fan of mass movements, I welcome the interaction that is brought about by shrinking our world. One can see this changing trend even within the relatively short space of time that I have been in the teaching profession. For, when I started my academic life in Cambridge in the late 1960s, our only guide (in English) to foreign law was the already dated (but) excellent manual of German law written by the late Professor Cohn. Matters were not really much better for French law even though in the post-war years the intellectual contacts with that country were very strong. For here, too, we basically had one book in English—the attractive but increasingly out-dated little book of the late Professors Amos and Walton. Even the bible of contemporary comparatists—Zweigert and Kötz's *An Introduction to Comparative Law*—had not yet seen the light of day in the original let alone in English. I need hardly give illustrations of how much the scene has changed; and changed not only in the classroom but even in the courtroom where the use of foreign material, though not an everyday occurrence hardly raises an eyebrow any longer. This is no mean achievement for those of us who have fought for this change.

Secondly, our task in disseminating legal ideas will be facilitated if we abandon the habit of a particular breed of comparatist who saw the subject largely (if not exclusively) as one which pursues a *mission civilisatrice*. This approach nearly killed off the cultivation of a subject that had been taken to such heights, mainly in the late 1920s and 1930s, by the *Kaiser Wilhelm Institute* of Berlin. This contributed to an almost unforgivable decline of the subject in the 1970s—certainly in France, Italy, and our country—though, of course, honourable exceptions can be mentioned.[106] Instead, we must put the method to the service of practitioners and judges and persuade them that it can improve the quality of their work, especially where local law does not possess a clear and convincing solution to a particular problem. A learned judge recently admitted that this could work. He thus said: "If the advocate can show that in other legal systems which we respect the problem facing the court is solved by the use of a concept which, while novel here in the relevant context, is a practicable one to adopt, then he may find that the court welcomes the stimulus which this can provide."[107]

Thirdly, though I see many areas of private law—mainly connected with the topics of court structures, procedure, and restitution—still offering many topics worthy of comparative discussion, I think the time is ripe for English comparatists to shift their attention to public law. By this I mean not only French Administrative law which, for years, has been a wonderful source of inspiration (and controversy) but also German and Italian public law. Re-reading Maitland convinced me that such a switch of emphasis is right. For, in one of his little-remembered essays[108] I noted that he perceived (and praised) the 19th century as the era of codification of private law. This started me thinking what would he have said if he were writing at the close of our century? I feel reasonably confident that the growth of administrative law would have attracted the attention of the great historian. And that must be right because the most notable feature of our century

[106] In France, for instance, the names of Denis Tallon and André Tunc spring to mind. In Italy we have the ubiquitous Rodolfo Sacco who literally changed the Italian landscape by introducing comparative law as an undergraduate course in most Italian Universities. In my own country the towering figure of Tony Honoré must be mentioned alongside the very sui generis contribution made by Tony Weir, mainly through his elegant translations of numerous foreign texts. In my view, only Germany escaped this decline as it can boast an impressive array of comparatists such as Zweigert, Lorenz, Stoll, Drobnig, Kötz, Schlechtriem, Grossfeld, Lutter, Schwartze, Zimmermann, Coester-Waltjen, von Bar, Muller-Graff, Ebke and others.

[107] Lord Justice Schiemann reviewing in 114 (1998) *LQR*, 515, at p. 523, my two-volume work *The German Law of Obligations* (co-authored with Professor Werner Lorenz and Dr. Gerhard Danemann) (1998). The learned judge, emphasising the utility of the comparative method, continued: "Future editors of English [sic] text books on contract, restitution or tort owe it to their readers to take the time to absorb these books and, at the very least, to incorporate the appropriate references in their footnotes . . ." Lord Goff expressed similar views in his Child lecture, reprinted in 1987 *Denning Law Review* 79 at 94. Thus he wrote: "If, as I hope and expect, [the English jurist] extends his vision to the study of those subjects as treated in other systems of law, his statement of English law can, and should be, set, . . . in a comparative context. In this way, practitioners in common law countries, and especially judges in those countries, will be exposed to new ideas which will not only enrich their understanding of their own law, but may influence them to develop it in ways which previously might not have been thought possible."

[108] "A Survey of the Century", a lecture delivered in 1901 and republished in *The Collected Papers of Frederick William Maitland* (ed. HAL Fisher) vol. III (1911), 432*ff.* See, also—in the same volume at pp. 474*ff.*—"The Making of the German Civil Code".

has been this switch from rules regulating horizontal relationships (citizen with citizen) to rules dictating how the vertical relationships (state and citizen) should be ordained. My guess is that in the years to come we will be forced to look at a new variant of this problem—new to us but not our German friends—and that is why I have started stressing the need to include German public law within our purview.[109] This inquiry, incidentally, leads us to another aspect of public law: human rights. But this is not where our comparative inquiries should stop. I think another area in which political events will force us into comparative study will be variations of federalism or, to put it less provocatively, constitutional problems resulting from conflicts that are bound to arise between the central government, the states and their variously independent regions. In both these areas of public law I think our German and Italian colleagues have much information and, I would add, ideas, to impart.[110] We should be ready to look at this with interest rather than take the easy way out and say, if federalism becomes an issue, the American or Australian models can provide us with all we need and more. The urge to opt for that easier option will, of course, be strengthened by the fact that studying American, Canadian or Australian law requires no particular linguistic effort. But, once again, I am sure that the onward rush of political developments in Europe will make the move towards studying Continental European public law more widely felt.

Fourthly, I think we must recall, especially in the context of what I have said in the previous section of this paper, that what we are primarily interested in is the broader ideas rather than the concepts, the organising categories, or the systems of analyses. The evolution of our administrative law supports my thesis and predilection. For pause and think how our administrative law came about. For, having started in the shadow of the Dicey legacy, it was mercilessly and unfavourably compared to the French *droit administatif* for most of the 1950s and early 1960s. Then came the work of some influential scholars, such as Sir William Wade, and some great judges, such as Lords Reid, Denning, Diplock and Wilberforce. And our law, finally, more than redeemed its original deficiencies by coming up with its own, native, solution: a *droit administratif à la anglaise*, as the Master of Rolls—himself a leading scholar of the subject—put it so felicitously. This blend of local features with foreign and indigenous ideas seems to me to hold the key to the way forward as far as the new study of comparative

[109] For instance in my Wilberforce Lecture entitled, "Privacy, Freedom of Speech and the Horizontal application of the Human Rights Legislation" (1999) *LQR*, 47*ff*.

[110] I am encouraged to see that leading American comparatists share this view. Thus, see: Kommers, "Kann das deutsche Verfassungrechtsdenken Vorbild für die Vereinigten Staaten sein?" *Der Staat*. 37 *Zeitschrift für Staatslehre, öffentliches Recht und Verfassungsgeschichte* 1998, 335*ff*. Another topic, which I recently—1999—discussed with Professors JB Auby, D Coester-Waltjen and Dr S Deakin is the *Tortious Liability of Statutory Bodies*—an area of English tort, which is increasingly affected by the case law of the Strasbourg court.

public law is concerned. But it will require more than a passing acquaintance with European legal thought. In this area of the law I think we can say that this "new awareness" already exists to an impressive degree. For never before in our history can I find so many judges writing about matters of administrative law and human rights and demonstrating in their writings such a predilection for wider, jurisprudential and comparative material. Listing the names of some of those who have written such pieces—Lord Scarman,[111] Lord Woolf,[112] Lord Bingham,[113] Lord Browne-Wilkinson,[114] Lord Hoffman,[115] Mr Justice Laws,[116] Mr Justice Sedley,[117] Madame Justice Arden,[118] and, indeed, the current Lord Chancellor, Lord Irvine of Lairg,[119]—amply makes my point. This material will require a continued willingness to comb it for ideas when faced with problems that are new to us.

Fifthly, we must redouble our efforts on the language front. The aforementioned achievements of our judges are not, in themselves, enough to bring the cultural re-orientation that I wish and recommend. For a time, language differences and difficulties will still cause insurmountable difficulties. Some of our indigenous authors have, in fact, expressed their scepticism about our ability to overcome this hurdle.[120] Again, however, I remain optimistic. And I ask my readers to ponder three developments, all linked with what has been happening in Europe since the Second World War. In my view, all point in the direction that I wish us to take.

Thus, first, we already have, by my own reckoning, at least half a dozen senior judges who are proficient in German (more, if we add other lan-

[111] Most noteworthy, of course, is his Hamlyn Lecture, *English Law: the New Dimension* (1974)—the *fons et origo* of much of the contemporary debate on the need to acquire a human rights legislation.

[112] *Protecting the Public: A New Challenge* (1990). See, also, "Droit Public—English Style", the text of the FA Mann Lecture, [1955] *Public Law*, 51*ff*.

[113] "The European Convention on Human Rights: Time to Incorporate", The Denning Lecture, *Human Rights in the United Kingdom* (ed. R Gordon and R Wilmot-Smith) (OUP 1966), 1*ff*.; "Should there be a Law to Protect Rights of Personal Privacy?" [1996] *European Human Rights Law Review*, 450*ff*.

[114] "The Infiltration of a Bill of Rights" [1992] *Public Law*, 397*ff*.

[115] "A Sense of Proportion in Community Law in English Courts" in *Public Law in the UK and EC* (ed. F Jacobs and M Andenas) (1998).

[116] "The Ghost in the Machine: Principle in Public Law" [1989] *Public Law*; "Is the High Court the Guardian of Fundamental Constitutional Rights?" [1993] *Public Law*, 59*ff*.; "Law and Democracy" [1995] *Public Law*, 72*ff*.; "The Constitution: Morals and Rights" [1996] *Public Law*, 622; "The Limitations of Human Rights" [1998] *Public Law*, 254*ff*.

[117] "The Sound of Silence: Constitutional Law Without a Constitution" (1994) 110 *LQR*, 270*ff*. "Human Rights: A Twenty First Century Agenda" [1995] *Public Law*, 386*ff*.

[118] "The Future of the Law of Privacy" (not yet published).

[119] "Judges and Decision-Makers: The Theory and Practice of Wednesbury Review" [1996] *Public Law*, 9*ff*.; "Response to Sir John Laws" [1996] *Public Law*, 636*ff*.; "The Development of Human Rights in Britain" [1998] *Public Law*, 221*ff*.

[120] Weir, "Die Sprachen des europäischen Rechts: Eine skeptische Betrachtung" (1995) 3 *Zeitschrift für Europäisches Privatrecht*, 368*ff*., convincingly refuted by Professor Zimmermann in his "Savigny's Legacy" etc., 112 *LQR*, 595–6.

guages) and who are giving increasing signs that they are prepared to use this linguistic expertise in their work. Secondly, over the past ten or fifteen years, through a handful of published works, English-speaking jurists have acquired translations of over five hundred leading cases in contract and tort alone. Extracts, often lengthy, from almost as many decisions of the German Constitutional Court are also now available provided one knows how to look for them! Thus, in volume terms there is more German material available in English than the average English student would ever read using his English casebooks on contract, tort or constitutional law. The language problem is not thus insurmountable; and with the passage of time it will be proved to be an excuse but not a reason for not studying foreign law. Thirdly, and most importantly, we have a growing itinerant student population which will go on increasing in numbers and which, in twenty years' time or less, will be on stream as senior practitioners, civil servants, and judges. Their European experiences, enriched by study leaves and training programmes in various European countries, are bound, in my view, to be reflected in the law they pass, administer, or adjudicate on, as past experience with similarly educated young lawyers clearly shows.

Sixthly, I wish to stress the need for greater intellectual honesty when it comes to transplants of ideas. This is, in one sense, such an obvious proposition that I would not have felt the need to make it all. Yet recently, the readers of the *Law Quarterly Review* will have read a learned piece by a Scottish colleague in which he documented the extent of borrowing from Scottish law that took place in shaping some of the leading cases of contemporary English law.[121] Yet some of the readers of this learned article may have been impressed more by the fact that this borrowing from the civil law had to be concealed than it did happen at all. There may have been good reasons why such "loans" had to be suppressed. But the temptation to do so in the future would, in my view, be a dangerous concession to a legal kind of chauvinism, which is neither attractive nor likely to prove viable during the next millennium.

So I come, finally, to my seventh and last proposition which, because it trespasses on Professor von Bar's paper I shall keep brief.

I said this before and I repeat it now: comparative law is not a one-way street. The question that occupies me most is where can we make our greatest contribution? In my opinion, our contribution to the emerging new Europe will spring from our main strengths, which I find not in dogmatic analysis of the law but in our procedure, advocacy, pragmatism, and preference for a properly understood notion of incrementalism. To these I would add our teaching of the law, not least because it involves all of these attributes, which over the years I have come to admire. These we are well advised

[121] R Evan-Jones, "Roman Law in Scotland and England and the development of One Law for Britain", 115 (1999) *LQR*, 604.

to combine with the intellectual strengths of our neighbours and partners; and history suggests that such a combination of foreign and indigenous ideas can be made to work. For as Professor Simpson put it so felicitously, "in the history of Western European legal tradition of private law successful creative work consists in a combination between intelligent plagiarism and systematisation of what is lifted from others".[122] If it worked for private law—and the 1980s and 1990s have shown how fruitful the comparative methodology has been in the area of contract and tort—I see no reason why it should not work for public law. And I have already stressed that it is here that I think lies much of the future of comparative law.

So, I conclude this paper with two statements from two eminent judges whom I greatly admire and, I hope, I can even refer to as friends: Lords Goff and Bingham. In his Child Lecture[123] Lord Goff predicted that "... we are bound to see an enrichment of our legal culture on an unparalleled scale through the increasing study of comparative law ..." In his Mann Lecture Lord Bingham looked forward to the day when "England joined, or more accurately rejoined [sic] the mainstream of European legal tradition ..."[124] Sufficient time has elapsed since these statements were made to describe them both as prophecies. And, despite this, neither of their authors have met with the fate usually reserved for prophets. That must be a good sign!

122 *Op.cit.* n.6 above, at p. 254.
123 "Judge, Jurist and Legislature" 1987 *Denning Law Review*, 79 at p. 93.
124 *Op.cit.* n.3 above at p. 528.

2

Foreign Law and Foreign Ideas in the English Courts

INTRODUCTORY REMARKS

English lawyers are sometimes thought of as being as Europhobic as some of their politicians. As heirs to a long, original and, on the whole, successful legal tradition they would, many would argue, be perfectly justified in wishing to safeguard their system and not being anxious to replace it except where it was *shown* to be in need of reform.[1] Most German and French lawyers would, I suspect, take the same line; though representatives from smaller or "derivative" legal systems might show a greater interest in change and compromise. In my submission, the reality in England does not correspond to this image. Take, for instance, the English legal education. In many respects it is more open to European ideas than is that received by young French or Greek students, to give but two examples from systems which I happen to know at first hand. Thus, many Universities in my country still provide during the early stages of a legal education introductory lectures to Roman Law. This is an immensely useful course since it provides students not only with an overview of an entire legal system (which they will not get of their own until their second or even the third year of their studies) but also makes them realise that the problems of daily life may be susceptible to different answers or similar answers reached by means of differing reasoning processes. In that sense courses of this kind thus do for law what the study of Latin does for languages: it introduces English speakers to the "peculiarities" of the definite and indefinite articles declension, grammatical problems linked to gender and the like. Such an instruction can hardly be described as insular; and the open-mindedness which it embodies does not stop there. For the study of Roman law is followed by European Community law which is, nowadays, a compulsory subject for anyone who wishes to practise as either a barrister

[1] I have, myself, attempted to do this on several occasions. Thus, see, the Essays reproduced in my *Foreign Law and Comparative Methodology: A Subject and a Thesis*, (1997) *passim*. Nor is this a predilection found only in academics. Thus, *cf.* Lord Goff's remarks in his Wilberforce Lecture entitled "The Future of the Common Law" 46 *ICLQ* (1997) pp. 745 *ff*.

or a solicitor. Courses in French and German law or Comparative Methodology have also proliferated in recent years; and, what is just as remarkable (and praiseworthy) is that this trend has not come from our two oldest Universities (Oxford and Cambridge) but has been championed by London, Birmingham, Bristol, Durham, Exeter or Warwick, not to mention Edinburgh which, under the guidance of the late Professor John Mitchell, first appreciated the importance of European Community law.

The breadth of the educational approach is reflected in later life for those who join one of the major City firms of solicitors, which have offices in most capital towns in Europe. Indeed some, like Clifford Chance, have transformed the structures and cultures so as to be truly multi-national firms rather than English firms with branch offices in Brussels, Paris, Dubai or Hong Kong. This, too, has involved a "mentality revolution" of sorts, which should not be under-estimated.

On the political level, the UK also has one of the best records for observing Community Directives. The well-known reluctance to accept European initiatives, at least not before a proper debate has taken place, is not matched by a reluctance (found in other Community members) to observe and apply to the letter what has been agreed upon. Let us not forget that this, too, forms part of the "record" which has not received adequate recognition.

Any of these broad areas could be used as the basis of a paper which wished to discuss the growing importance of European law in the United Kingdom. But in this presentation I would like to focus on a completely different aspect of what I once called the Europeanisation of English law.[2] In particular I wish to look briefly, because of lack of time, at two areas of the law—human rights law and pure, private law—in order to suggest that the thinking patterns of English judges as well as their attitudes towards foreign decisional law may be undergoing a slow but profound change. I intend to discuss the first topic in section 1 of this paper, while in section 2, I would like to look at the "optional"[3] use of foreign judgments by some recent decisions of the House of Lords. In the last section—section 3—I shall wrap up this survey with some thoughts about the effect which these developments may have on comparative methodology and the use of foreign law by national courts, be they English or Continental European.

[2] *The Gradual Convergence: Foreign Ideas, Foreign Influences and English Law, on the Eve of the 21st Century* (1994), chap. one.

[3] I have borrowed the terminology and the idea from Professor Drobnig's "The Use of Comparative Law by Courts" in *Rapports Généraux XIVe Congrès International Athènes 1994*, pp. 68*ff*. The best example of "necessary" application of foreign law is found in the systems of most Continental European countries which give priority to generally recognised rules of public international law over national law.

1. THE HUMAN RIGHTS REVOLUTION

This is a vast subject so, again, I shall limit my observations to the *indirect* impact which the case law of the Court of Human Rights in Strasbourg has had on English law and, more generally and, in my view more importantly, on English legal culture as a whole.

The impact of the European Convention has, of course, been *indirect* since for a variety of economic/political reasons (which we all now know[4]) the Labour Government of the early 1950s[5] frustrated all attempts to incorporate the Convention into English law and this even though England had played a prominent part in its drafting and was the first country to ratify it. There is, thus, something of an irony in the fact that it is a Labour Government which, some forty-seven years later, is remedying one of the most unfortunate and expensive (for litigants) consequences of our attachment to the dualistic approach to international law. This foreign influence, though indirect, has, especially in the course of the last five years or so, become very significant as our judges, judicially and extra-judicially, have shown a growing interest in the potential of this foreign source of ideas. Four points in particular need to be stressed here for the benefit of a non-English readership.

First, the number of court decisions which have, in one way or another, relied on the European Convention on Human Rights, (and less so, the International Covenant on Civil and Political Rights, and the Universal Declaration of Human Rights) thus far exceeds four hundred and seventy. To a French lawyer, accustomed to some fifteen thousand *pourvois* to his *Cour de cassation* per annum, this may seem as an infinitesimally small number of decisions. But before he reaches this conclusion he should remember that in England the Court of Appeal hears not more than 1,500 cases *per annum* and the House of Lords roughly 100 (covering both civil and criminal matters). Needless to add, the bulk of these cases do not involve human rights issues.

There is another reason why this figure is substantial. Foreign readers in particular must not forget that in the United Kingdom the Commission's right to receive individual appeals was not acknowledged until 1966. The case law references in fact did not start until the early seventies; and as Mr. Murray Hunt, the author of an outstanding recent monograph on the subject has shown, over half of these judgments date from the last five years alone.[6] From an English perspective, therefore, this numerical figure is

[4] They are mentioned and discussed by Lord Leicester, "Fundamental Rights: The United Kingdom Isolated?" *Public Law*, Spring 1984, pp. 46 *et seq.* and, more recently, Geoffrey Marston "The United Kingdom's part in the Preparation of the European Convention on Human Rights, 1950" (1993) *International and Comparative Law Quarterly*, pp. 796 *et seq.*

[5] With the valiant exception of the then Foreign Secretary Ernest Bevin.

[6] *Using Human Rights Law in English Courts* (1997), 127 and Appendix One.

impressive. More importantly, perhaps, the figures deserve note because they almost certainly suggest a trend.

Secondly, one must note the acceleration of this trend in the most recent past. This flight into the Convention sometimes happens in an "honest" i.e. open way, for example by stating that it is permissible to refer to the Convention whenever our law was (or is) in a state of flux or uncertainty, while in others it prompts our judges to discover (or re-discover) that the Common law has always been as good as the Convention and thus there is no need to have open recourse to the provisions of the Convention.[7] Though this tendency to claim that one's own law is just as good as the regime established by the international conventions can be found in other systems, as well,[8] in our case at least I do not find it very convincing. For, as Lord Bingham, the Lord Chief Justice, recently pointed out: "If in truth the Common law as it stands were giving the rights of United Kingdom citizens the same protection as the Convention—across the Board and not only in relation to Article 10—one might wonder why the United Kingdom's record as a Strasbourg litigant was not more favourable."[9] Yet, this criticism notwithstanding, the linking of the Common law to the Convention has meant that our judges could, by adapting the Common law, go beyond the doctrine of *ultra vires* which, essentially, permits judicial intervention when powers conferred by the legislature are exercised contrary to their intended purpose.[10]

Thirdly, and this aspect of the problem was explored at a conference which the Oxford Centre for the Advanced Study of European and Comparative Law organised in London late in 1997 in association with the

[7] Thus, *All. Gen* v. *Guardian Newspapers Ltd (No 2)* [1990] 1 AC at pp. 283–4 (per Lord Goff); *Derbyshire County Council* v. *Times Newspapers Ltd.* [1993] 2 WLR 449.

[8] For instance Italy, where the Italian Supreme Court first justified the protection of human privacy by reference to the Convention but then shifted its position and held that the "new" right could be found secreted in the Italian Constitution. On this see Professor Alpa's lecture at the Centre for the Advanced Study of European and Comparative Law in the University of Oxford entitled *The Italian Law of Privacy*, published by the Centre in 1997.

[9] "The European Convention on Human Rights: Time to Incorporate" in *Human Rights in the United Kingdom*, (Richard Gordon QC and Richard Wilmot-Smith QC, eds) (1996), 9. Thus, as another great jurist observes in the same collection of essays, "Since 1965 twice as many petitions have been lodged against [Britain] as against any other member, and it has lost more serious cases than any other nation." Ronald Dworkin, "Does Britain need a Bill of Rights", in *ibid.*, at pp. 59, 63.

[10] This shift was made possible by pronouncements such as the following from the former Master of the Rolls Sir Thomas Bingham in *R.* v. *Ministry of Defence, ex. p. Smith and Others* [1996] 1 All ER 257, at 263 where he said: "The more substantial the interference with human rights, the more the court, will require by way of justification before it is satisfied that the decision is reasonable . . ." The impact of the Convention on judicial review is discussed, *inter alia*, by Beloff and Mountfield, "Unconventional Behaviour? Judicial uses of the European Convention in England and Wales" in 1996 *European Human Rights Law Review*, 467*ff.* and the current Lord Chancellor, Lord Irvine of Lairg in "Judges and Decision-Makers: The Theory and Practice of *Wednesbury* Review" in [1996] *Public Law*, 59*ff.*

multi-national firm of Clifford Chance, is the breadth of the impact which the Convention has (and will have) on many branches of our law, once it is finally incorporated. This is likely to go far beyond the traditional topics which we tend to discuss under the heading of human rights such as sexual and racial discrimination, immigration, and administrative law and is going to affect (even more than it does at present) other areas of the law such as corporate law, the law of contracts, torts and crimes. I make this point here not only because I believe that we have not yet fully appreciated the full effect of the (imminent) incorporation of the Convention into our law, but also because I wish to lay down a marker on another point, namely whether the incorporation of the Convention will make our lawyers as sensitive (or hypersensitive) to real or imaginary human rights issues. If this does occur, and to some extent I think it is bound to do so,[11] American (and Canadian) human rights law will also be cited with greater frequency. And if the Canadian experience is anything to go by, arguments turning on the Convention may bring a different kind of literature, a different kind of argument in court, and a different kind of judicial reasoning in the final judgment.[12] All this, however, is little more than speculation which must be addressed more seriously in another essay but which I raise here merely to suggest that further developments in this field of the law are bound to bring more foreign law, more foreign ideas, and more foreign methodology into our system. More about this point in the last section of this essay.

Fourthly and finally we must take note of the fact that the Convention has acted as a kind of catalyst for growing extra-judicial utterances by some of our most respected judges. Thus, in a way which is unusual by English tradition, many of our leading judges such as Lord Scarman,[13] Lord Woolf,[14] Lord Bingham,[15] Lord Browne-Wilkinson,[16] Lord Hoffmann,[17] Mr

[11] Even though I do not foresee the American type of excesses coming to my country under the guise of human rights law. I thus do not share the apocalyptic picture painted by two colleagues, Professors Ewing and Gearty, in "Rocky Foundations for Labour's New Rights" [1997] *European Human Rights Law Review*, 146*ff*.

[12] On this see Mr Justice Gerald La Forest's essay "Who is Listening to Whom? The Discourse between the Canadian Judiciary and Academics" in *Law Making, Law, Finding and Law Shaping: The Diverse Influences* (ed. BS Markesinis) (1997), 69*ff*.

[13] His seminal Hamlyn Lectures, *English Law the New Dimension* (1974), could be credited for having started this whole debate in its contemporary form.

[14] *Protection of the Public: A New Challenge* (1990), Hamlyn Lectures. See, also, his FA Mann Lecture entitled "Droit Public—English Style" [1995] *Public Law* 57 *et seq.*

[15] "The European Convention on Human Rights: Time to Incorporate", The Denning Lecture, reprinted in *Human Rights in the United Kingdom* (ed. Richard Gordon and Richard Wilmot-Smith) (1996) pp. I–II; "Should there be a Law to Protect Rights of Personal Privacy?", [1996] *European Human Rights Law Review*, 450*ff*.

[16] "The Infiltration of a Bill of Rights" [1992] *Public Law*, pp. 397*ff*.

[17] "A Sense of Proportion" in *Community Law in English Courts* (F Jacobs and M Andenas eds) (1998).

Justice Laws[18] and Mr Justice Sedley[19] and, indeed, the current Lord Chancellor, Lord Irvine of Lairg,[20] have joined a growing number of academic writers in producing a stream of articles and public speeches, which draw heavily on the human rights material and often have a strong missionary tone about them. That their prescribed remedies differ is, of course, something that should be expected and, to the extent that it provokes wider debate, welcomed. But these differences have also resulted in the production of a literature which is comparative in outlook as it is jurisprudential (and, often, missionary) in tone. These are characteristics, which one would not normally associate with the work of English judges; and they could, with a minimum of good will, be expanded one day beyond human rights and Community law to include the study of foreign rules of a purely domestic character. Lords Goff[21] and Bingham[22] have, in fact, already taken this step; and the indications are that more judges are having their interest in foreign law awakened by this new material.[23]

2. IDEAS AND CASE LAW EMANATING FROM EUROPEAN NATIONAL SYSTEMS AND COURTS AND REFERRED TO BY ENGLISH COURTS

From my perspective as a comparative private lawyer this is an even more important recent development and one, which may even put my country ahead of most other countries[24] on the European Continent in terms of open-mindedness and intellectual curiosity.

[18] "The Ghost in the Machine: Principle in Public Law" [1989] *Public Law*, pp. 27*ff*.; "Is the High Court the Guardian of Fundamental Constitutional Rights?" [1993] *Public Law* pp. 59 *et seq*.; "Law and Democracy" [1995] *Public Law*, pp. 72 *et seq*.

[19] "The Sound of Silence: Constitutional Law Without a Constitution" (1994) 110 *Law Quarterly Review*, pp. 270 *et seq*. "Human Rights: A Twenty-First century Agenda" [1995] *Public Law*, pp. 386 *et seq*.

[20] "Judges and Decision-Makers: The Theory and Practice of *Wednesbury* Review", [1996] *Public Law*, 59*ff*.

[21] For instance in "Judge, Jurist and Legislature", (1988) 2 *Denning L Journal* 79; "Comparative Law: The Challenge to the Judges" in *Law Making, Law and Law Shaping: The Diverse Influences* (Markesinis ed.) (1997), 37*ff*. and, most recently, in his Wilberforce Lecture entitled "The Future of the Common Law", published in 46 *International and Comparative Law Quarterly* (1997), 745*ff*.

[22] "There is a World Elsewhere—The Changing Patterns of English Law" (1992) *International and Comparative Law Quarterly*, 513*ff*.

[23] See, for instance, the comments of Lord Woolf, Master of the Rolls, in his Foreword to my book *Foreign Law and Comparative Methodology: A Subject and a Thesis* (1977), vii–viii.

[24] Certainly Italy seems to lag behind England in the judicial use of foreign law. See Professor Taruffo's comments in "The Use of Comparative Law by Courts" in *Rapports Nationaux Italiens au X1Ve Congrès International de Droit Comparé, Athènes 1994*. (Giuffrè 1994.)

In this essay, I shall look at six leading cases[25] and make a few, brief, observations under three headings. First, I shall sketch the problems with which these cases were concerned. Secondly, I shall look at the legal issues they raised from a comparative angle. Finally, I shall put forward a few thoughts about how we should try and interest English courts in the foreign material (and, for clarity's sake, I repeat that my observations here are limited to private law cases which raise no conflict of laws issues). This sub-heading will appear on its own as paragraph 4 of this paper since it contains in summary form the basis of what I have been advocating for a very long time but also because it needs further refinement and improvement.

(a) Our six examples

Chronologically, the first important case of recent vintage is *Smith* v. *Littlewoods*.[26] The dispute was the result of vandals entering a disused cinema in the centre of a Scottish town without, apparently, the owner's knowledge. During one of these entries a fire was started, which spread to adjoining premises, causing damage to, *inter alia*, the plaintiff's property. The court took the view that the defendant owner of the "invaded" premises was not liable for the damage suffered by the plaintiff, owner of the adjoining premises, though the reasoning given by the two main judgments was not the same. Lord Mackay thus thought that liability could, on occasion, arise if the defendant's negligence was proved.[27] Lord Goff on the other hand took the view that this was a case of omission[28] and that liability could not be imposed under English law unless the facts of the case fell—which they did not in this instance—under one of the narrowly recognised list of exceptions.[29]

Kay v. *Robertson*[30] came next. This was a case of invasion of privacy. A well-known actor had been involved in an accident, which attracted the attention of the media. The defendant, the proprietor of a pornographic newspaper, sent his agents to "interview" the plaintiff. Pretending to be nurses, they gained access to the intensive care unit of the hospital where Mr Kay was being treated, photographed him using flash light (which was,

[25] But other examples do exist, for example, from Criminal law. See, for instance, *R. Reid* [1992] 1 WLR 793, 811. See, also the most recent decision of the Court of Appeal in *R.* v. *Chief Constable of the North Wales Police* [1998] 3 WLR 57.

[26] [1987] 1 AC 241.

[27] [1987] 1 AC 241, esp. 270.

[28] *Ibid.* at pp. 271 *et seq.*

[29] [1987] 1 AC 241, at pp. 272–3. *Cf.* BGH 23.10.1975, BGHZ 65, 221, 224 and Dalloz, *Répertoire de Droit Civil*, vol, vii, no 656 *et seq.*

[30] [1991] FSR 62; also reprinted in the Calcutt Report.

apparently, prohibited given the plaintiff's severe cranial injuries), and proceeded to take an interview of sorts with the semi-comatose plaintiff. An attempt to stop the publication of the picture and the interview failed, the plaintiff only gaining some minor concessions from the Court (e.g. a declaration that the interview and picture were published without his consent).

Woolwich Building Society v. *IRC*[31] came next. A Building Society paid money to the tax authorities pursuant to regulations issued by the Inland Revenue. It did so even though it questioned the legal validity of the said regulations. Subsequently, as a result of legal action taken by the Society, these regulations were declared to be *ultra vires* and the Revenue repaid the sums received. But the tax authorities refused to pay interest, which the plaintiffs claimed was payable from the moment these sums had been paid to the Revenue. The House of Lords, expanding existing categories of the Common law (which included recovery of sums paid under a mistake of fact or limited categories of compulsion) allowed the plaintiffs' claim where its payment had been made pursuant to an *ultra vires* demand by a public authority.

Henderson v. *Merrett*[32] is our fourth case. Its facts are extremely complicated to summarise here. Suffice it to say that: (a) the dispute arose because of the well-publicised economic crisis which hit Lloyds of London in the early nineties and (b) that the case raised the issue if and when a duty of tort could be excluded by the underlying contract which existed between the parties to the action.

White v. *Jones*[33] came close thereafter and, for our purposes, it is the next significant case. The dispute arose because a testator asked his solicitor to alter his will in a way that would benefit some of his descendants (whom he had excluded by a previous will). The solicitor negligently delayed to execute the instructions and the testator died before the alterations were effected. His estate thus devolved under the rules of intestacy and the disappointed beneficiaries claimed their loss from the negligent lawyer. Their action was successful.

Finally, in *Hunter* v. *Canary Wharf Ltd*[34] the action was in the tort of nuisance (the tort which, in the French terminology, regulates problems of neighbourhood). It was brought by the owners of small homes whose television receptions were seriously affected by the subsequent building of a very high tower block in the newly developed area of Canary Wharf, east of Central London. The actions failed.

[31] [1993] AC 70.
[32] [1994] 3 WLR 761.
[33] [1995] 2 WLR 187.
[34] [1997] 2 WLR 684.

(b) Their legal issues from a comparative angle

All these cases deal with factual configurations which have equivalents or close analogies in the modern civil law systems.[35] The French or German reader will notice them immediately, so copious citations are unnecessary. Thus, the *Kay* case has facts similar to those in the *Gérard Philippe* case;[36] one finds exact equivalents to *White* v. *Jones* in France[37] and Germany;[38] and *Hunter* finds a precise analogy in a decision of the German Federal Court Of 21 October 1983.[39] I have always maintained that finding exact factual equivalents facilitates the teaching of foreign law and the receptions of foreign ideas simply because it puts the foreign user of such material at ease. For, it takes him out of the theoretical and conceptual discussion, which is appropriate to one system but not to another, and puts him at a factual level where the similarity of the problems and the answers can be tested in a very tangible way. Often, the underlying policies pursued by the different systems can also be easily discovered hidden behind the conceptualism appropriate to each system and shown to be the same across national borders. This means that you can help put the external ideas into the kind of language and habit of mind that is acceptable to an English judge. The fact that British judges used foreign material in the above cases lends credence both to the idea and the suggestion made here (and repeated in the last paragraph of this essay). Equally, however, these are early days for this trend which I am here both describing and applauding. One must, therefore, be careful not to read too much in these first and tentative attempts to use foreign law.

Turning now to the results reached by the English courts we note some interesting variations from Continental case law, which in turn, can lead the teacher (and, at some subsequent date, perhaps another judge) to consider these differences further. We note, for instance that in *Henderson* Lord Goff considers the problem known in French law as "cumule des actions". Thus, after accepting what some British authors have called the "elegance" of French law[40] and also attempting a brief *tour d'horizon* of Australian and New Zealand law,[41] the learned judge reached the conclusion that

[35] Compare, for instance, *Smith* v. *Littlewoods Ltd* to BGH 3.2.1987, VersR 1987, 1096. The German action, based on what we would call the torts of Negligence (para. 823 1 BGB) and Nuisance. (para. 906. 2 BGB), also failed.

[36] Paris 14 mars 1965, JCP 1965, II, 14223.

[37] Thus, see, Dalloz, *Jurisprudence* 1979, 19242 Cass civ. 23 Nov. 1977; *Jurisprudence* 1982, 19728, Cass civ. 14 Jan. 1981.

[38] BGH 6 July 1965, NJW 1965, 1955.

[39] BGH 21.10.1983, BGHZ 88, 344.

[40] Weir, *International Encyclopaedia of Comparative Law*, vol xi, chap. 12, para. 55.

[41] Especially on pages 786–7.

". . . in the present context, the common law is not antipathetic to concurrent liability, and that there is no sound basis for a rule which automatically restricts the claimant to either a tortious or contractual remedy. The result may be untidy; but given that the tortious duty is imposed by the general law, and the contractual duty is attributable to the will of the parties, I do not find it objectionable that the claimant may be entitled to take advantage of the remedy which is most advantageous to him, subject only to ascertaining whether the tortious duty is inconsistent with the applicable contract . . ."[42] The citation and, indeed, the judgment as a whole, form an excellent tool for a comparative discussion of the French and German attitudes towards this problem of concurrence of actions as well as of the underlying causes (limitation periods,[43] exclusion clauses, as well as structural deficiencies in Codes etc.[44]) which have led foreign lawyers and judges to allow litigants to get out of contract into tort or vice versa. Incidentally, Lord Goff was aware of the German approach, which he (rightly) added appears to have caused "no perceptible harm"[45] to the German system.

While in *Henderson* the result thus went the German rather than French way, in *Kay* the solution reached by the Court of Appeal—it should be stressed with great regret—showed English law to be different from both French and German law. The comparison of the respective case law has been attempted by this author[46] elsewhere so we shall add nothing more here. It is, however, worth stressing two features of that case.

Thus one must first note how English judges try to use (if not abuse) existing torts, usually devised to protect persons from physical interference or land from different types of intrusions, to protect human personality and privacy. This method, close to the English mentality (found in both private and public law), that the best way to tackle new problems is not to devise new institutions but to pervert existing ones, does not, however, always achieve satisfactory results as the *Kay* judgment clearly shows. Secondly, the *Kay* case, especially when compared with the French and German case law, reveals English courts at their most timid, wishing for legislative intervention to extricate them from their present difficulties. By contrast, the French arid German law on this subject is based on cases, which have prag-

[42] [1994] 3 WLR 788.

[43] On which see Professor Andrew Burrows' inaugural lecture "Solving the Problem of Concurrent Liability," (1995) *Current Legal Problems* 103*ff*.

[44] In Germany in particular the restrictive provision of para. 831 BGB which makes employers liable for the harm caused by their servants only in cases where the employers have been guilty of culpa *in eligendo* or *vigilando* has pushed German courts into enlarging the area of application of contract law in order to take advantage of the wider rule contained in para. 278 BGB. For details on this see Markesinis *The German Law of Obligations*, v. *II*, *the Law of Torts*, 3rd ed. with corrections and additions (1997) pp. 686 *et seq*.

[45] [1994] 3 WLR at p. 779.

[46] Thus, see "Our Patchy Law of Privacy—Time to do Something about it" 53 *Modern Law Review* (1990) pp. 802 *et seq*. as well as the articles reprinted in my *Foreign Law and Comparative Methodology: A Subject and a Thesis* (1997).

matically, and on a case by case basis, handled this complex new problem. One would have, therefore, thought that there is plenty more room here for comparative work and inspiration.

Space prevents us from attempting a similar sketch of the other decisions mentioned here even though they can all be used as springboards for further exploration of foreign law. Thus, to give but one last illustration, the difference between English law on the one hand and almost all the other systems on the other on the question whether tortious liability should be imposed for culpable omissions can—and, indeed, has been—the subject of many articles, books and, even, colloquia.[47] But the point that I would like to raise for some future discussion is a different one, namely, do the foreign systems, which impose a civil liability for inactivity, really enforce this philosophy through their courts? Are people really sued (civilly and criminally) for failing to help endangered fellow citizens? Are such actions brought with any discernible consistency? And have they finally achieved their proclaimed educational role? Discussions of this topic have tended, I think, to be limited to the philosophical or legalistic position adopted by a particular system but have not, to my knowledge, yet shown how the different systems work in practice.

3. INTERESTING THE COURTS IN FOREIGN LAW AND COMPARATIVE METHODOLOGY

The citation and use of foreign legal material in *purely*[48] private law matters by English courts is a new phenomenon. Like the case law, which deals with the European Convention, and to which we alluded in the first part of this essay, it really is not older than ten years or so. Moreover, it is associated with a few only of our most senior judges such as Lords Bingham, Goff, Steyn, and Cook. The way these judges have used foreign law has also, on the whole, been limited to re-enforcing a decision based on purely Common law material and reached through the usual common law ways of reasoning. Finally, one should add that more often than not, the use of the Continental European material has been accompanied by understandable pronouncements about the dangers which accompany the use of foreign law.[49] Yet despite all these limitations and caveats, this phenomenon

[47] See, for instance, *The Good Samaritan and the Law* (ed. J Ratcliffe, 1966).

[48] I use the term to refer to the six types of cases which I discussed earlier on but, in reality it is not an exact term since many "private" law cases are increasingly affected by the Convention or by other principles of constitutional law—a phenomenon which I once described as the "constitutionalisation of private law". The *Derbyshire* case, discussed in several sections of this essay is a good example of this view trend.

[49] Thus, in *White* v. *Jones* [1995] 2 WLR 187, 202 he said: "I hesitate to embark in an opinion such as this upon a comparison, however brief, with a civil law system; because experience has taught me how very difficult, and indeed potentially misleading, such an exercise

arguably marks the beginning of a trend, which is *real, new, original* and one, which should be *encouraged*. I have italicised a number of words in this last sentence because I think they bear a very important significance.

This trend is thus first *real* in the sense that though the judicial decisions which have included references to foreign law may not exceed one dozen in all they evince a distinct interest of some of our most imaginative judges in things European in general. I believe this conclusion is supportable because of the growing number of extra-judicial pronouncements, speeches, lectures that these (and other judges already mentioned) have made in recent times.[50] Taken as a whole, therefore, the volume of material is significant, and it is even impressive in so far as it suggests a slow change in judicial mentality. Indeed, we must not forget that the new judicial trend to take more active account of the European Convention both in Human Rights law and our administrative law more generally was, largely, *foreshadowed* by such extra-judicial writings, starting with Lord Scarman's Hamlyn Lectures. The judges, who first expressed these views extra-judicially, then came back to them in an official capacity (or, again, extra-judicially in order to refine them); and few would deny that this trend is here to stay.

Now, while it would be too facile to ignore the fact that the "European invasion" has occurred mainly in the area of Human Rights, administrative law, and European Community law, it would be wrong to ignore the fact that English law as a whole is influenced by all these factors and is thus, understandably, faced with new challenges. No doubt, in *pure* private law matters this challenge and this trend are still in their infancy. Yet, as stated earlier on, the incorporation of the Convention will increasingly and openly affect almost all branches of our domestic law and, in my view, generate its own dynamics for further Europeanisation of other parts of our law.

As stated, this internationalist trend is not only real; it is new, at least by reference to judicial attitudes, which have prevailed during this century. One thus has to go back to the 18th century (Mansfield) or the latter half of the 19th century (Blackburn, Jessel, Wills) to find such internationally minded judges as the ones we have today (though the interests of the earlier generations lay mainly in Roman law and the *lex mercatoria*). Individual characteristics apart, however, one has to note that this new trend is under-

can be". Further down, however he added—and this is crucial for the concluding remarks of this essay—"Exceptionally, however, . . . thanks to material published in our language . . . we have direct access to publications which should sufficiently dispel our ignorance of German law and so by comparison illuminate our understanding of our own." *Ibid.*, 202.

[50] In fact this tendency has alarmed the current Lord Chancellor sufficiently to lead him (while he was still shadow Lord Chancellor) to fire a warning shot across the bows of such judicial prolixity. See his "Judges and Decision-Makers: The Theory and Practice of *Wednesbury* Review" [1066] *Public Law* pp. 59 *et seq.* as well as his speech in the House of Lords of 5th June 1996, HL 50 Deb, vol 572, cols, 1254–1313.

standable since our current judges have been active in an era of intense European debates, enhanced European travel, and increased European contacts.[51] The fact that in the years to come our judiciary will be drawn increasingly from the ranks of students who have studied European law, studied law in Europe, and (probably) had enhanced business contacts with European clients during the practising phase of their careers, can only help strengthen these tendencies further and decrease the Europhobia which some of our politicians of the Right have in recent times so irresponsibly tried to encourage.

The trend is, finally, original in that I, at least, have not encountered it (or encountered it to such an extent in the purely private law sphere) in either Germany or France. Though I cannot claim to have attempted for the purpose of this article a thorough, lexis-type search of judicial decisions for these two jurisdictions, my feeling is that in neither do we find similar references to foreign law (outside their own legal family). To be true, the statement would have to be qualified as far as French law is concerned by the proviso that to be meaningful the search would have to be extended to include the opinions of the Advocate Generals and the *arrêtistes* rather than be limited to the decisions of the highest courts which are notoriously opaque as to the sources which have influenced their decisions.[52] But German decisions, which are longer and much more explicit than the French, confirm my gut feeling. I can thus recall only five judgments of the *Bundesgerichtshof*[53] where references have been made to Anglo-American material though, obviously, more frequent references can be found to Austrian and Swiss cases and academic writings emanating from these Germanic systems. If I am right in this assertion, then my courts are leading in this field and claims to the effect that "... countries like the United Kingdom ... *are much less open* to genuinely foreign

[51] Particularly noteworthy was a judicial conference of British and German judges organised in Germany a few years ago by Professor Christian von Bar. An account of its proceedings can be found in 58 *RabelsZ* (1994) pp. 421–464.

[52] Though at the aforementioned Meeting of the International Academy of Comparative Law in Athens in 1994 Professor Légeais was reported to have claimed an "increased frequency of references to comparative law by French courts, particularly the Court of cassation ...". See Professor Fatouros' "Summary of the Session" reproduced at the end of Drobnig, *op.cit.*, note 3, above, at p. 86.

[53] BGH 18.1.1983, BGHZ 86, 240 = JZ 1983, 447 = JuS 1984, 434. (Wrongful life and wrongful birth action; references to English and Californian law); BGH 27.2.1992, NJW 1992, 1463, 1466–7 (rule against self incrimination in criminal law; references to American, English, French, Dutch, Italian and Austrian law); BGH 30.6.1987, BGHZ, 101, 215, 223 (causation/rescue doctrine; references to American law); BGH 23.5.1984, BGHZ, 32, 345, 352 and 356 (criminal prosecution, doctrine of entrapment; references to American, English and Austrian law); BGH 16.9.1987, BGHZ, 101, 337, 342–3 (breach of contract; references to Uniform Commercial Code and to American law through the work of Professor Schlechtriem). A fuller and more systematic presentation of the German material can be found in Drobnig, "The Use of Foreign Law by German Courts" in *German National Reports in Civil Law Matters for the XIXth Congress of Comparative Law in Athens 1994* (1994) pp. 5–24.

law . . ."[54] may need to be toned down. In any event, the picture I have attempted to describe is something of a paradox given the Europhobic image which my country has on the European Continent—one among many other paradoxes, which I said in a French *Festschrift*[55]—one encounters when studying foreign law.

Finally, this trend must be encouraged. From what I have said it is obvious why I believe this; and, again, I feel, the senior judiciary of my country is openly giving me this encouragement.[56] The problem is how we do this, and to this last and important topic I devote the few remaining paragraphs of this essay.

To answer this question one must remember that the real creators of English law are its judges. They always were and still are, though the ascendancy of the legislator and the increased volume of statutory law has provoked much discussion as of late. However significant this trend for more legislation may be, for our purposes trying to make legislators sensitive to foreign ideas is a thankless task. Indeed, I would, with few exceptions apart, also add that it is useless since legislators rarely act where there are no votes.[57] With legislators then "out of the way", one is left with the judge as the only *effective* receiver and subsequent communicator of new ideas.[58]

The idea that you can inspire the judge to innovate through learned monographs or voluminous treatises died in me thirty years ago when I crossed the Channel. For the English judge is, in this sense, very different from the German or the Greek. This is not because the German judge has more time to read his legal literature than his English counterpart has but because the former *has* to inform himself of the law and the various arguments in favour and against applying it to the facts before him. The European judge has thus been deprived of the invaluable research and other supportive services which the English barrister gives to his judge. But, useful though barristers have been to British judges, traditionally one did not expect (nor obtained) from them *ideas* that were derived from any source other than the constant distillation of previous case law. Thus, until recently, one rarely expected English barristers to cite academic literature, have recourse to foreign law, or be inspired by such "external" legal documents as the Convention for new ways of presenting their case. The

[54] Drobnig, *op.cit.*, note 3, above, at p. 83. Emphasis added.

[55] *Mélanges Christian Mouly* (1997), under the title "Les paradoxes dans la loi".

[56] See, for instance, Lord Woolf's Foreword to my recent book *Foreign Law and Comparative Methodology: A Subject and a Thesis* (1997), pp. vii–viii.

[57] The spectacular inactivity towards the vast majority of Law Commission proposals, procured at great public expense and waste or much intellectual effort supports the assertion in the text.

[58] By contrast, the German legislator, both during the 19th century and during ours, has made frequent use of the comparative method. On this see, *inter alia*, Drobnig, "Die Nutzung der Rechtsvergleichung durch den deutschen Gesetzgeber", *RabelsZ* 46 (1982) pp. 253–307.

Derbyshire litigation offers an excellent illustration since it demonstrates how for decades its facts were seen as raising nothing more than technical points connected with the law of defamation and precedent.

Carter Ruck on *Libel and Slander*, for decades the bible of defamation lawyers, underscores the point. The question whether a local authority had the right to maintain an action for damages in defamation in respect of its governmental and administrative reputation was thus seen as depending on two old, and contradictory, tort cases and was resolved on the most technical of arguments: the dicta of the highest authority prevailed.[59] The free speech aspects of the case were not noticed by any practitioners' treatise[60] and only one academic author raised the issue[61] to get short shrift by the judge at First Instance in *Derbyshire*[62] because he had done so in his inimitable, stimulating personal style. Then came the judgment of the Court of Appeal with its invocation of Article 10 of the Convention.[63] The tort case suddenly acquired constitutional dimensions (as twenty five years earlier the famous American decision of *New York Times* v. *Sullivan*[64] had done for USA law) and, as a result our law of defamation may be on course for more changes than the books on the subject have yet been able to predict.[65] Our entire law of defamation may thus be on the verge of an unprecedented reformulation of its basic principles in the light of foreign influences.

The way to effect change—foreign-inspired change—is thus to make judges aware that foreign law provides new ideas and new approaches to old and new problems alike. If this "awareness" can be induced through Counsel (as was the case in *White* v. *Jones*) so be it; if it comes about through contacts with academics at the Inns of Court (as happened with the late Sir Arthur Goodhart, one of those few academics who had exercised a great influence on British judges) that is acceptable, as well. Or if it can be done through personal connections with foreign academics or judges that, too, will come to be accepted.[66] And I say this because I believe that the intellectual curiosity of the new type of judge coupled with an unparalleled willingness also to try his hand on the lecturing circuit will make this receptivity greater than ever before. I stress this belief of mine because

[59] *Libel and Slander* (4th ed. 1992), p. 73.

[60] For instance, Gatley, *Libel and Slander* (8th ed. 1981) §§ 958, 9; Clark and Lindsell *On Torts* (16th ed. 1989), §§ 2–43, 21–181, 21, 25.

[61] Weir, "*Local Authority* v. *Critical Ratepayer*—A Suit in Defamation" (1972) CLJ, 238.

[62] *Derbyshire County Council* v. *Times Newspapers* [1992] 770 at 785.

[63] Especially by Balcombe and Butler Sloss LJJs.

[64] 376 US 254 (1964).

[65] Another defamation case *Rantzen* v. *Mirror Group Newspapers* [1994] QB 670 confirms the above as it displays a tendency to use the Convention beyond the resolution of ambiguities in primary or subordinate legislation.

[66] Lord Goff has admitted to such contact on at least two public occasions. Thus, see his Wilberforce lecture and his contribution to the Second Clifford Chance lectures. Those of us who have helped create such contacts would now wish to see them work in the reverse direction as well!

I have followed carefully and with keen interest the growing interest which some of our very best judges have been developing in foreign and comparative law. And I expect them to continue on this path as our new Bill of Rights will force them to consider matters (such as the idea of the *Drittwirkung die Grundrechte*), which has a long pedigree in Germany but has not yet captured the imagination of the English lawyers. Of course, such new trends will put the full-time comparatists under a special responsibility: to supply the relevant material to their judges in an easily digestible way. This means more than finding it and translating it; but it also means another article![67]

[67] Some of my ideas on this can be found in my *Foreign Law and Comparative Methodology: A Subject and a Thesis* (1997).

3

The Familiarity of the Unknown

1. INTRODUCTORY REMARKS

Foreign implies unknown; and we often make the mistake of assuming that unknown means different, even bad and dangerous. One should not be afraid of differences. For real differences, be they in language, aesthetic values, or the law, provide the kind of contrasts and yardsticks which allow one to understand and rethink one's own ideas, rules, and institutions and, on occasion, be converted to the alien ones. Take ancient Rome, medieval Granada, the Renaissance, and nineteenth-century Britain. They all show that the quality of any civilisation can be seen not only by its indigenous products but also by its ability to graft new shoots on its own trunk to stimulate new growth and achieve richer and more differentiated products. The willingness to look elsewhere and to borrow is thus a sign of strength and confidence of a particular society and not of weakness. Yet in our law, especially during the twentieth century, differences—real or perceived—have tended to frighten lawyers away from foreign legal systems. The reasons for such an attitude could be many: innate conservatism, lack of time to study the foreign material, or a realistic appraisal of the (undoubted) difficulties of using foreign law in their own setting.

The learned judge honoured by this volume has always been aware of the difficulties of using foreign law in his daily work;[1] but his intellectual curiosity, which has also made him an erudite jurist, has also led him to

[1] Thus, in *White* v. *Jones* [1995] 2 AC 207, 263, he said: "I hesitate to embark in an opinion such as this upon a comparison, however brief, with a civil law system; because experience has taught me how very difficult, and indeed potentially misleading, such an exercise can be." However, he then went on to say why such an exercise is worthwhile provided certain conditions have been satisfied. He thus added: "Exceptionally however . . . thanks to material published in our language . . . we have direct access to publications which should sufficiently dispel our ignorance of German law and so by comparison illuminate our understanding of our own." In an excellent monograph entitled *Using Human Rights Law in English Courts* (Oxford, 1997), Murray Hunt has thus encapsulated perfectly the challenge, which full-time comparatists face in Britain today. "The problem", he argued (at p. 260), "is one of legal culture, and in particular the predominant tendency of English judges to absorb any external influences into familiar habits of mind." If comparatists manage to serve foreign law in a digestible way, its use by English courts is destined to rise in matters of pure private law as it has in the areas of human rights, administrative law, and Community law.

take a great interest in foreign, especially modern, civilian systems. This tendency has increasingly become a hallmark of his judicial[2] and extra-judicial[3] work; and in his list of contributions to the science of law it must rank second only to the unique role he has played in the creation of an English law of Unjust Enrichment. It is thus appropriate that Lord Goff's interest in foreign law and comparative methodology should be noted in a Festschrift published in his honour even if this present tribute, by force of circumstances, is bound to be inadequate.

What I would like to do in this short essay is to suggest that the study of foreign law often reveals interesting paradoxes. The type of paradox I would like to highlight lies in the fact that often foreign systems, which here should be taken to refer mainly to the modern German and French legal systems—have displayed the kind of characteristics which we associate with the common law but not with them. Indeed, my thesis will be that at times the civilian systems have displayed these features even more emphatically than the common law has done in comparable situations. Indeed, in the situations that will be examined in this essay, the (English and American) common law will be shown to have displayed the type of attitudes and characteristics that its lawyers commonly attribute to the modern civil law. If this is true in the cases mentioned in this essay—and it is submitted that the observations contained here apply to a much wider range of situations—then the fear of consulting foreign law because of the perils of the unknown should be diminished. For the unknown will soon prove to be more familiar than hitherto imagined; and familiarity will not breed contempt but excite interest and, even, inspire the outside observer. This, then, is an essay on legal paradoxes of a certain kind. I shall call them "constructive paradoxes" since their revelation and understanding does not lead to estrangement and division but encourages *rapprochement* and understanding.

The identification of these (legal) paradoxes is, at first instance, best left to comparatists. For comparatists, accustomed to looking at legal phenomena from a wider angle, are, it would seem, well placed to notice these oddities, probe them and perhaps even explain their existence more easily. For, unlike national lawyers, who may treat such phenomena as part and parcel of their everyday life and leave them unquestioned, the comparatist

[2] The examples where he has referred to foreign systems include the following cases: *Smith* v. *Littlewoods Corp* [1987] AC 241 at 271; *R* v. *Reid* [1992] 1 WLR 793, 811; *Woolwich Equitable Building Society* v. *IRC* [1993] AC 70 at 174; *Henderson* v. *Merrett Syndicates Ltd* [1995] 2 AC 145 at 184, 193–4; *White* v. *Jones* [1995] 2 AC 207, 254–5, 262–4; *Hunter* v. *Canary Wharf Ltd* [1997] AC 655, 686.

[3] Thus, see "Some Comparative Reflections", in BS Markesinis (ed.), *The Gradual Convergence: Foreign Ideas, Foreign Influences and English Law on the Eve of the 21st Century* (1994), pp. 128 *ff.*; "Comparative Law: The Challenge to the Judges" in *Law Making, Law Shaping and Law Finding*, The Clifford Chance Lectures, vol. 11, ed. BS Markesinis (1997); and, most recently, in his 1997 Wilberforce Lecture "The Future of the Common Law" (1997) 46 ICLQ 745.

will be struck by their very existence and feel the need to explain them. In this essay I shall focus on five such paradoxes—three taken from French law and two from German, which I shall then compare to English and American law. What they have in common is that they all deal with fairly narrow legal institutions or rules, which on the whole produce fairly similar answers. Yet these instances reveal more than a similarity in results. For they suggest that the foreign systems are not as structurally and methodologically different from ours as we have always been led to believe. Realising this fundamental point may, in the fullness of time, help us approach foreign systems in a different mood. For we need, I think, to encourage the study of the law in a way which helps bring us together rather than perpetuates divisions of the past. Our times demand nothing less.

2. OUR FIVE PARADOXES

For our first paradox we have to go back one hundred years.

The 1880s were an important decade across Europe. In Germany, for instance, the social legislation of Bismarck was completed, soon afterwards generating considerable interest among lawyers in New York. In France, too, 1888 proved an important year since the *Cour de Cassation*, in the case of *Depress c Wannenbroucq*[4] was forced to grapple with the problem of the life insurance contract. Article 1121 of the *Code Civil* did not offer much help given that it allowed the "beneficiary" to sue directly the *promettant* only if the *stipulant* had a (pecuniary) interest in the performance of the promise. Taken literally, as was the practice of that time, he had not. But the *Cour de Cassation* adopted a more flexible interpretation of the wording of the Code by accepting that a *profit morale* was sufficient. As Colin, Capitant, and Juillot de la Morandière pointed out later in their classic treatise:[5] "It would be impossible in our view to find in the case reports the trace of a single decision in which a stipulation for the benefit of a third party has been held invalid as being contrary to Articles 1119 and 1121 of the Civil Code."

Thus, the French courts managed to transform what was, clearly, meant to be an exception to the rule of privity into the rule, itself, providing one of the best examples of judicial creativity at the height of nineteenth-century positivism.

A comparable but not identical innovation had taken place in England six years earlier; and the same social problem—the need to validate life insurance contracts—also lay behind the English developments. But in England it was the legislator who brought about the change in the

[4] Cass civ 16 Janvier 1888. S 1888.1.121.

[5] *Cours élémentaire de droit civil français*, Dalloz 10th edn. (1948), No 204.

law[6] and did so using slightly more words than the French judges had done, though nowhere near as verbosely as the most recent attempt by the Law Commission to dilute the English doctrine of privity.[7]

Our second paradox is of the same kind but this time it comes from the comparison of English and German company law. Thus, in our country, for well over a century the rule in *Foss* v. *Harbottle*[8] supported the proposition that English courts are not allowed to become involved in internal conflicts between shareholders or minority shareholders on the one hand and directors on the other. Only a limited number of exceptions to this rule were allowed, among them the right to apply for a winding up of the company (or against a decision of the meeting of shareholders) on the ground that it was contrary to law or the Articles of Association. This position was changed by section 210 of the Companies Act 1948 (now sections 459–61 of the Companies Act 1985) which, *inter alia*, gave shareholders the right to apply to a court for (appropriate) relief for such matters as mistreatment, misuse of company assets, oppression, etc.[9] Thus, in our law, the alteration of the legal position concerning "internal conflicts" was, yet again, largely achieved through the intervention of the legislator.

By contrast, in German law the position that there exists a special *Rechtsverhältnis* (legal relationship) which gives rise to mutual rights and duties (*Treuepflichten* = fiduciary duties) between shareholders enforceable by courts was reached through decisional law. Thus, the first stirrings in favour of minority rights can be found in a decision of the *Reichsgericht* of 1931.[10] The real turning point, however, came with the famous *ITT* decision of the *Bundesgerichtshof* of 5 June 1975,[11] which set in train

6 See s. 11 of the Married Women's Property Act 1882.

7 The proposed Bill contained in the Law Commission's most recent (and learned) Report (Law Comm no 242 of 1996), consists of seven long clauses, which run to 165 printed lines.

8 (1843) 2 Hare 461.

9 For details see R Pennington, *Company Law*, 7th edn. (London, 1995), chap. 17, esp. pp. 885*ff*.

10 RG 31.3.1931, RGZ 132, 149, 163. The next important step was taken by BGH 9.6.1954. BGHZ, 14, 25, 38.

11 BGHZ 65, 15. The defendant owned two companies. The first—company X—was a service company wholly owned by him, which provided services to some 300 other companies. In the second company—a *Gesellschaft mit beschränkter Haftung* (GmbH)—he was the majority owner and the plaintiff was the minority owner to the tune of 15%. The main purpose of the *GmbH* was to manage two *Kommandit-Gesellschaften* (henceforth *KGs*) in which the *GmbH* owned the majority of the capital while the plaintiff owned the minority. The defendant used his influence as majority owner of the *GmbH* to persuade the two *KGs* to enter into a highly profitable service agreement with company X. The plaintiff, who as stated was minority owner of the *GmbH* and of the two *KGs*, complained that the defendant had misused his power as majority holder of the *GmbH* to achieve this result (which benefited his other company, X). As the law then stood, a minority partner could not force the *KGs* to claim the over-payment to company X (on grounds of unjustified enrichment). Nor could he sue in his own right (for his own, indirect, loss as partner of the *KGs*) since in tort pure economic loss is not recoverable under §823 1 BGB. Nevertheless the BGH, creating the aforementioned *Treuepflichten* between partners of *GmbH* companies, allowed such a claim against the defen-

the development of a whole range of new rights given to one partner (and, later, shareholder) against another. The impression one gets from this case law is that in its results it is at least as supple as that which flows from the discretion which the British statute has given to its judges.[12] This example thus shows that civilian systems rely regularly on their courts (and not their parliaments) for (both) the updating and the significant reorientation of their law in order to meet new needs in their rapidly changing societies. Moreover, this judicial activity is not limited to matters of contract and tort but runs across the whole range of private law including family law and, as our example shows, company law as well.

The third paradox took rather longer to take shape. In France it started in 1895,[13] when two decisions of the *Chambre Civile* of the *Cour de Cassation* and the *Chambre de Requêtes*[14] decided to improve the lot of widows whose husbands had died in industrial accidents by introducing a form of strict liability. The judicial intervention was prompted by the growth of industrialisation and the corresponding need to tackle the legal consequences of what became known as the *accidents anonymes de travail* where proving the fault of the defendant/employer was almost impossible in practice. The French legislator, paralysed until that moment by internal political problems, intervened soon after these seminal judgments were handed down and put the problem of accidents at work on a statutory basis. But a new social problem—increasing car accidents—gave the courts the chance to have a second bite at the cherry and reintroduce in an expanded form strict liability into a Code which was, for all intents and purposes, squarely based on the fault principle. The turning point came in 1931 when a young girl, Lise Jand'heur, proved a tenacious enough litigant to push the *Chambres Réunies* to hand down its homonymous, historic judgment which was based on the unpromising few words of Article 1384 CC. Despite eloquent

dant/majority owner of the *GmbH*. Some ten years later the new *Treuepflichten* were, again through court activity, extended to shareholders of *Aktiengesellschaften*. See BGH 1.2.1988, BGHZ 103, 184 and, most recently, BGH 20.3.1995, BGHZ 129, 136.

[12] On the whole subject see Lutter and Hommelhoff, *Kommentar zum GmbH-Gesetz*, 14th edn. (1995), para. 14 GmbHG, Rn 15*ff*. I am grateful to Professor Lutter for alerting me to this interesting (but complex) case law which he has discussed, not only in his *magnum opus* cited in this note but also in numerous Arts. which have appeared in the periodical literature: See *AcP* 1980, 84, 115, 117; ZHR 1989, 464*ff*., JZ 1995, 1053.

[13] An earlier Belgian attempt, initiated by a courageous puisne judge, fizzled out by the early twentieth century. For details see: Mazeaud and Mazeaud, *Leçons de droit civil* II, part 1, 6th edn. by F Chabas (1978), pp. 538*ff*.

[14] Cass 16 June 1896, DP 1897.1.433; Req 30 March 1897, S 18981.71 = DP 1897.1.441. The Conseil d'État, 21 June 1895, DP 1896.3.65 had, in fact, blazed the trail a year before the Cour de Cassation. An even earlier, and not dissimilar, attempt in Belgium to give independent status to the celebrated lines of Art. 1384 CC was overtaken by legislation (which then stunted all further growth of the law). See, Mazeaud and Mazeaud, *Leçons de droit civil*, II, part 1, 6th edn. by F Chabas (1978), pp. 538*ff*.

disapproval by some eminent academics,[15] further expansive efforts took place in 1964,[16] 1966,[17] and 1982—this last year being that of the famous *Desmares* decision,[18] which was soon thereafter supplemented by legislation. Thus, less than a century after it had begun, a legal heresy in an important part of private law had become the new orthodoxy; and it was the judges who had written and spread the new gospel.

In England, strict liability has taken a rather different and, some would say, sadder path. In 1862 one of the greatest judges of the common law—Blackburn J—facilitated its birth (or rebirth) with a judgment[19] which became famous not only for the boldness of its analogies but also because of the judge's strength of conviction.[20] But the boldness of one judge was undermined by the reserve of a successor;[21] and, most recently, the initiative was almost totally laid to rest by the judge we honour in this volume.[22] Indeed, Lord Goff, a keen student as we have seen of foreign law, even suggested that, if strict liability were to be introduced at all, it should be done by means of specifically devised statutes, each dealing with a particular kind of risk.[23] For the third time in his judicial career,[24] the great judge was thus going down a Germanic path;[25] though one cannot tell whether the imitation was in this case a conscious one or not.[26]

[15] E.g. Ripert, D 1930.1.59. The strange decision of the Court of Appeal of Grenoble of 4 Déc 1978, JCP 1980.2.19340, though not on Art. 1384 CC, very nearly vindicates Ripert's fears while showing how objectively *faute* is understood.

[16] Cass civ 18 Déc 1964, D 1965. J 191 and, esp. the conclusions of M Avocat Général Schmelck.

[17] Ch mixte 20 Déc 1968 (three decisions) D 1969, 37.

[18] D 1982. 449.

[19] *Rylands* v. *Fletcher* (1866) LR 1 Ex 265; (1868) LR 3 HL 330.

[20] See, Wigmore, *Selected Essays in the Law of Torts* (1924), 78 *ff.* See, also, Bohlen, *Studies in the Law of Torts* (1926), 359; Green, "Tort Law Public Law in Disguise", 38 *Texas L Rev* (1959), 1; Pound, "The Economic Interpretation of the Law of Torts", 53 *Harvard L Rev* (1940), pp. 365 *ff.* The best account is by Professor Simpson in "Bursting Reservoirs and Victorian Tort Law: *Rylands and Horrocks* v. *Fletcher*" (1868), repr in *Leading Cases in the Common Law* (1995), 163 *ff.*

[21] *Read* v. *J Lyons and Co Ltd* [1947] AC 156 at 168 per Lord Macmillan.

[22] Lord Goff in *Cambridge Water Co* v. *Eastern Counties Leather plc* [1994] 2 AC 264 at 305.

[23] [1994] 2 AC 264 at 305.

[24] Thus, see, *Leigh and Sillavan* v. *The Aliakmon Shipping Company Ltd* [1985] QB 350; *Henderson* v. *Merrett Syndicates Ltd* [1995] 2 AC 145; *Cambridge Water Co* v. *Eastern Counties Leather plc* [1994] 2 AC 264.

[25] The Germanic predilection for individually drafted statutes of strict liability is described in Markesinis, *The German Law of Torts: A Comparative Introduction*, 3rd edn. (1994), 692–720; but this approach is not without its critics. Thus, see Kötz, "Empfiehlt sich eine Vereinheitlichung und Zusammenfassung der gesetzlichen Vorschriften über die Gefährdungshaftung im BGB?" in *Gutachten und Vorschläge zur Überarbeitung des Schuldrechts* (1981), 1779.

[26] This author always treated Lord Goff's theory of "transferred loss" as an English adaptation of the German notion of *Schadensverlagerung*, which lies at the centre of the legal notion of *Drittschadensliquidation.* Most recently, however, Lord Goff has denied this extra-judicially and maintained that he became aware of the German notion only *after* he had shaped his own theory in *The Aliakmon.* On this see his "Comparative Law: The Challenge to the Judges", in BS Markesinis (ed.), *Law Making and Law Shaping: The Diverse Influences* (1997), chap. 3.

Our fourth paradox displays some of the features of the other two. We find it in the law of privacy, developed by the French courts on a case-by-case basis (often only faintly linked to Article 1382 CC) and then consolidated by the introduction of a typically laconic provision in the Civil Code.[27] Our courts, on the other hand, despite the fact that they had created the raw material which two famous American academics used to fashion a right of privacy,[28] remained faithful to their narrowly understood doctrine of precedent. The English belief that when new needs arise it is better to deal with them by perverting existing institutions rather than creating new ones has remained intact.[29] When the doubtful wisdom of this attitude was tested in a real case,[30] it was found to be sadly wanting. Thus, a strong Court of Appeal chose to complain about the state of English law, to imply that German law might be better but, in the end, also felt obliged to leave it to the legislator to do something to rectify the injustice. But our legislator is busy, as most legislators are; and in this instance it is also terrorised by our press, which sells papers (and thus makes money) by publicising the misfortunes of others. So many of us feel that our law on the subject lags behind that of France and Germany with academics being the only champions of those who see their lives ruined by a sleazy press.[31]

The fifth and final paradox is a complex one and difficult to analyse within the confines of a *Festschrift* contribution. Yet it may well be one which will be with us for years to come as our courts come to grapple with our new Human Rights legislation. In any event, it deserves to be mentioned briefly, if only to show that my thesis of "constructive paradoxes" developed here straddles the public/private law divide (to the extent that it still holds out the appeal that it once did). The paradoxical features of the phenomenon in fact become obvious if we look at it first from a theoretical or dogmatic point of view and then study it as it appears in litigated cases. So, let us turn to theory first.

German jurists, those acknowledged masters of the elaborate dogmatic structure, have a notion known as *die Drittwirkung der Grundrechte*. Rendering the notion into English as "the third-party effect of constitutional rights" makes the underlying idea marginally more intelligible but if anything, less acceptable. For we all know that Human Rights were developed to protect individuals against state intrusions and that, therefore, they were

27 Art. 9 Code Civil.

28 Warren and Brandeis, "The Right to Privacy", 4 *Harvard L Rev* 193 (1890).

29 Yet this does not always work, as the speeches in the House of Lords showed in *Hunter* v. *Canary Wharf* [1997] AC 655 when dealing with the majority judgments in *Khorasandjian* v. *Bush* [1993] QB 727. Interestingly enough, the social problem which led the Court of Appeal to twist the tort of nuisance in order to protect privacy was taken care of by the subsequent, narrowly conceived Harassment Act 1997.

30 *Kay (Gordon)* v. *Andrew Robertson and Sports Newspapers Ltd* [1991] FSR 62.

31 On this see the collection of essays published under the title *Protecting Privacy*, *The Clifford Chance Lectures* vol. IV, ed. BS Markesinis (1998).

designed to work in a "vertical" manner. Giving them a "horizontal" effect, so as to enable them to regulate the relations between private entities as well, runs the risk of undermining private autonomy on which our private law has for so long been based. Any talk about "privatising Human Rights"[32] thus poses serious philosophical problems, especially for those who believe that the state should interfere as little as possible with private autonomy. But this debate need not be pursued further. For it is clear that any investigation along these lines is bound to drag us into inconclusive discussions of a jurisprudential and political character. This is not, of course, to deny their interest or validity. But it is unlikely to lead to the discovery of information that an English practitioner or judge would wish to use in court and it is the latter that has always attracted my attention as a comparative lawyer anxious to demystify his subject.

Yet, despite these difficulties and dangers, an attempt must be made to understand the Germanic material. For, once the new Human Rights legislation is in force, the originality and *relevance* of the German ideas will prove indisputable.[33] This is particularly true of the aspect of the problem that concerns me here. For "It would, indeed, be a poor sort of 'incorporation' which exempted private individuals and bodies from respecting the fundamental rights of their fellow-citizens and drove them back to Strasbourg with all its costs in time and money—the very evil which 'incorporation' is supposed to remedy."[34] So the horizontality issue, which is what the *Drittwirkung* debate is all about, will be one of the more thorny ones to confront our judges once the new legislation begins to affect our case law. It is, however, equally undeniable that this (Germanic) material will be difficult for common lawyers (and not only English but also American common lawyers) to assimilate. That is why I think it is important to cast aside, at least in the beginning, the theoretical debates about autonomy and ask whether the *Drittwirkung* phenomenon can be found, in substance if not by name, even in those systems which appear to be totally incompatible with its underlying notions. The system that, therefore, cries for comparison with the German is that of the United States. For if the idea (if not the methodology) can be found in the most market-orientated country in the world then, perhaps, our conservative ideologists might not have to worry too much about its adoption in our own country.

[32] The expression belongs to Andrew Clapham, who is one of the few British lawyers to address the problem of horizontality with much originality—most recently in "The Privatisation of Human Rights" (1996) 1 EHRLIZ 20.

[33] See my "Privacy, Freedom of Speech and the Horizontality of the Human Rights Bill" *1998 Wilberforce Lecture*, 115 (1996) LQR 47*ff*. See also "The Applicability of Human Rights as between Individuals under German Constitutional Law" (with Dr Stefan Enchelmaier), in BS Markesinis (ed.), *Protecting Privacy* (1998), chap. 8.

[34] Sir William Wade, "Human Rights and the Judiciary", Judicial Studies Board *Annual Lecture 1998*, 5.

In my opinion a glance at both systems goes some way towards making my thesis plausible if not acceptable to all. For it reveals speech disputes that arose in a private employment relationship that raise the same issues and achieved (or came close to achieving) analogous results. Thus, in both instances, the plaintiffs/employees indulged in a political activity that did not meet with the approval of their (private) employers. Both the employers' attempts to dismiss the employees was countered by the argument that such an action would, in the *final* analysis, conflict with basic Human Rights enshrined in the Constitutions of the two countries.

It was, *precisely*, this kind of factual setting that in Germany launched the expression *unmittelbare Drittwirkung* (*direct* third-party effect)[35] in the sense that the Human Rights Articles of the Constitution *directly* governed such disputes. The idea was laudable; the means used to implement it went too far. Four years later in a seminal judgment the Constitutional Court[36] adopted a more subtle variant propounding the view that Constitutional provisions had a "radiating effect" (*Ausstrahlungswirkung*) on private law, "influencing" rather than "directly governing" its relationships. Much ink has flowed in America[37] to show that—rightly or wrongly, this is not the point here—the parallel American doctrine of "state action", extended to its furthest[38] reach in *Shelley* v. *Kraemer*,[39] comes close to the German doctrine. Yet whatever may be the right answer the fact is that a *few* American courts, in the context of the factual situation here examined, have had little difficulty in adopting a *basic* stance which is very similar to the one found in Germany. What is interesting about this case law is that it allowed the constitutional law to penetrate the private law dispute not through the "state action" doctrine but through another amorphous notion, that of "public policy". Methodologically, therefore, the desired results were the same in both systems though the way they were pursued was done through the concepts that were most pliable to each. In *Novosel* v. *Nationwide Insurance Company*[40] we thus find the perfect illustration. For in this case

[35] BArbGE 1, 185 (1954). The judgment of the Court, presided over by judge Hans Carl Nipperdey, draws heavily on his earlier writings as an academic, notably his seminal "Gleicher Lohn der Frau für gleiche Leistung. Ein Beitrag zur Auslegung der Grundrechte", in *Recht der Arbeit* (1950), 121*ff*. As is explained in what follows in the text, the theory that now prevails allows the constitutional rules to have an indirect, overarching effect on private law relations but denies to them any direct applicability.

[36] BVerfGE 7, 195 (1958).

[37] Professor Peter Quint has collected the references in his excellent "Free Speech and Private Law in German Constitutional Theory" 48 *Maryland L Rev* 247 (1989).

[38] But see *Sullivan* v. *Barnett*, 139 F 3d 158 (1998), petition for cert Pending No 97–2000. That the problem is not going away can be seen in the discussion of Siegel, "The Constitution and Private Government: Toward the Recognition of Constitutional Rights in Private Residential Communities Fifty Years After *Marsh* v. *Alabama*" 6 *William and Mary Bill of Rights Law Journal*, 461 (1998).

[39] 334 US, 1 (1948).

[40] 721 F 2d 894 (1983). The (predictably adverse) reactions to *Novosel* are discussed by Professor Perritt: "The Future of Wrongful Dismissal Claims: Where does Employer Self-

the Court of Appeals of the Third Circuit took the view that the concern for rights of political expression, which animated First Amendment *public*[41] employee cases, was also applicable to *private* employees under Pennsylvania law.[42] The Court was thus able to state in distinctly Nipperdeian terms[43] that "the protection of important political freedoms . . . goes well beyond the question whether the threat comes from state or private bodies."[44]

Other cases, which have followed this line of argument, could be quoted.[45] Yet it will suffice to mention but two since they relate to the right of privacy, which is likely to cause most of the headaches when the new Human Rights legislation comes into force. Thus, in the Californian case of *Semore* v. *Pool*[46] the Court of Appeal of the Fourth District held that the right of privacy in the California Constitution prohibits a private employer from conducting arbitrary drug testing and that the dismissal of the employee for failing to submit to the proposed test violated the public policy of the state. The position was reaffirmed four years later by the (state) Supreme Court in *Hill* v. *National Collegiate Athletic Assn*[47] where the court held that the privacy clause of Article 1, section 2, of the State Constitution, "creates a right of action against private as well as government agencies".[48] Accordingly, when a private employee's contract is terminated

Interest Lie?" in 58 *U Cin L Rev* 397, esp. pp. 402*ff.* (1989), where the author describes the *Novosel* doctrine as "an important model for possible future expansion of the public policy tort into *a constitutionalisation of private employment*" (emphasis added).

[41] Thus, to stick with the same State, see *Hunter* v. *Port Authority of Allegheny County* 419 A 2d 631 (1980): Employer's right to dismiss employee of an "at-will employment" is circumscribed by requirements of public policy which may be derived directly from First Amendment of the US Constitution and sec 7 of the Pennsylvania Constitution.

[42] In *Borse* v. *Piece Goods Shop, Inc* 963 F 2d 611 (1992) the court refused to extend the *Novosel* ruling to a dismissal of an employee who refused to submit herself to urine analysis screening for drug use. Significantly, however, it refused to hold "that a constitutional provision may never serve as a source of public policy in . . . wrongful discharge actions [taking place in a private workplace]". It is precisely this last point which brings the two systems closer together than they are commonly believed to be.

[43] See n. 35 above.

[44] *Novosel* (n. 40 above), at p. 900.

[45] E.g. *Devlin* v. *North Shore Door Co* 1995 WL 277, 110 (Ohio App. 8 Dist): "Clear 'public policy' sufficient to justify an exception to the employment-at-will doctrine . . . may be discerned by the Ohio judiciary based on sources such as the Constitution of Ohio and the United States."

[46] 217 Cal App. 3rd 1087, 266 Cal Rptr 280 (1990).

[47] 7 Cal App. 4th 1, 26 Cal Rptr 2d 834, 865 P 2d 633 (1994). This has been followed in different contexts. See e.g. *Pettus* v. *Cole* 49 Cal App. 4th 402, 57 Cal Rptr 2d 46. (Employee made prima facie case showing that disclosure to employer of detailed medical information by psychiatrists in connection with request for disability leave violated his constitutional right to privacy as he had legally cognisable interest in preserving privacy of his medical history and psychological profile.)

[48] Once again, the generality of this statement is of especial significance for the wider comparative point that I am trying to make. One must, however, also note two further points. First, in n. 20 (p. 869) of the *Hill* judgment, the court expressed doubts as to the continued validity of the *Semore* ruling. Secondly, courts, as we already noted when mentioning the *Borse* judgment in n. 42 above, are reluctant to apply these principles in drug-testing cases. Thus,

on the ground that he refused to take a random drug test, the employee may invoke the public policy exception to the "at-will termination" doctrine to assert a violation of his constitutional right of privacy.

We shall return to the lessons that can be drawn from these cases in the next section but, clearly, they are both many and interesting.

3. WHAT DO OUR PARADOXES TELL US ABOUT THE ENGLISH COMMON LAW AND THE MODERN CIVILIAN SYSTEMS?

The differences (such as they are) in the substantive solutions of the systems compared in this essay are, in one sense, the least worthy of note. After all, Europhobia is, in this country, built on emphasising (and often caricaturing[49]) our differences with the Continent of Europe and then convincing ourselves that where differences do exist, our solutions are always better (which, as a general principle, is clearly untenable). I have no doubt that in France and Germany as well one can find colleagues with a similar kind of mentality, quick to praise their system and to deride ours. Biased people will never be convinced, even when confronted by overwhelming evidence.

In reality, therefore, what examples such as these reveal about the foreign systems as a whole is more interesting. Here I shall point out five differences and attempt to highlight their wider import.

First, let us note or, rather, re-emphasise, that, as our examples clearly show, French law is not only largely found in judicial decisions. It has also developed through judicial activity. Methodologically one could further add that this often displays only the slightest use of a deductive syllogism that is considered one of the hallmarks of the modem civil law systems.[50] But that point is too important to be made here just in passing so it will have to receive a more detailed treatment in some future piece. The famous French expression that the judge is nothing more than "la bouche de la loi" is thus unconvincing. For, as the late Jack Dawson once felicitously observed,[51] the French decisions demonstrate that, if the phrase has any meaning left to it, it is only as an example of expert judicial ventriloquism!

This decisional nature of French law, though obviously known to legal experts, is none the less worth repeating. For it has escaped the full atten-

in *Jennings* v. *Minco Technology Labs Inc* 765 SW 2d 497 (1989), a Texas court not only held that employers can require drug testing (and dismiss employees of "at-will" contracts if they refuse to comply); it also slapped the employee with attorneys' fees for even raising the issue.

[49] Probably the best example of this tendency is the widely held belief—in this country as in the USA—that in French law the accused is guilty until he is proved innocent!

[50] Lord Macmillan, "Two Ways of Thinking", in *Law and Other Things* (1938), 76.

[51] *The Oracles of the Law* (1968), 411.

tion of some important common law judges.[52] Moreover, if it were fully understood and digested it would, I think, reduce their reluctance to pay much attention to the modern civil law since they ascribe to it a degree of generalisation which is only partially there. Incidentally, most of the above observations are also true of German law. For, though this system is endowed with a newer and more carefully drafted civil code than that found in France, it has allowed its judges room for some spectacular developments in contract, tort, labour, corporate, and family law to mention but five important areas of private law.

Secondly, not only have French (and German) *courts* been active; they have also opted for "flexibility" and "pragmatism" and shown less concern for doctrinal legitimacy and consistency than we, on this side of the Channel, tend to attribute to them (along with their alleged tendency for generalisations). Again, one tends to think of the Holmes aphorism that "the life of the law has not been logic; it has been experience"[53] as being restricted to the common law until one encounters numerous French and German decisions which, tacitly if not openly,[54] proceed from the same assumption. Once again, therefore, one wakes up to the fact that the theoretical differences between the two systems drummed into one's pliable mind during law school days are seriously attenuated in practice. To put it differently, the Continental (especially judicial) attachment to wide and amorphous principles is seriously tempered by feelings of pragmatism and gradualism as well as an aversion to any kind of misplaced judicial adventurism. In my submission these features of Continental case law have escaped the attention of many common lawyers. The examples given from the area of contracts in favour of third parties, shareholder disputes, strict liability, privacy, pre-contractual liability (which so worries English common lawyers[55]) and the like, all support this assertion. Many more could be given to force a reappraisal of our view of the modern civil law.

And that is not all. The English (but not American) tendency to stick to statutory reform has proved more rigid and restrictive, which explodes the view commonly held by modern civilians that our law is more flexible than

[52] E.g. Lord Scarman, "Codification and Judge-Made Law", offprint of a lecture delivered on 20 Oct. 1966 to the Law Faculty of the University of Birmingham, p. 19.

[53] OW Holmes, *The Common Law* (1881), 1. Rudolf von Jhering, whom Holmes had read but quoted less than he deserved, also came very close to this position. So Holmes's attack on the German theorists is more aptly directed at some of them—such as Puchta—whose influence, however, had already, at the time that Holmes was writing, begun to wane. But that is another and complicated issue!

[54] Though Goethe, at least, provides a forerunner to Holmes's aphorism in *Faust* (II 2038–9): "Grau teurer Freund, ist alle Theorie, Und grün des Lebens goldener Baum."

[55] Lord Ackner's concerns in *Walford* v. *Miles* [1992] 2 AC 128 is an example. For a forceful Continental reply see Kötz and Flessner, *European Contract Law*, trans Tony Weir (1997), 34*ff.* esp. 41.

theirs. Compare, for instance, the *Despretz* judgment, which does not limit recovery to spouses and children, with the English Act of 1882, which does just that. The result is that in English law, where other beneficiaries are envisaged by the life insurance contract, they can only recover if they can successfully invoke the trust mechanism. This, as one insurance expert once claimed, can work "considerable injustice".[56] It has also meant that quite a few other statutes have had to be passed to fill some of the gaps left open by the first legislative intervention.[57] The paradox thus is that the flexibility often attributed by French and German lawyers to the common law is found in their own system rather more frequently than in that of their neighbours! Indeed, one could argue[58] that the doctrine of *stare decisis*, combined with the currently prevailing understanding by English courts of the Australian-born[59] notion of "incrementalism", makes it very difficult for our legal system to adapt effectively and sufficiently quickly to the social and economic changes of our times.

The third point follows from the other two; and it can be seen at work most clearly in our example concerning the developing law of privacy. French (and, indeed, German) law has moved with the times; English law has struggled to keep abreast. The standard English tort textbooks even refuse to discuss the issue except in a most cursory manner. The way the struggle has been shaped by the courts could, of course, be described as both ingenious and ingenuous as old torts have been pressed into new uses, often only to come to grief. But the resulting gaps, as evidenced by the *Kay* case,[60] also speak against the common law. For such cases demonstrate conclusively that the high ideals invoked by the British press in favour of the *status quo* are nothing but smokescreens since they are really totally inappropriate to instances such as the one that confronted the Court of Appeal in that famous case. As stated, the legislature,[61] paralysed by overt threats from sections of the press has, moreover, refused to oblige. So we shall remain at an impasse until a courageous judge is given the chance

[56] Colinvaux, *The Law of Insurance*, 5th edn. (1984), 361.

[57] See e.g. Marine Insurance Act 1906, s. 14(2); Law of Property Act 1925, s. 47(l); Road Traffic Act 1972, s. 148(4).

[58] As Sir Arthur Goodhart did in "Precedent in English and Continental Law" (1934) 50 LQR 40.

[59] *Sutherland Shire Council* v. *Heyman* (1985) 60 ALR 1, at 43–4 (per Brennan J). It is submitted that subsequent case law has proved Lord Cooke right when, while still wearing his New Zealand judicial hat, he had pointed out how incrementalism can be used to support opposite conclusions. See *South Pacific Manufacturing C6 Ltd* v. *New Zealand Security Consultants & Investigations Ltd* [1992] 2 NZLR 282, at 295.

[60] Where a well-known actor, who was photographed against his will while in hospital, found himself, essentially, without a remedy against the offending paper which had published the photograph along with an interview which he never gave.

[61] In England but not in the USA. Thus, see the recently enacted legislation in the State of California, which makes it a tort to take photographs of people (or record their conversations) more or less on lines similar to those advocated by the recent "Caroline" decisions in Germany.

through an appropriate case to take the bull by the horns and, with the help of the new Human Rights Act, do what has hitherto not been possible.[62] Thus, in all matters where law reform involves no votes, the reform of the law in England relies on the stubborn litigant who, often against the advice of his professional adviser, is prepared to test his rights to the limits. Lawyers must be eternally thankful to the likes of Lise Jand'heur and Mrs Donoghue.

Fourthly, when legislation is finally proposed—which does not mean that it will also be enacted[63]—it is likely to adopt a drafting style, which would make Portalis turn in his grave.[64] Of course, it could be objected, why should an English draftsman be concerned about a dead Frenchman's views about drafting techniques? But one answer to this is that if we wish to exert an influence over future developments in Europe and elsewhere we must make our ideas exportable; and our drafting techniques are anything but that. A second and more important argument for changing our drafting techniques is that our detailed way of drafting statutes is, in this area of the law, more likely to lead to more and not less litigation. All these ideas may strike national lawyers, especially English lawyers, as rather odd if not even dangerous. However, as I stated in the beginning of this essay, it is the task of comparative lawyers to force their national brethren to reconsider the wisdom of their own solutions and not allow them to bask in a state of self-induced satisfaction, reinforced by years of inertia.

My final, general observation refers to the *Drittwirkung* cases found in German and American law and discussed earlier on. What these cases suggest is that sometimes in comparative law what matters is not what the courts (and academics) say but what they do (or can do with a minimum of ingenuity). Nor does it really matter if they do what they do by relying on the notions and concepts that are most familiar to them but not to us. Thus, in the unfair dismissal cases discussed above, constitutional ideas entered the private law dispute through the notion of public policy circumscribing the employer's rights in the "at-will" employment contracts. The German starting point was thus achieved without any reference to *Drittwirkung*, *Wechselwirkung*, *Ausstrahlungswirkung* and the like, which are both so intriguing and so off-putting to the common lawyer's mind. But the absence of the almost metaphysical terminology does not mean that the seed developed in Germany nearly sixty years ago, namely that human

[62] And that is why the horizontality debate is so important.

[63] The pitiful record of implementing the Law Commission's well-thought-out proposals is a glaring example of waste of public funds and intellectual effort. Again, one suspects that legislation does not follow because there are no votes in these topics.

[64] For his views see Fenet, *Recueil complet de travaux préparatoires du Code civil*, 1 (1836), 470, 475. Examples of ponderous English statutes, which have created serious problems of interpretation, include the Animals Act 1971, the Defective Premises Act 1972, and the Unfair Contract Terms Act 1977. The Germans, notorious for composing difficult legal texts, surpass us in complexity only in the case of the last example.

rights are under threat from private entities as much as the State, cannot germinate in the common law soil. The basic idea is a valid one; and it is the foundation stone of any theory of horizontality however one chooses to call it.

The above discussion (and the American case law given in the notes) also reminds us of the dangers of comparative methodology. For the lack of a solution that is uniformly acceptable to the fifty American jurisdictions could be taken as presenting us with an insurmountable obstacle in formulating precise comparative conclusions. The diverse case law thus shows that the wider *Novosel* doctrine—that the Constitutional texts can help shape the public policy exceptions to the doctrine that "at-will contracts" can be terminated by the employer for any reason or no reason—has had a mixed reception. The reasons for this can be many, and this is not the place to explore them in detail. In particular, the drug-testing cases, which seem to have shown the greater reluctance to use this technique, may in part be explicable by the general desire to fight the drug war with all means available, setting aside what are seen as legalistic niceties. A more general explanation for rejecting the *Novosel* approach may be linked to the wider debate concerning the desirability of taking such powers away from the legislator and giving them to the (unelected) judiciary. But, in my view, the validity of my thesis remains unaffected by these attempts to keep the judicially created exceptions to the employment "at-will" doctrine to a minimum. For what the *Novosel* case law shows is that that the *Drittwirkung* doctrine is not technically inconceivable even in the United States in the sense that constitutional ideas can and will enter into the domain of a private law dispute. That in America the same result came about through the equally amorphous concept of public policy is, I submit, a matter of relative detail. What does, however, matter is the realisation that human rights are, nowadays, as seriously threatened from powerful private entities as they are by the State. A theory of horizontality of some kind is thus called for. How, precisely, we implement it must, however, be left to the techniques used and the philosophies prevalent in each system that has to face this problem.

Finally, one must not bring this discussion to an end without noting that *Novosel* in the USA, despite all its imperfections, achieved what eluded the *Bundesarbeitsgericht* in Germany. For the latter court, despite its grandiloquent declarations, failed to do justice to the employee who was dismissed simply because his political views differed from those of his employer whereas the reverse result was reached by *Novosel*. But then, perhaps we can come back to the point alluded to earlier on: the inescapable conclusion that these cases do not only involve legal arguments but also political choices. Thus we should not, perhaps, forget that the German case involved a communist sympathiser at the time when the cold war was gaining in virulence. This may suggest much about the result; but it might also give us some intriguing clues (and I do not put it stronger than that) as to why in the drug-testing cases in the USA the *Novosel* (wider) doctrine failed to gain a foothold. It is thus plausible to suggest that the legal decision must be seen against the political realities that prevail at the time that the dispute reaches the court. The final conclusion of the German court, that limiting the speech rights of the dismissed employee is permissible if it serves to protect some other competing legal value (*Rechtsgut*), can thus be seen as a sham that clothes in legalistic language a decision of political expediency. That such a (harsh) interpretation is not entirely fanciful can be seen from the fact that the court found no constitutional text on which to peg such an approach but, instead, chose to trump the constitutionally protected speech rights by relying on previous court practice and academic writings.[65]

4. A CONCLUDING COUNTER-POINT

From what has already been said it will be clear that I have not suggested in this essay (or any of my other writings) that French or German law are in all cases better than my own. I could give many examples to show where Anglo-American law has, arguably, thought out more particular problems than French or German law has done, but two will suffice.

The first deals with the actions for so-called "wrongful life" and "wrongful birth" which are (typically) brought by a child and its parents respectively against a negligent doctor who failed to diagnose the mother's rubella during her pregnancy and thus deprived her of the chance to abort the foetus. The brevity of my observations hardly does justice to a topic which raises ethical and legal issues of the highest order. Yet even the few words I will say about these cases can give the discerning reader some idea of what I have in mind. Indeed, I have elsewhere suggested that the cases on this subject lend themselves to comparative analysis.[66]

Three recent French cases, two from the *Cour de Cassation*,[67] and the other from the *Conseil d'État*,[68] suggest, to a foreign observer at least, that

[65] BArbGE 1, 185, 194–5 (1954). A second constitutional challenge was based on the idea that the dismissal violated Art. 3(3) of the Constitution, which prohibits discrimination on grounds of political opinion. Though the Court held that this constitutional provision also had a horizontal effect it, again, held that it had not been violated in this instance. Subsequent case law has, however, shown greater sensitivity to the employee's political views, especially if the facts of the case suggested that the employer had, by dismissing the employee, overreacted to the latter's stance. Thus, see BArbGE 47, 363 (1984).

[66] For further details see my "Reading through a Foreign Judgment", in P Cane and J Stapleton (eds.), *The Law of Obligations: Essays in Celebration of John Fleming* (1998), chap. 10.

[67] Cass 26 mars 1996, Bull Civ 1996, 109 and note Jourdain in 1996 *Rev trim dr civ* 623.

[68] Conseil d'État, decision of 14 Feb. 1997 (transcript). For a summary and a discussion see *Le Monde* 17 Feb. 1997, particularly useful in that it contains the *conclusions* of the *Com-*

the law in France is in a state of flux.[69] Uncertainty gives academics the chance to try out creative solutions; but it also encourages litigation and, surely, French citizens have enough of that. But that is not my only complaint about the French decisions. What I found most disturbing in the French case law is the lack of a clear distinction between "wrongful life" cases and "wrongful conception" cases (where an unwanted but healthy child is born) since, both ethically and legally, they raise different issues. Just as disconcerting is the absence of any attempt to reconcile contradictory decisions. The lack of clarity as regards the headings of damages—who was being compensated and for what—is also worrying, especially to those who like myself may be asked to advise litigants about foreign law. The comparison of these contradictory (and opaque) French cases with the decision of the Supreme Court of New Jersey in *Procanik* v. *Cillo*[70] is thus both instructive and illuminating. Personally, I also believe that a French law student is likely to find the American discussion infinitely more informative than his own case law. And, I think this remains true even after these decisions are read in conjunction with the observations of the *arrêtistes* who, in practice, do so much towards making the published French judgments more usable. The late Advocate General Touffait and Professor Tunc were thus right to propose, in a seminal Article published over twenty-five years ago, the need to motivate French judgments to become more explicit.[71] Clearly, their thesis ran so much against long-standing French habits[72] that their advice was never heeded. But from a comparative point of view, time has done nothing to make it less attractive.

A comparative lawyer reading judgments of the highest French courts thus misses the clarity and analytical rigour that he expects from his own judgments. This makes the spreading of French ideas abroad more difficult since the foreign observer, whether judge or student must undertake a much fuller examination of the (often inaccessible, secondary) French material before even starting to find the analysis and policy arguments most needed. In that sense, therefore, one can go even further and claim another paradox,

missaire du Gouvernement Mme Péresse which give the real (and well-known) reasons for denying the child's claim.

[69] Since the decisions of the Cour de Cassation accepted the child's claim for damages and the (slightly) more recent decision of the Conseil d'État did not. A Common lawyer will find the latest decision of the Conseil d'État difficult to understand not so much because it seems to run counter to the earlier decision of the same court of 27 Sept. 1989, GP 1990, 421. For it does not—as Professor Moreau stressed in his note to the latest decision published in 1997 *La Semaine Juridique*, 22828—but because it is so completely incompatible with the philosophical position adopted by the Cour de Cassation.

[70] 97 NJ 339, 478 A 2d 755 (1984), where a doctor's negligent failure to diagnose that the mother had been infected by rubella led to the birth of a seriously sick child and the issuing of tort actions by both the handicapped child and its parents.

[71] "Pour une motivation plus explicite des décisions de justice, notamment de celles de la Cour de cassation", *Rev trim dr civ* 1974, pp. 487*ff.*

[72] Described in the classic monograph by Mimin, *Le Style Judiciaire* (1958).

namely that, contrary to the prevailing view in this country, the German decisions (subject to the point already made about the difficulties associated with German theorising) may be more usable by our courts than the French. Yet our academic curriculum does not reflect this reality.

Notwithstanding my last comment, I believe it is also true to assert that the "informational" value of the foreign decisions is less than that of the decisions of the common law. The German equivalents of *White* v. *Jones*—a case mentioned here partly because it is so well known in this country and partly because the judge honoured in this volume played such a leading part in it—offer as good examples as any for this, my second point. Thus, despite the fact that the Germans faced and solved the *Ross* v. *Caunters*[73] problem a good fifteen years before we even addressed it, and despite the fact that the German contractually flavoured solutions have, in my opinion (but not in that of others), much to commend them, none of these German judgments provide a match to their two English counterparts[74] in terms of thoroughness of discussion of the underlying issues. Indeed, no decision of the German Federal Court has, to my knowledge, come close to reflecting the kind of intellectual duel which we find in *White* v. *Jones* in the opinions of Lords Goff and Mustill.[75] Nor have I found a German judgment on this issue, or come to that any tort dispute, which can match the extensive comparative discussion which Lord Goff undertook in his opinion in *White* v. *Jones*. No wonder, then, that Lord Goff's judgments and extra-judicial writings (like Lord Denning's before him) are regularly given to German students of comparative law for discussion and enlightenment.[76]

So, after all, comparative law is a two-way street and my system may also be able to *teach* foreign lawyers a thing or two. The word teach is, deliberately, printed in italics, not only because it is the most important role a teacher can perform, but also because it suggests yet another paradox. For my point is really quite simple. Modern civilians stand to learn most from us not by studying the odd legal institution or solution to a particular problem[77] but by learning to appreciate the way our judgments are con-

[73] [1980] chap. 297.

[74] *Ross* v. *Caunters* [1980] chap. 297 and *White* v. *Jones* [1995] 2 AC 207.

[75] In Germany this would, of course, be found in the academic literature.

[76] See Professor Odersky's observations in his foreword to Markesinis, Lorenz, and Dannemann, *The German Law of Contract and Restitution* (1997). Professor Odersky was, until the autumn of 1996, President of Germany's (supreme) Federal Court.

[77] Though that could help them as well. Thus, the German law of "breach of contract", an amalgam of statute and case law, is inordinately complicated, as is their law on limitation. Many Germans also think that their law of vicarious liability (and its accretions) could also be simplified. German law also ignores the benefits that may arise from the doctrine of undisclosed agency, the institution of *Kommissionär* only partly rectifying the effects of this omission (see §§392 1 and II HGB). Other areas of law, in which we may have something to offer our German colleagues, include the law of undue influence. On all these matters see Markesinis (with Lorenz and Dannemann) *The German Law of Obligations* (1997), vol. I, chaps. 2 and 6, vol. II, chap. 3. On this recent trend, see Professor Stephan Lorenz's "Arbeitsrechtlicher

structed. They can also learn from the way we use our cases in the classroom in order to make our students think, hypothesise, even let their imagination run wild. Given that so much of modern European law is now secreted in decisions, this may not be as heretical a suggestion to make as it may at first sight appear. Case law books may, for the time being, be more frequently used in Germany than in France; but in the years to come I think the practice will spread further in both these countries. In the meantime, as far as French law is concerned, decisions of Courts of Appeal may well serve as a better source of information for those of us who know (or suspect) the full richness and ingenuity of the French spirit and wish to know what the French judges really think about certain issues of common interest. I thus maintain that our Socratic method (reflected in judicial opinions) remains more pragmatic, analytical, policy-orientated, interdisciplinary, and revealing and should thus be studied more carefully by our friends on the Continent of Europe. Not surprisingly, this last-mentioned strength of the common law received pride of place when Lord Goff delivered the 1997 Wilberforce Lecture.[78] And this must be another example of his "give and take" philosophy which is the characteristic attribute of the true comparatist and which can easily be put into practice if one even glances at the list of topics given in notes 77 and 79.

But let me return to my main point. For us to claim that we can *teach* European colleagues how to *teach* law is, as I suggested above, another true, if not outrageous, paradox (hence the italics) since we simply do not have the same long and respectable tradition in academic education as Continental European universities have. This, then, is a paradox in the sense used in this essay, namely, an oddity that proves a common assumption about a foreign system wrong. And the assumption here is that the common law is the system of pure problem-solvers and not system-builders and thus is best admired for its pragmatic solutions rather than its analysis and reasoning process.

In the light of the above I would be tempted to formulate the following proposition. French and German judgments would become clearer to their own nationals and more exportable to foreigners if they were more explicit in giving their true reasons and more willing in trying to reconcile their rich case law. This richness would be further enhanced if they took a leaf out of the book of our best judges and started studying and using more frequently the common law.

Yet even if we fail to convince our European neighbours of the advantages which they will gain by studying our law and legal techniques, we

Aufhebungsvertrag, Haustürwiderrufsgesetz und 'undue influence'" in JZ 1997, 277*ff*. and, more fully, his *Der Schutz vor dem unerwünschten Vertrag-Eine Untersuchung von Möglichkeiten und Grenzen der Abschlußkontrolle im geltenden Recht* (1997). Examples could, of course, be multiplied.

[78] "The Future of the Common Law" (1997) 46 ICLQ 745.

must continue, come what may, to try to understand them better than we currently do. For such growing understanding will help our practitioners and businessmen deal better with neighbours and major trading partners. It will also assist our judges and jurists to solve problems, which our neighbours may have encountered (and even solved) before us.[79] Such a study of foreign law may often reveal that law to be more advanced and, at times, even more transplantable than we assume it to be. Lord Goff's rich and pioneering work demands that we go on probing the unknown so as "to dispel our ignorance of German [and French] law and so by comparison influence our understanding of our own".[80]

[79] Thus German law addressed—through cases—the problems of pre-conception injuries (to the mother) a good twenty years before we came up with our answers through legislation. See e.g. BGH 20 Dec 1952, BGHZ 8,244 = NJW 1953, 417. The German law of nervous shock in many respects has foreshadowed the more liberal position towards which our law seems to be moving. For instance, RG 21 Sept. 1931, RGZ 133, 270. And in the area of family law (redistribution of property after divorce, equality of spouses, equal and fair treatment of legitimate and illegitimate children) German law came up with more liberal and modern solutions before we did. See, *inter alia*, KJ Gray, *Reallocation of Property on Divorce* (1977), passim. "Proportionality", slowly becoming fashionable in this country, also has old roots in German (and Dutch) administrative law; and, just as topically, German scholars have done much more work on third-party effects of fundamental rights (*Drittwirkung der Grundrechte*) than we have and could thus provide us with some guidance in this developing area of the law. The list of examples could be enhanced further to prove that comparative law is a two-way street.

[80] *White* v. *Jones* [1995] 2 AC 207 at 263.

4

Reading Through a Foreign Judgment

INTRODUCTORY REMARKS

At the height of the so-called "Beef Crisis" in 1996 Mr. D. F. Williams, the Secretary General of the European Commission and Britain's most senior Civil Servant in Brussels, warned against the Europhobic sentiments, which were being whipped up by certain politicians and the press.[1] He stressed the importance which the market of the European Union presented for Britain and the wider opportunities, which "Europe" offered to the British. While some English politicians bicker, as they try to shape a Europe *à la carte* which will allow them to profit from the European Union while also competing with it or, even undermining it, businessmen and law firms have long grasped the significance of the opinions contained in Mr. Williams's speech.[2] The same cannot be said of academic lawyers who only grudgingly came to recognise the importance of Community law in the late seventies and, more so, in the eighties; and, arguably, still pay inadequate attention to the significance of the rulings of the Court in Strasbourg and even less to the Supreme Courts in the major continental systems.

The current "rush" to complete legal studies through abridged courses also means that for the bulk of our law students there is simply no time for even trying to understand our major partners, their legal systems, and their way of thinking. Not surprisingly, therefore, in this country the level of research into and study of foreign law fell—with few notable exceptions[3]—to a rather low point in the 1970s and 1980s. The contrast with countries such as Germany could thus not be more striking. A recent prolonged stay in Munich, as the guest of their University's Institute of Comparative Law,

[1] At a speech given in York on 7 June 1996 to the Solicitors European Group Annual Conference.

[2] "Britain exports more to Belgium and the Netherlands than to the United States; its exports to Germany equal those to the United States and Japan combined; it exports as much to France as to the whole of the Commonwealth." Extract from Mr Williams' speech, kindly provided to the author.

[3] Such as at Oxford and King's College, London.

frankly left me envious of the extent to which younger colleagues there were "shadowing", each in their respective area, developments in the Common Law. Not even in an old and wealthy University such as mine, can we rival them in their interest in and knowledge of foreign law or in their library equipment. Even a committed "European" like myself cannot help but feel a pang of envy at this superiority of the best of Germany's institutions.

The scholar to whom this volume is dedicated is, however, one of those shining exceptions to whom I have alluded; and this country can lay some claim to his work because of his past association with King's College, London, and Brasenose College, Oxford. A piece on how one should try to approach and understand foreign judgments is thus a fitting if modest tribute to his work which has combined so forcefully Germanic scholarship with the eclecticism and willingness to speak one's mind which characterise the flourishing legal cultures of his two adopted countries: Australia and the USA. This piece is addressed mainly to teachers of law whose work might, one day, influence our judges, the senior partners of the law-making process in this country; but otherwise it forms part and parcel of my life-long effort to give the study of foreign law the place it deserves in our law curriculum.[4]

The problems which this essay will look at arise in actions, which in the Common law world, have become known as actions for "wrongful life" and "wrongful birth".[5] Since the way the teacher selects cases for discussion in the classroom can determine the breadth of his sweep, it is important to explain why this subject has been chosen. Five reasons at least can be given for this choice. They are the following.

First, similar relevant decisions can be found in almost all systems. *Secondly*, these decisions reveal clearly the areas where the systems are similar and where they are different. *Thirdly*, the decisions show how the wider legal background affects the style of reasoning as well as the final outcome of the case; and this, incidentally, also points to some of the dangers of legal transplants. *Fourthly*, the approach in some of these cases does not depend on the inductive versus deductive way of reasoning which, we have been told time and again, differentiates the two ways of thinking: the English and the Continental. *Finally*, they show how relatively insignificant are the

[4] On which see my recent *Foreign Law and Comparative Methodology: A Subject and a Thesis* (1997).

[5] Since these terms have not been used consistently, especially in the American literature, it may be desirable to state that in this essay the first—*wrongful life*—is used in a way which refers to actions brought by the handicapped child and can include, among other things, claims for emotional harm and the cost of medical expenses. *Wrongful birth* actions are brought by the parents of the affected child and, likewise, can include claims for moral and pecuniary damages. *Wrongful conception* cases, including claims for the birth of a healthy but unwanted child, are not discussed in this paper though, as we shall see further down, the distinction is not always clear in the French judgments.

legal concepts used by jurists, at any rate for the purposes of comparing the results reached by the various systems. Let us look at these points in turn, focusing, because of lack of space but also out of deference to our honorand, on German and American law though, occasionally, also drawing attention to French law.[6]

SIMILAR LITIGATION FOUND IN MOST COUNTRIES

At the outset the discussion requires two or three general qualifications.

The first is the obvious one, namely, that we are talking here of the countries which were once described as belonging to the "Western World" but nowadays are best described as advanced or industrialised countries. For, clearly, the less "developed" countries do not have the same level of litigation for these types of cases, partly for technological reasons and partly because their inhabitants are accustomed (perhaps with greater maturity) to treating many of these incidents as part of the normal vicissitudes of life which are best handled through family cooperation rather than through state help or litigation.

Secondly, even within this group of "industrialised" countries with which we are concerned, indigenous factors may account for a lack of case law. For example, strong religious beliefs on the morality of abortion, coupled with criminal legislation on the subject, which may vary in its breadth in significant details, affect the existence of case law on our subject.[7] Belgium is a good example of a country where no case law of any significance was found for the reasons given above; the Republic of Ireland is another, and that is one reason why they have been totally excluded from the purview of this essay.[8] Overall, however, one must note a degree of similarity in the social, economic, and political backgrounds of the countries which are looked at in this essay with the consequence that the transplantability of particular legal solutions can be considered with profit.

[6] Italian law offers interesting analogies—for instance Cass Civ. 22.11.1993, n. 11503, 1994 *La Nuoava Giurisprudenza Civile Commentata* 690, with note by Professor Vincenzo Zeno Zencovich—and so do mixed jurisdictions such as Louisiana. For reasons of space, however, their consideration must be omitted from this paper.

[7] In *Trib. grande inst. Evreux*, 21 déc. 1979, *D*. 1981. 185 the mother's first and unsuccessful abortion took place in France. By the time the mistake was discovered, the time limit (ten weeks from the moment of conception) for having a legal abortion in France had passed; but it was still possible for her to have a legal abortion in England, which she did. The (culpable) defendant was held liable for the extra costs of this second operation.

[8] This is also true of French law, though it does not figure in the opaque judgments. (Abortion was first legalised by the "experimental" *loi Veil* of 17 January 1975 and took its definitive form with the *loi Pelletier* of 31 December 1979.) For Professor Le Tourneau, note to Cour d'Appel de Riom of 6 July 1989, *DS* 1990, 284, 286, French law does not recognise a right to abortion but merely "tolerates" it in certain circumstances.

There is a third factor, which may affect the levels of litigation. It is really a variant of the previous one: the Constitution and its interpretation[9] can also have a bearing on these cases. An illustration of this can be found in the recent German case law. Thus, the re-affirmation by the German Constitutional Court that "the child's existence cannot, in law, be classified as damage",[10] effectively continues to bar all direct claims by the child itself.

In America the "constitutionalisation" of private law can be seen by the effect which *Roe* v. *Wade*[11] had on this branch of the law.[12] More ominously, one might wish to speculate on the fate of the wrongful life/birth actions if abortion rights are restricted as a result of the recent and politically orchestrated reactions of the "pro-life" movement. Though one may take heart from the fact that the moods of the American public are often transient, it must be admitted that the current picture, from the claimants' point of view, is bleak if one is to judge from a series of statutes passed by many American States in the eighties limiting or totally eliminating such causes of action.[13] This trend (though not the reasoning) stands in marked contrast to the two most recent decisions of the *Cour de cassation*,[14] which may be heralding an expansion of plaintiffs' rights. We shall return to some of these ideas later on.

SIMILARITIES BETWEEN THE SYSTEMS

Let us first start with the most elementary observation. Many students (and some courts) have had difficulty in deciding what harm the doctor/defendant has caused in these cases. Both the landmark German and New Jersey cases in this field clarify this point at the outset; and do so using almost identical language. Thus, the German court states that ". . . the defendant did not cause the child's deplorable condition . . . However, in breach of his obligation towards the mother to treat her, he failed to prevent by means of an abortion the birth of a child, the health of which was severely endangered and in whose person the danger materialised in a severe form."[15]

[9] Which may remain consistent or alter over a period of time. Thus, in the United States, changing attitudes about the constitutionality of abortion, have affected the availability and ambit of the tort actions of "wrongful life" and "wrongful birth".

[10] BVerfGE 88,203, section D.V.6. Article 2 (2), which protects "the right to life", is, of course, the one mainly considered in these cases.

[11] 410 US 113, 93 S. Ct. 705.

[12] See, for instance, the frank admissions, which *Procanik* v. *Cillo*, 97 NJ 339, 478 A. 2d 755 (1984), contain on this matter.

[13] A summary can be found in B.S. Markesinis, *The German Law of Torts: A Comparative Introduction*, 3rd (ed.) (1994).

[14] *La Semaine Juridique* (JCP) 1996, 156. Contrast, *Conseil d'Etat*, 14 fév. 1997, *La Semaine Juridique*, 22828.

[15] BGHZ 86, 240, 250. This elementary point was, apparently, misunderstood by the *Cour administrative d'appel de Lyon* and its decision was thus quashed by the *Conseil d'Etat* of 14 fév. 1997, *Semaine Juridique*, 22828 (with approving note by Professor Moreau).

While in *Procanik* the court said: "In the present case, the plaintiffs do not allege that the negligence of the defendant doctors caused the congenital rubella from which the infant plaintiff suffers . . . The essence of the infant's claim is that the defendant doctors wrongfully deprived his mother of information that would have prevented his birth."[16]

Moving next to more important matters, we notice that both systems also reach the same (negative) result concerning the most difficult claim in these actions, namely the child's claim for general damages for being born.[17] The American judgment, reviewing early case law, states simply that ". . . policy considerations have led this court in the past to decline to recognise any cause of action in an infant for his wrongful life".[18] The German court likewise takes the same view and states: ". . . this Division believes that in cases such as the present the limits within which claims can be adjudicated according to law have been reached altogether and even exceeded."[19] A long line of subsequent cases has not budged on this point.[20]

Thirdly, both systems are *at idem* in so far as they make sure that the child's basic needs will be taken care of through damages given to the parents. Could this solution be running counter to the philosophical stance taken by those courts which have argued that life cannot be damage and cannot justify the award of damages? It is very tempting to give an affirmative answer to this question. But this would produce an overall result, which would be too harsh for most. The decision of 16 November 1993 of the *Bundesgerichtshof*[21] ingeniously wriggles through the (puritanical) obstacles laid before it by the Constitutional court.[22] This section of the judgment of the *Bundesgerichtshof* thus concludes with the following peroration:

[16] *Procanik* v. *Cillo* 478 A. 2d 755, 760 (1984).

[17] The position of French law is, probably, the same despite the recent two important decisions of the *Cour de cassation*, which we discuss further down in the text.

[18] *Procanik* v. *Cillo*, n. 16 above, at p. 760.

[19] BGHZ 86, 240, 254.

[20] In BGH NJW 1994, 788, an attempt to argue this point on appeal was abandoned, obviously because it was hopeless. Likewise, BGH NJW 1996, 2432, which involved an attempted abortion of twins, which succeeded in the case of one but left the other fertilised egg alive. The most recent case—BGH 4. 3. 1997, NJW 1997, 1639, reached the same conclusion by stating, somewhat blandly, that the child was not included within the protective scope of the contract between mother and doctor. This continuing case law is also giving rise to interesting literature with the result that Germany is no longer following the American debate but, in one sense, leading it. Thus, see: Cramer, "Pränatale Diagnostik und Fetaltherapie. Auswirkungen auf die Rechtsprechung des Bundesgerichtshofes zur Zeugung oder Geburt eines genetisch geschädigten Kindes als Schadensfall ("wrongful—birth action")", *MedR* 1992, I, 14; Deutsch "Das Kind oder sein Unterhalt als Schaden—Eine methodische Grundfrage des geltenden Rechts", *VersR* 1995, 609.

[21] BGHZ 124, 128; NJW 1994, 788; BGH NJW 1997, 1639.

[22] BVerfGE (Second Division) 88, 203, section D.V.6. Four years later the First Division of the Constitutional Court handed down a judgment which went the other way and upheld a civil court's decision to award damages in wrongful birth and pregnancy cases covering even the costs of maintenance of a healthy child: BVerfG 12 November 1997, NJW 1998, 519. In between 1993 and 1997 some lower courts, under the influence of the 1993 decision of the

"This Division is rather of the opinion that, especially in cases such as this, granting compensation not only has no detrimental effect on this child [honestly, how could it!] but can rather be beneficial to it, since it improves its financial situation and possibly even its standing within the family. The shifting of the maintenance burden to the attending doctor appears especially satisfactory where, due to his faulty consultation, he is co-responsible for the economic burden which, if a severely handicapped child is in constant need of care, can even threaten the family's existence.[23] As this Division has previously stated . . . even in cases where the doctor is fully liable for all extra expenditure calculated by means of an economic comparison, the parties are still burdened with the total personal care of the child and also with a certain amount of financial losses and sacrifices which they cannot transfer to the person who created the damage. The Court fails to detect any constitutionally objectionable attack on the honour of the child from this partial economic alleviation of the parents' burden."[24]

The teacher who uses material such as this in the classroom can, of course, digress here and refer to the cat and mouse jurisdictional game which the Constitutional and Federal Court play from time to time, as the latter shows signs of "irritation" by the generalised fiats which the former sends down from its Olympian heights. Indeed, the discerning teacher/reader obtains a clear glimpse (from judgments such as that of the *Bundesgerichtshof* of 16 November 1993) of how the Federal Court handles these "directives"; and can, thereby at his discretion, add further dimensions to his exposition of foreign law.

DIFFERENCES BETWEEN THE SYSTEMS

The appreciation of the two systems comes more into relief when we look at the differences between the approaches of the two courts. They lie in three areas.

Constitutional Court, had refused to award maintenance damages to a healthy child. The way such lower courts managed to evade the aforementioned decision of the Federal Supreme Court (BGH NJW 1993, 788) was by distinguishing it on the ground that it had decided a claim from a handicapped child. Thus, see: LG Düsseldorf, 2 December 1993, NJW 1994, 805. But not all courts agreed; and the case law showed signs of confusion that seemed to be encouraged by the 1993 decision of the Constitutional court. Thus see: OLG Düsseldorf, 15 December 1994, NJW 1995, 788 awarding maintenance damages to a healthy child. The chances that the Constitutional court would thus, once again, be drawn into the dispute were enhanced and, indeed, this happened in 1997 though this time as a result of the First Division (with a more liberal tradition) entering the fray. The possibility of the two Divisions of the Constitutional court delivering contradictory opinions is explained by Kommers, *The Constitutional Jurisprudence of the Federal Republic of Germany*, pp. 16–22, 2nd ed. (1997) but the outcome does not seem satisfactory, at least in the eyes of a foreign observer. An attempt to refer the differences to the plenum of this court to resolve this "internal dispute" was rejected: BVerfG 22 November 1997, NJW 1998, 519.

[23] This point, as well, is made by the *Procanik* decision at p. 762.

[24] BGHZ 124 at p. 144.

First, style. As I have discussed this elsewhere[25] little need be added here. Special note, however, must be taken of two features of the cases. The first is how each court uses its respective case law; and let it be noted that, yet again, we are confronted with an area of the law which in almost all countries but England has found its answers through cases and not statutes. The second is the use of the comparative method in the German case (albeit here, unfortunately, displaying a mistaken appreciation of American law).[26]

Secondly, methodological approach. For reasons, which have again been explained elsewhere,[27] German law often resorts to contract to perform what we would regard as tort functions. Thus, here, too, the remedies of the various plaintiffs are seen as stemming from the main contract made by the mother of the affected child with the hospital. This part of the German reasoning makes little sense to a common lawyer so little more need be said on this point.[28]

The last area of difference can be found in the substantive answers given; and here we note two major differences.

First, in German law the mother is not allowed any damages for pain and suffering except for that which "exceeds the inflictions which accompany a birth without complications". If, for instance, she was forced because of the damage to the foetus, to have an *abortion*, a small sum would be claimable under this heading. More importantly, "no pecuniary damages can be awarded . . . in respect of a violation of the right to plan a family as an emanation of the general right to one's personality."[29] By contrast, the American case allows such claims; indeed, *Roe* v. *Wade*[30] is the *fons et origo* of the developments in this part of the law.

Secondly, the cases differ in the way they deal with the affected child's claim for special damages. Unlike the New Jersey court in *Procanik*, the German court refuses the child's claims, (for what we would call general *and* special damages), and this irrespective of whether the claim is based on contract (the child being seen, as stated above, a third party beneficiary of the contract made by the mother and the hospital) or in tort. On the other hand, both parents are, as already noted, compensated to the tune of all living and medical expenses incurred for the handicapped child.[31]

25 "A Matter of Style" 110, *LQR,* 607 (1994).

26 BGHZ 124 at p. 251.

27 See, for instance, *The German Law of Torts: A Comparative Introduction*, 3rd ed. (1994), 46 *et seq*.

28 The recent double decision of the *Cour de cassation* of 26 mars 1996—*Bull Civ*. 1996, 109—also chose to base liability on art. 1147 CC, i.e. a contractual rule but this has puzzled some French commentators. See for instance, Professor Jourdain's observations in *Rev. trim dr. civ*. 1996, 623, 4.

29 BGHZ 86, 240, 248. Point re-confirmed by BGH NJW 1994, 788.

30 410 US 113, 93 S.Ct. 705.

31 BGHZ 86, 240, 247. The Federal Court recently stressed forcefully that the damages must include both normal and extra-ordinary expenses: BGH NJW 1993, 788. See, also. BHG

Despite this last-mentioned similarity, the American decision remains more generous than the German in that damages for "medical and other expenses" are given to the parents *and* the child. Though the American court is quick to clarify that such damages are not "doubled",[32] in the sense that the damages to the child become payable only when the parental obligation to maintain ceases, the difference is significant since it means that in New Jersey law (but not in German law) the child can go on receiving compensation in the event of surviving its parents. In one sense, however, the extent of this generosity may be exaggerated: statistics suggest that victims with serious injuries rarely live beyond their majority.

THE INFLUENCE OF LEGAL BACKGROUND ON THE OUTCOME OF THESE CASES

Professor Fleming made this the central theme of his excellent comparative analysis of the American legal system entitled *The American Tort Process*.[33] There he showed how the differences between American and English tort law lay not in the concepts or values adopted by the two systems but on the impact that backdrop factors such as the presence or absence of a written constitution, a Bill of Rights, juries, the welfare state, a differently trained and organised legal profession and the like had on the final outcome of the cases. His pioneering study has not yet been replicated at a Continental European level; but it is submitted that his main ideas hold true also for the comparison of English, American, and German law. This further and significant dimension to the study of the law is well illustrated by the two cases discussed in this paper.

Thus, first, we note how the German court categorically asserts that "Human life . . . is a legally protected interest of the highest order deserving absolute protection. No third party may determine its value".[34] The court goes on to hold that "it is impossible to determine . . . whether a life affected by serious handicaps as an alternative to absence of existence can be regarded at all in law as damage . . ." Significantly the court alludes to its not so distant past and states ". . . generally, having regard to the experience under the National Socialist regime of lawlessness, the practice of the courts in the Federal Republic does not permit, with good reason, any legally relevant judgment about the value of the lives of others."[35] Consid-

NJW 1997, 1639. In France, on the other hand, the lower courts are less generous since they limit damages to extra-ordinary expenses incurred on behalf of the "abnormal" child. See cases cited by Le Tourneau in *DS* 1990, 287.

[32] *Procanik* v. *Cillo*, n. 16 above at p. 762.

[33] (1988).

[34] BGHZ 86, 240, 252.

[35] BGHZ 86, 240, 252.

erations such as these have led the German courts, as we have already noted, to deny the child/plaintiff any legal redress.

But there is another, more contemporary and pragmatic argument for denying the child special damages; and it is one, which in Professor Fleming's terminology, is dictated by the different national background. A hint of this comes towards the end of the German judgment where the court states that its solution to grant the parents special damages may not be enough "once the duty to maintain [the child] comes to an end, as for instance, when they die".[36] Here as stated, the American solution appears, if not preferable, certainly more generous to the child; that is until one notes the way the German court completes the above-mentioned thought. "In all these cases" says the court "a fateful development takes place the interruption of which cannot be demanded by the child and the effects of which must be made good by the community within the bounds of the possible."[37] An admission here, that the social security net (effectively absent in the USA) will thus take over, but also a very important explanation for the fact that American tort law is so often more generous than its European counterparts. That this will provide only a limited relief—"within the bounds of the possible"—and will be less generous than the tort/damages system of compensation, is an undoubted fact. But as Frederick the Great said over two centuries ago: "*Der Mantel des Königs ist Warm aber Kurz*".[38] One could not better this summary of one of the advantages and drawbacks of the social security versus the tort method of compensation!

The way the American court deals with some of the philosophical points of the case is also instructive. With regard to the child's claim for special damages, the court said:

"We need not become preoccupied . . . with . . . metaphysical considerations. Our decision to allow the recovery of extraordinary medical expenses is not premised on the concept that non-life is preferable to an impaired life, but it is predicated on the needs of the living. We seek only to respond to the call of the living for help in bearing the burden of their affliction".[39]

[36] Note here that in German law the obligation to maintenance continues for life and does not, as in many American jurisdictions, come to an end upon the child attaining majority. This difference in the family law rules may thus explain the lesser generosity of the German tort rules. To put it differently: in the English Common law, tort law often makes up for the defects of the law of contract, family and succession. Yet, in German law at the end of the day a difference still remains at the expense of the child. For what happens to it when the parents die? The solution, as we explain in the text, is found in German social security law.

[37] BGHZ 86, 240. In BGH NJW 1997, 1639, the Federal Court refused the child's claim on the ground that the child was not included within the scope of the contract made by its mother and the doctor. Why this is so is not explained, though a few lines further down the court alludes to the dangers of enlarging un-necessarily the extent of medical liability.

[38] The cloak of the King is warm but small.

[39] *Procanik* v. *Cillo* 478 A. 2d 755, 763 (1984).

Without too much distortion one can read into these lines the idea that something must be done about these unfortunate victims of human errors; and, in the absence of any social security provisions in the USA, tort law must perform this function. This agenda was clearly in the minds of such eminent American scholars as Fleming James Jr. who advocated with such passion the expansion of American tort law in the fifties and sixties.

If true, this is an important new optic for looking at American tort awards for it suggests that to the extent that they deal with future medical expenses they are rightly more generous than their European counterparts. Additionally, one must also bear in mind that a large slice of the damage award will, in America, go to counsel under the contingent fee system which, in one respect at least, is nothing more than a way of financing litigation, alternative to but just as defective as our legal aid system.

The judgment in the New Jersey court in *Procanik* becomes even more interesting when it comes to give its reasons for denying the child's claim for general damages. The relevant section deserves to be quoted in full not least because it provides an open admission of how the jury system has affected the operation of tort law in practice. It said:

"Underlying our conclusion is an evaluation of the capability of the judicial system, often proceeding in these cases through trial by jury, to appraise such a claim. Also at work is an appraisal of the role of tort law in compensating injured parties, involving as that role does, not only reason, but also fairness, predictability, and even deterrence of future wrongful acts. In brief, the ultimate decision is a policy choice summoning the most sensitive and careful judgment. From that perspective it is simply too speculative to permit an infant plaintiff to recover for emotional distress attendant on birth defects which the plaintiff claims that he would be better off if he had not been born. Such a claim would stir the passions of jurors about the nature and value of life, the fear of non-existence, and about abortion. That mix is more than the judicial system can digest."[40]

This is a pragmatic and admirable assessment of conditions in the jury room, especially the context of contemporary American politics. Arguably, it is also a more convincing explanation for denying damages than resorting to philosophical or metaphysical statements, which even when proclaimed with great conviction, do not enjoy unanimous support.

INDUCTIVE AND DEDUCTIVE REASONING

In his perceptive lecture entitled "Two Ways of Thinking"[41] Lord Macmillan suggested that the Scots and Continental Europeans opt for a deductive

[40] *Procanik* v. *Cillo* 478 A. 2d 755, at p. 763.

[41] Reproduced in his book *Law and Other Things* (1938) 76 *et seq.*

way of reasoning while the Anglo-Saxons prefer the inductive approach. "To proceed from principles to instances is the characteristic of the one school [continental European] to proceed from instances to principles—or perhaps not to proceed beyond instances—is the characteristic of the other [common law]." This central theme, however, failed to bring out the fact that the two worlds, though starting from different positions, tend to meet in the middle.[42] For our purposes, therefore it is interesting to note that one can find abundant German case law, which goes from its starting premise to its conclusion, without really using the one or the other way of reasoning.

The "wrongful birth" and "life" cases we have been comparing offer such an illustration; and to the extent that they do not follow the reasoning pattern one expects of them, but proceed to the finishing point in a very similar fashion, they can help bridge the gap between the two major legal families of the world by showing that even their so-called cardinal difference—their different ways of thinking—is not as omnipresent as one has been led to believe. For one must stress the fact that there are large areas of German law where the same holds true. This tends to happen where the statutory material in the Code is slender; and the pegging of the result on a codal provision tends to be more a formality than a logical necessity.

Here only a few instances of this can be given; but in all of them one can attempt the kind of interpretation/analysis of the decisional law, which we have tried in this piece.

From the German law of torts we thus note that the development of contractual ways of circumventing the tort rule of vicarious liability can be included in this group.[43] This tendency to move away from the strict codal reasoning can also be seen in the judicial development of the general right to one's personality. The deductive reasoning which one finds here derives its force from the hierarchically superior Constitution; and that is as far as deduction goes. Yet even here one is left with the impression that the courts are trying to do justice to a problem which has become more acute in our times than it was when the Code was drafted and less concerned to pursue the Code's merciless logic to its end. In that sense, therefore, one could apply to these cases the American dictum that "Law is more than an exercise in logic, and logical analysis, although essential to a system of ordered justice, should not become an instrument of injustice."[44]

The absence in any meaningful way of any deductive or inductive logic is even more obvious in important areas of contract law, which have been transformed over the last century by the courts, the result being dictated by

[42] To be fair to the great jurist he does say that in Scotland "the edges of distinction have been blurred by constant contacts" with England.

[43] This "peculiarity" of German law is extensively discussed in Markesinis *The German Law of Torts. A Comparative Introduction*, 3rd ed. (1994) pp. 685*ff*. and pp. 774*ff*.

[44] *Procanik* v. *Cillo* 478 A. 2d 755 (1984).

purely practical considerations or iniquities of the codal solutions. This is progressively obvious in the slow enlargement of the codal notion of impossibility of performance, which culminated in the ability of German courts to readjust (*Ausgleichsanspruch*) the contractual obligations of the parties. Here, a mere perusal of the judgments shows how the reference to the Code—§ 242 BGB—amounts to little more than paying lip service to the notion that the courts are applying statutory law and hardly disguises their creative powers, often prompted by little more than the desire to do justice during a period of drastic dislocation of the German economy. How creative this power can be, can be seen not only by the courts' ability to move away from the wording of the contract chosen by the parties but also in the extent of their power to re-draw the contract, the entire process finding but the slightest of justifications in the Code. A number of interesting illustrations of this are given in *The German Law of Contract and Restitution*,[45] co-authored by this writer with Professor Werner Lorenz and Dr. Gerhard Dannemann. Two can be mentioned here as illustrations of the point we are trying to make. In these decisions the scant reference to codal provisions, coupled with the insistence, commonly found in cases turning on § 242 BGB that they each turn on their facts, demonstrate that neither deductive nor inductive reasoning is dominant here. Instead, the result is dictated by the court's feeling of fairness, at times coupled with an economic analysis of the circumstances of the case before it.

In 1966 the *Bundesgerichtshof*[46] heard a case involving a city dweller that had decided to live in the country and was offered the possibility of a lease of land on which the defendant/builder was to erect for him a prefabricated house. When, to the surprise of both contracting parties, the local authority declined to give building permission for the works to proceed, the plaintiff sought to recover his down payment from the builder. In such a case and in accordance with the traditional application of the doctrine of impossibility, the defendant would have been excused his obligation and the plaintiff entitled to recover the pre-paid amount by way of restitution.[47] Yet the court went down a completely different path. For the defendant builder argued that he could build a house on another piece of land, lying near by and having the same characteristics as the first plot (view, clean air etc.). This land belonged to a different land owner who, argued the builder, was willing to grant the plaintiff a similar lease of it as the one the plaintiff had originally obtained of the first piece of land. The BGH was of the view that if these assertions could be proved—as it was left to a lower court to verify them—the substitute performance should be allowed to go ahead.

[45] O.U.P. (1997).

[46] BGH JZ 1966, 409.

[47] Subsequent decisions have shown a greater reluctance to order substitute performance. See OLG Karlsruhe JZ 1972, 120.

In our view, it is entirely unconvincing that this bold result flowed deductively from any codal provision even though it was, on the face of things, based on the mundanely-phrased provision about good faith of that enactment.

A more recent decision of the *Bundesgerichtshof*[48] shows the extent of praetorian powers which the German courts have arrogated to themselves when solving a case through the good faith provision of the Code (§ 242 BGB). Talk of deductive reasoning once again serves no meaningful purpose in such cases.

The litigation arose after the recent re-unification of Germany when the old "West" swallowed up the bankrupt "East". The case involved a buyer (defendant) and a seller (plaintiff) of a machine originally acquired from Austria. Both parties operated within the state controlled economy of communist (former) East Germany. The two Germanys agreed to unite in 1989 and the currency of East Germany ceased to exist in July 1990. East German marks (for brevity EDM) were converted into West German marks (WDM) at a rate of 2 : 1. The purchase price of the sold object was 1.7 million EDM; and before the disappearance of the EDM, the plaintiff had paid 400,000 EDM. The BGH took the view that the two parties should share the cost of the fiscal disruption to the transaction, which the unexpected political and economic changes had wrought. Pegging this result on § 242 BGB was only the first step. The way the court thought the sharing of the costs should be undertaken is even more intriguing; and, again, it bears no connection to deductive or inductive reasoning.[49] Arguably, the result is thus not really based on any kind of "legal principle" but on the court's desire to make some kind of economic sense of a transaction, which had been completely falsified by the unexpected political developments that shook Germany during the late 1980s.

Cases such as the above are not, of course, the norm. In our aforementioned *The German Law of Contract and Restitution* my German co-

[48] BGH NJW 1993, 259. Some of the post reunification cases are discussed by Ebke "Legal Implications of Germany's Reunification" (1990) 24 *Int. Lawyer* 1130.

[49] The BGH calculation was as follows. 1.7 EDM (purchase price) minus 400,000 EDM (deposit already paid) left 1.3 EDM unpaid. Exchanged for WDM this meant 650,000 WDM, half of which—i.e. 325,000 WDM should be paid by the defendant (buyer). This may sound as very much less than the originally agreed purchase price of 1.7 EDM but, in fact, it may have been too generous to the plaintiff (seller). For the 1.7 EDM were based on the unrealistically inflated price of EDM and Austrian schilling (from where, it will be remembered, the sold object was originally acquired). If one used the WDM/schilling market exchange rate, the purchase price would have been 380,000 WDM. Now it will be recalled that the plaintiff was allowed to claim 325,000 WDM; and he was allowed to keep the deposit already received (which was 400,000 EDM or, at a 2:1 exchange rate, 200,000 WDM). This means the plaintiff (seller) ended up with a total of 525,000 WDM for a machine which, realistically priced, was worth 380,000 WDM. That covers its cost; and leaves a profit of about 40%. That the court would have used its adjusting powers under § 242 BGB is understandable and, possibly, even fair; that it should been so generous to the plaintiff is, however, more open to doubt.

authors and I discuss the kind of case which involves the typical German deductive syllogism which will take the judge through a series of paragraph chains before coming up with the result desired by the Code.[50] But not all decisions display these characteristics; and to the extent that one uses as teaching tools decisions, which do not depend on deductive or inductive reasoning, one can take the comparisons of different systems even further. For in such cases the methodological differences between Common and Civil law are attenuated and thus the mental block, which discourages consultation of each other's law, should also, in theory, be correspondingly weakened.

CONCEPTS: VERBAL DEVICES WHICH FORMULATE JUDGMENTS BUT DO NOT REALLY EXPLAIN THEM

The starting idea is, again, Professor Fleming's. To be sure, it was formulated in the context of the Common law and posited that there was often considerable equivocation between such legal concepts as duty, remoteness, foreseeability, and the like.[51] In later years, another imaginative tort scholar repeated this idea in somewhat more colourful language by maintaining that "it is a question of aesthetics as much as anything else whether one feels that the acceptable solution is better produced by emphasizing causation or duty or damage."[52] But all this can also be applied with profit to the comparative study of foreign law.

If we return to our wrongful life/birth cases and look at them from a broader comparative perspective than we have done so far, namely by bring in French material,[53] we shall see that the results remain broadly similar even though they are justified through the use of different concepts. The French judgments in particular thus seem to be almost pre-occupied with whether the notion of causation is satisfied in these cases. Whether this is a convincing way of handling their facts is not really the issue. But what these decisions do show, especially when compared with the American or German case law, is that in Professor Fleming's words the concepts are only "the means of formulating conclusions but do not often dictate them".[54] The comparisons of the four systems we have been looking at in

[50] Markesinis, Lorenz, and Dannemann, *The German Law of Contract and Restitution*, chap. 1 (1997).

[51] "Remoteness and Duty: The Control Devices in Liability for Negligence", 31 *Can Bar Rev*. 471 (1953).

[52] T. Weir in Catala and Weir, "Delict and Torts: A Study in Parallel" 34 *Tulane L. Rev*. 701, 705 (1965). However, this is not always true. Thus, in *Rondel* v. *Worsley* [1969] 1 AC 191 for instance, the expressed policy aim of the court could not have been achieved through the mediums of causation, carelessness, or damage.

[53] Italian law, not discussed in this essay because of reasons of space, confirms the validity of most of the above general statements.

[54] *Supra*, note 51 at pp. 497–8.

this essay confirm this; for though the concepts differ the results are broadly speaking very similar. But let us at this stage of the discussion turn briefly to French law since its study reveals a different set of difficulties when studying foreign law.

The first problem with French law is finding out precisely what the courts allow in such cases. Sir Frederick Pollock is said to have written that "this [i.e. Britain] is the only country in Europe where quite a large portion of important affairs, from the Constitution downwards, are worked by just doing the thing you want and saying as little as possible about it even to yourself".[55] This statement could apply with equal force to the decisions of the highest French courts.

Until March 1996 and February of this year (1997) the French law was basically to be found in two decisions of the *Conseil d'Etat*[56] and one of the *Cour de cassation.*[57] The following dense statement from the latter, denied any *damnum* to the mother "given that the birth of a child conceived by her could not, *in itself*, amount to a juridically recognisable harm to her, even if the birth followed an unsuccessful attempt at abortion." The italicised words supply the only visible clue that the legal position is not as simple as the key statement implies at first glance; and even when the reconstruction of the picture has progressed—with the aid of the *arrêtistes*, the *conclusions du Commissaire du Gouvernement*, and the published versions of the decisions of the lower courts[58]—it is not as complete as the one which we have obtained from the German and American judgments. As instruments of teaching the law, the value of the French judgments is thus very low indeed. So, that observation apart, what is the picture, which emerges from this puzzle?

The first decision of the *Conseil d'Etat* and that of the *Cour de cassation* of 1991 dealt with the mothers' claims. We have no clue whether any claims were advanced on behalf of the children, though given that in both cases the children born were healthy, the probable answer is that none were made.[59] The italicised words of the judgments ("in itself"), alluded to above, have nevertheless allowed the *arrêtistes* to argue that the mother's position might be different if *she* could prove that she had suffered "une souffrance morale spéciale", for instance because the child was conceived as a result

[55] Cited by Lord Macmillan, "Two Ways of Thinking" in *Law and Other Things* (1938), 82.

[56] Of 2 July 1982, DS 1984, 425 and of 27 September 1989 GP 1990, 421.

[57] Of 25 June 1991, DS 1991, 566.

[58] We are lucky that in the present cases we have all three. In most instances, however, one or more of these "clues" will be missing, making the reconstruction of the case very difficult. This, for instance, is the case of the very latest decision of the *Conseil d'Etat.* I have only seen extracts of the revealing *conclusions* of the *Commissaire du Gouvernement* in the *Monde* of 17 February 1997.

[59] In German law the doctor's liability is, in such cases, limited to that of a natural father. It is fixed by means of tariffs and tends to be much less generous than when tort law methods of compensation are used.

of rape;[60] or because the child was born with grave deformities.[61] However, this last-mentioned decision of the *Conseil d'Etat* was not, really, a case of "wrongful life/birth" but concerned a claim for damages for injuries inflicted by a negligent doctor to a living foetus. Thus, despite some academic[62] and journalistic dicta[63] to the contrary, the better view would appear to be that it cannot be used as a "precedent" in genuine "wrongful life" cases in order to justify any claim by the affected child. The validity of this view was recently confirmed by the *Conseil d'Etat*, which re-stated its opposition to allowing the child (in contrast to its parents) any damages whatsoever.[64]

Thus far, the reconstruction of the French law has brought it closer to the American and German judgments than its opaque judgments would suggest at first sight. Though we cannot say how substantial this approximation is, since we do not have a comparable, settled list of compensatable headings of damage,[65] the overall picture is quite similar, especially since the most recent cases have made it quite clear that the parents' claims for their pain and suffering and the child's cost of maintenance are recoverable.[66] Finally, this picture of similarities is completed by the fact that (until recently) there was nothing in these judgments, which could be taken to support the view that any sum could be given to the child for it being born. Indeed, the repeated insistence that life, in itself, cannot be seen as damage made this difficult to accept in any form.[67]

[60] Cour d'Appel de Riom, *DS* 1990, 284. It is interesting that the decision of the Court of Appeal stressed that the plaintiff's only complaint seemed to be that the birth of her (healthy) child would make it impossible for her to lead the ordinary life of a young girl! Incidentally, there is no clue as to why she had allowed herself to become pregnant; nor indeed that she had been contributorily negligent in failing, despite medical advice, to have timeously an echo test to verify the successful conclusion of the abortion. At First Instance, this claim had led a more sympathetic court to reduce her damages by half.

[61] As is shown by Conseil d'Etat, *GP* 1990. 2. 421. In this case the liability of the hospital, which was held responsible for the doctor's negligence, amounted to just over 1 million FF, 400,000 of which had to go to the Social Security for medical expenses etc. and 600,000 to the child for "des souffrances physiques et du préjudice esthétique" which he suffered "ainsi que des troubles dans ses conditions d'existence".

[62] Le Tourneau, DS 1991, 567.

[63] Alluded to by Professor Moreau in his note to *Conseil d'Etat*, 14 fév. 1997, *Semaine Juridique* 1991, 195.

[64] *Conseil d'Etat*, 14 fév. 1997, *Semaine Juridique*, 1997, 22828.

[65] The cost of a new abortion, to complete the first and unsuccessful attempt has been consistently allowed. See, for instance, *Trib. grande inst. Evreux*, 21 déc 1979, *D*. 1981, 185. Extraordinary expenses seem allowable; but what amounts to "circonstances particulierment inopportunes ou exceptionnelles" is left to the courts of First Instance and access to their decisions is not always easy.

[66] In *Conseil d'Etat* 14 fév. 1997, *Semaine Juridique* 1997, 22828, a proper case of "wrongful birth" claim, the court denied the parents' claim for 2 million FF for pain and suffering and gave them, instead, a paltry 200,000 FF. Additionally, the parents were given 5,000 FF per annum for as long as the child lived to cover the child's annual expenses.

[67] Indeed, pro-life authors such as Professor le Tourneau wax lyrical about this. In his most helpful comment on the decision of the Court of Appeal of Riom he thus states (*DS* 1990,

Yet this picture of trans-border uniformity of the law may have been shattered by two recent (1996) decisions of the *Cour de cassation* which seem incompatible with American, English, and German law and, indeed, irreconcilable with the even more recent (1997) decision of the *Conseil d'Etat* to which we have already referred.

The first of these decisions of the *Cour de cassation* was the result of an action brought against a "geneticist" who advised a couple who consulted him to go ahead and procreate assuring them that the symptoms of neurological disorder that concerned them were not likely to be transmitted to any child which the mother conceived.[68] The second case concerned the familiar rubella drama. In both instances, the claims of the impaired *children* succeeded—the argument that life, itself, could not be considered as *dommage réparable* being reformulated to allow a pro-plaintiff result.[69] Once again, however, there is no complete clarity as to who is suing (the judgments only deal with the claims of the children). Opaqueness also exists as to what is being compensated. All that we have here is the almost meaningless generality "dès lors leur décision [of les juges du fond] condamant le médecin à réparer les conséquences dommageables définitives des troubles de l'enfant est légalement jusitfiée."[70] Notwithstanding these uncertainties, to foreign eyes at least, these decisions can only herald a further liberalisation of the law in the direction of more extensive compensation rights in addition to being in serious conflict with the pronouncements of the *Conseil d'Etat*.

Before we close this brief survey of French law it should be repeated that beyond the general and conclusionary statements alluded to above, the French decisions also display a particular approach to the issue of the existence of a causative link between the doctor's negligence and the harmful event. This, of course, is inevitable for a system that has no device such as own "duty of care" under which it can subsume all the wider policy issues raised by the case. The consequence is that the notion of causation is understood in an overtly normative manner to end up with a result, which we

288): "La vie même penible, est un don, peut être une grace . . . Toute notre civilisation nous souffle cet axiom et nous pousse à la chanter." This view was, again, re-asserted by the *Commissaire du Gouvernment* in the recent decision of the *Conseil d'Etat* of 14 fév. 1997 where Madame Pécresse said: "Nous ne pensons pas qu'un enfant puisse se plaindre d'être né tel qu' il a été conçu par ses parents, même s'il est atteint d'une maladie incurable ou d'un défaut génétique, dès lors que la science médicale n'offrait aucun traitment pour le guérir in utero. Affirmer l'inverse serait juger qu'il existe des vies qui ne valent pas la peine d'être vécues et imposer à la mère une sorte d'obligation de recourir, en cas de diagnostic alarmant, à une interruption de grossesse." *Le Monde*, 17 February 1997. It is noteworthy that the judgment, itself, makes no allusion whatsoever to this important policy reason.

[68] *Bull Civ*. 1996, 109—decision of 26 March 1996.

[69] ". . . le dommage ne consiste pas à naitre, mais à naitre atteint des séquelles graves et irréversible d'une maladie contractée avant la naissance." Jourdain, *Rev. trim. dr. civ*. 623, 4.

[70] *Bull Civ*., 1996, 109.

would also adopt relying on a different conceptual methodology. This point is made very clearly in the second decision of the *Conseil d'Etat* where the trier of fact held that the obstetrician's negligence did not take place in the operating room but consisted of failing to check after the operation was over whether the whole of the foetus had been extracted from the mother's womb. The *Commissaire du Gouvernement* thus continued: "Ainsi, peut-être certains d'entre vous trouveront-ils que le préjudice n'est pas du tout en relation avec la faute reprochée, mais bien plutôt avec la façon dont l'opération a été conduite ou avec la décision d'y recourir, c'est à dire avec des circonstances qui ne peuvent être imputées à faute à l'hôpital". The concluding statement is full of meaning when the *Commissaire* proceeded to say that ". . . nous hésitons à vous proposer d'adopter un raisonnement où le droit paraît s' écarter de la justice."[71]

THE UTILITY OF STUDYING FOREIGN LAW IN A COMPARATIVE WAY

For some authors the major advantage of studying foreign legal systems is a cultural one. Professor Jolowicz, for instance, when asked to contribute a paper to a conference held in Paris under the general heading "Les professions juridiques et le droit comparé" responded that "le droit comparé ne s'avère pas de grande utilité pratique du point du vue d'un membre d'une profession juridique".[72] Like many French authors he attributes to comparative law (a misleading term encompassing in this country foreign law and comparative methodology) "une valeur . . . essentiellement culturelle". That such a function exists, and must be encouraged, especially now that Roman law seems—unfortunately—to be in terminal decline in this country,[73] cannot be doubted. But this writer at any rate has seen much more in his subject than the cultural icing to a "black-letter" law cake; and the benefits gained from this subject, in these days of increased legal borrowings or legal harmonizations, are ones which, he feels, should be stressed more loudly.

Yet this view has yet to gain full acceptance in England. Thus, one learned contemporary writer who, because of his provenance, should have shared this view of a closer co-existence of the common and civil law worlds has,

[71] *GP* 1990, 422.

[72] 1994 no 3 *Revue Internationale de Droit Comparé*, 747.

[73] In Germany it has been "saved" because it has been combined with the study of German legal history (increasingly viewed within the wider context of European culture) and comparative law. Thus, see, Reinhard Zimmermann "Roman and Comparative Law: The European Perspective (Some Remarks apropos a Recent Controversy)", *Legal History*, vol 16, No 1 (1995) 21, and see esp. 27. This approach was put into practice in that author's magisterial treatise *The Law of Obligations, Roman Foundations of the Civilian Tradition* (1992).

nevertheless, expressed doubts as to whether comparative law can achieve its full potential in the real world of practice. That these predictions appear to be partly prompted by (his openly admitted) resentment that comparative law may nowadays be taking good minds away from his own subject (Roman law) is no reason to pay these doubts any less attention or leave them unanswered.

Lord Rodger of Earlsferry, the author of such pessimistic predictions,[74] makes them even more poignant by linking them to Lord Goff's judgment in *White* v. *Jones*.[75] He thus states specifically:

"I still wonder whether comparative law will achieve the kinds of practical results which are claimed for it. Certainly it will not do so if it is used as a substitute for analysis. . . . quoting chunks of law from other jurisdictions . . . can be really useful only as an aid to the proper analysis of the question before the court . . . references to the general principles adopted by Civil Law systems will usually have only a limited impact, especially since the approaches of those systems may very often diverge from one another. For this reason even Lord Goff . . . seems to have been able to draw only rather limited and inconclusive assistance from looking at Civil Law material on the concurrence of actions in *Henderson* v. *Merrett Syndicates Ltd*.[76] In *White* v. *Jones*[77] Lord Goff invokes German, French and Dutch law—along with Commonwealth and American authority—as support for the view that negligent solicitors should be held liable to disappointed beneficiaries. But when it comes to the actual analysis of the legal basis for any such liability, despite a fairly detailed discussion of two German doctrines, Lord Goff eventually falls back on an extension of *Hedley Byrne* as the actual foundation for his decision."[78]

This writer, who was involved in the *White* v. *Jones*[79] litigation as a very junior counsel, finds part of this criticism convincing; but he also feels that it misrepresents the respondents' efforts in that litigation.

First, no one advocated (in this or comparable cases) the introduction of "general principles" of the civil law. What my side (the successful respondents in the case) wished to indicate, through the use of the abundant foreign material which it assembled, were three things: first, we wished to stress the fact that liability was imposed on such facts in the vast majority of legal systems. A rule which enjoys such wide recognition cannot be as bad as the

[74] "Savigny in the Strand", John Maurice Kelly Memorial Lecture of 1994 (printed by University College Dublin in 1995 at p. 24). Dr. Jane Stapleton has also expressed similar doubts in her learned contribution entitled "In Restraint of Tort", published in *The Frontiers of Liability* (ed. P. B. Birks 1994) II, 83, 101.

[75] [1995] 2 WLR 194–5.

[76] [1995] 2 AC 145.

[77] [1995] 2 WLR 187, 194*ff*.

[78] *Op. cit*., note 74, above, at p. 25.

[79] [1995] 2 WLR 187.

appellants made out. Secondly, we wished to indicate that the rule had not caused an insupportable insurance crisis.[80] Finally, we felt that this material, so presented, could properly be taken into account by their lordships when considering English law, more precisely the heading of what is "fair and reasonable" in the duty of care phase of the enquiry.

Is any of the above so revolutionary? In the view of this writer, the answer is clearly negative. Nor, in the light of this particular case, is it convincing to argue that the use of comparative material would *inevitably* add to the cost and length of litigation since the material which we introduced in the *White* v. *Jones* hearing took less than an hour to present to their Lordships compared to double the time that it took Counsel for the Appellants to read extracts of the judgment of the judge at first instance.

Secondly, Lord Goff may not, on one reading of his judgment, have made as full use of this material as my side, at least, had hoped;[81] but merely by citing it he surely made lawyers of all kinds more aware of what another eminent British judge has described as another "world elsewhere".[82] We may not be ready to profit fully from that other world out there yet; but, as a result of changes in our legal education, we soon will be; and the earlier we start familiarising English lawyers with the potential significance of the foreign material, the better.

Thirdly, that this material was not used as a "substitute for analysis" can be seen in Lord Mustill's judgment and the effect it had upon it. To be sure, the learned judge's opinion did not adopt the German reasoning. Yet, it is submitted, if carefully read, the opinion shows how influenced the learned judge was by the Germanic debates about the contract/tort divide and the consequences which this entails. This view is reinforced if one reads Lord Mustill's opinion in conjunction with his thought-provoking article "Negligence in the World of Finance".[83] The doctrinal setting may thus be different in Germany; but forcing an English lawyer to try to understand it may, at the very least, be forcing him to rethink his own law.

It is thus at least arguable that because Lord Mustill refrained from openly citing the German material he admitted to using, many English lawyers may have been quick to underestimate the effect this had on his thinking process.

[80] An important point given that in this case counsel for the appellants produced a series of examples from cases which the Law Society was expecting to flood the courts if the plaintiffs won in this case. Though the discussion over these cases took the better part of a morning, on closer analysis most turned out not to possess the particular features of *White* v. *Jones* and to be able to produce their own answers in different ways. I have argued elsewhere, that this prolonged discussion offered a good example of wastage of judicial time.

[81] Though he did refute the appellants' contention that a pro-plaintiff ruling would lead to unbearable insurance consequences; [1995] 2 WLR 187.

[82] Sir Thomas Bingham M.R. "There is a World Elsewhere: The Changing Perspectives of English Law", 41 *Int. Comp. L. Quart.*, 513 (1992).

[83] 5 *The Supreme Court Journal*, 1–41 (1992).

Two additional points must be made to conclude this counter-thesis to Lord Rodger's views.

First, in his aforementioned article Lord Rodger states that what is needed is the supply of more detailed knowledge of foreign law. In this short piece and elsewhere, this author has always argued along similar lines, condemning René David's approach in his "Les grandes systèmes du droit cotemporain". My two-volume work entitled *The German Law of Obligations*[84] goes as far as the book of any one author can go in supplying over two hundred and fifty German decisions in translated form—almost as many extracts as any English law student is likely to read in his preferred English case book on contract and tort—and accompanies them by over one thousand pages of commentary and annotations. More importantly, if one looks at the number of works, translations, articles and monographs by other scholars, published in the last ten years and compares this situation with the three books my generation had when I started as a law teacher,[85] one must admit to great progress having being made in this area of the law. We would not have had this "New Wave" had my generation not made the crucial shift from (old) civil law (i.e. Roman Law) to modern civil law (i.e. Continental European law); and the scholar honoured in this *Festschrift*, admitted as much in an oft-cited book review.[86]

A further point, related to the above argument, must also be stressed. The new (translated and annotated) material does not merely describe the foreign systems but facilitates more active use of their case law; and in this piece I have tried to suggest ways of "milking" this material of its rich contents. Thus, I have tried to show how, starting from decisions, we can come to appreciate the common factual backgrounds and the remarkable similarity of solutions. I have also suggested that studying foreign law through cases also gives the teacher the chance to compare judicial styles, reflect on the sources of law and the use made of them by various courts, and also look at the relationship of the civil courts to the constitutional jurisdictions which are growing ever-more powerful in most Continental countries. With slightly more effort on the part of the teacher, delays in litigation, levels of compensation, and the inter-relationship of tort awards and social security awards can also be discovered through this material. A "lecture" on one

[84] Volume I, co-authored with Professor Lorenz and Dr. Danneman, is entitled *The German Law of Contract and Restitution*; vol II is entitled *The German Law of Torts*. Both are published by the Oxford University Press (1997).

[85] Cohen's *Manual of German Law*; Amos and Walton's *French Law* and von Mehren's *Comparative Law*.

[86] "Comparative Law of Torts", 4 *Oxf. J. Leg. Stud.* 235 (1984) where, referring to the Roman material which had been included in a book coauthored with the late Professor F. H. Lawson, he wrote: "... the whole retention of the Roman law relic surely owes more to nostalgia than to functional justification." The book reviewed is entitled *Tortious Liability for Unintentional Harm in the Common Law and the Civil Law* (1982) and is a revamped edition of Professor Lawson's classic *Negligence in the Civil Law*, published in 1950.

case and its parallels in two or three jurisdictions, can thus easily be spun out over two or three hours; and if the same is done systematically over a forty or sixty hour course on, say, foreign tort law or contract law, my experience has shown that the teacher will have imparted a great deal of knowledge on foreign law to his autochthonous student. More importantly, that material will already be in a shape and form that will make it more user-friendly to others who may subsequently wish to refer to it. All this, I suggest is both interesting and useful; and, as I already said, methodologically it is very different in style to what was available some twenty-five years ago.

This brings me to my last point: the receptivity of the judges of the future. I regard this as a very important issue and, again, regret to sense a difference of views between such an eminent jurist as Lord Rodger and myself. I am, however, encouraged to take issue with the learned Lord not only because I find comfort in the fact that others, as eminent as Lord Rodger, have differed with him on this issue. Thus Professor Koopmans, Advocate General of the Dutch Supreme Court and former (Dutch) Judge at the Court of the European Communities, recently confirmed that what I have been advocating for a very long time is, actually, already happening in foreign supreme courts.[87] And if to this statement my English readers retort, "yes, it may be happening abroad but it cannot happen here", let me explain why I think that such an assertion will be proved wrong.

First, some of Lord Goff's contemporaries and most of his successors are likely to have a University *legal* education behind them, something which was not true as recently as thirty years ago. It is logical, therefore, to expect such judges, nourished on textbooks as never before, to share a greater receptiveness to academic doctrine than their predecessors did.

Secondly and more importantly, we must soon be approaching a new crop of judges who will have visited Europe, not as part of some grand tour during their youth of the kind that was fashionable in the 18th and 19th centuries, but as participants in some kind of short or more sophisticated Erasmus-type programme. Take, for instance, the four year double degree, which King's College London has been running for years with Paris One. It attracts students at least as good as the best Oxbridge recruits; and it supplies them with a truly first class double training, accompanied by a technical linguistic proficiency in both languages. Will lack of languages be an obstacle to such a generation of judges? And if knowledge of the French and German languages is likely to become more widespread, will the same reluctance to look at foreign material continue? The truth of the matter is that there is out there a whole new generation of excellent legal minds waiting to come "to power" without any of the hang-ups (cultural or political) of the older generation but, on the contrary, conscious of the

[87] "Comparative Law and the Courts" 45 *The Intern. and Comp. L. Quart.* 545 (1996).

respective strengths and weaknesses of a number of European legal cultures.

We are creating such a generation of European lawyers in Oxford; and to anyone who argues that it will be a long time before they have the influence on our law that I am predicting, I say that I am prepared to wait. And, while waiting, I will go on trying to devise better ways of introducing these new recruits to the mysteries and fascination of foreign law and enticing them to visit the foreign countries and work in them. What adversity in life gave to John Fleming, we would like to supply in a more normal and congenial manner to the young Oxonians of today in the hope that this might give them a mind as agile and as open as his.

5

Why a Code is not the Best Way to Advance the Cause of European Legal Unity

A. INTRODUCTION

For someone who, like myself, feels not only English, Greek, Italian but also European, a conference such as this presents a dilemma as well as a challenge. The challenge, quite simply, is how to avoid the dilemma of choosing between the English and the Continental European point of view or, if you would rather see things in more legal terms, the common law—particularly the English common law—versus the civil law attitudes towards codification. One solution I can find to this dilemma lies in a theory, which I expounded, in the different context of how to teach foreign law to one's own lawyers. There I advocated that you must first "deconstruct" and then "re-construct" the foreign ideas to make them more acceptable to your own environment. In the present context, this means first telling you why I think the topic of our conference is, in my opinion, unrealistic (at least for the foreseeable future) and then telling you how I think some of the underlying ideas about closer European co-operation, which I find attractive, can be pursued.

B. THE QUEST FOR UTOPIA

I note, first, that what we are debating is not supported by history. The legal unification, which codes purport to promote, has I think, almost uniformly followed—(a) economic union and (b) political unification of some sort. Even if the first pre-condition can be taken to be sufficiently satisfied by the end of this millennium—a big if I hasten to add—the second point seems, realistically speaking, to be even further away on the horizon.

I note secondly that the drafting of codes has, in all but one instance—that of the French *Code Civil*—taken a long or very long time. The Netherlands' own record of 43 years is hardly an encouraging omen. And if that is the picture in the national context, I think the overall prognosis is bound to be even more grim in the supra-national context we are considering. I note, incidentally, that this is also true of "private" attempts to unify small parts of the law—and I am here thinking of the Lando project for which I have much time and admiration. I confess that in my own life, I spend little time thinking about death and God: in the first case because I can do nothing about it; in the second because I understand so little about Him—not least since the feminist movement has managed to remove from Him even the one attribute which for centuries has been taken for granted namely, that He is masculine! Frankly. I feel the same sense of frustration with our topic: a frustration which is increased by the realisation that in the crowded European agenda the enactment of a uniform code must, surely, rank as a very low priority. Thus, I would rather be discussing with you today ways to promote some of the *underlying ideas*, which I find attractive. Ideas which help to promote greater mutual understanding; ideas which strengthen our consciousness of our common heritage and demolish the prejudices which we so often find in our national Press; ideas which help to promote the greater mobility of persons and good ideas which are connected with the harmonisation of those parts of the law where harmonisation is truly needed and not merely undertaken for the sake of creating a uniform legal culture. More about these points in the second part of this brief Report.

I note, thirdly, that these days the idea of codification is not as widely favoured even by academics as it was, say, one hundred years ago. To be sure, those in favour will be quick to remind us that since the Second World War some fifty states have adopted codes, but without in any way sounding arrogant, I see little chance of the Codes of Egypt, Jordan, Algeria, the Seychelles, Columbia, Bolivia, or Paraguay, to give but some instances, serving as serious models for inspiration for our work, even assuming it were to take off which, I repeat, I do not think it will. Professor von Bar is one of the colleagues who have expressed an interest in studying the legal systems of the smaller countries. Personally, and despite an understandable personal predilection in the same direction, I am only partially persuaded by his arguments. For, if accepted, his ideas would only add to the complexity of our task and prolong the "gestation" period of our proposed child.

I am, fourthly, daunted by the task itself. What daunts me are three things in particular; and they have to be discussed in turn.

First is the fact that in a good code its different parts, sections and books, call them what you will, must be well interconnected. Take one instance. Many of us have argued how similar our laws on tort are or, more accurately, how similar they can be made to look with the help of some skilful (and well-meaning) manipulation. But in a code you cannot focus simply on the tort section—on which you have mainly asked me to speak: you must see this, adapt it, and reformulate it in conjunction with the law of contract, restitution, property and, indeed, other parts of the law such as criminal law, family law and the law of succession. I shall not bother you with examples though, I am sure, many spring to the minds of you all. Not many of us are polymaths, so I wonder whether we could ever make up a commission or commissions that could undertake such a complex task and, more crucially, eventually, try to bring the various national parts together. In any event, like Professor Bonnell, I cannot see my German colleagues abandoning large parts of their law of tort or contract in order to adopt the English or French approach for no better reason than creating a uniform code.[1] I know that, and do not merely suspect it; for a few years ago I attended a conference in Paris where there was some talk of extending the new French regime about traffic accidents and insurance to the rest of Europe—a modest and, some would argue, sensible proposal; and I recall Professor von Bar (and two German insurers who were also present at the Conference as observers) threatening to walk out if it came to that! Nor do I take any encouragement from the Lando project and its interesting attempts to weave compromises given that it has, so far, only covered a very small part of the law and even that has required more than fifteen years to reach fruition. No doubt, the admiral project leader will tell us more about his optimism which is now prompting him to move beyond the realm of "model laws" to full-blown codes. I confess in advance that even his formidable tenacity and ability to keep a team together leave me sceptical about the precedental value of his project outside the important area on which he has chosen to concentrate. Nor, if I may repeat this again, is the political climate propitious for such initiatives. On the contrary, raising such projects may give ammunition to those philosophically opposed to a more closely integrated Europe to harden their opposition towards this idea. It would be too facile to say that this group is composed only of Englishmen!

Secondly, I am daunted by the fact that those who, like Professor Zimmermann, tell us that in the old *ius commune* we can find part at least of our salvation may be seeing only part of today's very complex picture. I stress this because I feel they may lead less observant lawyers who talk of codification to see private law in isolation from the public law environment. For what we have today is a complicated amalgam of private

[1] Where German law has been deemed to be defective, for instance the area of "irregularities of performance"; reform proposals have been put forward. It is interesting, however, to note that even these limited reforms have not been implemented almost ten years after they were proposed.

and public law—I have elsewhere described the phenomenon as the constitutionalisation of private law—informed by a very different ideology than the one that shaped our traditional private law with its Roman origins. I am thus not only thinking of modern labour law, and how it has affected traditional contract doctrine, but also of insurance and social security law and how complex they have made the overall system of compensation of wrongfully inflicted harm. For, to return to my narrow topic of torts (on which I was originally asked to concentrate), surely my colleagues are not envisaging the harmonisation of the law of delict without at least an attempt to accompany it with a harmonisation of the social security rules and the attendant rights of subrogation. I regret that in my earlier paper on the law of torts I failed to stress this factor adequately, for I think one of the most urgent things that have to be done is the greater co-ordination of tort law and social security law—two systems which have experienced parallel but un-coordinated growth in each national system. Real harmonisation, if that is our true aim, can hardly be advanced if underlying differences in the social security systems are allowed to distort the effects of harmonised tort rules. This "combined" harmonisation of tort and social security rules is a Herculean task to achieve in one system let alone many.

Let me then move to my third concern; our different drafting techniques—a topic, which has received little attention during this conference. German lawyers may feel proud that, partly at least because of the work of academics, their ideas on contractual privity are now spreading to the English common law. Yet is that enough? Compare, for instance, the length and complexity of the legislation which the Law Commission has proposed, essentially bringing the English law of privity closer to that of the continental European systems. Can you imagine this being done over the whole area of the code? Or can Professor Lando really convince us that such a drafting technique would ever be accepted by European countries or, conversely, that his article-type presentation of the "compromise product" is likely to become acceptable in mine in the foreseeable future? Even allowing for the fact that some amending legislation to the German Code has, in recent times, shown signs of English verbosity, thus suggesting a certain convergence in drafting styles—and I am here referring to the Law on Standard Conditions of Business, one of the most inelegant pieces of modern legislation I have encountered—I still do not believe that the time is ripe for such a common endeavour. I note, incidentally, that even those of my colleagues who are more enthusiastic about the codification idea than I am, tend to think in terms of one, or two, or more generations before it can become a reality. Prophesying the future is neither my forte nor my professional duty so I again refuse to spend time on an endeavour, which strikes me as being riddled with so many uncertainties.

C. ALTERNATIVE WAYS OF FOSTERING GREATER CO-OPERATION AND UNDERSTANDING: A MULTI-TRACK APPROACH

Why continue the task of demolishing a topic, which was designed to bring us together, especially since the careful reader will have noticed that this "demolition work" was done—subtly of course but no less assuredly—by most of the contributors to the volume *Towards a European Civil Code*[2] (and, indeed, most of the speakers at this conference). Let us, instead, switch to a more pragmatic mode and see whether there are other ways through which some of the European objectives that I share can be achieved. This pragmatism is, I think, one of the most attractive features of the common law.

A law teacher has, of course, much sympathy with the ideas and work of Professor Zimmermann, subject to the kind of qualifications, which I mentioned earlier on. But my sympathy for such an approach is not prompted by loyalty to my branch of the legal profession. On the contrary it is, I hope, provoked by a pragmatic appraisal of today's realities, strengthened by the lessons of history. For certainly in Europe in the 17th century and in Germany for most of the 19th, a lack of a central government or, even, an effective central court, made academics the obvious legal *honoratiores*—to use Max Weber's (and, later, Max Rheinstein's) well-known expression. The current American experience is, if anything, more instructive since it shows that an effective free trade area can survive and, indeed, thrive, despite a considerable degree of legal diversity. But this illustration also shows how the fragmentation of a homogeneous culture into a multitude of small jurisdictions has been reduced through the activities of the national law schools which focus on the law which applies *everywhere* across the country but which, as such, is not in force *anywhere*. The focus of these studies is, thus, the core of what is common to all state laws namely, their tradition, their basic features, their common values and, above all, their methodology. I venture the guess that the same techniques will be used to facilitate trade for those states which have joined NAFTA. Thus, those who under-estimate the potential influence which the academic profession can have on the development of a legal system conveniently forget the role of the German or North American academics in the shaping of the law of their respective countries.

I see an additional advantage to this approach in that it provides us with a much-needed *organic synthesis and development of principles*, which bind together the existing, growing, patchy, and uncoordinated attempts at unification. I am referring, of course, to the harmonising effects of Direc-

[2] Hartkamp et al. (Eds.), *Towards a European Civil Code*, 1994.

tives, which as I said in my earlier piece, could continue the work of harmonising part of modern liability law. Areas that, I think, are susceptible to such "patchy" treatment include traffic accidents, some kinds of accidents at work, and problems of environmental liability, especially on the transnational scale. I hope that both these things happen (i.e. patchy harmonisation and an academic development of synthesising general principles); and I am not worried by the argument that such an approach will be slow in evolving, since I have already said that the one proposed by those who are raring to start drafting a code is no more likely to be quicker.

Directives and other forms of conventions are not the only ways of achieving a greater degree of harmonisation. As stated, my proposals to promote some of the underlying aims are based on a multi-track approach. Providing businessmen with a set of unofficial rules, which they can, if they wish, incorporate into their transactions, has many of the advantages of a code or codes without some of their disadvantages. This path, too, must thus be pursued. Such "model laws" if they are adopted by the parties, will be adopted because they have devised a clear and workable regime and not because they have been imposed from above by some remote, supra-state legislator striving for funded solutions. Such model laws do not have to conform to national drafting techniques and thus are likely to arouse less opposition. And if they prove unworkable or, with the passage of time are in need of fine tuning, that could be done in the unofficial way in which they were born in the first place. That, I think, is the best accolade one can give to the Lando project.

A parallel practice of our highest courts could also be encouraged to develop, especially if materials could become more widely available and ideas and solutions could be made to travel more easily. This is the third track and there are some signs that this is already happening in my country. The habit could grow—I predict will grow—more if the European Union continues to assist student and teacher mobility, takes measures to encourage the organic growth of a European consciousness, and makes foreign material more readily available to our national courts. In this context, allow me to refer briefly to the work that we are carrying out at my Institute in Oxford, which is guided by these principles.

In Oxford, we recently established the nucleus of "roving" European professors by having every year with us at my Centre four Professors from Germany, three from France and (most recently) one from Italy. All these colleagues teach their own law in their own language to those of our students who have chosen to take part in our four-year courses (one of which is spent abroad). But, at the same time, we try to integrate our foreign visitors into our English classes and in this way are now giving even our English students a taste of foreign law, be it German, French or that of any other country as part of the instruction they receive in English law. It would be a mistake to conceal the fact that we are facing teething problems in this new venture; but, overall, I think it is a good start since it helps bring carefully selected students together who are then often employed by multinational firms and thus prolong their co-operative work in the practical field. If I were a central European agency, I would pump more money into such ventures, provided they were carefully selected and rigidly meritocratic in their aims and in the human resources they depended upon. I think, in other words, there is room for a more advanced and more selective version of the Erasmus or Socrates types of schemes—though I know that governments on the Continent of Europe tend to baulk whenever one even mentions meritocratic criteria or the pursuit of excellence.

Another way in which mentalities can change, co-operation be fostered, and understanding improved, is through the writing of European textbooks and case books. I have already said how this could help our courts borrow ideas from each other and help our students shed some of the prejudices with which they have been allowed to grow up. Professor van Gerven is leading one such project: and I have, myself, (with two German colleagues) tried my best with a two-volume comparative presentation of *The German Law of Obligations: Contract, Restitution, and Tort.* Professor von Bar's monumental *European Law of Delict* is another example of this effort, as is Professor Kötz's erudite and inspiring latest book entitled *European Law of Contract.* The advantage of such works is that they can be as complete as codes but much more flexible in their contents. They can also be used by practitioners and even judges when seeking inspiration on a novel or difficult problem—a point I mentioned earlier but which I repeat because I regard it as very important.

Against this background, I have little to add to what I wrote a few years ago about the law of torts in particular. I believe the Dutch Presidency is right to feel proud of its new code. But in my respectful opinion, it will leave a much more profound mark on the matter in hand if it could find ways to foster more contacts between our students, our law teachers, our practitioners, and our judges in order to discuss not the drafting of codes but a different set of topics. Here are some. Though they are mentioned indicatively, they are sufficient to show you the direction I would like us to take.

1. Funding of common research posts and projects on "manageable" topics, including the study of differences in civil procedure.
2. Common vocational programmes, including advocacy.
3. Fostering a greater understanding of how the law works in practice, perhaps through exchange apprenticeship schemes. Law firms should be asked to assist such programmes since they stand to benefit financially from them.
4. Fostering of closer links between academic institutions and practising lawyers.

If my ideas strike you as strange, I readily admit it is because we British have kept ourselves out of the mainstream of legal events in Europe for too long and thus failed so far to demonstrate to you that we have something to offer in almost all of the above areas. I think that if some of these ideas get on your agenda you will discover that we are ready to teach as well as to learn so long as our feet remain firmly on the ground. The idea of a European code, however, belongs to the "Paradise of Legal Ideas" that would have appealed to some Pandectists but leave most of us on my side of the Channel sceptical to say the least.

6

Der wachsende Einfluß der Menschenrechte auf das englische Deliktsrecht[1]

HOMAGE AN HANS STOLL

Drei der größten Rechtsvergleicher unterrichteten in Freiburg, und mir war es vergönnt, sie alle kennenzulernen. Es handelt sich um Ernst von Caemmerer, Hans Stoll und Peter Schlechtriem. Ich habe Vorlesungen von allen dreien gehört; außerdem hatte ich die Ehre, die beiden letzteren an meinem Institut in Oxford zu Gast zu haben. Dort lasse ich keine Gelegenheit aus, meine Studenten (und meine Kollegen) daran zu erinnern, welche geistigen Schulden wir in England beim deutschen Rechtsdenken haben. Das verdankt sich zum größten Teil den Schriften von Kollegen wie Hans Stoll, dessen Werk gründlich, eindringlich und anregend ist. Es war mir deshalb eine Ehre, um einen kleinen Beitrag zu diesem Band gebeten zu werden, der nicht nur den Mann ehrt, sondern auch seine Rechtsordnung, von der ich selbst so viel gelernt habe.

EINLEITENDE BEMERKUNGEN

Seit der Zeit nach dem Zweiten Weltkrieg haben die Menschenrechte immer wieder für Schlagzeilen gesorgt, in Deutschland wie in England, aber mir soll es hier nur um die Lage in England gehen. Teils will ich meinen Beitrag nicht ausufern lassen, teils fehlen mir vertiefte Kenntnisse im deutschen Recht.[2] Es gibt aber noch einen weiteren Grund, der das englische Recht

[1] Für Hilfe bei der Übersetzung seines Vortrags aus dem Englischen dankt der Verfasser Herrn Dr. Stefan Enchelmaier, stv. Direktor des Instituts für Europarecht und Rechtsvergleichung und Herrn Hannes Unberath, Worcester College, Oxford.

[2] In verschiedenen Schriften habe ich meine Überzeugung geäußert, daß das deutsche Recht gegenüber dem englischen oft ausgefeilter ist, sowohl was einige seiner Grundbegriffe angeht, wie auch einige seiner Lösungen in der Praxis; siehe, z.B., BS Markesinis 'Five Days in the House of Lords: Some Comparative Reflections on *White* v. *Jones*' 3 *Torts Law Journal*

für eine vergleichende Untersuchung empfiehlt. Seit rund fünfzig Jahren hat das englische Recht in diesem Bereich mehrere Standortverschiebungen erfahren, die sich festzuhalten lohnt.

Außenpolitische Gründe waren es zunächst, derentwegen wir die Europäische Menschenrechtskonvention nicht umsetzten, obwohl wir maßgeblichen Einfluß auf ihre Entstehung genommen hatten. Dabei ging es um die schrittweise und manchmal zögerliche Auflösung des Britischen Weltreichs. Es ließ sich nur schwer rechtfertigen, daß wir zuhause Menschenrechte verkündeten und schützten, während wir sie im Ausland unterdrückten. Die Umsetzung der Konvention mußte daher verschoben werden.[3] Später traten die Unruhen in Nordirland an diese Stelle und ließen die Regierung mit einer Klärung der Menschenrechtslage zögern. Als Ergebnis erlitt unsere Rechtsordnung einige peinliche Schlappen in Straßburg. Die Verantwortlichen waren aber offenbar der Meinung, dies sei ein Preis, den es sich zu zahlen lohne. So mußten britische Bürger, die sich von ihrer eigenen Rechtsordnung ungerecht behandelt fühlten, über lange Zeit Rechtsschutz im Ausland suchen. Kurz gesagt, nach dem Zweiten Weltkrieg wurde die erste günstige Gelegenheit, einigen Teilen unserer Rechtsordnung, die noch aus dem neunzehnten Jahrhundert stammten, neues Leben einzuhauchen, verschiedenen politischen Bedürfnissen der unmittelbaren Nachkriegszeit untergeordnet.

In Deutschland dagegen war die politische Lage Ende der vierziger, Anfand der fünfziger Jahre ganz anders. Infolge der militärischen Niederlage traten die Menschenrechtsverletzungen während der Zeit des Nationalsozialismus in vollem Umfang zutage. So wurde das Bestreben, die Menschenrechte zu achten, und allen voran die Menschenwürde, zum Grundstein der deutschen Verfassungsgeschichte der Nachkriegszeit. Im Unterschied dazu fand sich England, das sich in dem Ruhm sonnte, einen "gerechten Krieg" gefochten zu haben, weniger unter Druck, seine Einstellungen wie auch den Schutz der Menschenrechte zu modernisieren, obwohl beides sehr vonnöten war.

169*ff.* (1995); "Some Comparative Reflections on the Right of Privacy of Public Figures in Public Places" (zusammen mit Dr. Nico Nolte) in *Privacy and Loyalty* (Hrsg. P.B.H. Birks) (1997) 113–131; "Privacy, Freedom of Speech and the Horizontality of the Human Rights Bill" *1998 Wilberforce Lecture*, 115 (1999) *LQR*, 47–88.

[3] Zur Rechtfertigung seiner Ablehnung eines Rechts auf Individualbeschwerde erklärte der seinerzeitige Kolonialminister in einem Rundschreiben: "Die Einführung eines solchen Systems der Anrufung internationaler Behörden würde erhebliche Mißverständnisse und politische Unruhe in vielen Kolonialgebieten schaffen. Der Großteil der Menschen in vielen Kolonien ist nach wie vor politisch unreif, und die Grundlage guten Regierens über solche Menschen ist die Achtung vor einer einzigen, ungeteilten Autorität, die sie als verantwortlich für ihre Angelegenheiten anzuerkennen erzogen worden sind. Die Verwirrung[, die sich aus einer Umsetzung der Konvention ergeben würde], würde die Autorität der Kolonialregierung aushöhlen, Ergebenheit würde erschüttert, die Verwaltung würde erschwert und Aufwiegelung erleichtert." Zit. nach Lord Lester, "Fundamental Rights: The United Kingdom Isolated?" (1984) *Public Law* 46, 50.

Dieser Zustand konnte nicht für immer anhalten. Ende der sechziger, Anfang der siebziger Jahre entwickelte sich zunehmender Druck auf das Verwaltungsrecht und den Menschenrechtsschutz in England. Zunächst wurden Ombudsleute eingeführt. Dies geschah mit dem Ziel, krasse Beispiele von Rechtsverletzungen der Verwaltung zu korrigieren. Dann begann der Staat sich verplichtet zu fühlen, die Opfer von Gewalttaten zu entschädigen, deren Täter nicht ausfindig gemacht werden konnten. Nicht zu vergessen ist schließlich das zunehmende Streben nach besseren Beziehungen zwischen den Rassen und nach Gleichheit der Geschlechter, das Menschenrechtsfragen breiten Bevölkerungsschichten zu Bewußtsein brachte. Es war nicht mehr genug, solche Fragen als gefährlich für unsere Außenpolitik oder als bedeutsam nur für eine einzige unruhige Provinz abzutun. Der innere Druck—soziale Gleichheit, Gleichheit der Geschlechter und der Rassen—ging uns näher, und weil diese Probleme auch das Wahlverhalten beeinflußten, konnten die Politiker jedwelcher Ausrichtung sie nicht unbeachtet lassen. Diese Fragen erwiesen sich daher als die wirksamsten Triebkräfte der Veränderung. Einige bemerkenswerte Äußerungen hochrangiger Richter[4] gaben dieser Bewegung weitere, juristische Glaubwürdigkeit. Sie wurde nun auch in dem neuen Zusammenhang mit Europa gesehen, nicht nur mit dem Europa Straßburgs, sondern auch mit dem Luxemburgs, insbesondere nachdem letzteres sich die Grundsätze zueigen gemacht hatte, die das Fallrecht des ersteren bestimmten. Die traditionelle englische Abneigung gegen Grundsatzerklärungen blieb jedoch. Die Betonung einer pragmatischen, minimalistischen und schrittweisen Herangehensweise hatte zur Folge, daß die "neuen Fragen" hauptsächlich mit punktuellen Gesetzen behandelt wurden statt auf eine mehr ganzheitliche Weise. Obwohl beteutende Richter, ungewöhnlich für das englische Recht, zunehmend die Vorzüge einer systematischen Entwicklung des Rechts priesen,[5] ergaben sich die Veränderungen im Bereich der Menschenrechte in der üblichen schrittweisen, pragmatischen und nicht immer widerspruchsfreien Weise.

In jüngerer Zeit hat ein anderes Rechtsgebiet—das Deliktsrecht—begonnen, sich von Menschenrechtsfragen beeinflussen zu lassen. Unzufriedenheit mit unserem deliktischen Schutz gegen Ehrverletzungen (*law of defamation*), insbesondere seine Tendenz, die Freiheit der politischen

[4] Insbesondere Lord Scarman, dessen Hamlyn Vortrag *English Law: The New Dimension*, (1974) sich als Katalysator des akademischen Schrifttums (in den 1970ern and 1980ern) und der Rechtsprechung (in den 1980ern und besonders in den 1990ern) erwies.

[5] ZB Lord Mustill in seiner abweichenden Meinung in *White* v. *Jones* [1995] 2 WLR 187, 228E; Lord Hoffmann in *Hunter* v. *Canary Wharf Ltd* [1997] 2 WLR 684, 709F. Der einflußreichste auf dem Gebiet der Menschenrechte war ursprünglich Lord Scarman. In jüngerer Zeit gehörten zu den Unterstützern dieses Trends unter anderen der Lord Chancellor, der Lord Chief Justice und Lord Lester of Herne Hill (einer der führenden Praktiker was Menschenrechtsfragen angeht).

Meinungsäußerung zu ersticken, und die oft übertriebenen Entschädigungssummen, ließ Juristen die Möglichkeit in Betracht ziehen, diesen Entwicklungen dadurch Einhalt zu gebieten, indem man sie dem Grundrecht der Meinungsfreiheit unterordnet. Amerika hatte in den frühen sechziger Jahren diesen Weg gewiesen, aber erstaunlicherweise brauchten seine Ideen länger als sonst, um sich nach Osten zu verbreiten. Als es darum ging, anhand des Rechts der Meinungsfreiheit die Grenzen der persönlichen Ehre abzustecken, kam anfänglich Article 10 der Menschenrechtskonvention zum Einsatz. Diesmal hatte das Problem jedoch nichts mit Außenpolitik, Nordirland oder ähnlichem zu tun. Wie die Probleme der Gleichheit der Geschlechter oder der Rassen war es hausgemacht. Es entsprang der ungewöhnlichen Strenge des englischen Beleidigungsrechts und der wachsenden Unzufriedenheit damit.

In diesem Aufsatz soll es darum gehen, wie es dazu kam, daß Menschenrechtsfragen das Deliktsrecht durchdrungen haben. Hat diese Entwicklung ihren Höhepunkt erreicht? Wird sie sich auf weitere Gebiete des Deliktsrechts ausdehnen? Wie werden die Rechtsanwender auf die neue Herausforderung reagieren? Ich kann hier nur auf einige wenige Fragen zu sprechen kommen; eine umfassende Darstellung würde das Format eines Buches erfordern. Eins scheint jedoch klar: Das Deliktsrecht entwickelt sich zum Haupteinfallstor für die Menschenrechte in die englische Rechtsordnung, so sehr dies auch überraschen mag. Dieser Trend hat sich unlängst durch das *Osman*-Urteil des Europäischen Gerichtshofs für Menschenrechte noch verstärkt.[6] Wenn das Gericht seinen Ansatz im *Osman*-Urteil im schwebenden Verfahren *X* v. *Bedfordshire*[7] bestätigt, könnte unser gesamtes Deliktsrecht seine wichtigste Neuausrichtung durchmachen, seit seine moderne Phase mit der Grundsatzentscheidung des House of Lords in *Donoghue* v. *Stevenson*[8] begann. Das ist nicht nur für Anwälte von Interesse, die in den Menschenrechten neue Angriffs- und Verteidigungsmittel entdecken. Es ist auch für Rechtsvergleicher interessant, die immer schon von der Ausstrahlung und Rezeption von Ideen gefesselt waren, und vielleicht auch vom wachsenden Einfluß des öffentlichen auf das private Recht.

Solche umwälzenden Veränderungen ereignen sich nur selten im Leben eines Rechtsgelehrten. Es liegt daher auf der Hand, daß sie in einem begrenzten Rahmen wie hier nicht alle genannt oder gar erörtert werden können. Zwei Punkte möchte ich jedoch für den Leser hervorheben.

Auf den ersten habe ich schon vor beinahe zwanzig Jahren aufmerksam gemacht. Ich habe ihn die "Konstitutionalisierung des Privatrechts"

[6] Urteil vom 28. Oktober 1998, *The Times* 5. Nov. 1998, (1998) BHRC 293, ECtHR.

[7] [1995] 3 WLR 152. Es gibt Anzeichen dafür, daß das Gericht seinen Ansatz bestätigen wird, siehe die Meinung der Komission in den Anträgen Nr. 29392/95 vom 10.9.1999 (*Z* v. *U.K.*) und Nr. 28945/95 vom selben Tag (*T.P. und K.M.* v. *U.K.*).

[8] [1933] AC 562.

genannt.[9] Er verdiente die vermehrte Aufmerksamkeit aller Juristen, vor allem aber die der Rechtsvergleicher. Letztere haben den Gegenstand ihrer Untersuchungen nämlich hauptsächlich beim Privatrecht eingeordnet und den wachsenden Einfluß weitgehend außer acht gelassen, den das öffentliche Recht auf das Privatrecht hat. Im Zusammenhang des Deliktsrechts wirft dies zahlreiche Probleme auf. Ist beispielsweise unsere Hierarchie der Werte der deutschen oder der amerikanischen näher? Schon diese Frage wird die meisten meiner Landsleute entsetzen. Wie kann ein englischer "common lawyer" einem deutschen "civil lawyer" näher sein ? Es geht mir jedoch darum: Teilen wir in England die amerikanische Auffassung, daß die Meinungsfreiheit als ein Wert *jederzeit* allen anderen vorgeht? Oder wollen wir uns lieber dem deutschen Recht anschließen und die widerstreitenden Werte sorgfältig (ich meine, mit aller nur erdenklichen Sorgfalt) abwägen? Der Umstand, daß unsere Gerichte mehr amerikanische als deutsche Urteile zitiert haben, bedeutet meines Erachtens nicht, daß sich die Frage gar nicht stellt, oder gar schon in der einen oder anderen Weise entschieden wäre. Diese Auswahl der Bezugnahmen bedeutet, meine ich, nicht mehr, als daß das deutsche (oder französische oder italienische) Gedankengut aus sprachlichen Gründen noch nicht die gebührende Aufmerksamkeit gefunden hat. Mit dieser vorläufigen Erklärung soll es hier sein Bewenden haben.

Ein zweiter Punkt soll hier nur kurz erwähnt werden, weil er sich mit dem weiteren Problem der Methodenlehre beschäftigt, auf die sich in zunehmendem Maße meine Bemühungen richten.[10] Ich möchte hier die Wirkungen beschreiben, die Menschenrechtsfragen in jüngerer Zeit auf das Deliktsrecht gehabt haben. Ich möchte auch darüber nachdenken, wie die englischen Juristen mit den Veränderungen zurechtkommen werden, die ihnen aus Straßburg aufgezwungen werden. Meine eigene Vermutung ist, daß es zu keiner einheitlichen Reaktion kommen wird, und daß sie, schlimmer noch, ängstlich sein wird, und so die Gelegenheit verpassen wird, breitere menschenrechtliche Grundsätze für das Deliktsrecht zu entwickeln. Sollte dies eintreten, so wird diese Neuausrichtung des englischen Rechts vor allem denjenigen Rechtsanwälten zugute kommen, die das Klagenpotential ausschöpfen, wenn nicht ausbeuten wollen, das unsere neue Menschenrechtsgesetzgebung zusammen mit der Straßburger Rechtsprechung bieten wird.

DIE UNTERWANDERUNG DES BELEIDIGUNGSRECHTS

Im englischen Recht ist Beleidigung (*defamation*) eine unerlaubte Handlung, und nur selten eine Straftat. Dies ist so seltsam, wie es wichtig ist. Es ist

[9] Ich habe den Begriff zum ersten Mal in meinem Shimizu Vortrag verwendet und erläutert, veröffentlicht in 53 [1980] *MLR* 1 *ff.* Seitdem hat ihn u.a. Professor Christian von Bar in seinem monumentalen *The Common European Law of Torts,* vol. I (1998), 569 *ff.* aufgegriffen.

[10] Siehe dazu mein *Foreign Law and Comparative Methodology: A Subject and a Thesis* (1997). Ich hoffe, daß bald ein zweiter Band mit Aufsätzen zum öffentlichen Recht folgt.

seltsam, weil Beleidigung vor Geschworenen verhandelt wird.[11] Es ist aber auch wichtig, weil das Beleidigungsrecht von der Notwendigkeit beherrscht ist, widerstreitende Werte in Einklang zu bringen: die persönliche Ehre und die Meinungsfreiheit. Unser Recht hat bisher seine urspünglichen Züge bewahrt, daß es nämlich a) sich geweigert hat, von der Geschworenenverhandlung abzugehen, und daß es b) anders als die USA immer noch deutlich die persönliche Ehre der freien Rede vorzieht. Die jüngere Gesetzgebung und Rechtsprechung haben den ersten Zug nicht unberrührt gelassen. Meines Erachtens wird der zweite Zug bald demselben Druck nachgeben,[12] aber diese Entwicklung steht noch aus, und das amerikanische Vorbild, so interessant es auch sein mag, ist nicht ideal für England.

Der Fall *Rantzen* v. *Mirror Group News Papers*[13] stützt meinen ersten Punkt. Die Zeitung als Berufungsklägerin beschwerte sich, die £250.000 Schadensersatz, zu denen sie verurteilt worden war, laufe auf eine Beschränkung oder Bestrafung ihrer freien Meinungsäußerung hinaus. Sie forderte den Court of Appeal auf, von seiner neuen Kompetenz[14] Gebrauch zu machen, Geschworenenurteile abzuändern. Das Gericht hatte diese Möglichkeit, wenn der ausgesprochene Schadensersatz "exzessiv" war. Darunter hatte man bislang einen Schadensersatz verstanden, der so hoch war, daß er keinerlei Wirklichkeitsbezug mehr erkennen ließ. Bei der Beratung des Gesetzes im Oberhaus hatte der Lord Chancellor hervorgehoben, die neue Bestimmung solle den Gerichten eine *gesetzliche* Grundlage für das Aussprechen eines anderen Schadensersatzes geben. Sie verfolge jedoch *nicht die Absicht, die Gründe zu erweitern, aus denen ein Geschworenenurteil abgeändert werden durfte*. Die Berufungskläger argumentierten jedoch—und das Gericht schloß sich dem an—daß die Möglichkeit des Gerichts, Geschworenenurteile abzuändern, sich nach Article 10 der Europäischen Menschenrechtskonvention (EMRK) in der Auslegung durch den Europäischen Gerichtshof für Menschenrechte (EGMR) in Straßburg bestimme. Zwar war die EMRK nicht Teil des englischen Rechts, wie das House of Lords unzweideutig im *Brind*-Fall befunden hatte.[15] In einem

[11] Hinsichtlich anderer Besonderheiten unseres Beleidigungsrechts, s. Markesinis und Deakin, *Tort Law*, 4. Aufl. 1999, S. 643–5.

[12] Damit meine ich die politische Meinungsfreiheit und das Bestreben, sie stärker als bisher zu schützen. Siehe dazu die Aufsatzsammlung von Professor Ian Loveland, *Importing the First Amendment. Freedom of Speech and Expression in Britain, Europe and the USA* (1998); siehe auch dessen *Political Libels* (1999). Aus Platzmangel werde ich auf diese wechselseitige Beeinflussung von Menschenrechten und Beleidigungsrecht nicht näher eingehen. Sie ist jedoch potentiell noch bedeutender als die Schadensersatzproblematik, die ich im folgenden erörtern werde.

[13] [1994] QB 670.

[14] § 8 (1) und (2) des Courts and Legal Services Act 1990.

[15] *R.* v. *Secretary of State for the Home Department ex. parte Brind* [1991] 1 AC 696. Dabei handelte es sich nicht um einen Beleidigungsfall, sondern um eine Klage von Journalisten, gestützt auf Art. 10 EMRK, gegen den sog. Nordirischen Rundfunkbann, nach dem der IRA und ihren Unterstützern keine direkte oder indirekte (durch Interviews oder Berichter-

anderen Fall[16] hatte das House of Lords jedoch durch Lord Goff ausgesprochen, daß

> "wo es um die Redefreiheit geht, Article 10 einen weiteren Anwendungsbereich [hat], und zutreffend als ein Ausdruck von Grundsätzen [angesehen werden kann], die dem Common Law zugrundeliegen."

In seiner Besprechung des *Rantzen*-Falls hat Murray Hunt darauf hingewiesen, daß der Court of Appeal damit
"nicht nur in die Lage versetzt war, gesetzliche Bestimmungen und Common Law im Licht der EMRK [auszulegen], sondern weitergehend auch die Frage aufwerfen konnte, ob nicht das Fehlen einer Anleitung für Geschworene beim Bemessen von Schadensersatz mit der EMRK insofern unvereinbar war, als danach Einschränkungen der Meinungsfreiheit gesetzlich bestimmt sein müssen."[17]

Der geschickte Gebrauch der Meinungsfreiheit in *Rantzen*, größtenteils gestützt auf ausländische Rechtsquellen, senkte auf diese Weise die hohe Schwelle, die das Common Law vor eine Änderung von Geschworenenurteilen durch die Gerichte gesetzt hatte. Beleidigungsfäle im Anschluß an *Rantzen* haben die mittelbare Wirkung bestätigt, den die EMRK auf die englischen Gerichte hat. Die Fiktion verlor an Einfluß, man brauche die Konvention nicht wirklich, weil das englische Recht im Ergebnis, wenn auch nicht im Vorgang der Entscheidungsfindung, auf dasselbe hinauslaufe.

Der Gebrauch, den das *Rantzen*-Urteil von Straßburger Gedankengut machte, war mutig, aber es steht darin nicht mehr allein. Der spätere *Elton John*-Fall,[18] in dem wieder der Court of Appeal *punitive damages* (Schadensersatz mit Strafcharakter) erheblich herabsetzte, bezog sich zur Begründung auf die EMRK. Der Human Rights Act 1998 wird diese wechselseitige Befruchtung voraussichtlich noch beschleunigen, und der Lord Chancellor wird es, entgegen seiner ständigen Mahnung zur Zurückhaltung, schwer finden, Richter wie Lord Bingham,[19] Lord Woolf,[20] Lord Justice

stattung) Gelegenheit gegeben werden durfte, im Rundfunk ihren Standpunkt zu vertreten. Das Gericht befand, mangels irgendwelcher Auslegungsspielräume im Gesetz komme die Anwendung von Art. 10 EMRK nicht in Frage.

[16] *Attorney General* v. *Guardian Newspapers (Spycatcher) (No 2)* [1990] 1 AC 109; aufgegriffen von Lord Keith im späteren Fall *Derbyshire County Council* v. *Times Newspapers* [1993] AC 534 (550).

[17] *Using Human Rights Law in English Courts* (1997), S. 198.

[18] *John* v. *Mirror Group Newspapers Ltd* [1993] 2 WLR 953. In diesem Fall wurde der ursprüngliche Schadensersatz iHv. #$#350.000 (für die Beschreibung des gleichnamigen Popsängers als bulimisch) auf die immer noch erkleckliche Summe von #$#50.000 herabgesetzt.

[19] "The European Convention on Human Rights: Time to Incorporate", The Denning Lecture, abgedruckt in *Human Rights in the United Kingdom* (Hrsg. Richard Gordon und Richard Wilmot-Smith) (1996) pp. 1–11; "Should there be a Law to Protect Rights of Personal Privacy?" [1996] *European Human Rights Law Review*, 450*ff*.

[20] *Protection of the Public: A New Challenge* (1990), Hamlyn Lectures. Siehe auch seine FA Mann Lecture "Droit Public—English Style" [1995] *Public Law* 57*ff*.

Sedley,[21] Lord Justice Laws[22] und andere zu zügeln, die in ihren Urteilen wie in Aufsätzen ein bisher ungekanntes (und höchst willkommenes) Interesse an der Rechtsvergleichung zeigen. Bevor ich mich meinem zweiten Punkt zuwende, möchte ich hervorheben, was ich für den wichtigsten Gesichtspunkt der genannten Fälle halte.

Es ist nicht die Tatsache, daß der Anstoß zu dieser Wandlung ganz klar "von außen" kam. Interessanter noch erscheint mir, daß englische Richter versucht haben, die Fiktion aufrechtzuerhalten, solche "Anstöße aus dem Ausland" seien gar nicht nötig gewesen. Das englische Recht habe schon immer die Menschenrechte betont und berge in sich selbst den Stoff für seine weitere Erneuerung.[23] Lord Goff hat diese Überzeugung, wie immer in der eingängigsten Weise, in seinem zweiten *Spycatcher*-Urteil in dem folgenden, oft zitierten Absatz wiedergegeben:[24]

> "Ich erlaube mir die Bemerkung, daß ich keinen Widerspruch zwischen dem englischen Recht in diesem Feld und Article 10 EMRK sehe. Dies mag kaum überraschen, können wir uns doch glücklich schätzen, daß die Freiheit der Rede hierzulande jedenfalls ebenso lange, wenn nicht länger als in irgendeinem anderen Land verbürgt war. Article 10 EMRK, in Übereinstimmung mit seinem erklärten Zweck, verleiht ein Grundrecht und schrönkt es dann ein, während wir in unserem Land (wo es im Rahmen der Gesetze jedem freisteht zu tun, was er will) eher die Redefreiheit zum Ausgangspunkt nehmen und das Gesetz nur dazu dient, die Ausnahmen niederzulegen."

Nicht nur seine Eleganz ist bezeichnend für dieses Urteil. Es hebt auch das Gewicht hervor, das das englische Recht[25] auf Rechtsbehelfe und Rechtsverletzungen[26] legt, statt wie die modernen zivilistischen Rechtsordnungen auf Rechte abzuheben.[27] Unglücklich an Lord Goffs Aussage ist jedoch, daß sich im Anschluß an sie viele englische Juristen der Illusion hingegeben haben,

[21] "The Sound of Silence: Constitutional Law Without a Constitution" (1994) 110 *Law Quarterly Review*, pp. 270*ff*.; "Human Rights: A Twenty First century Agenda" [1995] *Public Law*, pp. 386*ff*.; und unlängst *Freedom, Law and Justice*, (1999) Text seiner Hamlyn Lecture aus dem Jahr 1998.

[22] "The Ghost in the Machine: Principle in Public Law" [1989] *Public Law*, pp. 27*ff*.; "Is the High Court the Guardian of Fundamental Constitutional Rights?" [1993] *Public Law* pp. 59*ff*.; "Law and Democracy" [1995] *Public Law*, pp. 72*ff*.

[23] Einer der beredtsten Vertreter dieser Schule war Lord Browne-Wilkinson; seine Gedanken dazu finden sich (außer in seinen Urteilen) in "The Infiltration of a Bill of Rights" [1987] *Public Law*, 397*ff*.

[24] *A.G.* v. *Guardian Newspapers (No 2)* (Spycatcher 2) [1990] 1 AC 109, 283.

[25] Ich betone das "englisch," weil in vielerlei Hinsicht interessante Abweichungen zwischen englischem Common Law einerseits, und demjenigen der USA und Kanadas bestehen. Letztere stehen dem kontinentaleuropäischen Recht oft näher als das englische Recht.

[26] Dies wiederum erklärt, warum unser Recht so oft verfahrensrechtlichen Ursprungs ist, und warum wir von Kläger und Beklagtem sprechen, wenn unsere kontinentalen Kollegen die Ausdrücke "Gläubiger" und "Schuldner" benutzen.

[27] Die geschichtlichen Gründe für diesen Unterschied hat der inzwischen verstorbene Prof. Harry Lawson in seinem Cooley-Vortrag *A Common Lawyer Looks at the Civil Law* (1953), pp. 138*ff*., beschrieben.

sie stimme für die ganze Bandbreite der Menschenrechte. Bei allem Respekt für Lord Goff, ich meine, sie trifft nicht mehr zu, wenn wir erst einmal den Bereich der Redefreiheit verlassen, in dessen Zusammenhang sie ausgesprochen wurde. Ich möchte mich daher dem Lord Chief Justice, Lord Bingham of Cornhill, anschließen, der geschrieben hat:[28]

> "Dem House of Lords zufolge gibt es, was die Meinungsfreiheit angeht, keinen grundsätzlichen Unterschied zwischen englischem Recht und Article 10 EMRK. Auch Lord Goff of Chieveley hat dies in einem der *Spycatcher*-Urteile ausgesprochen. Die früheren *Spycatcher*-Urteile desselben Gerichts hat man jedoch für Verletzungen der Konvention gehalten, wie auch andere Entscheidungen der Lordrichter. Wenn tatsächlich das gegenwärtige britische Recht den Bürgern des Vereinigten Königreichs denselben Schutz gewährte wie die Konvention—in ihrer ganzen Bandbreite, nicht nur im Hinblick auf Article 10 –, dann muß man sich wundern, warum das Straßburger Sündenregister Großbritanniens so lang ist."

Der Versuch Lösungen als hausgemacht darzustellen, die in Wirklichkeit auf Anstöße von außen zurückgehen, deutet nicht nur auf einen gewissen, verständlichen Nationalstolz; er unterschlägt auch einige Gefahren. Normalerweise folgt einer solchen Lösung nämlich ein Fallrecht, das den Neuzuwachs (oder die Reform des Bestehenden) eng einschnürt und eine systematische Weiterentwicklung des Rechts unmöglich macht. Anders ausgedrückt, die bloße Möglichkeit, daß Straßburg ein Urteil umstürzen könnte, zwingt zu größerer Sorgfalt. Meines Erachtens bestätigt das *Barrett*-Urteil[29]—die erste wichtige Entscheidung des House of Lords seit *Osman*—diese Beobachtung, aber es deutet auch auf die genannten Gefahren hin. Wie ich gegen Ende näher ausführen werde, werden wohl dieselben einschränkenden Auslegungsmethoden auf *Osman* angewandt werden. Wie gut das funktioniert, wird davon abhängen, in welcher Form sie zur Anwendung kommen.

DIE AUSWIRKUNG DER MENSCHENRECHTE AUF DIE DELIKTISCHE FAHRLÄSSIGKEITSHAFTUNG

(a) Vorbemerkungen zur Fahrlässigkeitshaftung im englischen Recht

Die Haftung aus dem Deliktstatbestand "negligence" ist unser engstes Gegenstück zu §823BGB. Ein wesentlicher Unterschied ist jedoch, daß sie nur unsorgfältiges, und nicht vorsätzliches Handeln erfaßt. Aus geschichtlichen Gründen fällt letzteres weitgehend, wenn auch nicht auss-

[28] "The European Convention on Human Rights: Time to Incorporate" in *Human Rights in the United Kingdom* (Hg. R. Gordon und R. Wilmot-Smith) (1996) 1, 9. (Fußnoten sind ausgelassen).
[29] *Barrett* v. *Enfield London Borough Council* [1999] 3 WLR 79.

chließlich, unter spezielle Deliktstatbestände für vorsätzliche Schädigungen (sogenannte "nominate intentional torts"). Ein weiterer Unterschied besteht in den Tatbestandsmerkmalen der *negligence* Haftung. Sie unterscheiden sich dem Augenschein nach (und auch in der Sache) ganz erheblich von denen des §823BGB. Einerseits erfordern beide Verschulden (Fahrlässigkeit und / oder Vorsatz, je nach dem oben Gesagten), Kausalität (wobei beide nach tatsächlicher und rechtlicher Ursache unterscheiden) und einen Schaden. Andererseits weisen sie eine Reihe von Tatbestandsmerkmalen auf, die sich von der Warte der jeweils anderen Rechtsordnung auf den ersten Blick befremdlich ausnehmen. So hat es etwa den *Anschein*, daß das englische Recht, anders als das deutsche, nicht einen von vornherein festgesetzten und eng ausgelegten Kreis von Rechtsgütern schützt. Auch *scheint* es nicht vom Römischen Recht die Voraussetzung der *iniuria* geerbt zu haben, die in Deutschland unter dem Stichwort der *Rechtswidrigkeit* erhebliche theoretische Meinungsverschiedenheiten ausgelöst hat. Dem aufmerksamen Leser wird der Kursivdruck nicht entgangen sein. In Wahrheit erfüllt nämlich im englischen Recht der rechtspolitisch aufgeladene Begriff der "duty of care" dieselbe Aufgabe wie die genannten Begriffe im deutschen Recht. Die Übersetzung mit "allgemeine Sorgfaltspflicht" oder die Behandlung als eine Entsprechung zu den deutschen "Verkehrspflichten" hilft der Rechtsvergleichung nicht viel weiter und soll hier nicht verfolgt werden. Stattdessen sollte man eingestehen, daß der Begriff der "duty of care" das Hauptmittel der englischen Richter ist, diejenigen Beziehungen und Interessen einzugrenzen, die unter dem Schutz der Rechtsordnung stehen. Damit tritt der englische Richter in die rechtspolitische Abwägung ein, die im deutschen Recht der Gesetzgeber des BGB selbst vorgenommen hat. Letzterer hat damit den Richter vor der Schwierigkeit bewahrt, ihm aber auch die Freiheit beschnitten, die Grenzen des Deliktsrechts immer neu zu bestimmen. In der Praxis unterscheiden sich die Ergebnisse beider Ansätze nicht so sehr. Dies kann man am besten an der Frage des reinen Vermögensschadens sehen, den keine der beiden Rechtsordnungen dem Grundsatz nach erstatten will, dem aber beide, wenn auch in verschiedener Weise, erlaubt haben, "durch die Maschen zu schlüpfen."

Ein solcher Vergleich *der Funktionen statt der Begriffe* kann uns vieles über die beiden Rechtsordnungen lehren; er würde jedoch über den Rahmen eines Festschriftenbeitrags hinausführen. Ich möchte deshalb zuletzt nur eine einzige Frage anschneiden, auf die es für das Verständnis meiner Hauptaussage entscheidend ankommt, insbesondere für ihre Zusammenfassung am Ende meiner Ausführungen.

Nur kurz möchte ich die folgende Frage erörtern: Wie entscheidet der Richter, ob den Beklagten dem Kläger gegenüber eine "duty of care" trifft? Nach viel "Hin und Her" haben die englischen Gerichte vier Fragen entwickelt, die nacheinander zu stellen sind. "War der Schaden des Klägers für den Beklagten voraussehbar?" "Stand der Beklagte dem Kläger nahe (im rechtlichen Sinne)?" "Ist es fair, gerecht und vernünftig (*fair, just, and rea-*

sonable), den Beklagten haften zu lassen?" und, wenn wir alle diese Fragen bejaht haben, "sprechen irgendwelche rechtspolitischen Gründe (*policy reasons*) *gegen* die Haftung?"

Es ist leicht zu erkennen, daß (a) diese Begriffe biegsam sind und (b) einander überschneiden, was zu Wiederholungen in der rechtlichen Untersuchung führt. Außerdem wurde das dritte Erfordernis—ob es *fair, just* und *reasonable* ist, den Beklagten haften zu lassen—von seinem ursprünglichen, engen Anwendungsbereich, dem reinen Vermögensschaden,[30] ohne größere Diskussion auf Eigentumsverletzungen übertragen.[31] Als ob diese Schwiergkeiten nicht schon ausreichen würden, selbst den erfahrendsten Juristen zu verwirren, kommt eine weitere Schicht hinzu, wenn es um die Haftung von Hoheitsträgern geht: Ob nämlich eine Verletzung gesetzlicher Pflichten oder Kompetenzen zivilrechtiche Haftung auslöst (in Ergänzung zu einer möglichen Haftung aufgrund des verletzten Gesetzes), und ob es eine deliktische Haftung unabhängig von einer Gesetzesverletzung gibt. Auch dies kann hier nicht weiter erörtert werden; statt dessen verweise ich den Leser auf eine rechtsvergleichende Untersuchung, die jüngst unter dem Titel *Tortious Liability for Statutory Bodies: A Comparative and Economic Analysis of Five English Cases* erschienen ist.[32] Es reicht hier die Feststellung, daß die Klage von Anfang an keinerlei Aussicht auf Erfolg hat, wenn der Richter aus irgendeinem der genannten Gründe zu der Auffassung gelangt, daß keine "duty of care" besteht. Der Beklagte kann vor diesem Hintergrund einen Antrag stellen, die Klage wegen Unschlüssigkeit abzuweisen (*motion to strike out*), über den das Gericht dann als eine rein rechtliche Vorfrage entscheidet, ohne in eine Untersuchung der Tatsachen,[33] des Verschuldens, oder des Ursachenzusammenhangs einzutreten.

(b) Der Osman-Fall

Die Ursprünge des *Osman*-Falles reichen bis in die Mitte der achtziger Jahre zurück. 1987/88 verkündete das House of Lords sein wichtiges Urteil in Sachen *Hill* v. *Chief Constable of West Yorkshire*.[34] Dieser Deliktsrechtsfall

[30] Dort sind die Zweifel an der Erstattungsfähigkeit am größten. S. dazu *Governors of the Peabody Donation Fund* v. *Sir Lindsay Parkinson & Co. Ltd* [1985] AC 210, 241C (per Lord Keith), und auch *Caparo Industries Plc* v. *Dickman* [1990] 2 AC 605.

[31] *Marc Rich & Co A G* v. *Bishop Rock Marines Ltd* [1995] 3 WLR 227. Der Versuch, diese Überlegungen zwei Jahre später auf Fälle der Körperverletzung anzuwenden, stieß auf die entschiedene Ablehnung eines einstimmigen Court of Appeal, s. *Perret* v. *Collins* [1998] 2 Lloyd's Rep. 255.

[32] Ein gemeinsames Projekt der Professoren Dagmar Coester-Waltjen, Jean-Bernard Auby, Simon Deakin und *des Verfassers*, erschienen 1999 bei Hart Publishing.

[33] Die Tatsachen werden so unterstellt, wie es am günstigsten für den Kläger erscheint. Dennoch haben viele Richter ihr Unbehagen darüber zum Ausdruck gebracht, daß sie ihr Urteil auf der Basis von bloß angenommenen und oft nicht eindeutigen Tatsachen bilden müssen und so der Gefahr Vorschub leisten, daß dicta der Urteilsgründe in Folgefällen mißbraucht werden.

[34] *Hill* v. *Chief Constable of West Yorkshire* [1988] 1 WLR 1049.

war das Nachspiel der Verurteilung des Sereinmörders und—vergewaltigers, der als der "Yorkshire Ripper" bekannt wurde. Den Zivilprozeß hatte die Mutter des letzten Opfers gegen die Polizei von Yorkshire angestrengt. Der Fall wurde unter dem Gesichtspunkt der *motion to strike out* verhandelt. Die Mutter stützte sich im Rahmen des Vorverfahrens auf die unterstellte Fahrlässigkeit der Polizei, die den "Ripper" als einen der zahlreichen Verdächtigen während der Mordserie vernommen, ihn später aber wieder freigelassen hatte. Mit umfänglichen Begründungen wiesen der Court of Appeal und nach ihm das House of Lords die Klage ab. Dafür waren rechtspolitische Überlegungen (*policy considerations*) ausschlaggebend, nämlich das Bestreben, die Polizei nicht unter zusätzlichen Ermittlungen, Verzögerungen und Kosten zu erdrücken, und sie nicht dadurch von ihrer Hauptaufgabe abzuhalten, der Verbrechensvorbeugung und der Festnahme von Kriminellen. Anders ausgedrückt, es sei besser, die vorhandenen, begrenzten Mittel auf die Ermittlung von Verbrechen zu verwenden statt auf die Ermittlung von Fehlern bei der gewöhnlichen Polizeitätigkeit. Dieser Hinweis auf den wirksamsten Mitteleinsatz diente als Grundlage für viele spätere Urteile, in denen sich die Richter streubten, eine Vielzahl öffentlich-rechtlicher Körperschaften—Gemeindebehörden, Polizei, Staatsanwaltschaft, Feuerwehr usw.—für behauptete Verstöße gegen ihre gesetzlichen Befugnisse haften zu lassen.

Trotz einiger Ausnahmen kann man sagen, daß die *Hill*-Regel[35] *ihrer Wirkung nach* "der Polizei eine Blanko-Immunität für Handlungen oder Unterlassungen bei der Ermittlung und Bekämpfung von Verbrechen" verleiht. Dies ist offensichtlich eine attraktive Lösung für eher konservative Juristen, die (wahre oder eingebildete) Gefahren für die Zahlungsfähigkeit jedweder öffentlich-rechtlichen Körperschaft sehen, sollte sie jemals für die Folgen ihrer Fehlleistungen zur Verantwortung gezogen werden. Die Verfechter dieser Denkrichtung sahen auch keinen Wert in der Abschreckung, die sich aus der möglichen Haftung für die Polizei ergeben könnte. Schließlich hatte bis vor kurzem auch niemand die Möglichkeit erwogen, daß ein solcher uneingeschränkter Haftungssausschluß eine Rechtsversagung für den Kläger bzw. das Opfer darstellt, das seine Klage aufgrund des Begriffs der "duty of care" abgewiesen sieht. So jedenfalls stellte es sich dar, bis der Europäische Gerichtshof für Menschenrechte schließlich einen Fall entschied, der die englischen Gerichte vor nahezu sechs Jahren beschäftigt hatte.

Der tragische Fall, der diesen Gang nach Straßburg auslöste, war *Osman v. Ferguson*.[36] Das Drama entfaltete sich, als ein Lehrer 1987 eine "ungesunde" Besessenheit für einen seiner Schützlinge entwickelte.[37] Der Junge, der diese Annäherungsversuche abwies, und seine Eltern beschwerten sich

[35] [1988] 1 WLR 1049.

[36] [1993] 4 All ER 344.

[37] Daß über zwölf Jahre vergehen mußten, bevor so etwas wie Gerechtigkeit walten konnte, stellt selbst eine ernsthafte Verurteilung unseres Systems dar. Es ist auch ein greifbares Beispiel dafür, wie die Heimführung der Menschenrechte durch den wenig zurückliegenden Human

bei der Schule und ihrem Direktor. Dies führte zu einer Reihe von Gesprächen mit dem Lehrer, der sich ungebührlich verhielt. Er wurde immer feindseliger und bedrohte den Jungen und seine Familie. Die Polizei wurde über das Verhalten des Lehrers informiert, blieb aber offenbar untätig, auch nachdem bekannt geworden war, daß der depressive Außenseiter, der der Lehrer war, gedroht hatte, er werde ein "Hungerford" anrichten.[38] Ein Jahr später, als sich die kriminellen Gewalttaten häuften, stellte die Polizei offenbar eine Akte zusammen in der Absicht, den geistig verwirrten Lehrer zu verfolgen. Aber wie zu befürchten war, handelte der Lehrer als erster, tötete den Vater und verwundete den Bruder des Jungen. Der Richter weigerte sich, die Klage in einem Vorverfahren wegen Unschlüssigkeit abzuweisen, aber diese Entscheidung wurde vom Court of Appeal aufgehoben, der sich auf das *Hill*-Urteil berief, obwohl er in diesem Fall den Nähefaktor zugunsten des Klägers eingreifen sah, der in *Hill* abgelehnt worden war.

Als die Sache vor den Straßburger Gerichtshof kam, entschied dieser,[39] daß eine solche Blanko-Immunität eine "nicht zu rechtfertigende Beschränkung des Rechts eines Klägers darstellen kann, im Fall begründeter Ansprüche gegen die Polizei einen Urteilsspruch in der Sache zu erhalten." Der Gerichtshof urteilte also, daß "alle Gesichtspunkte der Klage auch der Sache nach erwogen werden, und nicht automatisch durch eine Regel ausgeschlossen werden sollten, die einem Haftungsausschluß für die Polizei gleichkommt." Dies führte zu der einstimmigen Entscheidung, daß im vorliegenden Fall die Anwendung der Ausschlußregel (aus dem Fall *Hill*) eine "unverhältnismäßige Einschränkung des Rechts des Klägers auf Zugang zu einem Gericht darstellte und aus diesem Grund eine Verletzung von Article 6 Abs. 1 EMRK vorlag."

WIE WERDEN DIE ENGLISCHEN JURISTEN AUF OSMAN REAGIEREN? EINIGE ABSCHLIEßENDE GEDANKEN

Die Menschenrechte und das Beleidigungsrecht sind nun eine interessante Symbiose eingegangen. Weitere Veränderungen werden sich daraus in den

Rights Act den Streitbeteiligten Zeit und dem Land die Blamage ersparen kann, von einem ausländischen Gericht über die Mangelhaftigkeit der eigenen Rehtsordnung belehrt zu werden. Das ist aber wieder eine andere Angelegenheit!

[38] 1987 richtete in Hungerford ein bewaffneter Mann ein Blutbad an, der in eine Schule eingedrungen war, sechzehn Personen tötete und dann Selbstmord beging. Die genauen Worte des Täters in diesem Fall waren Gegenstand einiger Kontroversen im Fall.

[39] Ich übergehe die Ausführungen des Gerichts zu Art. 6 der Konvention, mit denen es sein Tätigwerden in dieser Sache begründete. Einerseits mangelt es hier an Platz, andererseits möchte ich nicht die Aufmerksamkeit des Lesers von der erheblichen Wirkung ablenken, die diese Entscheidung der großen Kammer auf das englische Recht haben wird, obwohl sie strenggenommen für unsere Gerichte nicht verbindlich ist. Diese Wirkung wird noch größer sein, falls, wie zu erwarten ist, Straßburg in seinem Urteil in dem derzeit anhängigen *Bedfordshire*-Fall derselben Linie folgt.

nächsten Jahren ergeben. Der eigentliche Gezeitenwechsel wird aber in unserer wichtigsten unerlaubten Handlung eintreten, der Fahrlässigkeitshaftung aus *negligence*. Darin sehe ich die mögliche große Bedeutung des *Osman*-Urteils. Falls, wie zu erwarten ist, das Gericht in Straßburg diese Linie in seinem Urteil *X* v. *Bedfordshire* fortsetzt,[40] wird die willkürliche Anwendung des Begriffs der *duty of care*—der seit dem bahnbrechenden Fall *Donoghue* v. *Stevenson* ein Begriff von überragender Wichtigkeit war—eingeschränkt, vielleicht sogar beseitigt. Wie auch immer es weitergeht, das Deliktsrecht ist mit einer anderen Welt in Berührung gekommen—Menschenrechte mit internationalem Anwendungsbereich—und es wird womöglich für immer verändert sein. Aber was wird geschehen? Wir wollen dieser Frage in vier kurzen Unterabschnitten nachgehen: (a) Die Bedeutung der *motion to strike out*; (b) Versuche, *Osman* einzugrenzen; (c) Versuche, die Bedeutung von *X* v. *Bedfordshire* durch Abgrenzung von Folgeentscheidungen auf Tatsachenebene einzuschränken; und (d) Wie sollen die Gerichte weiter vorgehen?

(a) Die Abweisung einer Klage wegen Unschlüssigkeit im Vorverfahren (striking out actions). Zwar klagen Richter oft über die Gefahr, daß weitreichende Aussprüche im Zusammenhang mit der Abweisung von Klagen wegen Unschlüssigkeit in Vorverfahren in späteren Fällen mit unglücklichen Folgen angewandt werden. Alles in allem aber gebrauchen sie das Werkzeug der *striking out motion* recht oft. Sein großer Vorzug ist, daß es eine volle Verhandlung vermeidet und so dringend benötigte Justizzeit spart. In einem Land mit einem Bruchteil der Vollzeitrichter, die andere Länder vergleichbarer Größe und rechtlichen Niveaus aufweisen, ist dies kein unerheblicher Zweckmäßigkeitsgesichtspunkt. Auch den Parteien selbst sollte dieses Mittel eigentlich zusagen, weil es die verhältnismäßig schnelle Klärung der wesentlichen rechtlichen Gesichtspunkte erlaubt und mit geringeren Kosten verbunden ist als eine volle Verhandlung. Andererseits darf man nicht übersehen, daß dieses Mittel den Beklagten begünstigt, nicht zuletzt weil es einfacher ist, die Klage aus rechtlichen Gesichtspunkten abzuwürgen statt im Rahmen einer vollen Tatsachenerhebung. Verbunden mit der zunehmenden Schwierigkeit, Gerichtskostenhilfe zu erlangen, macht dies es für den Kläger zu einer Herkulesarbeit, eine Klage gegen die meisten öffentlich-rechtlichen Körperschaften auch nur in Erwägung zu ziehen. Nach meiner Einschätzung haben solche Überlegungen den Straßburger Gerichtshof beeinflußt. Die Beteuerungen der britischen Seite, daß das englische Recht in Wirklichkeit doch keine grundsätzliche Haftungsfreizeichnung für Polizisten vorsieht, haben ihn unbeeindruckt gelassen. Wir sollten uns jedoch abschließend daran erinnern, daß diese einschneidenden

[40] Und die Komisssion hat sich schon in der Hinsicht geäußert, siehe Fn. 7, oben.

Wirkungen nur möglich sind, weil den Richtern dieses grobe, aber sehr wirksame Mittel der *duty of care* zur Verfügung steht, das, wie die Redensart geht, die Verhandlung "im Keim erstickt."

(b) Versuche, Osman einzugrenzen. Eine der ersten Entscheidungen des Court of Appeal nach *Osman* war *Palmer* v. *Tees Health Authority.*[41] Die Umstände dieses Falles brauchen uns nicht lange aufhalten. Die Klage wurde angestrengt von der Mutter eines Opfers einer Sexualstraftat. Sie verlangte Schadensersatz für ihre eigenen post-traumatischen Störungen und für den Tod ihrer Tochter. Letztere war von einem Geisteskranken ermordet worden, der in der Krankenanstalt der Beklagten behandelt worden, dann aber entlassen worden war, obwohl der Klägerin zufolge bei ihm Anzeichen vorlagen, daß er vermutlich wieder schwere Straftaten begehen würde, was auch tatsächlich geschah. Die Klage wurde schon wegen Unschlüssigkeit im Rahmen der *striking out motion* abgewiesen weil angeblich kein Klagegrund vorlag. Der klägerische Anwalt wandte ein, daß die *Barrett*-Entscheidung im Licht von *Osman* solche frühzeitigen Klageabweisungen nahezu unmöglich mache.

Der Court of Appeal schloß sich dieser Auffassung nicht an. Einerseits gebe es im *Palmer*-Fall, anders als in *Barrett*,[42] keine Nähe zwischen der Krankenanstalt und dem Opfer, einer unbeteiligten Dritten. Vor allem aber verbiete *Osman*, Klagen aus den Gründen abzuweisen, daß es nicht "fair, just and reasonable" sei, den Kläger haften zu lassen, so daß es gar nicht erst zur vollen Verhandlung kommt. Nicht verboten sei es, in einem Fall wie dem vorliegenden, wegen des fehlenden Näheverhältnisses auf der Basis einer *motion to strike out* die Klage abzuweisen. Trotz Lord Justice Stuart-Smiths Versuch, diese Unterscheidung anhand einiger Passagen des *Osman*-Urteils[43] zu rechtfertigen, wird sich diese Auslegung wohl, bei allem Respekt, nicht dauerhaft durchsetzen. Denn einerseits haben wir schon gesehen, daß die Tatbestandsmerkmale der englischen Fahrlässigkeitshaftung ineinander übergehen. Deshalb ist es unhaltbar und auch nicht wahrscheinlich, daß dieser Versuch durchgehalten werden wird, die beiden Fälle voneinander abzugrenzen. Tatsächlich hat auch Lord Justice Pill, der dritte an der *Palmer*-Entscheidung beteiligte Richter, eingeräumt, daß Erwägungen eines gerechten Ausgleichs ("fairness and justice") in die Entscheidung eingehen, ob dem Näheerfordernis genügt ist. Andererseits unterliegt es keinem Zweifel, daß den Richtern in Straßburg, unangesehen

[41] Derzeit noch unveröffentlicht. Ein verkürzte Wiedergabe der Entscheidung findet sich in *The Times Law Reports*, 5.7.1999. Das neueste Urteil in diesem Bereich folgt *Palmer* und zeigt ähnliche Tendenzen auf: *Jarvis* v. *Hampshire County Council*, Urteil vom 11.11.1999, siehe *The Times Law Reports*, 23.11.1999.

[42] In *Barrett* hatte der Kläger, ein Kind in der Obhut einer örtlichen Behörde, gegen die Behörde geklagt, weil ihm deren Nachlässigkeit Schaden zugefügt habe. Hier gab es mit anderen Worten keinen Zweifel, daß dem Näheerfordernis Genüge getan war.

[43] Insbesondere Rnr. 142 und 157.

der Unbestimmtheit einiger Passagen im *Osman*-Urteil, die "unverhältnismäßigen Wirkungen" der englischen Praxis der *striking out actions* "mißfielen" und daß es ihnen wichtig war, diese negativen Auswirkungen einzugrenzen. Ihr eigenes Urteil zu verfeinern und neu zu definieren, wie es der Court of Appeal getan hat, liegt natürlich in der Natur der Abgrenzungstechniken, derer sich der englische Richter bedient und die er schon in seiner Studienzeit erwirbt, in der allerdings die Studenten auch dazu erzogen werden, dem Schrein der unkritisch hingenommenen Behauptungen zu huldigen. Demgegenüber liegt die Bedeutung *Osmans* für jedermann sichtbar zutage, und Lord Browne-Wilkinson tat recht daran aufzudecken, daß ihm *Osman* vorschwebte, als er—zögernd, wie wir annehmen dürfen—sein Urteil in *Barrett* verkündete.[44] Deshalb scheint es wenig wahrscheinlich, daß Straßburg es jemals zulassen würde, daß seine Entscheidung über den wesentlichen rechtspolitischen Gesichtspunkt des *Osman*-Falles durch solche Argumente unterwandert wird.

(c) Versuche, die Bedeutung von X v. *Bedfordshire durch eine strikte Abgrenzung der Folgeentscheidungen einzuschränken.* In *Barrett* v. *Enfield* versuchten Lords Slynn und Hutton, *Osman* zu umgehen, zumindest übergingen sie den Fall in ihren Urteilsreden. Praktisch spielten sie aber auch die Bedeutung von *X* v. *Bedfordshire* herunter indem sie den Fall eng abgrenzten. Letzterer Fall hatte eine ausgefeilte Rechtfertigung für die Abweisung von Klagen wegen Verletzung gesetzlicher Pflichten auf der Grundlage der *motion to strike out* geliefert. Wie unterscheiden sich also die beiden Fälle?

X v. *Bedfordshire* war ein Fall aus einer ganzen Reihe von Fällen, in denen Gemeinden verklagt worden waren, weil sie fahrlässig versäumt hatten, Kinder in ihrer Obhut vor sexuellem Mißbrauch zu bewahren, oder aber sie überstürzt der Obhut ihrer leiblichen Eltern entzogen zu haben, um sie vor Mißbrauch zu bewahren. In beiden Fällen mag die Behörde nicht mit der nötigen Sorgfalt gehandelt haben, und in beiden Fällen mag die Entscheidung in der Sache sehr wohl falsch gewesen sein. Die Frage nach dem Vorliegen einer *duty of care*—unabhängig von einer gesetzlichen Bestimmung—wurde jedoch ablehnend beantwortet, und zwar aus einer Reihe von rechtspolitischen Gründen.

Diese Gründe und ihre zweifelhafte Überzeugungskraft sind anderswo untersucht worden.[45] Auf verschiedene Weise sind sie alle mit der Forderung

[44] "Angesichts der Entscheidung im Fall *Osman* ist es jetzt schwer vorhersehbar, wie der Fall ausgehen würde, wenn wir die *striking out order* aufrechterhielten. Ich halte es jedenfalls für wahrscheinlich, daß der Fall dann nach Straßburg getragen würde." [1999] 3 WLR 79, 85. Ohne eigene Urteilsreden zu halten, schlossen Lord Nolan und Lord Steyn sich dem Vorredner an was das Ergebnis anbetrifft. Es läßt sich annehmen, daß sie sich auch diesem Hinweis anschließen.

[45] S. Markesinis, Auby, Coester-Waltjen, and Deakin, *Tortious Liability of Statutory Bodies: A Comparative and Economic Analysis of Five English Cases*, (1999) Kap. 2 und 3.

nach ökonomischer und verwaltungstechnischer Effizienz verknüpft. Diese Effizienz, so zumindest die These, würde aufs Spiel gesetzt werden, könnten Gerichte solchartige Verwaltungsentscheidungen im Hinblick auf eine deliktische Haftung nachprüfen. Hier wollen wir nur diejenigen Gründe betrachten, die die Rechtfertigung der Abgrenzung der *Barrett-* und *Bedfordshire*-Fälle abgaben.

Der erste Grund, im *Bedfordshire*-Fall die Haftung der örtlichen Behörden abzulehnen, war die sachgebietsübergreifende Natur der Entscheidung, das Kind in amtliche Obhut zu nehmen, an der eine Anzahl verschiendener Behörden teilgenommen hatten. Die Haftung einer Behörde allein aufzuerlegen, wäre schwierig; sie allen aufzuerlegen, unfair. Wie diese Art von "Zwickmühle" es rechtfertigen soll, daß der Schaden am glücklosen Kläger hängen bleibt, ist in keiner Weise klar. Dieses Problem trat jedoch im *Barrett*-Fall nicht auf, in dem die umstrittenen Entscheidungen von einer Behörde allein gefaßt worden waren.

Das zweite Argument im *Bedfordshire*-Fall für die Haftungsfreistellung war, daß den Klägern andere Rechtsbehelfe zur Verfügung standen, um ihrer Beschwernis abzuhelfen. Dies ist theoretisch wie praktisch ein sehr zweifelhaftes Argument, und Lord Hutton hat es, meines Erachtens zu Recht, in seinem Urteil in *Barrett* entschieden abgelehnt. Man mag jedoch zweifeln, ob dies reicht, um dieses Argument der Vergessenheit anheimfallen zu lassen, berufen sich doch englische Richter bedauerlicherweise oft darauf.

Das für unsere Zwecke letzte Argument in *Bedfordshire* für die Haftungsfreistellung hat in der Rechtsprechung seit *Hill* einen festen Platz behauptet. Es beschwört die "Abwehrhaltung," die die Behörden vorgeblich einnehmen angesichts der Möglichkeit einer Haftung, und die sie entscheidungsunwillig werden lasse. Auch dieses Argument ist bei mindestens zwei Lordrichtern auf Ablehnung gestoßen, Lords Slynn und Hutton, die sich statt dessen der Bemerkung Lord Justice Evans` vom Court of Appeal anschlossen. Dieser hatte ausgeführt:

> "wenn das Verhalten [der Behörde] einen Gegenstand betrifft, der sich an vernünftigen Maßstäben messen läßt, ist mir nicht ersichtlich, warum das öffentliche Interesse aus der Warte des Rechts nicht verlangen sollte, daß diese Maßstäbe eingehalten werden."[46]

(d) Wie sollten die Gerichte weiter vorgehen? Es ist, meine ich, zwecklos, den Argumenten im einzelnen weiter nachzugehen, mit denen die Lordrichter ihren Fall von dem in *Bedfordshire* abgrenzen und ein vorzeitiges Abweisen der Klage wegen Unschlüssigkeit vermeiden wollten. Ein solches Vorgehen mag in bestimmten Tatsachenkonstellationen angemessen sein, in anderen versagen. Vor allem aber scheut es eine offene Auseinandersetzung

[46] [1997] 3 WLR 628 at 638; bestätigt in [1999] 3 WLR 79, 94; 114.

mit der Tatsache, daß die rechtspolitischen Gründe mit denen das englische Recht die Haftungsfreizeichnungen für Behörden rechtfertigt, nach *Osman* schlichtweg unhaltbar geworden sind. Ein Fallrecht, das auf Ausweichmanövern und Haarspaltereien beruht, und daß zu den wesentlichen Problemen, wie ich sie oben angesprochen habe, nichts zu sagen hat, wird niemandem nutzen außer Praktikern, die ihren Lebensunterhalt mit feinen Unterscheidungen verdienen. Eine weitaus besser vertretbare Lösung könnte etwa wie folgt aussehen.

Statt ihr Erstaunen über den schöpferischen Gebrauch zu äußern, den der Straßburger Gerichtshof von Article 6 EMRK macht, sollten englische Richter diesen Gebrauch nutzen, um sich aus der Falle zu befreien, in der sie sich mit den Entscheidungen in Sachen *Hill*, *Stovin*[47] und *Bedfordshire* selbst gefangen haben. Sie sollten, kurz gesagt, eingestehen, daß ihre übermäßig beschützende Haltung gegenüber öffentlich-rechtlichen Körperschaften nicht mehr in unsere Zeiten gesteigerter Verantwortlichkeit paßt. Sie sollten die Rechtslage in Frankreich oder Deutschland betrachten, um sich zu überzeugen, daß die befürchteten Folgen behördlicher Haftung anderswo nicht eingetreten sind. Wie und warum dies in anderen Ländern funktioniert hat, sollte Gegenstand sorgfältiger Untersuchung sein, und dies sollte ergänzt werden um eine weniger grobe Anwendung ökonomischer Analyse, wie sie in den Urteilen einiger Richter schon angeklungen ist.

All dies muß nicht ein Brechen der Dämme nach sich ziehen, außer vielleicht für die nötige kurze Zeit, bis der juristische Markt sich wieder im Gleichgewicht befindet.[48] Die Haftung ließe sich ohne weiteres mittels der Begriffe der Fahrlässigkeit, des Ursachenzusammenhangs und zusätzlich mittels angemessener und nicht übertriebener Schadensersatzbeträge begrenzen. Die Gerichtskostenhilfe, die selbst immer geiziger wird, wird ebenfalls helfen, einen Ansturm auf die Gerichte zu verhindern. Maßvolle, aber spürbare Schadensersatzbeträge können dazu beitragen, das Problem auf eine angemessene Größenordnung zu beschränken. Außerdem hätten die Kläger und beklagten Behörden nach einigen richtungweisenden Urteilen die notwendige Orientierung, um zu entscheiden, in welchen Fällen eine Schlichtung, und in welchen ein gerichtliches Austragen angezeigt ist.

[47] *Stovin* v. *Wise* [1996] 3 WLR 388. Die Tatsachen sind denen sehr ähnlich, die BGH NJW 1980, 2194 zugrunde liegen, außer daß das englische Gericht mehrheitlich zugunsten des Beklagten entschied.

[48] Wenn eine Akzeptanz *Osmans* eine Zunahme von Rechtsstreiten bewirkt, wie die Befürworter des *status quo* behaupten mögen, kann man die Vorhersage wagen, daß eine solche Zunahme nur von kurzer Dauer sein wird. Dafür lassen sich viele Beispiele aus der neueren Geschichte unseres Deliktsrecht anführen: Haftung des "trespassers", Haftung für fahrlässige Behauptungen, psychiatrischer Schaden etc., bei denen ein Brechen der Dämme vorausgesagt worden war (aber nicht eintrat), wann immer eine Liberalisierung unserer Deliktsregeln in Angriff genommen wurde.

Für das Ende jedes Jahrtausends ist es offenbar bezeichnend, daß Propheten des Untergangs auftreten und das Ende der Welt vorhersagen. *Osman* wird nicht dazu führen. Im Gegenteil, der Fall wird englische Richter daran erinnern, daß ihr Recht nicht mehr ausschließlich davon bestimmt wird, was innerhalb der geographischen Grenzen Englands geschieht. So verhält es sich in ihrem Wirtschaftsleben, in ihrem nationalen Geschmack, der sich anderen annähert (in allem von Kaffee und Tee bis zur Musik) und, wie ich meine, im Recht. Außer rechtlichem Konservativismus gibt es keinen Grund anzunehmen, daß die fortschreitende Europäisierung des englischen Rechts entweder vermeidbar oder schlecht sei.

7

Privacy, Freedom of Expression, and the Horizontal Effect of the Human Rights Bill: Lessons From Germany

I. INTRODUCTORY OBSERVATIONS

No country, other perhaps than the USA, has considered the problems of horizontal application of Human Rights as thoroughly as Germany; and when it comes to balancing competing values, German jurists have, in my view, constructed one of the most sophisticated and rational systems that has ever been devised. This essay will attempt to discuss in a comparative way some of these complex issues which, to make matters even more difficult, straddle the traditional divide between public and private law. Comparison, however, requires knowledge of at least two systems, which one then proceeds to compare with each other. Knowledge of German law, the system that, for reasons, which I shall explain later, I have chosen to compare to ours, I cannot assume to be generally available even among a knowledgeable audience and readership. So, in the first part of this essay I shall attempt to cover some of its salient points, especially in so far as they refer to speech rights and privacy. In the second part my aim will be to show how this foreign experience could be relevant to what we do with our law at this crucial moment of its history. Before turning to these issues, however, it might be useful to sketch out some of the key points, which underlie my subject since they may make German law more digestible.

The debates about whether human rights articles should regulate the relations between private individuals raises at least four complex and interrelated issues all of which have been tackled by German law and, to a lesser extent, by other Common law jurisdictions but not ours.

First, given that it has always been thought that the primary purpose of human rights protection is to safeguard the individual against the excessive power of the state, what justifies limiting the autonomy of private individuals in their relationships with one another? Secondly, what is the inter-relationship between public and private law (at least in those systems which recognise it as a key feature of legal taxonomy)? To what extent should the dictates of public law be permitted to encroach upon the development of private law? Embedded in this second question is also that of jurisdiction of different courts. Particularly in a system such as the German, where the jurisdiction of the Constitutional Court is clearly demarcated from that of the ordinary courts, on what grounds can the encroachment of this court on the field of private law be both justified and controlled? The third difficulty goes behind these initial questions and challenges the assumption of a watertight distinction between public and private law. On closer examination, the conflict may well be between the civil liberties of two individuals—either speech against speech or speech against privacy. In fact, the position of the privacy right as a human right, itself demonstrates that private and public law are inextricably linked. This is further demonstrated by the fact that most human rights documents include derogations or limitations permitting legislators or courts to restrict the scope of a right in specific circumstances. Seen from this perspective, the question is not whether private individuals should be subject to public law obligations, but how a legal system ought to balance the basic right of individual autonomy from state intervention against the rights of other individuals including their right of free expression. This leads us on to the fourth major issue viz., who should be entrusted to carry out the balancing exercise. For our purposes, the question becomes: should we entrust this task to the judges and why? The shifting attitudes evidenced towards this issue by our major political parties over the last thirty years or so have not made the answer to this difficult question any easier.

But to return to German law. To their credit, German judges and academics have addressed most if not all of these issues. The first, namely, the justification for extending human rights restrictions to actions of private individuals was addressed, as we shall see further on, as early as 1954 by Hans Carl Nipperdey when President of the Federal Labour Court. That his solution was not the final or, even, the best one is demonstrated by the evolving response to the second question namely, the justifiability of encroachment of public law (and with it the Constitutional Court) on private law. This seems to have been resolved by German law through the judicial development of three principles, which have permitted a flexible interaction between public and private law. Thus: (i) the constitutional order should "influence" rather than "govern" private law norms; (ii) there should be a reciprocal relationship between the Constitution and "general laws" found in the private sphere and (iii) the notion of "heightened scrutiny", which the Constitutional Court tends to reserve for the most "serious cases" but, otherwise, shows what a foreign observer would regard as considerable deference towards the decisions of the ordinary courts. The third issue namely, the shifting boundaries between public and private law, is recognised both in the Constitutional text (which in Articles 5(2) and (3) includes express derogations) and in the judicial development of a "balancing" approach. Furthermore, the issues raised in the case law have demonstrated how frequently the underlying conflict is between two human rights, particularly privacy as against expression. The result has been the creation of an almost unique amalgam of public and private law: the notion of a constitutional tort. Finally, the question of whether the judges can be "trusted" to perform these balancing exercises can only be answered by evaluating the results which, in the case of Germany, have, I believe, fully justified their role.

II. SOME BASIC FEATURES OF GERMAN LAW

1. Horizontal effect of Human Rights

(a) The text of the Constitution

Most German scholars agree that the text of the Basic Law (Constitution) is ambiguous on the question whether its Human Rights articles (mainly arts 1–19) are also meant to regulate the relations between private individuals. Apart from invoking the wider philosophical argument that it was not for the state to interfere with the rules of private law, which enshrine the belief in "private autonomy",[1] opponents of any horizontal extension also argued that where constitutional rules were meant to cover private relationships as well, the constitutional draftsman had said so explicitly.[2] But this argument cuts both ways; and the fact that a horizontal extension was not meant to be prohibited by the Constitution is reinforced by the positive and declarative form given to many of its key articles.[3] This point is backed by the discussions of the *Herrenchiemsee* drafting committee,[4] which are all the more significant given that the same debate (about hori-

[1] Dürig in Maunz/Dürig *Grundgesetz Kommentar*, Art. 1, Abs 3, Rdnrn 129–30. Criticism has thus been voiced at the increasing "constitutionalisation" of such areas of private law as landlord and tenant, surety, and employment law. See: Zöllner, "Regelungsspielräume im Schuldvertragsrecht", *AcP* 196 (1996), 1; Oeter, "'Drittwirkung' der Grundrechte und die Autonomie des Privatrechts", *AöR* 119 (1994), 529; Roellecke, "Das Mietrecht des BVerfG", *NJW* (1992), 1649; Medicus, "Der Grundsatz der Verhältnismäßigkeit im Privatrecht" *AcP* 192 (1992), 35.

[2] For instance Art. 9(3) GG.

[3] For instance Art. 2(1): "Everyone has the right to the free development of his personality . . ." Likewise with Art. 1(1).

[4] *Bericht über den Verfassungskonvent auf Herrenchiemsee vom 10. bis 23 August 1948*, 2 *Akten und Protokolle*, 513, 580. On the other hand Hermann von Mangoldt's authoritative *Das Bonner Grundgesetz*, vol. I (1953), 34–42, argues that the Constitutional Convention, which from 1st September 1948 continued in Bonn the work of the *Herrenchiemsee* Committee of experts, did not believe that the Basic Law was meant to apply to private law.

zontality) had plagued the previous Constitution of Weimar. Yet the underlying issues, as we are now coming to realise in our country, are not susceptible to unequivocal answers so it was thus not entirely surprising that a storm of protest broke out when, in 1954,[5] the Federal Labour Court, under the influence of its first President Nipperdey, seemed to jump the gun by declaring that freedom of expression had an *unmittelbare Drittwirkung*—i.e. a direct limiting effect—on the acts of private parties.

(b) The Lüth *theory of constitutional "influence" and the rejection of the "direct effect" approach*

Veit Harlan was a film director who became notorious during the Nazi period for directing anti-Jewish films. After the War he was convicted for his anti-Jewish activities but was subsequently acquitted because the tribunal felt unable to disprove his assertion that he had made the films under "compulsion".[6] In 1950 Erich Lüth, a press official in the City of Hamburg, was incensed by Harlan's re-appearance on the public scene with a new (and un-controversial) film. He believed fervently that Harlan's past would revive old controversies, hinder contemporary efforts to re-build links between Christians and Jews—a task which took up much of his own time—and harm Germany's rehabilitation on the world scene. So, acting in a private capacity, he called for a boycott of Harlan's film. The civil courts, holding that the boycott contravened § 826 BGB,[7] granted Harlan an injunction against Lüth. The Constitutional Court overturned the injunction in the first and, arguably, most important freedom-of-expression case in its post-War period.

The Constitutional Court began by accepting the fact, especially in the light of the recent Nazi experience, that "The main purpose of Basic Rights is to protect the individual's sphere of freedom against encroachment by public power; these rights are the citizen's bulwark (*Abwehrrechteo* = defence rights) against the state."[8] But, the court continued, their primary

[5] Nipperdey the judge was, in fact, only following Nipperdey the scholar who, four years earlier had, in a seminal and still cited article argued in favour of direct horizontality. Thus see "Gleicher Lohn der Frau für gleiche Leistung. Ein Beitrag zur Auslegung der Grundrechte", *Recht der Arbeit* 1950, 121*ff.* The literature, which followed the decision of the Federal Labour Court, was enormous. Sharply critical was Ehmke in *Wirtschaft und Verfassung*, 78 *ff.* (1961). But Nipperdey struck back in "Grundrechte und Privatrecht", *Festschrift Molitor*, 17–33 (1962).

[6] BVerfGE 7, 198, 222–26. Post-war de-Nazification proceedings, usually reserved for middle-ranking supporters of the Third Reich, also "exonerated" Harlan. In a later decision the *Bundesgerichtshof* prohibited the showing of Harlan's most famous, anti-Jewish film: BGHSt 19, 63 (1963).

[7] "A person who willfully causes damage to another in a manner *contra bonos mores* is bound to compensate the other for the damage."

[8] BVerfGE 7, 198, 204 (1958), translated in BS Markesinis, *The German Law of Obligations*, vol II, *The Law of Torts: A Comparative Introduction* 3rd ed. with corrections and additions (1997), 355.

function did not exhaust itself with the granting of such protection. On the contrary, one could see in the Basic Rights an "objective order of values" ("*eine objektive Wertordnung*"), which pervaded the entire legal system and affected especially strongly those areas in which the law prescribed binding rules (*ius cogens*) that displaced the will of the parties.[9] These objective values were essential for the public good and should thus be protected from encroachment whatever its source—public or private.[10] This was particularly true of the "basic right to freedom of expression, the most immediate aspect of the human personality in society [which] is one of most precious rights of man. [This right] is absolutely essential to a free and democratic state, for it alone permits that constant spiritual interaction, the conflict of opinion, which is its vital element. In a certain sense it is the basis of freedom itself . . ." And then came the court's peroration, taken from Mr. Justice Cardozo's opinion in *Palko* v. *Connecticut*[11] and cited in the original: "[freedom of expression] is the matrix, the indispensable condition of nearly every other form of freedom." Thus Nipperdey's idea that "The basic right to free expression . . . would be rendered largely ineffective . . . if . . . *individuals and others with economic and social power . . . were in a position by virtue of that power to restrict it at will*"[12] resurfaced in a modified form. For though it was no longer claimed that the Human Rights provisions had a *direct* effect on private relationships, the Court argued that the constitutional order "*influenced* rather than *governed* private law norms".[13] Thus, in a way that bears some resemblance to the struggles between our courts of Equity and Common law, a *modus vivendi* began to emerge between Constitutional and ordinary courts, one which would not denature the civil law elements of the dispute but would, nevertheless, leave room for Constitutional principles to "flow" and "radiate" (*Ausstrahlungswirkung*) into the civil norms and affect their interpretation.

2. Textual cross-referencing

This short sub-section is really meant to introduce the reader to the next two as part of developing the themes mentioned thus far. It is also meant

[9] Passim, pp. 203–7. English translation at p. 355.

[10] The idea is prominent in the *Wallraff* case (discussed below) where the Constitutional Court said: "Free press depends on editorial confidentiality and this can be violated just as much by the state as by individuals or societal forces." BVerfGE 66, 116, 135 (1984). This point is picked up again in III, 3, (a), below.

[11] 302 US 319, 327 (1937).

[12] BArbGE 1, 185, 192*ff*. The italicised section demonstrates, once again, the belief that not only the state can infringe basic rights. Twenty years later similar ideas were put forward in France by Jean Rivero. See, for instance his "La protection des droits de l'homme dans les rapports entre personnes privées", in René Cassin, *Amicorum Discipulorumque Liber*, (1971), vol III 311*ff*.

[13] BVerfGE 7, at p. 205.

to remind him that the systematic bent of the German legal mind means first, that their statutory texts, especially important ones such as the Civil Code and the Constitution, are drafted with great care and an elaborate system of cross referencing and, secondly, that in their interpretation techniques the Germans are used to moving from one section of a statute to another in a certain logical sequence. In the first volume of *The German Law of Obligations* my co-authors and I gave a number of illustrations of this tendency in the area of civil law; here one should note that the difficulty is, if anything, greater since one has to move between two texts which, though they stand in a hierarchical order the one to the other, in reality they influence each other and the final result almost in equal measure. This interplay of texts has given judges considerable room for creativity, and has enabled them, once again, to work in concert with their academic brothers in a common effort to make the system work. The above must also prompt us to consider to what extent Germanic ideas are exportable to systems which do not share the same basic structures. In the view of this writer, the quick answer is a positive one; but more will be said about this in section III, below.

(a) Article 5(1) and (2) GG (speech)[14]

Unlike the First Amendment of the Constitution of the United States, which with great brevity has left it to the courts to discover and protect the various facets of speech-related freedoms, the Germans have chosen to spell matters out more clearly and meticulously. One consequence of this is the limits to freedom of expression found in Article 5(2). On the face of it this provision could be seen as containing a serious set of limitations and, indeed, this is how it has worked in the hands of many ordinary courts. But, as we shall note below, this is not how the Constitutional Court has allowed matters to develop.

(b) Article 5(3) GG (artistic creation)[15]

The intriguing feature of this provision is not so much that it treats art, science, and research separately from the other (speech) freedoms found in Article 5(1) but that it does not subject art to the restrictions of Article 5(2).

[14] Art. 5 (Freedom of Expression):
"(1) Everyone shall have the right freely to express and disseminate his opinion by speech, writing, and pictures and freely to inform himself from generally accessible sources. Freedom of the press and freedom of reporting by means of broadcasts and films are guaranteed. There shall be no censorship.
(2) These rights are limited by the provisions of the general laws, the provisions of law for the protection of youth, and by the right to inviolability of personal honour."

[15] Art. 5(3): "Art and science, research and teaching, shall be free. Freedom of teaching shall not absolve from loyalty to the Constitution."

At first sight, therefore, artistic creation seems to receive greater protection than free speech. Once again, things are not what they appear to be since the courts have developed the technique of delimiting the ambit of one human right by testing it against others found in the Constitution, itself. As we shall see in sub-section 4, the check has been found in Article 1 of the Constitution—something, which once again, brings us back to the art of balancing in the process of finding the perfect equilibrium appropriate to the constitutional order.

3. The Constitution trumps civil law

In this section we shall look briefly at three examples. In the first speech trumps § 826 BGB, in the second it completes *praeter legem* the list of protected interests of § 823 I BGB[16] *and*, effectively, overturns the clear meaning of § 253 BGB.[17] Finally, in our last illustration, speech interests trump ordinary rules of contract. That the Constitution can, normally speaking, prevail over the hierarchically inferior Civil Code is not really so astonishing until we are reminded that these are all disputes between individuals and are thus examples of *Drittwirkung* in practice.

(a) Lüth's *theory of "reciprocal effect":* Wechselwirkung

Harlan's suit against Lüth was based on the latter's call for a boycott contravening § 826 BGB. It would be idle to deny that, at that time, Harlan's claim seemed a very powerful one. For not only was this a dispute between private persons which, on the face of it, left no room for the application of the Bill of Rights; the constitutional protection of free speech, enunciated in Article 5(1), is subject to the "qualifications" of the general law.

The Constitutional Court overcame the first hurdle in the way we have already described; but the second hurdle was no less serious since the wording of Article 5(2) makes it clear that the draftsmen always intended to allow the civil and criminal legislator the freedom to place some limits on the free expression of opinion. Of the words of this article which symbolised this freedom, two were particularly open-ended—"general laws"; and Lüth tried to argue that these only referred to rules of public law and thus excluded § 826 BGB. The Constitutional Court refused to accept this

16 "A person who willfully or negligently injures the life, body, health, freedom, property, or other right of another contrary to law is bound to compensate him for any damage arising there from."

17 "For an injury which is not a pecuniary loss compensation in money may be demanded only in the cases specified by law." The most notable example of such an exception can be found in § 847 BGB though this provision is silent on human dignity (including privacy). This, of course, is deliberate since the drafters of the Code had decided to exclude the protection of privacy form the ambit of § 823 I BGB.

(narrowing) interpretation but, mercifully, (for Lüth and speech rights in German law) was able to preserve much of the sanctity of freedom of expression through its ingenious theory of "reciprocal effect" (*Wechselwirkung*) which, in this instance, "neutralised" the effect of § 826 BGB.

At first sight the theory as much as the terminology seems Germanic and to common lawyers prima facie off-putting. Yet it posited a simple idea namely, that just as the "general laws" can, because of Article 5(2), affect the Constitution so does the Constitution, in its turn, affect them. So, when a judge determines the extent to which the general laws limit the Constitution, the laws themselves should be seen against the background of the entire legal order and the importance it attaches to free speech. To some extent this is recognised as being a circular argument[18] but, in the ultimate analysis, it amounts to little more than an invocation of the principle of proportionality (*Verhältnismäigkeit*). Subsequent decisions have, indeed, resorted to the balancing techniques of proportionality itself to test the limitations of governmental action. Thus, as a leading decision on proportionality put it in 1988, "General laws restricting expression are valid only if they are adapted (*geeignet*) to the achievement of a legitimate purpose, necessary (*erforderlich*) to that end, and the burden they impose is not excessive (*zumutbar*)[19] in the light of the achieved benefits".[20]

Once the court had reached that stage, Lüth was home and dry! For his motives in calling for the boycott were impeccable; indeed, his position seemed to cry out for the action he, in fact, did take. As for Harlan's countervailing economic interests, though important, they had to give way to the sanctity of political free speech. As the court put it, in a style that could be mistaken for a Cardozo or Brandeis aphorism, "When the formation of public opinion on a question of general importance is at stake, private and especially economic interests must take second place."[21]

(b) Political and economic speech compared: Blinkfüer

At this point, a brief excursus is needed. Not every call for an economic boycott receives such preferential treatment; the *Blinkfüer* case demonstrates this clearly.[22] The litigation was born of the cold war, which was intensified when the Berlin wall was erected in 1961. An important pub-

[18] See Roman Herzog in Maunz/Dürig/Herzog/Scholz, *Grundgesetz Kommentar*, Art. 5 Rdnr. 261 though the learned author, until recently President of the Federal Republic of Germany and prior to that President of the Constitutional Court, wisely adds (Rdnr. 262) that such reasoning may be inherent in the Constitution which, on the one hand, allows the ordinary law to place limitations on Basic Rights but, on the other, also prevents such limitations from interfering with the "essence of the Basic Right" in question: Art. 19(2) *GG*.

[19] This is taken to mean that no other means, less restrictive of free speech, are available.

[20] BVerfGE 78, 232, 245.

[21] BVerfGE 7, 198, 219.

[22] BVerfGE 25, 256 (1969).

lishing group—the Axel Springer group—instructed its dealers and distributors not to handle journals which contained information about television programmes made in what used to be Eastern Germany. Dealers who refused to comply with this instruction would, in future, be barred from selling Springer newspapers. The letter was mainly directed against *Blinkfüer*, a *small*, left-wing publication which immediately sued Springer, relying on § 823 I BGB and claiming that the call for a boycott was "unlawful" under that paragraph of the Civil Code.[23] Springer's defence, that the call for the boycott was constitutionally protected along the lines of *Lüth*, was turned down since his boycott was different from *Lüth*'s in so far as the latter "was simply an appeal to the moral and political responsibility of his audience".[24] Moreover, Lüth's call for a boycott "was incapable of directly and effectively restricting the human and artistic freedom of . . . Harlan, for Lüth [unlike Axel Springer] had no means of coercion at his disposal . . ." In the end, therefore, Springer's economic might, its "financial grip" over its distributors, and the threatening tone in which the letter calling for a boycott was written, all weighed against them as the court treated this self-seeking speech as worthy of no protection.[25] But the Court, true to its self-appointed task of weighing each case separately, refused to go as far as saying that all calls for economic boycott were worthy of constitutional protection. "The Constitution", reasoned the Court, "does not bar the economically more powerful from engaging in the intellectual struggle of opinion . . . provided the means employed by the person who calls for a boycott [are] constitutionally acceptable".[26] This would have been the case, for instance, had Springer called for a "reader" boycott rather than tried to exploit the economic dependence of the subjects of the boycott. Once again, the reasoning is nuanced and the result not that different from that reached in the U.S.A. where, for instance, courts have held that picketing aimed at encouraging consumers to boycott a secondary business does not enjoy First Amendment protection.[27]

If the court had stopped there and simply held that Springer's rights of free speech were not protected, the case would have provided an example of how the motives of the speaker can affect the extent of protection afforded to his speech. But the Court took one more step by holding that a private entity (Springer) had violated *Blinkfüer*'s speech rights. And not

[23] For details of this important tort heading see Markesinis, *The German Law of Obligations*, vol II, *The German Law of Torts*, 3rd ed. (1997), chap. 2.

[24] BVerfGE 25, at 267. Translation taken from Professor Kommers, *The Constitutional Jurisprudence of the Federal Republic of Germany*, 2nd ed. (1997), 374.

[25] The thrust of this reasoning has been followed since. See, for instance, BVerfGE 62, 230 (1982). A thorough analysis can be found in Lerche, "Zur verfassungsgerichtlichen Deutung der Meinungsfreiheit (insbesondere im Bereiche des Boykotts)", *Festschrift für Gebhard Müller*, 197*ff.* (1970).

[26] Translation from Kommers, *op.cit.*, p. 373.

[27] *NLRB* v. *Retail Store Employees Union Local 1001*, 447 US 607 (1980).

only that: the lower courts, by *not* ordering Springer to pay damages to *Blinkfüer*, had perpetuated the constitutional violation. The effect of this was the birth of a constitutional tort, along lines only known to Irish law, allowing one individual to sue another in order to enforce his constitutional rights. This aspect of the case will surface again in the next sub-section.

(c) Soraya*: The re-defining of § 823 I BGB and the "defeat" of § 253 BGB*

For our purposes the *Soraya* litigation[28] is the next important signpost because (a) it contains some carefully crafted dicta about the judge's power to adapt the law to changing socio-economic times; (b) it confirms the aforementioned new trend to create a new constitutional tort and, in doing so, completely re-adjusts the ambit of § 253 BGB; and (c) it brings into our lecture the law of privacy, confirming a prior and long-standing effort of the *Bundesgerichtshof* to fashion a general right of personality out of Article 1 of the Constitution. Because of lack of space we shall not discuss the first point, which deserves an article in its own right;[29] nor shall we elaborate on the second, since we have already covered this topic elsewhere.[30] The remainder of this sub-section will thus focus on the last of the aforementioned issues, the recognition of a *constitutional* right of privacy sounding in damages. In this context, three points need to be stressed.

Firstly, in *Soraya* the Constitutional Court gave its seal of approval to the *Bundesgerichtshof*'s basing of this new right of personality on Article 1 of the Constitution.[31] In the late 1950s and early 1960s, in the absence of binding precedent, the Federal Court's efforts had not passed without judicial doubts and academic criticism.[32] The imprimatur of the Constitutional Court put an end to this debate, retrospectively as it were sanctioning the judge-made general right of personality in the light of a prolonged parlia-

[28] BVerfGE 34, 269 (1973).

[29] We shall thus only reproduce the key sentence of the judgment since, intriguingly, it seems to come close to the interpretative obligation in cl. 3(1) of the Human Rights Bill. "Occasionally, the law can be found outside the positive legal rules erected by the state; this is law which emanates from the entire constitutional order and which has as its purpose the 'correction' of written law. It is for the judge to 'discover' this law and through his opinions give it concrete effect. The Constitution does not restrict judges to apply statutes in their literary sense when deciding cases put before them. Such an approach assumes a basic completeness of statutory rules which is not attainable in practice . . . The insight of the judge may bring to light certain values of society . . . which are implicitly accepted by the constitutional order but which have received an insufficient expression in statutory texts. The judge's decision can help realise such ideas and give effect to such values."

[30] Markesinis, *The German Law of Tort*, 3rd ed. (1997) pp. 63*ff*. 376*ff*.

[31] BGH May 25, 1954, BGHZ 13, 334. (*Schacht*).

[32] For instance by Löffler, "Die Grenzen richterlicher Rechtsfindung beim immateriellen Schadensersatz", *NJW* 1962, 225. But the fears expressed in articles such as this about the effect these decisions might have on free speech have not been materialised, as we shall explain further down in the text.

mentary inactivity similar, in many respects, to ours. The invocation of Article 1 of the Constitution,[33] protecting human dignity as the basis of this new privacy right bears, as we shall note further down, a notable resemblance with the Warren and Brandeis attempts to base an American general right of privacy on the idea of "an inviolate personality" (even though, in the end, matters developed differently in the USA).

Secondly, one should note that in German law damages (or injunctions) have been awarded for such varied violations of personality rights as "appropriation of likeness",[34] unlawful release of an insured person's medical record,[35] "neighbour snooping"[36], un-necessary publicity about an impending divorce of a member of the aristocracy,[37] the publication (by the *Stern* magazine) of a telephone conversation between two leading politicians (unlawfully recorded by unknown persons),[38] the unauthorised opening of sealed mail,[39] the unauthorised imitation of the voice (of a recently deceased actor) for the sake of advertising a product,[40] and, most recently, photographing a public figure in a public place.[41] That these results involved, as already stated, a re-appraisal of codal provisions which, in the event were found to be outdated, can only be seen as a sign of open-mindedness on the part of the German judiciary.

Thirdly the *Soraya* litigation arose as a result of a fabricated interview, which the former Empress of Iran never actually gave. In condemning fab-

[33] Art. 1 (Protection of human dignity):
"(1) The dignity of man shall be inviolable. To respect and protect it shall be the duty of all state authority." See, also, Art. 2 of the Constitution, note 67, below.

[34] BGH February 14, 1958, BGHZ 26, 349 (1958).

[35] BGH April 2, 1957, BGHZ 24, 72 (1957).

[36] OLG Köln 13 October 1988, NJW 1989, 720. (7,000 DM were awarded to the successful plaintiff whose privacy had thus been invaded.)

[37] OLG Hamburg 26 March 1970, *NJW* 1970, 1325. Since the case involved a member of the Hohenzollern family the court carefully considered (and, in this case rejected as inapplicable) the possible (statutory) exception, which applies to "persons of contemporary history". An injunction against publication was thus granted to the plaintiff. If the "private" information is already in the public domain, the courts will be reluctant to accord privacy protection. Yet even in such cases the courts will investigate whether a full identification of the complainant is necessary or, in effect, is part of a gold-digging operation on the part of the defendant/publisher. Thus, see, BGH 26 January 1965, *JZ* 1965, 411; BGH 24 November 1987, *NJW* 1988, 1984. But *cf.* BGH 15 April 1980, *NJW* 1980, 1790.

[38] BGH 19 December 1978, BGHZ 73, 120. The court decision is noteworthy for the detailed balancing of privacy rights versus speech rights. The conversation was between Helmut Kohl (at the time of writing Federal Chancellor) and Kurt Biedenkopf (Prime Minister of the State of Saxony). This is a rare Kohl legal action for the Chancellor, unlike the former Prime Minister of Bavaria Josef Strauss, has avoided recourse to the courts.

[39] BGH 20 February 1990, VersR 1990, 531. (The opening of the sealed letter violates the personality rights of both sender and receiver.)

[40] OLG Hamburg 8 May 1989, NJW 1990, 1995.

[41] BGH 19 Dec. 1995, BGHZ 131, 332 = *NJW* 1996, 1128 (third *Caroline* case). In a fourth and contemporaneous decision, known as the *Caroline Son* case—BGH 12. 12. 1995, BGH *NJW* 1996, 985—the court placed great emphasis on the defendant's obvious commercial motives in the taking of the prince's photographs.

ricated interviews, the Court more importantly set itself firmly against the idea that false facts deserved any constitutional protection. "An invented interview" said the court "adds not an iota to the formation of real public opinion".[42] The point, as we shall note further down, was repeated even more strongly in the subsequent *Böll* case[43], setting German law apart from a line of American cases[44] which, perversely one is inclined to say, have held that even deliberate falsification of quotations is insufficient to trigger off the "knowledge of falsity" requirement of the *New York Times* v. *Sullivan*[45] ruling which would make the publisher liable.

(d) Private employment contracts

This is the last example meant to show how the ideas emanating from public law have penetrated the domain of private law.[46] A decision of the Federal Labour Court of 1984 offers an excellent illustration.[47]

In that case a printer working in a private concern refused to take part in the printing of a book, which in his view, glorified war. Though his action was motivated by deeply held beliefs he was dismissed by his employers and sued for reinstatement. The Labour Court took the view that the case raised serious issues relating to Article 2 of the Constitution,[48] which guarantees freedom of conscience. This constitutional provision, for the reasons already noted in the area of free speech, exerts an influence on private law, which meant that the "reasonableness " of the employer's action had to be tested against the wider constitutional background. The court thus resorted to the by now familiar test of balancing. Since the employee's views were

[42] BVerfGE 34, 269, 283–4. This does not, however, shift the burden of proof for disputed facts (other than those deliberately made up) on those who express their opinion on matters of public concern. They may thus rely on reports by third parties that the other party has not expressly denounced: BVerfGE 85, 1, 22 (*Critical Bayer Shareholders* case).

[43] BVerfGE 54, 208 (1980) and re-confirmed in the (first) *Caroline* case: BGHZ 128, 1 = *NJW* 1995, 861. In the court's view this "forced commercialisation" (*Zwangskommerzialisierung*) warranted a large award of damages which did, in fact follow when the Court of Appeal of Hamburg fixed the amount (for three complaints consolidated in the first case) to 180,000 DM: OLG Hamburg *NJW* 1996, 2870. Whether restitutionary damages can and should be ordered is currently a subject of a heated debate. In favour of this view is Professor Schlechtriem in his case note to the first *Caroline* case, *JZ* 1995, 362*ff*.

[44] E.g. *Masson* v. *New Yorker*, 111 S. Ct. 2419 (1991).

[45] 376 US 254 (1964).

[46] It is in this area that one finds the greatest difference with the American "state action" doctrine though, again, the difference can be over-stated. Thus, for an exact parallel of BArbGE 1, 185 see *Novosel* v. *Nationwide Insurance Co.* 721 F. 2d 894 (1983) which I discuss in greater detail in "The Familiarity of the Unknown", *Essays in Honour of Lord Goff*, to be published by the OUP in 1999.

[47] BArbGE 47, 363 (1984).

[48] Art. 2: "(1) Everyone shall have the right to the free development of his personality in so far as he does not violate the rights of others or offend against the constitutional order or the moral code. (2) Everyone shall have the right to life and to inviolability of his person . . ."

deeply held, the book in question did, indeed, glorify war. More importantly, the Court held that the employer had over-reacted by dismissing the employee instead of assigning another employee to perform the said task. The Court thus came down in favour of the employee. Though the decision is interesting in that it used the *Lüth* reasoning,[49] in its results it is consistent with a long line of cases, which have used the Constitution to affect private law arrangements.[50]

4. Constitutional balancing

Three cases, among many, must be mentioned briefly in this section. They are *Mephisto*,[51] *Böll*,[52] and *Wallraff*.[53]

Mephisto is a dubious case in two respects. First, it marks a retreat from the *Lüth* position, which posited a strong constitutional review of the decisions of the ordinary courts. In that sense, it has been overtaken by later decisions of the Constitutional Court some of which will be discussed below. *Mephisto* is also dubious—at any rate to Common lawyers—since it concerns the granting of a damages action for the disparagement of the dead. Finally, *Mephisto* is an unsatisfactory or, at any rate, mysterious judgment since it was decided 3–3 with two judges (needed to make up the normal panel of eight) missing from the record! Yet *Mephisto* also has its rewarding passages.

The dispute concerned a *roman à clef* entitled *Mephisto—Roman einer Karriere*, written by Klaus Mann (son of the Nobel laureate Thomas Mann) and faintly based on the life of a great actor and Nazi supporter Gustaf Gründgens who had, for a short time, been married to Klaus Mann's sister Erica and had acquired a great reputation in his rendering of Goethe's

[49] Of "indirect" influence. The Labour Court's own jurisprudence has, starting with BArbGE 1, 185 (1954), always favoured a direct application of the Constitutional norms. The adoption of the *Lüth* approach in this case could be seen as an abandonment of the original position of "direct approach"; more likely, however, it is an indication that the theoretical niceties between the two approaches are not that important since, in practice, the results are very similar. On the other hand, the Labour Court still subjects trade union–employer agreements (*Tarifverträge*) to direct constitutional scrutiny since such agreements are seen as "substitute legislation" since the Federal Minister of Employment routinely declares them as having the force of law for all employment relationships in the industries covered by them: *Allgemeinverbindlicherklärung*—(declaration of universal applicability): BArbGE 71, 29, 35.

[50] Thus, BAGE 1, 185 (1954) condemned the firing of a (private) employee because his employer disagreed with the former's political statements. BArbGE 4, 274 (1957) invalidated a contractual provision, which allowed the employer to dismiss his employee if and when the latter married. Yet even these cases have some isolated American parallels.

[51] BVerfGE 30, 173 (1971).

[52] BVerfGE 54, 208 (1980).

[53] BVerfGE 66, 116 (1984).

Faust.[54] Mann committed suicide in 1949; and by the time his book was published in Germany,[55] Gründgens had also died. So the action was brought by Gründgens' adopted son against the publisher of Mann's book.[56] The action was for defamation; and the prime defence was that this was not a case involving speech but a work of art, and that artistic creations were not, according to Article 5(3) of the Constitution, subject to the defences of Article 5(2).

Why art receives such preferential treatment over speech is, to us at least, something of a mystery. At one stage the court, itself,[57] seemed to explain this preference because of the shabby treatment given to artists during the Nazi period. But artists were by no means the only ones who got a raw deal out of this darkest period of German history. Another explanation might be the importance traditionally attached in Germany to art and artistic creations compared to political debate, which became truly free only during this century. This, too, may be something of an over-simplification. What, however is not in doubt is the fact that the Court first defined art in what, in legal circles, has become a locus classicus.[58] Then it proceeded to state that even this, apparently unrestricted, freedom found its limits in other parts of the Constitution and, in particular, in the all-important Article 1.

Close on the heels of *Mephisto* followed *Soraya*, a case already referred to above. With its confident pronouncement that "An individual's dignity and personality rights . . . lie at the core of the value order reflected in the fundamental rights protected by the Constitution . . . It must be respected and protected by all organs of the state"[59] the court was re-affirming, if re-affirmation was needed, the centrality of human dignity in the German Constitution. *Böll*, which followed ten years later, was to return to the themes of both cases and shows how personality could, in appropriate circumstances, trump even speech rights.

[54] Extracts are still available on Deutsche Grammophon cassettes. Two years before his death, Gründgens produced in Hamburg the last three parts of Lawrence Durrell's *The Alexandria Quartet* to "great acclaim" much to Durrell's pleasure, a sign of Gründgens' continuing appeal in some circles. See Lawrence Durrell, *Spirit of the Place. Mediterranean Writings* (1969), 132.

[55] The book, written in 1936, was first published in Amsterdam by a small publishing house but, at that time, received little attention.

[56] Interesting information about the historical background can be found in K. Mann's *Der Wendepunkt: Ein Lebensbericht* published after his death in 1981.

[57] BVerfGE 30, 173, 192 (1971).

[58] "The essence of artistic endeavour lies in the free creative process whereby the artist, in his chosen communicative medium, gives immediate perceptible form to what he has felt, learnt, or experienced. Artistic activity involves both the conscious and the unconscious, in a manner not rationally separable. Intuition, imagination, and knowledge of the art all play a part in artistic creation; it is not so much communication as expression, indeed the most immediate expression of the artist's individuality." Markesinis, *op.cit.* note 8, above, at p. 361.

[59] BVerfGE 34, 281.

Böll, which American lawyers would describe as a "false light" case, was decided during the period when the "red brigades" were active in Germany. In a broadcast that came shortly after a terrorist assassination, a commentator laid the blame for the current unrest at the door of a number of notable social critics, including Böll, the Nobel Prize laureate. Böll, said the commentator, had described the State as "pile of dung"; in contemporary Germany, he saw nothing but "the remnants of decaying power"; and he had accused the State of "pursuing the terrorists in a pitiless hunt". Böll, it turned out, had never made the first statement. The statement about "decaying power" had been taken totally out of context; and as for the Government pursuing the terrorists pitilessly, what Böll had said was that sections of the Press (not the State) had pursued them pitilessly which, clearly, was not the same thing.

Personality rights included the right not to be misquoted, reasoned the Constitutional Court. "Among other things", continued the court, "this right includes personal honour and the right to one's own words. It also protects the bearer of these rights against having statements attributed to him which he did not make and which impair his self-defined claim to social recognition." The importance of judgments such as the above is not only that they show how one constitutional value—dignity—is pitched against another—speech; but also how the courts, through carefully chosen words, define the ambit of such notions as "human dignity" and "personality" on a case-by-case basis.

Wallraff is our last example of constitutional balancing. The decision reveals another reason why speech rights may have to give way to personality and privacy or, more accurately, to the speech rights of another individual.

Günther Wallraff, a well-known journalist, adopted a fictitious name and sought employment with the "Bildzeitung"—a right-wing tabloid, part of the Springer group, with a wide circulation in Germany. He used his employment with the *Bild* to obtain "inside" information about the *Bild's* editorial practices. The product of his "research" was then published in a book, parts of which the regional court, on an application by Bild, ordered him not to publish. The *Bundesgerichtshof* lifted the injunction on the grounds that, though Wallraff's methods had been illegal, his Article 5(1) rights could not be abridged. So *Bild* then took its case to the Constitutional Court.

The Constitutional Court, applying the heightened review, which it had re-adopted after the mid-seventies,[60] decided to review the entire file more thoroughly. Its conclusion was that "the right of editorial confidentiality" was a pre-requisite of a free press since it secured its independence. Such in-

[60] BVerfGE 42, 143 (1976) which marked a departure from the deferential approach adopted by *Mephisto* and a return to the *Lüth* principles. More on this in subsection 5, below.

dependence would, of course, be protected if it had been violated by the State; but a very thorough review of the facts showed that constitutionally protected rights could be just as easily and effectively infringed by an individual. The detailed "balancing" of interests then led the court to admit that though constitutional protection will, normally, be removed from the publication of information which was illegally obtained, the protection could endure if the publication served a socially useful function (e.g. revealed some illegality). But since Wallraff's revelations had failed to reveal anything illegal in the Bild practices but had, on the contrary, been themselves based on information obtained by deception, Wallraff's speech rights under Article 5(1) GG had to give way to Bild's rights to editorial confidentiality, which was also based on the same article of the Constitution.

5. Germany's constant search for an equilibrium between competing values. A contrast with American law?

In *Konigsberg* v. *State Bar*[61] Mr Justice Black said: "I believe that the First Amendment's unequivocal command that there shall be no abridgment of the rights of free speech and assembly shows that the men who drafted our Bill of Rights did all the 'balancing' that was to be done in this field . . ." Though this dictum appears in a dissent, and one can find, especially in earlier times, American justices arguing that "no constitutional guarantee enjoys preference"[62] over others, it would appear that Justice Black's statement succinctly states the dislike felt both by American judges[63] and academics[64] in balancing competing values against that of free speech.

In part, of course, this is due to the categorical phrasing of the First Amendment, which was born out of the American experience with seditious libel and its stark contrast with the text of the German Constitution, which reflecting a different (recent) historical experience, strives for a balancing of values, which it regards as equally important.

Though such concerns are not unknown in Germany,[65] the preference for balancing interests whenever they are in conflict has won the day. The

[61] 366 US 36, 61 (1961).

[62] *Ullmann* v. *United States*, 350 US 422, 428 (1956) (Frankfurter, J).

[63] See, also Hugo Black, "The Bill of Rights", 35 *N.Y.U.L. Rev.* 865, esp. 882*ff.* (1960).

[64] Thus, among the voluminous literature see: McKay, "The Preference for Freedom", 34 *N.Y.U.L.Rev.* 1182 (1959); Frantz, "The First Amendment in the Balance" 71 *Yale LJ* 1424 (1962); Mendelson, "On the Meaning of the First Amendment: Absolutes in the Balance", 50 *Cal. L. Rev.* 821 (1962).

[65] For instance, Steindorf, *Persönlichkeitsschutz im Zivilrecht*, 20 (1983); Tettinger, "Der Schutz der persönlichen Ehre im freien Meinungskampf" *JZ* 1983 317. Ossenbühl, "Medien zwischen Macht und Recht" *JZ* 1995, 633; Sendler, "Kann man Liberalität übertreiben?" *ZRP* 1994, 343. It is noteworthy, however, that much of this concern has been addressed to the danger that human dignity may not be accorded sufficient attention when pitched against speech interests.

English observer is thus well-advised not only to note the difference between German and American law but also to study the meticulous criteria which the German courts have developed over the last four decades to carry out this balancing task. Having done this, he may then wish to ask himself whether these German criteria are preferable to the ones which the accidents of litigation have imposed upon English law and which will be briefly mentioned further down. Thus, in cases where speech clashes with privacy we find German courts weighing such factors as: (a) the motives of the publisher[66] which, in the context of privacy protection, has been taken to mean that if the invasion was motivated by a wish to make money at the expense of the plaintiff damages should be assessed in a way that would deprive the tortfeasor of his ill-gotten gains;[67] (b) the importance of the speech e.g. does it advance knowledge and public debate or merely benefit the speaker financially;[68] (c) the way in which the information about the plaintiff was obtained: illegal means,[69] telephoto lens[70] (indicating to the "intruder" that the plaintiff wished to be left alone); (d) the extent of the dissemination of the information;[71] (e) the accuracy of the statement or whether it was fabricated by a news medium;[72] (f) the breadth of the restriction which the plaintiff wishes to place on the defendant's speech rights[73] (g) other, wider societal objectives which may be involved in the dispute[74] and so on.[75] The courts also take the view that a severe attack may justify an otherwise excessive counter-attack. (The *Gegenschlag* theory of speech).[76]

This balancing, evincing a strong desire on the part of the German courts to accommodate the competing values of free speech and privacy, as well

[66] Contrast BVerfGE 7, 198 (*Lüth*) with BVerfGE 25, 256 (*Blinkfüer*).

[67] See, for instance, BGH 19 September 1961, BGHZ 35, 363, 369*ff.* and, more recently and in a more elaborated manner, BGH 15 November 1994, BGHZ 128, 14–16. This introduction of "punitive" damages into German law has generated much (and not always favourable) comment from academic commentators. See, for instance, Stoll, *Haftungsfolgen im bürgerlichen Recht* (1993), 57–67; 79–82; 210*ff.*; Rosengarten, "Der Präventionsgedanke im Zivilrecht" *NJW* 1996, 1935–1938.

[68] BVerfGE 7, 198, 219 (*Lüth*).

[69] BVerfGE 66, 116 (1984) (*Bild-Wallraff*).

[70] BGH 19 Dec. 1995, BGHZ 131, 332. The overall damages for Princess Caroline's harassment were fixed at 180000 DM: OLG Hamburg, 25 July 1996, NJW 1996, 2870.

[71] BVerfGE 35, 202 (*Lebach*); OLG Saarbrücken NJW 1997, 1376, 1379.

[72] See: BVerfGE 34 269 (1973) (*Soraya*); BVerfGE 54, 208 (1980) (*Böll*); BGHZ 128, 1 (first *Caroline* Case).

[73] BVerfGE 42, 143 (1976).

[74] BVerfGE 35, 202 (1973) (*Lebach*).

[75] BGH 5 May 1964, NJW 1964, 1471 offers a good example of the position taken by German courts that not everything that interests the public can be published in the public interest. In that case, the defendant magazine wrote an article about a criminal prosecution brought against the plaintiff. In it, it also referred to his repeatedly adulterous life. The court stressed that, normally, such revelations will be treated as amounting to actionable instances of violated privacy. In this case, however, the revelation was left un-punished since the plaintiff had, in the past, held himself out as a moralist.

[76] BVerfGE 12, 113 (1961) (*Schmid-Spiegel*), re-confirmed by BVerfGE 54, 129 (1980) (*Art critic*).

as Constitutional norms and the rest of the legal order, is not only found in speech and privacy cases. We thus find the same tendency in other areas of civil liberties where the judges are, once again, willing to give guidance to future administrators and courts as to how to perform their tasks.

The *Brokdorf* decision of 1985,[77] concerning the right of assembly, offers a good example of both of these points though, because of lack of space it will be the only one we offer in this article. For there the court went beyond the procedural arguments which would have been enough to justify the setting aside of the civil courts' order enjoining citizens not to demonstrate outside a nuclear plant because there were indications that some of the demonstrators might turn violent. Instead, the court stressed the importance of demonstrations to a liberal democratic order, noted that the danger of violent acts by some demonstrators did not, of itself, justify the cancelling of the whole demonstration, and added poignantly that the answer to such threats lay in restraining those who threatened violence against the demonstrators and not the demonstrators themselves. The only concession made to the authorities was to insist that in the future they be given adequate notice of such assemblies so as to take all necessary precautions. It need hardly be stressed that in all these cases what matters is not whether one agrees with the final result reached by a particular court but the efforts made to develop usable and consistent criteria for resolving conflicts between legal values—a point to which we will have to return again and again in this paper. The search for an equilibrium between competing values and interests thus strikes me as a central and, I believe, commendable feature of German constitutional thinking.

6. Defining the limits of Constitutional scrutiny

Timorous souls will always find reasons to ignore foreign law even where it patently appears to be pregnant with ideas. Here we shall not rehearse some of the reservations usually put forward by introverted domestic lawyers—which will be addressed in section III, below—but only address one legitimate concern which may be voiced against the German practice of subjecting the ordinary courts to constitutional justification: how can we keep within workable bounds such expansion of constitutional control? The problem has occupied German literature and the courts extensively; so this item can serve as the last one to be included in this first part of this essay.

For the reader who is interested in figures the answer is re-assuring: a relatively small number of cases concerning matters of pure private law end up being subject to such review: the judicial exhortation which has ensured this is found in *Lüth* and will be cited more fully below. On the other hand,

[77] BVerfGE 69, 315.

for the reader who wishes to know more about the techniques used to achieve this controlled intervention, the following may serve as an introduction into what is, undoubtedly, a complex topic.[78] Our discussion will be attempted under four sub-headings.

(a) Lüth*: the dispute retains its private law character*

This point has been re-asserted many times since it was first enunciated in *Lüth*[79] and it basically means that the Constitutional Court will not be dragged lightly into private law disputes (and litigants know this); the main exception to this attitude, and this is of recent vintage, can be found in the area of speech rights—the subject of this essay. This stance also means that the private law values retain their potency and are not to be displaced easily by constitutional ideas. This stance, as subsequently refined by numerous cases, seems to go a long way towards appeasing many of the concerns voiced by lawyers[80] fearful of the effects of an indiscriminate application of any theory of *Drittwirkung*.

In *Lüth*, itself, this stance was expressed clearly and unequivocally when the Constitutional Court proclaimed that: "The Constitutional Court must determine whether the reach and effect of the basic rights in private law has been correctly ascertained by the regular courts. But this is also the limit of its investigation: it is not for the Constitutional Court to check judgments of civil courts for errors of law in general; the Constitutional Court simply judges the 'radiant effect' of the basic rights on private law and implements the values inherent in the precept of constitutional law . . . The Federal Constitutional Court is certainly not there to act as a court of review, much less overview, for civil courts . . ."[81]

[78] For further details see: Markesinis and Enchelmaier "The Applicability of Human Rights as Between Individuals under German Law" in *Protecting Privacy* (ed. Basil Markesinis), forthcoming in 1999.

[79] BVerfGE 7, 198, 205.

[80] For instance KJ Partsch in *Privacy and Human Rights, 3rd International Colloquy about the European Convention on Human Rights 1970* (ed. AH Robertson, 1973) where he wrote: "Relations between individuals are far more complex and versatile [than relations with the state]. It is not only a problem of power; the more differentiated problems of love and hatred, of affection and dislike, of envy and competition, of neighbourhood and living side by side, of common interest and diversity are involved, not to mention the particular situations of personal care, guardianship, educational influence, and all other influences connected with the different forms of dependency. Adequate care should be taken of all these elements of a common life in a social community if the idea of transferring fundamental rights and freedoms from the public to the social sphere is to be realized."

[81] Translation in Markesinis, *op.cit.* note 8, above, at p. 356. The idea has been stressed extra-judicially by Justice Hans van Rupp in "Judicial Review in the Federal Republic of Germany", 9 *Amer. J. Comp. Law*, 33 (1959). The reluctance of the Constitutional court to interfere with the way the Administration (in all its forms) has exercised its discretion can be seen from many cases. Thus, see, BVerfGE 49, 89 (*Kalkar* case: challenge of a decision to allow the construction of fast-breeding nuclear reactor on the grounds that the authorising statute was unconstitutional rejected); BVerfGE 56, 54 (noise pollution); BVerfGE 46, 160

So *when* will the Constitutional Court be drawn into a dispute (which, one must stress again, involves two *individuals*)? Since 1958 patterns have changed but, generally speaking, it is fair to say that *in the area involving speech and expression rights* the Court has shown a greater willingness to review a decision *if* one or more of the following factors are satisfied. Since what follows is based on a progressively built case law, it is best sketched under the headings of a handful of leading cases. One must, however, stress the fact that this recent willingness to review decisions of ordinary courts has sacrificed clarity and predictability to the desire to give heightened protection to speech rights.

(b) Seriousness of invasion justifies heightened scrutiny: Deutschland Magazin[82] *and* Echternach[83]

When a labour union press service described the *Deutschland Magazin* as *ein rechtsradikales Hetzblatt* (a right-wing radical hate sheet) the magazine publisher sued and obtained[84] an injunction against the defendants ordering them not to repeat the statement "in the same words or in words of similar meaning".[85] The Union's complaint that the order of the civil courts violated its speech rights was only partly accepted. For the Constitutional Court upheld the prohibition against the italicised words (because of their unusual severity[86]) but allowed the defendants the use of other, less inflammatory language, to convey the same idea. But the court, signalling its intention to return to a more searching constitutional review of the decisions of the ordinary courts (especially in matters of this kind) stressed that "When the intensity of the invasion [of the speaker's constitutional rights by the ordinary courts] is at its greatest, the court is fully empowered to replace the evaluation undertaken by the civil court with its own evaluation".[87] In this case, the "invasion" of the speaker's rights by the ordinary courts was,

(refusal to interfere with state's decision not to give in to the demands of his kidnappers); BVerfGE 18, 85 (decision of BPatG [Federal Patent Court] holding that certain information concerning the publication of information contained in a patent application was permissible and not subject to constitutional review).

[82] BVerfGE 42, 143 (1976).

[83] BVerfGE 42, 163 (1976).

[84] The basis of the claim was § 823 II BGB in conjunction with two paragraphs of the Criminal Code—paras. 185 and 186—which deal with various forms of defamatory statements.

[85] BVerfGE 42, 143, 144.

[86] The expression used, difficult to translate accurately, could suggest in German a hatred, which could lead to murder and other crimes against humanity. The Constitutional Court took the view that the words amounted to an accusation that the magazine was agitating for unconstitutional goals.

[87] A dissenting judge, Judge Rupp-von Brünneck, a great libertarian, would, apparently, have liked to have gone further than her brothers by establishing an automatic, heightened degree of review because of the chilling effect which decisions of ordinary courts can have on the Press: BVerfGE 42, 143, 156 (1976).

as already stated, found not to have been so great so the judgment of the ordinary courts survived the constitutional scrutiny.

Though *Deutschland Magazin* left some commentators doubting as to how the new "interventionist" tendencies would work in practice, the case that followed it—*Echternach*[88]—showed that only case law would gradually set the proper parameters of the Constitutional Court's willingness to interfere with the judgments of the ordinary courts. The "similarity" of the facts between *Deutschland Magazin* and *Echternach* gave the first clue as to how this task would be accomplished in practice.

In *Echternach* the defendant attacked the Deutschland Foundation,[89] described as a "nationalistic enterprise in democratic clothing", for improperly giving the name of Konrad Adenauer, Germany's first post-World War II Chancellor, to a prize, which they had just set up. The Foundation's action, based on § 823 II BGB succeeded, the court ordering the speaker to refrain from repeating the "remarks". Repeating the *Deutschland Magazin* formula, the Constitutional Court was, however, able to distinguish this second case from the earlier one on the ground that here the ordinary courts had prohibited the "expression of a certain thought content" and not merely the repetition of certain words. This, being a "limitation of the speaker's freedom of opinion, which affected the basic right at its core and not merely at its margins",[90] was impermissible, and triggered off a review of all the relevant facts by the Constitutional Court, itself.

(c) The severity of the sanction

The seriousness of the invasion of the complainant's constitutional rights by the decision of the ordinary courts is not the only reason which justifies a heightened review of the ordinary courts' ruling. Excessive sanctions, imposed by the ordinary courts, will also trigger off Constitutional intervention. The *Strauss Placard*[91] and the *Flag Desecration* cases[92] illustrate this heading.

The litigation in the first case was triggered off by a display of placards which referred to Bavaria's Minister President as a man "who protects fascists" and shields Hoffmann, "the Oktoberfest murderer".[93] The ordinary courts convicted the writer of the placards for the offence of "insult"

[88] BVerfGE 42, 163 (1976).

[89] Publisher of the *Deutschland Magazin*.

[90] BVerfGE 42, 163, 169.

[91] BVerfGE 82, 43 (1990).

[92] BVerfGE 81, 278 (1990). BVerfGE 81, 298 (1990) is a parallel case involving the parodying of the first two stanzas of the German National Anthem. Once again, the Constitutional court disagreed with the finding of the ordinary courts that this amounted to seditious libel.

[93] Hoffmann was convicted for setting off a bomb during the Oktoberfest killing and wounding a number of innocent revellers.

according to § 186 of the Criminal Code.[94] The Constitutional Court felt justified to intervene with the decision, which in the end, it set aside as violating speech rights. The result, which would probably be condemned by English law but would be applauded in the USA, is not really the point I wish to stress here. Indeed, in Germany, too, public opinion has been divided over the correctness of the decision. What is, however, more interesting is the Court's further attempts to define the reasons which would trigger off a heightened review of the constitutionality of the decision of the lower courts. Thus the Constitutional Court held that whenever the lower courts determined the content of the communication in a way that might have serious constitutional implications they would have to explain their reasons or expose themselves to constitutional review. Thus, serious legal consequences could flow from describing a statement as a factual assertion (*Tatsachenbehauptung*),[95] a value judgment (*Werturteil*),[96] or a formal insult (*Formalbeleidigung* as in this case) since the latter was an offence, which attracted criminal sanctions. In such cases the classification of the statement by the ordinary court might well affect the ambit of basic rights and was thus subject to review.[97]

The *Flag Desecration*[98] case makes the same point. It involved an absurd collage of photos on the back cover of a book, the top one of which showed (in black and white) a man urinating while the bottom one reproduced a picture (in colour) of soldiers saluting the German flag. Since a urine trail was noticeable behind the flag, the ordinary courts took the view that § 90a of the Criminal Code applied. This punishes with imprisonment of up to three years or by a fine "anyone who publicly . . . defames the colours, the flag, the coat of arms or the anthem of the Federal Republic or one of its States . . ."

The lower courts treated the publication as raising artistic not speech issues and, as noted, this means that according to Article 5(3) of the Constitution such rights cannot be limited by ordinary laws but only by countervailing *constitutional* norms. The countervailing value was, one must admit ingeniously, found to be enshrined in Article 22 of the Constitution, which adopting the colours of the abortive liberal uprising of 1848/9, lacon-

[94] § 186 Criminal Code:
"Whoever asserts or disseminates in regard to another person a fact which is likely to cause that person to be despised or to be humiliated in the opinion of the public, shall be punished for insult, unless this fact is proved to be true, by fine, custody or imprisonment not to exceed one year, and if the insult was committed publicly or by distribution of writings, pictures, or representations, shall be punished by fine or imprisonment not to exceed two years."

[95] Since facts are not protected unless true.

[96] Since value judgments enjoyed presumptive protection. In a subsequent decision—BVerfGE 85, 1, at pp. 14–15 (1991) the Constitutional Court said: "Every person may assert and disseminate his opinion irrespective of whether it is valuable, valueless, true, or false, well grounded or not, emotional or irrational. Sharp and exaggerated opinions are also protected."

[97] BVerfGE 82, 43, 51.

[98] BVerfGE 81, 278 (1990).

ically ordains that "the Federal flag shall be black, red and gold". For, from this description, the court opined, the Federal Republic has an interest in its citizens identifying with values symbolised by the flag. Artistic values thus clashed with the proper functioning of the state, which is itself, a prerequisite of the protection of human rights. Paragraph 90a of the Criminal Code thus did nothing more than incorporate in the field of criminal law this important constitutional value.

Thus far the reasoning would suggest that the interests of the state would prevail and the author of the absurd collage would lose his case. But the court, having asserted the principle it was anxious to establish, namely that artistic creation was not unlimited but could clash with the state's own interest in its symbols, then proceeded to weigh all relevant factors before deciding the final outcome of the case. From a conservative stance it thus swung to a liberal one and asserted that "the symbolic protection of the flag could not immunise the state from criticism." The case was thus remanded to a lower court to perform the balancing of competing interests, one reason for the court taking such a careful and interventionist approach being the severity of the consequences which would follow if the lower court's determination had been left unchallenged.

(d) Speech as a special case for heightened review: Stern-Strauss *case*[99] *and* Soldiers are Murderers II *case*[100]

As already stated, from the eighties onwards some liberal members of the Constitutional Court wished speech rights to provide a special reason for heightened constitutional review of the decisions of the ordinary courts.[101] This finally occurred in the 1990s with the result that the German protection of speech and opinion is one of the highest found in the civilised world. Two cases illustrate this and, indeed, suggest that press speech rights are more effectively protected in Germany than they are in this country. Once again, one may disagree with this result and, indeed, many in Germany have done so.[102] But whatever one's doubts, one cannot accuse German law of stifling free speech.

The litigation in the first case was triggered off when Ralph Giordano, a prominent Jewish writer and survivor of a concentration camp, gave an interview to the magazine *Stern* on the occasion of the death of Rudolph Hess. In it he stated that some German politicians were "opportunistic democrats" (*Zwangsdemokraten*). By this he meant that they had adopted

[99] BVerfGE 82, 272 (1990).

[100] BVerfGE 93, 266 (1995).

[101] BVerfGE 42, 143 at p. 154. (Justice Rupp von Brünneck who, incidentally, was the most powerful dissenter in the *Mephisto* case.)

[102] The leading cases and the difficulties, which they have created, are reviewed by Markesinis and Enchelmaier, *op.cit.* note 78, above.

democratic ideals by force of circumstance even though their own preference was for more authoritarian ways of running things. He regarded Franz Josef Strauss as "a personification of this type" though he also added that he wished to "depersonalize his comments" for his comments really referred to a type of person who was active in contemporary Germany and existed because of the "as yet un-resolved German longing for a strongman (*Sehnsucht nach dem starken Mann*) . . . and the Leadercult (*Führerkult*)".[103] Such characters, in Giordano's view, represented a danger to German democracy. Strauss sued for libel and the lower courts agreed and forbade the further use of his name to personify the term "opportunistic democrat".[104]

The Constitutional Court first referred to *Lüth* and the "reciprocal effect theory" in order to justify its review of how the "general laws" could operate to restrict the scope of constitutional values. In this process, the court continued, one should never forget the importance of speech freedoms and the fact that "Especially in public debate, criticism, even in exaggerated and polemical form must be accepted if one is to avoid limiting the process by which public opinion is formed."[105]

Thus, where speech freedoms were involved, the court would exercise heightened review of the decisions of the lower courts. The purpose of this was not to substitute its own judgment for that of the ordinary courts but simply to make sure that the procedure had been correctly followed, the characterisation and the meaning of the communication had been properly carried out, and the decisions of the ordinary court been fully explained. Applying the above guiding principles to the facts before it, the Constitutional Court took the view that the ordinary courts had given to Giordano's interview the worst possible interpretation and failed to see it as a sharp, albeit permissible contribution to the wider issues of the state of the democratic order in Germany. In so doing, the Constitutional Court thus, essentially, redefined the meaning of defamation for the purposes of Article 5 of the Constitution in that it suggested that intentional denigration and insult were not, of themselves, sufficient to constitute libel. Thus, the statement would remain unprotected if it defamed Strauss without serving any other substantive value; but it would receive protection, even if sharp and insulting, if it could be seen—as the Constitutional Court felt it should have been—as a contribution to a wider political debate. How workable these distinctions are in practice is a matter of speculation. The result of this case must also be in doubt from the point of view of English law. But the deci-

[103] BVerfGE 82, 272, 273–4. This is another topic, which can allow those who teach foreign law through cases to make wide-ranging, and it is submitted, interesting excursus into the impact, which a foreign culture can have on its law.

[104] The final resolution of this dispute took place after Strauss's death, the action having proceeded posthumously in accordance with the *Mephisto* principles.

[105] BVerfGE 82, at p. 282.

sion must serve as yet another illustration of the importance given to speech rights in Germany, something that our own press seems to underestimate every time it argues that recognition of privacy rights will have a chilling effect on speech.

Soldiers are Murderers II[106] is one of the most controversial decisions handed down by the Constitutional Court in its entire history. For those of us who believe that cases can be used as excellent springboards for the presentation to a student (and more mature legal) audience of points of law and history of a foreign country this protracted litigation is a model of sorts. Clearly, in the light of these statements what follows is only a crass summary of the points which form part of this presentation and the reader should consult the relevant literature for further details.[107]

The five cases consolidated on appeal all dealt with criminal convictions of pacifist demonstrators for defamation during the 1991 Gulf War. One involved a sticker which referred to "Soldiers as Murderers", where the T in the German word *Soldaten* had been replaced with a cross. Another sticker reproduced a well known "photo of a soldier being shot with the caption 'Why?'" Yet a third called people to "turn swords into ploughs". The ordinary courts interpreted the word "murderers" in the legal sense of the criminal code and the words "Why?" and "soldiers" as referring to the German Army. The communications were thus proscribed as insulting and hatred inciting. One notes in passing that since 1951[108] the *Bundesgerichtshof* has held that it is possible to defame a specific group of people. Once again, therefore, § 186 of the Criminal Code—a "general law"—appeared to have the effect anticipated by Article 5(2) of the Constitution of limiting free speech.

Both the (restricted) chamber that decided *Soldiers are Murderers I* (which decided one of the cases) and the full First Senate of the Court (which decided the consolidated appeals) in *Soldiers are Murderers II* would have none of this. Having re-asserted the oft-quoted belief in freedom of expression, it went on to elaborate that this freedom gave the speaker the right to choose how, when, and in what form to articulate his opinions, to that extent (apparently) eliminating the distinction between "form" and "content" of speech enunciated in the *Deutschland Magazin* case. Return-

[106] BVerfGE 93, 266 (1995). This decision of the full court (eight justices) was, in fact preceded by *Soldiers are Murderers I*, a decision of a section of the Court (three justices), which triggered off the public controversy. The first decision can be found in BVerfG NJW 1994, 2943. The title comes from a 1931 work of Kurt Tucholsky.

[107] For the difficulties inherent in the judgment see Herdegen, "Kommentar zu 'Soldaten sind Mörder'", *NJW* 1994, 2933 *ff*. For a discussion in English see: Eberle, "Public Discourse in Contemporary Germany", 47 *Case Western Reserve L. Rev.*, 797, 878 *ff*. For journalistic reactions in the USA see Stephen Kinzer's article in *The New York Times*, 15 January 1966. But the best guide of how high the feelings ran in Germany, on the whole, against the decisions, can only be gleaned from the study of the daily press of the period.

[108] BGHSt 36, 83. The legal system as a whole takes a particularly dim view of incitement of hate, especially on grounds of race. See, also, § 130–1 Criminal Code.

ing to a theme which the Court had adopted in the early nineties,[109] it then went on to link communication freedoms not only with the desirable idea of furthering the democratic process (which is the value that lies behind Article 5 of the Constitution) but also to treat them as an essential attribute of all human beings. In this way the court was linking speech rights to Articles 1 and 2 of the Constitution, which enshrine the sacred notions of human dignity and free development of personality. This, as already explained in our brief discussion of the *Stern-Strauss* case, did not mean the total eclipse of defamation law; but it does mean, somewhat along the lines of *New York Times* v. *Sullivan*,[110] its reduced importance, at least where the alleged libellous statement also serves some wider, substantive interest. In the light of the above the Court came to the conclusion that the statements in question should be seen as containing general, anti-war sentiments, rather than statements which dehumanized and denigrated the German Army.

Where these decisions leave German law is too early to predict with confidence. When one is attempting such an evaluation, especially if trying to work out the consequences in the context where speech clashes with privacy rights, one may have to take many factors into account. The fact that in *Soldiers are Murderers II* the full court split 5–3 in its final decision is an indication of the divided opinion in Germany on these issues and, particularly, the very recent trend to overemphasise speech values.[111] It is thus more likely that the German partiality for balancing values will continue to guide the courts in speech/privacy cases and save German law from some of the extremes which one finds in countries such as the U.S.A.[112] My own guess thus is that the German courts will continue to favour political speech and distinguish between speech which informs and speech which is mere gossip and is motivated by greed.[113] The distinction is laudable; and it is no less defensible because the dividing line may, on occasion, be difficult to draw. One might further hazard the guess that this greater willingness to review the constitutionality of the decisions of the ordinary courts (or, more

[109] Thus, in 1991 the Court had argued that "the reason why free expression received constitutional protection is because it is an immediate expression of human personality". BVerfGE 85, 23, 31.

[110] 376 US 254 (1964).

[111] See, for instance, Kriele "Ehrenschutz und Meinungsfreiheit", *NJW* 1994, 1897*ff.*; Ossenbühl "Medien zwischen Macht und Recht", *JZ* 1995, 633*ff.* But *cf.* Justice Dieter Grimm (a member of the panel that decided the first of the *Soldiers are Murderers I*) who subsequently defended it in "Die Meinungsfreiheit in der Rechtsprechung des Bundesverfassungsgerichts", *NJW* 1995, 1697, 1705.

[112] The most recent cases support this prediction. Thus, see, LG Berlin *NJW* 1997, 1155. See, also, the case concerning Prince Ernst August von Hanover, so far only reported in the *Frankfurter Allgemeine Zeitung* of 9 May 1998, and likely to end up in the Constitutional Court.

[113] The Constitutional Court has confirmed the accuracy of this prediction in its most recent judgment: BverfGE *NJW* 1998, 2887.

generally, the administration or, even, the legislature) is not likely to spread outside the area of speech rights and disturb the rather cautious pattern which seems to prevail in other types of cases and the Court's oft-proclaimed exhortation of "self-restraint", especially in matters with strong political overtones.[114]

One last thought should be mentioned. The purpose of this (second) section of this article was not to prophesy the future but to describe what its third part will claim to be a valuable source of ideas. Certainly, the idea that the intensity of the review will vary according to the extent to which human rights are threatened by the challenged decision can, despite all its uncertainties, find parallels in many judgments of British courts as they, too, have recommended a variable threshold of the *Wednesbury* review where speech is concerned.[115] The possibility of legal borrowings are thus there for all but the most insular. For what is at issue here is not the copying of the German concepts or solutions but the use of their ideas for local inspiration.

III THE HORIZONTAL EFFECT OF OUR HUMAN RIGHTS BILL

1. Is it possible?

Direct horizontal effect of the kind found in Irish law[116] was, clearly, not intended by the Bill, which not only excludes any reference to private individuals and entities but also, in clause 6 (1), makes it clear that only "public authorities" must act compatibly with the Convention. Whatever "public authorities" may mean, and despite the inconsistencies to which this different treatment may lead, the implication must surely be that *some* entities or persons do not have to act compatibly with the Convention. In the House of Lords the Lord Chancellor was very clear about this when he reminded his audience that "The convention had its origins in a desire to protect

[114] BVerfGE 36, 1, 14. Despite its pronouncements on "judicial self-restraint" this *Grundlagenvertrag* decision has been criticised by some authors as a purely political one. Thus, see Kriele, "Recht und Politik in der Verfassungsrechtsprechung", *NJW* 1976, 777, 778.

[115] See, for instance, Lord Bridge's views in *R.* v. *Secretary of State for the Home Department, ex p. Bugdacay* [1987] AC 514, 531 E-G; *R.* v. *Secretary of State for the Home Department, ex p. Brind* [1991], 1 AC 696, 748–749. Another important judgment, related to the ECHR, is *R.* v. *Secretary of State for the Home Department, ex p. McQuillan* [1995] 4 All ER 400, esp. 422 (per Sedley J) and, more recently, by Sir Thomas Bingham MR (as he then was) in *R.* v. *Ministry of Defence, ex p. Smith and Others* [1996] 1 All ER 257 at 263.

[116] E.g. *Meskell* v. *Coras Eireann* [1973] IR 121 at 132–3 (per Walsh J); *Lovett* v. *Gogan* [1995] ILRM 12. The Irish position bears considerable resemblance to the views of the German Federal Labour Court: BArbGE 1, 185.

people from the misuse of power by the state, rather than from the actions of private individuals . . ." He was thus right to conclude by re-stating that clause 6 "does not impose a liability on organisations which have no public functions at all".[117]

Yet neither clause 6 nor its accompanying statements must be seen in isolation. The debates in the House of Lords form as much part of the legal scenery, which must be surveyed by future interpreters of the Bill, as does the practice of the Court of Human Rights in Strasbourg (which will remain part of our legal scenery) and, indeed, the recent case law of our own courts. Seen in this way clause 6 must, as Mr Murray Hunt recently asserted, be taken to "preclud[e] *direct* horizontal effect, rather than as endorsing a vertical approach".[118] This nuanced statement makes particular good sense given the decision to include the courts in clause 6 (1). For if courts are bound to act compatibly with the Convention this will, surely, have some effect on the adoption of some variant of horizontality. This conclusion is reinforced by the fate reserved for Lord Wakeham's amendments, which were clearly aimed at precluding horizontality and "the development of a common law of privacy"[119] and the Lord Chancellor's response to such attempts.[120]

My reading of these statements[121] convinces me that our courts are authorised to "modify" and "develop" the Common law in order to achieve compatibility with the Convention. Where "development" ends and "judicial legislation" begins is, of course, another question though I do not feel it has to be addressed here, not least because of our courts' well-ingrained tendency to proceed in an incremental way. But what needs to be repeated here is that a form of horizontality is not barred. What form our own version of horizontality will take remains to be seen; but the German model, close as I see it to the Canadian[122] and to some views expressed in South Africa,[123] must make it an obvious source of inspiration. The view I am putting forward here is, I believe, also supported by current trends found in the European Commission and the Court of Human Rights which are both exploring new ways of applying the Convention to relations between

[117] HL Deb., 13 November 1997, cols. 1231–2.

[118] "The Effect of the Convention on the Law of Obligations" in *The Impact of a Bill of Rights on English Law* (ed. Basil S Markesinis) (1998), chap. 12.

[119] HL Deb., 24 November 1997, col. 772.

[120] HL Deb., 24 November 1997 at col. 783. Lord Williams of Mostyn made similar points. See, HL Deb., 24 November 1997, col. 759.

[121] See, also, the Lord Chancellor's comments in "Address to the 3rd Clifford Chance Conference on the Impact of a Bill of Rights on English Law" in *The Impact of a Bill of Rights on English Law* (ed. Basil S Markesinis) (1998) chap. 2 and Mrs Justice Arden's lecture at King's College, London, on 26 November 1997 entitled "The Future of the Law of Privacy" (not yet published).

[122] *Retail, Wholesale & Department Store Union, Local 580* v. *Dolphin Delivery Ltd.* [1986] 2 SCR 573; *Manning* v. *Hill* (1995) 126 DLR (4th) 129.

[123] *Du Plessis* v. *De Klerk* (1996) 3 SA 850.

private individuals.[124] In my view, the activities of our own courts during the last ten years or so to develop the common law outside of judicial review in a manner consistent with the Convention is also consistent with the above-mentioned German trends.[125] Finally, the argument in favour of horizontality becomes particularly strong if one bears in mind that the proposed legislation will operate under the shadow of the European Court in that a litigant whose claim might not be covered by the terms of the Act will still be able to take his case direct to Strasbourg. No wonder then that Sir William Wade, in his recent lecture to the Judicial Studies Board, felt able to claim that "It would, indeed, be a poor sort of 'incorporation' which exempted private individuals and bodies from respecting the fundamental rights of their fellow-citizens and drove them back to Strasbourg with all its cost in time and money—the very ill which 'incorporation' is supposed to remedy."[126] The question, which we shall thus have to face, is not *whether* we can privatise human rights but *to what extent* we should do so. So let us turn to some of the arguments advanced for and against such a move.

2. Arguments against such an extension

(a) Problems of "balancing"

Some journalists have expressed the "fear" that a horizontal effect of the Bill would force judges to balance the rights contained in Articles 8 and 10 of the European Convention (henceforth ECHR). At one level, this "fear" makes no sense at all since balancing will have to take place even if the Bill were to have only a vertical effect. So, if we are honest about this, the journalistic fear seems to arise in the context of balancing of Article 8 of the Convention against Article 10. Thus restated, the argument seems to conceal two concerns.

The first is that the idea of balancing is difficult if not conducive to perpetual uncertainty. The second is that such a balancing is bound to affect adversely speech rights. Neither of these fears is convincing.

Balancing of competing interests lies at the core of the judicial process; and our courts, with their incremental and pragmatic tendencies, are masters of the art. In the case of privacy and speech rights such balancing is both essential and unavoidable. For as Professor Jutta Limbach, the Presi-

[124] See, for instance, Clapham "The Privatisation of Human Rights" (1996) 1 *EHRLR* 20*ff*. For a recent case see: *A* v. *UK*, Report of the Commission, 18. September 1997, where the Court held the UK in breach of Art. 3 for its failure to provide laws to protect adequately a child subjected to corporal punishment by its stepfather.

[125] On which the best account is by Murray Hunt, *Using Human Rights Law in English Courts* (1997) pp. 39–40, 146–151.

[126] "Human Rights and the Judiciary", *Annual Lecture 1998*, 5.

dent of the German Constitutional Court, recently observed: "The conflict between freedom of the press and the right of privacy can only be decided in the light of the individuality of the case and its special circumstances."[127] One of our greatest constitutional authorities, Sir William Wade, was echoing similar statements when he said that "These rights [of privacy and free speech] will often pull in different directions and delicate balancing exercises will be demanded."[128] One of the main aims of this paper has been to suggest to English readers that in German law they will find excellent guidelines as to how such a balancing process should be carried out. Moreover, the Strasbourg case law, more palatable perhaps to those prejudiced against things German, comes close to the German model by also according some preference to (political) speech over privacy. That is why the present author regards the Home Secretary's statement[129] that in privacy cases courts should have regard to the countervailing freedom of expression as little more than a sop[130] to the Murdoch Press, which has been clamouring unconvincingly over this issue for the past ten years.

(b) Judges are the wrong balancers

Balancing depends on the balancer; and, so the argument goes, judges are not qualified to attempt it. This objection has found support mainly among academics from the left of the Labour party.[131] But it is the Murdoch press which has adopted it with the greatest vehemence in its consistently proclaimed faith in self-regulation. Thus, when the former Lord Chancellor produced a thoughtful White Paper on Privacy[132] recommending the adoption of a general rule, a former editor of one of the London-based tabloids expressed his concern by saying that privacy issues were too sensitive to be left to be decided by "clapped out judges". This message (if not the language) is repeated in the so-called serious broad sheets and makes their campaign suspect. Thus in its editorial of 25 January 1989 *The Times* wrote: "In the history of freedom won by the Press, restrictions have a general tendency to become wider in their compass, not narrower. Lord Alexander enjoins us[133] to put our faith in the judiciary. "*We would betray our duty to a free press to be so trusting of those who are themselves so fallible and*

[127] (Unpublished) speech delivered in Belfast on 11 May 1998 entitled "The Protection of Human Rights In Germany".

[128] *Op.cit.*, 12.

[129] *Hansard*, 16 Feb. 1998, col. 777.

[130] Sir William Wade, *op.cit.*, at p. 8, agrees with this assessment. A more meaningful "concession" was the prohibition of *ex parte* injunctions.

[131] For instance Professors Griffith, Ewing and Gearty.

[132] Consultation Paper issued by the Lord Chancellor's Department, July 1993 following the Calcutt Committee (*Report of the Committee on Privacy and Related Matters*, Cmnd. 1102, 1990.)

[133] *The Daily Telegraph*, 21 January 1989.

inconsistent."[134] If such doubts about the judiciary's ability to decide legal issues with political overtones had been expressed by any Labour supporter during the height of the miners' strikes in the 1980s *The Times* of that period would have lashed out against those who undermined our judicial institutions. That *The Times*, nowadays, often appears to be playing its part in achieving the same aim, while at the same time also undermining public faith in a host of other institutions, must not be forgotten. For one might be forgiven for thinking that faith in the judicial system appears to be linked with the critics' real or perceived interests. Thus, the Press's attitude varies on whether it is complaining about the law of defamation or privacy. In defamation, where juries have been known to award large damages against the Press, the demand is that the quantification should be left to judges. On the other hand, in privacy cases the danger that a judge might attempt to temper free speech in favour of human dignity leads to the opposite view: judges cannot be trusted and only the Press knows how to control the Press!

(c) A horizontal extension of the Bill of Rights will flood the courts with claims, especially claims founded on the new "tort" of privacy

Though this is, inevitably, a matter of speculation, Lord MacKay's White Paper did not, on balance, accept this to be a credible fear.[135] The Press Complaints Commission, said its Chairman fairly recently, "fears that the new Bill of Rights will subject its rulings to lengthy appeals that would render it ineffective".[136] Leaving aside the dubious assumption that the Press Complaints Commission (and its various predecessors) have been effective,[137] one wonders what tangible evidence one can produce in order to raise the spectrum of interminable appeals (and delays) caused by privacy claims. Once again, a cursory study of foreign practice would reveal that this floodgates argument is not supported by the experience of German and, come to that, French and Italian courts.[138] Why then would our country, burdened by sub-

[134] Emphasis added.

[135] Infringement of Privacy (1993), 6.36–6.40.

[136] *The Times*, 2 December 1997, p. 8.

[137] The constant issuing of new, "tighter", guidelines by the Press Complaints Commission can only imply that the regime, which they are meant to be improving, was not efficient enough in the first place. Yet while it lasted, the press in unison would tells us that their self-controlling mechanisms were perfectly adequate and that there was thus no need nor any room for legislative or judicial improvements.

[138] Reviewing the published case law of the decade 1985–1994 my German colleague Dr. Nico Nolte and I found only twenty-five published decisions of the Federal Court. See: "Comparative reflections on the Right of Privacy of Public Figures in Public Places" in *Privacy and Loyalty* (ed. Peter Birks) (1997), 113*ff*. It is noteworthy that the most recent spate of cases which have resulted from the *first Caroline* decision (false interview) are concerned with the measure (and juristic nature) of the damage award. By contrast, the *third Caroline* case (unauthorised photographing), despite its greater potential to widen the ambit of the tort, has not (yet) affected the volume of litigation.

stantially higher litigation costs than all its European counterparts, go down a different path? And why would our national character, which dislikes "making a fuss" about things, let alone resorting to litigation, alter so drastically if judges such as the Lord Chief Justice decide in their wisdom that cases like *Kay* v. *Robertson*[139] should not be left without a suitable legal response? Would our citizens really go beyond the Press Complaints Commission unless they felt that they had a real and un-addressed complaint?

(d) An increased amount of unsatisfactory casuistry

The point was made forcefully by *The Guardian* on October 25th 1997. "Lord Bingham" said its leader writer "suggested . . . that incorporating the European Convention would inevitably mean that the right of privacy would be established by judge-made law". Since our entire administrative law edifice has been constructed in this manner this opening statement could only have meant to strike fear in the hearts of the un-informed reader of the article. Unfortunately, its peroration is no more convincing: "The trouble with judge made law is that it would be established in a haphazard, *case by case basis* [sic], with no clear public interest defence or other entrenched safeguards the British media needs".

What is shocking about such statements is not that they reveal a rather dismal lack of understanding of the Common law system but that they ignore the fact that our own law is casuistic; that our casuistry is built around accidents of litigation rather than on rational criteria; and that, in its results, is often conducive to uncertainty. Thus, why is it right to fashion a remedy in *Tolley* v. *J.S. Fry and Sons Ltd.*[140] for amateurs and not afford the same protection to professionals who are more likely to have their pictures used by others for gain? Or why should the deserving claim of the plaintiff in the *Gordon Kay* case depend upon whether the tort of battery could be applied to the taking of a photograph by means of a flashlight? Or, finally, why should a person who has been spied upon by his neighbour have to prove that the requirements of the old tort of nuisance have been satisfied?[141] Compared to the German criteria,[142] our own way of muddling through seems positively primitive.

(e) An increased protection of privacy will stifle speech

This is a legitimate concern of the media; but one hopes that the little already said about German law has proved that this fear is exaggerated. I,

[139] [1991] FSR 62, CA.
[140] [1931] AC 333.
[141] The *Khorasandjian* v. *Bush* litigation offers another example [1993] QB 727, overruled in part by *Hunter* v. *Canary Wharf Ltd.* [1997] 2 WLR 684.
[142] Discussed above, II, 5.

for one, refuse to accept that our judges will prove less solicitous of the interests of free speech than their German counterparts so I shall not labour this point further.[143]

3. Arguments in favour of a horizontal effect

Even if the arguments against horizontality seem, on closer examination, to be weak can we think of any positive arguments in favour of such a move? After all, no one doubts that according to the traditional doctrine, Bills of Rights were meant to protect citizens against the power of the state. Why should such a tradition be abandoned?

(a) The dangers posed to human rights by private entities

Underlying the German idea of *Drittwirkung*, as a number of quotations and many cited cases have shown, is the belief that in our contemporary world individuals and private entities can interfere with human rights as extensively and, arguably, more frequently than the State can. The idea has not been without its supporters even in this country. Thus, speaking in the Commons in 1971, a Labour MP who subsequently became Solicitor General remarked that "there are other relationships, not only relationships between the individual and government, which can also blight lives, and which for many individuals can result in tragedy. Very serious distress can be caused by an employer, by a landlord, or by a neighbour. Not all wrecked lives are caused by governments."[144] These are precisely the examples, which Nipperdey had in mind when he launched his *Drittwirkung* campaign fifty years ago.

Of all the (private) oppressors, the press stands out most for criticism and as a source of concern. For though it has for long now been described as the Fourth Estate it has never been subjected to anything like as tight controls as the more traditional sources of power. Politicians must keep registers of their interests and comply with codes of practice, which if anything, are becoming more stringent. I do not believe I have ever even heard a call for such a similar register of interests to be set up for journalists. Certainly, journalists exercise more power than Members of Parliament and, I suspect, most Ministers. Newspapers also seem to escape most forms of

[143] It is also noteworthy that the three *Caroline* cases—BGHZ 128,1; BGHZ 131, 332 and OLG Hamburg *NJW* 1996, 2870, were not criticised by the serious press; indeed, the Association of German Journalists welcomed the award for the false interview case. See: *Frankfurter Allgemeine Zeitung* of 26. 7. 1996, at p. 12. See, also, the same paper of 2. 9. 1997, at p. 13.

[144] Peter Archer (now Lord Archer of Sandwell), HC Debs, 2 April 1971, cols 1861–2. See, also, Sir Gordon Borrie, "The Regulation of Public and Private Power" [1989] *PL* 552.

censorship. To allow such entities to destroy the reputations of citizens, as they tend to do with anyone who advances a view that conflicts with their interests, or disturb their anonymity and solitude without good reason is not fitting in a civilised society; and it is even more repulsive if it is done by shady means. Nor is it a fitting remedy to order the newspaper to apologise—often in an inadequate manner—long after its intermeddling has caused much suffering. The real question is thus not whether a certain group of professionals should enjoy more power and privileges than most of us, but how to control this power without impeding other freedoms—such as speech—which our society rightly values very highly.

(b) The unity of the legal system: avoiding irrational, discriminatory solutions

This is another good reason why our Human Rights Bill should, in appropriate circumstances, be given a horizontal effect. This is the result of the legitimate desire to avoid solutions which discriminatory regimes can create as a result of reasoning from different times. Such unwarranted discrimination can, in fact, emerge at three separate but theoretically interconnected levels.

Thus, first, if we limit the application of our Bill of Rights in a strictly vertical manner, we may end up creating a cleavage between our own, domestic, view about the applicability of human rights law and that which is now emerging in Strasbourg and which seems increasingly prepared to depart from traditional doctrine and "privatise human rights".[145] Out of the growing number of examples which one could cite, the case of *X and Y* v. *The Netherlands* strikes me as particularly significant. For it was given in the context of Article 8 of the Convention (which will play a crucial role to the strengthening of our law of privacy) and the court there noted that in addition to the negative obligations incumbent upon the state "there may be positive obligations inherent in an effective respect for family life . . ." These obligations—the court continued—"may involve the adoption of measures designed to secure respect for private life even in the sphere of the relations of individuals between themselves."[146]

Secondly, a rigid "public authority"/"private person" division is likely to cause problems in a world of deregulation which in the 1980s may have had a distinctive Conservative hue about it but which nowadays seems also to have become accepted by the new Labour orthodoxy.[147] Thus, to refer

[145] The expression was coined by Andrew Clapham, in his stimulating *Human Rights in the Private Sphere* (1993). He traces recent Strasbourg developments in "Opinion: The Privatisation of Human Rights", (1996) *EHRLR*, 20*ff*.

[146] Series A, vol 91, para. 23.

[147] The division has also figured in the Strasbourg case law. See, for instance, the corporal punishment cases in state (*Campbell and Cousins* v. *United Kingdom* Series A, No 48 (1982) 4 EHRR 293) and independent schools (*Costello-Roberts* v. *United Kingdom*, Series A, No 247-C, (1993) 19 EHRR 112).

to two well-known instances, let us not forget that before the judgment was given in *Malone* v. *UK*[148] on 2 August 1984, the relevant sector of the Post Office had become British Telecom. And before the "friendly settlement" was approved by the Commission on 8 July 1987 in *Baggs* v. *UK*[149] the British Airports Authority had become Heathrow Airport Ltd. Could this mean that a slight change in timing could mean the loss of the protective effect of the human rights law because of a change of status of the defendant whose conduct may cease to be covered by the Human Rights Bill?

Finally, "The Human Rights Bill will entrench a new hierarchy of rights in domestic law between public and private employees."[150] Thus, employees will acquire no direct actions against *private* employers when such freedoms as expression, privacy, or association are affected but will do so if they are employed by public authorities. Invoking the adverse effects that such an action might have on the (eroded) notion of private autonomy does not, in my view, provide a convincing argument for such results. Moreover, how are we going to distinguish between public and private employers, especially these days when so many authorities combine public and private functions? And what will the position be of recently privatised bodies which may be required to contract on special employment terms prescribed by statute or act under government directives?

(c) No real threat to private autonomy

This philosophical argument has, as stated, been well canvassed by German academics; and the attractiveness of the *Lüth* judgment was that by acknowledging that the Constitution exerts "an influence" on private relationships and, adding for good measure, that their resolution in cases of conflict, ultimately depends on the application of private law, has ensured that this concern has been properly addressed. For German law demonstrates that individual autonomy remains an important constitutional value since "private space" and "private choices" invariably survive the test of constitutional justification. For the German version of horizontality, as sketched in section II, above, shows how the test in justification takes place openly and publicly instead of suppressing all inquiry by arbitrarily limiting the scope of application of fundamental rights. It also shows that though not without its difficulties and uncertainties, it is more subtle than some of the Common law attempts to privatise "fully" the Bill of Rights.[151] Those

[148] Series A, vol 82. The English decision, which was the subject of complaint, was under the name of *Malone* v. *Commissioner for the Metropolis (No 2)*, [1979] Ch. 344.

[149] Applic. 9310/81.

[150] Hepple, "The Impact of Incorporation of the European Convention on Human Rights on Labour Law" in *The Impact of a Bill of Rights on English Law* (ed. Basil S. Markesinis) (1998), chap. 7.

[151] Though in fairness to authors such as Andrew Clapham one must note their attempts to enunciate guidelines, which will determine which private action will survive constitutional scrutiny and which should not be lightly tolerated.

who remain unconvinced would thus do well to consult more closely the debates, which have taken place across the Channel.[152]

(d) Traces of the German ideas already exist in the Common law systems

Those who believe in the idea of over-arching, basic values which affect the entire legal order and are also attracted by the balancing of competing values, so central to German law, may still feel daunted by Germanic concepts and structures. Yet German doctrine is inherently interesting, of venerable antiquity, and is increasingly traceable in many Strasbourg ideas. The argument for studying it seems unanswerable if for no better reason than to understand fully what is coming to us via Strasbourg. The question thus is not *whether* one should study German law but *how* best to use its experience. To stress its significance, we shall discuss it under three subheadings, which I believe, flow from the *Lüth* innovation: (i) Is the wider reach of the German doctrine of *Drittwirkung* comparable to the American doctrine of State Action? (ii) Is the creation of a constitutional tort sounding in damages allowing one individual to sue another? (iii) We must ask ourselves whether the dogmatic differences between the systems really matter given that in practice the results seem to converge more than is commonly appreciated.

(i) Both American and German law accept, certainly more clearly than English law,[153] the distinction between public and private law. Both, likewise, acknowledge that their respective Bills of Rights exercise their maximum influence in cases involving the state. One difference,[154] however, which has to be mentioned here briefly is the full extent of the American "State Action" doctrine, which comes close to accepting that in *some instances* the Constitution can extend its reach to regulate private relationships.

Approximating the German and American doctrines through a wide interpretation of what counts as the "state" or "public function" offers little help since one is left with the impression that American courts have, on the

[152] Thus Professor Dürig, one of the severest critics of the *unmittelbare Drittwirkung* theory, seems well content with the *Lüth* theory of influence, which he does not regard as posing a significant threat to private autonomy. Common lawyers have also argued that horizontality is not incompatible with personal autonomy. Thus see: Butler "Constitutional Rights in Private Litigation: A Critique and Comparative Analysis" (1993) 22 *Anglo-American Law Reports*, 1 and, more recently, Clapham, "The Privatisation of Human Rights" (1996) 1 *EHRLR* 20.

[153] Though in a procedural sense, since *O'Reilly* v. *Munkman* [1983] 2 AC 237, English administrative law has recognised a dichotomy in that purely public law challenges must be brought by way of judicial review.

[154] The other difference flows from the *Blinkfüer* case, BVerfGE 25, 256 (1969) and others, which have followed it, and is the judicial creation of a constitutional tort by one private person against another. We shall return to this briefly in section 3.2 below.

whole, taken a restrictive view on this matter.[155] By contrast, much more interesting are the attempts of American courts to treat court decisions in disputes between *private* individuals as involving the exercise of a possibly unconstitutional state function. The famous case of *New York Times Co.* v. *Sullivan*[156] offers an example; *NAACP* v. *Claiborne Hardware Co.*[157] another, though less known in Europe.[158]

Yet what is crucial in these decisions, and marks them apart from the *Lüth* doctrine, is the fact that the court decision was seen as an act of state *because the rule which the courts applied had been fashioned by the state.* Thus, the crucial element is not the fact that *the dispute is between individuals* but the *provenance of the applied rule*, which was formulated (through statute or common law) by the state. The only exception which we thus find in American law which brings it really close to the German position is that enunciated in *Shelley* v. *Kraemer*[159] where the United States Supreme Court set aside a court order which enforced a racially restrictive covenant drafted by *private parties and used in a private dispute*. But subsequent courts[160] seem to have made little or no use of the *Kraemer* innovation; and though the reasons for such restrictive attitudes have varied, and subsequent attempts to distinguish the cases have not left everyone impressed,[161] the result is not in doubt: German law has a more over-arching effect that touches private law in a wider but, as already stated, balanced manner.

(ii) If the above observations underscore the point that German and American law retain their distinctiveness they also suggest that on a number of occasions American law was given the chance to expand in the direction taken by the German courts. That it did not do so is, in one sense at least, less important than the fact that it could have done. For this demonstrates that if the German ideas seem alien to us, it is because

[155] For instance, *Rendell-Baker* v. *Kohn*, 457 US 830, 842 (1982). For a summary of the American doctrine see Nowak and Rotunda, *Constitutional Law* (1995), chap. 12. For a comparative discussion with Europe see Clapham, *Human Rights in the Private Sphere* (1993), pp. 150–163. The position in Hong Kong seems fairly similar. See: *Tam Hing-yee* v. *Wu Tai-wai* [1992] 1 HKLR 185 applying the Hong Kong Bill of Rights Ordinance No 59 of 1991.

[156] 376 US 254 (1964).

[157] 458 US 886 (1982).

[158] Concerted trade boycott by blacks anxious to force white merchants to pursue non-discrimination in their community led to tort damages. Reversing, the Supreme Court took the view that the state court's decision violated the first and fourteenth amendment rights of organisers of the boycott.

[159] 334 US 1 (1948).

[160] E.g. *Gordon* v. *Gordon*, 322 Mass 197, 124 N.E. 2d 228, cert. denied 349 US 947 (1955) (will discriminating on grounds of religion); *Rice* v. *Sioux City Memorial Park Cemetery*, 245 Iowa 147, 60 N.W. 2d 110 (1953), cert dismissed 349 US 70 (1955) (discrimination on ethnic grounds in burial contract).

[161] E.g. Professor Wechsler, "Toward Neutral Principles of Constitutional Law", 73 *Harv. L. Rev.* 1 (1959).

of their "clothing" which puts off all but the most curious of Common lawyers.

We can reinforce this statement by looking at the second point, which the *Blinkfüer* and *Soraya* litigation logically developed, out of *Lüth*. This, it will be recalled, was the creation of a constitutional tort available to one individual against another. Thus, in their famous article Warren and Brandeis had envisaged the creation of a tort of privacy as a by-product of the notion of "inviolate personality".[162] That this was *not* impossible in constitutional terms even in the United States can be seen from a handful of undoubtedly interesting decisions which felt able to create a tort action sounding in damages out of constitutional provisions and the precepts of natural law.[163] That in the end such efforts stumbled over the American insistence that constitutional rights are not normally directed against individuals only takes us back to our earlier observation that our American colleagues *chose* to keep constitutional law out of the domain of private law. But the reverse would not have been a legal or logical impossibility. At a different time and, perhaps, in a different geopolitical situation, America might well have gone down the path taken by the Germans or, indeed, the Canadians or the South Africans.

(iii) The same kind of thoughts must be tested against the doubts expressed by American jurists who, having noted the similarity of results between German and American law, have found the reasoning of the German courts precarious. Thus Professor Quint[164] sees the reasoning of the German court in the *Flag Desecration* case as being "fragile" because the German court found that "the government has a constitutional interest in prohibiting flag desecration in order to protect the authority of the state and the free democratic order" even, one might add using the American terminology, in the absence of a "clear and imminent danger". Yet, in my view, the German cases make sense in the light of the notion of "militant democracy"—a cardinal notion of the Constitution of 1949—which seems understandable if not justifiable given: (a) recent German history and (b) the immediate threat (real, not only perceived) which Germany (but less so the USA) faced during most of the cold war period. But even in the light of the more liberal and tolerant American attitude towards most forms of seditious libel, the German doctrine is not that "odd" if we recall what opposition was reserved for the (majority) American (flag) decisions of the 1990s which were based on a more absolutist doctrine of free

[162] "The Right to Privacy", 4 *Harv. L. Rev*. 193, at 205–7 (1890).

[163] *Melvin* v. *Reid*, 112 Cal. App. 285, 291, 297, P. 91, 93–4 (1931); *Pavesich* v. *New England Life Ins*. Co. 122 Ga. 190, 197, 50 S.E. 68, 71 (1905).

[164] "The Comparative Law of Flag Desecration: The United States and the Federal Republic of Germany", 15 *The Hastings International and Comparative Law Review*, 613 (1992).

expression.[165] And even this difference is attenuated in practice when we remind ourselves that, in the end, even the German courts came down in favour of free speech. In the light of all this it seems to me difficult to assert that the American system is *objectively* preferable to the more nuanced German counterpart. All one can do is to record a personal preference.

In the end, therefore, I suppose that if one were to try and develop a common thread for all these (different) observations it could be this. When comparing systems one is ultimately faced with the problem of characterising a glass which is 50% filled with water. Should one call it half full or half empty? Since both descriptions are accurate, the temperament of the speaker will determine the final choice. I grew up in an era when it was still fashionable to stress (undoubted) differences. My belief in a more integrated legal world has led me to look for similarities between systems as part of my strongly-felt conviction that the time has come for us to proclaim our common, legal heritage[166] as a first step for working out our common future. Seen through such spectacles the problem I have been discussing here has received analogous and often identical solutions in systems which cut across the Common and Civil law divide. Certainly, the dogmatic debates found in learned articles in Canada or South Africa and, more recently, in our country, contain nothing which would strike a German jurist as incomprehensible. If I am right in this, the reverse must also be true (subject only to language difficulties). The use of German ideas in our debates can thus only be stopped by mental blocks but not by weaknesses in the arguments or by insurmountable structural differences. For those interested in comparative methodology, this is a crucial point to make.

IV CONCLUSIONS

(a) The Bill of Rights: The dawn of a new era in judicial thinking and techniques

During a recent legal conference Lord Browne-Wilkinson spoke of the effect that the Human Rights Bill would have on judicial reasoning and, in this context, touched upon was the recourse to foreign law. The experience with the Canadian Charter suggests that the borrowing of ideas will increase

165 *Texas* v. *Johnson*, 491 U.S. 397, 400 (1989). See, also *United States* v. *Eichman*. 110 S. Ct 2404 (1990). In both cases the Justices were divided five to four.

166 For similar views see: Reinhard Zimmermann's magisterial "Savigny's Legacy. Legal History, Comparative Law and the Emergence of a European Legal Science" 112 *LQR* (1996), 576.

dramatically.[167] And, in this country, the growing number of lectures given by our judges on this subject indicates that they are mentally ready for such a broadening of their horizons. It is thus perfectly legitimate to predict that interest in the case law of the European courts will also increase since the case law of the Strasbourg court, which will also become an even more important part of our legal heritage, owes a great deal to French, German and Dutch law. In so far as it encourages the study of the decisions of the national courts of the major European states this article does little more than follow the current trend.

The difficulties inherent in my suggestions will lie in two areas: one is overcoming the obstacles of language; the other is in discovering how the ideas rather than the structures can be used to provide inspiration. Little need be said about the former since, in my view, with the passage of time, and with the increase in the number of students pursuing further legal studies in Germany (and other European universities), the problem will diminish even if it does not disappear altogether.

(b) Does the "transplantability" of the German ideas depend on the existence of a written Grundnorm?

This is the second difficulty to which I have alluded; and in this paper I tried to take the first step namely, to make colleagues, especially judges, aware of the enormous wealth of the German material. If, in the fullness of time, they come to share my view that a way must be found to tap this repository of human knowledge and experience in order to protect human rights more effectively, then a series of secondary questions will arise. One of them will be whether the complex German approach depends on an edifice, which is simply lacking in our country? To put it differently, can their ideas be transplanted into a system, which lacks a hierarchically superior *Grundnorm*, and a Constitutional Court created to safeguard its (measured) prevalence in the area of private relationships? The trap is not as dangerous as it may appear if we can start our thinking process by banishing concepts from our minds and look at the ideas, which lie behind them.[168]

I do not have to enter the debate on parliamentary sovereignty which, dare I say it in a public forum, strikes me as becoming rather dated.[169] For, once again, the substance matters more than the form; the substance, which the new Human Rights Bill has given us, is of a hierarchy of norms however

[167] *Cf.* Mr. Justice La Forest in "Who is Listening to Whom? The Discourse between the Canadian Judiciary and Academics" in *Law Making, Law Finding, and Law Shaping* (ed. Basil S Markesinis) (1997), 69*ff*.

[168] A theme, which I have tried to develop in different legal contexts. See my *Foreign Law and Comparative Methodology: A Subject and a Thesis* (1997).

[169] See Murray Hunt, *Using Human Rights Law in English Courts* (1997), chap. 2.

we wish to call it or qualify it. For once the Bill proclaimed that courts have the right to test subsequent legislation against its basic tenets and, if found to be incompatible refer the matter to the Government to do something about it, the signs were there for all of us to see: compatibility with the (hierarchically superior) Bill and its values is part of future legal life.[170] The question, which thus remains to be addressed, is whether our courts will extend the application of the values contained in the Bill to private relationships. I have already given some reasons why, in my opinion, this is not foreclosed—many would argue, positively intended—by the wording of the Bill or the debates in the House of Lords. I also gave my reasons why I think that such a step should be taken.

Yet even if my predilection for horizontality were to be adopted, the question remains who will do this "second testing"? In Germany as we have seen the task is, on the whole, performed with commendable restraint[171] (though, perhaps with some uncertainty at the fringes) by the Constitutional Court. But, one could object, we do not have a Constitutional Court; and no one has yet seriously proposed that we should. Once again the quandary that this statement leads to is caused by excessive attachment to concepts and structures rather than the substance of the matter.

I referred earlier in my presentation to the very English combination of law and equity. There was, of course a time when the courts of Equity would step in after the Common law procedures had been exhausted and then attempted to apply their own panoply of remedies. In substance if not in name they were performing a task not so dissimilar to that undertaken by the German Constitutional Court though the topics they dealt with were not quite the same.[172] The division, of course, between Common law and Equity no longer exists in any formal sense; and the recourse to the two sets of remedies is had by one and the same court. However, don't we have here the seeds of an idea that could solve our problem as well?

So let me pull my various threads together and suggest the following.

Even our Human Rights Bill can be subjected to the *Lüth* analysis and pronounced to contain an "objective set of values" of particular significance to the entire legal order. If these values were not so *unusually* important,

170 The Lord Chancellor would, of course, counter-argue that the declaration of incompatibility device is there precisely to avoid the Convention being given a hierarchically superior status.

171 Dr. Stephan Enchelmaier recently reviewed the 2614 decisions of the *Bundesverfassungsgericht* published in the first 94 volumes of the official reports and found that the *Drittwirkung* theory had only been invoked in 166 decisions.

172 I stress *quite the same* for we find judgments of the German Constitutional Court, which try to limit the rigours of the ordinary law, performing the task which equity carried out for our law. See, for instance, BVerfGE 81, 242 (1990) where the Constitutional Court in effect controlled the validity of a "restraint of trade clause". Likewise, BVerfGE 89, 214, (1993), the court held that the guarantee of private autonomy implicit in Art. 2(1) forbade enforcement of an unconscionable surety agreement between parties of unequal bargaining power—in our optic an "undue influence" case.

why introduce the requirement, unique in our system,[173] that subsequent statutes must be tested against the Convention? The unusual features of the Human Rights Bill must surely point to the fact that it is an enactment with superior moral if not legal content.

If we accept this and the equally Germanic idea that no legal value has, a priori, a superior force over others, then we can come to this conclusion: when a court of law is adjudicating a dispute on the basis of private law it must, of course, be conscious of the fact that it is this corpus of law and its more individualistic philosophy which is primarily to be used to solve the dispute. But courts must also remain conscious of the fact, as indeed the Human Rights Bill expects them to, that beyond a certain point the application of private law may become offensive to the basic values contained in the Human Rights Bill. If it does, and in the German examples we have encountered numerous illustrations of when and how this can happen, the court deciding the dispute or, if necessary an appeal court, must ask itself whether the results dictated by private law do not offend the overarching values of the Human Rights Bill. I think something along these lines would not offend any basic principles of our legal system but, on the contrary, be consistent with the spirit of our Human Rights Bill. Nor would it lead to an un-necessary and costly "constitutionalisation of private law" if, again, our courts absorb the German experience and embark upon this task of "constitutional legitimation" with restraint.

(c) Why German law?

So I am left, I think, with one last important question to answer. Why have I focused on German law? Like Maitland, Pollock, Anson, Holmes, Roscoe Pound and Llewelyn I, too, admire German legal culture; but to their well-known views I would like to add some riders of my own.

First, the ingenuity of German legal thinking did not come to a halt with the drafting of the Code almost a hundred years ago. Germany's post-World War II *Wirtschaftswunder* is well known; the parallel *Rechtswissenschaftswunder* has not, however, been noticed to the same degree. This is a particularly apt observation for my subject at a time when so much of the contemporary Common law writing is busy constructing theories to bring human rights into the private sphere. For in the German doctrine and case law we find the usual ability to theorise and analyse but born out of a disastrous immediate past. The theorising in other words has gone hand in hand with the desire to redeem as far as humanly possible unforgivable errors of the past and the determination never to repeat them. So this is not ivory tower theorising but a serious attempt to reflect on problems, which

[173] One could, of course, argue that the interpretative obligation of cl. 3 (1) of the Bill is not so different from that found in s. 2 (4) of the European Communities Act 1972.

are common to us all. I firmly believe that this universality of legal problems, especially of problems related to human rights, never escaped the attention of the justices of the German Constitutional Court since so many of them have spent so much time abroad—especially in England and America—either as refugees, students, or visiting Professors. ". . . Our German neighbours have [thus] brought their law up to date, and are facing modern times with modern ideas, modern machinery, modern weapons." These are Maitland's words, not mine;[174] and though they refer to the enactment of the German Civil Code, they are, I feel, equally appropriate to German constitutional law developments in the post-World War II period.

Secondly, the study of German law reveals our Press, and those who have blindly advocated its interests, as being at best ill informed and at worst deliberately misleading. The study of German law shows that a more widely perceived protection of human privacy need not impair speech rights nor have an inhibitive effect on investigative journalism as *The Times* argued it is bound to have.[175] Indeed, if anything, I find some of the German decisions have gone too far in allowing un-necessarily offensive speech though, for present purposes, this is beside the point. The empirical study of German law also proves that their courts have not been flooded by frivolous claims.

Thirdly, whether we like it or not, our country and our law is about to enter a new era. When one enters uncharted territory, guidance must always be welcome though, of course, it need not be accepted unquestionably. German constitutional law is not only the product of a dialogue between theory and practice; it has also evolved within a context of a federal structure, which, dare I say it, we do not have *yet*. It has also taken into account the European dimension of contemporary politics and law and skilfully blended it with its own, indigenous features. The resulting amalgam is both complex and rich. To decipher it and make it usable by our lawyers will take more than a lecture; it may well take a generation. But what I tried to do tonight was nothing more than what the present Lord Chief Justice did in his Francis Mann lecture namely, to remind my learned audience that "There *is* a World Elsewhere"[176] and to add my own advice: "Study it comparatively". For, as the great Thomas Mann put it in his famous epic novel *Josef und seine Brüder*, "Denn nur durch Vergleichung unterscheidet man sich und erfährt was man ist, um ganz zu werden, was man sein soll."[177]

174 "The Making of the German Civil Code" reprinted in The *Collected Papers of Frederick William Maitland* (ed. by HAL Fisher), (1911), 474 at p. 485.

175 Leader of 28 November 1989.

176 "There is a World Elsewhere—The Changing Pattern of English Law" (1992) 41 *I.C.L.Q*. 513.

177 "For only by comparison does man distinguish and learn what he is in order to become what he should be." Vol III, *Josef in Ägypten* 1936, (trans. by HT Lowe-Porter, Minerva ed., pp. 754–5).

8

The Applicability of Human Rights as between Individuals under German Constitutional Law

1. PRELIMINARY OBSERVATIONS

In German law, as it is well known, the general right of privacy is largely the product of the ordinary courts working under constitutional inspiration. Yet in many if not most instances its violation comes about as a result of the activities of individuals or the Press and not the State. Such intrusions often reveal a clash of interests again between individuals—the interest to be let alone and the interest to speak one's mind; and, the sparring individuals frequently seek their protection in the Constitution and its human rights provisions. But how did the human rights provisions come to be involved in such disputes between private persons? Is such an "intrusion" of public law into the realm of private relationships possible and, if it is, how can it be controlled to ensure that it does not get out of hand and undermine the concept of private autonomy which lies at the roots of private law? This is a question that has figured in many privacy cases but goes well beyond them as the first of us has explained elsewhere.[1] Since two chapters in this book deal with detailed aspects of the German law of privacy, we have decided to devote this, its last one, to this wider issue. This essay is thus not so much concerned with *which* human rights are protected under the German Constitution of 1949 (*Grundgesetz* or *GG*)[2] but with the question against *whose* incursions

[1] "Privacy, Freedom of Expression, and the Horizontality of the Human Rights Bill: Lessons from Germany", *LQR*, winter 1999.

[2] The employment of the unusual term "Basic Law", instead of the more traditional "Constitution", was meant to highlight the document's temporary character. As the original preamble—it was rephrased after unification in 1990—made clear, the Germans in the Western *Länder* (formed on the territory of the former Western zones of occupation) considered that they had no authority to act also on behalf of those in the Eastern (Soviet) zone to enact the definitive Constitution. A definitive constitution for the whole of the German people acting in free self-determination could, according to the *GG*, come into being either by extending the geographical scope of application of the *GG* to "other parts of Germany" (Art. 23 as unamended), or by creating an entirely new constitution to be adopted, this time, by the whole of the German people (Art. 146 as unamended). In 1990 the first option was chosen and by

these rights are protected. Since our own Human Rights Bill will give rise to the problem of horizontality, it is important that British lawyers are given ideas and as much information about foreign law as is possible. For soon they will need all the inspiration that they can get.

Not that long ago the question we just posed would have appeared to most observers as odd. For according to traditional theory, public authorities (of various levels: supranational, national, regional, local) were considered as the sole, proper recipients of complaints concerning violations of human rights. This traditional view still holds good today for a large number of cases. Increasingly, however, other entities are proving themselves to be just as threatening to the "life, liberty, property" and other basic rights of citizens. The example of the Press—the "fourth estate"—hunting down prominent or, even, ordinary individuals who happen to achieve temporary notoriety in its perpetual quest for sensational stories, readily springs to mind.

Nowadays, therefore, the new paradigm of a human rights violation may be that of an "individual" (to be understood here as referring to any natural or legal person which is not acting with public authority) encroaching upon the freedom of another individual. The application of human rights in this context is variously described as having a "horizontal" (as opposed to the traditional, vertical) application. In Germany the term "third party effect of Basic Rights" *(Drittwirkung der Grundrechte)* is more in use, though both these terms refer to the same phenomenon. Although the issues associated with it have received some attention in some common law systems, notably Canada, Ireland, and South Africa, the problems of horizontality were first addressed in a systematic way by German scholars. Thus, already during the Weimar Constitution of 1919 one finds the first attempts to tackle some of its most troublesome aspects,[3] though the study of this aspect of human rights did not really start in earnest until the early 1950s.

2. THE PROBLEM

(a) The early beginnings: the German *Bundestag* procrastinates on women's rights

Most of the human rights acknowledged by the Basic Law can already be found in the Weimar Constitution of 1919 (though, unlike its predecessor, the Basic Law chose to place the human rights articles at the very begin-

then no need was felt to alter the well-established and respected text. Indeed, in 1993 the *Verfassungskommission* set up immediately after the 1990 reunification to review the entire Basic Law had, on the whole, given it its unequivocal approval.

[3] For instance, Art. I I I § 1, 2nd sentence, of the 1918 Constitution provided that free speech must not be hampered by any employment relationship and no one should be disadvantaged for exercising such rights.

ning of the Constitution to symbolise their importance). Prominent among them is the principle of equality before the law.[4] The Basic Law considers this a right citizens can invoke in the courts and which binds, among others, the legislature.[5] This becomes apparent from the reading of Article 1 (3) GG according to which basic rights "shall bind the legislature, the executive, and the judiciary as directly enforceable law". The equality provision of the Weimar Constitution—Article 109 (2)—which provided that in principle men and women had the same rights and duties as citizens, was more in the nature of a constitutional exhortation than a binding rule of law. But, as the greatest commentator of the Weimar Constitution observed,[6] the fundamental rights enumerated in the text were "only guidelines for prospective legislation" and thus had no "immediate relevance and applicability". *De iure* and *de facto*, therefore, women experienced manifold inequalities with the constitutional ideals remaining largely a dead letter.

In order to make Article 3 *GG* more effective and, at the same time, to give the *Bundestag* (the German Lower House) time to make the necessary changes in the various laws, Article 117 (1) *GG* stated that legislation which was inconsistent with the 2nd para. of Article 3 would remain in force until adapted to the new requirements of the Basic Law. This exemption from the scope of the new Constitution did not, however, extend beyond 31 March 1953. In effect therefore, the 1949 Constitution gave Parliament a breathing space within which it had to adapt the old law to the requirements of the new order.

Discrimination against women, however, continued to occur until well into the 1970s[7] (and different treatment still persists, where biological reasons make it "compelling")[8] broadly in two guises.

[4] Art. 3 GG § I states "All persons are equal before the law." § 2 proclaims that "Men and women shall have equal rights", while § 3 concludes with the statement "No one may be disadvantaged or favoured because of his sex, his parentage, his race, his language, his homeland and origin, his faith, or his religious or political opinions."

[5] Under the Weimar Constitution basic rights limited only the executive and judicial branches of government.

[6] Gerhard Anschütz, *Die Verfassung des Deutschen Reiches*, 14th edn. (1933), 514*ff*.

[7] For instance, equal pay in the workplace did not come into force until 1980 (see § 612, 2 BGB); and this was more due to the pressure exerted by Community legislation (e.g. The Equal Treatment Directive 1976/207) than Art. 3 GG. It must be said, however, that this is a somewhat unusual way of bringing about an enhanced protection of human rights in Germany since "[its] jurists in general seem convinced that [their] system establishes such a high standard of protection for individual rights guaranteed in the Basic Law that international human rights law could hardly offer any improvement." Simma, Khan, Zöckler, and Geiger "The Role of German Courts in the Enforcement of International Human Rights" in *Enforcing Human Rights in Domestic Courts* (eds. Conforti and Francioni) (1997), 71 at 108. This does not mean that German law has not been found to be deficient compared with the ECHR. The decisions in the *Luedicke* case (28.11.1978, Ser. A, No 29), the *König* case (28.6.1978, Ser. A, No 27), the *Eckle* case 15.7.1982, Ser. A, No 51) the *Pakelli* case (25.4.1983, Ser. A, No 64) and the *Oztürk* case 21.2.1984, Ser. A, No 73) and others prove that the record is not unblemished.

[8] BVerfGE 39, 169, 185–6 (1975). *Compulsory* military service is one example: BVerfGE 12, 45, 52*ff*. But the Constitutional Court also seems to be moving towards a kind of affirmative

First, there were statutory provisions which directly denied women rights or treated them less favourably then men. This was true of the provisions of family law (Fourth Book of the Civil Code—*Bürgerliches Gesetzbuch* or BGB which was extensively reformulated between 1958 and 1976) embodying, at the time when the new Constitution came into force, an almost purely paternalistic notion of the family. Secondly, one was faced with an important body of rules which discriminated against women but emanated from private law, namely in the area of conditions of employment. To this day, this area of German law (at least to the extent that it is formally enacted by Parliament) remains patchy. Usually, the *Bundestag*[9] follows (on those occasions when it acts at all) long-established agreements between trade unions and employers' federations, as upheld and interpreted by judges. This practice suggests that, in effect, the legislature has, to a large extent, delegated the creation of labour law to the parties concerned. Typically, at the time when the 1949 Constitution came into force, women earned less money for equal work than men did. To make matters worse the first *Bundestag*, elected in 1949, was in no hurry to improve the legal status of women whatever the wishes of the consitutional legislator. As the late Professor Max Rheinstein observed,[10] irrespective of their political background, the members of the new *Bundestag* "tend[ed] to identify the Christian pattern of family and society with the ancient pattern of the patriarchal family and general male dominance . . . [and] they were [thus] not overly zealous to implement a command that happened to find expression in the Constitution". They were, in other words, believers of what subsequent German case-law described as the *Hausfrauen-und Versorgungsehe:* housewife and maintenance marriage principle (i.e. the proper place of women was in the house!).[11]

It was not long before the situation described above gave birth to two legal problems. The first was related to the meaning of the term *Recht*[12]

action by having allowed, for instance, women the right to opt for earlier retirement than men, BVerfGE 74, 163 (1987). A few years later, the Court came back to this idea of restrained reverse discrimination by stating that "actual disadvantages typically affecting women may be compensated for through preferential regulations because of the requirement of equality in Art. 2 sec 2 GG," BVerfGE 85, 191, 207. In 1994 a Constitutional amendment to Art. 3 added to sec 2 the words "The State *promotes* [sic] actual implementation of the equality of women and men and acts to eliminate existing disadvantages"; but this has been seen as being programmatic in nature and not as creating individual rights to specific state behaviour.

[9] Federal competence in this field is not exclusive but, according to Arts. 72 (1), 74 No. 12 *GG*, federal legislation takes precedence over state legislation on identical matters (concurrent legislation).

[10] "The Law of Family and Succession", *Gesammelte Schriften* (ed. G. Leser) (1972), 212 at 219*ff*.

[11] The early (but revolutionary) case-law which radically changed this unfavourable treatment has been reviewed by Professor Inga Markovitz in "Marriage and the State: A Comparative Look at East and West German Law", 24 *Stanford Law Review*, III (1971).

[12] In German the term can denote law in general, (including natural law) as opposed to statutory law *(Gesetz). Thus* see Art. 20 (3) *GG:* "The executive and the judiciary shall be

in Article 117 *GG*. The second, and not unconnected with the first, was whether Article 3 *GG* applied only to Parliamentary enactments or extended to private relationships. The latter subquestion, of course, touches upon the question of horizontal effect of human rights. In 1950, Professor Hans-Carl Nipperdey of the University of Cologne set out to answer these questions in an article that informs the discussion to this day.[13]

The first question proved fairly easy to answer. Article 117 *GG* applies only to laws passed by the *Bundestag* and the *Landtage* (state parliaments). Only these were granted a period of grace before they adapted their laws to correspond to the requirements of the new legal order. This makes perfect sense. Altering private arrangements is not nearly as cumbersome as the legislative process; and the issues tend to be less complex. Moreover, wage agreements expire after a fixed period of time and, in any event, need regular re-negotiating. Another reason for this interpretation was the fact that the term *Recht* can be found in Articles 123–126 *GG* which deal with the continued application of laws pre-dating 1949 (so-called pre-constitutional law). Since Article 117 *GG* refers to a comparable problem, and the word *Recht* here is widely accepted to have the meaning given above, one must assume that the constitutional draftsman did not intend to employ it in a different way in the case of Article 117.[14]

Next came the crucial question, namely, the article's direct application to relationships between private parties. Nipperdey answered this in the affirmative. Two broad arguments lead him to this conclusion. One concerned the heightened importance of human rights under the *GG*; the other was derived from the wording of some of the constitutional provisions.

In its barest outlines the first argument posits that since the eighteenth and nineteenth centuries new threats have arisen to human rights. Whereas before the industrialisation of our society the function of human rights was to protect the freedoms of the individual from incursions by the state, by the time the twentieth century had arrived new forces[15] had established themselves within society that were often as powerful as the state itself, and equally able to determine (adversely) people's lives. This was certainly true of large employers. In parallel with industrialisation, the democratisation of society and the rise of popular sovereignty had changed the role and scope of constitutions. For, where formerly they had been "granted"

bound by *Recht und Gesetz*" [i.e. law and justice]—the juxtaposition here denoucing legal positivism. On the other hand, the term can also refer to the rights which one person has against another or a public authority, be they contractual or statutory in origin (*subjektives Recht*). The term also covers any provision in any piece of formal enactment of general application not conferring such rights (*objektives Recht*).

13 "Gleicher Lohn der Frau für gleiche Leistung. Ein Beitrag zur Auslegung der Grundrechte" in *Recht der Arbeit*, 1950, 121 *et seq*.

14 Nipperdey, *op.cit.* (n. 13 above), 126.

15 In the words of Hugo Sinzheimer, pioneer of employment law in the Weimar Republic, "*soziale Gewalten*".

(oktroyiert) by the monarch (or, in the traditionally decentralised Germany, the college of reigning princes), constitutions were now seen as the freely agreed fundamental norm which regulated all life in society. Constitutional provisions, therefore, had to be given the widest possible application. In principle, therefore, no area of life could be exempt from their scope.[16]

Nipperdey's second argument pointed out that in some cases the Constitution itself expressly provides for the horizontal application of human rights.[17] Article 9 (3) *GG* is a case in point: "Agreements restricting or intended to hamper [the right to form associations in order to safeguard and improve working and economic conditions] shall be null and void; measures to this end shall be illegal." The open-ended wording of Article 3 (3) *GG*—"*no one* shall be prejudiced . . ." —could be taken to point to the same conclusion: what is illegal need not expressly be declared void. Moreover, in the light of what immediately preceded the Constitution of Bonn was it possible for discrimination based on race, political opinion, faith, or sex, to be accepted under any circumstances? In any event, as the state nowadays employs decreasing numbers of civil servants, and the majority of the population work in the private sector, to exempt the terms of private employment from the application of the relevant article would reduce its significance to an unacceptable level.[18] If this sounded convincing in 1950 it is all the more so now, as the century is drawing to a close.

The latter (teleological) argument is reinforced rather than contradicted by the provisions of Article l *GG* which is, by its position at the beginning of the Constitution no less than because of its content, marked out as the bedrock of the whole Constitution: "(1) Human[19] dignity is inviolable. To respect and *protect* it is the duty of all state authority. (2) *The German people* therefore uphold human rights as *inviolable and inalienable* and as the *basis of every community*, of peace and justice in the world." These sonorous proclamations conclude with the more pragamtic order contained in § (3) of this article which states that "The following basic rights shall *bind the legislature, the executive, and the judiciary* as directly enforceable law."[20]

Since the judiciary is, according to Article 1 (3) *GG*, bound by Article 3 (3) *GG* it cannot, Nipperdey argued, uphold contracts or unilateral acts discriminating on grounds outlawed by the Constitution without itself violating its provisions. The fact that the German *people*, not merely the German *state*, uphold human rights as the basis of their community, must

[16] Nipperdey, *op.cit.* (n. 13 above), 124.

[17] Though this argument counts both ways since one could counter-argue that where horizontality was envisaged the Constitutions said so expressly.

[18] Nipperdey, *op.cit.* (n. 13 above), 124, 125.

[19] The German text here uses a word—*Mensch*—which denotes both male and female human beings.

[20] Our italics.

also mean that each and every individual must respect the human rights of others. Similarly, given that the state has to protect human dignity, from which all specific human rights flow, no public authority could endorse any practice that violated human dignity. The same is true of agreements between private parties; as human rights are inalienable, they must not be abrogated by contract.[21]

These conclusions are not, however, limited to Article 3 (3) *GG* and the principle of equal pay for equal work. Every single human right protected by the Constitution has to be scrutinised with a view to determining whether it is directed exclusively against the state. This would certainly be the case where incursions by private parties are inconceivable. For instance, individuals can neither grant nor withdraw citizenship.[22] Where, on the other hand, this is not the case but, on the contrary, freedom needs protection against wider societal forces, the basic rights have to inform private law relationships as well.[23]

(b) A bold move by the Federal Labour Court

When the German Supreme Courts of the various branches of the judiciary were established in accordance with Article 95 (1) *GG*,[24] Nipperdey became the first President of the Federal Labour Court. From this position he masterminded the first official pronouncement of a Supreme Court on the question of the horizontal applicability of human rights. Before this happened, however, the *Bundesgerichtshof* had acknowledged the general right to one's personality[25] as being protected under the law of torts. In that case. however, it had not been necessary to decide the question of horizontal

[21] Nipperdey, *op.cit.* (n. 13 above), 125.

[22] Retention of which is protected under Art. 16 (1) *GG*.

[23] Nipperdey, *op.cit.* (n. 13 above), 125.

[24] Germany has 5 supreme courts, each specialising in different matters. These are: The Federal Court for Civil and Criminal matters (*Bundesgerichtshof* henceforth BGH), Administrative law (*Bundesverwaltungsgericht*), Labour law (*Bundesarbeitsgericht*, henceforth BArbG), Social matters (*Bundessozialgericht*), and Financial law (*Bundesfinanzhof*). Though in one sense at least "superior", the Consitutional Court (*Bundesverfassungsgericht*, henceforth BVerfG) stands separately from the above 5 courts. For a diagram and commentary giving more details, see Markesinis, *The German Law of Obligations, vol. II, The Law of Torts*, 3rd edn, 1997, ch. I (henceforth referred to as Markesinis).

[25] BGHZ 13, 334 = NJW 1954, 1404. This right is derived from Arts. I and 2 *GG*, taken as a whole, although it is not explicitly mentioned in either Article. This "holistic" approach is a subdivision of teleological interpretation: where lacunae are discovered in the law that would endanger the discernible aim of existing provisions, any number of such provisions can be taken together to derive from them rules that would overstretch the interpretation of each of them individually. In other words, one plus one may sometimes equal three if two is not enough for the purposes of the interpreter of the Constitution. For details see Markesinis, *op.cit.*, ch. 2.

application of human rights: the Constitution was merely used to influence the interpretation of a provision of the Civil Code. To put it differently, the outcome of the case did not turn on the direct application of provisions of the Constitution to acts of private parties.[26] In a case decided by it in December 1954,[27] however, the Federal Labour Court felt compelled to take a stand on this issue.

In that case a (private) employer (defendant) had dismissed one of his employees (the plaintiff) because the latter had, before the general election of 1953, disseminated in his workplace propaganda for the Communist Party. The defendant invoked the need to maintain order in the workplace by keeping political controversy out of it as far as possible. The plaintiff challenged his dismissal in the labour courts, claiming that it violated his right to free speech. His claim was that in reality he was being punished for his Communist sympathies.

The Federal Labour Court (*BArbG*) found that the conditions for a lawful dismissal, as set out in the applicable statutes, had been fulfilled.[28] It did, however, go on to examine whether the dismissal, though in accordance with employment law, violated Article 3 (3) *GG* which prohibits discrimination on grounds of political opinion, as well as Article 5, which protects free speech.[29] In order to do the above, the *BArbG* had to acknowledge the horizontal application of basic rights even though its citation of opposing opinions[30] makes it clear that it was fully conscious that by doing this it was addressing a controversial issue.

Referring to the writings of Nipperdey (and others) the court held that some (but not all) basic rights should be taken to afford the individual protection exclusively against the state. Others, however, contained guiding principles for the good structuring of society and social interaction (*Ordnungsgrundsätze für das soziale Leben*). As such, they were directly relevant to legal relationships among citizens. The *BArbG* then reiterated Nipperdey's argument that the guarantees contained in the Constitution would be considerably weakened if they did not also apply to relationships between individuals. This was especially true of the right to free speech. If societal and economic forces were free to curtail it at whim, without being subject to the constraints of the Constitution, the said right would not be

[26] BGHZ 13, 334 at 338 (May 1954) with reference to a book by Nipperdey; translation (excerpts) in Markesinis at 376–80. A similar, albeit vaguer, reference to Art. 6 *GG* (protection of marriage) had already been made in BGHZ 6, 360 at 365 (June 1952) in a case where a husband had had his mistress move into the family home which his wife would not allow.

[27] BArbGE 1. 185*ff*. Comparative lawyers may wish to compare this decision with *Novosel* v. *National Insurance Company* 721 F.2d 894. More about this in the conclusions.

[28] *Loc.cit.* 188–91.

[29] The latter provides, in so far as is here relevant: "(1) Everyone has the right freely to express and disseminate his opinions by speech, writing, and pictures . . . (2) These rights are subject to limitations embodied in the provisions of the general laws . . ."

[30] BArbGE, *loc.cit.* at 192.

able to play its key role in establishing and maintaining a liberal and social political order.[31]

Having established that the dismissal of the plaintiff by the defendant had to be measured against the yardstick of Article 5 (1) *GG*, the *BArbG* then turned to a possible justification under § (2) of the same article, namely, that expression rights can be limited by the "general laws". The court held that the term "general laws" (*allgemeine Gesetze*) was meant to exclude laws (but also contracts and unilateral acts such as a dismissal) which prohibit or hamper the expression of an opinion *solely* [emphasis in the original] because of its political or other aim and its intellectual effect upon others. The limiting of speech rights was, however, admissible where it served to protect some other value recognised under the law *(Rechtsgut)*. Among these values were peaceful relationships in the workplace *(Betriebsfieden)*.[32] Such relationships could, therefore, be protected in the way the existing legislation did protect them. Nevertheless, this justification would not be available for acts that amounted to humiliation *(Maßregelung)*, arbitrariness, or other abuses on the part of the employer that were unreasonable *(unbillig)* and excessive (*unsachlich*, literally: bearing no relation to the underlying subject matter; out of proportion).[33]

Applying these criteria to the instant case the *BArbG* found the dismissal justified. The plaintiff had repeatedly and despite clear warnings from the employer disturbed the peaceful relationships in the workplace, including those with the defendant. Thus the statutory provision which gave the right to dismiss the employee could be properly regarded as falling within the concept of "general laws" as defined above which, in appropriate circumstances, allowed the curtailment of free speech under Article 5 (2) GG.[34]

Having disposed of the speech issues, the court then had to turn to the question whether the defendant's conduct had violated the provision prohibiting discrimination on grounds of political opinion (Article 3 (3) *GG*). The court held that this article, too, was horizontally applicable. However, the court was also concerned that its strict application to legal relationships among individuals could excessively burden the contractual autonomy of the parties. For this autonomy, as well, was recognised and protected under the Constitution. The principle of non-discrimination, therefore, ruled out only acts which lacked any reasonable and acceptable sense *(die jedes verständigen und zu billigenden Sinnes entbehren)*. As a "rule of reason" [sic], which is required by the nature of the conflict between two individuals each

[31] *Ibid.*, 193–4.

[32] This finding was not deduced from any text. The court rather chose to provide extensive references to the effect that this position had always been accepted by the judiciary as well as by academics.

[33] BArbGE 1, 194–5.

[34] *Ibid.*, 195–6.

invoking human rights, a violation of Article 3 (3) *GG* could only be deemed to have occurred where the differential treatment was specifically and exclusively based on one of the criteria listed as inadmissible in Article 3 (3) *GG*. In the instant case, however, the dismissal of the plaintiff by the defendant was based on the latter's repeated and intentional disrespect for the defendant's reasonable demands. Thus, on this ground as well, the legality of the dismissal was upheld by the *BArbG*.[35]

At this point it may be worth reiterating the structure of the court's argument since, as we shall note below, it applies a reasoning which is, essentially, different from that later adopted by the Federal Constitutional Court *(Bundesverfassungsgericht* or *BVerfG)* in the *Lüth* case.[36]

The *BArbG* starts its inquiry by checking whether the dismissal is in keeping with the ordinary laws. This is an important, albeit a preliminary assessment: had the employer been found at this stage to have been at fault, the court would not have had to examine the highly complex and controversial issues that followed. It is, however, noteworthy that in the course of the detailed discussion of the provisions governing dismissal, the question is not raised whether they are compatible with the Constitution. The interpretation, at this stage, leaves aside the constitutional issues altogether. These are discussed only later in a more detailed manner. It is only at this subsequent stage that the *BArbG* points out the paramount importance of the right to free speech (Article 5 (1) *GG*) and highlights the danger that the available justifications (Article 5 (2) *GG)* might be abused. It is thus forced to work out the criteria which distinguish justified use from abuse. Within these limitations, it does, however, accept the decision of the legislature to determine how precisely to regulate a situation where one finds competing values. On a straightforward interpretation of the statutory provisions it thus found the dismissal lawful.

The next step in the court's reasoning was crucial. After discussing the arguments for and against a *direct* horizontal application of human rights, the *BArbG* came down in favour of the first option. In doing so, however, it did not fail to address one obvious danger which is inherent in this approach, namely, that it might stifle private autonomy and initiative. In particular note was taken of the fact that the principle of non-discrimination might destroy the desirable flexibility of economic and social relationships. The remedy offered—the "rule of reason"—consists of an adapted interpretation of the human rights invoked in a given conflict between indi-

[35] BArbGE 1, 196.

[36] To complete the picture it should, however. be mentioned that in BArbGE 47, 363 at 373–5 (Dec. 1984), the court held that as a rule, no *direct* application of human rights was called for and solved the case before it—a case involving a printer and conscientious objector who was sacked because he had refused to print a book that allegedly glorified war—by interpreting the provision governing an employer's right to assign specific tasks to employees in the light of Art. 4 (1) *GG* (freedom of conscience). The court expressly adopted the doctrine of *indirect* influence of human rights on private law (*mittelbare Wirkung der Grundrechte im Privatrecht*), *cf. loc.cit.* p. 373, bottom, and has stuck to it in subsequent cases.

viduals: arbitrariness and proportionality are, respectively, the negative and positive criteria. These criteria apply in a uniform and coherent manner to the right of free speech and the prohibition of discrimination and, presumably, to other human rights as well.

The direct application of human rights thus neatly separates the material interpretation and application of statutory law from the assessment of its constitutionality. Problems are disentangled and discussed systematically, each in its turn. If the dismissal is lawful (under ordinary law) the statute allowing the employer to have recourse to it has to be checked under the relevant article of the *GG*. More precisely, what must be checked is whether the provision in question serves to protect a recognised value or, in the case of alleged discrimination, whether illicit criteria are employed. These choices are, at first instance, left to the legislator to make; and the court presupposes that, when making them, the latter will take cognisance of the importance of free speech.

In the final step of the process the court ascertains whether an abuse has occurred and applies the "rule of reason" in the case of private law relationships. This last step consists of comparing the concrete act of the individual concerned (i.e. the dismissal itself) against the basic right and checking its compatibility with the Constitution—bearing in mind, however, the fact that the statute that permits the dismissal has already been subjected to the same test (*cf.* above).[37]

This solution creates one obvious problem. The implied, reverse side of the adaptation mentioned above is that, apparently, stricter standards have to be applied where a public authority allegedly encroaches upon an individual's liberties since here the "rule of reason" is not applicable. In other words, double standards (between cases involving the state and cases where only private individuals are concerned) are unavoidable. Coherence is achieved only within one area, not between them. On the other hand one must note that the problem of double standards only occurs with regard to the assessment of the concrete act; the problem is thus confined to the last step of the (admittedly) complex reasoning process.

3. TENTATIVE BEGINNINGS IN THE FEDERAL CONSTITUTIONAL COURT: FROM (SUBJECTIVE) RIGHTS TO (OBJECTIVE) VALUES

The ground for the *BVerfG*'s approach, enunciated in the seminal *Lüth* judgment of 1958 (and discussed briefly in the next section),[38] was prepared by a decision on the joint taxation of spouses. In principle, under German tax law each income-earner is taxed on their own returns. At the time of

[37] One of the most eminent critics of the judgment of the BArbG—Professor Canaris, "Grundrechte und Privatrecht" *AcP* 184 [1984] p. 201 at 213—seems to underplay the fact that the court had already undertaken the constitutional control of the underlying statute.

[38] BVerfGE 6, 55 (1957).

the judgment, however, spouses were taxed jointly. Due to the progression in the tax band the combined income of the spouses, in cases where both partners were earners, attracted a higher taxation than the individual incomes would have had if they had been taxed separately. A married couple from Munich challenged their tax demand, *inter alia*, on the grounds that the statute ordering joint taxation violated Article 6 (1) *GG*[39] and Article 3 (1) *GG*.[40] The Munich tax court accepted this argument and referred the matter to the *BVerfG* to rule on the constitutionality of the said provision of the income tax code (§ 26 *EStG* 1951).[41]

The *BVerfG* started by considering Article 3 (1) *GG*. The point here was that married earners were treated less favourably than single persons. As the court pointed out, this provision ruled out arbitrary differentiations between comparable situations. But it also required the legislature to respect other norms which embodied the decision of the Constitution to uphold certain fundamental values in law and in society at large.[42] In appropriate cases, such values were the primary yardstick by which to test the constitutionality of a statutory provision. In such circumstances, the general prohibition of discrimination did not apply.[43]

The *BVerfG* went on to identify Article 6 (1) *GG* as such a norm embodying a fundamental value. The protection of marriage not only served to fend off direct coercion by the state: beyond this classical function of human rights, Article 6 (1) *GG* fulfilled other roles which were closely related and shaded into each other. Applying teleological reasoning, the court held that constitutional interpretation had to realise the legal potential of a given norm to its fullest when applying it to a concrete case. Thus, in a *positive* sense, "protection" meant that the state had to shield marriage and family from harm inflicted by third parties. On the other hand, "protection" in a *negative* sense meant that the state, itself, had to abstain from harming or impairing marriage and family. The latter point implied that even provisions which unintentionally put married couples at a disadvantage had to

[39] "Marriage and family shall enjoy the special protection of the state."

[40] "All people are equal before the law."

[41] This was a reference to the Consitutional Court in accordance with Art. 100 (1) *GG*: "Where a court considers that a law on whose validity its ruling depends is unconstitutional it shall stay the proceedings and . . . seek a ruling . . . where it holds this Basic Law to be violated, from the Federal Constitutional Court." In Germany, every judge has the duty to check the compatibility with the Constitution of statutes they are called upon to apply. Only the *BVerfG*, however, has the right to declare such statutes void if it finds them in violation of the Constitution. Such decisions are published in the *Federal Law Gazette* and have, themselves, the force of law according to § 31 (2) of the Law on the Federal Constitutional Court. Statutory orders, administrative acts, and rules created by autonomous bodies vested with public authority enjoy less protection than parliamentary statutes. They can be set aside by any judge who finds them unlawful.

[42] "*Grundsatznormen, in denen für bestimmte Bereiche der Rechts—und Sozialordnung Wertentscheidungen des Verfassungsgebers ausgedrückt sind.*" BVerfGE 6, 55, 68.

[43] BVerfGE 6, 55 at 71.

be subjected to the same scrutiny. Thus, constitutional scrutiny did not depend upon whether the harmful consequences were deliberate and intended.[44]

The provision in question was meant to skim off some of the financial benefits of marriage, for instance money saved as a result of economies of scale due to a joint household. The reasons for doing so, however, were untenable in the light of Article 6 (1) GG. The legislature had, in short, contravened its "negative" duty. The court, therefore, had no difficulty in finding that the said provision of the income tax code fell foul of Article 6 and hence declared it void.[45]

Two points should be highlighted about this judgment; and both reappear with varying degrees of regularity in subsequent case-law.[46]

First, it extends the classical ambit of fundamental rights beyond the relationship between individual and state. The positive "protective function" *(Schutzfunktion)* of the fundamental rights described above obliges the state to protect individuals from incursions into their liberties by *fellow citizens.* We shall return to this point in section 5 below.

Second, the controversial tax provision did not hinder any couple from marrying. It did not even make marriage itself disadvantageous. What possible deterrent there was resulted purely from the fact that non-married couples were treated relatively more favourably. Naturally, other married couples were not to blame for this. The situation, therefore, neither came under the paradigm of the classical *defensive* function of human rights (as against the state), nor the newly-proclaimed *protective* function (as against individuals). The Constitution, however, did not protect marriage and family simply because they were nice things to have, like public libraries or golf courses. Rather, in the view of the *BVerfG*, marriage and family were protected because they were the nucleus of any society of responsible and independent citizens.[47] Their protection should, therefore, be comprehensive. It should also encompass burdens that are merely incidental to provisions pursuing other, legitimate aims. These provisions should, therefore, be screened for such consequences. This approach was to prove seminal to the *BVerfG*'s definition of its own standards of constitutional control of the activities of both legislature and the ordinary courts.

44 *Ibid.*, 71, 72, 76, 77.

45 *Ibid.*, 77, 84.

46 The *BVerfG* later revised its position on the applicability of Art. 3 (1) *GG*. It now uses basic rights granting freedoms as criteria to flesh out the general prohibition of discrimination rather than reading a prohibition against discrimination into the former as it arguably did in the taxation of spouses case. Also, the court subsequently clarified that not every indirect incumbrance, however light, is prohibited by the basic rights. Rather, there has to be a substantial impairment. On both points, see Hans Dieter Jarass, "Bausteine einer umfassenden Grundrechtsdogmatik", *AöR* 120 [1995], 345 at 348, 364 with further references.

47 BVerGE 6, 71.

4. A CLASSIC: *LÜTH* AND THE INDIRECT HORIZONTAL EFFECT OF HUMAN RIGHTS

In January 1958, roughly a year after the "spouse taxation" case, the *BVerfG* defined more clearly its position on horizontality in the *Lüth* case. In that case, the eponymous plaintiff[48] was, at the material time, head of the press department of the State of Hamburg. In a purely private capacity he issued two statements warning against the professional comeback of the film director Harlan.[49] In these statements Lüth also called upon film distributors, cinema owners, and the public at large to boycott Harlan's latest (and non-offensive) film in order to protect the moral reputation of the German cinema both at home and in the eyes of the world at large. The production and the distribution companies involved in the making and showing of the film invoked § 826[50] of the Civil Code and obtained a judgment in the regional court of Hamburg against Lüth enjoining him from repeating his call for a boycott. Against this, Lüth appealed to the *BVerfG*.

The *BVerfG* took as its starting point the question whether, in arriving at its judgment, the Hamburg court was obliged to take into account the plaintiff's human rights. As stated, in the opinion of the regional court, Lüth's call for a boycott met the conditions for tortious liability under § 826 BGB. The application of this norm to Lüth's statements obviously curtailed his freedom of speech. Whether the judgment violated Article 5 (1) *GG* (i.e. curbed free speech in an unlawful way) depended on the *BVerfG* deciding two issues in favour of Lüth. The first arose because the dispute was between two individuals. Did the human rights provisions of the Constitution have any influence on such relationships and, if so, how was this manifested? The second issue was more technical but just as crucial to Lüth's claim. Article 5 (2) of the Constitution expressly allows for speech rights to be "limited by the provisions of the general laws, the provisions of law for the protection of youth, and by the right to inviolability of

[48] This time, the action was a constitutional complaint under Art. 93 (1) No. 4a *GG* which may be filed by anyone claiming that one of their basic rights has been violated by public authority. The latter term comprises, among others, the courts of all branches of the judiciary. Thus, individuals can appeal to the *BVerfG* to check the compatibility of judgments with the Constitution. As to the limited scope of this examination, which does not amount to another instance of revision, see below. The procedure is set out in more detail in §§ 90–96 of the Law on the Federal Constitutional Court. Where legal action against the violation is admissible, § 90 (2) requires the plaintiff, as a rule, to exhaust all available judicial remedies. An exception applies only if, as in *Lüth*'s case, this exhaustion would entail a serious and irreparable disadvantage for the complainant. If, according to § 95 (2), a complaint against a decision is upheld, the *BVerfG* quashes the judgment and refers it back to the competent court for retrial.

[49] Harlan had, between 1933 and 1945, been the director of, among others, one of the most notorious anti-semitic movies to be made during these years.

[50] "A person who wilfully causes damage to another in a manner *contra bonas mores [entgegen guter Sitten]* is bound to compensate the other for the damage."

personal honour." § 826 was just such a "general law". In legal terms, Lüth's position thus did not appear to be strong.

The Court began by examining the first issue. After acknowledging the existence of two extreme positions—an exclusively vertical application of human rights (i.e. that human rights had no bearing whatsoever on relationships between individuals) and an unfettered horizontal application—the court stated that it did not deem it necessary to enter into this debate in full. Rather, it felt able to confine itself to two statements.

First, it accepted that the basic rights were, in principle, defences of the citizen against the state. This was mirrored in the fact that constitutional complaint, as the remedy specifically intended for the safeguarding of these rights, was available only against public authorities. Secondly, the *Grundgesetz* was not neutral about fundamental values (a charge commonly levelled at the Weimar Constitution). Rather, it had established, in its chapter on human rights, a system of objective values *(objektive Wertordnung)* which was specifically meant to reinforce the effectiveness of human rights. This system permeated the entire area of private law. No private law provision running counter to it could be upheld; the interpretation of all had to be informed by it.[51]

Although, therefore, a conflict between individuals remained governed by private law,[52] human rights "influenced" the application of the provisions of private law. This was especially true of those provisions that could not be abrogated by private parties (*ius cogens*, mandatory provisions) and were thus akin to provisions of public law. Under this heading came the BGB's general clauses and, especially, § 826 with its reference to *gute Sitten*, which could not be disregarded with impunity. *The general clauses were thus treated as the "inroads" (Einbruchstellen) through which basic rights entered private law and influenced the outcome of the private*

[51] *Loc.cit.* at 204, 205. The court later explained this by the fact that the *GG* was but the highest-ranking part of the entire legal order. This order had to be understood as a *Sinnganzes*, i.e. a system in which every part was referential to every other with the values as embodied in the constitution inspiring and informing the whole, BVerfGE 75, 201 (April 1987), at 218 (Adoption). This principle can be seen in action in a case upholding the granting by the ordinary courts of monetary compensation for a violation of the plaintiff's (Princess Soraya, divorced wife of the Shah of Persia and at the time a darling of the yellow press) general right to her personality through a fake interview. The ordinary courts had overridden § 253 BGB which ruled out compensation in such cases but, thereby, deprived private law of its most effective and sometimes the only sanction for such offenses. BVerfGE 34, 269 (Feb. 1973) at 274, 280, 281. As Art. 2 (1) *GG* (from which the general right to one's personality is derived, see above) is the *lex generalis* of all the other, specific basic rights granting freedoms, the violation of any such right entitles the harmed to compensation, see Canaris, "Grundrechte und Privatrecht" *AcP* 184 (1984), 201 at 208. On *Lüth, Soraya* and related cases, see Markesinis, at 31.

[52] As the court later made clear, the involvement of a judge adjudicating the matter as an organ of public authority does not alter this position, BVerfGE 73, 261 (April 1986) at 268 (social protection for laid-off workers provided for in a trade union–employer agreement).

dispute.[53] According to Article 1 (3) *GG*, therefore, the ordinary courts were obliged in each case to consider whether the provisions of private law which they had to apply to the case before them were shaped or affected by fundamental rights. If the ordinary court failed to do so, not only did it violate the law—*objektives Recht*; in addition, every citizen had a *subjektives Recht* against the court for his basic rights to be taken into account in this way.[54]

Having thus disposed of the first problem, the Constitutional Court then turned its attention to the second issue mentioned above. Harlan's suit against Lüth was based on the latter's call for a boycott contravening § 826 BGB. It would be idle to deny that, at that time, Harlan's claim seemed a very powerful one. For, as stated, the constitutional protection of free speech, enunciated in Article 5 (1), is, because of Article 5 (2), subject to the "qualifications" of the general law.

For Lüth this second hurdle was no less formidable than the first since the wording of Article 5 (2) makes it clear that the draftsmen of the Constitution always intended to allow the civil and criminal legislator the freedom to place some limits on the free expression of opinion.[55] Of the words of this article which limited this freedom, two were particularly open-ended—"general laws"; and Lüth tried to argue that these only referred to rules of public law and thus excluded § 826 BGB. The Constitutional Court refused to accept this (narrowing interpretation) but, mercifully for him (and the subsequent fate of free speech in German law), was able to preserve much of the sanctity of freedom of expression through its ingenious theory of "reciprocal effect" *(Wechselwirkung)*.

At first sight the theory as much as the terminology seems Germanic and to Common lawyers off-putting. Yet it posited a simple idea, namely, that just as the "general laws" can affect the Constitution so does the Constitution, in its turn, affect them. So, when a judge determines the extent to which the general laws limit the rights granted by the Constitution, the laws themselves should be seen against the background of the entire legal order

[53] *Loc.cit.* at 205, 206. In the court's subsequent jurisprudence, this passage has been reiterated on numerous occasions and applied to the most diverse cases; see recently, e.g., BVerfGE 94, 1 (Feb. 1996) at 8 (defamation); 90, 27 (Feb. 1994) at 33 (reception of Turkish programmes by tenant through satellite dish); 89, 214 (Oct. 1993) at 229 (credit guarantee by relatives without means); 86, 122 (May 1992) at 128 (apprentice not taken on after training because he allegedly advocated political violence in an apprentices' magazine). Cases in these areas will be examined in the second part of this paper. Comprehensive references to the court's jurisprudence with regard to all basic rights thus applied: Classen, "Die Drittwirkung der Grundrecht in der Rechtsprechung des BVerfG", *AöR* 122 [1997], 65 at 89–92.

[54] BVerfGE 7, 195 at 206. 207. Whatever the nature of this right is, the court later made it clear that the indirect horizontal application did not oblige the judge himself directly to apply to a case human rights that did not, after all, bind the parties *inter se;* the judge merely had to respect these rights' "radiating effect" (*Ausstrahlungswirkung*, a term already used in *Lüth*) on private law, BVerfGE 73, 261 at 269.

[55] This approach had, in fact, a long pedigree since we find a similar provision in Art. 118 of the Weimar Constitution of 1919.

and the importance it attaches to free speech. In effect this is an invocation of the principle of proportionality *(Verhältnismäßigkeit);* and subsequent decisions have, in reality, resorted to the balancing techniques of proportionality itself to test the limitations of governmental action. Thus, as a leading decision on proportionality put it in 1988, "General laws restricting expression are valid only if they are adapted *(geeignet)* to the achievement of a legitimate purpose, necessary *(erforderlich)* to that end, and the burden they impose is not excessive *(zumutbar)* in the light of the achieved benefits."[56]

Once the court had reached that stage, Lüth was home and dry! For his motives in calling for the boycott were impeccable; indeed, his position seemed to cry out for the action he, in fact, did take (though, as stated, he took it acting in a private capacity). As for Harlan's countervailing economic interests, though important, they had to give way to the sanctity of political free speech.[57] As the court put it, in a style that could be mistaken for a Cardozo aphorism, "When the formation of public opinion on a question of general importance is at stake, private and especially economic interests must take second place."[58]

This approach has been accepted in principle by the vast majority of commentators. Thus, it has been stressed that Article 1 (1), 2nd sentence *GG* speaks of the duty of "all state authority"—not individuals—to protect and respect human dignity. This is reiterated in Article 1 (3) and Article 20 (3) *GG*. According to Article 3 (1) *GG*, all people are equal "before the law", which is thus addressed to the legislature. Also, the clauses in most of Articles 1 to 19 *GG*, authorising the legislature to limit the exercise of certain freedoms or to spell out the details of such freedoms that require legislation (e.g. property and marriage), point in the same direction.[59] Several lines of criticism have, however, been put forward.

One criticism fears that basic rights are diluted if they are not applied outright but merely "radiate" out as "objective principles".[60] Such a "dilu-

[56] BVerfGE 78, 232, 245–7.

[57] This does not, however, mean that a boycott is under all circumstances a legitimate means of public controversy; contrast the *Blinkfüer* case. There, a market-dominating publisher tried to quash a small publishing firm from printing East German television programmes which, indisputably, published mainly Communist propaganda. The publisher calling for a boycott used its economic might rather than the force of argument in order to deter distributors from handling the issues of *Blinkfüer.* The ordinary courts condemned this practice and the *BVerfG* upheld their decision: BVerfGE 25, 256 (Feb. 1969) at 266, distinguishing *Lüth* at 267. For further details see Markesinis, "Privacy, Freedom of Expression and the Horizontal Application of the Human Rights Bill", 1999 *LQR* (forthcoming).

[58] BVerfGE 7, 198, 219.

[59] Medicus, "Der Grundsatz der Verhältnismäßigkeit im Privatrecht", *AcP* 192 (1992), 35 at 43.

[60] Jarass, "Grundrechte als Wertentscheidungen bzw. objektivrechtliche Prinzipien in der Rechtsprechung des BVerfG", *AöR* 110 [1985], 363 at 377, 378; Quint, "Free Speech and Private Law in German Constitutional Theory" [1989] *Maryland L Rev.* 247 at 262.

tion" might even make sense for, as the *BVerfG* itself once remarked, a basic right might have to be more narrowly circumscribed when it is invoked to inform relationships between individuals, "given the special features which characterise these relationships", than when it is used as a defence against an intrusion of individual freedoms by the state.[61] The general practice of the *BVerfG*, however, does not seem to substantiate this either as a fear or as a practice. For, when ruling on cases involving private parties only (or rather, on the ordinary courts' judgments in such cases) the *BVerfG* routinely refers to judgments involving public authorities and individuals and vice versa.[62] In both areas, therefore, the court seems to assume that basic rights have the same ambit.

Another criticism is that, although acknowleging that basic rights are inappropriate to govern legal—particularly contractual—relationships between individuals, the *BVerfG* is reluctant to acknowledge the full effect of the principle of contractual autonomy. The concept of "objective values", therefore, is nothing but a ruse to allow it to meddle with private contracts.[63] There may be some force in this argument, especially if it is seen against the background of some recent decisions. As a generalisation, however, the statement strikes one as too sweeping and thus unconvincing. Here, suffice it to point out, as Nipperdey did in 1958,[64] that Article 123 (1) *GG* provides that "law in force before the first meeting of the Bundestag shall remain in force in so far as it does not conflict with the Basic Law". If private law is instrumental in guaranteeing the contractual autonomy of individuals and if, furthermore, the Constitution apparently assumes that such law, like any other, can be in conflict with the Basic Law, then it is difficult to deny that private contractual relationships are to some extent subject to constitutional influence.[65]

Whatever the force of such criticisms, the Constitutional Court has frequently repeated its *Lüth* formula. However, though the possibility of a constitutional review will not be given up, the chances of the court exercising it in private law disputes is, in all but the speech cases, rather limited. The

[61] BVerfGE 66, 116 (Jan. 1984) at 135 (*Wallraff* decision). For details of the case see Markesinis (n. 1 above).

[62] Numerous examples of this: Hager, "Grundrechte im Privatrecht", 1994 *JZ* 373 at 375, fn. 23.

[63] Zöllner, "Regelungsspielräume im Schuldvertragsrecht" *AcP* 196 [1996] 1 at 7–9.

[64] Nipperdey, "Boykott und freie Meinungsäußerung", [1958] *Deutsches Verwaltungsblatt* 445 at 447 (right column).

[65] That leaves the question open as to what is subject to scrutiny: the individual's action or the statutory provision the individual bases their claim on. Canaris, "Grundrechte im Privatrecht" *AcP* 184 [1984] 201 at 222, accused the court of denying this distinction; yet he himself gives examples of the court subjecting provisions of private law directly to scrutiny under basic rights (which is what he advocates) on p. 212. This distinction will be discussed in s. 5 below on the state's protective duties.

"patent case" of 1964,[66] frequently cited in the years that followed *Lath*, can serve as a good illustration of such a deferential attitude towards the decisions of the ordinary courts.

In Germany an inventor, in order to obtain a patent, has to apply for his invention to be registered with the Federal Patent Office in Munich. If the office deems the invention to be patentable, it publishes the application and invites third parties to raise objections. The applicant had applied for a patent on a self-tanning lotion containing certain new ingredients. The office objected to some of them and, as a result, the applicant withdrew his request to patent the said ingredients. Then a competitor requested access to the file in order to decide whether to challenge the patentability of the remainder of the application. Initially, the office refused to grant this in respect of the ingredients withdrawn from the application but, upon appeal, the Federal Patent Court (*Bundespatentgericht* or *BPatG*) granted the request, based on a procedural provision in the Law on Patents (§ 24 *Patentgesetz* or *PatG*).

The applicants brought the matter before the *BVerfG*. They claimed the interpretation of § 24 *PatG* by the *BPatG* violated their right to property: Article 14 (1) *GG*.[67] They claimed that the ingredients mentioned in the original application could still be made patentable; now, however, their secrets had been revealed to a competitor who could use this knowledge and thus save research and development costs. By withdrawing the application in so far as it concerned these ingredients, the knowledge had also been withdrawn from the public domain.

The *BVerfG* first turned to the question whether the provision allowing the patent office to grant access to its files was compatible with the Constitution. The court found that § 24 *BPatG* adequately balanced the conflicting concerns.[68] Then, the *BVerfG* turned to the main complaint, namely, that the *BPatG* had applied the provision in a way which violated basic rights of the applicant. Citing *Lüth* the court held that the ordinary courts, when applying provisions of private law, had to take into account the influence which basic rights had upon them. If they failed to do so, their judgments would have to be quashed.[69] On the other hand, continued the court,

[66] BVerfGE 18, 85. In other instances, however, the Constitutional Court has not shown such restraint and, as a result, not escaped serious academic criticism. See, for instance BVerfGE 89, 1 (1993) where the court invoked the right to property in order to intervene in a dispute between landlord and tenant.

[67] It reads: "Property and the right of inheritance shall be guaranteed. Their substance and limits shall be determined by law."

[68] It should be noted that the constitutionality check of a law limiting a basic freedom, apart from the material considerations peculiar to each basic right, extends also to whether it has been adopted following the correct procedure, BVerfGE 6, 32 (*Elfes*) at 41 (Jan. 1957). The problems stemming from the *BVerfG*'s checking the balancing done by the legislature will be discussed in more detail further on in this chapter.

[69] BVerfGE 18, 85 (1964) at 91, 92.

this did not mean that the *BVerfG* could be seised of a dispute each time a flawed judgment possibly encroached upon basic rights. Conducting the procedure, ascertaining and assessing the facts, interpreting and applying the law to the facts of each case, were activities exclusively within the realm of competence of the ordinary courts and lay outside the jurisdiction of the Constitutional court. Only in so far as constitutional law (*spezifisches Verfassungsrecht*, a somewhat pleonastic expression) had been infringed, would the *BVerfG* quash a judgment following a constitutional complaint? This it would do where basic rights and their influence on the law of inferior rank had been ignored (*Nichtbeachtung von Grundrechten*). Such ignorance occurred where either the judge had been obviously unaware that basic rights influenced the way he had to arrive at his judgment or where he had misapprehended in principle the significance and ambit of a basic right and where this misapprehension had some bearing on the case. It was not sufficient that he had merely attached too much or too little weight to the concerns of one side or the other.[70] By applying this standard, the decision of the *BPatG* was upheld, the *BVerfG* reconfirming its reluctance to interfere lightly with the decisions of the ordinary courts.

More recent case-law has shed further light on the question whether and when the Constitutional court should intervene. In its 1990 "commercial agent's" (*Handelsvertreter*) case, which we shall examine further below, the *BVerfG* drew together many loose threads which will be noted in the sections that follow while redefining in one respect the *Lüth* judgment.

5. A NEW FOUNDATION: THE STATE'S PROTECTIVE DUTIES

By the 1970s, and while the above developments were being consolidated, a new paradigm was beginning to emerge. The *BVerfG*, building on some earlier dicta,[71] was busy developing the concept of the state's "protective

[70] BVerfGE 18, 85 (1964) at 92, 93. The court added in a later case, BVerfGE 30, 173 (*Mephisto*) at 197 (Feb. 1971), translation in Markesinis (n. 24 above), 359–65, that the same applied where the limits had to be drawn to the basic rights of one party *vis-à-vis* those of another. This is, in essence, already contained in the last sentence of the earlier formula.

[71] It will be remembered that in the taxation of spouses case (BVerfGE 6, 55) the court extracted from Art. 6 (1) *GG* the (positive) duty of the state to protect marriage and family from impairments by "other (societal) forces" (*loc.cit.* at 76). But the real beginning of this trend should be traced back to the "Television case" of 1961—BVerfGE 12, 205—where the central government's attempt to set up a new broadcasting network was defeated by the Court on the grounds that it trespassed on the powers reserved for the *Länder*. More significantly for present purposes, the guarantee of broadcasting freedom contained in Art. 5 (1) *GG* was found to go beyond the traditional right to be left alone by the state and was taken to include a positive duty on the part of the state to ensure that all significant interest groups had a chance to influence the governing bodies of such broadcasting institutions. A summary of the arguments can be found in Professor Currie's highly compressed but readable account of *The Constitution of the Federal Republic* (1994), 37–8 and 229–233.

duties". Though some of the cases that follow are governed by public law, German lawyers have taken the view that their principles are easily transferable to private relationships affected by human rights issues since the underlying problems are materially the same. Thus, an emission of, say, fumes or radiation can, for instance, be in principle scrutinised both under public law (e.g. the Federal Law on the Protection Against Emissions: *Bundesimmissionsschutzgesetz* = *BImSchG*) or under private law, namely, §§ 906, 1004 of the Civil Code.[72]

The first significant opportunity to develop the concept of the protective duties of the state came with the first abortion case.[73]

Up until the coming into force of the Abortion Reform Act in 1974 abortion was illegal but could, under certain narrowly defined circumstances, be justified or excused. The 1974 reform of the law (§§ 218 *et seq*. of the Penal Code—*StGB* = *Strafgesetzbuch*) made it legal to have an abortion within the first twelve weeks of pregnancy (so-called time-limit solution or *Fristenlösung*) so long as the pregnant woman had given her consent and the abortion was carried out by a licensed physician. The opposition, the Christian Democratic party in the *Bundestag*, along with the governments of five *Länder*, thought this legalisation—though limited in time—was incompatible with Article 2 (2), 1st sentence *GG*.[74] Its validity was thus challenged before the Constitutional Court. Three days after its enactment, (21 June 1974) the application of the new statute was suspended by the Constitutional Court by means of a "preliminary injunction" (*einstweilig Anordnung*) pending the final decision. This came with the publication of the full judgment of the court one year later.

The first problem which confronted those who challenged the Act was, obviously, whether an unborn child could invoke the constitutional provision which guarantees life and physical integrity since after only twelve weeks no foetus is viable outside the womb. Relying on the records of the Constitutional Convention the *BVerfG* had no doubt that life began before birth—certainly not later than the fourteenth day after conception.[75] But

[72] The former reads: "(1) The owner of a piece of land is not entitled to prohibit the intrusion of gases, vapours, smells, smoke, soot, heat, noises, shocks and similar interferences emanating from another piece of land to the extent that the interference does not or only immaterially prejudice the use of his piece of land." As to the latter, see above. The *BImSchG* *is* designed to refine this rather rudimentary provision and to bring the public interest into play by involving the authorities to varying defrees according to the seriousness of the emissions.

[73] BVerfGE 39, 1. This was yet another type of action before the court, this time based on Art. 93 (1) no. 2 *GG:* "[The Federal Constitutional Court shall rule] in case of disagreement or doubt as to the formal and material compatibility of federal . . . legislation with this Basic Law . . . at the request of the Federal Government, a Land government or one third of the members of the Bundestag" (so-called "abstract" review of norms as the applicants need not allege a violation of their (subjective) rights).

[74] "Every one has the right to life and physical integrity."

[75] BVerfGE 39, 37. The objective value principle thus lay at the core of the state's affirmative duty to protect life. Most academics have stressed this point. Thus, see Dürig,

this was not the conclusive argument. It need not be decided, held the court, whether the *nasciturus* comes within the ambit of Article 2 (2) *GG* or whether it "merely" (emphasis in the original) benefits from the objective side of this norm. The court had, since the *Lüth* judgment, consistently held that the basic rights not only granted individuals defensive rights as against the state; they also constituted a system of "objective values" (*objektive Wertordnung*) which, as fundamental decisions of the constitution, guide legislators, the administration, and the judiciary. This was sufficient to determine whether and to what extent the state had a duty to protect unborn children.[76]

The next problem concerned the material scope of the guarantee of life and physical integrity: no public authority had, after the enactment of the *GG*, ever encouraged, let alone forced, any woman to have an abortion. Rather, abortion had been considered in Germany as a punishable evil that could only under certain circumstances be tolerated. Instead, what was sought by the applicants was the protection of the state from attacks against life by private parties—the woman who sought the abortion and her doctor. The legal situation thus became triangular—which is no surprise: if Article 1 (1), 2nd sentence *GG* mentions "protection",[77] in this case the dangers human dignity has to be protected from can only emanate from private individuals. For any dangers caused by the state itself were already caught by the "respect" side of the wording of the article.[78]

The question that confronted the court was, therefore, whether the legislature had, through the (reforming) 1974 Act, done enough to protect life, More specifically, the question was whether, with the reform of § 218 StGB, the legislature had exhausted its duty to protect life in accordance with the dictates of the Constitution. This question, too, was given a familiar answer by the *BVerfG*.

From Article 2 (2) *GG*, held the court, followed a duty to protect human life.[79] This finding was strengthened by invoking Article 1 (1), 2nd sentence *GG*: any form of human life, born or unborn. as a result of its existence alone, shares in the fundamental human dignity, whether or not it is conscious of this dignity and capable of defending it.[80] Therefore, while it was true that the pregnancy, the birth, and the upbringing of an unwanted child could affect in some respects the mother's life, abortion destroyed the child's life altogether. The latter's right to life, therefore, took precedence over the

Maunz/Dürig, *Grundgesetz Kommentar*, Art. 1, Rdnr. 102: Grabitz, "Freiheit der Person", 6 *Handbuch des Staatsrechts* 109, Rdnr 14–15.

[76] *Loc.cit.* at 41, 42.

[77] "To respect *and protect* [human dignity] shall be the duty of all public authority."

[78] Claus-Wilhelm Canaris, "Grundrechte und Privatrecht", *AcP* 184 [1984], 201 at 226.

[79] Reaffirmed by the second abortion decision of 1993: BVerfGE 88, 203, 251.

[80] BVerfGE 39, 1 at 41, 42.

mother's right to self-fulfilment (Article 2 (1) *GG*)—irrespective of any time limit.[81]

From this, it followed that the enacted legalisation was unconstitutional for it fell short of the condemnation of abortion that was required by the Constitution. Indeed, the new Act made abortion even appear as a legitimate alternative to contraception. Yet maintaining the illegality of abortion, by punishing those who carry it out, was not enough. In every case, prevention is better than repression. The protection of the unborn also required helping the mother accept her child. What could be done in this respect was, however, largely for the legislature to decide and, in principle, exempt from the scrutiny of the Constitutional Court.[82] The German Parliament almost instantly complied with the ruling of the court and abortion has since—as it was before the 1974 Act—been possible only for medical, eugenic, ethical, and serious social reasons.[83] Thus, abortions during the first twelve weeks reverted to being illegal, subject to one important concession made by the second abortion decision of 1993: a woman (and her physician) who has gone ahead with an abortion during the first twelve weeks of *pregnancy despite counselling designed to change her mind* could not be criminally punished. In essence, this seems to be based on the belief, already voiced by the dissents in the first abortion case, that the duty of the state to protect the *nasciturus* was best fulfilled by trying to "educate" the pregnant woman rather than by threatening her with criminal sanctions.[84]

This is an important judgment; and it offers great scope for a comparative examination of the underlying issues.[85] For our purposes, however, two points are particularly noteworthy.

First, the court had to weigh two competing concerns, each backed by a

[81] *Ibid.*, 43. Translated extracts of the decision can be found in Kommers, *The Constitutional Jurisprudence of the Federal Republic of Germany*, 2nd edn. (1997), 336*ff.* where the subsequent fate of this controversial debate is also discussed with admirable clarity. See also Currie, *op.cit.*, 310–14.

[82] BVerfGE 39, at 44.

[83] This regime has, essentially, survived post-unification attempts to harmonise the more liberal law of the former Eastern Germany with the tougher law of the West. On this see the Second Abortion case, BVerfGE 88,203 (1993)—a monument to judicial prolixity. (The two dissents alone cover 163 pages of the official reports!)

[84] This latest twist in the abortion saga has helped reduce the otherwise irreconcilable philosophical differences between the German and American position as expressed in *Roe* v. *Wade,* 410 U.S. 113 (1973).

[85] Professor Mary Ann Glendon has done this in her *Abortion and Divorce in Western Law: American Failures, European Challenges* (1987). The provocative subtitle indicates how the comparative material can be used to question national law. See also, Kommers, "Liberty and Community in Constitutional Law: The Abortion Cases in Comparative Perspective" 1985 *B. Y U. L. Rev.* 371; Brugger, "A Constitutional Duty to Outlaw Abortion? A Comparative Analysis of the American and German Abortion Decisions" 36 *JöR* (n. F.) 49 (1987). The second abortion case is discussed by Kommers "The Consitutional Law of Abortion in Germany: Should Americans Pay Attention?", 10 *Journal of Contemporary Health Law and Society*, 1*ff.* (1994); Walther, "Thou Shalt not (but though mayest): Abortion After the German Constitutional Court's 1993 Landmark Decision", 36, *German Yearbook of Internatioonal Law* 387 (1993).

basic right. On the one hand; we have the mother's right to decide that a child would not fit into her life style—a right protected by Article 2 (1) *GG*[86]—and on the other hand the court is faced with the ***nasciturus***'s own right to life based on Article 2 (2) *GG*. German courts have perfected the art of balancing competing interests and values.

Many examples could be quoted to illustrate how this works in practice.[87] Citing the guiding principles is all that we can do here. Thus, in an earlier case, the court had described this balancing as reciprocally applying the principle of proportionality in order to realise each right as far as possible.[88] Subsequently, in a speech case, the Constitutional Court described the essence of proportionality in this way: "General laws restricting expression are valid only if they are adapted (*geeignet*) to the achievement of a legitimate purpose, necessary (*erforderlich*) to that end,[89] and the burden they impose is not excessive (*zumutbar*) in the light of the achieved benefits."[90]

The second, important point of this decision is its willingness to give wide discretion to the legislature to fulfill its duty of protection. This point can, in fact, be found in both of the abortion cases (1975 and 1993); but it was also expanded in the following case which will be used to show how the proposition just cited—willingness to review but within limits—works in different areas of the law in order to determine the precise scope of such affirmative duties. It deals with the equally controversial subject matter of environmental pollution.

In December 1972, the authorities of the *Land* of North Rhine-Westphalia had granted a private power-generating company permission to build a nuclear power plant near the village of Kalkar. This plant was designed to try out the novel technology of "fast breeding", that is, the reactor produced new nuclear fuel while it burnt the original fuel rods. A farmer from the vicinity of the proposed site challenged this permission. He lost his case in the administrative court of first instance; but the court of second instance agreed with him that the provision on which the permission to build the reactor was based (§ 7 of the Law on the Peaceful Exploitation of Atomic Energy and on the Protection Against its Dangers—*AtomG*) was unconstitutional in so far as it was applicable to this case. The court alleged that,

[86] It reads: "Everybody has the right to self-fulfilment in so far as they do not violate the rights of others or offend against the constitutional order or against morality."

[87] On this, see Markesinis, "Privacy, Freedom of Expression, and the Horizontal Effect of the Bill of Rights: Lessons from Germany", 1999 *LQR* (forthcoming).

[88] BVerfGE 35, 202 (*Lebach* murder case) at 221 (June 1973), see Markesinis (n. 24 above), 390–8. It should be noted that this position was later refined, although the proportionality test is still part of the balancing. In the instant (abortion) case this process is somewhat obscured by the fact that on one side, it is all or nothing: the child cannot give up part of its life.

[89] This means that no other way exists to achieve the desired aim without restricting speech. On the necessity principle see BVerfGE 39, 156, 165.

[90] BVerfGE 78, 232, 245–7. For a fuller discussion see Hirschberg, *Der Grundsatz der Verhätnismässigkeit* (1981).

among other things, § 7 was incompatible with Article 2 (2) *GG*. It thus referred the question to the *BVerfG* under Article 100 (1) *GG*.[91]

Invoking, once again, the objective side of the basic rights—in this case Article 2 (2) *GG*[92]—and citing, in particular, Article i (i), 2nd sentence *GG*, the court held that whether the authorities had to act or not depended on the specific factual and legal situation. The proximity and gravity of the possible dangers, the rank of the interests to be protected, and the pre-existing legislation, all had to be combined in order to determine whether, when, and by what means the legislature had to take precautions. Applying these criteria, the court did not find § 7 *AtomG* to be in violation of Article 2 (2) *GG*. Looking at the *AtomG* in its entirety the court came to the conclusion that Parliament had done its utmost to prevent all reasonably foreseeable danger.[93] In the circumstances the court was unwilling to use the process of constitutional review to substitute its own value judgment for that of the administration.

The facts of this case illustrate the new facet of our problem. For, once again, the question was not whether *public authorities* actively threatened the lives of citizens. The question was whether they were permitting private individuals to harm other citizens through (unintended) consequences flowing from their own activities. The impairment of the fundamental right of the complainant was, therefore, only indirect and arose from the special factual circumstances of this case. As in the abortion case, the objective side of the basic right thus served to extend its ambit far beyond the classic defensive paradigm. For under the latter theory the state had to encroach upon the rights of an individual directly and by legally binding *fiat* before the human rights complaint procedure could be set in motion.

There is, however, one caveat to the above innovations. The court's application of the mentioned criteria suggests that, in cases of *indirect* harm, the burdens imposed on individuals must be of substantial weight before the court decides to intervene in their favour. In modern societies, where many spheres of life are interdependent, to do otherwise would lead to a paralysis of the legislature. It is factually impossible (and legally unnecessary) to take into consideration even the slightest inconveniences of every individual who may be affected by a given piece of legislation—as long as it is not intended to curtail his rights. § 7 *AtomG* (as all the other provisions of that law) was, on the contrary, specifically meant to protect individuals from the dangers of nuclear power as far as this was possible. Since what risks remained could be seen as being both inevitable and reasonable, the state

[91] On this procedure, see above, note 41.

[92] It should be added that all basic rights are but specific emanations of the fundamental principle of human dignity, see BVerfGE 93, 266 ("Soldiers are murderers II") at 293 (Oct. 1995). What the court here deduces for the objective side of Art. 2 (2) *GG* is equally true for all other basic rights.

[93] BVerfGE 49, 89 (*Kalkar*) at 141, 142 (Aug. 1978).

had discharged its protective duty. If, on the other hand, the dangers had been grave, and the existing legislation had offered insufficient protection, it would not have been allowed to remain inactive without this amounting to a violation of the objective side of basic rights. Thus, whether or not action is called for is a matter for the legislature to decide. As Professor Currie has put it: "The extent of the state's affirmative obligations in practice seems to depend less upon the reigning theory than upon the aggressiveness or deference with which it is applied."[94] The *BVerfG* had no doubts about this; and it explained its position once again in another case, this time touching on the question of noise pollution.

Environmental legislation involves most complex questions of a factual nature, often calling for forecasts based on probability. Usually, several solutions can be envisaged to any given problem. In this situation, which solution is chosen is a matter of political aims and priorities and the availability of suitable (not least financial) means. According to the democratic principle, and in keeping with the doctrine of separation of powers, these are matters which should be left to Parliament to judge. In such situations, said the Constitutional court, its role is reduced to checking whether the legislature chose an obviously faulty path or remained inactive altogether where protection of important constitutional values was required.[95] Summing up its jurisprudence in an even later case the court was thus eager to add that the legislature had a wide discretion. Especially where conflicting interests of several individuals had to be balanced the one against the other, the Constitution merely provided the framework for this but did not dictate any particular outcome.[96]

What has so far been said with regard to the legislature applies with equal force to the administration. It too, has a (considerable) margin of discretion when it comes to fulfilling its protective duties which the Constitutional court will be slow to invade. This was clearly brought home by the *Schleyer* case.

In *Schleyer* the eponymous applicant, president of the "German Employers' Federation", had been abducted by terrorists who threatened to kill him unless some of their comrades were released from prison.[97] Schleyer sought from the *BVerfG* an order instructing the Federal Government and the governments of those *Länder* where terrorists were imprisoned, to give in to the kidnappers' demands. Again, this was a triangular situation, with

[94] *Op.cit.* (n. 71 above), 16–17.

[95] BVerfGE 56, 54 (Aviation noise) at 80, 81 (Jan. 1981). This case confirms *Lüth* to the effect that individuals can invoke the state's protective duties as their own subjective rights: the ruling was on a constitutional complaint and the *BVerfG* wasted no time with the question of admissibility of the action.

[96] BVerfGE 92, 26 (Merchant vessels' register) at 46 (Jan. 1995).

[97] The application was lodged in his name by his son. Likewise, BVerfGE 66, 39, 60 (1983)—decision concerning the stationing of nuclear weapons on German soil: the question how best to defend the country should be left to the government.

the state called upon to come to the assistance of one of its citizens. The court declined to make an order: the administration had to have discretion as to how to react in cases such as this. In particular, the public at large had an interest in the government not allowing itself to be blackmailed and terrorist methods not being seen to pay off.[98]

From these and other cases some general patterns become discernible.

First, basic rights have a *negative* side to them. They are "negative norms of competence";[99] they tell the state what it must not do. This comes into play when the state imposes burdens on individuals or takes rights away from them. Seen in this way, basic rights stipulate duties of omission. But basic rights also have a *positive* side which applies when an individual encroaches upon the liberties of another individual and the state is called upon to assist the latter. In this context, basic rights stipulate duties to act.[100] As these situations are as manifold as the possible remedies—sometimes they may go beyond the state's influence altogether—the state, as a rule, has a choice whether and how to react. But though basic rights have both "negative" and "positive" sides, both of these are co-extensive, that is, they have the same personal and material scope. In both cases the meaning of "everyone", "nobody", "life", "free speech", or "association" does not change. The protective duty is, however, susceptible to gradation according to the urgency and feasibility of the state's response. There is thus no unconditional duty to act to "protect" as there is an unconditional duty to "respect" human rights (Article 1 (1), 2nd sentence *GG*).

Secondly, a common feature of both sides of basic rights is the required balancing of interests involved. In the sphere of public law, these are public interests (or the public's endorsement of private pursuits such as the construction of, say, a railway or an open-cast mine). In the sphere of private law private concerns, as backed up by a basic right,[101] have to be weighed individually the one against the other.

Metaphorically speaking, this balancing implies a mutual give and take. More precisely, what happens is an application of both the subjective and the objective side of human rights respectively. To the extent that one side

[98] BVerfGE 64, 160 (*Schleyer*) at 165 (Oct. 1977).

[99] Jarass, "Bausteine einer umfassenden Grundrechtsdogmatik" *AöR* 120 [1995] 345 at 347.

[100] Contrast Judge Posner's dictum that the US Constitution is "a charter of negative rather than positive duties": *Jackson* v. *City of Joliet* 715 F.2d 200, 203 (7th Circ. 1983). This view was affirmed by the US Supreme Court in *DeShaner* v. *Winnebago County Dept. of Social Services*, 489 U.S. 189 (1989) where the court said: "[N]othing in the language [or history] of the Due Process Clause . . . requires the State to protect the life, liberty, and property of the citizens against invasion by private actors . . . Its purpose was to protect the people from the State, not to ensure that the State protected them from each other." *Cf.*, however, Heyman, "The First Duty of Government: Protection, Liberty and the Fourteenth Amendment", 41 *Duke L.J.* 507 (1991).

[101] If no specific freedom applies, the right to self-fulfilinent (Art. 2 (1) *GG*) does, i.e. the right to do everything that is not forbidden.

(*A*) is barred by law from doing something that could impair the interests of the other side (*B*), the defensive side of human rights comes into play with regard to that law. Consequently, the principle of proportionality is applied to gauge the constitutionality of the statutory prohibition. To the extent that *B* is protected, the protective duty applies. The question then is not whether *A*'s concrete action is compatible with *B*'s basic rights. Actions of private parties are not bound by the basic rights, *viz. Lüth*. Rather, the question is whether the state has evidently failed to grant *B* "adequate" protection, understood on a sliding scale and within a wide margin of discretion. As long and in so far as this minimum of protection is granted, the details are left for the state to determine.

Both sides, taken together, produce the following: if limited protection of *B* is sufficient, it will not excessively curtail *A*'s rights. The same is true if essential interests of *B* are at stake. "Too much protection" of *B* can, however, amount to an excessive burden on *A*, for example, where *B*, having worked for *A* for forty years, could not even be sacked for gross misbehaviour. The formula to be applied, therefore, is the following: has the state provided at least a minimum of protection for *B* without, at the same time, encumbering *A* in a way which exceeds what is necessary for *B*'s interests? This abstract reasoning will be seen in action in the *Handelvertreter* case to be considered in the next section.

Thirdly, German courts, in a manner reminiscent of the practice found in our own, are not unwilling to state their ability to intervene—in the case before us, when human activity affects the human rights of other individuals. But *ability* to intervene does not automatically translate into *eagerness* to intervene and substitute their own value judgments for those of the administration. In many situations the contrary is true, especially where the issues before it have strong political overtones; indeed, in such cases the court has, itself, made use of the term "judicial self-restraint".[102] This, it is submitted, is a healthy approach and its only blemish is that the complexities of life and litigation have led German courts to make some important inroads into it, sometimes as a result of judicial refinements and in others as a result of an application which has courted political controversy. Even though one is tempted to dismiss both these tendencies (excessive refinement or dubious application) as inevitable, one must, nevertheless, say something about these greyer areas of the law, if only to make the reader aware that the final evaluation of German law requires much subtlety.

[102] For instance in BVerfGE 36, 1, 14, where the Court had to review the 1972 Treaty between West and East Germany which, for the first time, recognised the East as an independent state. The Treaty, challenged on the grounds that it contravened the provisions of the Constitution which envisaged the reunification of Germany (which in fact occurred in 1990), was upheld by the Court but not without provoking a political storm and a flood of academic literature, much of it critical. See. for instance. Kriele, "Recht und Politik in der Verfassungsrechtsprechung", *NJW* 1976, 777.

6. REFINING THE *LÜTH* JUDGMENT

It will have been noticed that all of the above cases (including *Lüth*) concerned situations where individuals faced a situation they had, from the outset, not wished to get into: unborn babies do not, presumably, wish to be aborted; the farmer at *Kalkar* would not, himself, have wished to build any potentially dangerous installation in his vicinity; *Schleyer* was abducted and held to ransom against his will; *Lüth* was, arguably, anxious to provoke some reaction to Harlan's re-emergence on the public scene, but not eager to be dragged to court over his warning against this event. The bulk of everyday legal relationships, however, consists of contractual relationships. These involve at least some voluntary element on behalf of the parties. It was to that paradigm that the *BVerfG* turned its attention in the *Handelsvertreter* case[103] in which the justices, for the first time since *Lüth*, had occasion to reflect on the doctrinal foundations of the question of horizontal effect and to re-address the basic issue of constitutional "interference" with the decisions of the ordinary courts.

The defendant of the action in the ordinary courts had from 1977 to the end of 1979 worked as a (freelance) commercial agent of the plaintiff, a wine company. In November 1979 he terminated his contractual relationship (freelancers and commercial agents are not employees covered by the usual protective labour laws) because he had found a better-paid post. The plaintiff, however, offered him improved conditions so the defendant withdrew his resignation only a week after he had tendered it. Nevertheless, in the course of the following January, he also took up the new post with another company.[104] When this came to the attention of the plaintiff, the latter terminated the contract with immediate effect.

So far, the case seems usual enough. Complications, however, arose from a restraint of trade clause which the two parties had included in their contractual agreement. Such agreements are governed by § 90a of the Commercial Code (*Handelsgesetzbuch* or HGB).[105] In accordance with this

[103] BVerfGE 81, 242 (Commercial agent), (Feb. 1990).

[104] Again, due to his status as a freelancer, he hoped this would go unnoticed.

[105] The provision reads as follows:

"(1) An agreement which restricts the commercial agent in the pursuit of his trade after the termination of the contractual relationship (agreement on competition) . . . may not be concluded for longer than two years from the termination of the contractual relationship. The contractor is obliged to pay the commercial agent a reasonable compensation for the period of restriction of competition.

(2) The principal may waive in writing the restriction of competition before the termination of the contractual relationship, so that upon the expiration of six months following the declaration he is discharged from the obligation to pay compensation. *If the principal terminates the contractual relationship for serious cause owing to the culpable conduct of the commercial agent, the latter is not entitled to compensation* [our italics].

(3) If the commercial agent terminates the contractual relationship for serious cause owing to the culpable conduct of the principal, he may denounce the agreement on competition . . .

provision, the parties had agreed that for two years after the termination of the contractual relationship the defendant would be barred from working in any capacity for any competitor of the plaintiff. Furthermore, in the event that culpable behaviour on the part of the defendant brought about the termination of the contract, the parties had agreed that the defendant would not be entitled to any compensation. Accordingly, the plaintiff sued the defendant seeking an order restraining him from any competition.

The *Bundesgerichtshof* held that the agreement on competition was valid. As a self-employed and professionally and economically independent merchant[106] the defendant had been free to weigh the risks and advantages of the contract as a whole. He was, therefore, bound by the agreement on competition.

The defendant thought this decision violated several of his basic rights. In reality, he argued, he had had no choice but to accept the contract he had been offered. The agreement constrained him unduly as it deprived him of all income; being self employed, he was also not entitled to any unemployment benefits. He argued that § 90a HGB was unconstitutional as it provided, in sub-paragraphs 2 and 3, utterly divergent sanctions depending upon whose conduct had caused the contract to be terminated.

The *BVerfG* began by pointing out that the defendant had consented to the contract. To be sure, by doing so he had limited his professional freedom; nevertheless, that was but one possible exercise of this freedom. In principle, the state had to respect the autonomous arrangements made by private parties. Citing *Lüth*, however, the court pointed out that private autonomy was only granted within the confines of the law; ordinary law had, in its turn, to respect basic rights.[107]

Some constitutional constraint was necessary as private autonomy was based on self-determination. The latter, however, pre-supposed certain conditions which were not fulfilled where one side was so dominant as to be able to dictate to the other the terms of a contract. If, as a result of such circumstances, the weaker party had agreed to limit his freedom, the law was obliged to restore the parity and ensure that basic rights were protected. This would only help realise the fundamental decisions (*objektive Grundentscheidungen*) of the Constitution, as embodied in the chapter on human rights. To be sure, when enacting such protective norms, the legislature enjoyed an especially wide margin of discretion. In particular, it was free to provide for typical cases only. However, it was also obliged to take into consideration the fact that protection for one side meant curtailing the freedoms of the other. The competing concerns had to be balanced, again

(4) Agreements providing otherwise, which are disadvantageous to the commercial agent, may not be concluded."

[106] Which is what commercial agents are according to the HGB.

[107] BVerfGE 81, 242 at 254.

within a wide margin of discretion. Where there were no specific norms governing the situation, the general clauses of the Civil Code applied and the task of discharging the protective duty shifted to the judge.[108]

Applying these general considerations, the *BVerfG* acknowledged that often the commercial agent had but little negotiating clout. This was especially true for those working for one principal only. The latter had, on the other hand, a legitimate interest to prevent competition from his former agents. § 90a (1) HGB was designed to regulate this conflict. Thus para. (4) was designed to prevent circumventions of the general rule while para. (2), 1st sentence, dealt with exceptions to these principles. Thus, the validity of the agreement between the parties depended on the constitutionality of § 90a (2), 2nd sentence. The legislature had not overstepped its discretion when it assumed that commercial agents generally needed protection. In this sense, the granting of compensation was disproportionate neither with regard to the freedoms of the principal (which were reined in) nor to the degree of protection needed by the agent. The exception contained in § 90a (2), 2nd sentence HGB, however, was disproportionate given its generality and maximum duration, particularly since § 628 (2) BGB[109] granted the principal damages in such cases. The legislature either had to allow for differentiations through a general clause or it had to create differentiated provisions.[110] As the provision was, therefore, unconstitutional, the agreement based on it collapsed and the case was referred back to the court of second instance for re-determination. The arguments employed by the *BVerfG* are in accordance with what has been decided by earlier case-law: the agreement on competition as such is not to be gauged against the basic rights of the parties as they are not directly bound by each other's human rights. The commercial agent, however, needs protection because the agreement is apt to take away his livelihood by depriving him of his job for two years while also depriving him of the protection offered by the welfare state (objective side of his freedom of occupation, Article 12 GG). The state is, therefore, under a duty to protect him. The legislature has wide discretion how to do so: it had for this purpose inserted a special provision in the Commercial Code.

This provision—not the agreement based upon it—should then be assessed in the light of the basic rights of the parties. Such an examination leads to the conclusion that the provisions of § 90a (1), (2), first sentence, (3), and (4) HGB live up to the requirements of the typical situation. They

[108] BVerfGE 81, 242 at 255, 256.

[109] It reads: "If the notice [of termination of a contract of service by the principal] is occasioned by the conduct of the other party in breach of the contract, the other party is bound to make compensation for *any* [our italics] damage arising from the termination of the service relationship": commercial disadvantages can, therefore, not justify denying all compensation from the agent.

[110] BVerfGE 80, 242 at 260–2.

ensure a livelihood for the agent: if he can do better in another job, he can renounce the agreement, thereby losing the compensation accorded by para. (3), and so can the principal, thereby ridding himself of the obligation to pay much to an agent whose competition he does not fear: para. (2), first sentence. Any other arrangements, however, operating to the detriment of the agent, are invalid pursuant to para. (4). Thus, these provisions also respect the concerns of the other party (subjective side of the principal's right to property and professional freedom, Articles 14 and 12 *GG*).

The same cannot be said of § 90a (2), 2nd sentence HGB. The principal's rights are still not infringed (his burdens are even alleviated); but the exception makes the whole provision fall below the minimum standard of protection owed to the agent (objective side of his freedom of occupation). The offending provision removed, parity is restored and the case can be retried on a constitutionally sound legal basis. Ideally, the *Bundesgerichtshof* should have listened to the defendant's arguments about the unconstitutionality of § 90a (2), 2nd sentence HGB and, under Article 100 (1) *GG*, asked the *BVerfG* to rule on this question before deciding the dispute.

The decision is remarkable in that it brings together the various developments in the doctrine of protective duties and applies them in a coherent way. It does not supersede *Lüth:* where there are no specific, protective provisions the general clauses still serve as "in-roads" for human rights to permeate private law; and the case where not even these clauses help is not even mentioned. Even so, the test to be applied is laid out much more clearly. Above all, the competences of the legislature, ordinary judiciary, and Constitutional Court are now, in principle, much more sharply defined. The reservation is apt, since in the absence of special provisions, the ordinary courts still play the role assigned to them in *Lüth*. Hand in hand with this goes some uncertainty about the standards the *BVerfG* applies when checking the courts' judgments as to whether they have adequately heeded the human rights of the parties. To this problem we will now turn.

7. NO "SUPER-REVISION"—BUT (IN SOME INSTANCES) SOMETHING WHICH COMES QUITE CLOSE

(a) Understandable interventions

It must be clear by now that though in *Lüth* the *BVerfG* held that it was its task to check whether the courts had acknowledged and correctly assessed the influence of human rights on private law it had also tried to set limits to this role. The cases we have examined show that, on the whole, the *BVerfG* is slow to intervene with a decision of the legislature, the administration, or the courts unless they have shown a serious misunderstanding of the human rights position. Such reluctance has been particularly pronounced in the area of the state's protective duties—something which has even led eminent American comparatists to observe that "in practice [the] differences between the two countries in respect to positive duties should not be exaggerated."[111] This observation should not, however, be overstressed. For, though the German Consitutional court has stuck to its moderate view with a fair measure of consistency, it has not given up its right to intervene and review decisions of other organs of the state where the circumstances demand this. In this sub-section we shall thus mention a few instances where such intervention strikes us as reasonable while in the next sub-section we shall look at some recent examples of constitutional review which, in the eyes of many commentators both in Germany and abroad, seem to have gone too far.

That the deference was never meant to be seen as total submission can be seen from the "Expert Witness" decision of 1978. The decision was concerned with the case-law of the *Bundesgerichtshof* dealing with false testimony given by expert witnesses. According to a long-standing case-law of the BGH such witnesses were only liable to compensation when they had *intentionally* given false testimony and, as a result, some person had suffered damage. This case-law thus gave considerable protection to expert witnesses. Under § 823 (1) BGB[112] (the general clause of the German law of torts), negligence is sufficient for a person to incur civil liability provided the other requirements of this paragraph are also satisfied. The *Bundesgerichtshof* purported to protect expert witnesses in their capacity as aides to the judge since the witnesses were effectively seen as fulfilling a civic duty. Additionally, the *Bundesgerichtshof* was also anxious to encourage legal certainty: cases might have to be retried more often if it were easy to challenge the validity of crucial evidence.

Yet this reasoning could also lead to grave injustice as the facts of the instant case plainly demonstrated. For the person who lodged this constitutional complaint had been placed for several weeks in an institution for the mentally ill because an expert witness had *negligently* found him mentally disturbed. The applicant alleged that his general right to his personality as well as his personal freedom had been violated by the decision which flowed from this testimony. He did, however, find himself barred from obtaining any compensation as a consequence of the case-law of the *Bundesgerichtshof* to which reference has already been made. This, the *BVerfG* held, ignored that provisions such as § 823 1 BGB on compensation for violations of the right to one's personality and of personal liberty, fleshed

[111] Currie, *op.cit.* (n. 71 above), 16.

[112] It reads: "A person who, *wilfully or negligently* [our italics], unlawfully injures the life, body, health, freedom, property or other right of another is bound to compensate him for any damage arising therefrom." For an extensive review of this provision. see Markesinis, *op.cit.* (n. 24 above), ch. 2.

out Article 2 (2), 2nd sentence *GG*.[113] To be sure, the legislature had some discretion how to translate its protective duties into provisions of private law. In particular, it could discharge these by providing sanctions on violations. Though the courts had a task to develop and, where necessary, supplement the law with their own case-law, the discretion of the legislature could not be pre-empted by them. Provisions on sanctions could, therefore, not be waived with regard to certain persons, whatever the motives for doing so, without thereby violating of Article 2 (2) *GG*.[114] On this occasion, therefore, the case-law of the *Bundesgerichtshof* was condemned as unconstitutional.

A 1995 decision of the *BVerfG* offers another illustration. There the court was asked to consider the following problem.[115] The applicant, a works counsellor, had distributed in his workplace information leaflets which came from his trade union. For this, his employer formally reprimanded him. The applicant desired that the reprimand be deleted from his personal record but his efforts to achieve this result failed before all three instances of the ordinary (labour) courts. The *BArbG* in particular had held that the activity of distributing leaflets did not come under the guarantee of the freedom of association according to Article 9 (3) *GG* even though recruiting new members did. To allow such a distribution to take place would either require a statutory rule or an industry-wide agreement to this effect. Neither of these, however, existed. While re-affirming the principle that it was for the ordinary courts to interpret the contract of employment,[116] the *BVerG* disagreed with the *BArbG*. The Labour court's reading of Article 9 (3) was in this instance found to have been too narrow and its decision was, in the event, quashed. The consitutional intervention was justified only because the judgment of the ordinary court had shown a serious misunderstanding of the human rights aspect of the case.

Another case—the Adoption case[117]—shows how subjective rights and objective principles blend when both concepts come into play in a given case. The question there was whether it was sufficent to show that there was a high likelihood that a child would *not* suffer from the severance of its links with its biological family before it could be placed in an adoptive family. The court held that in this context absolute certainty was not required; a high likelihood to that effect was enough. Family matters such as adoption, despite the (intense) involvement of the authorities, are governed by private law. It was, if anyone, the biological parents who had failed

[113] This and the following sentence read: "Personal freedom is inviolable. [This right] may not be encroached upon save pursuant to a law."

[114] BVerfGE 49, 304 (Expert witnesses) at 319, 320 (Oct. 1978).

[115] BVerfGE 93, 352 (Trade union promotion) at 360, 361.

[116] In the light of the general clauses of the law of obligations and by taking into consideration the influence of basic rights on the latter.

[117] BVerfGE 75, 201 (Adoption) (April 1987).

in their parental role (rather than the adoptive parents who took the child into their family) and brought about the child's suffering. The authorities merely ascertained that the biological family provided no adequate home and that the adoptive family was capable of doing so. Their role was, therefore, essentially a protective one.

This general point was brought home even more clearly in a case concerning § 611a BGB.[118] A female fitter, who had applied for an advertised post, failed to be hired. The job went, instead, to a male fitter, supposedly because it was physically too demanding for a woman. The *BVerfG* pointed out that its scrutiny was not limited to situations where the defensive side of human rights came into play. When the ordinary courts had to interpret and apply provisions meant to discharge protective duties, the *BVerfG* checked whether they had fundamentally failed to implement the protective aim of the provision. This aim was delineated by the basic right.[119] Such a violation had, indeed, occurred since the woman was turned down on the basis that the man hired had longer working experience—a criterion which operates against women with regard to traditionally male occupations. Indirect discrimination had, therefore, taken place. The case shows, *inter alia*, how the formula devised in the patent case (discussed above) works in cases concerned with the "protective" aspect of human rights. For when giving effect to this, the courts have the same discretionary powers which they have when weighing the competing concerns which exist in "defensive" actions.

Cases such as these, especially if combined with some of the earlier ones discussed above, show that the standards of the Consitutional Court are not rigidly fixed. Rather, they evince a kind of sliding scale which leaves the *BVerfG* some leeway, enabling it to take account of the peculiar features of each situation.[120] Thus, the more a judgment encroaches upon basic rights, the more thorough the constitutional check will be,[121] regardless of whether the matter is governed by private or criminal law.[122] Where concerns of paramount importance are involved, even small flaws in the interpretation of statutory law will not escape the scrutiny of the *BVerfG*.[123] This certainly seems to have become the case with a wide variety of cases which have one thing in common: they all deal with different aspects of speech. These decisions, however, have been very controversial so they justify a heading of their own.

[118] This rather lengthy provision is (predominantly) aimed at protecting women against discrimination by their employer (or would-be employer in case the person concerned is denied employment on discriminatory grounds). It shifts the burden of proof to the employer (para. (1)) and grants the person compensation if the employer fails to establish that no discrimination has occurred (para. (2)).

[119] BVerfGE 89, 276 (Female fitter) at 286 (Nov. 1993).

[120] BVerfGE 75, 201 (Adoption) at 221 (Apr. 1987).

[121] BVerfGE 61, 1 (*NPD Europas*') at 6 (June 1982).

[122] BVerfGE 86, 1 ("*Cripple b. Murderer*") at 10 (Mar. 1992).

[123] BVerfGE 79, 51 (Adoption) at 63 (Oct. 1988).

(a) A step too far?

The change began to manifest itself in the attitude of the Constitutional Court in the mid/late 1980s; and in this case-law we find the court going beyond previous pronouncements and checking even the finding of the facts by the ordinary courts. More precisely, the Constitutional Court began to ask itself whether the ordinary court had ascertained the content and circumstances of an expression in a way adequate to the basic right.[124] The *BVerfG* thus came to check in full whether the demands of Article 5 (1) *GG* on the interpretation of an expression have been met, especially in the case of criminal conviction for defamation.[125]

At the stage of interpreting the norms to be applied, Article 5 (1) *GG* thus requires, on the one hand a balancing of the importance of free speech and, on the other, the countervailing value in whose interest free speech is being curtailed. At the stage of applying the law thus interpreted to a given case, Article 5 (1) *GG* calls for a weighing of the detractions suffered by personal honour and free speech respectively. Since all circumstances of the case have to be taken into consideration, the result of such weighing is not predictable in advance.[126] What is crucial is neither the intention of the person issuing the statement nor the understanding of the person who sees himself as being thereby affected. What counts, instead, is the understanding of a sensible and unprejudiced public. The wording of (the whole of) the expression is, in this respect, not the definitive yardstick; its external circumstances also have to be taken into account.[127] The latter serves to ascertain the meaning of a statement.

The next (still preliminary) step is to subsume the statement under the terms of the law. Whether an expression made in public (*öffentliche*), contains value judgments (*Werturteil*), or asserts facts (*Tatsachenbehauptung*), will determine to what extent it comes within the ambit of the right of free speech as well as the degree of protection that it receives, for, in German law, facts are sacred while opinion remains free. Which category the statement comes under is also important when free speech has to be balanced against other values protected by the Constitution. The *BVerfG*, therefore, checks the categorisation of the facts made by the ordinary court to ensure that the judgment of the ordinary court does not have a deterrent effect, suppressing admissible criticism. In order to assess an expression correctly, the ordinary court has to grasp its proper meaning. If it fails to do so, especially when imposing a criminal sentence for the expression, its decision

[124] Just as an aside it may be noticed how little is left of the assertion by the court that it was no instance of super-revision: fact finding is distinctly the task of the lower instances.

[125] BVerfGE 93, 266 ("Soldiers are Murderers" II) at 296 (Oct. 1995).

[126] *Ibid.*, 292, 293. 27.

[127] *Ibid.*, 295.

will be reviewed and, probably, overturned for this is exactly what Article 5 (1) *GG* is designed to avoid. Moreover, such suppression would have a deterrent effect on others who share the opinion but see themselves barred from expressing it with impunity.

For this reason, the right to free speech not only informs the interpretation of laws curtailing it, but also guides the interpretation of expressions. Where various interpretations are conceivable, the courts may not suppose a punishable meaning without having before ruled out other alternatives with convincing reasons. In this respect, an expression must not be isolated from its context where the latter helps define its true sense.[128] These considerations, too, are checked in full by the *BVerfG*. It does not, however, decide the case on its own. This remains the task of the ordinary court[129]—though just how much of a task is left for the ordinary court to perform *after* the above review has taken place is open to question!

Of the many cases which illustrate this speech-protective way of reasoning two can serve as illustrations, for they apply this reasoning to the full.

The first is known as the *Stern-Strauss* case.[130] In that case, Ralph Giordano, a prominent Jewish writer and survivor of a concentration camp, gave an interview to the magazine *Stern* on the occasion of the death of Rudolph Hess. In it he stated that some German politicans were "opportunistic democrats" (*Zwangsdemokraten*). By this he meant that they had adopted democratic ideals by force of circumstance even though their own preference was for more authoritarian ways of running things. Giordano regarded Franz Josef Strauss, then Minister President of Bavaria, as "a personification of this type of politician", though he also added that he was anxious to "depersonalise" his comments which he intended to refer to a type of person who was active in contemporary Germany and existed because of the "as yet un-resolved German yearning for a strong man . . . coupled with the Nation's leader-cult mania (*Führerkult*)".[131] Such characters, in Giordano's view, represented a danger to German democracy. Strauss sued for libel and the lower courts accepted his claim and forbade the further use of his name to personify the term "opportunisitic democrat". The Constitutional Court first referred to *Lüth* and the "reciprocal effect theory" in order to justify its review of how the "general law"—here the criminal law of defamation—could, in accordance with Article 5 (1) *GG*, be allowed to curtail the freedom of speech. In carrying out this evaluative process, reasoned the court, one should not forget the importance

[128] The dissenting opinion on "Soldiers are Murderers" (No. 2) pointed out that it could not be expected that the ordinary courts would have followed up on each and every interpretation the *BVerfG* later found conceivable. BVerfGE 93, 266 diss. op. at 315 (Oct. 1995).

[129] BVerfGE 94, 1 (*Deutsche Gesellschaft für humanes Sterben*) at 8, 9 (Feb. 1996).

[130] BVerfGE 82, 272 (1990).

[131] BVerfGE 82, 272, 273–4.

that speech played in public debate. If the process of formation of public opinion were to remain unfettered, even "exaggerated and polemical" speech should be tolerated. The court was thus anxious to examine whether the ordinary court had properly characterised the meaning of communication and had fully explained its decision in accordance with the reasoning process described above. In its view, this had not occurred, the ordinary court plumping instead for the worst possible interpretation of Giordano's speech instead of seeing it as a contribution, sharp but none the less permissible, to the debate of wider issues relevant to contemporary Germany. For this reason, the Constitutional Court felt it had no option but to quash the decision of the ordinary court and, in so doing, it essentially redefined the law of defamation in the context of political debate.

The National Anthem case[132] is one of two decisions[133] involving desecration of national symbols which has proved just as controversial. The constitutional appeal was launched after the applicant was condemned by the ordinary courts for violation of the criminal law[134] for having ridiculed the National Anthem in a poem which became known as the *Deutschlandlied 1986*. The poem, written in a rhythm that roughly followed that of the original poem, parodied the first two stanzas by describing the Federal Republic as a country where brutal force and primitive sexuality prevailed. For good measure, it also added that the poem should be recited in suitable circumstances such as "when having a crap or before a fuck".

The Constitutional Court quashed the lower judgments on the grounds that they had not approached the constitutional issues raised by the case in the right way. The poem, said the Court, reflected the author's views about "everyday experiences in Germany". Since quality was not an essentail criterion for satisfying the term "art", it could be treated as a work of art in a legal sense, attracting the protection of Article 5 (3) GG. The question then was whether the judge of the ordinary court had interpreted it adequately (*werkgerechte Interpretation*). To be sure, it was a satirical poem which, at first sight, represented a "wild concoction of negative and offensive expressions"; but there was more to the poem than that. In the court's view, the author had tried to convey the view that there was a great gap between constitutional ideals and everyday life in Germany. By using the

[132] BVerfGE 81, 299 (1990).

[133] The other, BVerfGE 81, 278 (1990), involved a photo-collage ridiculing the national flag. The case is discussed by Markesinis, "Privacy, Freedom of Expression, and the Horizontal Application of the Bill of Rights", 1999 *LQR* (forthcoming) and, in more detail by Quint, "The Comparative Law of Flag Desecration: The United States and the Federal Republic of Germany", 15 *Hastings Intern. and Comp. L. Rev. 613* (1992).

[134] Paragraph 90a of the German Criminal Code punishes with imprisonement or a fine anyone who publicly "defames the colours, the flag, the coat of arms or the anthem of the Federal Republic".

metre of the original and by echoing its phonetics,[135] the idealisation of the original had been turned into the exact opposite. By opting for the worst possible interpretation of the words, the ordinary court had failed to inquire whether, through the realistic depiction of the cruelties of life, the poem had not, in fact, brought out more clearly the ideals of the original. No case had thus really been made out in favour of the view that the anthem had been desecrated; and in the absence of such evidence, the *BVerfG* could not consider whether there were any countervailing constitutional values capable of limiting the freedom of artistic expression. The decision of the ordinary court was thus quashed.

8. APPRAISING FROM AFAR: SOME TENTATIVE CONCLUSIONS

Any summary of such a complicated area of (foreign) law is bound to be crass; it also runs the risk of being misleading through over-simplification. Yet, as already stated, German law seems to have considered many of the points which will become relevant to English law as well, after the enactment of our Human Rights Bill. Someone thus has to make a start in explaining German law to British lawyers and suggesting why and how they stand to learn from its longer experience with some of these issues and its well-known ability for theoretical analysis. This essay does not pretend to be doing anything more than that. The remaining part of it will therefore try to assess whether the type of horizontality adopted by German law and the limits imposed upon it in practice have actually worked.[136] In particular, we shall try to evaluate the criteria developed by German courts that determine the limits of constitutional review. It must be admitted straightaway that such a critical assessment is not easy.

Four broad objections may thus be raised against the current attempts to delimit the role played by the constitutional and ordinary courts.

First is the resulting uncertainty. The combined scrutiny of applicability (constitutionality of the law applied) and application (compatibility with the basic right of the method of arriving at the judgment), as enunciated in the Patent case discussed earlier, coupled with the sliding scale of the thoroughness of the review exercised by the *BVerfG* can, at times, make the

[135] The original was composed by August Heinrich Hoffmann better known as Hoffmann von Fallersleben in 1840–1 and became known as *Das Lied der Deutschen.* Its beautiful music, composed by Haydn for the Austrian Emperor Franz Josef (and known as the theme in the second movement of the String Quartet in C major Opus 76.3), predates the poem by about 43 years. The poem's third (and French-inspired) verse remains (since 1952) Germany's National Anthem while the first verse, with the misunderstood words "Deutschland über Alles", no longer forms part of the Anthem because of its association with the Nazi regime.

[136] Whether it is transplantable into our own system is discussed by Markesinis, *op.cit.* (n. 1 above).

results of this scrutiny unpredictable. One would have thought that where the applicable law raises some concerns but is not obviously unconstitutional, this should lead to a restrictive interpretation and application of constitutional intervention. To what extent such a constitutional intervention is necessary depends on the gravity of the concerns the *BVerfG* entertains about the law. However, this gravity and its causes are not always predictable *to the judge hearing the case before it reaches the constitutional court* by way of a constitutional complaint (which, as we know, requires the prior exhaustion of all available judicial remedies). That must contribute to the overall uncertainty which cannot be welcome either to litigants or to the law in general.

Secondly, there is the onerous task that the current procedure places on the shoulders of lower courts. For even supposing a puny judge has doubts about the applicability of constitutional principles to his case, he lacks the time and the sophistication to include in his judgment the kind of learned excursus into constitutional law which the Constitutional Court seems to expect of him.[137] Thus, the chances are that he will, in all probability, proceed to decide the case without any sophisticated reference to the constitutional material. He is therefore unlikely to be explicit about his doubts or, if they did exist, in which way and to what extent they influenced his interpretation of the law and led him to restrict its application out of deference to human rights law. By failing to do so, however, he runs the risk of showing that he was not "sensitive" enough to the significance of human rights for the case of the losing party. It would then be up to the Constitutional Court to decide whether or not to uphold his judgment. It would, in any case, be impossible to pin down the limits of what was tolerable and what was not: the criteria of each stage in the assessment are imprecise from the outset (as, to some extent, they must be); and their influence on each other creates even more uncertainty.

Thirdly, the current process does not seem to reflect adequately the different backgrounds and talents possessed by the different judges who may become involved in one and the same dispute or, indeed, the differences (sometimes significant) in constitutional and ordinary statutory interpretation.[138] For even if—a big if—the tests under constitutional law were subject

[137] What is required in this respect can be seen from a judgment on landlord/tenant law representative of many similar judgments. When applying the BGB's provision on the justified interest of the lessor in the notice of termination (§ 564b), the *BVerfG* held, the ordinary courts have to take into consideration the guarantee of property for both landlord and tenant. They have to bring to life (*nachvollziehen*) the legislature's balancing of these interests and avoid excessive burdens on either side; BVerfGE 89, 1 (Tenancy as property) at 9 (May 1993)—no small beer for the judges sitting on their own in local courts hearing hundreds of cases a year.

[138] The literature is vast, but see Ernst-Wolfgang Böckenförde, "Die Methoden der Verfassungsinterpretation-Bestandsaufnahme und Kritik", *NJW* 1976, 2089*ff*. See also, Gust, *Parlamentarischer Gesetzgeber und Bundesverfassungsgericht* (1985).

to mathematical precision, the way a particular case may be handled may largely be influenced by who is handling it: a judge of the ordinary jurisdiction or a member of the Constitutional Court. This problem stems from the differences in outlook (in turn caused by the different backgrounds) between the normal judiciary and the members of the Constitutional Court, however blurred these may have become in some instances in recent times. For the judges (and clerks) at the Constitutional Court are not as intensely preoccupied with the doctrinal details of a given area of the law as the ordinary judges seem to be. Of necessity, the former tend to adopt a broad-canvass approach to the various factual situations which come before them. All the judges of the Constitutional Court can do is apply the rather crude instrument of a balancing of conflicting basic rights to single, isolated cases that reach them in a way that must strike some as somewhat haphazard. Thus, they seem to assume the role of the ordinary judge without actually having the means and, at times, the training to fulfill it. It cannot, however, be the task of a Constitutional Court to correct results which it does not like in the style of a parliamentary committee on petitions.[139] On the whole, the judges of the Constitutional Court would probably accept this proposition.

Finally, it could be argued that the predictability of litigation has been further reduced by the recent trend to allow heightened review in cases involving free speech. Summing up the position, therefore, some contemporary critics of the *BVerfG*—especially those who come from a private law background—have taken the view that the crucial question remains to this day without a definitive answer.[140] Quite simply, this question is when and to what extent the judgments of the ordinary courts are open to scrutiny by the *BVerfG*. Since "Spezifisches Verfassungsrecht" is, essentially, a blank formula, one could, once again, voice the concern that the law lacks precision. In this context it might be worth noting that this opaque term tends to be used when the Constitutional Court declines to scrutinise a judgment in some respect or other.[141]

Yet, weighty as these criticisms may be, they do not seem to be conclusive. This feeling is reinforced by the fact that the *status quo*, despite its critics, probably has an even larger number of supporters and, on the whole, seems to have served Germany well for nearly fifty years now. Just as remarkable for our purposes is the fact that, despite the ambiguities mentioned and even stressed in this paper, the constitutionalisation of private law has not got out of control. To put it differently, the adoption of horizontality has not flooded the Court with an unmanageable number of applications. Thus, judging from the nearly 3,000 published decisions

[139] Oeter, "'Drittwirkung' der Grundrechte und die Autonomie des Privatrechts", *AöR* 119 [1994] 529 at 557, 559, 560.

[140] Ossenbühl, "Medien zwischen Macht und Recht", JZ 1995, p. 633.

[141] Ossenbühl, "Medien zwischen Macht und Recht", JZ 1995, pp. 638, 640.

reproduced in the first 96 volumes of the Court's Official Reports we find less than 200 of them arising out of *purely* private law disputes. Stripped of the political emotion understandably generated by some of these decisions, the overall picture may thus be more positive than appears if the doubts expressed in the text (and mainly advanced by critics of the speech cases) are taken too seriously. Why should that be so? We offer four reasons.

First, it is tempting to suggest that uncertainty and unpredictability are, to some extent, endemic in a subject such as the control of constitutionality of the acts of the Administration and the Legislature since the Constitutional Court—indeed, any court placed in its position—has to strike a workable balance between the independent performance of its task and the need not to challenge in an excessive or aggressive manner the competence of the elected legislators or officials. The desire to strike this balance can be seen in the many decisions of the Constitutional Court which, while declaring a statute to be unconstitutional, have either stood back from declaring it void, asked the legislature to reconsider the point at issue, or occasionally, itself, proposed temporary solutions.[142] The fact that the court has, even in such cases, been blamed by one party or the other can only underline the thankless nature of its task!

Secondly, and more closely to the point discussed in this paper, despite its multiple criteria, ponderous phrases, metaphysical terms and, at times, vague tests, the Constitutional Court has stuck to its view that its interventions must be limited and its work not seen as an overview of the work of the ordinary courts. In that sense the measured pronouncements of the *Lüth* judgment have—a number of glaring contrary examples apart—survived the test of time. Just as importantly, this message seems to have reached those who could avail themselves of the services of the Constitutional Court. The relatively small number of judgments which deal with private-law issues supports such a conclusion even though those who have "interfered" with private autonomy have generated a heated debate. It is, perhaps, these more obviously "private law" cases—such as the "surety case"[143]—which have most attracted the wrath of the private-law lawyers,[144] though a Common-law comparatist may be allowed to ask whether, in these instances, the Constitutional Court was really trying to invent ways which would soften the harshenss of "pure private law" more or less as our system of equity mitigated, over the centuries, the rigours of the Common law. All these are, of course, genuinely controversial issues and one is only restating the obvious when one states that it would be utopian to expect academic unanimity as to how they should be handled.

Thirdly, among the case-law one can find many instances where the German courts seem to draw a distinction between the tendency to draw

[142] See, for instance, BVerfGE 33, 303 at 346; 37, 217 at 260–2; 37, 324 at 325.

[143] BVerGE 89, 214.

[144] For instance, Professor Zöllner in *AcP* 196 (1996), 1*ff*.

private individuals into the sphere of obligations created by the various provisions of the *GG* and the substance of the obligation which, in practice, they then tend to dilute. This seems to have happened with the leading decision of the Federal Labour Court which started the modern phase of this entire debate.[145] For there, it will be recalled, while the Court favoured the plaintiff's attempt to consitutionalise his dispute with the defendant, in the end (ingeniously or ingenuously) decided the case against him. Both the decision and its result thus deserve to be compared with and contrasted to the American case of *Novosel* v. *Nationwide Insurance Company*[146] where the opposite result was reached in factual circumstances which are very similar to those of the leading German case. For those of us who have been arguing for a long time for the desirability of teaching comparative law through parallel cases, this "similarity" is neither surprising nor unwelcome. Yet what really is interesting about this American decision is its key motivation, which can be found in the Court's assertion that "The protection of important political freedoms . . . goes well beyond the question whether the threat comes from state or private bodies."[147] For comparative lawyers the significance of decisions such as the above—and this is by no means an isolated instance—is twofold. First, they show that though American law does not *appear* to recognise a horizontal effect of Constitutional rights beyond the rather narrow confines of *Shelley* v. *Kraemer*,[148] in practice it is often very similar[149] to German law in that it duplicates if not, indeed, goes beyond the latter's actual results. Secondly, as the first of us has explained elsewhere,[150] this undiscovered and often underplayed similarity between two apparently very different systems means that the transplantability of ideas from one to the other is far from impossible provided the proper precautions are taken to understand and handle particular rules within their wider socio-political context.

Finally, notwithstanding the criticisms voiced above, the net result has given Germany impeccable democratic credentials in the period since the end of the Second World War. This is certainly true of the speech cases which, despite their undoubted controversial aspects, have managed to accord speech rights protection levels similar to those found in the United States while also protecting personality and privacy rights in a way which

[145] BArbGE 1, 185, discussed above in section 2 (b).

[146] 721 F.2d 894—the United States Court of Appeal for the Third Circuit upholding Plaintiffs complaint for unlawful dismissal against his (private) employer because he refused to support the latter's lobbying efforts and had privately stated his opposition to the company's political stand.

[147] 721 F.2d 894, at 899.

[148] 334 U.S. 1 (1948).

[149] The first of us had made this point in a number of articles, most recently in "The Familiarity of the Unknown", *Liber Amicorum Robert Goff* to be published by Oxford University Press in 1999.

[150] See n. 1 above.

American law has not managed to do. This could be seen as achieving the best of both worlds and should thus not pass unnoticed, especially in Britain where concern has been voiced about the effect that increased privacy protection could have on speech rights. The German experience would appear to dispel completely this fear.

The overall conclusion may well be that we are here faced with a complex and controversial part of the law where human efforts can never achieve a perfect result, but one which German lawyers have managed to approximate to a satisfactory degree. What lessons this experience may hold for English lawyers is another and more complex issue. Clearly, they will be discovered if we try to understand what the German courts are trying to do rather than just try to translate their terms or transplant their concepts and theories. In this context one must re-emphasise one of the major concerns of modern German law: how to protect human rights against intrusions which are no less serious for not emanating from the state itself. Nipperdey in Germany (and some twenty years later Rivero in France) fully appreciated this danger. With few exceptions. one does not find a similar awareness in this country on the eve of the enactment of our Human Rights Bill. Sooner or later the horizontality of this document will thus become an issue in our country as well. We shall be able to handle it more effectively if we have done our homework better and studied how our neighbours solved problems which are common to us all.

9

Tortious Liability of Statutory Bodies

I. A FIRST LOOK AT THE FIVE CASES AND THE PROBLEMS THEY RAISE

1. Introductory comments

One does not have to be either an advanced or sophisticated lawyer to appreciate the importance of our subject; but it might not be out of place to remind the reader of its complexities and how we tried to confront them. These stem from factors which one could describe as both philosophical and methodological. The philosophical factors ultimately turn round the model of justice one thinks most suited for the law of torts—corrective or distributive—and the way these starting points inevitably colour one's feelings that the contemporary law of torts is either becoming too mean or too generous. One can debate this to eternity; but, like most philosophical issues, it is, we feel, incapable of a definitive answer.

The methodological problems are easier to explain, although again, not subject to one, obvious solution. Here are some reasons for this statement.

First is the fact that our subject straddles tort law and administrative law and, thus, when one is proposing solutions, one must bear in mind constantly the different philosophies, type of remedies and procedures that obtain in these two branches of the law. Secondly, and more controversially, this is one (of the many) areas of tort law that could benefit from both conceptual and empirical studies concerning the economic and insurance consequences of imposition of liability. That such studies are rare cannot be doubted (although the gap is slowly being filled, especially in the common law world). More regrettable, however, is the fact that for many traditional lawyers and, more so for judges, the desirability of adopting such an approach has not yet been proved beyond all reasonable doubt. Our view on this particular point is that some British judges have attempted such analyses, but in a manner that strikes us as being essentially intuitive. Continental courts are, if anything, even further behind ours in this respect (although this observation is subject to what we say below about German academic literature). We welcome the growing use of economics in the English courts and recognise that, since this development is still in its infancy, there is bound to be some degree of experimentation in the way the courts use this type of material. However, we will argue below that the courts should be aiming for a more principled approach to economic reasoning and to the assessment of economic evidence. Finally, one must note the added complexity introduced by our wish to discuss our subject in a comparative manner. Such a dimension is, we feel, essential if we are to assert, as we do in this book, two things: first, that English law is not only in an unsatisfactory state but is also set on a course of conflict with the law coming out of Strasbourg; and secondly, that the ideas and experience of French and German law which, arguably, lie at the heart of the Strasbourg approach, suggest that the liberalisation of the tort rules that Strasbourg might provoke will not entail catastrophic consequences in any economic or practical sense.

The need to add a comparative aspect to our study does not blind us to the dangers that come with any compressed presentation of foreign law and the ease with which this can (unintentionally) lead to distortions. On the contrary, because we are conscious of these dangers, we have tried to overcome these methodological difficulties by concentrating on five specific factual configurations which are not only important in daily litigation practice but have also revealed exact parallels in our three models: the English, the French and the German. This focused approach inevitably underplays (but does not ignore) other important features (e.g. level of damages, procedural devices) that affect the broader picture. To that extent our study can only, and with caution, support any wider theory about tort liability of public bodies in general. But legal theories, like buildings, are not constructed in one fell swoop but are the result of the careful positioning of one stone after the other in a fairly planned way. Thus, to change metaphors, we are confident that if the seeds of our research take root, and more colleagues—practising or academic—look at how different legal systems have coped with similar factual situations, more elaborate and differentiated products can eventually grow out of such efforts. This, then, is as much an essay on comparative methodology as it is a critique of the solutions adopted by English law.

It is also with methodology that we wish to close this section of preliminary observations. In this book, what will be particularly criticised is not so much the actual result reached by our courts in the five instances we have selected for discussion—although we readily confess our dislike of it—but the growing tendency to exclude liability through the utilisation of the notion of "duty of care". This concept, which has no real parallel in any of the modern civil law systems, is exceptionally vague and blunt. Its vagueness can either be used to conceal all meaningful discussion of the policy arguments that underlie these disputes or, conversely, turn the judicial process into an open-ended and unsubstantiated debate over value judgments. Either way, it seems to be encouraging our courts to impose, in practice if not in theory, blanket immunities, effectively preventing future litigants from asserting that the facts of their dispute justify a different legal outcome. For a long time English law has tolerated this essentially "unjust" result in the interests of what one could broadly describe as "administrative convenience". The growing constitutionalisation of private law, especially through the medium of human rights legislation, and the need for growing accountability, may, however, be about to defeat this peculiarity of English law. Not everyone will weep for the possible demise of a notion of duty of care which, fifty years ago, one great jurist[1] called the "fifth wheel of the coach" and which, nowadays, at least one contemporary specialist[2] has openly condemned as a superfluous cause of confusion. But if that occurs—a big "if" at present—it will have been facilitated by influences which emanate from outside the area of private law and, more interestingly, outside the state boundaries of the English legal system. This line of thought will bring us back to our starting point about the overlap of public and private law—this time in the form of mutual interaction. But it will also place us within the realm of comparative law as we discover yet another pressure point for the growing convergence of the common and civil law systems. The last section of this book may thus, contrary to what was said earlier, justify some observations that extend beyond the specific facts of our five factual configurations.

2. Tort law and economic analysis: some general considerations

This work is not only comparative in nature. We thus also make use of the techniques of economic analysis to throw light on the legal issues under discussion. Since such an approach to law is not widely recognised in our three models, it might be useful, at the outset, to clarify some issues relating to the use of economics in legal scholarship. This is the aim of this section.

Economic analysis can be used in a number of ways to help us understand and evaluate decisions of the courts in relation to the tort of negligence. "Positive" economic analysis aims to identify the economic purpose and function of rules of legal liability, and to predict possible effects of changes in those rules. This is done, initially, by making certain behavioural assumptions about the responses of individual actors to rules of law. Individuals are assumed to act "rationally" in response to legal rules in much the same way as participants in market transactions respond to changes in

[1] Buckland, "The Duty to Take Care" (1935) 51 *LQR* 637.
[2] Hepple, "Negligence: The Search for Coherence" (1997) 50 *Current Legal Problems* 69*ff*.

prices. Legal rules, like prices, send signals about the likely consequences of behaviour, to which the parties are assumed to be capable of adjusting. By affecting the costs and benefits, which attach to conduct of particular kinds, liability rules can influence both the "supply" of and "demand" for certain activities.

The precise nature of the initial assumptions upon which this type of reasoning depends is a matter of some dispute among law and economics scholars, many of whom would reject the notion that individuals always act with perfect rationality in the way that many textbook models of market behaviour imply. This is not the place to enter into this methodological debate;[3] it is sufficient for our purposes to note the claim made by the economic analysis of tort law—namely, that legal rules have behavioural consequences which can be modelled and predicted with varying degrees of confidence depending on the context in question.

"Normative" economic analysis seeks to evaluate legal rules against criteria of economic efficiency. The meaning of "efficiency" needs to be carefully considered in this regard. Essentially, an outcome is said to be economically "efficient" if the *overall wealth or well being* of society is enhanced. The branch of economics known as "welfare economics" has developed a range of sophisticated techniques for determining when this is or is not the case. A first step is to regard the welfare of society as synonymous with the aggregate welfare of its individual members. Situations can then be ranked according to how far a move from one to another involves an increase or decrease in the welfare of the individuals involved. A "Pareto efficient"[4] move is one in which at least one person is made better off and no one is made worse off; a "Pareto-optimal" allocation is a state of affairs in which no further improvements of this kind can be made. A move is "potentially Pareto-efficient"[5] if the resulting allocation of resources increases the aggregate or overall welfare of the group, even if, as a consequence, some individuals are left worse off.

In all this, the notion of "value" used by economists refers to the subjective preferences of individuals as revealed by their conduct and behaviour in situations of bargaining and exchange. Stated slightly differently,

[3] These methodological issues are considered by S Deakin, "Law *versus* Economics? Reflections on the Normative Foundations of Economic Activity", in M Richardson and G Hadfield (eds.), *The Second Wave of Law and Economics* (1999). For a valuable recent overview of the law and economics movement by two of its leading exponents, see L Kaplow and S Shavell, "Economic Analysis of Law", National Bureau of Economic Research Working Paper No. 6960 (1999).

[4] The expression "Pareto-optimal" refers to the origin of this criterion of efficiency in the work of the Italian economist Vilfredo Pareto. For an important discussion of the use of the Pareto criterion in modern law and economics, see G Calabresi, "The Pointlessness of Pareto: Carrying Coase Further" (1991) 100 *Yale Law Journal* 1211.

[5] Potential Pareto efficiency is also known as "Kaldor-Hicks efficiency" in the economic literature. See, e.g., R Posner, *Economic Analysis of Law*, (4th ed. 1993), chap. 1.

value is a function of the expressed "wants" of individuals. The reasons for the use of this definition are tied up with the historical development of economic methodology and with the rejection of attempts to derive indicators of value by reference to certain supposedly fundamental "needs".[6] Again, we must pass over some important methodological debates, which have called this predominant approach into question.[7] It is enough for present purposes to seek to clarify exactly what is being claimed when law and economics scholars refer to efficiency in the context of tort law. What they normally mean by "efficiency" is that a legal rule induces a reallocation of resources from less highly valued to more highly valued uses, thereby increasing the total welfare or well-being of all the individuals concerned. If this is done without diminishing the well-being of any particular individual, the outcome is Pareto-efficient; if some individuals lose out, but aggregate well-being is increased, there is potential Pareto efficiency.[8]

How is this general approach applied to tort law? The economic theory of law sees tort law as a means of reducing the overall costs of "accidents" and other causes of harm in society. As Calabresi puts it in his seminal work, *The Costs of Accidents*: "apart from the requirements of justice, [it is] axiomatic that the principal function of accident law is to reduce the sum of the costs of accidents and the costs of avoiding accidents".[9] According to Calabresi, accident costs are of three main types: (1) the costs to victims in terms of injury, lost earnings and other damage; (2) the costs incurred by both potential plaintiffs and potential defendants in taking precautions to avoid harm; and (3) the costs of administering the system of accident compensation, in terms of the processing of claims, the adjudication of disputes and the distribution of payments. Calabresi's point is that from the perspective of economic efficiency, the aim of the law should be to minimise the sum total of these costs. Minimising the costs of harm to victims may not be possible without curtailing other activities which society values. Similarly, the goal of full compensation for all victims of harm would imply an increase in certain administrative and organisational costs.

In short, the economic analysis of tort law tells us that hard choices are unavoidable when considering the degree of care to be demanded of the

[6] This is discussed in S Deakin, "Law and Economics" in P Thomas (ed.), *Legal Frontiers* (1997).

[7] See S Pratten, "Needs and Wants: the Case of Broadcasting Policy" (1998) 20 *Media, Culture and Society* 381.

[8] The emphasis in the study of the liability rules of tort law is on allocative efficiency as described in the text, but there are other notions of efficiency which do not depend on there being a redistribution or reallocation of resources which may be important in other contexts (such as company and commercial law): see S Deakin and A Hughes, "Economic Efficiency and the Proceduralisation of Company Law" (1999) 3 *Company, Financial and Insolvency Law Review*, forthcoming.

[9] At 26.

perpetrators of harms or the level of compensation payable to victims. The standards set by the law of tort are not just an indication of those types of action or activity which society finds reprehensible; they also tell us what level and distribution of harms society is prepared to tolerate in return for achieving some other end or goal. Against this background, the "positive" economics of tort seek to tell us how potential plaintiffs and defendants are likely to respond to rules of a particular kind, what the resulting degree and incidence of harm will be, and what knock-on effects are likely to flow from the attempts of the parties to adjust to particular liabilities (or to the absence of liability). This is a task which, while it can make a certain amount of progress using axiomatic reasoning based on the model of the "rational" economic actor, can ultimately only be carried forward through empirical analysis. Fortunately for tort lawyers, the volume and quality of empirical research on the practical effects of liability rules have both increased in recent years, so that we do now have firm evidence on many matters which were previously the subject of speculation and hunch.[10]

The task of "normative" economics, in evaluating tort law against the criteria of efficiency, is in many ways much more problematic. To be completely sure that a particular outcome was allocatively efficient, we would have to engage in calculations of the costs and benefits of using the law to shift resources within and between particular groups. Because of the inherent complexity and difficulty of this type of calculation, law and economics scholars tend to fall back on a number of conceptual devices, which substitute for a more specific analysis. Here, the way in which liability rules are seen as countering "externalities" is a central issue. An "externality" is simply an external cost or benefit which is conferred or imposed on an individual as the result of the conduct of another. Put slightly differently, externalities are unbargained-for effects; they result from the inability of the parties concerned to bargain over the possible consequences for each other of their future conduct. An externality gives rise to a "social cost", which in this context refers to a category of cost that reduces the overall well-being of society. Externalities are thereby a cause of inefficiency in the allocation of resources.

This is the issue dealt with in R H Coase's classic article, "The Problem of Social Cost".[11] Coase argued that rules of private law, including what we now think of as "property rules" and "liability rules",[12] could operate in such a way as to offset externalities, by imposing liabilities upon those

[10] See, generally D Dewees, D Duff and M Trebilcock, *Taking the Facts Seriously. Exploring the Domain of Accident Law* (1996).

[11] (1960) 3 *Journal of Law and Economics* 1; reprinted in Coase, *The Firm, the Market and the Law* (1988).

[12] The distinction between property rules and liability rules was introduced and systematised by G Calabresi and D Melamed, "Property Rules, Liability Rules and Inalienability: One View of the Cathedral" (1972) 85 *Harvard Law Review* 1089.

responsible for inflicting unbargained-for harms upon others. However, it is essential to bear in mind here the distinction between "social cost" and "private cost". Coase was not arguing that it was always and everywhere efficient to compensate the victims of tortious harm. Not all private costs or harms give rise to a social cost. A true externality arises only when the parties are prevented from reaching a consensual solution by obstacles to bargaining, or "transaction costs".

The importance of transaction costs in tort law can be seen through an example. When a court imposes liability on a polluter, the issue for the economist (according to Coase) is whether the value of production in society as a whole is increased or decreased as a result of the court's intervention. This is because the imposition of liability on the polluter will cause a loss to him, which may outweigh the gain to those who were harmed by his activities. Seen purely from the viewpoint of efficiency (and leaving aside other, non-economic considerations which might be expected to influence the court), the issue turns on which of the two parties places the highest value on the right in question. If it were possible to bargain at low or zero cost, the court might assume that the victims of the pollution did not value their freedom from pollution very highly—otherwise they would have "bought out" the polluter. On this basis, it would opt for a finding of "no liability".

On the other hand, the court might take the view that the barriers to a transaction of this kind were in practice very considerable, with the result that there was no realistic prospect that bargaining would take place. (This would be a reasonable assumption in many cases of pollution where the threat of "free riding" deters coalitions of pollution victims from banding together to negotiate a solution with the polluter.) Under these circumstances, the solution most consonant with efficiency would be for the court to assign the right to the party who would have purchased it but for the existence of high transaction costs. If this would have been the pollutee, the court will impose liability on the polluter.

The search for efficiency in tort law is thus bound up in practice with attempts to conceptualise the related concepts of "externalities" and "transaction costs". Since much of tort law is concerned with liability between strangers, among whom bargaining is either expensive or impossible, the notion of externality is often highly relevant. However, externalities can also arise in many situations where the parties are known to each other in advance but where one can find incomplete information or similar barriers to efficient contracting. Here, liability rules may play an important role in promoting efficiency, and it may be largely a matter of legal history and accident that such rules are often grouped together under the heading of the tort of negligence rather than taking a contractual form. The "rigidity" of the English law of contract in respect of the protection of third party rights is thus one explanation for the existence of duties of care in tort which relate to pure economic loss.[13] In other areas where the tort–contract boundary is more fluid, as in the case of the rules governing the employment relationship, tortious duties overlap very closely with implied contract terms.[14]

Applying these ideas to the context of the liability in tort of public bodies, we are faced with a range of possible uses for the economic analysis of law. From a "positive" perspective, economic analysis can be used to tell us what the effects of decisions on liability might be in the three areas identified by Calabresi: the costs of harmful actions and activities; the costs of precautions taken to avoid harm; and the costs of administering claims for compensation. In other words, we may get a clearer idea of whether the imposition of liability is likely to lead to greater care being taken by public bodies, and whether this is at the expense of excessive precautions and/or high administration costs. From a "normative" perspective, economic analysis may be able to provide some indication of whether or not reallocations of resources, which result from liability rules, enhance efficiency. Is society better off if public bodies are held responsible for the consequences of their action or inaction over a wide range of matters affecting the individual citizen, or would well-being be enhanced if individuals themselves were left to take the necessary precautions (through insurance or otherwise) to safeguard their interests?

In all this, it is just as important to be aware of what economic analysis cannot do. A first caveat of this kind relates to the role of positive or predictive economics. As we saw above, axiomatic reasoning of the kind used by economists to generate predictions or hypotheses is, strictly speaking, only the preliminary stage in a process of inquiry which should lead on to empirical studies of various kinds. In the absence of empirical research, which examines the operation of the law in concrete institutional and market settings, the predictions of purely conceptual economic reasoning would have to be treated with the utmost caution by the policy maker or judge.

A second caveat concerns the role of non-economic values in the process of policy formation and analysis. As we explained, welfare economics have developed a set of techniques, which help us in determining whether particular allocations of resources either enhance or diminish the overall wealth or well-being of society. Concepts such as "externalities" and "social cost" are aimed at providing a basis for understanding and resolving conflicts between private interests and the wider collective good. It is true that this kind of analysis would be of little value in certain societies and political contexts. This would be so, at one extreme, if society placed no value what-

[13] See BS Markesinis, "An Expanding Tort Law—the Price of a Rigid Contract Law" (1989) 105 *LQR* 104.

[14] See BS Markesinis and SF Deakin, *Tort Law* (4th ed., OUP, 1999), chap. 6.3.

soever on individual freedom and autonomy, or if, at the other extreme, it were completely indifferent to the consequences for third parties and for the wider community of private, self-interested behaviour. To that extent, therefore, the use of the techniques of welfare economics presupposes some agreement on a basic core of values in society; but we have no difficulty in suggesting that these are values which would be widely accepted in modern, liberal democratic societies.

In short, the criteria of economic efficiency cannot fail to be of interest and concern to judges and policy makers in societies such as our own. But this does not imply that economic efficiency is the only or sole set of values which should guide the law. What economic analysis cannot do is weigh efficiency in the balance against other, potentially competing values—such as equality in distribution, or respect for the dignity of the individual. In proposing the use of economic analysis, therefore, in the context of tort law, we must also insist that there is a proper appreciation of the limits—both methodological and normative—to this kind of reasoning. Without such an appreciation, economics can become a dangerous tool.

Consider, for example, the criterion of Pareto optimality, which we outlined above. In insisting that a move from one state of affairs to another cannot be deemed efficient unless it avoids making anyone worse off than they were before, the Pareto criterion appears to give maximum respect to individual autonomy: no one should be deprived of rights or resources against their will. But the Pareto criterion, in itself, is perfectly compatible with sets of allocations, which cannot be reconciled with liberal values. As the Nobel laureate Professor Amartya Sen has pointed out: "[a]n economy can be optimal in this sense, even when some people are rolling in luxury and others are near starvation, as long as the starvers cannot be made better off without cutting into the pleasure of the rich."[15] Whether a Pareto-optimal state of affairs is truly desirable is, in the final analysis, a question, that can be answered only by reference to values, which, as we have already indicated, lie beyond the scope of economic analysis.

An understanding of what economics can and cannot do in this context is all the more important because of the growing use of economic ideas by the judges themselves. Writers in the law and economics tradition have not sought to claim that the "inherent economic logic" of the common law is the result of explicit economic reasoning. Rather, they have suggested that "economic principles are encoded in the ethical vocabulary that is a staple of judicial language".[16] This is an important and interesting claim, although it is beyond the scope of our present discussion to consider it in any depth. Of more immediate concern to us are some signs that judicial antipathy to economic reasoning is weakening, and that some judges are increasingly

[15] A Sen, *Collective Choice and Social Welfare* (1970), 22.

[16] W Landes and R Posner, *The Economic Structure of Tort Law* (1987), 23.

prepared to make explicit reference to economic concepts when determining the scope of liability rules of private law. In the case of the tort of negligence, the foremost example of this is the judgment of Lord Hoffmann in *Stovin* v. *Wise*.[17] We return to a closer examination of Lord Hoffmann's use of economics, and to other references to economic reasoning in the five cases under review, in our discussion in the following chapters.

3. Tort liability of public bodies: the position in principle

(a) English law[18]

In this section we attempt a thumbnail sketch of the basic principles applicable to our three models, whereas in the next section we describe the five English factual configurations which have provided the parameters of this study. We must start by reminding ourselves that in this book we are concerned with a topic that straddles public and private law and that, in principle, a breach of a public law right will not give rise to a claim for damages unless the latter can also be based on a private law cause of action. It is further well settled that a breach of a statute, be it culpable or not, will not, of itself, give rise to a private law cause of action unless it is shown that the legislator, explicitly or by necessary implication, intended to create a private cause of action in favour of a class to which the plaintiff belongs. This matter ultimately becomes one of statutory construction; and it would seem that, outside the area of workplace legislation, such private law causes of actions are very rarely discovered or invented. But could the carrying-out of a statutory duty by the defendant create a relationship between himself and the plaintiff such as to give rise to a duty of care at common law?[19] It is clear that, both in theory and in practice, the co-existence of a common law duty of care alongside a statutory duty is possible. It is equally clear that liability in damages cannot arise when the public body is doing what Parliament has "authorised". This means that if the decisions complained of fell within the ambit of the statutory discretion they cannot be actionable at common law. If, however, the decision complained of is so unreasonable that it falls outside the ambit of the discretion conferred by the statute, then there is no *a priori* reason for excluding all common law

[17] [1996] AC 923, 941–58.

[18] For fuller discussions, see Arrowsmith, *Civil Liability and Public Authorities* (1992); Harlow, *Compensation and Government Torts* (1982); Street, *Governmental Liability* (1953)—full of ideas but out of date; Wade and Forsyth, *Administrative law* (6th ed., 1994); Weir, "Governmental Liability" 1988 *Public Law* 40*ff*.

[19] We do not discuss here the possibility of a duty of care being imposed upon the authority's servants in the course of performing the authority's statutory functions. The point was, however, considered by Lord Browne-Wilkinson in *X (Minors)* v. *Bedfordshire County Council* [1995] 3 WLR 152, 185*ff*.

liability. However, as Lord Woolf MR recently said,[20] the prospect of establishing this *Wednesbury*[21] type of reasonableness is "extremely remote". Yet only if this hurdle is surmounted will the court then proceed to examine whether a common law duty of care can be established by applying the tripartite test of *Caparo*:[22] forseeability, proximity and fair, just and reasonable. In this context, one must not forget that this test was introduced to act as a three-element controlling device. This is precisely what it has become, especially since the courts allowed themselves the right to determine what is fair, just and reasonable by taking into account "the statutory framework within which the acts complained were done"[23], i.e., bringing the public law tests into the private law phase of the enquiry. Thus, despite numerous qualifying sentences found in the opinions of our judges, the combination of public and private law criteria has drastically limited contemporary ability to seek damages from negligent statutory authorities.

(b) French law

It is impossible to proceed and compare specific cases before stressing how different French and English law are in their approach towards the question of administrative liability. A bird's eye view of the main differences between these two visions can be given in the following way.

First, in French law, it has been accepted since the end of the nineteenth century that administrative liability was not, as a rule, subject to the same rules as those applying to private liability. Thus, in one of the most famous French cases[24] the *Tribunal des Conflits* held that liability in the public services: "*cannot be governed by the principles which are laid down in the Civil Code for relations between one individual and another; that this liability is neither general nor absolute; that it has its own special rules which vary according to the needs of the service and the necessity to reconcile the rights of the state with private rights*".

Notwithstanding this statement, one must immediately stress that a considerable historical evolution has taken place since that decision was handed down defining the principles according to which administrative liability is

[20] *Barrett* v. *Enfield London Borough Council* [1997] 3 WLR 628, 634. Unlike the *Bedfordshire* case, which concerned the extent of the duty of care owed by a local authority to children *prior* to their being taken into care, *Barrett* concerned the extent of the duty owed *after* a child had been placed in the care of a local authority. In this case, as well, the conclusion was the same: no liability for the reasons given in *Bedfordshire*. This result was reversed, however, by a unanimous House of Lords (see [1999] 3 WLR 79) and the case was remitted for trial.

[21] *Associated Provincial Picture Houses* v. *Wednesbury Corporation* [1948] 1 KB 223.

[22] *Caparo Industries Plc.* v. *Dickman* [1990] 2 AC 605.

[23] See, for instance, *Stovin* v. *Wise* [1996] 3 WLR 388, 414–5, per Lord Hoffmann.

[24] *Tribunal des Conflits*, 8 février 1873, Blanco, *Recueil des arrêts du Conseil d'Etat*, 61, concl. David.

submitted to special rules—belonging to public law—which are different from ordinary rules on civil liability. When the principle was stated in *Blanco* it meant, in the opinion of the *Tribunal des Conflits*, that the administration would less easily and less frequently be held liable than individuals according to the rules of private law. Nowadays, however, the special nature of administrative liability law has acquired a totally different meaning. On the whole, therefore, one can argue that this part of the law has become more generous to plaintiffs and more ready to accept the existence of liability than is private liability law. This inversion has become most visible in recent times and the question is, "what provoked it?" At this stage of our analysis, suffice it to mention only two elements.

Sociologically speaking, it is clear that the growing influence of "administrative consumerism", as well as the idea of "socialisation of risks" caused the evolution. Technically speaking, the enlargement of administrative liability was achieved both by the administrative courts—especially in certain "sensitive" areas such as public hospital liability—and by the legislator, a number of statutes having been passed, mainly since 1980, dealing with the subject of state liability.

Secondly, unlike English law, French law on administrative tortious liability is based upon a general concept of fault. This characteristic is actually common to the whole French law of torts—both private and public. However, in the particular field of administrative law, it simply means that the administrative courts could—and still can—evolve their case law by reference to that general standard of what a "normal" operation of administration should and should not be. The solutions of the courts thus do not have to fit in some strictly delimited "pigeon-holes" like those found in English law. A French administrative court is even free to state that a public authority has committed a fault which leads to its liability—"*une faute de nature à engager sa responsabilité*"—without determining to which kind of fault that belongs.

Thirdly, it is very important to mention that in French administrative law the main kind of fault—indeed, the one most frequently sanctioned in practice—is illegality, and that any illegality is, by its nature, an administrative fault likely to give rise to civil liability if it directly causes damage. The equivalence between illegality and fault also applies to procedural irregularities subject, however, to an important qualification. A procedural irregularity will not lead to liability where it appears that the decision was, in substance, justified; in that situation administrative courts will consider that there is not a sufficient link of causation between the illegality and the damage, since the decision could have been taken in any event.

Fourthly, the main way in which French administrative courts have reduced the ambit of administrative liability is by admitting that, in some fields, such liability should be subject to a condition of gross fault—*faute lourde*. The rationale invoked to justify this special requirement is that the corresponding activities are particularly difficult to perform and that, therefore, simple faults, committed in their operation, have to be forgiven or at least ignored in any legal sense. That such a formula is vague and open-ended cannot, of course, be doubted. What, however, is even clearer is the fact that the list of activities that can engage liability only in the event that the *faute* is *lourde* has shrunk over the years.[25] Thus, nowadays, the list comprises only police activities (provided these are material activities and are not merely related to decision-making), activities related to tax services,[26] and activities which control local government and those public or private institutions which state authorities are legally expected to monitor.

Even though the condition of gross fault is an important limitation in the ambit of administrative liability, it is not the only obstacle that the courts have put in the path of liability. Two others are worth mentioning.

The first derives from the fact that administrative courts are sometimes reluctant to compensate certain categories of damages. Until 1961,[27] this was the case for mental anguish—"douleur morale"; and it is still the case for damages consisting in future economic losses, which administrative courts frequently refuse to compensate because they do not consider them as sufficiently certain.[28]

The second limitation can be found in the rigorous way in which French administrative courts deal with the problem of causation where the plaintiff has contributed through his own fault to the damage for which he is seeking compensation. Some planning law cases clearly reveal this strictness. Thus, where a developer has, for example, been granted an illegal planning permission and is adversely affected by certain consequences of that illegality—for instance, because he has to pay damages to the neighbours of the developed land—and then acts against the administration, he will generally be confronted with the argument that he, himself, has committed a fault when applying for an illegal permission, and that his fault counterbalances, totally or partially, the fault committed by the administration when granting the unlawful permission.[29]

Until recently another limitation on administrative liability came from the fact that administrative courts were usually very tight-fisted when deter-

[25] For instance, until recently, the list included a case of great practical importance—liability for medical and surgical accidents in public hospitals.

[26] Except that since 1990 the requirement of gross fault has been limited to situations in which those services meet special difficulties in the assessment of taxpayers' situations.

[27] *Conseil d'Etat*, Assemblée, 24 novembre 1961, Letisserand, *Recueil des arrêts du Conseil d'Etat*, 661.

[28] That attitude is often visible in cases concerning planning law. For example, a developer who has illegally been refused planning permission and who tries to get compensation for the sales profits or the rents he claims to have lost because of that illegal refusal will usually fail because the judges will not be convinced that the commercialisation would have been beneficial. See Jean-Bernard Auby, *Répertoire Dalloz, Résponsabilité de la puissance publique*, under *Urbanisme*.

[29] See *ibid*.

mining the amount of damages they would award to successful plaintiffs. Certainly, their attitude seemed stricter than that adopted by the ordinary courts when adjudicating on similar issues. This tendency, however, is less apparent today and many commentators would argue that it belongs in the past.[30]

Fifthly, and contrary to what was said above, French administrative law has, since the end of nineteenth century, accepted that in certain circumstances the administration might find itself liable even though it is guilty of no fault at all. This solution is admitted in two sets of cases.

In the first, the admission of "non-fault" liability stems from the idea of risk: the administration will have to compensate for the damage it has caused even if its behaviour was quite correct because its activity, by its very nature, created risks. A classic example is the accidental injury of a bystander through the use of firearms by the police.[31] Another example of where "no-fault" liability applies is where public works cause, or the presence of a public installation cause, damage to people who are not users but merely neighbours.

The second type of situation in which liability without fault may arise is based upon the idea of breach of equality. The rationale here is that even if the attitude of the administration was not unlawful or negligent, if it has caused a damage which appears to be both "special" and "abnormal" it will be liable. Nowadays, the prevailing view is that it would be unfair—more specifically, contrary to the principle of equality—to leave people who have suffered such damage without compensation. That theory has been applied by the *Conseil d'Etat* to damages caused by lawful administrative decisions,[32] and even to damages caused by statutes[33] or international treaties ratified by the French State.[34] However, it is worth noting that the

[30] See for example, L Neville Brown and John S Bell, *French Administrative Law* (OUP 1998), 200.

[31] *Conseil d'Etat*, 24 juin 1949, Lecomte et Daramy, *Recueil des arrêts du Conseil d'Etat*, 307.

[32] The main application of that theory concerns cases where the administration refuses the assistance of the police in enforcing a judicial decision—expelling, for example, a tenant who does not pay his or her rent because of a threat to public order. The important decision here is: *Conseil d'Etat*, 30 novembre 1923, Couiteas, *Recueil des arrêts du Conseil d'Etat*, 789.

[33] The landmark decision was *Conseil d'Etat*, Assemblée, 14 janvier 1938, *Société des produits laitiers La Fleurette*, *Recueil des arrêts du Conseil d'Etat*, 25. In that case a statute had been passed which implied the prohibition of a product, which was made only by the La Fleurette company. Notwithstanding the fact that the company obtained compensation, this kind of "legislative" liability is admitted in only a very small number of cases.

[34] As in legislative liability, there are only a few cases in which compensation has been effectively granted. In the first case, in which the principle of liability due to the ratification of a treaty was accepted, the damage was not considered as being special: *Conseil d'Etat*, Assemblée, 30 mars 1966, *Compagnie d'énergie radio-électrique*, *Recueil des arrêts du Conseil d'Etat*, 257. Compensation was, conversely, granted in the case of "*Dame Burgat*"—*Conseil d'Etat*, Section, 29 octobre 1976, *Recueil des arrêts du Conseil d'Etat*, 452—The claim came from a landowner, whose tenant was a diplomat, and who had found it therefore impossible to insist on rent being paid because of the tenant's immunity.

practical impact of this heading is rather limited: the requirement of a "special" and "abnormal" damage is a tight filter in contrast to liability without fault which is grounded on the "risk" rationale and which is frequently and successfully invoked.

(c) German law

In German law, tort liability of public bodies is widely discussed. Reform has been considered for over twenty years. Its unquestioned aim is a modern, unified responsibility for wrongs committed by public bodies—mostly, but not entirely, independent of fault, and based on statute. At present, however, most of the law is judge-made; it is secreted in many different kinds of causes of action, and it is not always clear.[35] In this book, however, we will concentrate solely on those situations where damages are sought for breach of an official duty (*Amtspflichtverletzung*)—comparable to the factual situations in our five English cases. This liability of public bodies flows from the combined application[36] of Article 34 of the Constitution[37] and § 839 of the BGB.[38] This means that public bodies are liable in damages to individuals injured by their own (or their employees') culpable failure to perform properly any official duty owed to the individual. Liability is excluded where, first, the breach of a duty is due to a negligent act only and the individual injured can obtain redress from another source

[35] For example: "expropriation" (*Enteignung*)—Article 14 of the Basic Law; "expropriation-like wrong" (*enteignungsgleicher Eingriff*); "expropriation-like act" (*enteignender Eingriff*); "special sacrifice" (*Aufopferung*); "sacrifice-like wrong" (*aufopferungsgleicher Eingriff*); and others. All these causes of action imply that the public body acts in a public function, not in a solely fiscal matter. In the latter case—as in other solely financial or private relationships of public entities (e.g., the Protestant churches, universities, state banks (*Bundesbank*, *Sparkassen*)—the liability for any wrong will be similar to that of private law entities (BGB, §§ 89, 31 or § 831).

[36] We will be dealing only with the liability of public bodies and not with the liability of their employees. The latter will result from BGB § 839 only if there is no liability of the public body according to the combined application of Article 34 of the Constitution and BGB § 839 and only if the employee has the status of a civil servant (*Beamter*). Other employees will be liable in accordance with BGB, §§ 823 *et seq.* where no state liability is envisaged.

[37] Article 34 states: "If any person, in the exercise of a public office entrusted to him, violates his official obligations to a third party, liability shall rest in principle on the state or on the public body which employs him. In the event of wilful or grossly negligent conduct, the right of recourse shall be reserved. In respect of claims for compensation and of the right of recourse, the jurisdiction of the ordinary courts must not be excluded."

[38] § 839 states: "(1) If an official wilfully or negligently commits a breach of official duty incumbent upon him as against a third party, he shall compensate the third party for any damage arising therefrom. If only negligence is imputable to the official, he may be held liable only if the injured party is unable to obtain compensation elsewhere.
(2) If an official commits a breach of his official duty in giving judgment in an action, he is not responsible for any damage arising therefrom, unless the breach of duty is punished with a public penalty to be forced by criminal proceedings. This provision does not apply to a breach of duty consisting of refusal or delay in the exercise of the office.
(3) The duty to make compensation does not arise if the injured party has wilfully or negligently omitted to avert the injury by making use of a legal remedy."

(BGB, § 839 I 2);[39] secondly, where the victim did not make use of any legal remedy which could have mitigated his damages (BGB, § 839) (III);[40] and, thirdly, where a statute expressly provides for such an eventuality.[41] Here, it will suffice to draw the reader's attention to two elements of the cause of action: "fault" and the fact that "the duty must be owed to the individual plaintiff" and not the public at large.

The requirement of culpability has to be seen against the code's historical background: BGB, § 839 was designed originally to cater solely for the liability of a public official himself.[42] The central idea was that such an official should fear liability in damages only where he is at fault. Individual responsibility is of less significance where the state takes over liability.[43] In the current debates, over reforms, German writers remain convinced that the fault requirement should be loosened, but there is considerable disagreement as to the extent that this should happen.[44] These debates should not, however, conceal the fact that the concept of fault in German civil law (in contrast to the concept of fault in criminal law) is already understood in a very broad way.[45] So, as in English law, the standard of care in cases of negligence is an objective one, concentrating on the reasonable person in general and—with regard to particular groups or professions—on the special high standard of care one can expect from such particular group or profession. In practice, the test thus often comes close to the notion of strict liability; and it has been demonstrated that in most litigation concerning breach of official duty the issue of fault is rarely an obstacle for plaintiffs.[46]

[39] For this restriction on state liability and its doubtful and limited effects, see below.

[40] There is another restriction with regard to judicial decisions and the liability of the judge respectively to judicial administration (BGB, § 839 II: *Spruchrichterprivileg*), which, however, would carry us outside the ambit of this comparative study.

[41] For example, BNotO (*Bundesnotarordnung*, which is the Federal Law on Notaries), § 19, which provides for the personal liability of the notary public; RBHaftG *Reichsbeamtenhaftungsgesetz* (Law on Liability of Civil Servants), § 5 No. 2, which excludes liability for certain political acts in the diplomatic service; for further discussion especially on the constitutionality of such restrictions on state liability, see Ossenbühl, *Staatshaftungsrecht* 5th ed., 1996, 79 *et seq.*

[42] The old (Roman law) principle—*si excessit, privatus est*—known also in English law, along with disputes over the legislative competence for state liability rules, induced the draftsmen of the civil code to refrain from any rule on public liability (leaving this issue to the member states), although not from rules on liability of public bodies acting fiscally (see BGB, §§ 89, 31). For further details, see *Entwurf eines Einführungsgesetzes zum BGB für das Deutsche Reich*, 1. *Lesung nebst Motiven*, (1888), 185.

[43] First introduced to the whole of Germany by the *Beamtenhaftungsgesetz* of 1 August 1909 (GS 691). This was later acknowledged in Art. 131 of the Weimar Constitution 1919.

[44] Compare Pfab, *Staatshaftung in Deutschland* (1997), passim.

[45] For details, see Markesinis, *German Law of Obligations*, Vol 2, *The Law of Torts, A Comparative Introduction* (3rd ed., 1997); Deutsch, "Der Begriff der Fahrlässigkeit im Zivilrecht" *Jura* 1987, 505.

[46] *Zur Reform des Staatshaftungsrechts, rechtstatsächliche Erkenntnisse in Staatshaftungssachen, Verwaltungserhebung und Gerichtsauswertung* (1976), edited by the Bundesministerium der Justiz, 34, 202—only 14.1% of the claims failed because of the absence of fault.

Secondly, discretionary acts of public bodies (or their employees) are, in Germany, subject to judicial review to a far greater extent than in English law. Thus, a German judge may rule on and find fault even where the official acted within the ambit of his discretion (as will be shown in detail below). The discretionary character of an act is not in principle, therefore, a bar to justiciability; nor does it hinder the proof of careless decision-taking within the ambit of the discretion. The test applied by German courts is much wider than the *Wednesbury*[47] test of reasonableness that prevails in English law.

If the requirement of fault is no real obstacle to state liability the same is not true of the second element, namely "that the duty must be owed to the individual to protect his interests". This serves as an effective filter to remove from all public wrongs those cases where the state itself might be liable in damages. The duty must not exist solely for the benefit of the general public, but must at least also protect the individual or a class to which the individual/plaintiff belongs. The claimant must thus be such a protected individual or a member of a protected group, and the duty must exist to protect especially those interests of the individual that have been injured. The parallels here with the English requirements of liability for breach of statutory duty are evident. Nevertheless, one must remain conscious of the dangers that would accompany any complete assimilation. Although there are many decisions on this issue leading to some uncertainty over the exact application of this requirement in given cases,[48] the approach of German law seems to be stricter than that found in English cases. Thus, where it is open for policy considerations to play a part in the outcome of a dispute, they tend to focus on the relevance and meaning of the official duty and not so much on the wider considerations of justice, fairness and economic efficiency which one finds in English decisions. One, therefore, starts with the premise that fairness and justice require the state to be held liable to the individual for public wrong, except where the official duty is owed only to the public at large. Although the element of "duty towards the individual" (*drittbezogene Amtspflicht*) is phrased as a requirement and not only in a negative form as an obstacle to the claim, the relation of rule and exception in English and German law seems to be the reverse.[49] This

[47] *Associated Provincial Picture Houses* v. *Wednesbury Corp.* [1948] 1 KB 223.

[48] Münchener, *Kommentar, Papier*, (3rd ed., 1997) § 839, n. 227; for proposals to streamline the discussion, see: BGB, *Ladeur*, "Zur Bestimmung des drittschützenden Charakters von Amtspflichten im Sinne von § 839 BGB und Art. 34 GG—insbesondere bei Aufsichtspflichten" *DÖV* 1994, 665.

[49] This is obvious in the decision of the Federal Court of Justice with regard to the banking control system, where the court inferred from the silence of the statutory rule that the duty was owed towards the individual: BGH 15 February 1979, BGHZ 74, 144, 147 = NJW 1979, 1354; BGH 12 July 1979, BGHZ 75, 120, 122 = NJW 1979, 1879. For doubts on the constitutionality of the amendments of the statute (*Kreditwesengesetz*, as amended on 20 December 1984), Münchener *Kommentar, Papier*, above at n. 48, § 839, nn. 250, 251.

may be illustrated by contrasting the indicators of such "duty towards the individual" with the requirements of state liability in English law laid down by Lord Browne-Wilkinson in the *Bedfordshire* case (see below).

It is well established that there is a "duty towards the individual" when the (particular) individual has a right to claim performance of that duty (*öffentlich-rechtlicher Erfüllungsanspruch*). Claim of and duty towards the individual are two sides of the same coin. For example, an applicant may claim the issue of a building permission where he has complied with certain requirements. If the permission is not issued, or is issued too late, or is (illegally) made subject to a supplementary condition, a private law cause of action will arise.[50] Of course, these situations are less problematic and do not arise frequently in practice because the individual may usually launch an appeal against the decision and thereby obtain what he or she is entitled to claim. Although not identical, this class of case comes close to those situations in English law where Lord Browne-Wilkinson referred to breaches of statutory duty *simpliciter*.[51]

Another instance giving rise to a duty towards an individual is where the public body and the individual have entered into a special relationship. The duties of protection and care arising from such relationship are owed to the individual and also to third parties included in the realm of protection (*Schutzwirkung zugunsten Dritter*).[52] For example, a school owes a special duty of care towards its pupils.[53] In addition, a school has the duty to prevent pupils from causing harm to others. Thus, if a pupil damages the car of X during a school excursion, the responsible body may be liable towards the car owner.[54] It is tempting here to draw parallels with the

[50] BGH 14 December 1978, NJW 1979, 641, 642; BGH 10 March 1994, NJW 1994, 1647; BGH 13 July 1989, NJW 1990, 505 (marriage officer arriving too late in the hospital for the marriage ceremony, one fiancée having died already); compare also BGH 6 May 1993, NJW 1993, 2303, 2304; BGH 24 February 1994, NJW 1994, 2091; Münchener *Kommentar*, *Papier*, § 839 n. 228; *Wurm*, JA 1992, 1, 2.

[51] *X (Minors)* v. *Bedfordshire County Council* [1995] 3 WLR 165, 166.

[52] BGH of 20 June 1974, NJW 1974, 1816, 1817—a slaughterhouse owed a duty towards the employee of the butcher, who had to use the slaughterhouse; this notion of third party protection is known not only in tort law but especially in contract law, where contractual duties may involve the protection of persons close to the parties. For further discussion of contracts which protect third parties, see Markesinis, Lorenz, Dannemann, *German Law of Obligations*, Vol. I, *Law of Contracts and Restitution, A Comparative Introduction* (OUP 1997), 276.

[53] BGH 27 April 1981, NJW 1982, 37, 38; BGH 10 March 1983, FamRZ 1984, 1211 (both concerning the negligent control of a school bus stop). In most cases there will be no liability of the school and its responsible body because damage will be covered by insurance against school accidents taken out by the schools. This exception will not apply, however, when violations of the right of personality (*Persönlichkeitsrechtsverletzungen*) are at issue and money compensation for pain and suffering is sought: OLG Zweibrücken 6 May 1997, NJW 1998, 995: the responsible body had to pay DM 1,600 to a pupil who had consistently been made fun of by his teacher in front of the class causing the pupil great psychological harm.

[54] LG Hamburg 26 April 1991, NJW 1992, 377; in that case a cause of action against the pupil himself would have been unsuccessful due primarily to his lack of means.

Dorset Yacht case, although one might also be inclined to compare this element of the "duty towards the individual" with the requirement of proximity found in the *Caparo* test.[55] There are also differences, however, insofar as, in general, the required proximity need not exist between the tortfeasor and the injured person but between the injured person and the person protected by a special relationship with the tortfeasor. In addition, this duty has been extended—in contrast to contract law—towards those individuals who come into contact with the person protected: the duty of the public body encompasses the duty to prevent harm from the entrusted person as well as to prevent that person from doing harm to others. Thus, the scope of the duty is much broader than the duty of care considered in the *Dorset Yacht case.*

A "duty towards the individual" will also arise where the public body directly infringes absolute rights of an individual, namely his life, body, health, freedom, property (and other rights or interests of comparable weight, for example the right of personality), but not his purely economic interests.[56]

If none of these indicators are present, a "duty towards the individual" may arise from the protective purpose of the rule (*Schutzzweck der Norm*[57])—the rule which imposes a certain duty on the public body—which must have been created, *inter alia* to prevent the mischief that occurred. But this need not necessarily follow from the express intention of the legislator; it suffices that such protection for the individual arises from the nature of public dealings and the circumstances of such dealings, even if the rule has been laid down primarily for the protection of the public in general. One indicator of the protective purpose of the duty is the availability of a public law remedy for an injured person; another indicator is the special danger for the life and health of an individual resulting from these dealings. If public dealings create a special situation where an individual can rely on the duty of care owed to him by a public body, this indicates that duties arising from public dealings also have the purpose of protecting individuals; but the extent of the protective purpose may be limited to certain goods, especially to absolute rights and interests.[58] This is especially the case, for example, with regard to the duty to ensure safe traffic on the roads

[55] *Caparo Industries Plc* v. *Dickman* [1990] 2 AC 605.

[56] BGH 1 February 1982, NJW 1983, 627, 628; Münchener *Kommentar, Papier*, § 839, n. 229.

[57] The theory was first adopted in relation to breaches of contractual duties, and was later accepted in the law of torts with regard to liability under BGB § 823; originally it modified the concept of causation in BGB § 823 I, and, subsequently, it influenced the definition of the "protective norm" (*Schutzgesetz*) in the sense of BGB § 823II (compare Markesinis, above at n. 52, vol. II, *The Law of Torts*, 101), and the application of BGB § 839 (compare Canaris, Schutzgesetze—Verkehrspflichten—Schutzpflichten, in *Festschrift Larenz* (1983) 30, 40.

[58] BGH 26 January 1989, BGHZ 106, 323 = NJW 1989, 976—Altlasten, i.e., planning and contamination of soil.

(*Straßenverkehrssicherungspflicht*), which duty exists towards every individual road-user,[59] but only with regard to life, body, health, liberty, property and other rights and interests of comparable weight; the duty does not extend to protection against economic loss.[60] Thus, if traffic lights are installed wrongly and, as a result, an accident occurs which causes injury to individuals and damage to property, the public authority will be liable for all these damages. However if, due to the wrong installation of traffic lights a traffic congestion occurs, no liability will arise towards individuals who suffered economic loss because they were caught in the resulting traffic jam.

If there is a duty towards the (respective) individual,[61] and the protected rights and interests of the individual have been injured, there will be no further room for policy arguments and the state will be held liable—provided, of course, that the other requirements mentioned above are fulfilled.

4. Five factual situations

(a) English law

The facts and legal issues raised by our five English cases are so well known that we could have dispensed with the need of stating them again. Nevertheless, we do so in bare outline, mainly in order to facilitate their comparative juxtaposition with the French and German cases the facts of which are given in subsections (b) and (c) below.

First, *Hill* v. *Chief Constable of West Yorkshire*[62] involved a claim by the mother of a deceased woman (suing for damages to her estate) against the police on the grounds that because of their (alleged) negligence they failed, during their investigations of the commission of a series of similar crimes, to apprehend their perpetrator. This failure allowed the criminal to remain at large for a further period of time, during which he murdered the plaintiff's daughter. The action failed.

Secondly, *X (Minors)* v. *Bedfordshire County Council*[63] was one of two "child-abuse" actions (consolidated and heard together with three other

[59] The German cases differ considerably from the English cases, as exemplified by *Ancell* v. *McDermott* [1993] 4 All ER 355.

[60] BGH 18 December 1972, NJW 1973, 463.

[61] No duty towards the individual, however, exists with respect to legislative acts, such as the failure to provide necessary laws or the violation of individual rights by virtue of unjust or improper laws. Legislative acts—in comparison to specific acts towards individuals or groups of persons—are owed only to the public in general and, thus, cannot constitute a duty towards an individual or a violation of an individual's rights, unless specified by administrative or judicial acts. Other principles, however, apply with regard to "legislative wrongs" under European law; see Joined Cases C-6 and 9/90 *Francovich* v. *Italy* [1991] ECR I-5357.

[62] [1988] 1 WLR 1049.

[63] [1995] 3 WLR 152.

cases not discussed in this book). It arose in connection with a claim that a local authority negligently and in breach of its statutory obligations failed to exercise its powers to institute care proceedings after it had received serious reports that the plaintiff/child had been the subject of parental abuse and neglect. The second case—*M (A Minor)* v. *Newham London Borough Council*—was the mirror image of the first, since it involved a claim for negligently removing the child from maternal care on the basis of an unfounded belief that the abuse had taken place by the mother's cohabitee and the conclusion that the mother was unable to protect her child.

The third case, *Elguzouli-Daff* v. *Commissioner of Police of the Metropolis*,[64] involved the Crown Prosecution Service. Tort actions were brought by two persons who were detained in custody for suspected crimes. After long periods in detention—22 and 85 days respectively—the Crown Prosecution Service (CPS) discontinued proceedings against them on the grounds that there was insufficient evidence. The plaintiffs' statements of claim against the CPS were struck out by the judge who held that they disclosed no reasonable cause of action. The Court of Appeal unanimously rejected the plaintiffs' appeal, on the ground that the CPS owed no duty of care to those it was prosecuting.

The chronologically fourth example can be found in *Stovin* v. *Wise*.[65] In that case a local authority failed to exercise its statutory power to direct a private landowner, on whose property lay an obstruction, to have it removed in order to improve visibility at a nearby road junction which was known to have caused traffic accidents in the past. The plaintiff, who was injured at this junction by the defendant's car, claimed damages against him for his injuries. The defendant, in turn, joined the council as a third party. The action against the defendant having been settled, the battle shifted to the council's potential liability. By a majority of three to two, the House of Lords ruled in favour of the council.

The final case is *W* v. *Essex County Council*.[66] Here, parents and their children brought an action against a local authority, which placed in their foster care a child who was known to be a sexual abuser. An action by the molested children against the local authority succeeded by majority; but the parents' action for nervous shock was dismissed.

(b) French law

Hill v. *Chief Constable of West Yorkshire*. No exact equivalent of *Hill* was found in French published case law. However, this does not mean that a failure by the police to react to certain situations where action was needed

[64] [1995] 2 WLR 173.
[65] [1996] 3 WLR 388.
[66] [1998] 3 WLR 534. At the time of writing, the case is listed for a House of Lords hearing, but we have not been given a date.

cannot lead to public liability. For example, in the case of *Ville de Perpignan*,[67] the municipality was held liable because the local police had been warned that a cinema show was about to take place in premises that were not safe for fire purposes. Fire broke out on the premises and the plaintiff was injured. His action for damages against the police succeeded.

The case of *Mme Garagnon*[68] can also be mentioned here. In that case, after a French woman and her Algerian husband divorced, the husband succeeded in taking their children to Algeria. This was contrary to a decision by the Minister of the Interior that had prohibited them being taken outside the French territory. The state was held liable to Mme Garagnon, the *Conseil d'Etat* accepting that the airport police, had they checked the relevant file properly, would have realised that the father was prohibited from taking the children outside the French jurisdiction.

In such cases, when public liability is accepted, it is because the omission by the police to do what they should have done is considered to amount to such a serious wrongdoing that it amounts to gross fault (*faute lourde*). Indeed, as we have already made clear, police activities are one of the fields in which the condition of gross fault is required before public liability can be admitted.[69]

The above cases illustrate that where the omission by the police is not serious enough to be considered as a gross fault the administration will not be held liable. An example of this can be found in *Société Le Profil*.[70] During a hold-up by robbers, the policemen charged with protecting money which was being transported failed to react when they should have. The lateness and the inefficiency of their intervention were not considered as constituting a gross fault, and the company, whose money was transported and stolen, could not obtain compensation for its loss.

One must conclude the above comments by returning to a point already made concerning the fluid nature of the principle of *faute lourde*. The few examples given above suggest that whereas the principle could be used as a device limiting the police's eventual liability, the dividing line between ordinary and grave fault is neither obvious nor great. At any rate, this is likely to be the reaction of an English lawyer in cases such as the above, for whom the concept's fluidity will appear more a potential source of uncertainty—which, in the last resort, can be resolved only by litigation—than an effective limitation device. Even if that is so, however, the potential liability rule does not seem to have caused any economic or practical problems for the French police.

[67] Conseil d'Etat, 29 juillet 1948, *Recueil des arrêts du Conseil d'Etat*, 213.

[68] Conseil d'Etat, 26 juin 1985, *Recueil des arrêts du Conseil d'Etat*, 254.

[69] At least, as was mentioned above, where material, "physical" activities are concerned. Where what is criticised is an illegal decision, liability is subject only to a condition of simple fault.

[70] Conseil d'Etat, 27 avril 1979, *Recueil des arrêts du Conseil d'Etat*, 171.

X v. *Bedfordshire County Council and M* v. *Newham London Borough Council.* There appears to be only one published case in which social services were held liable because of their negligence in the exercise of the powers vested in them for the purposes of protecting children in danger of family abuse. (This administrative duty is called *protection maternelle et infantile.*) In *Epoux Ouaras*[71]—a three-year-old girl had been sent, with the agreement of her parents, to stay with a foster family for three months. The foster family, which was not French, had been selected by an association devoted to children's care. The child was seriously maltreated. Her parents were granted compensation. The *Conseil d'Etat* considered that the administration was at fault for not having verified the reliability of the foster family carefully.

Another case offers a possible comparison with *Newham.* In *M et Mme Pillon*[72] the *Conseil d'Etat* held that a social service had committed no fault in not warning the authority able to institute care proceedings about the threat posed to the health of children entrusted in the care of a particular family. (Information collected by the agency pointed to such dangers, and the concern should have been even greater given that the family had refused permission to the social workers to enter their house and talk to the children.) To an English lawyer these facts would indicate the presence of fault, but we cannot labour this point too much given that the finding of fault depended on the facts in each case, and we do not have them before us as the court did. The outcome of the litigation could be seen as an illustration of how the controlling device of fault works in practice. However, one must also note the dangers that may arise from the fact that such determinations may only be possible *after* litigation has taken place. To an English lawyer this observation will not just be crucial, but also, arguably, a reinforcement for his view to dispose such disputes without the cost and delays of a full trial. Nevertheless, one must also repeat—perhaps with some degree of surprise—the paucity of litigated examples, something which must indicate that in *practice* the potential liability rule has not opened the floodgates of litigation.

Elguzouli-Daff v. *Commissioner of Police of the Metropolis.* In French law, the question of state liability to people who have been improperly detained before trial has, since 1970, been governed by statutory rules. Thus, a statute passed on 17 July 1970 gives persons who, after having been detained in custody, are not subsequently sentenced, the right to compensation. This right is not subject to proving the presence of any fault. Until 1996 it was subject to the condition that the damage was "manifestly abnormal and particularly serious"; this condition, however, was removed by a 1996 Act.[73] Thus, nowadays, on the basis of this legislation, about

[71] Conseil d'Etat, 23 septembre 1987, *Recueil des arrêts du Conseil d'Etat*, 290.
[72] Conseil d'Etat, 4 mai 1983, n. 22811.
[73] Loi du 30 décembre 1996 relative a la détention provisoire.

half of the people who claim compensation receive it every year. The average amount of the compensation is 63,000 francs—about £6,300 per claim.[74] The amount, once again, covers "moral damages" and a separate (and additional) claim can be made for provable economic losses.

Stovin v. *Wise*. No exact equivalent to *Stovin* v. *Wise* can be found in the published French case law. The problem which arose in that case could, however, be resolved by French law, since in the Road Code (*Code de la voirie routière)*, article L.114–1 we find provisions which entitle public authorities to take the kind of decision which was not taken in the *Stovin* case. The powers thereby given to the appropriate authorities belong to what French administrative law calls administrative police (*police administrative*) an area of the law in which, as was mentioned above, public liability is subject to a condition of gross fault (*faute lourde)*. Thus, the administration could be held liable if it could be shown that it had failed to direct a landowner to remove an obstruction in a situation in which such action was necessary.

There are two cases with which *Stovin* might, nonetheless, be compared. Both cases concerned circumstances in which what was criticised was the omission by the administration to use powers concerning road traffic, but both of which related to private properties (more precisely, private roads which were open to the public). Thus, in the first case, *Commune de Maisons-Laffitte*, the *Conseil d'Etat* stated that the local authority had committed a gross fault, leading to its liability, because it had failed to make sure that various obstacles and barriers had been properly visible through appropriate lighting.[75] In the second case, *Ville de Paris c. Marabout*,[76] the local authority was equally condemned for having neglected to act against illegal car-parking in a private road which was open to the public, but where parking was forbidden by a regulation issued by the same local authority. M Marabout, who lived at the bottom of the road and who was deprived of a normal access to his property, was thus granted compensation.

W. v. *Essex County Council*. The most recent cases concerning damages caused by children in foster care concerned damages suffered, not by the foster family, but by third persons. In one case decided in 1998 by the Administrative Court of Appeal of Bordeaux[77] (*Consorts Fraticola*) a seventeen-year-old adolescent, while staying with a foster family, killed another youngster during a fight at the local fair. The Administrative Court of Appeal granted total compensation *to the family* of the latter child of

[74] René Chapus, *Droit administratif général* (12th ed., 1998), n. 1481.

[75] Conseil d'Etat, 8 mai 1963, Commune de Maisons-Laffitte, *Droit administratif*, 1963, n°215.

[76] Conseil d'Etat, Assemblée, 20 octobre 1972, Ville de Paris c. Marabout, *Actualité Juridique Droit Administratif*, novembre 1972, 597.

[77] C. adm. Bordeaux, 2 février 1998, Consorts Fraticola, Les Petites Affiches, 12 août 98, p. 3, concl. D Peano.

approximately 160,000 francs or the approximate equivalent of £16,000. The amount may be considered as small; but an English lawyer might well reflect on the fact that in his own system there could be no fatal accidents claim whatsoever, the only amount of damages claimable being by the estate of the victim himself.

What has to be specified is that the Administrative Court of Appeal reached its conclusions by admitting that, in this kind of cases, a presumption of fault would apply. In that case, this meant that the plaintiffs did not have to demonstrate that a fault had been committed, either by the administration in the choice of the foster parents, or by the foster parents in the way they looked after the foster child.[78] On the contrary, it was up to the administration to demonstrate that its behaviour, and the behaviour of the parents, was correct. This it failed to do.

Although there is no recent case concerning this issue, it is probable that administrative liability for the damages suffered by the foster family itself, and not by third persons, is even wider. It is probably a liability without fault, this kind of regime being one which usually benefits all people harmed when acting in the public service.[79] One cannot be certain of this conclusion, however, since in older cases the *Conseil d'Etat* imposed liability only in cases of proven fault.[80] Even this result, however, would make French law different from English law since in the *Essex* case—and for a variety of reasons, which we shall examine further down—liability to the parents was denied.

It must finally be mentioned that, if the child in foster care was a juvenile delinquent—more often staying in centres, but sometimes placed with families—the damages that he or she would cause would have to be compensated on the ground of liability without fault,[81] whoever the plaintiff was—a member of the foster family or a third person.

(c) German law

Comparable to *Hill* v. *Chief Constable of West Yorkshire* is a German case[82] in which the plaintiff sued the state claiming damages because the police

[78] The same presumption of fault had in fact been previously accepted by the Conseil d'Etat in one particular situation where damages are caused by children whose parents are dead or who have been abandoned by their parents, and who are under state protection (*pupilles de l'Etat*): Conseil d'Etat, 19 octobre. 1990, Ingremeau, *Revue de droit public*, 1990–1866, concl. C de la Verpillière.

[79] See *Répertoire Dalloz de la résponsabilité de la puissance publique*, V Collaborateurs occasionnels.

[80] Conseil d'Etat, 30 mars 1935, Derue, *Recueil des arrêts du Conseil d'Etat*, 132-30 mars 1938, Derue, *Recueil des arrêts du Conseil d'Etat*, 332-11 décembre 1957, Dle Champel, *Recueil des arrêts du Conseil d'Etat*, 1022.

[81] Conseil d'Etat, Section, 3 février 1956, Thouzellier, Dalloz, 1956-597, note J M Auby.

[82] BGH 30 April 1953 LM (Lindenmayer/Möhring = collection of Reported cases), § 839 [Fg] BGB, no 5.

did not act to prevent a robbery even though they knew that X and Y, who perpetrated the robbery, were members of a band of robbers and were on the prowl. X and Y later broke into the plaintiff's house. The plaintiff's action against the police was successful.

Secondly, although an exact parallel to the first case in *X (Minors)* v. *Bedfordshire County Council* can be found only in criminal law,[83] the questions of law raised in the second case (*Newham*[84]) are comparable to those considered by a decision of the Court of Appeal of Hamm in 1996.[85] In that case a minor had asked the local youth welfare authority to take care of her because she was experiencing considerable difficulties with her mother and did not wish to live with her any longer. The authority heard the minor and the mother and then applied to the family court, which assigned the right to determine the minor's whereabouts to the authority. The authority sent the minor to a home for children where the minor stayed for about ten months before she returned to her mother. The mother sued the state for damages because she was deprived of her daughter through the alleged wrong acts of the youth welfare authority. She maintained that the youth authority should have attempted reconciliation before separating her from her child and, more seriously, that it had also influenced her daughter's statement before the family court. Evidence was taken and the case went to a full hearing. The claim ultimately failed, but only because the authority was not found to have acted negligently.

Elgozouli-Daff v. *Commissioner of Police of the Metropolis* may be contrasted to a German case decided by the Federal Court of Justice in 1997:[86] The plaintiff had been arrested on a charge of fraudulent conversion (March 1990). The state prosecutor had applied to the court for a warrant for arrest, which was granted on condition that the detention should be suspended. The state prosecutor successfully appealed and the plaintiff was kept in detention for several more weeks until the arrest order was suspended in May 1990 and, finally, quashed in November 1990. The criminal proceedings against the plaintiff were stayed in March 1991. The plaintiff claimed damages for false imprisonment. He alleged that both the prosecution and the arrest had been instituted without reasonable or probable cause given that at the time of his arrest it had already become obvious that the incriminating evidence of two witnesses could not be relied upon in the case against him. The court awarded the plaintiff damages for both his material and immaterial loss.

The facts in a decision of the Federal Court of Justice in 1980 come close

[83] OLG Oldenburg 2 September 1996, ZfJ 1997, 95. See also OLG Stuttgart 28 May 1998, NJW 1998, 3131, 3133, also a criminal case, where the social worker was held responsible for acting in a timely and diligent manner to prevent mistreatment of a child who, however, died from this mistreatment!

[84] *M (A minor)* v. *Newham London Borough Council* [1995] 3 WLR 152.

[85] OLG Hamm 20 November 1996, ZfJ 1997, 433.

[86] BGH 16 October 1997, NJW 1998, 751.

to those in *Stovin* v. *Wise*. A traffic accident happened because the visibility of a road junction was obstructed by a hedge separating the two carriageways. The council argued that its duty was merely to ensure safe conditions on the road and that it did not extend towards the plaintiff who should have taken more care. The argument was considered and rejected. The court granted damages to the plaintiff.[87]

In the final case, comparable to *W* v. *Essex County Council*, the local youth welfare authority placed a child for adoption with the plaintiffs. The plaintiffs had made clear that they wanted to adopt only a healthy child. In fact, the child was mentally retarded which the authority could have known had it acted diligently. The plaintiffs successfully claimed damages with regard to their support obligation towards the retarded child.[88]

II. HOW DIFFERENT COURTS HAVE HANDLED THESE CASES

1. The reasons given by the English courts for denying liability in negligence

(a) Legalistic reasons: duty, proximity, fairness, justice and reasonableness

We describe these as "legalistic" rather than legal reasons since, in our view, the concepts used to achieve the results are value-neutral on their surface only. Thus, as a rich case law amply demonstrates, all these concepts are fluid enough to justify whatever result the judge has decided to reach before turning to the question of how he should justify his conclusion to the general public. Our tort books are, of course, replete with examples showing how courts use these malleable concepts. In our five illustrations, however, the most recent judicial decisions have demonstrated fairly clearly that the concepts used are only legal smokescreens for a heavy dose of judicial social engineering. We reinforce our assertion that these concepts are, essentially, a smokescreen for disguising value judgments by referring our readers to some interesting extra-judicial utterances on this subject from Lord Mustill.[89] Our assertion that the judgments have recourse to legal smokescreens does not, however, mean that we prefer the concealment of

[87] BGH NJW 1980, 2194.

[88] OLG Hamm, FamRZ 1993, 704.

[89] "What do courts do?" (1995–96) 3 *Särtryck ur Juridisk Tidskrift*, 611, 620: "One cannot always be sure, as regards an individual judge, that the reasons published in a judgment are in fact his reasons for the decision. They may have been considered after the event to reconcile the decision with legal materials which appeared to stand in its way, and which played no part in his formation of the conclusion, or to call support from favourable materials for a decision arrived at without recourse to them (for example a decision made intuitively, or on grounds of policy)."

the true policy reasons which explain (if not justify) these decisions. On the contrary, we welcome this open discussion of policy even if we advocate its refinement and disagree with the results which its application, apparently, dictates. In our view, the current state of affairs which, on the whole, we find unconvincing, will never change, let alone improve, if we fail to test openly the validity of the policy arguments which have been advanced to support the current, restrictive case law. In this context, therefore, we note with satisfaction that as one moves from *Hill* v. *Chief Constable of West Yorkshire*[90] to the most recent cases one detects a greater willingness to justify the results by reference to the policy reasons found mainly in *X (Minors)* v. *Bedfordshire County Council*[91] and, to a lesser extent, *Stovin* v. *Wise*.[92] On the other hand, we also voice some concerns about the non-scientific way in which the policy-oriented debate is taking place since we do not believe that policy arguments can be put forward largely on the strength of hunches rather than verifiable evidence. A refinement of this trend is thus called for if it is to survive in the future. We hope both take place.

The *Hill* decision, which we have taken as the starting point of the current restrictive trend, is, from the "justification" point of view, still in orthodox company. The bulk of the judgments is devoted to the discussion of the usual ingredients of the notion of duty of care. Thus, there is talk of: no liability because of "no duty";[93] no proximity (thus distinguishing it from the *Dorset Yacht* decision);[94] foreseeability, alone, will not suffice for the imposition of liability;[95] no liability for the acts of third parties (who are neither servants or agents);[96] absence of special relationship between plaintiff and defendant;[97] and, finally, whether the imposition of liability would be "fair, just and reasonable".[98] Notably (and surprisingly) absent from this list of "technical" arguments is the fact that *Hill* involved an omission instead of a bad act. As we shall note below, this point which, arguably, could have on its own disposed of the *Hill* claim, emerged in a key way in the judgments of both the majority and the dissent in the *Stovin* case. It has been argued, not entirely unconvincingly, that the policy justifications given

90 [1998] 1 WLR 1049.
91 [1995] 3 WLR 152.
92 [1996] 3 WLR 388.
93 [1987] 2 WLR 1126, 1143, per Fox LJ; 1139B, per Glidewell LJ.
94 *Ibid.*, 1135 E-F, per Fox LJ; *Hill* v. *Chief Constable of West Yorkshire* [1988] 1 WLR 1049, 1053A, 1955, per Lord Keith.
95 [1987] 2 WLR 1126, 1134E, per Fox LJ; *Hill* v. *Chief Constable of West Yorkshire* [1988] 1 WLR 1049, 1052I, per Lord Keith.
96 [1987] 2 WLR 1126, 1133E, per Fox LJ; 1139 G per Glidewell LJ.
97 *Ibid.*, 1130G, per Fox LJ; 1139F, per Glidewell LJ. *Osman* v. *Ferguson* [1993] 4 All ER 344, discussed below, was one of the exceptional cases where a special relationship was held to have arisen between the police and the plaintiff/tortfeasor's victim. Nonetheless, the action failed.
98 [1987] 2 WLR 1126, 1136H, per Fox LJ; 1139H, per Glidewell LJ.

for the *Hill* result (and discussed below) may form part of *obiter dicta* and not an integral part of the *ratio decidendi* of the decision.[99]

In the *Bedfordshire* decision, which is our second focal point, the "technical", legal arguments connected with tort liability were limited to the enquiry whether the local authority owed a direct duty of care. Lord Browne-Wilkinson's remarks are brief on two of the usual requirements—foreseeability and proximity—largely because the local authority (wisely) chose not to challenge the fact that they were satisfied. Instead, he asserted (without discussion[100] and, some might argue, not so convincingly) that the requirement of "fair, just and reasonable", essentially introduced into our system by the *Peabody*[101] and *Caparo*[102] judgments, also applied to cases involving physical harm to the person. He then switched to the policy arguments, which in his view negated the presence of any duty. To these we shall return in greater detail in the next subsection since they represent both in substance and in form one of the most interesting innovations of the judgment.

The *Elguzouli* judgment[103] is notable for the almost complete absence of any discussion of the usual ingredients of the notion of duty of care. Thus, there is only a fleeting reference to "foreseeability"[104] and an unquestioned acceptance of the point already found in Lord Browne-Wilkinson's judgment that the *Caparo* requirement of "fair, just and reasonable" also applies to all cases of negligence liability. One technical argument, however, seems to have escaped Lord Justice Steyn's (as he then was) attention: *Elguzouli*,

[99] Tregilgas-Davey, "*Osman* v. *Metropolitan Police Commissioner: The Cost of Police Protectionism*" (1993) 56 *MLR* 732, 737.

[100] [1995] 3 WLR 152 at 183. This was, indeed, accepted by the majority in *Marc Rich & Co. A G* v. *Bishop Rock Marine Co. Ltd.* [1996] 1 AC 211—a case involving property damage. Two years later an attempt was made to transport this reasoning to cases of physical injury in *Perret* v. *Collins* [1998] 2 Lloyd's Rep. 255 but it was boldly repulsed by a unanimous Court of Appeal. Lord Justice Hobhouse (as he then was) had this to say (at 258) on this crucial issue: "What the second and third defendants seek to achieve in this case is to extend decisions upon 'economic' loss to cases of personal injury. It represents a fundamental attack upon the principle of tortious liability for negligent conduct, which had caused foreseeable personal injury to others. That such a point should be considered to be even arguable shows how far some of the fundamental principles of the law of negligence have come to be eroded. The arguments advanced in this case [*viz.* that the kind of wider policy considerations used in *Marc Rich* to justify the majority decision should also be used in this case and absolve the defendants from all liability] illustrate the dangers of substituting for clear criteria, criteria which are incapable of precise definition and involve what can only be described as an element of subjective assessment by the Court; such ultimately subjective assessments tend inevitably to lead to uncertainty and anomaly which can be avoided by a more principled approach."

[101] *Governors of the Peabody Donation Fund* v. *Sir Lindsay Parkinson & Co. Ltd.* [1985] AC 210, 241C, per Lord Keith. The idea can, however, be traced back to Lord Morris's judgment in the *Dorset Yacht* case in 1970.

[102] *Caparo Industries Plc* v. *Dickman* [1990] 2 AC 605.

[103] *Elguzouli-Daff* v. *Commissioner of Police of the Metropolis* [1995] 2 WLR 173, 179. Including the judgment of the deputy High Court judge which Lord Justice Steyn (as he then was) described (approvingly) as "robust".

[104] At 183, which the judge was willing to accept as being satisfied.

unlike *Hill*—which plays a pivotal role in Lord Justice Steyn's judgment—was not a case of omission but a case of (distinctly) negligent acts. Yet the policy arguments in favour of immunity were so obviously in the forefront of Lord Justice Steyn's mind that he not only cited *Hill* as providing an "instructive analogy",[105] but went even further in asserting that in *Elguzouli* the reasons for immunity were here even stronger. The decision thus provides an even clearer illustration of the current (post-*Anns*[106] and, certainly, post-*Bedfordshire* and *Stovin*) trend to resolve these disputes by an open *if not exclusive* appeal to policy.

The majority and dissenting judgments in *Stovin* are a gold mine of ideas and analysis. Most are related to the issue of tortious liability for breach of statutory rules; and, if combined with the *Bedfordshire* decision, must signal a definite move away from the days of *Anns* towards a very restrictive[107] regime of tort liability of public bodies. The majority clearly suggests that nowadays a court which is confronted with such matters is not only obliged to investigate whether the decision in question is justiciable (the policy/operation dichotomy increasingly going out of fashion) but also whether it was irrational in the *Wednesbury*[108] sense (i.e., so unreasonable that no public body could have taken it). Even if it is, a private law claim in damages will not arise unless the court comes to the conclusion that it is "fair, just and reasonable" to make such an award. In this respect, discovering (or inventing) the "policy" of the statute with regard to compensation will be crucial.

Purely from the point of view of the tort of negligence *Stovin* presents two particular points of interest: first, its prolonged discussion of the distinction between acts and omissions, which as we have already noted received little attention in the *Hill* cases and its successors; secondly, its adoption of the view—which one could argue slipped into the general law of negligence almost without discussion until the House of Lords accepted it in a (fairly) recent and controversial majority decision[109]—that "fair, just and reasonable" is a requirement that is also relevant to all types of harm and not just pure economic loss. Potentially, this represents a significant move towards restricting the ambit of the tort of negligence and is in keeping with other recent attempts[110] to confine the reach of tort law.

[105] At 181.

[106] *Anns* v. *Merton London Borough Council* [1978] AC 728.

[107] It is too early to predict whether *Barrett* v. *Enfield London Borough Council* [1999] 3 WLR 79 can, on its own, reverse this trend. Our own guess, amplified further down, is that *Barrett* will be used technically and cautiously. Thus, if a real change is to come about, it will be through European influences, acknowledged or concealed but, nonetheless, there.

[108] *Associated Provincial Picture Houses* v. *Wednesbury Corporation* [1948] 1 KB 223.

[109] *Marc Rich & Co. A G* v. *Bishop Rock Marines Co. Ltd.* [1995] 3 WLR 227.

[110] *White* v. *Chief Constable of South Yorkshire* [1998] 3 WLR 1510 (psychiatric injury).

Such an ebb and flow of ideas about the exact boundaries of tort liability is not, of course, anything new. On the contrary, the whole history of tort law can be seen as a constant struggle between the rights of the injured versus the rights of their injurers. But these trends do justify two immediate reactions. Thus, first, they render dubious assertions that the tort of negligence is galloping out of control.[111] Its expansive tendencies are at the expense of other torts—*Rylands*, nuisance, to some degree defamation—not its traditional defendants. Secondly, and more relevant to our work, it cannot justify any conclusion that this trend is irreversible. As sure as day will follow night, the current judicial thesis will, itself, give way to a new antithesis and should not thus be seen as anything more than a passing phase in the unending battle to find a workable compromise between these antithetic positions. However, it is also interesting to note that the current position is being achieved through the deployment of the "fair, just and reasonable" device which (a) was first introduced[112] in the context of cases dealing with pure economic loss and (b) was not—originally at any rate—seen as having the potential of overtaking so completely the normative effect of the other ingredients of duty, namely foreseeability and proximity.

The durability of these changes in judicial philosophy will, we think, depend on two prime factors: first, on how convincing the policy reasons nowadays are openly invoked to explain why a particular result is (or is not) fair, just and reasonable; and, secondly, upon whether it will, in the long run, prove politically acceptable to introduce such extensive immunities in an (almost) blanket manner. Decisions like the one handed down in the *Essex County Council* case—our last focal point—may well bring more into relief not only the difficulty of applying wide *dicta* coming from "striking out" cases, but also the essential unfairness of the current trends which, it could be said, sacrifice justice so completely to the altar of financial good management. We must thus move on to examine the policy reasons given for these results and then superimpose a new influence, which has not yet been felt by our law: the human rights aspect of these extreme decisions. In our view, it is this kind of approach that is likely to reveal the unproved assumptions of the current conservative judicial trends. They will be shown to be even weaker when tested against the solutions adopted by some other legal systems which share the same economic and social characteristics as our own.

(b) Policy reasons

One should start by reminding the reader that in many of these cases—certainly the most recent vintage—liability was denied mainly by invoking the

[111] Weir, "The Staggering March of Negligence" in Peter Cane and Jane Stapleton (eds), *The Law of Obligations. Essays in Celebration of John Fleming*, (1998), 97*ff*.

[112] Subject to the point made earlier that one might be able to trace this idea in *one* of the judgments in the *Dorset Yacht* case.

public law/statutory duty powers arguments mentioned earlier. But in some decisions a number of unproved and, perhaps, unprovable policy propositions were also used—in some instances, such as in *Stovin*, "thrown in" at the end—in order to support the view that it was not fair, just and reasonable to find a duty of care. Although our judges are conscious of the fact that these arguments merge into each other and, more crucially, have not placed decisive reliance on any of them in isolation but looked at their cumulative effect, we shall here consider them separately. The arguments are basically four: (i) imposing liability on the public bodies in question would make bad economic sense; (ii) liability would inhibit the freedom of action of these bodies; (iii) it would be inappropriate for the courts to control elected bodies and tell them how to exercise their discretionary powers; and (iv) the victims in these cases had alternative remedies which make a tort remedy not only dangerous but also superfluous. We must examine these arguments in turn.

(i) Imposing liability on the public bodies in question would make bad economic sense

We call this set of reasons the "economic arguments" and note that in the English literature, it appears in a number of forms.

In the first, economic reasoning is invoked to explain why, in general, liability is not imposed in cases of pure omissions. As Lord Hoffmann put it in his judgment in *Stovin* v. *Wise*, the imposition of a duty of affirmative action upon a public body may result in its being required to confer an "externality", or unbargained-for benefit, upon a third party, in circumstances where this would lead to allocative inefficiency.[113] This rather technical economic explanation is examined in more detail in the next chapter. It seems not to have played a major part in Lord Hoffmann's reasoning in *Stovin* since he accepted later in his judgment that the "externality argument", while it might be of general relevance to the question of liability for omissions, did not really apply to public bodies since not only did they have the resources to act for the protection of third parties, they were also under pre-existing public law duties to act in any event.

In the second form, the emphasis is on the fact that a liability rule would force the public body in question to divert resources from other, potentially more important projects, to investigating its own actions or protect itself against possible claims. In *Hill* this argument appeared as a variation of the *Rondel* v. *Worsley*[114] argument: "The trial of such actions would very often

[113] [1996] 3 WLR 388, 406.

[114] [1969] 1 AC 210. It is, of course, interesting to note that this case is also currently under review by the European Court of Human Rights.

involve the retrial of matters which had already been tried . . . While no doubt many such actions would fail, preparing for and taking part in the trial of such an action would inevitably involve considerable work and time for a police force, and thus either reduce the manpower available to detect crime or increase expenditure on police services."[115] In the House of Lords, Lord Keith was of the same opinion when he said: "A great deal of police time, trouble and expense might be expected to have to be put into the preparation of the defence to the action . . . the result would be a significant diversion of police manpower and attention from the most important function, that of the suppression of crime."[116] The argument, understandably, resurfaces in the *Elguzouli* case where Lord Justice Steyn (as he then was) felt that an imposition of a duty of care would: "introduce a risk that prosecutors would act so as to protect themselves from claims of negligence. The CPS would have to spend valuable time and use scarce resources in order to prevent lawsuits . . ."[117]

The argument also appears in *Stovin*, where Lord Hoffmann took the view that the imposition of liability would divert resources from other needs such as education and social services.[118] A few lines further down he put the economic argument in a slightly different way when he allowed himself the luxury of speculating that "one of the consequences of *Anns* . . . and the spate of cases that followed was that local council inspectors tended to insist upon stronger foundations than were necessary".

A third argument relates to insurance, and is again to be found in the judgment of Lord Hoffmann in *Stovin* v. *Wise*. Essentially, this is an argument to the effect that the losses incurred in cases involving maladministration by public bodies can most often be dealt with through insurance carried either by the victim of harm or by some other party. Hence, in the context of the *Stovin* case, Lord Hoffmann argued that: "denial of liability does not leave the road user unprotected. Drivers of vehicles must take the highway network as they find it . . . It is primarily the duty of drivers of vehicles to take due care. And if . . . they do not, there is compulsory insurance to provide compensation to the victims."[119]

(ii) Liability would inhibit the free action of these bodies (the "inhibition argument")

In *Hill*, Lord Justice Glidewell put this argument in the following way: "if the police were liable to be sued . . . actions in this field would not be

[115] [1987] 2 WLR 1126, 1140, per Glidewell LJ.
[116] [1988] 1 WLR 1049, 1056.
[117] [1995] 2 WLR 173, 183.
[118] [1996] 3 WLR 388, 419.
[119] *Ibid.*

uncommon. Investigative police work is a matter of judgment, often no doubt dictated by experience and instinct. The threat of a decision which, in the end, proved to be wrong and might result in an action for damages would be likely to have an inhibiting effect on the exercise of that judgment."[120] In the House of Lords Lord Keith echoed the same view when he said: "In some instances the imposition of liability may lead to the exercise of a function being carried on in a detrimentally defensive frame of mind."[121] In the *Bedfordshire* case we again see this argument resurfacing in Lord Browne-Wilkinson's judgment when he stated that: "if a liability were to be imposed, it might well be that local authorities would adopt a more cautious and defensive approach to their duties. For example, as the Cleveland Report makes clear, on occasions the speedy decision to remove the child is sometimes vital. If the authority is to be made liable in damages for a negligent decision to remove a child (such negligence lying in the failure first to investigate the allegation) there would be a substantial temptation to postpone making such a decision until further inquiries have been made in the hope of getting more concrete facts. Not only would the child in fact being abused be prejudiced by such a delay: the increased workload inherent in making such investigations would reduce the time available to deal with other cases and other children."[122]

(iii) It would be wrong for the courts to second-guess public bodies in the exercise of their discretion (the "second-guess argument")

This clearly overlaps with the first and second policy arguments discussed above; but in the judgments it also appears as an independent policy heading. It thus plays a significant part in rejecting any idea of court interference where the decision of the public body lies in what was once termed the policy area. As Lord Browne-Wilkinson put it in the *Bedfordshire* case[123] "a common law duty of care in relation to the taking of decisions involving policy cannot exist." But an intervention by the court might become possible if the allegation of carelessness relates not to the taking of a discretionary decision but in the practical manner in which that act has been performed. The dividing line, however, between policy and operation (or, as some nowadays prefer it, justiciability) is sometimes more easily stated in theory than applied in practice. In some groups of cases, e.g., the police cases, the courts do not seem to have explored this distinction with any

[120] [1987] 2 WLR 1126, 1140.
[121] [1988] 2 WLR 1049, 1055. See also *Olotu* v. *Home Office* [1997] 1 WLR 328.
[122] [1995] 3 WLR 152, 184–5.
[123] *Ibid*., 173.

degree of thoroughness choosing, instead, to rely more heavily on the "scarce resources" argument in order to deny the imposition of any duty of care and, thus, any civil liability.[124]

(iv) In all these cases, the victims had alternative means of redress, which makes the tort remedy superfluous (the "alternative relief argument")

This argument also made its first appearance in the *Hill* case where the availability of some monetary compensation to the plaintiff through the Criminal Injuries Compensation Scheme was noted by both Lord Justice Fox[125] and Lord Justice Glidewell.[126] The very same alternative remedy was noted as being available to the children in the *Essex County Council* case by Lord Justice Steuart Smith;[127] and this may have been a significant reason why he, unlike the other two Lord Justices, refused to recognise a tort duty towards the children. But in other cases, the *Bedfordshire* and the *Elguzouli* cases in particular, the judges came up with a veritable barrage of alternative remedies which, in their view, influenced their answer as to whether it was "fair, just and reasonable" to create a tort duty and thus a damages remedy in those cases. In this section we shall simply list these alternative remedies and later we shall review their effectiveness.

(a) Even where a duty of care can permissibly be imposed, its ambit and scope are significantly influenced by the statutory regime. If this provides a special complaint procedure, this will militate against the availability of an additional damages remedy.
(b) The imposition of a common law duty of care may cut across a complex statutory regime, often interdisciplinary in nature and requiring the participation of many different professions. To make one group of experts or civil servants liable instead of another would be wrong; to make them all liable, would be unfair.
(c) The decisions taken under the statutory regime may be subject to judicial review.
(d) The tort of malicious prosecution may be available to the plaintiff/victim. Alternatively, an action for misfeasance in public office may exist.
(e) A claim under the Criminal Injuries Compensation Scheme may be available to the victim.

124 See, for examples, the cases cited below at n. 162.
125 [1987] 2 WLR 1126, 1137
126 *Ibid.*, 1140.
127 [1998] 3 WLR 534, 549.

2. The reasons given by the French law in reaching its (contrary) conclusions

(a) The attitude of French law towards the policy arguments used by English decisions

(i) The "economic argument"

One cannot find in either French case law or doctrine any visible trace of the "economic argument" used in English law in any of its three forms. The interesting question is to determine why this way of reasoning is so manifestly absent from French writings. The reasons are likely to be the following.

Over the years, the French system of public liability has become mainly compensatory in nature and is deeply focused on the plaintiff and the reparation of his or her damage.[128] As a result, the *Conseil d'Etat* has, in recent years, regularly enlarged the scope of public liability for the sole purpose of protecting citizens who happen to be harmed by administrative activities. One way of doing this has been, as already stated, by reducing the number of situations in which a condition of gross fault is a prerequisite of liability. The most remarkable example of that evolution took place in 1992 when the condition was removed in cases involving liability of public hospitals.[129]

In the light of the above it would thus appear right to claim that French administrative law is more inspired by the idea of "risk socialisation" under which the law tends to admit that when citizens suffer damage of a certain type and size it is the duty of the state to compensate them even if it is not possible to link them with something which could be called misadministration. This vision explains that, in the recent past, several pieces of regulatory legislation were put into place in order to grant people compensation—from the state budget—for damages having sometimes no relation—or at least without the need of demonstrating any relation—to any administrative action or omission. We could thus mention here as illustrations a 1990 Act for victims of terrorist acts as well as a 1991 Act concerning people affected by by transfusions of blood contaminated by the AIDS virus.

Once the above "philosophical stance" is noted—even if not accepted—one can see why French judges are unlikely even to consider the cost that a liability rule might entail for public authorities whose liability is the

[128] See, for instance, Christophe Guettier, *La résponsabilité administrative* (1996), 139; Michel Paillet, *La responsabilité administrative* (1996), 6.

[129] *Conseil d'Etat*, Assemblée, 10 avril 1992, Epoux V., *Recueil des arrêts du Conseil d'Etat*, 171, concl. H Legal.

subject of litigation. Somewhat more surprisingly, the idea that such resources might be better used in another "public" context equally does not seem to be considered. Thus, in the kind of consumerist vision of public liability which has become predominant in French law, compensating the damages suffered by citizens because of administrative activities can never be a wrong use of public money; on the contrary, it may even be seen as the best possible use of public money when it is viewed as serving the principle of equality by avoiding a result that means that people who have randomly been affected by administrative action remain without compensation.

As to the second form of the "economic argument", based upon the consideration of insurance, its absence seems to have the following explanation. In some cases, the damage suffered is not compensated by any insurance; in others, it would certainly not be considered as compatible with the principles described above if the insurers could not recover from the administration the money they had paid to citizens harmed by its activity.

(ii) The "inhibition argument"

The "inhibition argument" is not unknown in French theory of public liability but it certainly plays a secondary part. This is so because, apart from its fundamental compensatory function, public liability is also viewed as a way of disciplining the administration: in that role, it complements judicial review, by imposing payment of compensation, whereas the former provides the annulment of illegal decisions.

However, it is clear that consideration of a possible inhibition that liability could cause in administrative action has exercised a certain influence, and is still exercising some influence, in certain cases in which liability is subject to the requirement that a gross fault be committed. This is particularly clear in the field of police and local authority activities, illustrated by the cases we mentioned as comparable to *Hill* and *Stovin*. Thus it is precisely because French administrative judges still think that the admission of liability for a simple fault would make the police (or local authorities) too cautious—and, therefore, less efficient—that they have maintained gross fault as a condition of liability—a precondition which, as already stated, has been abandoned in other areas of liability. The fluidity of the notion of "gross fault" and the consequences that may flow from it must, however, be repeated here.

(iii) The "second-guess argument"

Will a French administrative judge sometimes refrain from imposing public liability because he thinks that it would mean that he has second-guessed the public body in the exercise of its discretion? Such an approach would hardly strike a French judge as a natural one. The reason is the following. In practice, in a large majority of cases in which the administration is held liable the fault, which has been identified, is an illegality. Illegality, in other words, is the most ordinary form of administrative fault.

This strong relation between fault and illegality has the consequence that the adjudication of administrative liability largely mirrors judicial review of administrative legality. The judges' attitude, when faced with questions of discretion, is the same in both cases. This means that judges have no reason to think that accepting liability would be especially impinging upon administrative discretion: they respect it, and review it to the same extent that they would otherwise do when reviewing questions of legality.

This does not mean that the "second-guess argument" plays no role at all. It is obvious that some of the cases in which French administrative law has, as we have specified, accepted liability without fault, have been so treated because it allowed the judge to grant compensation without having to assess state behaviour, in fields where the public action is particularly difficult, and where it appears that decision-makers must be left with a large amount of discretion. It is partly in order to avoid a "second-guess" debate on the decision by which a person is detained in custody before trial that the 1970 Act mentioned above stated that State liability would arise without fault where a person detained is not ultimately sentenced. The "second guess" argument is thus turned on its head insofar as it seems to lead to an expansion, not a restriction, of liability.

(iv) The "alternative relief argument"

It seems that in none of the cases we have mentioned, as comparable to the five paradigm English cases, could the consideration of an alternative relief have led the judges to exclude liability. In fact, there appears to be very few situations in which French administrative law could provide an adequate substitute to compensation granted on the ground of liability where damage has been suffered—the only example could be where somebody claims that he or she was refused by the administration a payment that he or she was entitled to receive, since that person can opt either for an action in liability or merely for the annulment of the refusal, with similar consequences if he or she succeeds.

Theoretically, there could be another alternative. In certain cases, the victim of damage caused by an administrative course of action can opt to act against civil servants instead of challenging the administration itself. This is so where the civil servants have committed what French law calls a personal fault—*faute personnelle*—and which corresponds to a very serious or intentional fault. In fact, however, this possibility will never be treated as "alternative relief" in the sense that its existence could lead the administrative judge to set aside administrative liability and direct the plaintiff towards private liability of a civil servant himself. Indeed, it has been ruled for a long time that, as far as the fault committed (be it a personal fault or not) has a link with the service, victims can act against the administration, which could then try to recover its money from a civil servant if he has committed a personal fault, and will not be driven towards the alternative of acting against the civil servant concerned.

(b) The actual reasons given by the French courts for the decisions

(i) Cases comparable to Hill

The way French decisions are worded shows clearly how free French administrative courts—compared to their English counterparts—are to act when they determine that an administrative fault has been committed. As mentioned above, French administrative courts operate within a very general and abstract concept of fault, which they apply with great flexibility. This appears from the fact that in two of the cases mentioned above, *Ville de Perpignan*,[130] and *Société Le Profil*,[131]—the *Conseil d'Etat* not only did not feel obliged to characterise the duty which the administration might have neglected, it did not even state which statutory or regulatory rule had laid down the duty! In the third case, *M et Mme Garagnon*,[132] the infringed duty was identified more precisely. It was to be found in the rules that determine the special surveillance airport police must exercise when minors are taken abroad. However, the statutory or regulatory rules defining that duty were not specified by the *Conseil d'Etat.*

Another interesting aspect of these cases is the way they consider whether or not there has been a gross fault. Administrative courts usually solve that problem by using three kinds of criteria.[133] These are: the importance of the duty which was not properly fulfilled; the obviousness of the fault, illustrated by its repetitiveness; and the size of the damage, which is sometimes a sign of how serious the fault is.

In none of the three cases is the criterion used made explicit. The case in which the reason why a gross fault was identified is most evident in *M et Mme Garagnon*—clearly, it was the importance of the duty to ensure that children are not taken abroad illegally.

(ii) Cases comparable to X *v.* Bedfordshire

In *M et Mme Pillon*[134] the exact nature of the duty which should have made the social service more careful in the placement of children was not specified. On the contrary, in *Epoux Ouaras*,[135] the *Conseil d'Etat* referred to

[130] Conseil d' Etat, 29 juillet 1948, *Recueil des arrêts du Conseil d' Etat*, 213.
[131] Conseil d' Etat, 26 avril 1979, *Recueil des arrêts du Conseil d' Etat*, 171.
[132] Conseil d' Etat, 26 juin 1985, *Recueil des arrêts du Conseil d' Etat*, 254.
[133] Michel Paillet, *La responsabilité administrative* (19''), 122.
[134] Conseil d' Etat, 4 mai 1983, No. 22811.
[135] Conseil d' Etat, 23 septembre. 1987, *Recueil des arrêts du Conseil d' Etat*, 290.

certain provisions which, in the Public Health Code (*Code de la Santé Publique*) require that social services supervise the health of all children under a certain age.

(iii) Cases comparable to Stovin

Three aspects of *Commune de Maisons-Laffitte* and *Marabout*[136] are worth mentioning. The first is that only in *Commune de Maisons-Laffitte* do we find an indication of the statute from which the administrative duty derived. The reference, however, is actually very wide as it is more a reference to the general powers local authorities have over traffic and car parking, than to a particular provision which would define a precise obligation.

The second aspect is that in *Marabout* the *Conseil d'Etat* expressed the view that the local authority should have acted in order to free the street from illegal car parking "by a regulatory decision, or by direct action" *(prendre des mesures appropriées, réglementaires ou d'exécution)*. Indeed, unlike English law, French administrative law on liability does not draw the distinction between policy and operation. Liability can arise either from wrong policy decisions—or the absence of them—as well as for wrong operational decisions—or the lack of them.

The third aspect is that, as the reader will already have realised, French administrative law on liability does not make a distinction between acts and omissions. Omission (*carence*) is a frequent cause of liability, and there are no signs in case law that it would, in any intellectual sense, be treated in a different way than negligent acts.

(iv) Cases comparable to Essex County Council

For our comparative purposes two points should be made about the case of *Consorts Fraticola*.[137] Once again, in that case neither the legal source of the neglected duty, nor its precise content, are made explicit. We are given to understand that social services are under an obligation to look after children placed in foster families, and that these families are also obliged, on behalf of social services, to look after the children. But this is nowhere made clear in the judgment; and no statutory basis is mentioned.

The case also shows how the presumption of fault works in practice. As the *conclusions du commissaire du gouvernement*[138] show, the plaintiffs

[136] Conseil d' Etat, Assemblée, 200F 1972, *Ville de Paris c. Marabout, Actualité Juridique, Droit Asministratif*, novembre 1972, 597.

[137] C. adm. Bordeaux, 2 février 1998, *Consorts Fraticola, Les Petits Affiches*, 12 août 98, 3, concl. D Peane.

[138] Opinion given by a member of the court, who will not adjudicate in the sense that he or she will not vote when the decision is taken. In spite of the way this person is called, he or she does not represent the Government in any capacity.

were not able to demonstrate that either social services or the foster family had not been careful enough in looking after the child. The *commissaire du gouvernement*—and apparently the court after him—were satisfied that it was not fair to leave the burden of proof on the plaintiffs; instead, this burden had to be shifted to social services.

3. German law

(a) The German attitude towards the kind of policy reasons advanced by the English courts in order to reject these claims

All of the arguments advanced in English decisions against the imposition of liability have also been considered by the German legislator, courts and academics and, generally speaking, found wanting. For instance, the four policy considerations discussed above had already been considered at the time when BGB, § 839 was being enacted one hundred years ago. It would be wrong to think, as some scholars often do, that such policy-orientated discussions represent a novel form of reasoning found only in the common law. If there is any novelty in the use of such arguments it lies mainly in the fact that they appear prominently in the judicial decisions, themselves, rather than that they have been identified as useful, additional tools in the reaching of the final decision. More important, however, is the observation that these policy concerns, which hold such sway in the minds of one or two of the highest English judges, have been steadily losing their appeal in contemporary German literature and judicial practice. The similarity with France is thus obvious, although the depth of the discussion that has taken place in Germany seems to be substantial.

The first two arguments—the "economic and inhibition arguments"—proved extremely controversial at the end of the last century.[139] It was thus stressed (as it is nowadays in England) that potential liability might make civil servants act too cautiously or expeditiously. But it was felt that even if this were to happen, and there were doubts whether in practice this would be the case, it would be better than any careless or less diligent behaviour on the part of the civil servants.[140] The same arguments also carried much weight with regard to the *personal* liability of the civil servant being sued. Thus, because of these considerations, it was *originally* argued that the civil servant should be liable *only* if he had acted maliciously or if his act

[139] Mugdan, *Materialien zum BGB*, Vol. II, 1305; *Protokolle*, Vol. I, 609, 611; "liability would cause an unforeseeable heavy burden on the state". *Motive zu dem Entwurf des BGB*, Vol. II, 824.

[140] *Protokolle*, Vol. II, 662.

amounted to a criminal offence.[141] In the event, however, the legislator decided not to adopt such a severe limitation of liability but, instead, chose to restrict the *personal* liability of the civil servant to solely negligent (but not intentional) acts whenever the injured person could obtain redress from another source (see discussion above). This limited restriction on liability was enacted in 1900 to secure that a person acting in an official function would not be inhibited by the fear of liability.[142] This argument carries little weight, however, if the public body is, itself, liable, an issue which had already been stressed in the consultations of the Committee which drafted the Civil Code. Liability of the state itself was thought to avoid the inhibition argument; but it was felt that this was not a matter for the Commission since the matter pertained to public law.[143] Besides this question the financial burden on the state had also been of great concern, especially with regard to certain categories of civil servants.[144] There was always the feeling, however, that it would be grossly unfair to leave a person affected by misconduct without recourse.[145] In addition, it must be stressed that the restriction does not play an important role in the present law, especially because courts have created many exceptions to the rule.[146] Only in a small percentage of cases can state liability be reduced, and in those cases the amount of money involved is negligible.[147] There is, therefore, unanimous acceptance of the view that this restriction should be abolished when the law is reformed (in accordance with what was said earlier in the book).

The danger that valuable time and resources might be spent in contesting the liability of public bodies has been raised as an argument against a general form of liability, i.e., a liability of the state even when all diligence had been observed (*generelle verschuldensunabhängige Haftung*). The argument has not been used, however, in the context of state liability where there has been a public wrong caused by a negligent act, where the protection of the individual is an issue, or where constitutionally guaranteed basic rights (such as life, health, liberty) are at stake.[148] In the latter cases in particular the argument is neutralised by the strong belief that an individual should be compensated for harm caused by a public body. This belief is regarded as an indispensable principle of the modern democratic state,

[141] Compare *Staudinger and Engelmann*, *BGB*, (1st ed., 1901), § 839, n. 2; *Motive*, above at n. 51, Vol. II, 822. For a critical view of this restriction on the liability of the state, see "Bettermann, Vom Sinn der Amtshaftung", (1961) *JZ*, 482, 483; HJ Vogel, "Die Verwirklichung der Rechtsstaatsidee im Staatshaftungsrecht" *DVBl*, 1978, 657, 659.

[142] Vogel, *ibid.*

[143] Protokolle, Vol. II, 662.

[144] *Jakobs and Schubert*, *Beratungen des BGB, §§ 652–853* (1983), 1024.

[145] *Motive zu dem Entwurf des BGB*, Vol. II, 736 *et seq*.

[146] See Münchener, *Kommentar*, *Papier*, n. 296 and below.

[147] Compare *Zur Reform des Staatshaftungsrechts* (1976), 12, 69.

[148] Vogel, above at n. 53, 657, 662.

and is taken very seriously.[149] Nor, finally, is this attitude affected by the distinction between "bad acts" and "omissions" which, again, seems to have weighed heavily in the minds of some senior English judges. *Hill* and *Elguzouli*, as well as their respective German parallels, thus show that harm can be caused by the public authority either when it fails to take the necessary decision to arrest a criminal promptly or where laxness results in an innocent person being kept in detention. The same would be true of the two child-neglect cases in *Bedfordshire*. For in the first of these the authority wrongly declined to act, in the second it acted wrongly.

The above-mentioned argument (the "inhibition argument") was relied upon by the district court (*Landgericht*) in the *criminal* prosecution of a social worker in the German equivalent of *Bedfordshire*.[150] The Court of Appeal reversed the decision of the *Landgericht* (which held the worker to be immune) because social workers are expected to decide, and in fact do decide, how to act according to their professional knowledge and experience and not because of fear of possible criminal sanctions.[151] Whatever one may think about this policy in criminal law, the situation with regard to the liability of the *state* for a public wrong is completely different.[152] Thus, on this matter German law lies closer to the view expressed by Lord Reid in the *Dorset Yacht* case[153] and has thus refused to adopt the argument that the imposition of liability could tempt civil servants to postpone vital decisions.

The argument that a liability rule might entail enormous financial consequences for the state has fared no better. A thorough empirical study, undertaken in connection with the reform proposals alluded to above, revealed that the financial burden of state liability (including all causes of action and not only breach of official duty) amounted to only 0.015% of the total budget.[154] This may, in part, be due to the relatively modest amount of damages which are awarded by German Courts,[155] and to which

[149] *Zur Reform des Staatshaftungsrechts, Gemeinsame Arbeitsgruppe des Bundes und der Länder zur Neuregelung der Staatshaftung* (1987), 10; Ossenbühl, *Staatshaftungsrecht* (5th ed. 1998), 6.

[150] LG Osnabrück 6 March 1996 in Mörsberger und Restemeier, *Helfen mit Risiko*, 121, see also 7.

[151] OLG Oldenburg of 2 September 1997, ZfJ 1997, 57; see also Oehlmann and Austermann *op.cit.*

[152] For the problems with regard to the duty to give warnings according to the new law on product security, see Tremml and Nolte, "Amtshaftung wegen behördlicher Warnungen nach dem Produktsicherheitsgesetz", *NJW* 1997, 2265.

[153] [1970] 2 WLR 1140, 1151: "It may be that public servants of the State of New York are so apprehensive, easily dissuaded from doing their duty and intent on preserving public funds from costly claims that they could be influenced in this way. But my experience leads me to believe that Her Majesty's servants are made of sterner stuff."

[154] *Zur Reform des Staatshaftungsrechts* (1976), 5, 71.

[155] For example, the sum of DM 5,000, was awarded in 1988 for unlawful detention in a psychiatric institution for seven days. This amount, however, was only meant to provide compensation for non-pecuniary damages and did not include compensation for possible economic losses. OLG Oldenburg, *VersR* 1991, 306. We return to this point in part 4.

we shall return below when we draw our comparative conclusions. At this stage, however, we will suppress the temptation of many English lawyers to dismiss the relevance of German law because of this difference in the level of awards. We must thus stress that, although the level of money compensation—especially for non-pecuniary damages—is not likely to be high, affected plaintiffs do at least receive some satisfaction from the imposition of tort liability. More importantly, they can claim and do, in fact, receive, substantial compensation for economic losses which flow from the administrative action. Thus, readers will recall that in the German equivalent to the *Essex*[156] case the adopted parents received full economic losses, namely the cost of rearing and caring for the handicapped child (for life) whom they had been misled into adopting.

By contrast, the third policy argument—the "second guess argument"—for a time played an important role in German decisions. The *Reichsgericht* constantly held that the courts should not interfere with discretionary decisions of public bodies.[157] The courts could only decide in cases where the public body acted outside the ambit of its discretionary power.[158] Thus, only arbitrary actions and decisions which show an obvious error on the record can give rise to liability in tort. Like the policy/operational test, the non-use of discretion could also give rise to liability. Thus, in an early case comparable to *Elguzouli* the court held that the state prosecutor had a duty (not a discretionary power) either to end the proceedings or to institute proceedings before a court.[159] Yet the extremely restricted control has increasingly been considered to be excessive and, in addition, outdated with regard to notions of justice in a modern democratic state, in which public bodies, even when they have discretionary powers, are bound by the law. This means that they must make use of their discretion according to the purpose of the respective rule.[160] If a statutory rule thought to protect the interests of individuals also gives discretion to a public body, justice requires that negligent use of the discretionary power causing harm to an individual should give rise to liability. Therefore, the restriction has been relaxed considerably—first with regard to judicial review of administrative acts by administrative courts,[161] and, subsequently, in public wrong cases raising issues of civil liability.[162] A discretionary decision may thus be reviewed by

[156] OLG Hamm, *FamRZ*, 1993, 704.

[157] For reasons of simplicity we shall make no distinction between the two categories of discretionary power in German law, namely "Ermessen" and "Beurteilungsspielraum", which have slightly different demarcations and are subject to different ambits of judicial control.

[158] RG 15 December 1939, RGZ 162, 273; RG 8 November 1938, JW 1939, 239, 240; see also BGH 17 January 1952, BGHZ 4, 302, 313 = NJW 1952, 583, 584.

[159] BGH 8 March 1956, BGHZ 20, 178, 182.

[160] BGH 15.2.1979, BGHZ 74, 144, 156 = NJW 1979, 1354, 1356.

[161] Here one started with distinguishing between discretion and non-appliance of discretionary powers, misuse of discretion and reduction of discretion to only one possible decision.

[162] BGH 15 February 1979, BGHZ 74, 144, 156 = NJW 1979, 1354, 1356; BGH 12 July 1979, BGHZ 75, 120, 124 = NJW 1979, 1879.

a court in a public wrong case even if it is within the ambit of discretion.[163] However, the court will not go into the question whether the decision taken by a public body was "right" (*Richtigkeitsprüfung*) but only whether the decision seems plausible (*vertretbar*).[164] The test of plausibility allows far more control than was sanctioned in the past, but it still does not mean that the court is substituting its own judgment for that of the administrative authority. Thus, in a case that provides a close analogy to *Elguzouli* the court scrutinised the decision of the state prosecutor even though a court had approved the prosecutor's application for the warrant. This attitude must again be viewed in connection with the principle that public bodies are bound by the law (Article 20 II of the Constitution), that they must respect the law diligently,[165] and that these principles might not be surrendered for the sake of mere administrative convenience. The difference with English law is, thus, once again notable. More interestingly, however, experience shows that the liberalisation of judicial review has not entailed serious (let alone catastrophic) consequences in any economic or practical sense (e.g. an increase in volume of litigation). What common lawyers would thus describe as the "floodgates argument" has, in practice, proved to be an imagined (or invented) fear, but not a real problem.

Let us now move to the "alternative relief argument". Although the sum of money involved in state liability cases can, as already stated, be relatively small,[166] it is, in most cases, the only redress that the affected individual may have. In Germany, as in England, special compensation systems may in certain instances give some relief, as, for example, the Criminal Injuries Compensation Scheme in England or the payments under the German Law on Compensation for Criminal Prosecution.[167] Between those systems on one hand, and tort liability on the other, there is, however, a notable difference, namely that in the latter case the injury was due to a careless act of the public body. In matters of justice the individual who has suffered a wrong can expect to be treated in a different way than someone who suffered misfortune.[168] In addition, the restriction on state liability in BGB,

[163] The discretion concerned in the following examples should be translated accurately as "*Beurteilungsspielraum*", not "*Ermessen*". Even if the errors involved do not give cause for appeal of an administrative decision (compare VwVfG, § 46) (*Verwaltungsverfahrensgesetz*) (Law of Administrative Procedure) the discretionary decision may give rise to a tort claim because it might not be unlikely that without the errors the discretionary decision would have been different, Münchener *Kommentar/Papier*, § 839, n. 203.

[164] BGH 27 September 1990—BGHR-BGB, § 839 Abs. 1 s. 1 Staatsanwalt 3; see also BGH 21 April 1988, ZIP 1988, 921.

[165] Ossenbühl, *Staatshaftungsrecht* (5th ed., 1996), 42.

[166] At least insofar as non-pecuniary damages are concerned. But see our observations in chap. 4.

[167] Which grants compensation for economic loss and—as far as detention is concerned—moral damages not exceeding DM 20 per day: StrEG, § 7.

[168] In German law the claims under the Law on Compensation for Criminal Prosecution are independent of a faulty act of the public bodies concerned and may exist parallel to the

§ 839 I 2 has, as already mentioned, little practical significance; it was relevant only with regard to 5.06% of all damages claimed.[169] The Federal Court of Justice thus described this rule as out of date, because the state should not conceal its liability behind possible payments made by others, such as private individuals.[170] Thus, exceptions to the exception regarding liability have been developed, namely with regard to certain kinds of redress and wrongs. If, for example, an employee of a public body travels with other road users, the alternative redress argument cannot be raised, because the public body is in the same position as other users.[171] The same can be said with regard to the duty of public authorities to take care in their daily activities (*Verkehrssicherungspflicht*).[172]

More interesting for our purpose are the kinds of redress held irrelevant to state liability. Payments under the social security system as well as those under private insurance taken out by an injured individual (or somebody else other than the tortfeasor) are not regarded as "alternative redress". In the first case this is because social security should be able to recover damages paid by the tortfeasor so that the community of insured persons does not bear the costs of a public wrong.[173] With regard to private insurance it is considered that the injured person (or somebody else) has paid for that benefit and this should not be to the advantage of the tortfeasor.[174] More significantly, redress against other *public bodies* (in the form of alternative administrative remedies) is also held to be irrelevant for the purpose of BGB, § 839 I 2. This follows the principle accepted by German law that public bodies are considered a unity.[175] Thus, we may summarise that in German law the alternative redress argument is regarded neither as an efficient nor a just restriction on state liability.

tort claims as well as to claims under Art. 5V of the European Convention on Human Rights, which concerns an unlawful (but not necessarily culpable) detention (BGH 31 January 1966, BGHZ 45, 58; BGH 29 April 1993, BGHZ 122, 268 = NJW 1993, 2927); Meyer, *Strafrechtsentschädigung und Auslagenerstattung*, (4th ed. 1997), 36; BGH 29 April 1993, VersR 1993, 792 = MDR 1993, 740.

[169] *Zur Reform des Staatshaftungsrechts* (1976), 12, 95.

[170] BGH 16 April 1964, BGHZ 42, 176 = NJW 1964, 1895; however, the court felt bound by the words of the statutes; only later groups of exceptions have been established (see below).

[171] BGH 27 January 1977, BGHZ 68, 217, 220 = NJW 1977, 1238.

[172] The Federal Court of Justice applies the exception to the exception here: BGH 10 July 1980, NJW 1980, 2194 (parallel case to *Stovin*); BGH 1 July 1993, BGHZ 123, 102, 104 = NJW 1993, 2613, 2616 (stability of trees—parallel case to *Ancell* v. *McDermott* [1993] 4 All ER 355; for critical remarks on this exception, see Münchener Kommentar, *Papier*, § 839, n. 310.

[173] BGH 20 November 1980, BGHZ 79, 26 = NJW 1981, 623; BGH 17 March 1983, NJW 1983, 2191; for the exclusion of continued payment of salary by the employer or the social security system see also, BGH 20 June 1974, NJW 1974, 1767, 1860.

[174] BGH 17 March 1983, NJW 1983, 2191; BGH 28 October 1982, BGHZ 85, 230, 233 = NJW 1983, 1868; BGH 2 April 1987, NJW 1987, 2664.

[175] BGH 12 April 1954, BGHZ 13, 88, 100.

(b) Reasons given by the German courts reaching their conclusions

In the comparable case to *Hill* the main issue was whether the police owed an official duty towards the individual. With regard to the Public Prosecutor's Office such duty is owed towards the accused (and other persons involved in the investigation). Otherwise, however, German law has, in a long line of decisions, accepted that the duty of care is owed only to the state. The reason given was that the Office has duties only towards the community at large.[176] However, the same has not been held to be true of the police, which have repeatedly been held to owe a duty towards individuals. Thus, the police have been held to be under a duty to prevent the commission of criminal acts,[177] to trace stolen goods,[178] and to avoid the commission of torts.[179] It is said that this differentiation between police and public prosecution services is due to the different structure of their respective duties. The police are thus seen as the guardians of good order, and this is taken to mean that they must protect individual citizens as well. On the other hand, the Public Prosecutor is there to enforce the criminal law (*staatlicher Strafanspruch*[180]); and such a duty can be owed only towards the state. Although in the case discussed here the result seemed very clear because the police officers had acted with gross negligence,[181] the result did not depend on the fact that the police acted intentionally. In recent decisions concerning the Public Prosecutor the Federal Court of Justice has stated expressly that an action against the police would not fail in a comparable situation, because the police owed such duty to the individual.[182]

The existence of such duty had also been the central point of discussion in the parallel cases to *Stovin*[183] and *Essex*,[184] although the question arose whether there was any duty at all. Unlike *Stovin*, the distinction between omission and bad act did not play any role in the German decision. If there is a duty to make traffic safe, this duty can equally be breached through bad acts or omissions. Neither did the court consider that the public author-

[176] RG 16 October 1923, RGZ 108, 249; RG 24 March 1937, RGZ 154, 268; BGH 28 March 1996, NJW 1996, 237, affirming OLG Düsseldorf 7 August 1995, NJW 1996, 530, affirming LG Düsseldorf 2 January 1995, ZIP 1995, 282; the state prosecutor, however, may have a duty of care towards a third party, if this individual has been involved in the investigation process: LG Trier 13 January 1994, VersR 1994, 810. See, also, BGH 16 October 1997, NJW 1998, 751.

[177] RG 26 February 1935, RGZ 147, 144; see also LG Landshut 14 September 1993, RuS 1994, 454.

[178] OGH Br.Z. Köln 22 September 1950, NJW 1951, 112—contrary to *Alexandreou* v. *Oxford* [1993] 4 All ER 328.

[179] BGH 29 June 1989, BGHR BGB vor § 1/*Beweislast Amtshaftung* 1.

[180] Steffen, "Haftung für Amtspflichtverletzung des Staatsanwalts" (1972) *DriZ*, 152.

[181] They had been lying before the court in order to protect the robbers.

[182] BGH 28 March 1996, NJW 1996, 2376.

[183] BGH 10 July 1980, NJW 1980, 2194.

[184] OLG Hamm 15 July 1992, FamRZ 1993, 704.

ity had any discretionary power. The authority could make only one decision, namely to ensure that visibility at the road intersection was not obstructed.

If the source of any danger is identified—which it was both in the English and German cases—it is the duty of the responsible authority to act in a timely manner.[185] The question whether the authority has acted in a timely manner, or whether there has been unnecessary delay, does not relate to the duty per se, but rather to the question of whether there has been any breach of this duty. Where it is impossible for the public authority to remedy all dangerous situations in a timely manner, such action would fail. The reason for its failure to impose liability would be lack of fault, and not reasons relating to discretion, policy, or administrative expediency.[186] It is very likely that in German law the decision would remain the same even if the obstruction of visibility were caused by an object on an adjoining land, as was the case in *Stovin*.[187] Because of the importance of safety in traffic, the court had no doubt that the general duty for the safety of the roads (for every user) included the duty to ensure visibility at that intersection.

In the *Essex* parallel case the court argued that the duty of proper information, although not expressly provided for in a statute, resulted from the nature of the dealings and was laid down at least by the directives of the board. There was a fundamental duty towards the parents, and its breach caused considerable damage.[188] The contrast with the English case could thus not be more pronounced.

The problem that the exercise of discretion restricts judicial review was discussed, to some extent at least, in the parallel case to *Elguzouli*. For the reasons given above it did not, however, stop the court from imposing liability. As the discretionary decision taken by the public prosecutor—at that state of the investigations—was not plausible but, on the contrary, rendered carelessly, the court held that it was a negligent act justifying the liability of the state. A similar result was achieved in a case where a person was kept in a psychiatric asylum as a result of an expert opinion concerning the

[185] This is contrary to *Ancell* v. *McDermott* [1993] 4 All ER 355.

[186] See LG Berlin 18 August 1994, VersR 1996, 603; LG Berlin 24 June 1993, VRS 88, 1995 7; OLG Sachsen Anhalt 28 June 1996, VerkMitt 1996 No. 124—all concerning bad road conditions in former East Germany; see also OLG Düsseldorf 23 October 1997, NVwZ-RR 1998, 708, which concerned icy roads.

[187] Compare BGH 28 May 1962, BGHZ 37, 165, 168, which held that a public authority is liable for dangers resulting from special street designs which adjoin rivers, ditches and so on; compare also with regard to tree branches above the road that might damage high lorries: OLG Sachsen Anhalt 5 February 1997, DAR 1998, 18. However, it must be mentioned that a hedge obstructing the view in the twin case to *Stovin* (as well as the dangerous memorial in BGH 28 May 1962, BGHZ 37, 165) was owned by the state.

[188] The Court of Appeal of Frankfurt argued in the same way in a recent case, but denied damages because of lack of fault: OLG Frankfurt 22 January 1998, OLG-Rp Frankfurt 1998, 243. See also BGH 2 April 1987, FamRZ 1987: 904—the official guardian (*Amtspfleger*) had not warned the employer of the ward that the employee was likely to be a pyromaniac.

state of his mind.[189] As well as detention, the discontinuation of criminal proceedings might also render a public authority liable if the decision is not "plausible".[190] In other instances, however, the courts have taken the view that the decisions were "plausible" and thus denied liability on the grounds that there was no fault.[191] Thus, from the point of view of German law, the important issue is that the Public Prosecutor has a duty of care towards the person charged with an offence and must thus pay due respect and consideration to the legitimate interests of the person charged.[192]

In the case cited as parallel to *Bedfordshire* the topic of discretion was not raised because the statute was clear on this point: there was a duty to act in a certain way[193] and that duty was performed diligently.[194] If there had been any negligent act (or omission) on the part of the youth authority, liability in damages would have arisen (though it is an open question, whether *moral* damages would be granted in such a (*tort*) action).[195] But there are many cases where the local youth authority caused economic loss to the child through negligent acts and in these cases the state was held liable because the youth authority owed a duty of care towards the child.[196]

[189] OLG Oldenburg 20 May 1988, VersR 1991, 306.

[190] BGH 21 April 1988, NJW 1989, 96, 98.

[191] BGH 22 February 1989, BGH-DAT Zivil; BGH 27 September 1990, BGHR BGB, § 839 Abs. 1 s. 1 Staatsanwalt 3.

[192] For example especially with regard to the information given to the public: OLG Hamm 15 July 1992, NJW 1993, 2109. This applies also to the police: BGH 16 January 1961, BGHZ 34, 184; BGH 19 January 1989, 1989, 1024; OLG Hamburg 2 November 1978, NJW 1980, 842. Of course, this role of the state prosecutor in German law differs from the English adversary system considerably. In German criminal procedure there is no adversary proceeding and the prosecutor is obliged also to reveal facts and circumstances which are in favour of the accused (§ 160 II) (see also BGH 8 March 1956, BGHZ 20, 178, 180), but this was not the vital point in the decisions cited above.

[193] Lakies, "Vorläufige Maßnahmen zum Schutze von Kindern und Jugendlichen nach §§ 42, 43 Kinder- und Jugendhilfegesetz (KJHG)", *ZfJ* (1992) 49 at 51.

[194] Were the facts exactly as in *Newham* there would arise the question in German law of whether the expert himself would be liable; compare BVerfG 11 October 1978, NJW 1979, 305.

[195] BGB, § 847 in combination with BGB, § 253 restrict moral damages to injuries of body, health and liberty; serious infringement on the right to personality (*Persönlichkeitsrechtsverletzungen*) has been held to give rise to moral damages (BVerfG 14 February 1973, BVerfGE 34, 269, NJW 1973, 1221; compare Markesinis, *The Law of Obligations, Vol. II, The Law of Torts*, 927), but here it would be questionable whether the same applies to parental rights (which are also protected in BGB, § 823 I) and, if not, whether the negligent act also injured the right of personality of the mother.

[196] OLG Celle 18 September 1996, NJW-RR 1997, 135, concerning advice with regard to maintenance; OLG Köln 10 January 1991, FamRZ 1991, 1098—the guardian gave days of grace for maintenance payments to the father; the Federal Court of Justice also awarded damages to the guardian, because the local youth authority had caused economic loss, BGH 15 June 1989, DAVorm 1989, 864. There has been some controversy over whether a local youth authority or an official guardian (*Amtspfleger*) acts in the exercise of a public office (denied by OVG Münster 6 March 1978, NJW 1979, 1220, 1221), but the overwhelming opinion especially in liability cases affirms this—see, for example, OLG Celle 16 August 1996, NJW-RR 1997, 135, expressly affirming the official function of the official guardian: BGH 5 May 1983, FamRZ 1983, 1220. There may also be liability of the state for the negligent act

The same is true with regard to negligent acts of a family court judge when authorising dealings of the guardian or the parent.[197] Had there been any tort case comparable to the first case in *Bedfordshire*, there is little doubt that a German court would have gone into the matter in detail and would have allowed evidence on the question of carelessness. That the criminal proceedings against the social worker (in the comparable German case) were finally stayed,[198] should not be taken as indicating that a tort action would fail; at the very least, it would have been tried and not, as in England, been struck out.[199] There is thus a duty of care on the local youth authority to protect neglected or misused children,[200] as soon as the authority obtains knowledge of the neglect or misuse.[201] It is another question, however, in what situation the conduct of the social worker will amount to a breach of that duty and it is a further and very delicate question of when it should be regarded as negligent.

III. A CRITIQUE OF THE ENGLISH REASONS

1. How convincing are the English arguments?

Since the five English cases discussed in this book have reached, as we have seen, their conclusions predominantly by reference to a number of openly stated policy factors, the continued viability of their results will depend upon whether future generations of practitioners, with or without the assistance of academic writers, are able to challenge the validity of their arguments. Of course, practitioners acting for aggrieved plaintiffs, may also try to avoid the restrictive results of these decisions by falling back on the time-honoured way of distinguishing their own case from an apparently binding and adverse older ruling. There are some signs that in the area of police

of the guardian towards third parties, for example the employer of a ward, who should have been warned by the guardian that the ward was a pyromaniac (this case is comparable to the *Essex* case): BGH 2 April 1987, FamRZ 1987, 904.

[197] BGH 31 March 1960, BGHZ 33, 136, 140—no proper control of guardian; BGH 20 November 1967, VersR 1968, 172—no proper representation of child.

[198] After the OLG Oldenburg, ZfJ 1997, 55, had allowed the appeal, the *Landgericht* stayed the proceedings because, if there had been any fault of the accused, it was only a minor fault (stop, § 153).

[199] For the problems resulting especially from criminal proceedings against social workers, see Mörsberger/Restemeier, *Helfen mit Risiko* (1997).

[200] The law, however, does not give a right to claim performance of that duty (*öffentlich-rechtlicher Erfüllungsanspruch*): Gerauer, "Die Struktur der Jugendhilfe im neuen Kinder- und Jugendhilfegesetz (KJHG)", *DAVorm* (1990) 495, 497.

[201] Hauck-Haines and Mainberger, *Sozialgesetzbuch* (SGB VIII) 23 (loose-leaf-service 1998), K 42, n. 15, K 51, n. 23, K 53, n. 13, K 55, n. 55. The Court of Appeal of Oldenburg (ZfJ 1997, 55) even held that a social worker has the role of a guarantor towards a child (*Garantenstellung*), i.e., in criminal law a role which obliges the social worker to act when the life and well-being of a child is endangered.

powers this has already happened.[202] However, in this context one must also note that the chances of this being accepted is becoming increasingly difficult as dicta from various "striking out" cases are piling up in a direction that is consistently favouring defendants.[203] This accumulation of such pro-defendant authority thus makes it nearly impossible for impecunious but deserving plaintiffs even to contemplate asserting in a judicial context that their case justifies being treated as an exception to the immunity trend. Indeed, one of the authors of the *Hill*[204] judgment admitted as much in one of his subsequent judicial opinions.[205]

On the other hand, practitioners will also have to take increasing note of the fact that Strasbourg is showing signs of unease over such blanket immunities which it sees, not without cause, as capable of amounting to a denial of access to justice under Article 6(1) of the European Convention of Human Rights. To the extent that this is correct, the European Court of Human Rights is prepared to voice some disapproval[206]—a disapproval which we venture to suggest will grow as our own Human Rights Act begins to exert a serious influence over the entire range of private law. Since, on the whole, we would welcome this development, we must now turn to examine the validity of the policy reasons advanced by our judges against tort liability in the hope to prove them unconvincing.

At first glance the policy arguments advanced by our courts seem overwhelming. The prestige of the judges who have advanced them—for instance, Lord Browne-Wilkinson, Lord Steyn and Lord Hoffmann—coupled with the confident style in which these policy views have been presented to the legal public—seem to confer upon them an aura of inevitability. These very same features, however, can also lead lawyers to forget that in some of the leading cases the final outcome of the litigation was opposed by most of the judges who heard the case. Of course, in precedental terms, what matters is the final count in the House of Lords. Analytically, however, pointing out the fact that there already exists serious

[202] Thus, *cf. Swinney* v. *Chief Constable of Northumbria Police Force* [1996] 3 WLR 968 with *Olotu* v. *Home Office* [1997] 1 WLR 328.

[203] We consider later on the effect that *Barrett* v. *Enfield*—[1999] 3 WLR 79—may have on this trend. Here, it is sufficient to state our belief that *Barrett* (in the Lords) would not have happened if it had not been for *Osman* and the kind of arguments we are advancing in this work.

[204] *Hill* v. *Chief Constable of West Yorkshire* [1988] 1 WLR 1049.

[205] *Alexandrou* v. *Oxford* [1993] 4 All ER 328, 340: "the observations . . . in *Hill*'s case in relation to the effect on the police of their being potentially liable in negligence were general, not limited to the facts of that case." Although this must now be read in the light of the observations in *Swinney* v. *Chief Constable of Northumbria Police Force* [1996] 3 WLR 968, the immunity granted to the police is, in practice, a blanket one; and this is how the Strasbourg court considered matters in its *Osman* judgment.

[206] We return to this issue below but note here that English lawyers are likely to see *Osman* as an impermissible example of judicial activism. Even if that is so, however, in our view they will have to learn to live with it.

division in judicial opinion can only strengthen the conviction that if these policy reasons can be challenged head on, the outcome they have produced may not be as unshakeable as may appear at first sight. This argument is further strengthened by the realisation, supported by growing judicial and extra-judicial pronouncements, that the philosophical starting point of our judges is no longer as uniform as it may have been fifty or even thirty years ago.[207] Our point is thus really this: the doctrine of binding precedent may, for the time being, be giving the impression that our law has taken an irreversible turn towards defendants, but this does not imply that this change is here to stay. Our belief in the opposite conclusion lies in our conviction that the policy reasons given by our judges are, on closer examination, much less convincing than their proponents make them out to be.

We will divide our analysis into a number of sections. We will thus consider first the group of reasons that are based on economic arguments. Secondly, we will analyse a set of justifications, which could be thought of as being broadly constitutional in nature: these refer to the division of powers between the executive and the courts and to the possibility of obtaining alternative remedies. Thirdly, we will examine the question of how far the reasoning in these cases has led to inconsistency of treatment in the application of the law. We will conclude by looking at the relationship between tort law and human rights.

(a) Economic reasoning

As we saw in Chapter Two, three broad types of economic arguments were offered. These relate, respectively, to externalities, defensive practices, and insurance. We will consider them in turn and then analyse a fourth reason not cited explicitly by the courts but referred to somewhat indirectly by Lord Hoffmann: this we call the "defendant of last resort" argument.

[207] That these philosophies may be radically different can be seen from the starting point adopted by two of our most learned judges. Thus, in the *Bedfordshire* case (*X (Minors)* v. *Bedfordshire County Council* [1994] 2 WLR 554, 572F) Sir Thomas Bingham MR (as he then was) said: "If [the child] can make good her complaints . . . it would require very potent considerations of public policy, which do not in my view exist here, to override the rule of public policy, *which has first claim on the loyalty of the law: that wrongs should be remedied.*" (emphasis added). In *Stovin* v. *Wise* [1996] 3 WLR 388, on the other hand, Lord Hoffmann seemed to adopt a different starting point when he said "the assumption from which one starts makes a great deal of difference . . . The trend of authorities has been to discourage the assumption that anyone who suffers loss is prima facie entitled to compensation from a person . . . whose act or omission can be said to have caused it. *The default position is that he is not*," (emphasis added). Most judges, however, would not take such a clear stand, even if in the end they leaned in Lord Hoffmann's direction. Thus, see Lord Browne-Wilkinson's views in the *Bedfordshire* case [1995] 3 WLR 152, 183B.

(i) Economics opposes the imposition of duties of affirmative action where this would lead to externalities in the form of unbargained-for benefits

This argument was very clearly expressed by Lord Hoffmann in the following passage in *Stovin* v. *Wise*:

"In economic terms, the efficient allocation of resources usually requires that an activity should bear its own costs. If it benefits from being able to impose some of its costs on other people (what economists call 'externalities') the market is distorted because the activity appears cheaper than it really is. So liability to pay compensation for loss caused by negligent conduct acts as a deterrent against increasing the cost of the activity to the community and reduces externalities. But there is no similar justification for requiring a person who is not doing anything to spend money on behalf of someone else . . . So there must be some special reason why he has to put his hand in his pocket."[208]

As Lord Hoffmann indicates, a general rule imposing liability for omissions could well lead to inefficiency. Just as an activity which causes negative externalities without incurring liability for them receives, in effect, a subsidy from tort law, so activities which give rise to obligations of affirmative action in the absence of any reciprocal benefit are being penalised by the legal liability system. We would therefore expect there to be underprovision of the activities in question.

Important and helpful *in general* though this passage in Lord Hoffmann's speech may be, it does not particularly help his own argument against the imposition of liability upon public bodies. Lord Hoffmann himself recognised that it has no application in situations of reliance or interdependence between plaintiff and defendant: "[t]here may be a duty to act if one has undertaken to do so or induced a person to rely upon one doing so". The exchange of reciprocal benefits or burdens between the parties may make it appropriate for an affirmative duty to be imposed, since the element of one-sided subsidy no longer exists. In fact, most of the situations in which English law imposes a duty of affirmative action are either like this (liability rarely arises between strangers) or involve the imposition of liability on the party who has the resources to deal with a particular threat of harm (such as an occupier or landowner).

In *Stovin* v. *Wise* the relationship between the parties was that of strangers;[209] at least we can say that there was no relevant, pre-existing relationship between the plaintiff and the council. Such was clearly not the case, however, in *W* v. *Essex County Council*[210] (which in any event is hard to

[208] [1996] 3 WLR 388, 406.
[209] The point is considered at length by Lord Hoffmann, *ibid.*, 406*ff.*
[210] [1998] 3 WLR 534.

see as an omission case). Not only were the parties known to each other prior to the harm occurring; the council had given an undertaking not to do the very thing it then did. In *Osman* v. *Ferguson*[211] the parties were known to each other and there was, arguably, an element of reliance by the deceased on the police with regard to his own safety as well as that of his son.

There are other reasons for treating the act/omission distinction with scepticism in the context of cases such as *Stovin* v. *Wise*. We shall offer two.

First, public authorities do have the resources to act in such a way as to obviate dangers to third parties. Thus, they are not excluded from liability by virtue of the need, as stated by Lord Wilberforce in *Goldman* v. *Hargrave*,[212] to take into account the actual resources available to a defendant upon whom a duty of affirmative action might be imposed. As Lord Hoffmann himself said:

"It is certainly true that some of the arguments against liability for omissions do not apply to public bodies like a highway authority. There is no 'why pick on me' argument: as Kennedy LJ said [in the Court of Appeal[213]], the highway authority alone had the financial and physical resources, as well as the legal powers, to eliminate the hazard."[214]

Secondly, in cases involving public authorities, the defendant is normally under some kind of pre-existing public law obligation to act. Where this is the case, we cannot speak of an affirmative obligation being created *de novo*. Nor would it be possible to argue that the imposition of liability would lead to the under-provision of the service or activity in question. This point was recognised by Lord Nicholls in *Stovin* v. *Wise* when he said:

"If there were a common law obligation in the present case, sounding in damages, the extent of the obligation would march hand in hand with the authority's public law obligations. This is a cardinal feature of the present case. The council's public law obligation was to act as a reasonable authority. The common law obligation would be to the same effect."[215]

(ii) Imposing liability on public authorities will lead to inefficiency in the form of "defensive administration" and the diversion of expenditure

In his judgment in *Stovin* v. *Wise*,[216] Lord Hoffmann argued that:

"The creation of a duty of care upon a highway authority, even on grounds of irrationality in failing to exercise a power, would inevitably expose the authority's budgetary decisions to judicial inquiry. This would

211 Supra, at n. 97.
212 [1967] 1 WLR 645.
213 [1994] 1 WLR 1124, 1139.
214 [1996] 3 WLR 388, 408.
215 *Ibid.*, 398–9.
216 *Ibid.*, 419.

distort the priorities of local authorities, which would be bound to try to play safe by increasing their spending on road improvements rather than risk enormous liabilities for personal injury accidents. They will spend less on education or social services. I think that it is important, before extending the duty of care owed by public authorities, to consider the cost to the community of the defensive measures which they are likely to take in order to avoid liability."

As we saw above, similar arguments were made by Lord Browne-Wilkinson in the *Bedfordshire* case, by Lord Justice Steyn in *Elgozouli-Daf*,[217] and by Lord Keith in *Hill*.

The claim that negligence liability leads to "defensive practices" is often made in this and related contexts. However, the evidence on which it rests remains slim. Some US studies have found evidence that expenditure on bureaucratic and administrative procedures designed to avoid liability for medical negligence, such as various kinds of form-filling and checking, has grown considerably in recent years and now amount to billions of dollars across the system as a whole.[218] No similar studies have been carried out for the United Kingdom or the public service elsewhere.

Lord Hoffmann's suggestion that, after *Anns*, local inspectors insisted on "stronger foundations than was necessary" is therefore just speculation. We could answer Lord Hoffmann's hunch, with a counter hunch namely, that while it is possible that the post-*Anns* regime led to unnecessarily strong and expensive foundations, the post-*Murphy* situation may be encouraging sloppy verification of building calculations. What the law must, surely, be striving to achieve is neither excessive caution nor unnecessary sloppiness; and the latter may well follow a signal from the courts that they are opposed to any form of civil liability. Legal arguments cannot be solved, and litigation cannot be determined, on the basis of hunches, however eminent and experienced their source may be. Moreover, hunch or intuition, the dividing line between what is prudent and what becomes excessive is a fine one. At present, we do not have enough empirical evidence to guide us in the matter of foundation inspections; and what we do have from another area of the law—medical malpractice—may suggest that one person's excessive caution is another's prudent practice. In another case,[219] Lord Hoffmann was prepared to be more candid and admit that the absence of empirical evidence makes it difficult to predict the economic consequences of a pro-liability decision; so why not show the same candour here and avoid alarmist statements? In short, we submit that an economic analysis of a decision requires more than our judges have so far been able to produce.

[217] *Elgozouli-Daf* v. *Commissioner of Police of the Metropolis* [1995] 2 WLR 173.

[218] Dewees, Duff and Trebilcock, *Exploring the Domain of Accident Law*, n. 10 above, chap. 5, reviews this evidence.

[219] *White* v. *Chief Constable of South Yorkshire Police* [1998] 3 WLR 1510, 1556.

What is also problematic for this argument is that it could apply with equal force to well-established areas of tortious liability, such as employers' liability and product liability. The argument is not unique to the liability of public authorities. Indeed, from this point of view the case for granting immunity to public authorities (via the concept of duty of care) is weaker still, since they are not subject to the forces of competition, nor to the same damaging reputational effects of litigation which affect private sector organisations.

In other contexts, the courts have been sceptical of arguments about the inhibitive effect that civil liability would have on the actors. In *Dorset Yacht*, Lord Reid had no time for such arguments.[220] In *Spring*, the House of Lords unanimously rejected a variant of this argument, and the sky has not yet fallen on our heads. Yet another variant of this point appeared in *Rondel* v. *Worsley*[221] and there it won the day. The signs are that Strasbourg, again, may remind us that continental European advocates are also subject to duties towards their courts and judges along with their duties to their clients. Their potential liability for negligent conduct has not caused them to be less honest, less forthright, or less effective than our barristers; and compulsory insurance has ensured that they have not suffered financial ruination as a result of a liability rule. Our brief comparative survey suggests that the potential of civil liability has not made continental police, local authorities or social security agencies less prompt, less efficient or less effective. The judges' arguments that apocalyptic consequences would follow if our system went the same way may thus sound attractive on paper but, in their extreme form, they are, once again, unsupported by any empirical evidence. The most recent pronouncement on this type of case—*Barrett* v. *Enfield London Borough Council*[222]—may provide some evidence that this point is getting through to some judges. Thus, in *Barrett* Lord Hutton opined that he "would not give this consideration great weight".[223] This statement was preceded, however, by the words, "In the circumstances of this case", and this could be seen as an important proviso given that Lord Hutton was keen to stress that the *Bedfordshire* arguments carried "insufficient weight" in the case which he was actually deciding. On the other hand, the learned Lord coupled his "dislike" of the "inhibition argument" with an express approval of a wider *dictum* by Lord Justice Evans in the Court of Appeal phase of the *Barrett*[224] hearing, and this could give a wider significance to Lord Hutton's phrase.

[220] [1970] 2 WLR 1140, 1151.
[221] [1969] 1 AC 191.
[222] [1999] 3 WLR 79.
[223] *Ibid.*, 114.
[224] There, the Lord Justice had argued that "if the conduct in question is of a kind which can be measured against the standards of the reasonable man, placed as the defendant was, then I do not see why the law in the public interest should not recognise those standards to be observed" ([1998] QB 367, 380).

(iii) First party insurance is a more effective way of spreading the loss than imposing liability upon public bodies

As we saw earlier, insurance arguments feature in Lord Hoffman's judgment in *Stovin* v. *Wise* as well as in some of the other cases under consideration here. The broader case for reducing the role of liability and, by extension, of liability or third party insurance, in favour of loss or first party insurance, has been made by Professor Patrick Atiyah. In *The Damages Lottery*, Atiyah argues that the liability system *is* both inefficient, because it gives rise to wasteful double insurance—first party and third party—and regressive, in the sense that higher prices and inefficient public services hit the poor hardest. First party insurance, he claims, would be preferable because only those who considered it worthwhile to insure would pay the premiums to do so.[225]

It is often assumed that the existence of liability insurance creates waste within the third category of accident costs identified by Calabresi, those relating to the administration of the system, while doing little to promote efficient precautions in relation to the second category. However, there is some empirical evidence to suggest that the abolition of liability and its replacement by private loss insurance lead to an increase in accident rates. This can be seen from "before and after studies" that looked at jurisdictions which abolished liability in tort for road traffic accidents and replaced it with a system based on first party insurance. In Quebec, the rate of increase in accidents was, according to various accounts, between 10% and 30%.[226] Insurance can, it seems, have a deterrent effect if premiums and bonuses are related to the experience of individual policyholders. This is true even of first party insurance. If first party insurance is "experience rated"—in other words, the less experienced pay higher premiums—the system incorporates an incentive to improve the standard of care.

In general, it is not at all clear from the present state of research in this area that we should prefer a tort regime in which fault plays no role. The system of fault plus liability insurance will often be a more effective deterrent than a no-fault scheme. Liability insurance is important from an economic point of view because it attaches implicit prices to dangerous activities. In this way, "the direct incentives of the liability system may be translated into the terms of insurance policies".[227] Insurers have an incentive to monitor the activities of the insured and set premiums according to

[225] *The Damages Lottery*, (Hart, 1997) 134.

[226] Dewees, Duff and Trebilcock, *Exploring the Domain of Accident Law*, (OUP, 1996) 25, citing M Gaudry, "The effects on road safety of the compulsory insurance, flat premium rating and no-fault features of the 1978 Quebec Automobile Act", in Osborne Commission, *Report of Inquiry into Motor Vehicle Accident Compensation in Ontario* (Toronto: Queens' Printer); R Devlin, "Liability versus no-fault Automobile Insurance Regimes: An Analysis of the Experience in Quebec" PhD Thesis, University of Toronto.

[227] Shavell, "Economic Analysis of Law" (1999) *NBER Reporter* (Spring), 12, 13.

how far they act to reduce the risk of harms to third parties. While this implicit pricing will not work well if insurance societies operate on the basis of "knock for knock"—effectively allowing claims to cancel each other out—this practice is, it seems, fading away in Britain for the very reason that it involves the cross-subsidisation of dangerous activities by the less dangerous, and hence is not in the long-term interests of insurance companies.[228] Hence, it is not necessarily the case that defendants can simply pass on the costs of liability if they have third party insurance. It seems that both the level of activity and the degree of care taken by defendants can be affected through the operation of liability when coupled with insurance.

This is demonstrated by the studies of North American workers' compensation schemes. In such schemes, it is the employers who have to take out insurance, not the employees. Insurance premiums end up being varied by industry and, more rarely, by firm. The most carefully constructed empirical studies—those which cater for the fact that the introduction of no-fault compensation leads to an increase in the number of injuries which get *reported*—found that increases in workers' compensation benefits led to a reduction in injury rates, and that the reduction was most substantial for high-risk industries and high-risk firms.[229] This evidence supports the claim that risk-related liability insurance helps reduce accident rates, in addition to providing for a degree of loss spreading.

In short, to argue that liability insurance necessarily involves waste and inefficiency within the system of accident compensation as a whole is to fail to understand the complex economic effects to which this form of loss-spreading gives rise. The optimal or ideal form of insurance depends in practice on a range of factors which include the relative wealth of the parties concerned (how effectively can they meet claims in the absence of insurance?) and the ability of insurers to observe and verify the risk-reducing activities of the insured. In some circumstances, it may be economically efficient to impose a statutory obligation on certain parties to take out liability insurance, as is currently the case in many areas of accident law. This would be so, for example, if those taking part in risk-creating activities would not, in the absence of insurance, have the means to meet claims against them. In some cases, economists suggest that the legislator should intervene to make liability insurance unlawful—this would be efficient where insurers could not effectively monitor risk-reducing activities and

[228] This has been extensively reported in the insurance and financial press. See, for instance, N Richardson, "Motor Insurance. Myth Hits the Crash Barrier", *The Independent*, 23 March 1996. We are grateful to Mr David Howarth of Clare College, Cambridge, for this reference and for a most helpful discussion on this point.

[229] M Moore and WK Viscusi, *Compensation Mechanisms for Job Risks: Wages, Workers' Compensation and Product Liability* (Princeton: Princeton University Press, 1990); Dewees, Duff and Trebilcock, *Exploring the Domain of Accident Law*, above at n. 10.

vary premiums accordingly. The legislator also has an interest in regulating attempts by potential defendants to render themselves "judgment-proof" by various devices aimed at evading liability (we return to this point below in the context of our discussion of the "defendant of last resort" argument).

To resolve these questions is a complex matter. As Professor Steven Shavell has suggested: "[t]o understand when and how to regulate liability insurance, these points need to be explored, and data needs to be developed and analysed on the nature of the judgment-proof problem and of liability insurance coverage in various areas of risk".[230] These are issues which probably require the kind of systematic consideration of policy options which only the legislator can effectively engage in. What, then, is the message for the courts? The issue for them is not whether and how to regulate liability insurance, but whether to create a demand for this type of insurance in the first place by imposing liability. As we have seen, the economic arguments for and against liability insurance are finely balanced; but they certainly do not point towards it being necessarily inefficient and wasteful. On the contrary, it may play a vital role in signalling to potential defendants the means by which they can reduce risks of harm to third parties.

This insight is just as relevant to the behaviour of statutory bodies and public authorities as it is to manufacturers, occupiers, and employers. Where public bodies carry third party insurance, we would expect insurance companies to monitor their internal processes for assessing and managing risk, in this way contributing to improved effectiveness in the delivery of public services. Where, alternatively, public bodies operate on the basis of self-insurance—in other words, carrying sufficient funds to meet potential claims—they have just as strong an incentive to avoid incurring liability for negligence. As David Howarth has pointed out,[231] negligent local authorities in this position will either have fewer recourses to meet their policy objectives, or will have to raise taxes to make up the difference and explain to voters why they are doing so. If, therefore, the courts were to grant sweeping immunities to public bodies, they would, in effect, be negating one of the principal mechanisms by which overall costs within the accident compensation system—not just the costs of accidents themselves but also the costs of precautions and the costs of administering compensation—are minimised.

This is not to suggest that the practice of liability insurance is always efficient. However, the answer to inefficiency, in this context, lies not in the abolition of liability, but rather in the regulation of insurance practices, as we have just explained. The history of liability insurance suggests that the

230 "Economic Analysis of Law", above at n. 227, 14.

231 D Howarth, review of PS Atiyah, *The Damages Lottery*, in *The Times Literary Supplement*, February 1998.

legislator is ready to intervene to make insurance compulsory where this is socially and economically desirable. There is no good, economic reason for courts to short-circuit this process by denying liability on the part of whole classes of defendants through the use of the duty concept. Indeed, from an economic viewpoint there is every reason for them not to take this step.

(iv) Public bodies need special protection as "defendants of last resort"

An argument which did not figure prominently in the judgments of the five cases we are considering here, but which has been discussed in the context of the academic debate and is implicit in some of Lord Hoffmann's comments in *Stovin* v. *Wise*, is the idea that public bodies are at risk of speculative litigation in a way which most individuals and private-sector companies are not. The idea is that public authorities are liable to become "defendants of last resort" since they are unable to escape liability in ways which are open to other types of defendants. The most obvious way in which other defendants do this is through bankruptcy or insolvency. Strategies for avoiding liability through the use of shell companies which protect the parent company from legal claims are well advanced in the United States, to the extent that commentators there have referred to the prospect of the "death of liability" if current trends continue.[232]

This practice does not appear so widespread in Britain, but we are certainly familiar with the idea that public authorities may end up as residual defendants when all else fails. Thus it has been suggested that the difficulty which home owners have in tracking down and obtaining damages from negligent builders explains why, in the line of cases culminating in *Murphy* v. *Brentwood District Council*,[233] it was local authorities which bore the force of litigation in respect of defective premises. Even where a builder can be traced and has sufficient assets to be worth suing, contribution between joint tortfeasors means that the builder's negligence is, to some extent, underwritten by the resources of the local authority: the activities of negligent private-sector defendants are then subsidised by the public purse.[234]

In our view, this is the *only* "economic" argument, which could justify treating public authorities as a special case through the device of the duty of care. All the other arguments considered here either fail to stand up to close economic scrutiny (such as the insurance argument), or, insofar as they survive such scrutiny, could be applied with equal force to cases involving private-sector defendants (such as the defensive administration argument).

[232] See L LoPucki, "The Death of Liability" (1996) 106 *Yale Law Journal* 1.
[233] [1991] 1 AC 398.
[234] See T Weir, "Governmental Liability" [1989] *Public Law* 40.

However, in accepting that the danger of speculative litigation against public bodies is a real one, we do not need to accept a near-blanket denial of liability of the kind which the law appears to have reached after the decisions in *X (Minors)* and *Stovin* v. *Wise*. Control devices may continue to be available to the courts even if the possibility of a duty of care in some cases is admitted. A control device is clearly present in the form of the special pre-tort relationship which existed in each of the *Essex*, *Osman*, and *Elguzouli-Daf* cases, where there were clear elements of reliance and (in the *Essex* case) of undertakings given by the defendant to the plaintiff. In none of these cases could the need to discourage "last resort" litigation realistically be invoked as a reason for defeating the claim.

Stovin v. *Wise* was not a case involving a pre-tort relationship; there was no element of specific reliance and no undertaking given by the defendant to the plaintiff as an individual. Lord Hoffmann's concerns about the implications of joining highway authorities to litigation involving road traffic accidents raise similar issues to those which we have considered under the heading of "last resort" litigation. Was the majority correct, therefore, to reject the possibility of liability in this case? There are in fact several features of *Stovin* v. *Wise* which make it a special case and which could have been used as control devices. As Lord Nicholls of Birkenhead explained in his judgment, the defendant not only had the resources to take the action necessary to remove the hazard, but had failed to do so only because of internal mismanagement, and not because of a decision of policy concerning the allocation of resources. It is true that, in this case, the result of making the highway authority liable would have been to benefit the first defendant's liability insurers. From an economic point of view, however, there may have been nothing wrong with this. As we suggested earlier, where liability follows fault, the workings of the insurance system can ensure that a price is attached to negligent activity (or non-activity), thereby providing incentives for it to be minimised. It is far from clear that the *full* consequences of the accident in *Stovin* v. *Wise* should have been borne by the first defendant's liability insurance, given that the situation of danger in this case was one for which the highway authority was to a certain degree responsible.

In many ways the *X (Minors)* case is the most complex and difficult one from the point of view we are considering here. Nevertheless, it is possible to see how this case, like *Stovin*, could have turned on the presence or absence of fault, rather than being decided on the issue of duty of care (with the result that the issue of fault was never considered). The decision to initiate childcare proceedings (or not) is, in nearly all cases, one involving a high element of professional judgment which the courts could review only with some difficulty. Very similar issues therefore arise as in the context of other situations where the courts must assess whether professional negligence has occurred; and here, as there, it does not seem implausible to suggest that some protection against frivolous claims could have been achieved by the application of the *Bolam*[235] test.

(b) Constitutional factors

(i) The division of powers between the courts and the executive

A further category of reasons relates to the division of powers between the courts and the executive when controlling the activities of public bodies. In our view, the current talk of the need to shield public bodies may be going too far in the direction of stating that the only real control is political and not legal. As one leading public lawyer has observed in his classic textbook,[236] "Public authorities, including ministers of the Crown, enjoy no dispensation from the ordinary law [of the land] This is an important aspect of the rule of law". Echoes of this can be found in Lord Nicholls' dissent in *Stovin* where he reminded us that "The law must recognise the need to protect the public exchequer as well as the private interests".[237] In the light of what will be said below about the validity of the "alternative remedies" argument, one might be forgiven for believing that our judges seem to be losing sight of this aspect of the matter. This is becoming particularly apparent where serious human rights are being violated as a result of this protective stance. All that such statements really betray is the fact that for as long as we do not have a set of morally (if not legally) superior rules, there is a serious risk that human rights values will be sacrificed to traditional tort reasoning. In this context it is interesting to note the contrast with the law in France and Germany where judicial control of public bodies is seen as a legitimate way of additional control and not as a dangerous and unacceptable interference with their decisional powers.

(ii) The existence of alternative remedies

The question of alternative remedies is also relevant in this context. In a few instances, newly invented remedies—for instance an Ombudsman's report—have provided remedies to wronged victims which the tort system could either not produce or might produce after a lengthy and costly litigation. In a handful of other cases, from the group here reviewed, the non-liability rule can be justified by the existence of *truly* alternative and *effective* remedies.[238] We submit, however, that these cases are, in numeri-

[235] *Bolam* v. *Friern Hospital Management Committee* [1957] 1 WLR 582; Markesinis and Deakin, *Tort Law*, (4th ed. OUP, 1999), 164–5.

[236] Sir William Wade in Wade and Forsyth, *Adminstrative Law*, (7th ed. OUP, 1994), 763.

[237] At 397.

[238] *Olotu* v. *Home Office* [1997] 1 WLR 328, where the remedy of *habeas corpus* was available to the illegally (over)-detained plaintiff and where, one also finds hints that he might,

cal terms, very much the exception.[239] So, how serious are judges when they tell us that a poor, under-privileged and, probably, uneducated citizen who has found himself unjustly held in custody for over three months can bring a successful action for malicious prosecution or misfeasance in public office? It is not just that his social and economic position makes it almost impossible for him even to contemplate taking on the governmental apparatus responsible for his misery—especially in these days of reduced generosity on the part of the Legal Aid Board; it is also that the torts in question have ingredients that make it very difficult to invoke them with any real chance of success. Finally, the availability of purely administrative law type of remedies (e.g., judicial review) are attractive only in theory. In practice, they hardly achieve any (moral) satisfaction; they promote no deterrent function; and they bring about no compensation whatsoever. On the contrary, the conclusion reached in cases such as *Elguzouli* and *Essex County Council*, to the extent that they are (partially) justified by the argument that in all of these instances there is an alternative remedy, can only provoke moral outrage, even among hardened lawyers.

Although this way of testing the validity of "the alternative remedy" argument is not shared (yet?) by the majority of our judges, the *Barrett* decision in the House of Lords provides some signs that not all judges are convinced by the prevailing argumentation we are here criticising. Thus, it is submitted that Lord Hutton was right to go beyond what we are stating, and not merely test the effectiveness of the alternative remedy (as we are suggesting) but assert boldly that "the jurisdiction of the court should not be excluded because of the existence of other measures of complaint".[240] As stated, this argument becomes even stronger when one bears in mind the exceptional paucity of "alternative remedies" asserted to be open to disgruntled plaintiffs. Because of its strong human rights implications, *Elguzouli* is the case that stands out most clearly in our minds.

additionally, have grounds for complaint against those who failed to alert him as to his possible remedies. Similarly, in *Hill* v. *Chief Constable of West Yorkshire* [1988] 1 WLR 1049 the availability of compensation under the Criminal Injuries Compensation Board obviously weighed on the minds of some of the judges. In this context, however, one must note two things: first, the generosity of the Criminal Injuries Compensation awards are, nowadays, considerably reduced so the effectiveness of this "alternative" remedy must be looked at very carefully; secondly, in many of the cases reviewed in this book this particular alternative remedy was simply not available.

[239] The Ombudsman's report in the Barlow Clowes affair is, possibly, one of the finest example of such intervention since it led to the government paying out to investors who lost their life savings a sum in the order of £16 million. Several ombudsmen schemes are currently in operation and are described briefly by Professor Peter Cane, *Tort Law and Economic Interests* 2nd ed. (OUP, 1996), 366*ff*.

[240] [1999] 3 WLR 79, 114.

(c) Inconsistency in the development and application of the law

(i) Bringing the law of tort into disrepute

Conservative lawyers tell us that the imposition of liability in some cases brings the law into disrepute since it insults its dignity. The principle is hardly debatable (although some of the examples given[241] to illustrate its application in practice, e.g., psychiatric injury, are debatable). If the dignity of the law, however, is invoked to condemn decisions which award compensation to victims and which most ordinary folk would regard as deserving, why is the same not happening when the denial of liability produces results which affront most citizens' sense of justice? Thus, statements to the effect that one "must not yield to an argument based on the protection of civil liberties" but opt instead for a (subjective) assessment of what serves best the interests of the "whole community"[242] in no way enhance the dignity of the law. Thus, those who regard the dignity of the law as a proper factor for determining the discovery of a duty of care should invoke it with greater consistency than is currently evidenced from their writings.

(ii) The misapplication of broad dicta

Broad *dicta*, in striking out actions, are used subsequently to justify judgments in different factual configurations. The policy reasons given in the *Hill* judgments had this effect on almost all cases that followed it. Few subsequent cases picked up the fact that the immunity rule in *Hill* was supportable on the ground that the harm flowed from an omission and not a bad act (as it did in *Elguzouli*). Few of the subsequent cases[243] also failed to explore the reality that their facts, unlike those of *Hill*, arguably involved mistakes made in the operational areas of police activities and not in the traditionally excluded area of policy. To the extent that this proves convincing—and, of course, in legal matters there is always room for argument—it suggests that the "preservation of scarce resources argument", first enunciated in *Hill*, has ruled the day and has in practice led to a blanket immunity. Thus, many will have been struck by the way the *Bedfordshire* pronouncements were used, almost verbatim, to strike out the parents' claims in the *Essex* case. What remedy was available to them, either as aggrieved parents or aggrieved ratepayers, against their local authority? Some lawyers may also be unhappy with the fact that the "fair, just and

[241] For instance, the award of damages to sufferers of psychiatric injury. See, Professor Stapleton's feisty "In Defence of Tort" in P Birks (ed.), *The Frontiers of Liability* (OUP, 1994), Vol. 2, 83*ff*.

[242] *Elguzouli* [1995] 2 WLR 173, 183.

[243] As, for instance, *Alexandrou* v. *Oxford* [1993] 4 All ER 328; *Osman* v. *Ferguson* [1993] 4 All ER 344; *Ancell* v. *McDermott* [1993] 4 All ER 355.

reasonable" requirement was introduced in these cases and utilised as a further means of limiting liability. The extension in *Marc Rich* by a divided House of Lords of such an "uncomfortably loose test for the existence of a legal duty"[244] from cases concerning pure economic loss to a case involving a property damage to a vessel is debatable. But it is literally unjustified, if not also unjustifiable, where abhorrent invasions incidents, such as those found in the *Essex* case, are at issue. Thus, it can be argued that in their recent judgments our courts have taken the rationale of *Hill* too far, moving from a position which was understandable, perhaps even justifiable, to one which even hardened lawyers may find difficult to accept.

(iii) Inconsistency in the treatment of professionals

A further result of the five cases we are considering here is a marked difference in the treatment of different categories of professionals. For instance, why are we willing to second-guess doctors but not willing to attempt the same with local authority officials? Is it because the courts are better equipped to perform the former rather than the latter task? Is it because we are more anxious to protect the anonymous civil servant from the eponymous doctor? Or is it because insurance practices work differently in the one case but not in the other? The same objections apply to the other argument advanced in favour of police and local authority immunity: liability would make them more timid and more hesitant to act. But why are actions against local authorities or the police any more likely to make them hesitant than malpractice actions made doctors over-defensive? (The contrary assertion, although often made, has never, to our knowledge, been proved empirically.) Until reliable answers are given to the above questions, one is thus bound to feel that the law treats the public body more leniently than the private defender. Even those who have favoured immunity in our cases have not advocated such a different treatment between public and private bodies.[245]

(d) Tort law and human rights

A further consequence of these decisions is the fact that our present law is bound to create friction with, at first instance, the Court in Strasbourg and, in due course, with our own human rights legislation. Lord Justice Steyn admitted as much in his *Elguzouli* judgment; and if we share the fear that such a conflict is looming ahead, we should do our uttermost to avoid it. Our submission has, all along, been that such conflict will be avoided only

[244] The words belong to Lord Nicholls in *Stovin* v. *Wise* [1996] 3 WLR 388, 396.

[245] "In the case of positive acts . . . the liability of a public authority in tort is in principle the same as that of a private person but may be *restricted* by its statutory powers and duties." *Stovin* v. *Wise* [1996] 3 WLR 388, 409.

if recourse to the notion of duty of care, as the device that produces blanket immunities, is abandoned. As stated, calls for degrading the use of this device in our law of torts are as old as the concept itself; but the need to do something about this is now becoming a matter of practical necessity and is no longer merely a topic fit for academic speculation. If such a change would take too bold a move, then our judges could, at least, make a start, by downgrading the requirement of fair, just and reasonable which they—wrongly in our view—extended to physical harms, and which has provided the entry point for so many of these conservative policies. The "fair, just and reasonable" device is young in age and can thus be remoulded more easily than the cardinal concept itself.

In this context, we must also ask the following, basic question: what is the state trying to achieve in all these cases? In general and abstract terms the answer must be that it is acting in a regulatory or supervisory function. Now, in some of the cases that can be brought under this broad heading, one could argue that the purpose of the norms which govern the regulatory function is to ensure that the (appropriate) rules laid down by primary or delegated legislation are observed by those who have to apply them. Such a definition could, for instance, be used to justify the non-liability rule reached in *Yuen Kun Yeu* v. *Attorney-General for Hong Kong*[246] where the regulatory regime concerned financial services and pension. Such an explanation/justification of the *Yuen Kun Yeu* case is not, of course, compelling in any legal or logical sense. We can see this both from studying other developed systems which have not followed this approach,[247] but we can also see it from the equally noteworthy fact that our system, as well, has ignored this "logic" of non-compensation by opting for a completely different solution *where public pressure is both large and organised.*[248] It does have the merit of not sharing the whole edifice of tort law but justifying a departure only where it can be argued that the primary aim of the regulatory function is to act in the interests of a weaker section of society. The *Bedfordshire*, *Barrett* and *Essex* cases could thus very plausibly be brought under this heading since here, as Professor John Bell, among others, has argued, "the idea of the protective norm suggests that [the state] should be liable to [those vulnerable people] for its failure to live up to expectations".[249]

[246] [1988] AC 175.

[247] E.g., the German system where the view taken by the courts is that state supervision of banking not only serves the public weal but also the interests of individual investors. Thus, see Markesinis, *The German Law of Obligations*, Vol. II, *The Law of Torts*, (3rd ed. OUP, 1997) 905 (with reference to BGHZ 68, 142).

[248] The Barlow Clowes affair offers an illustration of the point since £150 million was, apparently, paid out to those who suffered from the regulatory failure in that case. On this, see Gregory and Drewry, "Barlow Clowes and the Ombudsman" [1991] *PL* 192, 408. I The fact that the payment in that instance was *ex gratia* does not affect the argument in the text above.

[249] "Government Liability in Tort", *National Journal of Constitutional Law* 85, 101.

There is, in other words, plenty of room to argue that some of the cases we have encountered in this book can lay a strong claim to being decided differently than they have done thus far. Incidentally, in order to avoid frightening Germanophobes, we have so far deliberately spoken of the "scope of the norm" rather than the well-known German term of *Normzweck. But terms do not really matter.* What matters, instead, is the fact that this way of analysing legal problems was invented almost simultaneously (in the late-twenties) in Germany by Ernest Rabel, and in the United States by Leon Green. That, however, is only a detail!

Finally, we cite as a further reason the argument that can be culled from the experience of other, major, European legal systems. In the law of those countries we find a legal position, which casts grave doubts on the reality of the fears advanced by those who oppose the introduction of the tort rules in this part of the law. Such a different case law, unaccompanied by the apocalyptic consequences which the English detractors of tort law so often invoke, merits at least a closer study in order to discover why solutions which are deemed so unworkable in England have worked in France and Germany.

2. More doubts from abroad.[250] *Osman* v. *UK* and the growing impact of human rights law on English tort law

The *Hill* rule, achieving as it does immunity for the police through the use of the notion of duty of care, can, *in practice if not strictly speaking in theory*, be seen as conferring "a blanket immunity on the police for their acts and omissions during the investigation and suppression of crime". Until the Strasbourg judgment in *Osman* approached it from a different perspective no one, to our knowledge, had in this country even considered the possibility that such a blanket exclusion of liability could amount to a denial of justice for the plaintiff/victim who has his claim rejected through the use of the notion of duty of care. On the contrary, the case was seen as a simple example of a striking out action. As we shall see, the Strasbourg Court—with the concurrence of the English judge—did not share this optic at all but, on the contrary, took the view (in para. 139 of its judgment) that: "the applicants must be taken to have a right, derived from the law of negligence, to seek *an adjudication*[251] on the admissibility and merits of an arguable claim . . ."

[250] Andenas and Fairgrieve also point out the potential assistance that English law may derive from Community law. Thus, see "Sufficiently Serious? Judicial Restraint in Tortious Liability of Public Authorities and the European Influence" in Mads Andenas (ed.), *English Public law and the Common Law of Europe*, chap. 14. In the introductory chapter to the book the editor also rightly questions (at 3) whether the English courts will, in the long run, be able to operate two sets of rules, two types of remedies and two forms of reasoning "depending on whether the administrative action is based on a Community law measure or not".

[251] Our emphasis.

In the Court's view, the question of whether the restriction of that right (to have one's case heard) was compatible with Article 6(1) of the European Convention on Human Rights was to be determined later.

The tragic case that provoked this recourse to the Strasbourg court was *Osman* v. *Ferguson*.[252] The case involved a schoolteacher who, in 1987, developed an "unhealthy" obsession with one of his young charges.[253] Both the boy, who rejected these advances, and his parents, complained to the school and its head teacher. This led to a number of interviews with the teacher who became increasingly hostile and engaged in a series of menacing acts affecting the young boy's family. The police, who had been informed of the teacher's behaviour, apparently remained inactive, even after it became known that the dejected and depressed teacher "threatened to do a Hungerford".[254] A year later, as the acts of criminal violence increased, the police were, apparently, putting together a file with a view to prosecuting the mentally deranged teacher. But, alas, he acted first, by killing the father and injuring the boy's brother. The judge at first instance refused to strike out the plaintiff's action; but his decision was reversed by the Court of Appeal which relied on the *Hill* ruling even though in this case the proximity factor, contested in *Hill*, was found to exist in favour of the plaintiff. The Strasbourg Court, seised of the dispute, recently held[255] that such blanket immunities may "amount to an unjustifiable restriction of an applicant's right to have a determination on the merits of his or her claim against the police in deserving cases". Thus, the Court ruled that all the considerations relevant to the complainant's claim should also "be examined on the merits and *not automatically excluded*[256] by the application of a rule which amounted to the grant of an immunity to the police". This led to a (unanimous) decision that in the instant case the exclusionary rule (in *Hill*) "constituted a disproportionate restriction on the applicants' right of access to a court and for that reason there had been a violation of Article 6(1) of the Convention".

[252] [1993] 4 All ER 344.

[253] That over twelve years have been required to lapse before a semblance of justice could be achieved in this case is, itself, a serious condemnation of our system. It is also a tangible example of how the repatriation of human rights by our recent Human Rights Act should save litigants' time and the country the embarrassment of being told that its system of justice is deficient by a foreign court. But that is another matter!

[254] In 1987 Hungerford became the scene of a massacre in which a gunman ran amok, killing a number of persons. The exact words used by the assailant in this case were the subject of some dispute.

[255] *Osman* v. *UK*, (1998) *The Times*, 5 November (No. 87/1997/871/1083). In our discussion we say nothing about the Court's use of Art. 6 to justify its intervention in this case, partly because of lack of space but mainly because we do not feel that it is right to distract the reader's attention from the fact that this decision of the Grand Chamber, although not technically binding upon English courts, is likely to have an important impact upon our law. This impact is likely to be even greater if, as expected, Strasbourg follows the same path when it pronounces on the *Bedfordshire* case now pending before it.

[256] Our emphasis.

As already indicated, the significance of the decision just described goes far beyond its immediate facts. First, it is likely—ultimately, if not immediately—to provide a serious and, in accordance with what we have said above, well-deserved blow to the use of the notion of duty of care as a (blunt) device for effectively preventing damage claims against public bodies in general (and not just the police). If this leads to an increase in litigation, as the supporters of the status quo will argue, we submit that such an increase will be of a short duration (and could be further curbed by the award of small amounts, at any rate for non-pecuniary headings of damage). In support of this prediction we invoke the many instances (trespassers, liability for negligent references, psychiatric injury, etc.) found in our modern tort law where the opening of the floodgates was predicted—both in England and the United States—(but did not materialise)—every time an effort was made to liberalise or modernise our tort rules.

Secondly, we feel that the danger of frivolous claims being brought will also prove confinable through the use of other legal devices available to our courts including, of course, the burden of costly litigation and, as we suggested, the award of modest damages for the non-pecuniary parts of any such claims. In this context one must note the, as yet, unknown effect which the restriction of legal aid will have on the incidents of litigation. Moreover, we feel that even if it takes some time to achieve this type of litigation equilibrium, any temporary uncertainty that may ensue will be considered by many to be a small price to pay in exchange for ensuring that justice is not only done, but is also seen to be done.

Thirdly, we remind readers that other such cases are currently pending before the Strasbourg court. If the Strasbourg court follows its approach in *Osman* in cases such as *X* v. *Bedfordshire County Council* currently before it, it will bring about a significant rethinking in English tort doctrine. The outrageous facts of the *Osman* case (and, indeed, other cases such as *Elguzouli* and *Essex*) suggest that some of our judges, in their current "cerebral" mode, may be sacrificing traditional tort aims such as justice, deterrence and compensation to the altar of prudent management of admittedly scarce resources. The important point made in this book is that the current English approach to these problems is not the only realistic one available to any court of justice. The foreign experience, especially in Germany and France, suggests that other alternatives may merit more consideration, especially in the light of the fact that Europe is sending signals which we simply cannot *wholly* ignore. But our predictions to what may follow *Osman* are subject to the usual caveat that it is dangerous to prophecy about the future and, in any event, are less relevant for present purposes. What is more significant is to say a few words about the reactions that have thus far appeared with regard to the *Osman* case. Three, in our view, stand out for comment.

The first can be dealt with briefly since its discussion does not really pertain to this work but to those which specialise in the jurisprudence of the Strasbourg Court. It is based on a straightforward reading of the text of Article 6(1) of the Convention which provides that, "In the determination of his civil rights and obligations . . . everyone is entitled to a fair and public hearing. . . ." As Lord Browne-Wilkinson quite rightly put it:[257] "this would seem to require that the applicant has, under the local law, a right (right A) enforceable in the local court. Under Article 6 he is given as a separate right (right B) a right of access to the local courts to assert right A being a separate, free standing right. Thus one would assume that right A would consist of, for example, a contractual right or a tortious right not to be negligently injured. If a person is prevented from enforcing those rights that is not an infringement of right A but an infringement of right B i.e. the right of access to court." Lord Browne-Wilkinson then went on to state that, as far as he could see, *Osman* did not say that but, effectively, created a new right A for the plaintiff. His Lordship is, we submit, correct on this point,[258] with the result that the Strasbourg Court could be accused of having indulged in an interpretation of Article 6(1) of the Convention which is both novel and objectionable.

"Novel", we think it is, although in fairness it could also be seen as a continuation of a conscious decision to adopt a creative approach towards Article 6 which goes back at least until the *Golder* [259] decision of the same Court and, in our view, further expanded in the *Fayed* case.[260] But is it also "objectionable?" This brings us to the other two objections which, we indicated earlier, have already been levelled against *Osman*. Both are interrelated, and we shall look at them only to the extent that is necessary for the purposes of this book.

The prime objection would seem to be that Strasbourg cannot create *new* [261] rights for the United Kingdom; or, to put it differently, it should be

[257] *Barrett* v. *Enfield London Borough Council* [1999] 3 WLR 79, 84.

[258] Subject, we think, to the *caveat* that the right envisaged by the Court was, in essence, only a right to have whatever claim the plaintiff might have according to the law of torts adjudicated and not summarily (and routinely) dismissed in a striking out action. We read Lord Browne-Wilkinson's judgment in *Barrett* in the same light, since the learned Law Lord was anxious to say that in some instances such cases should be heard and this can only imply that there is an underlying basic right. We further see this as an important feature of the case since, in proximity terms, the *Osman* case differed from *Hill*.

[259] *Golder* v. *UK* (1975) EHRR 524.

[260] *Fayed* v. *UK* (1994) 18 EHRR 393 where, interestingly, the court said (para. 65): "it would not be consistent with the rule of law in a democratic society or with the basic principle underlying Art. 6(1)—namely that civil claims must be capable of being submitted to a judge for adjudication—if, for example, a State could, without restraint or control by the Convention enforcement bodies, remove from the jurisdiction of the courts a whole range of civil claims or confer immunities for civil liability on large groups or categories of persons".

[261] See P Craig and D Fairgrieve "Barrett, Negligence and Discretionary Powers"—unpublished paper delivered at a conference held at King's College, London, on 2 August 1999.

forced to respect the fact that this role belongs to the United Kingdom Parliament and courts. In principle, this is certainly correct, especially if we interpret the doctrine of parliamentary sovereignty in a very literal fashion. However, few would say that such an approach would nowadays tally with realities; and the reality we have in mind is the growing influence that human rights values are having on our law. This reality, in our view, means that the new human rights environment[262] may, on occasion, affect even the powers of the national legislator (or courts) to delimit the existence and contents of nationally recognised rights. Imagine, thus, the following series of examples.

Imagine first if Parliament were to pass a law saying that British Jews, because of their race, had no civic rights. Would such an enactment, even assuming that it surmounted the obvious political obstacles which would be put in its way, escape the control of the European Court (even if it had that of a British Court)? Could anyone dare to argue that national law recognised no rights and thus could bar such persons from going to courts? The answer must surely be "no" for the simple reason that the older doctrine of parliamentary sovereignty would have to yield to the growing influence that human rights law—both of the indigenous and imported variety—has on English law. In short, human rights will no longer tolerate crude race discrimination. A British Jew who thus found himself defeated by an English court would, undoubtedly, be able to complain that his Convention rights had been violated.

Now let us move a scale down and imagine another example, namely that a law was passed allowing only men to hold the office of Prime Minster of the United Kingdom. Such legislation would give no such right to a woman; but no English or Strasbourg Court would uphold it since, once again, it would run counter to another set of human rights values which has, in relatively recent times, become acceptable, and that is the equality between sexes. Human rights values would thus, once again, override internal legislation; and we assume that if an English court failed to grant a woman complainant an appropriate remedy on the grounds that the English Parliament recognised her no such right could, again, be overturned by Strasbourg on a number of grounds including violation of Article 6(1).

Let us finally move a notch further down and closer to the facts of the *Osman* case. Suppose that an English statute (or the courts) had proclaimed that a person who had suffered loss as a result of a careless act or omission of a statutory body was *never* to be allowed to seek redress before a court of law. Would such an enactment escape the control of the Strasbourg

[262] The impact of this new human rights (political) environment on traditional concepts of law—national and international—can be seen by looking at how the recent events in Yugoslavia/Kosovo have been handled from the point of view of public international law. The recent Pinochet rulings by the House of Lords can also be seen as reflecting a new appreciation of the impact of human rights on hitherto differently understood rules of law.

Court on the ground that no claim was recognised by English law? All kinds of human rights reasons could be invoked to argue in favour of a negative answer, and we think this is precisely why Lord Browne-Wilkinson, in his opinion in *Barrett*, stressed over and over again that "I find it impossible to say that all careless acts or omissions of a local authority in relation to a child in its care are not actionable".[263] However, if that is what he *said*, that is not what he and his colleagues have been doing in practice in *X* v. *Bedfordshire County Council*, *Osman*, *Elgozouli*, *Barrett*, and in so many other cases. In a series of cases, *which range over a very wide area of activities of different types of statutory bodies*, they have *effectively* been denying even to consider the issue of liability. Indeed, some leading judges (such as Lord Woolf in the Court of Appeal in *Barrett*[264]) have been particularly honest to admit that such actions will very rarely succeed in practice. In the light of this *practice*, is it really surprising that the Strasbourg Court took the view that a device of national law—the duty of care—which in the vast majority of cases blocks a litigant from having the merits of his case tested in court, leads to a denial of access to a court of law under Article 6(1) of the Convention? We submit that invoking the striking out practice as a defence and arguing that the Strasbourg Court misunderstood its aims is not really very convincing. For judges who begin, as the Strasbourg judges do, with the kind of liberal and philosophical assumptions we have tried to describe in this book this way of looking at things is unreasonable. More importantly, their concerns, if not their methodology, are bound also to influence the English approach. Indeed, less than one year after *Osman* was decided, it is already having some effect on English courts if one is to judge not simply by the result in *Barrett* but, just as importantly, the Senior Law Lord's desire to stress that a striking out action would not be—and should not be seen to be—a real and total block to having one's case tested before a court. How exactly the English courts will, in the end, square this position with the traditional use they have made of the duty concept remains to be seen. One can only foresee a compromise; but what comes out of such a compromise will undoubtedly have affected the traditional use and role of the notion of duty of care.

Which brings us to the last accusation hurled at *Osman*, no doubt in order to take it out of the human rights arena and avoid the abovementioned reactions. This came from Lord Hoffmann who, writing extrajudicially, tried to debase *Osman* even further by arguing that it was not really a human rights case at all. The learned Law Lord thus tried to explain *Osman* as being a case that involved no civil rights issues whatsoever but, merely, "[dealt] with the substantive civil law right to financial compensation for not receiving the benefit of a social service"[265]—in this case proper

263 [1993] 3 WLR 79, 82.

264 [1998] QB 367.

265 "Human Rights and the House of Lords" (1999) 62 *MLR* 159, 166.

policing of a particular community. This, in turn, made it easier for him to voice the concern (already addressed) that the *Osman* decision: "challenge[es] the autonomy of the courts and indeed the Parliament of the United Kingdom to deal with what are *essentially social welfare questions involving budgetary limits and efficient public administration.*"[266] Yet, as we have suggested time and again in this book, nothing could have been further from the minds of the judges in *Osman* who were, instead, challenging the blanket immunity which results in practice from the utilisation of the notion of duty of care, and doing this against a philosophical background which gives judges the right to control the administration in all its emanations. In their view, such an absolute and unchallengeable way of stopping the courts from even investigating the merits of a case was unacceptable in so far as it represented an interference with Article 6 rights as understood by the Court in its most recent jurisprudence. Thus, to present the case as "essentially involving welfare questions and budgetary limits" not only does injustice to the Strasbourg Court; it also prevents English lawyers from questioning the real consequences that flow from such open-ended and blunt notions as that of "duty of care" when used in cases such as these.

IV. COMPARATIVE CONCLUSIONS

As stated at the beginning of the first part, the tortious liability of statutory bodies has, in England and throughout this century, been the subject of only three monographs, erudite but on the whole brief, and one or two articles which one could be tempted to describe as feisty in style but not very convincing in substance. Surely such a state of affairs can no longer be tolerated. What cries out for a change and justifies further studies of this subject is first and foremost the change in political philosophy, which has led to a proliferation of statutory bodies charged with ever-growing powers that can affect our lives. Just as important are three other phenomena.

First, whether one likes it or not, it is a fact that many statutory bodies, including the police and local welfare services, are no longer seen as having a totally unblemished record. On the contrary, hardly a day goes by without the national press reporting some error committed by those bodies, often entailing considerably sad consequences. Secondly, on the more technical, legal side, there is a growing awareness that topics such as ours can no longer be studied within the insular settings of one single legal system. This is not only the result of comparatists urging their national colleagues to look abroad for inspiration; it is mainly due to the growing impact that the two European courts—in Luxembourg and Strasbourg—are having on the national legal systems of most of Europe. Finally, one could mention

[266] *Ibid.*, 164 (emphasis added).

the growing belief that the discovery of the best answer to the kind of problems which we have been discussing in this book can be facilitated by an interdisciplinary approach and should no longer be left to lawyers acting on their own and in isolation from other disciplines, especially that of economics. However, the complexity of the problems we have alluded to also means that one must accept from the very outset that, while few of our readers would question the validity of the above assertions, not all will share the way we have used these assumptions. We are even more conscious of the fact that not all of our readers will welcome our proposed remedies to the underlying problem which we see as a tendency to slide all too easily into the non-liability option. This tendency could not have been expressed more graphically than when Lord Hoffmann, using computer terminology, argued that "The default position is [that there is no entitlement to compensation from the person who has caused the harm]".[267]

Undeniably, there is something of a missionary in every academic. Understandably, therefore, we would be happy if the English courts were willing to shift their current position in the direction of our own beliefs. Yet, in writing this book, converting others to our preferred solutions has not been our main aim. What we have tried to do instead is bring together our combined knowledge on this subject and to present it in a form that might be digestible to English judges, who sometimes give the impression of being removed from the concerns of ordinary citizens. We feel this to be so when the merits or demerits of cases such as *Bedfordshire*,[268] *Essex*,[269] and *Elguzouli*[270] seem to be submerged in entangled distinctions (such as that between policy and operational decisions) on which even judges themselves seem unable to agree.[271] But there is another reason for targeting judges; and since it has been explained by the first of us on so many occasions[272] we feel that it would be wasting valuable space to elaborate on the basic belief on which this theory is based. Quite simply, it is our shared belief that the best way to serve our subject—comparative law and methodology—is to try to devise a method that makes it useful to those who *practise* law—be they judges or practitioners. As already stated, this book is thus as much a study in comparative methodology as it is an attempt to

[267] *Stovin* v. *Wise* [1996] 3 WLR 388, 411.

[268] *X(Minors)* v. *Bedfordshire County Council* [194] 2 WLR 554.

[269] *W* v. *Essex County Council, supra*, n. 66.

[270] *Elgozouli-Daf* v. *Commissioner of Police of the Metropolis* [1995] 2 WLR 173.

[271] Some judges admit as much themselves. Thus, see Lord Browne-Wilkinson's extra-judicial observation in "The X case: Implication for Educational Lawyers. An Address by Lord Browne-Wilkinson" (1996) *Education Law Association*, 3. (We are grateful to Dr. Mads Andenas of King's College, London, for bringing this unpublished paper to our attention.) We are similarly not convinced that the more modern discussion about "justiciability" will fare any better; but we leave this to administrative lawyers to sort out for themselves.

[272] His views can be found in a collection of essays published under the title *Foreign Law and Comparative Methodology: A Subject and a Thesis* (1998).

describe some basic rules about foreign—mainly French and German—law and suggest that English lawyers may be able to draw some lessons from them. A second, though no less important, consequence of our efforts is to encourage a greater co-operation between the academic and practising side of our profession.

Let us end the book, therefore, as we started it, namely with a few thoughts about comparative methodology.

What our survey shows is that however much one tries to narrow one's focus in order to sharpen it—and we did this by looking only at five, litigated, factual configurations—one cannot understand the working of legal rules unless one ultimately sees them within their wider setting. Thus, by narrowing our discussion to five concrete situations we could show that the problems were the same in all of our three models. However, we also quickly became aware that characterisation and appraisal of the foreign solutions was impossible without seeing them within their wider socio-legal context. The first lesson was thus that in any comparative study one must start by dispelling the instinctive fears one feels about "foreign law"; and the best way of doing this is often by presenting one's reader with narrow (and thus manageable) factually equivalent situations. Once this is done, however, one should then proceed to broaden the understanding of one's audience by analysing the particular solutions within the wider political and economic context of the foreign country being examined. If the socio-economic and cultural setting is broadly similar between the systems compared, one can then take the third and last step and attempt to draw conclusions from the foreign system with a greater degree of confidence than one otherwise might have had without this broader understanding. In our case this meant (a) looking at the facts of the cases chosen as examples and studying their solutions within the context of the *political* philosophy which prevails in the country whose system is being studied, and (b) studying them in conjunction with other, related *legal* rules.

Attempting (a) was in one sense easier than (b). For (a) confirms a point made not long ago by Professor John Bell (among others), namely that "European administrative law traditions remain very national".[273] In particular, it could be argued that the current, very generous position adopted by the French legal system is understood better if seen within the context

[273] "Mechanisms for Cross-fertilisation of Administrative Law in Europe" in Beatson and Tridimas (eds), *New Directions in European Public Law* (Hart, 1998), 147. However, this perfectly valid observation does not prevent Professor Bell asserting "that international interaction and collaboration at a practical and an academic level has and will continue to shape the development of specific national traditions" (*ibid.*, 147). In his view, such a cross-fertilisation is likely to be at its strongest in the area of "values" rather than "procedures". One must further note that scholars have already begun examining how cross-fertilisation and convergence of solutions can be encouraged even further. Thus, see Eivind Smith, "Give and Take: Cross-fertilisation of Concepts in Constitutional Law", and John F Allison, "Transplantation and Cross-Fertilisation" in Beatson and Tridimas (eds) *op.cit.*, chaps. 8 and 12 respectively.

of the political philosophy that has dominated the thinking of French governments during the last twenty years or so. This has been distinctly more "left" than that found in both England and Germany during the comparable period of time. This observation must be coupled with a parallel sociological evolution found, again, most strongly in France and known as the idea of the "société assurantielle" (risk socialisation). These phenomena in combination have, undoubtedly, taken "consumerism"—perhaps the single most important legal theme of this century—to new heights *and new areas*. Of these two phrases, "new areas" is, for our purposes, the most significant. For we all know how, during the last thirty years or so, the consumer movement has affected *private* law in all three countries studied here, and has done so in a fairly radical but similar manner. This, after all, is the period that saw the introduction in most European systems of similar hire-purchase and money-lending legislation, as well as analogous statutes protecting consumers from excessively rigorous exemption clauses or defective products or services. Cardinal notions of the liberal doctrine of contract were, for better or for worse—this is not our concern here—thus affected in a very significant manner. However, the little that has been said about French law on our subject shows that French administrative courts took the spirit of consumerism very much to heart and, as a result, shaped a philosophy and a set of solutions which, we hazard the guess, most English judges would regard as vague if not, arguably, dubious. To the extent that we are right in second-guessing their reaction to French political philosophy, we suspect that French law is unlikely to hold out much appeal immediately, at any rate to *practising* English lawyers. Yet, before one jumps to the other extreme and dismisses French law as completely irrelevant, one must also ask oneself two further questions.

The first, as already hinted, is philosophical. French administrative judges begin with the assumption that it is essentially unfair to impose on ordinary persons the burden of administration activities, which are achieved for the benefit of the whole of society. This factor seems, with some notable exceptions,[274] to be missing almost completely from the mental calculations made by the English judges. However, it is not entirely without merit. The French experience (and literature) thus deserve—at the very least—some consideration by the English side. We have already given instances—*Elguzouli*, *Essex*, and *Bedfordshire*—where we feel this factor is at its strongest. Yet, undeniably, it has been ignored by the English courts.

The second observation that is justified by looking at French administrative practices is something of a paradox. Thus, we see that despite the generous predisposition French law shows towards the kinds of claims considered in this book, it has, nonetheless, managed to work. What we mean

[274] Lord Bingham's reasoning in the Court of Appeal in *X* v. *Bedfordshire County Council* strikes us as an opposite illustration with which this kind of thinking may also attract supporters in England.

by this is that (a) the incidents of litigation remain limited; (b) the state, in all its forms and emanations, has not literally collapsed under the kind of economic pressures which instil such fear in the heart of Lord Hoffmann; and (c) academic (or intellectual) complaints against this state of affairs are neither loud nor numerous. How can all this be explained?

To such a question we readily admit that we have not been able to provide *conclusive and empirically* supported answers. We do not, however, believe that this book, which raises more questions than it can answer, has, for this reason, failed its purpose. First and foremost, making people think and consider is one of the primary tasks academics must perform. Additionally, however, we have also tried to understand what we found in the foreign systems and answer our own queries. Thus, where no obvious answers were to be found in the area of our *immediate* enquiry, we turned our attention to related areas of the law as a possible source of explanation. This approach explains our previously made statement that the operation of a particular rule can often be understood by studying some other set of norms, not always found in the same area or even branch of the law. To put it differently: the need to interrelate the various parts of whatever legal systems one is studying became, once again, very obvious. In this search we believe that we may have stumbled upon some interesting data which could be used as a source of inspiration for our system should it ever decide to re-orient itself in the way we are advocating.

For a brief moment we thus wondered whether the real answer to the French liability rule thus lay in the parsimonious tendencies of the French courts, already alluded to in our text, in fixing levels of monetary awards. Thus, although the condemnation of a statutory body could provide "satisfaction" for the aggrieved party (and also remain consistent with the philosophical tendencies alluded to above), a very low level of damages would not entail the economic ruination of the said statutory body. This, of course, is not a solution which would go down well with all English lawyers, some of whom would, we suspect rightly, not feel happy imitating a rule which encouraged delay in the settling of disputes and provoked high transaction costs for the sake of a token award amounting to a "rap on the knuckle" of a "misbehaving" authority. Be that as it may, this could still have been a (theoretical) explanation of sorts, accounting for the differences between these two systems and explaining why the French local authorities have not collapsed under the pressure of a generous liability rule.

Unfortunately, the paucity of available *empirical* data documenting the levels of French awards made such an explanation tentative though not implausible.[275] Moreover, the "comfort factor" provided by this "intuition"

[275] Those involved in transnational litigation know how important it is to back the widely held belief that European levels of damages are lower than, say, US levels with hard evidence. But the real crux of the matter lies in proving *how much lower* they are; and this is very difficult to do even in straightforward accident cases, which thus far have received the greatest attention.

was reduced further by the growing awareness, confirmed by consulting practising lawyers, that the level of damages is rising.[276] Thus, the only points on which there seemed to be no doubt were three: first, the philosophical belief of French administrative judges that such losses should be born by the community since the activities that caused them were carried out in the interests of the same community; secondly, the explanation that the French system "worked" solely because of the derisory measure of its damages was, if ever true, no longer sustainable; and, thirdly, that a proper evaluation of the economic thinking behind French judgments was impossible simply because so little of it appeared in any of the official or semi-official records. (Again, however, we note that there was a general debate about economic and insurance matters when the decision was taken to widen the liability of state hospitals.)

In some respects the position in Germany seemed more reassuring for our emerging conclusions, since the difficulties described above in connection with French law seemed to be attenuated. Thus, our German colleague was able to produce evidence of elaborate and long-standing discussions concerning the economic consequences of the liability rule, *some of it empirical in nature*. Indeed, what is so interesting about these German debates is that they have, in essence, preceded the current English discussions by about one hundred years and have now moved on to different levels which, philosophically, come closer to the French model than the English. Secondly, we noted that many of the policy arguments advanced in England against the imposition of liability had, again, been considered in Germany and had been rejected, in some cases many years ago. Thirdly, we noted that in this system, too, the measure of damages provides no justification of the liability rule, since, even though damages are, undoubtedly, modest when it comes to the *non-pecuniary* part of the award[277]—what Germans call

[276] Thus, not only was the original aversion of the administrative law judges to award "moral damages" (i.e., non-pecuniary damages) overcome, the amounts given under this heading have increased progressively from a derogatory FF 2,000 or 3,000 (£30 at 1999 rates of exchange) in the 1960s (see, for instance, Conseil d' Etat, 24 novembre 1961, *Recueil des arrêts du Conseil d' Etat*, 661) to over FF 50,000 (i.e., £5,000) in the late 1980s (Conseil d' Etat, 23 septembre 1987, *Recueil des arrêts du Conseil d' Etat*, 290), and then jumped to FF 2,000,000 (i.e., £200,000) in the most recent AIDS contamination cases (Conseil d' Etat, 9 avril 1993, *Recueil des arrêts du Conseil d' Etat*, 110). These figures may be lower than those that could be awarded by English courts, but they are no longer derogatory. Taken together with the German awards, they may also hold out a lesson for English courts. Incidentally, AIDS-related suits, brought against state hospitals (or state blood-transfusion agencies) and thus litigated before administrative courts, provoked an increase in monetary awards for non-pecuniary damages all over Europe. Examples are given by von Bar, "Schmerzensgeld in Europa" (1999) *Festschrift für Erwin Deutsch zum 70. Geburtstag*, 27*ff*.

[277] See, for instance OLG Oldenburg VersR 1991, 305, where the plaintiff's claim for DM 100,000 for being illegally incarcerated for five days was reduced from DM 100,000 to DM 5,000—at today's exchange rate roughly the equivalent of £1,700. Incidentally, although this figure is minuscule by comparison to sums given in the USA for these kind of torts, it is not much out of line of English awards made around the same time. Thus, see *Bishop* v. *Metropolitan Police Commissioner & Others* (1989) *The Times*, 5 December (£1,500 for malicious

damages which aim to provide "satisfaction" (*Genugtuung*) not "compensation to the victim"—the levels of compensation provided for provable economic losses can be substantial and, if anything, higher than the French.[278] If Lord Hoffmann's reasoning were right, the German liability rules would have brought in their wake considerable economic difficulties for all German statutory bodies subject to them. Yet nothing of the sort has happened. On the contrary, officially commissioned statistics have shown that the financial burden of state liability (including all causes of action, not just breach of official duty) amounted to only 0.015% of the total budget. Once again, therefore, one is forced to doubt the validity of the English fears or, at the very least, set them aside *until some figures can be produced to support them.*

These findings thus obliged us to seek explanations for the German results elsewhere. Our conclusion is that the system works, and there is no pressure to alter its basic structure. Our explanation is (tentatively) based on the *cumulative* effect of the following reasons: (a) insurance provides a workable framework; (b) liability makes civil servants more careful; (c) where the cost is, indeed, substantial, it is thought that it is right and proper to spread it among the community to which the statutory authority belongs; and, (d) finally, although the level of damages is not derisory, judges have never allowed it to reach the exorbitant levels that, say, US tort awards can reach. The *Bedfordshire* and *Essex* type of cases would seem to fall neatly within the above parameters; and the wider German thinking behind such an approach would, it seems, approximate the French philosophical stance mentioned above. Once again, however, we nourish no illusion that all our readers will agree with such an analysis. As such, we are putting forward these thoughts for further consideration by scholars who might be able and willing to test their validity *with the aid of further empirical data*. We feel confident, however, that our preliminary findings (or suggestions) cannot be rebutted merely by putting forward judicial intuitions. We consider this "request" to be entirely consistent with our belief that some areas of the law are best studied in an interdisciplinary way and cannot be handled properly through black-letter law concepts alone. We also feel that the English legal aid system, with its merit-testing procedures and financial

prosecution); *Barnes* v. *Commissioner of Police for the Metropolis* (1992) LAG, 14 (£2,500 for false imprisonment); *Linton* v. *EJ Parkinson & Son Ltd*, 11 May 1989 (£2,900: industrial tribunal award for discrimination). In *Noone* v. *NW Thames RHA* (1992) 41 EOR 20, the Court of Appeal suggested that the maximum award for injured feelings in such cases should be £3,000 (although some later cases have awarded double this amount).

[278] *Cf.* for example the German equivalent to *Elguzouli*—BGH 16 October 1997, NJW 1998, 751—where the damages claimed for pecuniary losses amounted to over DM160,990, or approximately £55,000: BGH NJW 1971, 751–52. Similarly, in the German equivalent to *Essex*—OLG Hamm, FamRZ 1993, 704—where the adoptive parents of an unhealthy child were granted the costs of looking after the child for life.

thresholds is, if anything, even more likely than its German counterpart to discourage frivolous and undeserving litigation.[279]

If, in accordance with the above, a *definitive* economic justification for the different solutions of foreign law remains elusive, the same is not true when we move to the wider philosophical reasons which lie at the root of these (foreign) liability rules. As already stated, we find both French and German law in broad agreement as to (a) the need to control statutory bodies, (b) their willingness to do this by using all possible means at their disposal including the courts, and (c) their complete contempt for the argument that such control would make the civil servants in question reluctant to act. All of us have much sympathy with these positions of principle; and we do not regard them as being fundamentally alien to the common law frame of mind. To support this assertion we rely on sections of Lord Reid's judgments given in the *Dorset Yacht*[280] case; Lord Bingham's most recent judicial work and, more precisely, his *dicta* in the *X* v. *Bedfordshire* case;[281] and, to some extent, Lord Hutton's strongly voiced doubts in *Barrett* about the validity of some of the arguments that led to the defeat of the plaintiff's action in *X* v. *Bedfordshire*. We thus feel considerable sympathy for the argument that it may be unfair to place, almost as a matter of course, the burden of administration activities carried out for the common weal on any individual person. On this count, therefore, we are inclined to think that the current English solutions—not, it must be stressed again, shared by all of our senior serving judges[282]—have been dictated by excessive caution and unconfirmed economic intuitions, rather than by any evidence, empirical or comparative, which makes such solutions incontrovertible.

Let us then move further from methodology and philosophy to substantive law.

Before we proceed to make more concrete observations on the current state of English law, we feel that it is necessary to stress the importance of the foreign material we have used in this book. Irrespective of whether or not the reader finds it convincing, the fact is that, on the whole, the views given above on French and German law reflect the state of thinking found in most of Europe. This means that this material is not only interesting in itself, but also goes a long way towards explaining the underlying suspicions the Strasbourg Court may have felt of the English judgments which, *de facto* if not *de iure*,[283] have, over the years, established wide-ranging

[279] Which is Lord Browne-Wilkinson's main worry. See his comments in his speech to the Education Law Association, cited above in note 262.

[280] [1970] 2 WLR 1140, 1145*ff*.

[281] In particular the tenor of his argument in his judgment in the Court of Appeal in the *Newham* and *Bedfordshire* cases [1994] 2 WLR 554.

[282] Thus, see, for example, Lord Nicholls' eloquent dissenting judgment in *Stovin* v. *Wise* [1996] 3 WLR 388, 392*ff*., especially 402*ff*., where he departs from Lord Hoffmann's approach in many significant respects.

[283] Before the Strasbourg Court, government lawyers attempted to emphasise a number of cases that showed which the immunity conferred on the police was not, in fact, a blanket

immunities for a wide range of statutory bodies. Seen in this context, what is of interest to us is not that the Strasbourg Court took the view it did in the *Osman* case, but that this view received the support of even the English judge. Thus, those who agree with Lord Hoffmann and who accuse the Strasbourg Court of not having understood how English law works, might wish to consider the possibility that their own preoccupation with "efficient allocation of scarce resources" may have led them to underestimate the wider political, legal and moral considerations that weigh so heavily in the minds of many leading European jurists. To imply that their views do not really matter any longer now that we have brought human rights "back home" is, with the greatest respect, totally unconvincing. For, not only does it ignore the continued influence that Strasbourg jurisprudence will have (even after the Human Rights Act 1998 comes into force) but also because it underestimates the wider infiltration of European thinking currently taking place in this country and is evidenced by the plethora of judicial and extra-judicial pronouncements of some of our most academically minded judges. Just as important is our conviction that if our understanding of the European position is accurate—at least in its philosophical undertones—we must be right in our assertion that Strasbourg will continue to abide by the position it adopted in *Osman*. This, too, is an important point, since it suggests that English judges may be disappointed if they try to "wish" *Osman* away.[284]

Secondly, we wish to stress that our criticism of English law is based on a combination of comparative material and economic analysis. With regard to the latter, the starting point may well be that this kind of (economic) reasoning may best be suited to specialist academics. This is not to say, however, that the judges are wrong to consider the wider economic implications of the imposition of liability upon public bodies or to try to add this weapon to their armoury. On the contrary, we feel that Lord Hoffmann's attempt in *Stovin* v. *Wise* to introduce a degree of rigour and clarity

immunity. However, of the five cases which they cited imposing liability on the police, only one—*Swinney*—is post-*Hill*. Thus, although these decisions may still stand on their facts, they do not seem to reflect the new trend in favour of immunity which was, if anything, reinforced by the cases considered in this book, especially the *Bedfordshire*, *Stovin* and *Elguzouli* decisions.

[284] We put forward this idea tentatively and in the light of two facts: first, we note that apart from Lord Browne-Wilkinson, the two judges who gave leading judgments in *Barrett* were able to dispose of the case without any reference to *Osman*; secondly, we recall how the House of Lords—unlike the Court of Appeal—tried in *Derbyshire County Council* v. *Times* [1993] AC 534 to argue—unconvincingly in our view—that the result reached in that case owed nothing to the background influence of the European Convention on Human Rights. We, therefore, respectively agree with Lord Justice Pill when, in his judgment in *Palmer* v. *Tees Health Authority* (1999) *The Times*, 6th July, he referred to *Osman* as a decision that "weighed heavily upon the decision in *Barrett*" in the House of Lords. (The quotation comes from the transcript of the, as yet, unreported decision.) The *Osman* influence can also be detected in *Brindle* v. *Commissioner of Police for the Metropolis*, 29 March 1999 (unreported at the time of writing) and *Swinney* v. *Chief Constable of Northumbria Police* (no. 2), *The Times*, 25 May 1999.

to the economic debate is to be welcomed and encouraged. However, Lord Hoffmann's formulation of the economic issues should—we hope—be seen as a most commendable effort to spark off a debate but, most assuredly, not as having concluded it. What is at issue here is not simply the conclusions he reached on the substance of the economic case (which we have considered above), but also his overall approach to the use of economics in cases of this kind. From this latter perspective, Lord Hoffmann's approach can be questioned for the excessive certainty with which predictions of the effects of liability rules were put forward. As we explained above, "positive" or predictive economic analysis should properly involve two stages, and the formulation of predictions or hypotheses using axiomatic economic reasoning is only the first of these. The second stage involves the testing of hypotheses using empirical research techniques. The fact that this is expensive and is rarely done (even by many law and economics scholars) is no reason to believe that it is not important. At the risk of repeating ourselves, this is not to suggest that the courts should completely eschew economic reasoning on the grounds that they lack the resources to test economic propositions in this way. However, we do suggest that the courts should treat economic predictions of the impact of liability rules with appropriate caution. In due course, it may be possible for the courts and counsel to develop procedures whereby the relevant economic literature on a given question is properly canvassed and assessed (as already happens in the context of competition policy cases and some others). Until that is done, however, care is needed in the way economic evidence is used.

A further and wider observation relates to the relationship between economic and non-economic values. As we showed above, it is essential to clarify what is meant by "economic efficiency" in this context. The criteria by which efficiency is judged—mainly, in the context of tort law, allocative efficiency—provide us with useful means for assessing whether particular outcomes are more or less likely to enhance the wealth or well-being of society. Even if they can be successfully deployed to this end, they do not tell us how to weigh economic efficiency against other values. Above all, they tell us nothing about how individual rights are to be weighed against efficiency in the case of conflicts between them. Economics can help to clarify the issues when such conflicts occur, so that we get a clearer picture of the nature and extent of the trade-offs which may be involved, but what it cannot do is provide us with an infallible calculus for resolving these trade-offs. In the final analysis, that involves judgments which lie beyond economics. The recent obsession of the courts with "budgetary issues" and "efficient government" to the exclusion of other values—a point which becomes particularly obvious when we compare contemporary English law with French and German—has not only prevented its advocates from exploring the possible deterrent value of holding the police and other statutory bodies liable for their negligent actions, it also means that the courts have failed to appreciate the significance of the not inconsiderable philosophical point, so dear to most European legal systems, that the courts are there precisely to effect this extra kind of control and keep the administration, in all its emanations, in check.

A substantial part of this book has also been devoted to making a number of more specific assertions above the current state of English law, some of which, we suspect, are more acceptable than others. The most incontrovertible assertion is that our courts have, in the space of the last ten years or so, shifted their justification process from a legal or legalistic one, to one which is distinctly more policy-oriented. We predict that this will have both welcome and unexplored consequences.

The reorientation will be welcome because it will make us all address real issues and concerns rather than use legal concepts in an excessively formalistic way to conceal the true basis for the court's reasoning (where the comparison with other systems may become relevant and even, give English law, the edge, if it makes proper use of this extra-legal material). But this approach also has consequences which, if we are honest about this matter, have yet properly to be fathomed.

Thus, how will practitioners henceforth proceed to distinguish their case from earlier ones when the argumentation brought into fashion by cases such as *X* v. *Bedfordshire* and the majority judgment in *Stovin* are so obviously different—in content and style—from the one that has prevailed for centuries? We can imagine at least three possible tendencies emerging from this current, unsatisfactory[285] state of affairs.

First, some judges will, no doubt, take their cue from the judgments of Lords Slynn and Hutton in *Barrett* and attempt to show that, what for brevity's sake we call the Browne-Wilkinson policy arguments in *X* v. *Bedfordshire* are inapplicable to the case before them. The merits of such tactics will be that they will avoid (or rather postpone) an *open* confrontation with Strasbourg. Such tactics may also offer barristers a sense of (false) security in that will make them feel that they are back on familiar turf arguing and distinguishing cases on the basis of ingenious distinctions and not banding about general and often un-provable policy assertions. The demerits of such an approach may, however, be even greater than the perceived advantages. For this way of proceeding will, undoubtedly, contribute to the increase in litigation, which—we must always remember—our judges fear most than anything else. More importantly, it will fail to address the core argument of the current orthodoxy. This is the theory of "economic efficiency" as enunciated most clearly by Lord Hoffmann but also consistently present in

[285] We call the current situation unsatisfactory not only because we are, ourselves, unhappy with the five cases we have discussed in this book, but also because we detect considerable judicial uncertainty as to how *Osman* should be handled. Thus, apart from *Barrett*, see *Palmer* v. *Tees Health Authority*, 2 June 1999 and *David Gower* v. *London Borough of Bromley*, 29 July 1999—both unreported at the time of going to press.

the judgments of those who have adopted his philosophy. Such a way of dealing with *Osman* will thus, in our view, be based on distinctions that will often cross the line that divides the ingenious from the ingenuous and thus will not be conducive to a principled development of the law.[286]

A second approach has been indicated by the recent decision of the Court of Appeal in *Palmer* v. *Tees Health Authority*.[287] What we see, here, especially in the two majority judgments, is an attempt to retain the "striking out" mechanism by saying that *Osman* only prohibited it through the use of the device of "fair, just and reasonable". Some admittedly vague pronouncements on this point in *Osman* thus allowed the majority in *Palmer* to argue that "striking out" was still possible on grounds of "lack of proximity". Those who like us believe that, foreseeability, proximity and "fair just and reasonable" all-too-easily slide into one another—and it would appear that Lord Justice Pill in *Palmer* is one of them—will find this way of "evading" *Osman* entirely unconvincing. For in our view, it runs so counter to Strasbourg's main philosophy as expressed overall in that judgment that any attempt to side-step Strasbourg in such a manner will be a new invitation to that court to intervene in our law. Once again, therefore, we see this as a half-baked response to clear signals from abroad that a real change is needed in our practices if further reversals by Strasbourg are to be avoided.

So this brings us to the third and most profitable way of proceeding. In our view this consists in first and foremost appreciating the reasons why Strasbourg reached the conclusion it did, rather than accusing its judges of not understanding our "strike out" procedures. This, as stated in this book, involves understanding the wider practice that prevails in Europe and which must surely be seen as "normal" by most of the Strasbourg judges. Secondly, it means weighing the kind of comparative and economic arguments we have presented in this paper and accepting that the basic economic philosophy that underlies our current (*ante Barrett*) judicial thought is at best not fully worked out and at worst flawed. Thirdly, it means devising a way for "keeping matters under control" that is workable in practice and methodologically acceptable to our judges. This must surely be by shifting their emphasis from "duty" to "careless breach" and "causation" and, in the end, rejecting unmeritorious claim on those grounds rather than through summary decision on the basis of assume facts. The fact that events are assumed to be as the plaintiff alleges them to be is of little use to him. For, as we have noted time and again, in practice if not in theory, the response of the courts has been almost constantly to hold that there is "no duty"

[286] Which some of our judges nowadays seem to think is highly desirable. See, for instance, Lord Mustill in his dissenting judgment in *White* v. *Jones* [1995] 2 WLR 187, 228E and Lord Hoffmann in *Hunter* v. *Canary Wharf Ltd* [1997] 2 WLR 684, 709F.

[287] *The Times*, 6th July 1999. Our comments are based on the as yet un-published full transcript of the judgments.

and thus no right to be tested and, if proved, enforced by them. Of course, friends of the *ante Barrett* status quo will be quick to point out that this way of proceeding may lead to an increase in litigation. We accept this as a risk but not as one that is greater than the increase of litigation that will be provoked by the *Palmer* or *Barrett* type of reasoning that we sketched above. Moreover, if such an increase in litigation does occur, we believe it could be short-lived. For, first, we are constantly reminded these days of how legal aid makes it increasingly difficult to resort to litigation. Secondly, we also feel confident that the first cluster of cases, if decided on the basis of clear and rational criteria (and not the ones that we rejected in the previous paragraphs), should be able to send clear signals to litigants as to which claims should be settled and which resisted. Thus, we suspect, few will doubt that the "careless breach" requirement is easily justified in, say, the *Essex* case; but not easily satisfied in cases such as *Bedfordshire* and *Barrett*. The assumptions we are putting forward will, in most disputes, be shared by Counsel who must realise (as law students do not) that the current victories won against the "strike out actions" approach, do not, necessarily, mean final victory for the plaintiffs. Proceeding with litigation will thus still remain the last resort, not to be undertaken lightly.

Secondly, we have suggested that in the material reviewed in this book our courts have moved slowly but steadily much further than the *Hill* facts (and judgments) originally called for. The almost complete shift from legal concepts to policy has made possible such a change in results. The multiplication of "affective immunities" has thus spread to cover not only the police but also welfare authorities, educational authorities, the public prosecution service and other emergency services in a way that in its amplitude has no real counterparts either in the Continent of Europe or, even, the US. Yet the legal outcome in some of the most recent decisions may be seen by many as an affront—in some cases a serious affront—to basic notions of justice. In short, paraphrasing Lord Justice Ward,[288] the pursuit of the greater public good at the expense of individual hardship can go so far and no further. If that is, indeed, the view which continues to prevail, these results will not prove long-lived. Justice—unquantifiable, immeasurable and vague though it may be—remains an important aim of the law in general, and of the law of torts in particular. The advocates of financial prudence and efficiency cannot use this virtue, however desirable it is, to trump so many well-established aims of tort law such as compensation, justice, deterrence,[289] and even retribution. A more measured result must be achieved

[288] *Swinney* v. *Chief Constable of Northumbria Police Force* [1997] QB 464, 487.

[289] We thus agree with Lord Justice Bingham (as he then was) when, in the Court of Appeal in *X* v. *Bedfordshire* [1994] 2 WLR 554, 662G he said, "I cannot accept, as a general proposition, that the imposition of a duty of care makes no contribution to the maintenance of high standards".

and, so far, all of us feel that this has eluded English law. Our reading of the Strasbourg decision(s) encourages us in the belief that this European influence will, along with others mentioned in this book, force the English courts to re-examine and, we hope, redefine (in an as yet unpredictable way) some of their absolute immunity rules.

Finally, we have described briefly two foreign legal systems. Although their structures and concepts are, as we have freely admitted, different to ours, the systems operate in political, social and economic environments, which are *broadly* similar (although with cyclical variations of emphasis from centre/right to centre/left and back again). The way these problems are handled in the judicial decisions (of Germany and, more so, France) may make some English lawyers feel proud of their judicial techniques and reasoning process. We think there is some truth in such an assertion. Equally, we feel that foreign judges might learn from studying the form and style of common law judgments. However, the foreign solutions (if not the judgments themselves) also suggest that the fears and arguments advanced in England to stunt the imposition of civil liability have not materialised abroad. Such a start contract, especially in what is the proper ambit of state responsibility, merits at the very least a more detailed study than we have managed to carry out so far in order to determine who is right: our neighbours or us. Such study will yield the incidental benefit of telling us something about our style of reasoning[290] and of our legal concepts—their weak and strong points—and their ability to survive in the future. More importantly, it will encourage our lawyers—students and practitioners alike—to keep the European dimension constantly in front of their eyes. The *Osman* decision suggests that Europe—love it or hate it—and its ideas will continue to be a source of controversy, irritation and, as far as we are concerned, inspiration for many years to come.

[290] Some authors have already carried out research which shows that, for instance, the French and English reasoning processes are more similar than they appear to be at first sight. Thus, see, J Bell, "Reflections on the Procedure of the Conseil d'Etat" in G Hand and J McBride (eds), *Droit sans Frontiers* (1991), 211*ff*. The value of this research and their conclusions are beyond dispute; but our examination of these cases also shows that, in this type of situation, the reasoning process and style are quite different. This can only confirm the widely held view that in comparative studies the warning against generalisations must be made constantly!

10

Judicial Style and Judicial Reasoning in England and Germany

1. THE NEED TO STUDY JUDICIAL STYLES: WHY PERSIST WITH THIS THEME?

My interest in this topic was recently re-kindled as a result of co-authoring a book with a German, French, and an English colleague.[1] Its title was "Tortious Liability of Statutory Bodies. A Comparative and Economic Analysis of Five English Cases".[2] This study focused on five factual situations which have been subject of litigation in England, France and Germany and revealed that English law produces different results from those found in French and German law. It also suggested that, under pressure from the Court of Human Rights in Strasbourg,[3] English law might be on the verge of a change. This would be neither surprising, at any rate to someone who has commented repeatedly on the "Gradual Convergence"[4] of common law and modern civil law, nor unwelcome. Nor is the "agent" for the change—the Strasbourg Court—surprising or unacceptable. For, again, I have long argued[5] that the two European Courts—Luxembourg and Strasbourg—are major engines for change, which have been inadequately accepted and understood in my country. But the interesting feature of these developments is that they are affecting the *substance* of the law, not the *reasoning process (and style)* by which this result is attained. In this area, as we shall see, English law remains—and is likely to remain—different. The point I wish to explore is thus "how different is it"? "What are the merits and demerits of these stylistic and reasoning differences?" And "what can they teach

[1] Namely, Professor Dagmar Coester-Waltjen of the University of Munich, Professor Jean Bernard Auby of the University of Paris II and Dr Simon Deakin of the University of Cambridge.

[2] Published by Hart Publishing in 1999.

[3] Mainly as a result of its decision in *Osman* v. *UK* No 87/1997/871/1083, recently increased by two Reports of the Commission in *Z and Others* v. *the United Kingdom* and *T.P. and K.M.* v. *the United Kingdom*, both adopted on 10 September 1999.

[4] This is the theme of a book I edited in 1994. Its full title is: *The Gradual Convergence. Foreign Ideas, Foreign Influences and English Law on the Eve of the 21st Century.*

[5] For instance in "Learning from Europe and Learning in Europe" in *The Gradual Convergence, op.cit.* above, pp. 1–32.

us about foreign systems and our own?" A preliminary answer to these questions is that any verdict must be a mixed one, i.e. one that suggests strengths as well as potential dangers in the English approach when it is compared to those found in France or Germany.

2. COMPARING LIKE WITH LIKE

The full benefit of comparing systems comes, I think, when one compares factually equivalent litigated circumstances. This, at least, must be the starting point though not the one with which one will end one's enquiry. The immediately obvious similarities encountered when one is comparing similar litigated situations makes the "foreign" reader feel reassured by what he is discovering rather than put off. For such a reader then easily grasps a problem which is familiar to him and notices with interest (and, perhaps, some amazement) that its answer, not infrequently, is analogous if not identical to the one he finds in his own system. The comparison of like with like also spares the foreign observer the trouble of dealing with concepts which are either untranslatable,[6] or relevant to one system but not to another,[7] or simply the products of structural differences or "oddities"[8] which exist in the "foreign" law but have no equivalent in his own. If these explanations are to be given, they can come at a later stage when they can also be better understood, especially if comparative methodology is combined with comparative legal history which I have always believed go hand in hand.

In our above-mentioned study, my colleagues and I adopted this method and compared a number of litigated cases exemplified by five leading English cases[9] which, we showed, have factual equivalents in both France and Germany.[10] Partly because of lack of space, but mainly because in this

[6] For instance *Weiterfresserschaden* or, insidious spreading loss—a concept which, in the context of damage caused to the product, has allowed the courts to resort to tort rules and by-pass contract law. Another such notion is that of *Drittschadensliquidation* or *Schadensverlagerung*, which, in recent times has entered into English law under the term of "transferred loss". Lord Goff, the creator of the English concept, though keenly interested in German law, has maintained that he created the notion independently from German law and later discovered the similarity. See: "Comparative Law: the Challenge to Judges" in *Law Making, Law Finding, and Law Shaping: The Diverse Influences* (ed. by Basil S Markesinis) (1997) pp. 37*ff*.

[7] Right of established and operating business: *das Recht am eingerichteten und ausgeübten Gewerbebetrieb*.

[8] The notion of contract with protective effects towards a third party—*Vertrag mit Schutzwirkung zugunsten Dritter*—is an obvious example.

[9] They were *Hill* v. *Chief Constable of West Yorkshire* [1988] 1 WLR 1049; *X (Minors)* v. *Bedfordshire* CC [1995] 3WLR 152; *Stovin* v. *Wise* [1996] 3 WLR 388; *Elguzouli-Daff* v. *Commissioner of Police of the Metropolis* [1995] 2 WLR 173; *W* v. *Essex County Council* [1998] 3 WLR 534.

[10] For references to this case law see our *Tortious Liability of Statutory Bodies* etc. (1999).

paper I am more interested in identifying the stylistic differences we find in the decisions, I shall here focus on only two of these cases. But the reader, who finds these observations of even marginal interest, would do well to read this paper in conjunction with our book.

The first of the cases worth studying is *Hill* v. *Chief Constable of Yorkshire*.[11] For me its interest lies not only in the fact that it spawned a number of subsequent decisions[12] but mainly because it influenced the style of their argumentation. The second case that we shall look at in this paper is *Stovin* v. *Wise*.[13] It deals with a local authority's potential liability for failing to remove obstructions on the highway, which then lead to traffic accidents. Their German counterparts are factually so similar[14] that, at this stage, one need do nothing more than merely give their references.[15]

3. DIFFERENCES IN STYLE AND REASONING

A judgment of the *Bundesgerichtshof* reveals much about German legal history, the kind of education German judges receive at University, the impact that a largely written/codified system has on the way German judges perceive their job, and much else besides.[16] Let us look briefly at these points under three different headings: history, legal education and the existence of a codal text.

(i) History. The first German judgment examined here refers to eight previous decisions whereas its English equivalent makes use of a far greater number. In Germany the frequency with which a German court will make use of earlier judicial work is, in fact even less significant that these figures suggests. This becomes obvious when, through careful reading of the judgments, one realises that the earlier case law is either quoted as an illustra-

[11] [1988] 1 WLR 1049.

[12] *Alexandrou* v. *Oxford* [1993] 4 All ER 328; *Ancell* v. *McDermott* [1993] 4 All ER 355; *Osman* v. *Ferguson* [1993] 4 All ER 344. Cf. *Swinney* v. *Chief Constable of Northumbria* [1997] QB 464—all dealing with the possible liability of the police towards victims of crimes which they failed to prevent.

[13] [1996] 3 WLR 388.

[14] Subject to one difference which is mentioned below and which distinguishes *Stovin* from its German counterpart.

[15] *Hill* can be compared with BGH LM § 839 [Fg] BGB no. 5; *Stovin* with BGH NJW1980, 2194.

[16] I shall not repeat here earlier comments about the abstract nature of the judicial language, the judges' courage to innovate, which is greater than it is often believed to be, and the way the collegiate nature of a German court, found even at first instance, manifests itself in the judgment. On these points see my observations in "Conceptualism, Pragmatism and Courage: A Common Lawyer looks at some Judgments of the German Federal Court", *Essays in Memory of Professor FH Lawson* Butterworths (1985).

tion of a particular view or as an example of an established practice. Rarely if ever, though, is this case law *scrutinised* in the way an English court would consider earlier decisional law. There is thus little or no evidence of the previous cases having been used as building blocks for the new decision. The reason for this different treatment is, of course, to be found on the combined impact that the three factors—history, legal education and codal background—have had on the nature of German judicial work. Equally important is the fact that for the German judge the primary building block is the Code that has to be applied, followed only by the academic exegesis to which this enactment has been subjected. Incidentally, I refer to the Code as the primary building block for two reasons. The first, and better known to English lawyers, is the fact that the judge's reasoning process starts by reference to a particular provision or provisions in the Code. But the second, less noticed yet crucial for present purposes is the fact that the codal text often spares the German judge the trouble of having to do and formulate some of the basic thinking that the his English colleague has to do for himself.

(ii) Legal education. The education received at law school is also different and, thus, both the result and the cause of the above-mentioned difference in the finished product. For at law school, the aspiring German judge will be taught how to use the codes, learn how to inter-link their various parts (and then combine the Codes with one another) and—to begin at least—to apply the texts he has been taught deductively.[17] In all this, he will be expected to make as logical and as consistent a use as he can of the many concepts that will be drummed into his head during a period of at least seven—if one includes the preparation for the second state exam—years of training. Though references to cases figure increasingly in legal courses,[18] the constant refining and re-defining of earlier case law, with the frequent use of the untested hypothesis, thus seem to me to be greatly lacking in a

[17] I have, however, argued elsewhere that there is a danger of exaggerating the differences produced by the civilian deductive method and the Common law inductive approach. See: "Reading Through a Foreign Judgment", *The Law of Obligations, Essays in Celebration of John Flemming* (eds. P Cane and Jane Stapleton) (1998), pp. 261*ff.*

[18] And, indeed, one encounters nowadays an ever-growing number of casebooks that approximate in appearance to their common law equivalents. See, for instance, Professor Haimo Schack and Dr. Hans-Peter Ackmann's *Höchstrichterliche Rechtsprechung zum Bürgerlichen Recht. 100 Entscheidungen für Studium und Examen*, 4th ed. (1997). But the casebook is not entirely a novel teaching tool, even in Germany. Indeed, in the hands of a grand master such as Rudolf von Jhering, it proved its success both in academic and commercial terms. Thus, his *civilrechtsfälle ohne Entscheidungen* had, by 1901, reached its ninth edition. The casebook method is now also used in Germany by those scholars who teach Common law and its methodology to German students. A good illustration is Professor Thomas Landmark's *Juristische Technik und Methodik des Common Law* (1998) (written with J Jones) and his *Common Law Tort and Contract*, Juristische Arbeitsbücher I, Münsterner Einführungen (1998).

legal training which is otherwise both long and very thorough. Thus, once again, the German judgment reflects this difference which merges very much with that mentioned under the previous sub-heading. For the same two reasons German judgments, as a rule, also make greater use of academic literature than their English counterparts,[19] though in the present instance recourse to academic literature was unusually restrained.

(iii) The Codal background. As stated under (i), the Code—and we are here concerned with the Civil Code—*and its preparatory works* has, in most cases at least, provided for the German judge some of the decisions of principle. Paragraph 823 I BGB has thus told him that pure economic loss is not included among the list of protected interests. The German judge thus does not have to search for wider—we could call them policy—reasons "of principle" that will lead him, as they lead his English counterpart, to the conclusion to "strike out a claim" for pure economic loss. The wider issues of concerning floodgates, insurability,[20] and the like will thus not be invoked (or even hinted) in the German judgment whereas they will play a major part in the Common law counterpart.[21] It is only when the latter feels that circumstances require a deviation from the basic, codal text that he will feel the need to start being inventive. Sticking with the same subject—pure economic loss—we thus see this where recovery has, despite the general rule, been allowed. This has necessitated either the creation of a new protected interest—e.g. the right to an established and operating business—or an ingenious (or ingenuous) use of some other concept in order to cover the perceived legal gap.[22] In the end, therefore, devices such as these have allowed "deviations" from the original position of the Code; characteristically, however, these innovations have not come about painlessly but, on the contrary, have caused much discussion and dispute in German academic and judicial circles.[23]

[19] For figures and an interesting discussion see Kötz, "Scholarship and the Courts: A Comparative Survey" in *Essays in Honour of Henry Merryman on his Seventieth Birthday* (1990) pp. 190*ff.*

[20] BGH 10 July 1963, BGHZ 40, 91 at 103–104, is, to my knowledge, one of the rarer cases which has referred to the wider questions of insurability and, somewhat indirectly, to the floodgates argument.

[21] Though many illustrations could be given no case brings home these points more clearly than the decision of the Canadian Supreme Court in *Norsk Pacific Co. Ltd.* v. *Canadian National Railway* [1992] 1 S.C.R. 1021.

[22] Such as that of *Weiterfresserschaden* or *Drittschadensliquidation*. It should be noted, however, that *Drittschadensliquidation* is one of the rare instances where the legislator left it to, or even encouraged the courts to fill the gap, see Mugdan, *Materialien zum BGB*, vol. 2, (1899) reprinted 1979, 517–18.

[23] See, for instance the reaction that followed BGH of 24. 11. 1976, BGHZ 67, 359. Thus, Hager, "Zum Schutzbereich der Produzentenhaftung", *AcP* 184 (1984), 413. But *cf.* Steffen, "Die Bedeutung der 'Stoffgleichheit' mit dem 'Mangelunwert' für die Herstellerhaftung aus Weiterfresserschäden", *VersR* 1988, 977; Kullmann, "Die Rechtsprechung des BGH zum Produkthaftpflichtrecht in den Jahren 1989/90", *NJW* 1991, 675.

Likewise, background differences—such as different history and different constitutional texts—largely explain the differences that exist between German and American law when it comes to the clash of free speech and reputation and privacy. In Germany, the statutory regime—Constitution and Code—have here encouraged the judge to seek an *ad hoc* reconciliation of the competing values and only occasionally has it given textually a hint as to which value should prevail. By contrast, the American Constitution has, in its First Amendment, made up the mind for all subsequent judges[24] by giving a predominant, some would say, exaggerated preference to the value of free speech and, effectively, deprived them of the opportunity even to attempt any balancing of values.

The same, in a sense, is true in the German cases that we are using here as models. Much of the discussion about the desirability of the courts second-guessing other parts of the Administration or weighing the economic consequences of a liability rule, was done for them by the legislator when the Code was drafted[25] or, more recently, when its revision has been planned.[26] The result of all this is that much of what appears in the English judicial opinion will not figure (and does not have to figure) in the comparable German judgment. But this does not mean that the issues that have occupied the English judges have escaped the attention of their German legal establishment; it only means that consideration of some of those issues might have taken place in a different forum and must be searched for in a different text. For those involved in the comparative examination of legal systems, this undoubtedly adds both an intellectual challenge and considerable complexity to their work. The scholar who studies a foreign legal system, though advised to start his research in a narrow and focused manner, is thus eventually forced to cast his research net more widely than he originally thought was necessary if he is to obtain a decent understanding of the foreign system.

4. SOME SPECIFIC ILLUSTRATIONS FROM OUR TWO SETS OF DECISIONS

Stovin v. *Wise* is one of the cases we have chosen to compare with its German law equivalent. They are, indeed, in factual terms almost identi-

[24] Thus in *Konigsberg* v. *State Bar*—366 US 36, 61 (1961) Mr Justice Black said: "I believe that the First Amendment's unequivocal command that there shall be no abridgement of the rights of free speech and assembly shows that the men who drafted our Bill of Rights *did all the 'balancing' that was to be done* in this field . . ." (Italics added).

[25] For instance, *Protokolle*, vol. II, at p. 662, about the value of the "economic-consequences argument" as a reason for not imposing liability. I am grateful to Professor Coester-Waltjen for this and the following reference.

[26] *Zur Reform des Staatshaftungsrechts* (1976), p. 5, 71

cal, the main difference between the two cases being that in the English case the obstruction that contributed to the injury did not lie within the property of the defendant's local authority. For our purposes, however, this is not an important point. By contrast, an important similarity found in both cases, that the defendants' fault consisted in not removing the obstruction—i.e. it was a case of omission—attracted very different treatment in the two systems. Thus, in the English case, it played an important part in the non-liability rule whereas in the German decision the German court did not feel that this point merited much attention. One explanation is, of course, the different approach taken by the systems when it comes to imposing tortious liability for omissions. The individualistic common law approach finds it difficult to reach this result save in factual situations which, broadly speaking, involve neighbouring landowners. But in this article, we are less concerned about the differences in substantive law and more interested in the style of reasoning used to achieve the different result. So here is how Lord Hoffman justified his refusal to make the local authority liable in the *Stovin* case. He said:

"In economic terms, the efficient allocation of resources usually requires that an activity should bear its own costs. If it benefits from being able to impose some of its costs on other people (what economists call 'externalities') the market is distorted because the activity appears cheaper than it really is. So liability to pay compensation for loss caused by negligent conduct acts as a deterrent against increasing the cost of the activity to the community and reduces externalities. But there is no similar justification for requiring a person who is not doing anything to spend money on behalf of someone else . . . So there must be some special reason why he has to put his hand in his pocket."[27]

In the next sub-section we shall ask ourselves whether this kind of argument is convincing. Here suffice it to stress that this kind of economic analysis is totally absent from the German judgment.[28] But it is not only this aspect of the case that was subjected to an economic analysis in the English litigation. Once again, Lord Hoffmann, had resort to economic arguments in order to argue that the imposition of liability on public authorities would lead to inefficiency since it would lead to unwelcome results. First, a diversion of scarce resources from good causes to defending legal suits and, secondly, to "defensive activities on behalf of the administration" as a way of

[27] [1996] 3 WLR, 388 at p. 406.

[28] However, in BGH 10.7.1980, NJW 1980, 2194 (2196) the judges seem to have dedicated at least some thought to the economic consequences of imposing an obligation to act on the council: "This *relatively simple and cheap* measure was to be expected of the defendant" (emphasis added). By comparing the cost of improving visibility to the costs resulting from accidents, the court was asking the right question from the point of view of economic efficiency.

avoiding future challenges to their decisions. He voiced this concern in the following way:[29]

"The creation of a duty of care upon a highway authority, even on grounds of irrationality in failing to exercise a power, would inevitably expose the authority's budgetary decisions to judicial inquiry. This would distort the priorities of local authorities, which would be bound to try to play safe by increasing their spending on road improvements rather than risk enormous liabilities for personal injury accidents. They will spend less on education or social services. I think that it is important, before extending the duty of care owed by public authorities, to consider the cost to the community of the defensive measures which they are likely to take in order to avoid liability."

This particular kind of economic argument has found much favour with many English judges in many different contexts of liability of statutory bodies since the seminal case of *Hill* was decided in 1987. Thus, Lord Justice Glidewell expressed it in the following way:

"If the police were liable to be sued . . . actions in this field would not be uncommon. Investigative police work is a matter of judgment, often no doubt dictated by experience and instinct. The threat of a decision which, in the end proved to be wrong might result in an action for damages would be likely to have an inhibiting effect on the exercise of that judgment."[30]

The careful reader will have noticed that the last quotations given have taken an essentially economic argument and re-shaped in a slightly different way. For instead of talking in terms of economic efficiency, and openly applying economic analysis with which judges usually feel uncomfortable, the argument is now put forward in what one could call a "constitutional sense". For in this form it now boiled down to this: Are the courts the suitable and able medium to second-guess the administration in the taking of its daily decisions? Put in this way, we shall see that the English courts are placing themselves very much against the grain of Continental European thinking which, by contrast, encourages the view that the courts should be

[29] [1996] 3 WLR 388 at p. 419.

[30] [1987] 2 WLR 1126 at 1140. In the House of Lords, [1988] 2 WLR 1049 at 1055, Lord Keith echoed the same view when he said "In some instances the imposition of liability may lead to the exercise of a function being carried on in a detrimentally defensive frame of mind." In X v. *Bedfordshire* [1995] 3 WLR 152, at pp. 184–5, we again see this argument resurfacing in Lord Browne-Wilkinson's judgment. He thus stated that "if a liability were to be imposed, it might well be that local authorities would adopt a more cautious and defensive approach to their duties. For example, as the Cleveland Report makes clear, on occasions the speedy decision to remove the child is sometimes vital. If the authority is to be made liable in damages for a negligent decision to remove a child (such negligence lying in the failure first to investigate the allegation) there would be a substantial temptation to postpone making such a decision until further inquiries have been made in the hope of getting more concrete facts. Not only would the child in fact being abused be prejudiced by such a delay: the increased workload inherent in making such investigations would reduce the time available to deal with other cases and other children."

given a wide range of control over the administration. This way of looking at things becomes almost a philosophical creed for the French administrative courts; and, in turn makes us wonder whether, by pursuing this line of approach, the Continental Europeans are unnecessarily ignoring the Common law concern for thrift and efficiency.

5. THE STRENGTHS AND WEAKNESS OF THE ENGLISH APPROACH

In the mind of this author many insights can be gained into judicial thinking and the differences between legal systems when one places judgments from two different systems next to one another and compares their style of reasoning as well as their substantive solutions in the way suggested above. Certainly this moving "to and fro" between texts to another makes one question the strengths and weaknesses of the arguments advanced. More significantly, one must be asked to consider the merits and demerits of thrashing out in a judicial decision wider policy points and giving the judge the task of not merely adjudicating but also trying his hand at social engineering. In this sub-section we shall consider briefly the first point and leave the other one to the concluding observations.

So how convincing is the economic/political argumentation of judges such as Lord Hoffmann?

Let us start by looking at his argument about the need to treat acts and omissions differently. Without going into the wider debate[31] alluded to above, let us offer two reasons why the distinction here between act and omission does not seem so appropriate.

First, public authorities do have the resources to act in such a way as to obviate dangers to third parties. Thus, they are not excluded from liability by virtue of the need, as stated by Lord Wilberforce in *Goldman* v. *Hargrave*,[32] to take into account the actual resources available to a defendant upon whom a duty of affirmative action might be imposed.

Secondly, in cases involving public authorities, the defendant is normally under some kind of pre-existing public law obligation to act. Where this is the case, we cannot speak of an affirmative obligation being created *de novo*. Nor would it be possible to argue that the imposition of liability would lead to the under-provision of the service or activity in question. This point was recognised by Lord Nicholls in his dissenting judgment in *Stovin* v. *Wise* when he said: "if there were a common law obligation in the present case, sounding in damages, the extent of the obligation would march hand

[31] That divides common law and civil law on this point. This is discussed in a comparative way by FH Lawson and BS Markesinis in *Tortious Liability for Unintentional Harm in the Common Law and the Civil Law*, vol. I (1982), pp. 71–80.

[32] [1967] 1 WLR 645.

in hand with the authority's public law obligations. This is a cardinal feature of the present case. The council's public law obligation was to act as a reasonable authority. The common law obligation would be to the same effect."[33]

So, on this point at least the German reasoning seems more convincing than the English.

But does Lord Hoffmann's second economic argument—the misuse of scarce resources—fare any better when looked at under the magnifying glass? Given the lack of space one can only refer the reader to the joint research project, which my foreign colleagues and I published some time ago. But our conclusion there was that the Hoffmann approach was at best arguable, at worst inadequately thought out.

Thus, first, the claim that negligence liability leads to "defensive practices" is often made in this and related contexts. However, the evidence on which it rests remains slim. Some US studies have found evidence that expenditure on bureaucratic and administrative procedures designed to avoid liability for medical negligence, such as various kinds of form-filling and checking, has grown considerably in recent years and now amount to billions of dollars across the system as a whole.[34] No similar studies have been carried out for the UK or the public service elsewhere and the point, as far as English law is concerned, must remain open.

Secondly, what is also problematic for this argument is that it could apply with equal force to well-established areas of tortious liability such as employers' liability and product liability. The argument is not unique to the liability of public authorities. Indeed, from this point of view the case for granting immunity to public authorities (via the concept of duty of care) is weaker still, since they are not subject to the forces of competition, nor to the same damaging reputational effects of litigation which affect private sector organisations.

Clearly, one could continue with this kind of analysis; and the more one developed these objections the more one would, I believe, become persuasive in voicing doubts about the *current*,[35] policy-oriented way of deciding judicial disputes. But space is at a premium so one should briefly look at the other side of the coin and enquire whether the Germanic type of reasoning is any more illuminating or more convincing than the English. Clearly, such doubts as one might voice on this issue one voices with trepidation, conscious of the fact that one is expressing a view about a system that is not only foreign but also highly sophisticated. The chance that a foreign observer may thus be treading on slippery ground is thus consider-

[33] [1996] 3 WLR, 388 at pp. 398–9.

[34] Dewees, Duff and Trebilcock, *Taking the Facts Seriously. Exploring the Domain of Accident Law* (1996), chap. 5, review this evidence.

[35] I stress current for in England at any rate the court never has the benefit of the kind of empirical information that can be provided by an *amicus curiae* or a *Brandeis Brief.*

able. Nonetheless, it is the task of comparative lawyers to go where others fear to tread! So here are some tentative thoughts on this vexed subject.

Overall, the Germanic approach strikes one as being much more legalistic and tied to the text of the statute which the judge has to apply. My feeling, however, is that such a view only represents the appearance and that the reality is not only much more complex but also, in an indirect kind of way, comes closer to the English than one is led to believe at the beginning of one's enquiry. Let me explain by offering two illustrations.

The first is the apparent total absence of any economic or policy discussion in the German decision. I stress apparent, for one soon realises the validity of the point I made earlier on, namely that the substance of these arguments has been considered by the German legal profession but that has happened elsewhere, not in the judgment, itself. Thus, the preparatory works of the Code reveal a complete awareness of the economic consequences of a liability rule;[36] and recent empirical surveys suggest that the imposition of liability has not led to the economic ruination of the local authorities,[37] which is so feared by the English judges. Why this is so is not entirely clear and, in my view, awaits an authoritative and empirically justified response. Until that comes, the fears expressed by English judges should not be entirely ignored by their German counterparts. Perhaps these fears are already discounted, not on the liability issue but on the levels of damages awarded by the courts. For the level of monetary awards may partly explain why their imposition can be carried without hugely adverse consequences. On the other hand, this may be, at best, only a tentative explanation; for the impression I obtain from the overall level of damages awarded by German courts is that they are not dissimilar to those found in England though they are lower than those awarded by American courts. Certainly, in the cases we are discussing here there have been some fairly substantial awards.[38]

The second point I would like to make is related to the preferred but not exclusive way used by German courts for accepting or rejecting this claim. This seems to me[39] to lie in the determination of the scope of the violated

[36] Mugdan, *Materialen zum BGB*, vol II, 1305; *Protokolle*, vol I, 609, 611, 622 where the legislator considered whether the imposition of liability might make civil servants too cautious and/or provoke "an unfortunate high burden on the state".

[37] *Zur Reform des Staatshaftungsrechts* (1976) 5, 71.

[38] For instance, OLG Hamm, FamRZ 1993, 704 (factually quite similar to our *W* v. *Essex County Council* [1998] 3 WLR 534). Likewise, BGH 16 October 1971, NJW 1971, 751 (analogous to our *Elguzouli-Daf* v. *Commissioner of Police of the Metropolis* [1995] 2 WL 173).

[39] See also Ossenbühl, *Staatshaftungsrecht*, 5th ed. (1998), 57: "Die Drittbezogenheit der verletzten Amtspflicht ist . . . ein ewiges Problem der Staatshaftung." (The scope of the violated rule, i.e. the extent to which it is meant to protect the particular person and harm suffered, is an everlasting problem of state liability.)

rule.[40] If the plaintiff or harm suffered was within the protective ambit of the statute, then recovery is allowed. But recovery is denied if the answer to this question is a negative one. To an English lawyer the approach is perfectly intelligible but it suffers from one grave flaw: how do we discover the scope or purpose of the statute in the absence of clear wording or sufficient evidence from the *travaux préparatoires*? The artful way in which German judges, applying a purposive interpretation, end up by discovering an official duty towards the aggrieved individual can, for instance, be seen in a decision of the Court of Appeal of Hamm[41] which factually comes very close to our *W* v. *Essex County Council.*[42] Both cases had to decide whether, *inter alia*, a local authority could be liable towards an adopting parent for negligently failing to communicate information about the physical and mental characteristics of the adopted child. (In the German case the parents had stipulated they would only adopt a healthy child. In the English case, the local authority gave for adoption a child with known criminal propensities despite the adopting parents' express wish that they were not willing to adopt a child with a propensity for sexual deviance.[43]) The German decision found for the parents, holding that the duties to which the Adoption Placement Authorities were subject to were, despite the absence of express wording, also due to the adopting parents. By contrast, our Court of Appeal, relying partly on our confused law about nervous shock reached the opposite result.

As stated, the German "adoption liability" case provides a good example of a skilful discovery of the "purpose of the violated rule". This author, however, feels less confident about the reasoning (but not the result) of the leading decision entailing the liability of the police for failing to arrest criminals who they knew were about to commit a robbery. The question whether the police's duty to apprehend such persons was also owed towards the victim (third party) of the thieves was handled in this way by the Federal Supreme Court:[44]

"According to the case law of the *Reichsgericht* [reference omitted], which the Senate followed in [reference omitted], the question of whether an official duty is owed by an official to a third party is to be adjudged taking into consideration the officer's official area of activity and the type of work which he is carrying out. In this connection the main emphasis is on the purpose which the official duty is to serve. If this is imposed on the

[40] A method also used in England where the possibility of a tort action for breach of a statute is being considered. For details, see Markesinis and Deakin, *Tort Law*, 4th ed. (1999), pp. 336*ff.*

[41] FamRZ 1993, 704.

[42] [1998] 3 WLR 534.

[43] For present purposes I ignore the fact that the claim by the English parents was further complicated by the restrictive English rules that apply to psychiatric harm.

[44] BGH LM § 839 {Fg} BGB no 5 of 30 April 1953. (Translation by Dr Raymond Youngs).

officer in the interests of individual persons, everyone whose interests are, according to the special nature of the official business, affected by it will be a third party. But if the purpose of the official duty is only the maintenance of public order or the interest which the state has in officials carrying out the responsibilities of their office properly, the official owes no duty to third parties, even if there is indirect intrusion into the interests of third parties by the exercise of this duty. *The task of preventing crimes is not however owed by the police in the interest of the general public alone, but, as to crimes which also intrude directly into the protected legal sphere of the individual, to the endangered individuals as well. If the police do not properly fulfil this task, this not only violates a duty owed by the police to the general public but also a duty owed by it to the endangered individuals.*"

Though, as I have said elsewhere,[45] this result is welcome, the reasoning given in the judgment, with the greatest respect, is not intellectually convincing. For its tone is conclusionary from the start (and especially noticeable in the italicised part of the extract); and the citation of earlier case law adds little to the persuasive power of the conclusion other than to show that the practice of the courts is constant. Seen from a different angle, one could ask how would a German judge react to the kind of arguments adopted by the English judges? Would he say that the basic position (allowing liability in principle) has already been determined by the legislator and that, therefore, he has no right even to contemplate the Hoffmann fears? Or would he reject them as being almost solely based on policy? Might he, alternatively, see some merit in the doubts voiced about holding the police (or local authority) liable? Could he in the end overcome these (English) doubts by invoking the kind of arguments that my colleagues and I invoked in our aforementioned book? Or, confronted with these (English arguments) would the German judge justify the "established" case law in some other way? In short, the discussion as it currently appears in the published decisions of German courts seems neither complete nor convincing.[46] The overall merits of the German position, and the reasons why this may be preferable to the English, become obvious only when the case is read in conjunction with the Code, its preparatory works, and academic literature. But the judgment, on its own, provides inadequate illumination for the jurist—be he English or German—who is studying it.

The same doubts about the reliability of the "scope of the rule approach" are reinforced when one reads the German judgments which, relying largely on the text of specific statutes, hold the police liable for the above-

[45] *Tortious Liability of Statutory Bodies* (1999) passim, co-authored with Professors Dagmar Coester-Waltjen and Jean-Bernard Auby and Dr. Simon Deakin.

[46] See also Professor Ossenbühl's comments in *Staatshaftungsrecht*, 5th ed. (1998), 58–9.

mentioned kind of faults but have refused, in many cases,[47] to hold public prosecutors liable for similar types of mistake.[48] The justification given for this different treatment of the two services—police/public prosecutor—has been found in the fact that the police are the guardians of good order; *and this is taken to mean* that they owe duties of protection even towards individuals.[49] On the other hand, the public prosecution office is there to make sure that criminal law is enforced and that has *not* meant—in most cases at least—that a duty was also owed towards individual citizens. Once again, the outside observer, burdened though he is with all the drawbacks of lack of local expertise, is nonetheless tempted to treat the pronouncements that justify these distinctions as a smoke screen, which conceals the real thoughts of the German judge. I, for one, though a long-standing admirer of German legal science, feel compelled to voice these doubts about some parts of the German judicial reasoning. And I do so because I wish to prompt my German colleagues to think about their own law in the light of the English reasoning. And, consistently with the theme of this essay, I think the comparison process can be enhanced precisely because the English judgments are, in their style and wording, so much more open and, arguably, more thought-provoking than the German.

I find further justification for my assertion that the "scope of the rule approach" is often a smokescreen for judicial "social engineering"[50] in the study of a large number of cases involving damaged electricity cables in circumstances very similar to those found in *Spartan Steel & Alloys Ltd.* v. *Martin & Co.*[51] For here in this case law I have, once again, found evidence of the same phenomenon namely, similarly phrased statutes in Germany, Switzerland, and Austria have in some systems justified an individual action under §823 II BGB whereas in others they have not.[52] Such antithetic case

[47] But not all. English readers must thus note that the immunity that prosecutors enjoy in German law is for the general discharge of their duties which, as stated in the text, above, is deemed to be owed to the community at large. On the other hand, towards the accused, or others involved in the prosecution, prosecutors enjoy no such immunity as a number of litigated instances clearly show. For a recent illustration see: BGH 16.10.1997, NJW 1998, 751.

[48] For instance, RG 16.10.1923, RGZ 108, 249; BGH 28.3.1996, NJW 1996, 2376.

[49] In addition to the leading case mentioned above, see RG 26.2.1935, RGZ 147, 144; OGH Br. Z. Köln 22.9.1950, NJW 1951,112.

[50] The term belongs to Lord Mustill. See, for instance, his "Negligence in the World of Finance" 5 *The Supreme Court [of Malaysia] Journal*, pp. 1*ff.* (1992). See, also, his "What do Judges Do?", *Särtryck ur Juridisk Tidskrift*, 1995–96, Nr. 3, pp. 611*ff.* Few judges have in my country been as frank as Lord Mustill in explaining how they think in private but my own hunch is that this does not mean that *they* reason differently. More interestingly, I suspect that much of what Lord Mustill confesses to doing in private, also applies to the thinking process of civilian judges. But proving the correctness of this personal hunch is almost impossible in the modern civil law setting where the French judge is cryptic by long tradition and the German judge is abstract as a result of a deeply ingrained predilection.

[51] [1973] 1 QB 27.

[52] I remind readers who have no clear recollection of these cases that the question there raised was whether a third party, who did not own the damaged cable, could claim damages against the tortfeasor for his resulting pure economic loss. Actions under § 823 I BGB having

law can only strengthen the suspicion that the concepts used by judges in the judgments provide the words that help them formulate them but give few clues as to the reasons that really lie behind them.

If I am right in these suggestions then the real difference between the two systems under comparison is that the style of one is to say what it thinks while the style of the other is to conceal it under a screen of apparently deductive reasoning and let the person in quest of the full truth search for it in a multitude of sources. This does not make the German judgment better or worse than its English counterpart; it just makes it less complete; and as a teaching tool, less effective an instrument of instruction.

6. SOME TENTATIVE COMPARATIVE CONCLUSIONS

I leave it for another occasion to discuss which of the two approaches sketched out at the end of the previous sub-section is preferable. Here I shall make only two final points.

First, as a teacher, I find the English judicial style and technique more informative than the German though I also feel that the policy arguments advanced by the English judges are either insufficiently developed or even unconvincing. I thus hope that more judges will follow Lord Hoffmann's attempts to analyse legal problems in an inter-disciplinary manner. I also hope that the arguments will be refined and increasingly based on evidence rather than judicial hunches. Such a development can, in my view, only take place in close co-operation with academics. For as Lord Goff once put it:

"... jurists are pilgrims with [the judges] on the endless road to unattainable perfection; and we have it on the excellent authority of Geoffrey Chaucer that conversations among pilgrims can be most rewarding".[53]

Secondly, it follows from the above that in my view German jurists—be they academic or practitioners—would also derive some benefit by studying how the judges in my country craft their judgments. But if the German judges may stand to gain from us by studying our style, for the reasons I

failed, ingenious litigants tried to justify their claims by relying on § 823 II BGB. Such an action would succeed if it could be shown that the violated statute—in these cases local by-laws protecting the integrity of the cables—could be construed as being "protective norms" in favour of not only the public at large but also the individual plaintiffs. As suggested in the text, above, the case law has been contradictory. On this see: Bürge, "Die Kabelbruchfälle", *Juristische Blätter* 1981, 57. In the late 1960s even German law dithered as to the right solution to this problem which can only go to prove that the statutory interpretation is, at the end of the day, greatly influenced by policy considerations. On this see: Taupitz, *Haftung für Energieleiterstörungen durch Dritte* (1981).

[53] *Spilada Maritime Corp.* v. *Cansulex Ltd.* [1987] 1 AC 460, 488.

have given elsewhere[54] I think we stand to benefit from them by looking at their substantive law and its techniques of keeping litigation under control. It would be gratifying if I were to be proved right in this conclusion for it would confirm my long-standing belief that we all stand to gain by studying each other's systems.

[54] *Tortious Liability of Statutory Bodies: An Economic and Comparative Analysis of Five English Cases.*

11

Developing an English Law of Privacy

THIS CHAPTER CONSISTS substantially of translations of German cases that deal (mainly) with the problems of privacy.[1] Five were produced by Dr. Raymond Youngs of the Southampton Institute,[2] an author of a learned casebook on German Law. Two come from the inimitable pen of Mr Tony Weir, of Trinity College, Cambridge.[3] Yet another,[4] was prepared by Mrs Irene Snook, who once taught at the Oxford Institute of European and Comparative Law. With the permission of Professor Hans Baade, one more[5] comes from that famous source book of foreign ideas and materials of the late Professor Rudolf Schlesinger,[6] while for the remaining four[7] the late Harry Lawson and (to some extent I) are responsible. The texts of the cases are printed in italics while the accompanying notes, written by me (except for the notes to the *Soraya* case), are printed in roman type. Privacy was chosen as a subject in the belief that it will be, if not one of the first to come before English courts, certainly one of the most important under our Human Rights Act 1998. The decisions reprinted here also provide excellent material to illustrate my ideas of how foreign law could be used before an English court. Only the last decision contained in this selection deals with the different and broader issue of *Drittwirkung* or, as it is now most commonly referred to in our country, the horizontal application of Human Rights. This case is included simply to give some idea of how the Germans see this thorny problem which has already given rise to some academic controversy in our country.[8]

[1] Six appear for the first time in the English language—cases nos six, seven, eight, nine and ten, while the summary of one—case no six—has already appeared in a leading American case book but is unlikely to be widely known in this country.

[2] Translations of cases nos seven, nine, ten, eleven and twelve.

[3] Case nos four and thirteen.

[4] Case no eight.

[5] Case no six.

[6] *Comparative Law*, 6th ed. by Baade, Herzog, and Wise (1998).

[7] Cases nos one, two, three and five.

[8] From the growing literature one thus notes that Sir William Wade ("Horizons of Horizontality" (2000) 116 *LQR*, 217*ff*. with references to his earlier works on the subject) and Murray Hunt ("'The Horizontal Effect' of the 'Human Rights Act'" [1998] *PL* 423) favour (some form) of the German doctrine being adopted by our law while Lord Justice Buxton

It is a well-known fact that the European Convention on Human Rights lies largely at the basis of our own recent statute. It would thus seem to follow that the case law and ideas of the major continental European systems that often lie under the surface of the Strasbourg case law are, sooner or later, bound to be noticed by those at least of lawyers who have an open and inquiring mind. The translations that follow are meant to help those who do not have access to the German originals to see what one of Europe's major and most sophisticated legal systems has done with this topic. But inviting English judges and practitioners to make use of foreign law raises a number of questions and entails a number of risks. Here are some and how, I believe, they can be minimised.

First, some of our judges and practitioners have in very recent times expressed doubts about the use of "unreported" judgments, or judgments coming from foreign courts—especially if these foreign courts are situated in non-American or Commonwealth jurisdictions with which our lawyers have little familiarity. The questions most frequently put to me as obstacles against such borrowings are the following. "How important are these decisions?" "How can we tell that they are important?" and "Are they still good law or have they been overruled?" In answering these questions the reader must, of course, be reminded of the fact that continental European systems do not adhere to the doctrine of binding precedent (except in a very few and narrowly defined situations). Nor are they accustomed to using the term "leading case" the way we do. Notwithstanding these caveats, all European systems—and henceforth the remarks will, for obvious reasons, be limited to German law—know full-well how to distinguish the important case from the one that turns purely on the facts of the dispute which the court had to resolve.[9] German courts are also slow to depart from a case law, which, with the passage of time, has become "constant". Thus, all the cases here reproduced are "important" or "leading" cases and, what is more, have not been overruled since their publication. The main thesis advanced in this section, however, is that German law has grown incrementally on a case by case basis. So these judgments, though important and illustrative of current German law, should be approached as English judg-

("The Human Rights Act and Private Law" (2000) 116 *LQR* 48) seems to regard it with suspicion given that human rights (originally at any rate) were meant to be protected against encroachments by the superior power of the State. An account (in English) of the German doctrine of *Drittwirkung* can, of course, be found in some of the essays reprinted in the earlier parts of this book. The Wade/Buxton controversy can, by the way, also be found in Israel where Chief Justice Barak, following the German cases, has introduced the *Drittwrkung* doctrine in Israeli contract law. On this, see Professor Shalev's comments in "Constitutionalization of Contract Law" in *Towards a New European Ius Commune* (eds A Gambaro and AM Rabello) (1999), 205 *ff*.

[9] Our French colleagues use the felicitous terms of *arrêt de principe* (which matters) and an *arrrêt d'espèce* (which goes no further that its facts).

ments would be. This means that, ultimately, they are building blocks that have to be carefully put together before the building is constructed or, in our case, an opinion on what the law is in a particular situation can be expressed.

The next concern English practitioners may have is how they can gain access to wider German material if they cannot read German. This can be an inhibiting effect on the use of foreign law since the interested person may not only wish to read the factually equivalent foreign case; he must also be able to place it within its wider context in order to appreciate its full significance and effect. Once again, however, one can say that the problem, though serious, is not entirely insurmountable, especially in the case of privacy. Thus, the English-speaking lawyer may wish to consult the works cited in the next footnote if he wishes to find out more about the continental European law of privacy in general and the German one in particular.[10] Clearly, the information available in the English language is considerable, though what conclusions the reader will draw from such a study will, to some extent, be determined by his own fears, impressions, predilections and wider philosophical positions about how to balance speech rights against privacy rights. It would, however, be difficult to deny five things that emerge from this literature about the current position of German law.

First is the fact that the German law has been built by the courts incrementally and on a case by case basis. The usual (English) fear that the foreign material will not be usable since it proceeds on a deductive rather than inductive way of reasoning[11] is thus not present in this part of German law. Thus,

[10] Thus see; Fleming, "Libel and Constitutional Free Speech" in *Essays for Patrick Atiyah* (1991), pp. 331*ff.* (eds P Cane and J, Stapleton); Handford, "Moral Damage in Germany" 27 *ICLQ* 849 (1978); Humphries, *Media and Media Policy in West Germany. The Press and Broadcasting since 1945* (1990); Krause, "The Right of Privacy—Pointers for American Legislation?" [1965] *Duke LJ* 481; Lorenz, "Privacy and the Press—A German Experience", *Butterworths Lectures 1989–90*, 79–119 (1990); Markesinis and Nolte, "Some Comparative Reflections on the Right of Privacy of Public Figures in Public Places" in *Privacy and Loyalty* (ed. by Peter Birks) (1997), pp. 113*ff.*; UNESCO Report: "The Legal Protection of Privacy: A Comparative Survey of Ten Countries", *UNESCO International Social Science J.* 1972, 417; Schlechtriem, "Some Thoughts on the Decision of the BGH concerning Princess Caroline of Monaco" and Stoll "The General Right of Personality in German Law: An Outline of its Development and the present Significance", both in *Protecting Privacy* (ed. Basil Markesinis) (1999) at pp. 131*ff.* and 29*ff.* respectively; Zweigert and Kötz, *An Introduction to Comparative Law* 3rd ed. (1998), (tr. by Tony Weir), § 43. A topic not discussed in this book is employee protection against violations of their privacy by their employers which has increased in recent times as computers enable employers to gather and store much personal information about their workers. German law is ahead of the law in both England and the United States; and it is discussed by Schwarz, "Privacy in German Employment Law" 15 *Hastings International and Comparative Law Rev.* 135 (1992)—an article with rich references to the relevant German literature. The literature in German is, of course, vast.

[11] Lord Macmillan made this the key difference in the thinking process of the English and continental mind in a lecture, which is a classic in the literature of comparative law. Thus see: "Two Ways of Thinking" in *Law and Other Things* (1938), pp. 76, 101.

though some important statutory provisions do exist,[12] most of the material is precisely of the type that an English lawyer would feel comfortable to use. The texts that follow support this assertion—such problems as may remain being attributable to difficulties associated with the art of translation which, invariably, is confronted by the twin perils of dull accuracy and flowing liberality. Incidentally, the reason why German law developed in the way just described is because in Germany, as indeed in our country, the Press managed to frustrate the two legislative attempts that were made to deal with this matter. One can thus only hope that our judges will prove as courageous in taking on the Press and as adroit as their German counter-parts in fashioning a workable compromise. For there is no doubt that the interests clashing here—speech versus privacy—are both sensitive and important and call for a compromise, not a total victory on either side.

Secondly, and this flows from my last remark, the protection of privacy in Germany has not been achieved at the expense of freedom of expression. The decisions cited here and elsewhere in this book prove that many cases, which in English law would have been caught by our law of defamation, have gone unpunished in Germany because of the high regard that the German Constitutional Court has for free speech. But the reader of this statement does not have accept it simply because it is (or seems to be) backed by many quotations. He can double check its veracity by reading what American "free speech" scholars have had to say about the current state of the German law. The writings of such American experts as Professors David Currie,[13] Donald Kommers[14] and Peter Quint[15] thus reveal a

[12] Two important provisions must be quoted here in full. First, of course, must come the relevant provisions of the German Constitution namely Arts. 1, 2 and 5. They read as follows;

Article 1 (Protection of human dignity)

(1) The dignity of man shall be inviolable. To respect and protect it shall be the duty of all state authority.

Article 2 (Rights of liberty)

(1) Everyone shall have the right to the free development of his personality in so far as he does not violate the rights of others or offend against the constitutional order or the moral code.

Article 5 (Freedom of expression)

(1) Everyone shall have the right freely to express and disseminate his opinion by speech, writing, and pictures and freely to inform himself from generally accessible sources. Freedom of the press and freedom of reporting by means of broadcasts and films are guaranteed. There shall be no censorship.

(2) These rights are limited by the provisions of the general laws, the provisions of law for the protection of youth, and by the right to inviolability of personal honour.

(3) Art and science, research and teaching, shall be free. Freedom of teaching shall not absolve from loyalty to the Constitution.

Also important are Arts. 22 and 23 of the Law of Artistic Creations of 1907 which are reproduced in the text of the decision of the Constitutional Court, case no eight, below. Additional articles in various statutes protect particular aspects of the human personality. Thus §12 of the BGB protects one's right to one's name.

[13] *The Constitution of the Federal Republic of Germany* (1994).

[14] *The Constitutional Jurisprudence of the Federal Republic of Germany*, 2nd ed. (1997).

[15] "Free Speech and Private Law in German Constitutional Theory", 48 *Md. L. Rev.* 247 (1989).

growing admiration for speech protection in Germany (even though they also point out to many areas of disagreement). This point is worth stressing for, if one were to believe what one often reads in the English broad sheets, on the speech front Germans suffer gravely compared to us. The reality is that they do not.

Thirdly, the recognition of privacy rights in Germany has not led to a flood of litigation. In the third edition of my *German Law of Torts* (pp 415–16 of the 1999 reprint), I collected the published citations of all the decisions of the superior courts and the total was meagre, indeed. The importance of these figures, which will be confirmed by the statistics I have collated up to the year 2000, is for us in England that much greater than one might think at first glance. For one must not forget the cheapness of going to court in Germany which must be compared with the much higher costs of litigation in this country. So why would a phlegmatic English litigant, burdened by one of the most costly legal systems in the world, become trigger-happy when his German counter-part is not? Having asked this question, however, I readily admit, that more research has to be done before we can offer a more definitive answer. The German way of handling—by all accounts both expeditiously and to everyone's (including the Press's) satisfaction—the urgent applications for preliminary injunctions, also deserves to be studied more closely.

The fourth point is both important but also difficult to make; but from the point of view of comparative methodology, it is most intriguing. Simply put it is this. The contrast of German (and English law) with that of the law of the United States is, on one level of philosophical dogma at least, complete. This is because in the United States, the First Amendment seems to preclude any balancing of the competing interests of speech and privacy by the courts. As Mr Justice Black put it in *Konigsberg* v. *State Bar*[16] "... the First Amendment's unequivocal command that there shall be no abridgement of the rights of free speech and assembly shows that the men who drafted our Bill of Rights did all the 'balancing'". Yet, some recent legislative[17] and judicial[18] attempts in the USA suggest that results similar to those found in Germany can also be reached in America and this despite the hostile (to privacy rights) environment created by the First Amendment. That such decisions still represent the exception rather than the rule is, to a comparative methodologist, a matter of relative insignificance. For to him what the decisions illustrate more than anything else is that solutions are transplantable even if the way of achieving them may be adapted to suit the legal environment of different jurisdictions. The possibility of protect-

[16] 366 US 36, 61 (1961).

[17] Cal. Civ. Code 1708 8 (a)*ff*.

[18] See, for instance, *Huskey* v. *National Broadcasting Co. Inc.*, 632 F. Supp. 1282, 1287–8 (N.D. Ill 1986); *Stressman* v. *American Black Hawk Broadcasting Co.*, 416 NW 2d 685 (Iowa 1987); *Sanders* v. *American Broadcasting Co. Inc.*, 978 P. 2d 67 (Cal. 1999). The rationale of the Iowa court thus comes very close to the view found in the *Caroline* case reproduced below.

ing human privacy by finding ways of punishing its intrusion rather than inhibiting the dissemination of the results of the intrusion—photos, recordings, etc.—may, in the long run, offer American lawyers new and intriguing ways round the "chilling effect" of the First Amendment.

The fifth and final point that emerges from the study of the German law may, on the eve of the application of our Human Rights Act 1998, be the most important one. For the study of German law arguably reveals it to be not just more effective in the protection it affords to human privacy and solitude but also more rational in the criteria it employs in the determination of the outcome of a legal dispute. Thus, as it is extensively shown in chapter seven, above, German judges will ask themselves a multitude of reasonable questions before deciding whether the plaintiff's privacy rights will prevail over the defendant's speech rights. So, if the real and main aim of the violation of the plaintiff's privacy was the defendant's desire to make a financial gain, the invasion will not be allowed to go scot-free. So, too, sanctions will follow if the information about the plaintiff was obtained through illicit means. Speech that advances knowledge or furthers public debate on legitimate issues will also get preferential treatment over fabricated material or scurrilous gossip. And as some American courts are now also accepting, information already in the public domain may become actionable if it is spread more than the circumstances warrant. The breadth of the restriction that the plaintiff wishes to place on the defendant's speech rights may also be taken into account in defining the latter's legitimate interests to speak and write his views. All this may, inevitably, be fuzzy at the fringes. But it has more logic in it than the haphazard way in which mediaeval torts have been developed by our courts in order to afford protection to an interest that has revealed its full vulnerability only in times which have facilitated the collection, collation and wide dissemination of private information. For cases like *Tolley*[19] show how defamation can protect the least deserving (the amateur) but not the most deserving (the professional); *Kaye*[20] shows (among other things) how self-regulation does not work with all sections of the Press; and the fate of *Khorasandjian*[21] in the Court of Appeal and subsequently in the House of Lords (when considered and partially overruled in the *Hunter* litigation) shows how disingenuous it is to try and handle such cases under the heading of private nuisance and its attendant (mediaeval) limitations. So the plea that authors such as myself make is not for a broad and amorphous new tort of violation of privacy but (a) an expansion of the protection of human privacy through (b) a rationalisation (and even incremental expansion) of the existing wealth of ma-

[19] *Tolley* v. *Fry* [1931] AC 333.

[20] *Kaye* v. *Robertson* [1991] FSR 62.

[21] *Khorasandjian* v. *Bush* [1993] QB 727, overruled in part by the House of Lords in *Hunter* v. *Canary Wharf Limited* [1997] AC 655.

terial. In my opinion, the Human Rights Act enables our courts to satisfy the first demand and in no way prevents them from doing so by adopting the second approach. The German material also demonstrates how one can achieve a workable balance by focusing the debate on rational criteria rather than making the outcome of litigation—hazardous and unpredictable at best—depend upon the ingenuous interpretation (or re-interpretation) of historical accidents. In my view, it also suggests a surer way of avoiding conflict with Strasbourg, which our new Act has not made irrelevant.

In the light of the above (as well as what follows) it might assist the reader to attempt a summary of German law in two matters.

First, in terms of subject matter German law has avoided the (arguably) unworkable distinctions favoured by American law between public officials, public figures, and ordinary mortals. The important position of principle is thus boldly asserted that all of the above, in the right circumstances, deserve to have their privacy rights respected. In the same breath, however, German lawyers will also add that the comfort given to the former group is less than the protection given to the latter.[22]

Secondly, the protection given to privacy is determined by reference to the location of the invasion. The following gradation thus seems supportable by the case law subject to the proviso that the dividing lines are not rigidly conceived. Thus:

The privacy of the home is highly regarded and its invasion, by means of parabolic microphones or telephoto lens deeply frowned upon. The case law further shows that the "home" is widely defined[23] to include a hospital, hotel, office and the like, with the result that cases such as *Kay* v. *Robertson*[24] would, in German law,[25] probably go in favour of the plaintiff. Further, German law would treat as actionable the photographing of the plaintiff inside the garden of her villa by means of a telephoto lens[26] or eavesdropping on the telephone conversation of a famous politician.[27]

The protection extends beyond the home, itself, to cover the area just in front of it, especially if the intrusion of the occupant's privacy is taking the

[22] For supporting references see: Jürgen von Gerlach, "Der Schutz der Privatsphäre von Personen des öffentlichen Lebens in rechtsvergleichender Sicht", *JZ* 1998, 741, 748 and note 95.

[23] Advocating this view, BVerfGE 32, 54, 75 in the context of Art. 13 of the Constitution.

[24] FSR (1991) 62 CA.

[25] And in French law, as well. See: Cour d'appel de Paris, *JCP* 1965 II 223; Cassation, *D.* 1967, Jur. 181.

[26] See, also, BGE 44 II 319 (Switzerland); Foro It. 1976, I, 2895 (Italy); Gounalakis and Glowalla, AfP 1997, 870, 874. The latter piece refers to a French court decision that allowed an action by the Duchess of York against a photographer who photographed her without her bikini top together with her alleged financial advisor while residing in a villa in the South of France. To my knowledge, this (in)famous incident was never the subject of litigation in this country, presumably because of the state of our privacy laws.

[27] BGHZ 73, 120 = JZ 1979, 349. It was, however, significant in this case that the subject of that conversation was not deemed to present an overwhelming public interest.

form of persistent surveillance by means of cameras and other such electronic means.[28]

Finally, protection is also given to public figures in public places though, as the cases reproduced below clearly show, for this to happen two requirements must be satisfied. First, the plaintiff must be in a secluded part of the public area and, secondly, it must be objectively clear to third parties that he was in a situation of private character. The way the courts have dealt with these requirements in the two *Caroline* cases reproduced each below is both illustrative of the balance which the German courts try to strike in these matters. The final result is thus one that openly depends on recognisable criteria, which even though not necessarily acceptable to all, attempt to be both logical and workable.

[28] BGH JZ 1995, 1115; BGH NJW 1998, 1237. Likewise, with eavesdropping: BGH JZ 1998, 528 = NJW 1997, 2189. For a French case, extending the protection to the entrance of a hospital see: Bulletin des arrêts, ch civ. 1987, 140 no 191. These decisions show that the private sphere does not end at the plaintiff's front door.

Case One
Federal Supreme Court,
First Civil Senate
25 May 1954
BGHZ 13, 334 = NJW 1954, 1404 = JZ 1954, 698

The D Company published on 29 June 1952 in its weekly journal . . . an article by K. B. with the title "Dr H.S. & Co." and the sub-title "Political considerations concerning the foundation of a new bank". The article contained a comment concerning the new Bank for Foreign Trade founded by Dr S in H, and expressed itself in that connection in opposition to Dr S's political activity during the national-socialist regime and the years after the war.[29]

On the instructions of Dr S the plaintiff, an attorney, sent to the defendant company a letter of 4 July 1952, saying, inter alia:

I represent the interests of Dr S. In terms of § II of the Press Act I hereby require the following correction of the above-mentioned article in your issue of Sunday the 6th instant:

1. It is incorrect that . . .

2. . . .

This claim for correction is made under the Press Act, in combination with the BGB, and also the law of copyright.

I ask you to inform me by telephone or in writing on or before midday Saturday 5 July 1952, of your confirmation of the unrestricted execution of the required correction, failing which legal proceedings will be taken.

The defendant company gave the plaintiff no answer. But in the issue of 6 July it published, along with sundry expressions of opinion by readers on K.B.'s article, the following under the heading "Letters from Readers".

Dr H.S. & Co.
To the . . . [name of journal]
I represent the interests of Dr H.S.

[29] At the risk of becoming repetitive one must stress that these judgments, and indeed the constitutional provisions mentioned above, can only be fully understood if one bears in mind the utter contempt shown towards human dignity by the Nazi regime. It was ironical therefore that the breakthrough decision of 1954 was indirectly connected with one of its former sympathizers. (BVerfGE 7, 198 and BVerfGE 30, 173 also involved former Nazis.) For the mysterious Dr S of that judgment, was Dr HHG Schacht, an undoubtedly distinguished economist and financier who played an important role in the restoration of a stable currency after the devastating German inflation of 1923. From 1923 to 1930 he served as President of the Reichsbank and became a supporter of the Nazi party. When Hitler came to power, Schacht played a leading role in the rearmament programme, though from 1938/9 onwards he was urging Hitler to reduce expenditure for armaments as the only way to balance the budget and reduce inflation which had begun to rise again. In July 1944 he was confined to a concentration camp until the end of the War and then he was one of the principal accused at the first Nuremberg trial. He was acquitted at the trial only to be brought subsequently before the German People's court at Stuttgart under the "denazification" laws. Sentenced to eight years' detention in a labour camp, Schacht appealed successfully against his conviction and, with his name "cleared", resumed a highly successful and respected career as a financier.

1. It is incorrect . . .

2. . . .

Dr M, Attorney

In the contents of 1 there was no reproduction of or extracts from the appropriate Nuremberg judgment concerning Dr S which the plaintiff had introduced in his letter of 4 July 1952. Otherwise they were unaltered.

The plaintiff sees in this kind of publication an injury to his right of personality. The publication of his letter, written in his capacity of attorney for Dr S, under the heading "Letters from Readers" and with its contents falsified by the omissions and the choice of title, constitutes a deliberate misleading of the public. The incorrect impression was thus created that this was a mere expression of opinion by a reader on the previous article on Dr S, as was the case with other readers' letters printed under the same rubric. The plaintiff, however, had kept clear of taking any political attitude and had acted only as an attorney within the scope of his instructions. From a professional standpoint alone the conduct of the defendant company was intolerable. An attorney must be able to ensure that demands for correction made in his client's name must not be circulated in a misleading manner.

The plaintiff demanded that the defendant company be ordered to recall in its next issue under "Letters from Readers" its statement that the plaintiff had sent a reader's letter to the defendant company in the matter of "Dr H.S. & Co.".[30]

The defendant company took the view that it was not bound to agree to the plaintiff's demand for a correction, because his letter did not conform to the requirements set out in § II of the Press Act. It lay therefore within its discretion whether and at what place in its journal to print the communication.

The Landgericht granted the claim under § 823 I BGB, in combination with §§ 186, 187 STGB. The Oberlandesgericht rejected the claim. According to the Court of Appeal's opinion there was, in the abbreviated publication of the plaintiff's letter under the rubric "Letters from Readers", no lawful disparagement of the plaintiff. The method of this publication certainly con-

[30] It is important to note that in this, first, important case of privacy the plaintiff attorney did not seek damages but only the insertion of a correction in the next issue of the defendant's newspaper. This failure to request a damages award was part of deliberate strategy of the plaintiff. For one must recall that at that time the plaintiff had to overcome two hurdles. The first was linked with the wording of § 823 I BGB—the leading tort provision of the Code—which had deliberately refrained from including privacy among the list of protected interests enumerated in that provision. The plaintiff's first and main hurdle (which, in the event, he overcame) was to establish a wider right in his personality that could then be subsumed under § 823 I BGB and its term "other rights". The next move, in the event accomplished in the *Gentleman Rider* case, reproduced as case number two, was to obtain a damages award. This, too, was not easy because of § 253 BGB which provides that "for an injury which is not an injury to pecuniary interests compensation in money may be demanded only in those cases specified by the law." Cases two and three, below, show how the German courts eventually overcame this hurdle and, once again, show how they will not flinch from adopting even a *contra legem* interpretation when changed circumstances demand this. The *Soraya* case, decision no 5, below, explains how the German judges have justified such boldness.

tained an incorrect statement of fact. The incorrect statement that the plaintiff had sent a reader's letter to the defendant company was, however, not apt to injure his credit, nor to bring him into contempt or lower his dignity in public opinion.

The appeal led to a restoration of the Landgericht's judgment for these.

Reasons

The Court of Appeal was in error in failing to examine whether the plaintiff's claim was justified on the basis of a disparagement of his personality rights. It dismissed the action only because it did not consider as proved the objective presuppositions (elements) of a delict in the sense of §§ 823 II, 824 BGB in combination with §§ 186, 187 STGB. This objection is rightly made in the appeal.

It can be left undecided whether the plaintiff's letter of 4 July 1952 was a written work in the sense of § I of the Copyright Act and hence fell within the protection of copyright. The Reichsgericht has, indeed, constantly made the protection of correspondence to depend on whether it showed the individual form required for the protection of copyright (RGZ 41, 43 1481; 6911 401 [403]). On the other hand it has been rightly pointed out in the academic literature that a need for the recognition of a personality right in respect of the use of one's own notes exists equally even when that protection cannot be derived from the personality right of the author, on the ground that they do not possess the form given by an individual intellectual activity . . . The Reichsgericht believed that it must deny such a protection of personality independent of copyright to publications of correspondence because the German law then in force contained no positive statutory provisions on a general personality right (RGZ 79, 397 [398]; 82, 333 b341; 94, 1; 102, 134; 107, 277 [281]; 113, 414; 123, 312 [320]). It has indeed, in many decisions on § 823 BGB, approved of the protection of personality rights (RGZ 72, 175; 85, 343; 115, 416; 162, 7), but in principle it has recognized personality rights with an absolute power of exclusion only for certain specified personality interests. In the literature, Gierke and Kohler had already pleaded for the recognition of a comprehensive personality right . . .

Moreover, now that the Basic Law [Constitution of 1949] has recognized the right of a human being to have his dignity respected (Article 1), and also the right to free development of his personality as a private right, to be universally respected in so far as it does not infringe another person's right or is not in conflict with the constitutional order or morality (Article 2), the general personality right must be regarded as a constitutionally guaranteed fundamental right. No further discussion is needed here of whether and how far the protection of this general personality right, the limitation of which requires a balancing of interests, is restricted in particular cases by justified private or public needs, which outweigh the interest in the inviolability of the exclusive sphere of personality; for in this present case it is not evident that the defendant company has any interests worth protecting, which it could use to justify the conduct objected to by the plaintiff. On the contrary, by the defendant company's choice of a way of publishing the request for correction, omitting essential parts of the letter, interests of the plaintiff in the nature of personality rights have been infringed.

Every verbal expression of a definite thought is an emanation from the author's personality, even when the protection of copyright cannot be attributed to its form. It follows that in principle only the author is entitled to decide whether and in what form his notes are communicated to the public; for every publication of the notes of a living person under his name is rightly regarded by the public as proceeding from a corresponding direction of his will. The nature of the notes and the method of their communication is subject to the criticism and valuation of public opinion, which draws conclusions from those circumstances about the author's personality. While an unauthorized publication of private notes constitutes—as a rule—an inadmissible attack on every human being's protected sphere of secrecy, a modified reproduction infringes the personality rights of the author because such unauthorized alterations can spread a false picture of his personality. In general, not only unauthorized omissions of essential parts of the author's notes are inadmissible, but also additions through which his notes presented for publication only for certain purposes acquire a different colour or tendency from what he expressed in the form chosen by him and the kind of publication he had allowed.

In so far as they concern works protected by copyright, those legal principles have long been inferred by the courts from the creator's enjoyment of the personality right of an author, which is only a particular phenomenon of the general personality right (RGZ 69, 242 [244]; 79, 397 [399]; 151, 50). As regards the protection of personality the interest of the author in notes which are protected by copyright is essentially the same.

In the present case the plaintiff had unambiguously sent to the defendant company only a demand for correction and, indeed, in his character as attorney for Dr S. Thereby the defendant company was only empowered by the plaintiff either to publish the text in an unshortened form or, restricting itself to the required correction, to make clear that there had been a demand for correction. Since the plaintiff does not ask for his original desire for correction to be carried out, it is unnecessary for the purpose of this decision to consider whether his letter of 4 July 1952 conformed to the conditions of the Press Act. If, in agreement with the Court of Appeal, this had to be denied, the only consequence would be that the defendant company had a right to refuse altogether to publish the letter. But it was not entitled to publish it under the rubric "Letters from Readers" and, moreover with the omission of the passages that would clearly show that the plaintiff was not putting forward his personal opinion in favour of Dr S but wished to obtain a correction under the Press law. The Landgericht's decision is to be approved, that this mode of publication—and also the placing of the correction side by side with five other letters on the article on Dr S published by the defendant company—was bound to produce the impression on an impartial reader that the plaintiff's letter gave his personal attitude to the controversy about Dr S. That misleading impression was also not dispelled by the literal reproduction of the plaintiff's introductory sentence; for that sentence, in its generally accepted character, told the reader only that the sender was Dr S's attorney.

It did not make sufficiently clear that the content also of the letter in question referred to his instructions as attorney and that it had been composed by him not as a private person but in the exercise of his profession.

Accordingly the Court of Appeal was not in error in holding that the publication of the letter of corrections in shortened form under the rubric "Letters from Readers" contained an untrue statement of facts. This also means that through the mode of publishing it, the letter acquired a meaning not in conformity with its original composition and that this form of publication did not correspond to what the plaintiff had alone given permission for, namely broadcasting to the public the letter of correction in the form he had chosen.

The Landgericht was right in regarding the publication complained of, which according to its findings had become known to an extraordinarily wide circle of persons, as a continuing disparagement and therefore that the demand for revocation was justified.

Case Two
Federal Supreme Court
First Civil Senate
14 February 1958
BGHZ 26, 349 = NJW 58, 827
(with a partially approving and partially critical note by Larenz JZ 1958, 571 and an
approving article by H. Coing in JZ 1958, 558).

The plaintiff is co-owner of a brewery in X. He is active as a gentleman show-jumper ("Herrenreiter").[31] *The defendant Limited Partnership is the manufacturer of a pharmaceutical preparation which is widely reputed as being able to increase sexual potency. To advertise this preparation in the Federal Republic, and in particular in K, it disseminated a poster with the picture of a show-jumper. Its basis was an original photograph of the plaintiff, which had been taken by a press agency at a show-jumping competition. The plaintiff had not given permission for the use of his portrait.*

The plaintiff claimed damages from the defendant for the damage which he suffered as a result of the dissemination of the poster. He alleged that in the given circumstances he could only claim as damages what he would have obtained if he had allowed the defendant to use his portrait. As his professional and social position did not allow him, and his financial means did not compel him, to dispose of his portrait for advertising purposes, and in particular for the defendant's preparation, he would have done this, if at all, only for a fair price, at a rough estimate DM 15,000 at the very least.

The plaintiff applied for an order that the defendant pay by way of damages a fair sum to be fixed by the court.

The defendant denied any fault and pleaded that, after touching up, the plaintiff's features were not recognizable in the poster; and that it had not itself designed or produced the poster nor obtained the portrait from S, but had ordered it from the H advertising agency, which it had trusted as a respectable, competent, and reliable firm, not to injure the rights of third persons. The defendant could not have known that the poster had been designed on the basis of a photograph, or that the photograph showed a "gentleman" rider. Only as the case developed did it discover that it really concerned a portrait of the plaintiff. Thereupon it prohibited without delay any further use of the advertisement.

The Landgericht ordered the defendant to pay DM 1,000 to the plaintiff by way of damages. The Oberlandesgericht ordered the defendant to pay DM 10,000 to the plaintiff. The defendant's further appeal was unsuccessful for these reasons:

1. The Court of Appeal, in agreement with the Landgericht, found that the depiction of the rider in the poster allowed the plaintiff's person to be recog-

[31] "Gentleman" (rider) is a literal translation of the German (*Herren*); but it should be understood as referring to an "amateur" and not a "professional" rider. The parallels with our own *Tolley* v. *Fry* [1933] AC 333, are thus obvious.

nized despite the retouching. It rightly concluded that the dissemination of the poster without the plaintiff's permission injured his personality rights, namely his right to deal with his portrait, and that the defendant must compensate him under § 823 11 BGB in combination with § 2 of the Act on Artistic Creations, if it was found to blame (cf. RG *JW* 1929, 2257; BGHZ 20, 345, 347 ff.*). The Court of Appeal came to that conclusion seeing that the defendant had not observed the care required in the circumstances, since it had obtained in the course of its business the poster prepared by the H advertising agency without making certain that the person depicted had agreed to the intended use of his portrait.*

The appellant's attacks on these findings must fail [further discussion not reproduced].

11. In awarding compensation to the plaintiff the Court of Appeal had in mind the licence fee which he could have demanded if a suitable contract had been arrived at between the parties. It held that it was justified in applying a method of assessing damages developed for breaches of copyright, because it was hard for the plaintiff to show whether and to what degree there had been any pecuniary loss. In contrast to the Landgericht, which had thought DM 1,000 to be sufficient, the Court of Appeal decided that DM 10,000 was the more appropriate figure.

Although the appeal is unsuccessful in the result, it must be conceded that the Court of Appeal's reasoning is not entirely appropriate to the peculiar facts of the case.

1. The appellant does not dispute that, even where there is an injury to the personality right to one's portrait, the damage can be estimated according to the payment that would presumably have been arranged if there had been a contract. Nevertheless the appellant argued that this method of assessing damages, which the Senate in its judgment of 8 May 1956 [BGHZ 20, 345 ff.*—Dahlke] declared admissible for the unauthorized publication of a portrait, could not be used if it was established that the person portrayed would, for special reasons, never have allowed his portrait to be used for advertising purposes.*

If in the case under appeal pecuniary damage had actually been in question, this attack would not have been well founded. For according to settled case-law and academic opinion, where a claim to an appropriate compensation is recognized, it is not a question of applying the general provisions of the law of damages but of its customary supplementation to make good injury to valuable exclusive rights, based on the equitable consideration that the defendant should not be better off than he would have been if his application for permission had been granted. The claim to appropriate compensation is therefore granted in all cases of unpermitted invasion of exclusive rights where permission is usually made dependent on payment and where, having regard to the kind of the right which has been violated, the invasion is habitually allowed according to the customs of daily life only—if at all—against compensation (BGHZ 20, 345, 353 ff.*). It is not at all necessary for a contract actually to have come into existence if the invader's conduct was otherwise unobjectionable.*

2. It must, however, be agreed that the Court of Appeal, by the method of assessment it chose, did not really try to work out the economic loss to the plaintiff, but rather to adjust the satisfaction due to him to his non-material disparagement. In particular the reasoning by which it arrived at the amount of the damage to the plaintiff shows that according to its opinion also he did not suffer any tangible pecuniary loss. In truth he claims not compensation for a non-existent pecuniary loss but an appreciable satisfaction for an unlawful attack on his personality protected by § 22 of the Act on Artistic Creations and Articles 1 and 2 of the Constitution. He demands satisfaction for the fact that a widely disseminated poster, by making him, one might almost say, "ride" for the purpose of advertising the defendant's tonic—and a sexual one at that—humiliated him and made him an object of ridicule. In such a situation it is absurd to award damages on the basis of a fictitious licence agreement. This way of estimating damage is appropriate only if one can start with the doing of some kind of pecuniary damage and all that is left is to alleviate the often difficult task of proving its amount. It fails if no pecuniary prejudice at all is in question. It fails also in the present case because it would assume that the plaintiff had done something that not only he, but all others of the same professional and social standing, must consider harmful and as a continuing degradation of his personality. It must convey an imputation that the plaintiff would, after all, voluntarily and for a large sum of money place himself in the unworthy position against which he is defending himself.

The plaintiff's claim therefore cannot be supported by the Court of Appeal's chosen method of assessment, helped out by the fiction of a loss of licence fee.

3. Moreover, basing the claim on unjustified enrichment is precluded because the plaintiff did not experience any pecuniary disadvantage and there is thus no pecuniary shift of the kind envisaged by §§ 812 ff. *BGB.*

4. If, therefore, the kind of assessment adopted by the Court of Appeal fails, and it is shown that the plaintiff in truth suffered no pecuniary damage, the decisive question comes to be whether he can demand compensation for the immaterial damage which he has suffered as a result of the invasion of his personality following the appearance of his picture in the advertisement. On the facts before it the Senate answers that question in the affirmative.

This Senate has already said in its decision in BGHZ 13, 334, 338 that the sacredness of human dignity and the right to free development of the personality protected by Article I of the Constitution are also to be recognized as a civil right to be respected by everyone in daily life, in so far as that right does not impinge upon the rights of others and is not repugnant to constitutional order or the moral law. This so-called general right to one's personality also possesses legal validity within the framework of the civil law, and enjoys the protection Of § 823 I BGB under the designation of "other right" (cf. *also BGHZ 24, 12* ff.*).*

Articles I and 2 of the Constitution protect—and indeed must be applied by the courts in the administration of justice—what is called the concept of human personality; they recognize in it one of the supra-*legal basic values of the law. Thereby they are directly concerned with the protection of the inner realm of the personality which, in principle, only affords a basis for the free and responsible self-determination of the individual and an infringement of which produces primarily so-called immaterial damage, damage expressed in a degradation of the personality. To respect this inner realm and to refrain from invading it without authorization is a legal command issuing from the Basic Law itself. And it follows from the Constitution that in cases of invasion of this sphere, protection must be given against damage characteristic of such an invasion.*

On the limited field of portrait protection this was established in 1907 by the special rules contained in §§ 22 ff. *of the Act on Artistic Creations, long before the Constitution came into force and at a time when the civil law did not as yet protect a general personality right. For the protection afforded by § 22, according to which portraits may be distributed or shown publicly only with the subject's consent, rests in essence on the fundamental principle of a person's freedom in his highly personal private life, in which the outward appearance of human being plays an essential part. The unauthorized publication of a portrait constitutes, as has long been recognized in legal literature, an attack on the freedom of self-determination and the free expression of the personality. The reason why a third person's arbitrary publication of a portrait is not allowed is that the person portrayed is thereby deprived of his freedom to dispose by his own decision of this interest in his individual sphere.*

Once the violation of the right to one's picture is seen as affecting one's personality it is possible to seek an answer to the question how to compensate immaterial damage in § 847 BGB. This allows an equitable compensation in money for non-pecuniary loss in cases of "deprivation of liberty". It is true that deprivation of liberty is here understood to mean deprivation of freedom of bodily movement, as well as compulsion to act, by means of force or threats, whereas § 22 of the Act on Artistic Creations deals with deprivation of the free and responsible exercise of will. Already, however, before the Basic Law came into force, the opinion was often expressed that any attack on the undisturbed exercise of the will was to be regarded as an injury to freedom in the sense of § 847 BGB. Now that the Constitution guarantees a comprehensive protection to the personality and recognizes human dignity and the right to free development of the personality as a fundamental value, it has done away with the dogma held by the original draftsmen of the BGB that there can be no civil law protection of general personality right; and since a protection of "inner freedom" without a right to compensation for immaterial damage would be in great part illusory, it would be intolerable to refuse compensation for that immaterial damage. Moreover, there is no obvious reason why § 847 BGB should not be extended by analogy to such attacks as injure the right to free exercise of the will, especially where that deprivation of intellectual liberty, just like deprivation of bodily freedom, renders natural restitution impossible. Where such blameworthy depreciations of the personality right are in question, the effective legal protection offered by the Constitution can, in the absence of any special legal provision, be attained only through its inclusion in the injuries mentioned in § 847 BGB, since their injurious consequences are of necessity primarily immaterial.

This view is not at variance with the sense of § 35 of the Act on Artistic Creations. Of course the injured party can claim under it a penalty for the injury to his right to his portrait, and with it to have his immaterial loss made good, only in criminal proceedings and on condition that the injury was intended; but that special provision shows only that as early as 1907 the legislator regarded an infringement of § 22 as so far-reaching and threatening that it was considered necessary to grant expressly to the injured party a claim to compensation for the disparagement. The restriction of the criminal law claim for a penalty to intentional injuries accords with the legislator's limitation of the threat of punishment for an infringement of § 22 to intentional interference. However, that does not mean that the same must apply to the civil law claims to compensation that are not regulated in the Act on Artistic Creations. On the contrary, since the Constitution now recognizes the general personality right as significant for civil law and has afforded a general civil law protection appreciably exceeding the narrow regulation of § 35 of the Act on Artistic Creations, the special provision of § 35 can no longer be cited in opposition to a more extensive civil law protection of the right to one's portrait. The general provisions of the BGB concerning delicts come into operation instead. That means that, at any rate since the Constitution came into force, by an analogous application of § 847 BGB, any blameworthy injury to the right to one's own portrait involves a duty to make good immaterial damage also.

In so far as the Senate, following the case-law of the Reichsgericht, decided in the Dahlke case (BGHZ 20, 345, 352 ff.*) that immaterial damage cannot give rise to a money claim in the absence of express legal provision, its opinion cannot be upheld in the light of the foregoing discussions. The statement was obiter, since the facts disclosed pecuniary damage, which could be estimated on the basis of the usual licence fee.*

111. The compensation to be paid to the plaintiff was fixed by the Court of Appeal at DM 10,000. Although starting from a possible assessment according to the satisfaction that might have been paid in a case of contract on the usual terms, the court's arguments fully apply also to fixing the amount of an equitable compensation under § 847 BGB. They also show that the court really awarded the plaintiff compensation for the immaterial damage that had resulted.

As the Grosse Zivilsenat explained in its decision of 6 July 1955 (BGHZ 18, 149), the claim for damages for pain and suffering offers the injured party an appropriate compensation for the depreciation of life (or personality) which is not of a pecuniary kind. But it also takes account of the notion that the doer of damage owes the injured party satisfaction for what he has done to him. It was emphasized in the decision that "satisfaction", which forms an integral part of the award for compensation for immaterial damage, must take into account all the relevant circumstances. This Senate adheres to this view in this present case. If one therefore moves on from that position, it follows that the Court of Appeal was not in error in taking all the relevant circumstances into account in fixing the amount of damages. In particular, that court explained that the fact that the plaintiff had never been ready to take part in any advertising must be a factor in deciding the amount to be paid. It con-

sidered it especially serious that the advertisement was for an aphrodisiac, and so was not to be compared with advertisements for other products. The court was right in taking the view that persons would be unlikely to allow their likeness to be used on a poster for this purpose and so run a risk of being recognized by a wider or narrower public exposing themselves to the innuendoes to which the defendant's preparation would give rise. The Court of Appeal *also took the plaintiff's social and business position into account, pointing to the fact that he moved in a social circle the members of which were for the most part known to each other and where the risk of making oneself an object to ridicule was especially great. When, after considering and giving weight to all these special circumstances relevant to amount of damages for pain and suffering, the* Court of Appeal *regarded the sum of* DM *10,000 as appropriate compensation (§ 287* ZPO*), it cannot be found to have acted contrary to law.*

Case Three
Federal Supreme Court, Sixth Civil Senate 19 September 1961

BGHZ 35, 363 = NJW 1961, 2059 (with approving notes by W. Rötelmann = NJW 1962, 736 and H. Hubmann = VersR 1962, 350, 562)

The plaintiff is a professor in the law faculty of the University of G at which he holds a chair of international and ecclesiastical law. From a stay in Korea he had brought with him a ginseng root, which he placed at the disposal of his friend Professor H, a pharmacologist, for research. The latter mentioned in a scientific article on ginseng roots that he had come into possession of genuine Korean ginseng roots "through the kind assistance" of the plaintiff. This led to the plaintiff being described in a popular scientific article, which appeared in the year 1957 in the H and W journal, along with Professor H and other scientists, as one of the best-known ginseng researchers of Europe.

The defendant company dealt in a tonic containing ginseng. In its advertisement for this tonic the plaintiff was referred to as an important scientist expressing an opinion on its value, and in an editorial note, printed in immediate connection with an advertisement in another journal, allusion was made to its use as an aphrodisiac. Both the advertisement and the journal were very widely distributed.

The plaintiff claimed that he had suffered an unauthorized attack on his personality right; and that the advertisement gave rise to the impression that he had, for payment, issued an opinion on a controversial topic in a department of knowledge not his own, and unprofessionally lent his name to advertising a doubtful product. He had suffered damage to his reputation as a learned man and been made an object of ridicule to the public and above all to his students. In reliance on BGHZ 26, 349 (Herrenreiter) he claimed DM 10,000 as satisfaction for the harm done to him.

The Landgericht awarded him DM 8000 as damages for pain and suffering. The appeals to both the Court of Appeal and the Bundesgerichtshof were unsuccessful.

Reasons

1. By invoking the plaintiff's scientific authority in its advertising to encourage belief in the effectiveness of its preparation for the mentioned purposes, the defendant company unlawfully disparaged his personality right (§ 823 I BGB). The reference to researches by the plaintiff, which lacked any objective foundation, was in the circumstances calculated to make him an object of ridicule in society and lessen his scholarly reputation. Moreover, he was bound to feel outraged by the way his name was used in advertising a preparation recommended as a sexual stimulant. The defendant company's conduct was also blameworthy. Before using the plaintiff's name for its advertisement it ought to have sought his agreement or at least to have ascertained whether and where he had stated what was asserted in its advertisement. The information in a popular article in the H and W journal ought in no way to have been adopted unseen; it was moreover substantially altered. The Court of Appeal rightly characterized the defendant's conduct as irresponsible. Likewise approval must also be given to the Court of Appeal's finding that the defendant company was also responsible for the note in the M journal which adopted in somewhat modified form the contents of the advertisement. Even if it was the advertising agency employed by the defendant company that caused the note to appear, the information contained in it depended on material supplied by the defendant company. At the very least, the defendant company had not supervised the advertising agency as was necessary.

*2. This Senate also agrees with the Court of Appeal's view that the plaintiff has a claim to compensation for immaterial damage. The case is, in its main lines, very similar to those decided by the Bundesgerichtshof and reported in BGHZ 26, 349 (*Herrenreiter*) and 30, 7. In both cases the way a product was advertised attacked the protected sphere of the personality right of persons who claimed compensation for the unlawful injury. In both the conditions for compensation for material damage were absent or at any rate not proved. If, in the circumstances, no permission to use a name or portrait for advertising purposes is in question, it is not possible to estimate pecuniary compensation on the lines of a licence fee according to the principles governing so-called unilateral acquisition without permission. The First Civil Senate awarded damages for pain and suffering to the plaintiff in the case decided by it and reported in BGHZ 26, 349 and also regarded an award of so-called "immaterial damages", with its function of satisfaction, as the adequate compensation that the law must afford to a plaintiff for the violation of his personality right. From the decision reported in BGHZ 30, 7 it must be taken that the standpoint of the Fourth Civil Senate is at least not at variance with that of the First Civil Senate.*

This Senate agrees with the First Civil Senate that satisfaction may be awarded to a person affected by the blameworthy infringement of his personality right. It is indeed stated in § 253 BGB that money compensation can be claimed for non-pecuniary damage only in cases expressly designated by the law. When the BGB established that enumeration principle, the high value of the protection of human personality and its special sphere had not received the recognition that it enjoys according to Articles 1 and 2 I of the Constitution. From the standpoint of the BGB, the protection of property interests always stood in the foreground, whereas the personal worth of a human being received only insufficient and fragmentary protection. In recognizing a general personality right of mankind and granting it the protection of § 823 I BGB, the courts drew for civil law purposes the consequences resulting from the rank the Constitution assigned to the worth of human personality and the protection of its free development. That protection, however, would be incomplete and full of loopholes if an infringement of the personality right did not give rise to a sanction adequate to the violation. Just as the restriction of protection by the law of delict to specific legal interests of a human being has proved too narrow to afford the protection of personality required by the Constitution, so a narrowing of immaterial damages, for immaterial loss to cover only injury to specifically mentioned legal interests, no longer conforms to the value-system of the Constitution. For Article 1 declares it to be an urgent obligation on the public power to protect the sacred dignity of the human being. Article 2 I puts the right of a human being to free development of his personality at the head of the fundamental rights. If the law of delict, in protecting the personality right in the non-material realm, retreated completely to a position where it merely protected the particular personality interests mentioned in Article 2 II, which are emanations from the personality right, the civil law would not be paying attention to the value-decision of the Constitution. The elimination of damages for immaterial loss from the protection of personality would mean that injury to the dignity and honour of a human being would remain without any sanction of the civil law, which deals with the disturbance of essential values and makes the doer of injury owe satisfaction to the victim for the wrong done to him. The law would then renounce the strongest and often only instrument calculated to ensure respect for the personal worth of the individual.

3. That does not mean that the legal consequences of injuries to body, health, and freedom on the one hand and the violation of the personality sphere on the other hand must be exactly the same or at least largely correspond to each other. A need for differentiation is already indicated by the fact that the factual aspect of an injury to a general personality right is much less specific than where body, health, or freedom is injured. That means that there are many marginal cases where the question is whether the case is one included in the generalized description of violation of the personality and whether, if it does, the unlawfulness is not excluded by the competing rights of the "offender", among which the right to free expression of opinion deserves particular attention. It is precisely where a so-called balancing of interest must take place that the limits of what is allowed are not always easy to fix. If for every overstepping of the limits, however petty, compensation for immaterial loss were to be awarded to the person affected, there would be a danger that unimportant injuries would be used inappropriately to make a gain. The purpose of awarding satisfaction would then be stultified. It must further be observed that it is more difficult to apply the general criterion of monetary value to measure immaterial injuries to the personality right than the consequences of bodily injuries. In injuries to the general personality right the satisfaction function of damages for pain and suffering advances into the foreground as that of compensation recedes. Hence it will always be necessary to look at the kind of injury to the personality right to see if the person affected, whose injury cannot otherwise be redressed, should be granted satisfaction for the wrong he has suffered. That will in general only be the case when the doer of damage is blamed for a serious fault or when an injury to a personality right is objectively significant. Only when such disturbances are serious may the civil law, taking seriously the protection of personality and its value as such, react against the injury by granting satisfaction to the person affected. Insignificant injuries do not call for satisfaction. Having regard to the special character of an injury to a personality right Swiss law, which has devoted greater attention than the BGB to legal protection of the personality (cf. Article 49 I of the Swiss Code of Obligations) also restricts damages for immaterial loss to serious cases.

4. The conditions for an award of immaterial damages especially occur when—as in a present case—there is a wanton attack on the personality right of another person out of a desire to increase the force of one's commercial publicity. Such an unfair attempt to succeed can be effectively countered only if it is burdened with the risk of an appreciable loss, and on the other hand, anyone who seeks to make money out of an unfair invasion of the sphere of another's personality must not feel hurt if he is forced to pay a money compensation. For the plaintiff the outrage inflicted—in particular since the object was recommended for specific purposes—was not at all insignificant, the more so because he ran the risk of readers assuming that he had lent his name for a money consideration. The award of a money compensation by way of satisfaction was justified by the seriousness of the attack as well as by the seriousness of the fault.

The amount of satisfaction to be given was for the judge of fact to assess. It could be attacked on appeal only if it rested on an incorrect finding of the applicable law or if the judge of fact overlooked essential points of view. No such defects, however, are here apparent. The Court of Appeal did right in attaching importance to the spread of publicity, which extended to Austria and Switzerland. It was also an essential factor in fixing the amount of the satisfaction that the defendant company continued the advertising complained of even after being warned by the plaintiff, thus displaying an especially reckless attitude. On the other hand, the Court of Appeal observed in the defendant company's favour that the mention of the name in the advertisement was not especially prominent, so that it might not have been noticed by the cursory reader.

Case Four
Court of Appeal of Hamburg, 21 May 1987
NJW 1988, 737

Facts

The plaintiff claims damages for immaterial harm resulting from a headline in the defendant's national daily newspaper. The Landgericht allowed the claim in part. The plaintiff's appeal was allowed in part, and the defendant's appeal was dismissed.

Reasons

I. *The defendant is guilty of a culpable invasion of the plaintiff's right of personality (§ 823 I BGB).*

1. The principal invasion of the plaintiff's right consists in the fact that the main headline in the 19 May 1986 issue of the defendant's newspaper B was so drafted as to suggest that the plaintiff would accept or had accepted DM 80,000 in return for being portrayed in the nude. This would be the impression received by any reader of this number of the newspaper who did not go on to read the full text of the article on the front page. The Landgericht was right to state that such readers would be very numerous. Headlines in this newspaper are set up in order to stimulate interest and curiosity about the article in question and induce readers to buy the paper. That is clear from the layout in this issue. The main headline can be read from quite a distance and can therefore be taken in by a person seeing the paper on a news-stand or being read by someone else.

The front page is so laid out that the reader learns the truth very gradually. The words "K Nude—DM 80,000" were readable from a great distance. Persons closer-to could see the text "K Nude. She wants DM 80,000." Adjoining the headline is a coloured picture of the plaintiff unclad down to the bosom; only closer inspection reveals this to be a drawing. Below the picture one sees, in somewhat larger letters, the words "No smile, the cool look—K in the P-Calendar". Even this does not tell the reader that there was no question of the plaintiff seeking a fee for publicity. The reader is throughout led to believe what the headline suggests. Only when the small print begins does the reader learn the truth, and then only if close enough to read it. The great majority of those unable to read this small print, especially those who do not buy the paper, will conclude to the discredit of the plaintiff that she was ready for a fee to display her body in the nude, partly because of what they have read, but partly also because they expect sensations from the B newspaper. Most readers will never learn the unsensational fact of the matter, namely that the plaintiff was actually claiming damages for having been so portrayed.

Even those who read the text below the drawing would have the same impression, for in the main they would conclude that the plaintiff allowed herself to be portrayed in the nude in the P-Calendar and was now demanding a fee for it. It is quite unlikely that anyone who did not have the paper in his hands would read the full text on page one and appreciate the truth of the matter, which was revealed only in its final sentence.

2. As drafted—and the defendant is responsible for its drafting—the headline invaded the rights of the plaintiff. It is true that any newspaper report is capable of being misunderstood by a cursory reader or of giving rise to false inferences. That is why this court has decided that one must put up with such negative reactions if a press report is accurate and not misleading; on a balancing of the interests involved, such invasions of the personality are not unlawful, for it would constitute a grave constraint on the basic right of freedom of the press if publishers were held responsible for misinterpretations which are, after all, hardly foreseeable. This applies particularly to readers who simply go by the titles of articles in the middle of a paper or journal and pay no heed to the text; the press need not concern itself with such cursory readers.

But it is different when headlines on the front page are calculated to excite the interest of people with no mind to read anything else in the paper, such as those who are wondering whether to buy the paper or glancing at a copy read by someone else in a train or a bus. Such a headline must be considered on its own, independently of the body of the article it heralds, for it can be foreseen that it will often be read cursorily in this way, and the press must certainly strive to avoid recognisable risks of likely misunderstandings, as indeed this court had already said. That is the case here.

3. The defendant was at fault. There was an obvious risk that the mention of the well-known plaintiff's name in conjunction with the idea of nudity and a sum of money would conjure up derogatory assumptions affecting her right of personality. Yet gravely at fault though the responsible editors were, it is not established with sufficient certainty that they deliberately intended to cause the harm.

*II. An award of damages for pain and suffering [*Schmerzensgeld*] is justified in this case.*

1. The Bundesgerichtshof has always held that even where there has been an unlawful and culpable invasion of the right of personality, the victim can claim money damages for immaterial harm only when the gravity of the invasion makes such a solatium *absolutely necessary. Whether such an invasion is sufficiently grave depends on all the facts of the case, including the seriousness and intrusiveness of the invasion, the dissemination of the publication, the duration of the harm to the victim's interests and reputation, the nature of and reasons for the defendant's conduct and the degree to which he was to blame.*

2. Given the very wide circulation of the B newspaper, the headline must have been taken in by a very large number of people who read no further. Thus the misapprehension we have indicated must have been very widely disseminated. The harm to the plaintiff's reputation as a public figure well-known at home and abroad was grave and long-lasting, and her name in the leading headline of the B paper, which would immediately command attention, placed her in a context highly prejudicial to her honour as a woman, diminished her seriousness as a politician and reduced her standing as a public figure. Apart from this, what was published in the B newspaper was not independently defamatory: it was the way the front page was laid out which induced the false impression of what the article went on to state.

The wrong was not, however, as great as might be expected from publication in the B newspaper, for anyone who read the whole of the front page would learn the truth of the matter.

The informational value of the fact that the plaintiff was claiming damages from P cannot be invoked here, for it was trivial. This fact could have been communicated quite explicitly without infringing the plaintiff's rights at all, but the fact that the infringement might have been avoided does not mitigate the infringement which occurred. It is, on the other hand, relevant that the B newspaper did publish a correction on the front page of its edition of 24 July 1986. This certainly amounts to an attempt to allay the consequences so far as those who were misinformed by the headline are concerned, but it cannot be said that it significantly diminished, much less neutralised, the effect of the publication in invading the plaintiff's rights: the correction was published in an unobtrusive manner which had none of the dramatic effect of the original publication, and in any case it can have reached only B's regular readers, and not the many other people who were affected by the original invasion of the plaintiff's right of personality.

3. The appropriate sum to award by way of solatium *is DM 10,000. The proven defamation is a weighty one, which set the plaintiff as a woman and well-known public person in a most degrading light. Those who read the headline and not the full article were left with the impression that the plaintiff was ready to let herself be portrayed in the nude for a fee—an impression quite at variance with the public esteem in which the plaintiff was held. This was calculated to do lasting harm to the plaintiff's reputation and standing. This needs no elucidation. It is equally obvious that because the plaintiff is a prominent politician, the adverse effect on her is much greater than it would be on a simple citizen known only to a few intimates. Finally, one must remember that those who drafted the headline must have been aware, had they been taking the proper care, of the grave risk of invading the plaintiff's right of personality. On the other hand, this invasion was not the result of a report which was actually false, as we have said above, and this also must be taken into account in determining the amount of* solatium. *Given that in this case the true facts were given to those who read the newspaper, the invasion was not as serious as it would have been had it resulted from false statements in* both *the headline* and *the text. Further, the de-*

fendant's published correction went some way towards reducing the damage. Taking all these points into consideration, we must say that the sum awarded by the Landgericht does not seem adequate compensation for the way the plaintiff's right of personality has been infringed. On the other hand, the plaintiff's demand for at least DM 30,000 does not seem appropriate on the facts of this case.

Case Five
Federal Constitutional Court (First Division)
5 June 1973
BVerfGE 35, 202

The petitioner had participated in an armed robbery of an arsenal of the German armed forces in the course of which several soldiers on guard duty were killed or severely wounded. The culprits were arrested after a prolonged search and were convicted. The petitioner was convicted as an accessory and sentenced to six years' imprisonment. A German television station commissioned a documentary play based on the crime, its planning, and detection and the background of the culprits, including the petitioner whose homosexual tendencies were stressed. The play showed a likeness of the petitioner and mentioned him frequently by name. The petitioner who had served two-thirds of his sentence and was soon to be released sought an injunction prohibiting the television company from broadcasting the play pending a decision on the merits of his claim that the play violated his right of personality.

The District Court of Mainz dismissed the action for an injunction on the grounds that the petitioner was "relatively a personality of contemporary history" and could therefore not rely on the right to the protection of his personality. The Court of Appeal of Koblenz [reference] affirmed this decision by weighing the respective interests of an individual to be protected against the unauthorized publication of his likeness in accordance with §§ 22 and 23 of the Act on the Protection of the Copyright in Works of Art and Photographs (henceforth cited as KUG) as a projection of the right to his personality covered by Arts. 1 and 2 I of the Constitution on the one hand and the need for objective pictorial information concerning persons in public life, which is recognized in § 23 KUG and must be interpreted in the freedom to express opinions and the liberty of broadcasting stations to provide information, protected by Art. 5 I of the Constitution on the other hand. The Court of Appeal held that in this conflict the right to provide information must prevail, especially since the trial had been concluded. The petitioner was "relatively a personality of contemporary history"; his interest in social reintegration had to give way to the interest of the public in general to receive a truthful account of the facts and the persons involved . . .

The German Federal Constitutional Court quashed the decisions of the two courts below on the ground that Art. 2 I in conjunction with Art. 1 I of the Constitution had been violated and issued a temporary injunction prohibiting the broadcasting of the play in question to the extent that it mentioned the petitioner by name and reproduced a likeness of him.[32]

[32] *Lebach* finds almost an exact equivalent in the decision of the California Supreme Court in *Briscoe* v. *Reader's Digest Association Inc.*, 483 P. 2d 34 (Cal. 1971). The similarity extends to the reasoning. This was in keeping with the trend that prevailed among California courts of that time to set out balancing criteria for weighing the speech interests against those of privacy. Thus, see, *Gill* v. *Curtis Publishing* Co. 239 P. 2d 630 (Cal Ct App. 1952). This trend was abandoned from the late seventies onwards, with the Californian courts increasingly adopting the arguments put forward by defendants that (a) their statements were in relation

Reasons

A. . . .

B. . . .

II. For the present case the Court of Appeal has held correctly that several fundamental rights affect the application of private law and that they lead in opposite directions. The right to one's personality guaranteed by Art. 2 I in conjunction with Art. 1 I of the Constitution conflicts with the freedom of broadcasting stations to provide information, in accordance with Art. 5 I, sentence 2 of the Constitution.

1. On the one hand, a televised broadcast of the kind in issue here concerning the origins, execution, and detection of a crime which mentions the name of the criminal and contains a representation of his likeness necessarily touches the area of his fundamental rights guaranteed by Art. 2 I in conjunction with Art. 1 I of the Constitution. The right to the free development of one's personality and human dignity safeguard for everyone the sphere of autonomy in which to shape his private life by developing and protecting his individuality. This includes the right "to remain alone", "to be oneself" within this sphere [reference], to exclude the intrusion of or the inspection by others [reference]. This includes the right to one's likeness and to one's utterances [reference] and even more to the right to dispose of pictures of oneself. Everyone has the right in principle to determine himself alone whether and to what extent others may represent in public an account of his life or of certain incidents thereof.

However, according to the constant practice of the Federal Constitutional Court, not the entire sphere of private life enjoys the absolute protection of the above-mentioned fundamental rights [references]. If an individual in his

to a matter of public concern or (b) was not sufficiently "offensive" to attract the sanctions of privacy law. The third most typical defence advanced by defendants was that the disputed statement (or picture) etc. was already in the public domain. This argument received powerful support from two important decisions of the United States Supreme Court in *Cox Broadcasting Corp.* v. *Cohen*, 420 US 469 (1975) and the *Florida Star* v. *B.J.F.*, 491 US 524 (1989). But in its most recent case law, California is displaying a certain swing back towards the older view of protecting privacy, for instance, by holding that excessive intrusion may become actionable even for facts which are already in the public domain. Thus, see, *Schulman* v. *Group W. Productions* 18 Cal. 4th 200 (1998); *Sanders* v. *American Broadcasting Co. Inc.*, 978 P. 2d 67 (Cal. 1999). And the legislature, under the pressure of the cinema industry, has also intervened to make instances such those discussed in the German *Caroline* cases actionable. Thus, see: California Civil Code § 1708 8 (b), (c), (e) and (k). Even among academics, invariably strong supporters of the theology of the First Amendment, one can nowadays find calls for a more balanced approach to these issues. Thus see Gielniak, "Tipping the Scales: Courts Struggle to Strike a Balance Between the Public Disclosure of Private facts Tort and the First Amendement" 39 *Santa Clara Law Rev.* 1217 (1999); Chemerinsky, "Balancing the Rights of Privacy and the Press", 67 *Geo. Wash. Law Rev.* 1152 (1999). For comparative lawyers, the true significance of these developments is not that they represent the dominant view in the United Sates—they do not—but that they show that much of the German thinking is (unconsciously) repeated in the United States. That must surely be a strong argument against those who—almost instinctively—dismiss Continental European material as being of little relevance to Common law courts.

capacity as a citizen living within a community enters into relations with others, influences others by his existence or activity, and thereby impinges upon the personal sphere of other people or upon the interests of communal life, his exclusive right to be master of his own private sphere may become subject to restrictions, unless his sacrosanct innermost sphere of life is concerned. Any such social involvement, if sufficiently strong may, in particular, justify measures of public authorities in the interest of the public as a whole—such as the publication of pictures of a suspect person in order to facilitate a criminal investigation (§ 24 KUG). However, neither the interest of the State to clear up crimes nor any public interest always justifies an infringement of the personal sphere [reference]. Instead, the pre-eminent importance of the right to the free development and respect of personality, which follows from its close connection with the supreme value enshrined in the Constitution, i.e. human dignity, demands that any intrusion of the right of personality which may appear necessary to protect such interest, must always be balanced against the protective rule laid down in Art. 2 I in conjunction with Art. 1 I of the Constitution. Accordingly, it must be determined in the individual case by weighing the particular interests whether the pursuit of the public interest merits precedence generally and having regard to the features of the individual case, whether the proposed intrusion of the private sphere is required by this interest in this form and extent, and whether it is commensurate with the importance of the case [references].

These principles, which were developed by the courts in respect of measures taken by public authorities, must be observed equally when the courts have to determine conflicting interests on the basis of private law. In the course of such a determination the courts are not precluded from taking into account the special position accorded to the media represented by broadcasting and television by virtue of their organization regulated by public law and their public functions.

2. In this respect the consideration is decisive, as the Court of Appeal has pointed out correctly, that the broadcast in dispute serves a function, the free exercise of which on its part is directly protected by a provision in the Constitution. Freedom of information by broadcasts in accordance with Art. 5 I, second sentence of the Constitution [freedom to broadcast], like the freedom of the press, of expression and information is a basic constituent element of a liberal-democratic order [references] . . .

Only when the exercise of the freedom to broadcast conflicts with other protected legal interests, the purpose of the individual broadcast, the manner of its presentation, and its actual foreseeable effect may become relevant. The Constitution has regulated possible conflicts between the freedom to broadcast and the interests of individual citizens, of groups and of the community as a whole, by referring to the legal system as a whole; according to Art. 5 II of the Constitution the emission of broadcasts is subject to the restrictions imposed by the general law. According to the constant practice of the Federal Constitutional Court the need expressed by this provision to take other protected legal interests into account must not render the freedom to broadcast a relative one; instead the laws which restrict the freedom to broadcast must in turn be interpreted in the light of the constitutional guarantee and must, if necessary, be equally restricted in order to ensure that the freedom of broadcasting is safeguarded adequately [reference]. Consequently the opposing protected legal interests must be balanced against each other in each individual case in the light of general and specific considerations.

III. 1. The general laws referred to by Art. 5 II of the Constitution include also the provisions of §§ 22, 23 of the Act on the Copyright in Works of Plastic Art and Photography of 9 January 1907 (RGBl. 1907) maintained by § 141 no. 5 of the Copyright Act of 9 September 1956 (BGBl. I 1273), which formed the basis of the judgment in issue before this court. These provisions, the wording and the original purpose of which related originally to the right to one's own likeness, have for a long time been interpreted by the courts and by writers to apply also to reproductions of one's likeness, whether accompanied by the person's name or not, as well as to the representation of a person by an actor on a stage [references]. The general approach to these provisions has changed since the Constitution came into force to the effect that the right to one's likeness is regarded as an aspect, as a special feature of the general right of personality which was derived from Arts. 1 and 2 of the Constitution [references].

These provisions are in accordance with constitutional law; their somewhat flexible character gives sufficient scope for applying them in keeping with the Constitution and it has been shown in practice that it is possible, in balancing the interest, as required by § 23 KUG, to take sufficient account of the reflex effect of the relevant fundamental rights. In this context, it is irrelevant from the point of view of constitutional law which factual element of § 23 KUG serves as the balancing factor [references].

2. In cases of conflict, such as the present, the general principle applies, on the one hand, that in applying §§ 22 and 23 KUG to televised broadcasts the freedom to broadcast must not be restricted excessively. On the other hand, as distinct from other general laws in the meaning of Art. 5 II of the Constitution, it is a special feature of the present case that the restriction of the freedom to broadcast serves in turn to protect an important concern of the Constitution; the interest of the person affected to prohibit the publication of his likeness or any representation of his person, which must be protected with the framework of § 23 KUG, is directly enhanced by the constitutional guarantee of the protection of personality. In solving this conflict it must be remembered that according to the intention of the Constitution both constitutional concerns are essential aspects of the liberal–democratic order of the Constitution with the result that neither can claim precedence in principle. The view of humanity taken by the Constitution and the corresponding structure of the community within the State require both the respect for the independence of individual personality and the guarantee of a liberal social atmosphere; the latter cannot be realized at the present time unless communications are unimpeded. In case of conflict both concerns of the Constitution must be adjusted, if possible; if this cannot be achieved it must be determined which interest must be postponed having regard to the nature of the case and to any special circumstances. For this purpose, both concerns of the Constitution, centred as they are on human dignity, must be regarded as the nucleus of the system of constitutional concerns. Accordingly, the freedom to broadcast may have the effect of restricting any claims based on the right of personality; however, the damage to "personality" resulting from a public representation must not be out of proportion to the importance of the publication upholding the freedom of communication [reference]. Furthermore it follows from these guiding principles that the required weighting of interests must take into account the intensity of the infringement of the personal sphere by the broadcast on the one hand; on the other hand, the specific interest which is being sensed by the broadcast and is capable of being thus served, must be assessed and examined as to whether and to what extent it can be satisfied even without any interference—or a less far-reaching interference—with the protection of personality.

IV. 1. In the light of these general principles the following criteria are relevant from the point of view of constitutional law in assessing televised broadcasts of the kind in issue here.

(a) A public report of a crime in which the name, a likeness, or a representation of the culprit is provided will always constitute a severe intrusion of his personal sphere, seeing that it publicizes his misdeeds and gives from the outset a negative slant to his person in the eyes of those to whom the report is addressed. It may be different if the report is designed to create sympathy for the culprit, as for instance in order to achieve a new trial, a pardon, or some other assistance . . .

(b) Disregarding the possibility of an additional infringement by the manner of the representation (polemics, falsification), even a report which seeks to be objective and factual, if televised, constitutes normally a much greater invasion of the private sphere than an oral or written report published in the press or over the radio. This is so, in the first place, because the visual impression and the combination of a picture and word is much stronger, but mainly because television commands a much greater audience than the cinema and the theatre, resulting in a special position. Consequently there is a special reason "for watching over the observation of the limits established by the law and to prevent an abuse [sic] of the right of personality which had become more vulnerable. In this respect the law must not give way to technical developments" [reference].

(c) If for the above-mentioned reasons alone a special need exists for protection against violations of the right of personality by televised broadcasts reaching such a wide audience, it must be remembered that the broadcast performance of a documentary play entails specific dangers . . .

In conclusion it can be stated that television broadcasts reporting on a crime naming, depicting, or representing the culprit, especially in the form of a documentary play, will normally constitute a serious invasion of his sphere of personality.

2. On the other hand weighty considerations suggest that the public should be fully informed of the commission of crimes including the person of the culprit, and of the facts which led to them. Crimes, too, are part of contemporary history, the presentation of which is altogether the task of the media.

Moreover the violation of the general legal order, the infringement of protective legal interests of the citizens involved or of the community, sympathy with the victims and their relatives, fear of the repetition of such crimes, and the desire to prevent them create a fully justified interest in receiving detailed information concerning the deed and the criminal. This interest will be all the greater the more the criminal act is unusual having regard to the special features of the object of the attack, the manner in which it was carried out, or the severity of the consequences. Where serious crimes of violence are involved, such as that represented in the play in issue, the interest to receive information is based not only on general curiosity and sensationalism but on serious reasons for asking who were the perpetrators, what were their motives, what was done to detect and to punish them, and for preventing similar crimes. For this purpose the desire to know only the facts will be predominant, but as time passes the interest increases to receive a more searching interpretation of the deed, its background, and its social setting. Not least is the legitimate democratic desire in determining to control the organs of the State and public authorities responsible for security and order, the prosecution and the criminal courts . . .

3. In balancing generally the interest in receiving information as circumscribed above by televised reporting within these limits against the invasion of the sphere of personality of the culprit which must follow inevitably, the interest in receiving information must generally prevail in so far as current reporting of crimes is concerned. He who breaks the peace established by law, attacks or violates by his act and its consequences his fellow citizens or legally protected interests of the community, must not only suffer the criminal punishment provided by the law. He must also accept, as a matter of principle, that the public interest in information caused by himself by his own deed is being satisfied in the usual manner in a community which observes the principle of freedom of communication. Moreover, the control of the prosecution and of the criminal proceedings which is assured thereby also benefits the culprit. However, the interest to receive information does not prevail absolutely. The importance of the right to personality, which is a corner-stone of the Constitution, requires not only that account must be taken of the sacrosanct innermost personal sphere [reference] but also a strict regard for the principle of proportionality. The invasion of the personal sphere is limited to the need to satisfy adequately the interest to receive information, and the disadvantages suffered by the culprit must be proportional to the seriousness of the offence or to its importance otherwise for the public. Consequently, it is not always admissible to provide the name, a picture, or any other means of identifying the perpetrator.

It is obvious that the right of personality is only postponed if the reporting is objective and if the interpretation is serious; it is different if the account seeks to be sensational, is intentionally one-sided or misleading. On the other hand, objective reporting of a serious crime justifies not only the publication of the name or of a likeness of the perpetrator; it also includes his personal life in so far as it is directly connected with the act, provides clues about his motive or the setting, and seems relevant for assessing the guilt of the perpe-

trator in the light of modern criminal law. The actual question as to where the limits are to be drawn in fact seeing that in principle the interest to receive information by reports of contemporary events must prevail, can only be answered having regard to the circumstances of the individual case.

4. The reflex effect of the constitutional guarantee of personality does not, however, allow the media of communication, apart from contemporary reporting, to deal indefinitely with the person of the criminal and his private sphere. Instead, when the interest in receiving information has been satisfied, his right "to be left alone" gains increasing importance in principle and limits the desire of the mass media and the wish of the public to make the individual sphere of his life the object of discussion or even of entertainment. Even a culprit, who attracted public attention by his serious crime and has gained general disapproval, remains a member of this community and retains his constitutional right to the protection of his individuality. If with the prosecution and conviction by a criminal court the act attracting the public interest has met with the just reaction of the community demanded by the public interest, any additional continued or repeated invasions of the personal sphere of the culprit cannot normally be justified.

5. (a) The time-limit when the reporting of current events which is admissible in principle becomes subsequently an inadmissible account or discussion cannot be stated generally; certainly it cannot be stated in months and years so as to cover all cases. The decisive criterion is whether the report concerned is likely to cause the culprit considerable new or additional harm, compared with the information which is already available.

(b) In order to determine the time-limit more clearly, the interest in reintegrating the criminal into society and to restore his social position may be treated as the decisive point of reference.

(c) Altogether a repeated televised report concerning a serious crime which is no longer justified by the interest to receive information about current events is undoubtedly inadmissible if it endangers the social rehabilitation of the culprit. The vital chance necessary for the existence of the culprit and the interest of the community to restore his social position must prevail in principle over the interest in a discussion of the crime. Whether and to what extent any exceptions are conceivable such as in the case of an overriding historical interest, of scholarly or other broadcasts which are addressed to a limited range of viewers need not be examined here.

V. 1. Examined in the light of the criteria of constitutional law, the decisions appealed against cannot be maintained. The district court has sought to balance the interests of the petitioner and the broadcasting station exclusively by reference to §§ 22, 23 KUG without taking notice of the reflex effect of the fundamental rights contained in Art. 2 I in conjunction with Arts. 1 and 5 I of the Constitution.

The Court of Appeal did realize that a conflict exists between the freedom to broadcast by virtue of Art. 5 I of the Constitution and the guarantee of personality by virtue of Art. 2 I and Art. 1 of the Constitution; in balancing, having regard to § 23 KUG, between the right to one's likeness and the inter-

est of the public to receive information it did take the reflex effect of these fundamental rights into consideration. In solving this conflict it did not, however, apply correctly the criteria which are to be derived from the existing constitutional provisions for the determination of cases such as the present, but have not been formulated hitherto by the Constitutional Court; above all, it did not attribute to the interest in rehabilitation the importance which it deserves from the point of view of constitutional law.

2. If sufficient account is taken of the effect of the provisions of the Constitution which are relevant in the present case upon the general law the conclusion must be reached that the petition of the complainant must succeed . . .

Case Six
Federal Constitutional Court in Proceeding Concerning the Constitutional Complaint of Publishing Company "Die Welt" and Mr. K.-H. V.
First Panel,[33] February 14, 1973.
BVerfGE 34, 269 = NJW 1973, 1221.

The plaintiff is Princess Soraya, the ex-wife of the Shah of Iran. At the time in question, after her divorce from the Shah, the plaintiff resided in Germany. The defendants are the publisher and chief-editor of an illustrated weekly paper, which is distributed throughout Germany and known to specialize in sensational society stories.

In April 1961, defendants' paper carried a front-page story purporting to be the transcript of an interview with the plaintiff. The interview, which appeared to reveal much of plaintiff's private and very private life, was wholly fictitious, i.e., it was totally and freely invented by its author, a freelance journalist. Defendants published the story without investigating whether the interview had actually taken place. In July, 1961, defendants' paper carried another story dealing with Princess Soraya, and as a part of that new story the defendants published a brief statement by the Princess to the effect that the alleged April interview had not taken place.

In the present action, plaintiff seeks damages for "violation of her personality rights." The Landgericht as court of first instance awarded her D.M. 15,000. The Oberlandesgericht (intermediate appellate court) and the Bundesgerichtshof (court of last resort in civil and criminal matters, abbr. BGH) affirmed, and the defendants brought the case before the Federal Constitutional Court by way of a constitutional complaint.

In order to understand the thrust of the defendants' constitutional arguments, we must take a brief look at the development and present status of the rules of substantive law which the plaintiff successfully invoked in the courts below.

Apart from a section protecting a person's right to his name, the German Civil Code contains no specific provisions concerning the subjects which we would label as defamation or invasion of privacy. In Germany, as in France, defamation traditionally has been thought of as a crime rather than a tort.[34] Under this traditional view, defamation actions normally have to be brought in the criminal courts, even though such an action ordinarily has to be prosecuted by the victim rather than the public prosecutor.[35] If the defendant is

[33] A case coming before the Federal Constitutional Court, unless summarily disposed, is heard by one of the two eight-judge panels.

[34] See BS Markesinis, "The Not So Dissimilar Tort and Delict", (1977) 93 *LQR* 78, 103–5; JF Murphy, "An International Convention on Invasion of Privacy", 8 *N.Y.U.J. Int'l L. & Pol.* 387, 422–23 (1976).

[35] See German Code of Criminal Procedure, § 374, 376. The public prosecutor brings such an action only if this is required in the public interest. German law generally vests the prosecutor with little or no discretion, and requires prosecution whenever there is reasonable cause to believe that the defendant has committed a crime. This general rule, however, is subject to exceptions in the case of certain relatively minor offenses, such as defamation.

convicted in such a criminal proceeding, he will be fined, or (in a very serious case) subjected to a jail sentence; but the victim cannot recover substantial damages in that proceeding.[36]

Until after World War II, attempts to bring civil actions for defamation or invasion of privacy found little favour with the German courts. The first paragraph of § 823 of the Civil Code authorizes tort recovery only if the plaintiff can show injury to his "life, body, health, freedom, property, or some other (similar) right". In order to bring cases of defamation or invasion of privacy within the ambit of this code provision, plaintiffs often argued that a person's interest in his reputation and privacy should be regarded as his "personality right" and should be protected as one of the "other rights" mentioned in § 823. But throughout the periods of the Empire, the Weimar Republic and the Third Reich, the courts essentially rejected that argument.[37]

A different judicial approach to the problem emerged after World War II, and after the adoption of the new West German Constitution, which contains the following provisions: [citation of articles 1 and 2 follows]

During the 1950s the BGH, explicitly invoking these constitutional provisions, gave up the former narrow interpretation of § 823 of the Civil Code and repeatedly held that a plaintiff's "personality right" is one of the "other rights" which are protected by § 823 against intentional or negligent infringement. This was an important development. It meant that—in contrast to prior law—the German courts now were treating injuries to a person's reputation or privacy as actionable torts.[38]

Even after this judicial breakthrough, however, a difficult issue remained to be resolved regarding the kind of damages for which recovery could be allowed under German law in cases of injury to the plaintiff's "personality right". The difficulty was caused by one of the Civil Code's provisions dealing with damages. [There follows the citation of some relevant provisions of the Code, including the one of § 253 given above.]

There are a few limited and narrowly defined cases in which an express provision of written law (within the meaning of § 253) permits the victim of a tort to recover money damages for an injury to non-pecuniary interests; the prime example is the case of personal injury, with respect to which § 847 of the German Civil Code explicitly authorizes the recovery of money damages

[36] Apart from other difficulties, German law until recently imposed a relatively low ceiling on the amount which the victim can recover in a criminal proceeding.

[37] It is interesting to note that in France the courts began much earlier than in Germany to employ tort remedies for the protection of privacy interests. The reason may be that Art. 1382 of the French Civil Code (see supra sec. 1), in contrast to German § 823, is of such generality that a French court, when granting tort recovery, could always claim to act on the authority of that Code provision. See WJ Wagner, "The Development of the Theory of the Right to Privacy in France", 1971 *Wash.U.L.Q.* 45, 49*ff.* Since 1970, moreover, tort remedies for invasion of privacy are explicitly authorized by the French Civil Code, Art. 9 (added by Law No. 70-643 of July 17, 1970). See also article 1916 (new) of the Civil Code of the Federal District of Mexico, and parallel revisions in the civil codes of many (but not all) Mexican States.

[38] For a full account, see Harry D. Krause, "The Right to Privacy in Germany–Pointers for American Legislation?" 1965 *Duke L.J.* 481, and most recently Karl-Nikolaus Peifer, "Persönlichkeitsschaden und Geldersatz", 96 *Zeitschrift für vergleichende Rechtswissenschaft* 74 (1997), also discussing parallel developments in Italy at 76–82.

for pain and suffering. The draftsmen of the Civil Code clearly regarded this provision of § 847 as an exception to the general rule laid down in § 253: that no money damages can be recovered for an injury to non-pecuniary interests.[39]

Neither the Civil Code nor any auxiliary statute provides for the recovery of non-pecuniary damages by a person whose "right of personality" has been injured. Thus when the tort of injury to a person's "personality right" was first developed by the German courts, it was initially thought that a plaintiff, while perhaps entitled to the publication of a retraction or to similar non-monetary relief under § 249, could not recover money damages without proof of what we would call "special damage," i.e., loss of his job, loss of customers, or the like. The plain language of § 253 indeed appears to preclude the plaintiff in such a case from recovering "general" damages for his soiled reputation and injured feelings.

In 1958, however, the German courts broke away from this restriction seemingly imposed by § 253. The occasion was the so-called *Herrenreiter* case (the case of the gentleman horse-back rider). That case involved a picture of the plaintiff, a well-known equestrian, elegantly positioned on horse-back while jumping over a hurdle. Without plaintiff's authorization, the picture was publicly and widely disseminated by the defendant as part of an advertisement promoting a sexual stimulant. The plaintiff's "personality right" was seriously injured by this advertisement, not only because it conveyed the impression that the plaintiff had sought to commercialize his great reputation as a sportsman, but also because it implied that he needed and used sexual stimulants.

The lower courts awarded the plaintiff a substantial sum of money as damages for the injury to his reputation and feelings. The BGH affirmed, essentially on the ground that § 847 of the Civil Code should be extended by analogy to cover the case at hand. This analogy argument was questionable, because the word "only" in § 253 explicitly prohibits an analogical extension of provisions, such as § 847, which engraft exceptions upon the general rule of § 253. Recognizing this, the BGH subsequently abandoned the analogy argument; but the result reached in the *Herrenreiter* case was reaffirmed in later cases, on the ground that in many situations the tort of injury to a person's "personality right"—a tort developed in response to value judgments expressed in the Constitution—would be without an adequate remedy if the victim of such a tort could not recover money damages for the violation of his non-monetary interests.

The BGH limited the breadth of these rulings by further holding that such a cause of action for money damages should be recognized only if (a) the injury to the plaintiff's "personality right" is substantial, and (b) the defendant's act is sufficiently culpable to justify the rendition of a money judgment in a sizeable amount. According to the BGH, both conditions, (a) and (b), are clearly satisfied in a case in which a defendant, by way of large-scale promotion of his own commercial interests, has wantonly violated the plaintiff's

[39] See Palandt, *Burgerliches Gesetzbuch*, § 847, Anno. la (53rd ed., 1994). Some additional exceptions are provided for in auxiliary statutes. See ibid.

"personality right." The repetition of such intolerable conduct, the BGH held, should be prevented by announcing a rule of tort law which makes it clear to would-be violators that such conduct is costly for them.

In the decisions dealing with this question, the BGH also pointed to the drastic technological and social changes that have taken place since the enactment of the Civil Code. The development of mass media, hardly predictable in 1900, makes the protection of an individual's personality right more important and more difficult in our day. Therefore, the BGH held, a court which takes the value system of the Constitution seriously can no longer feel bound by § 253 of the Civil Code insofar as that provision denies recovery for non-pecuniary damages even in cases of grave injuries to an individual's personality right.

The lower courts, after some initial reluctance on the part of some of them, generally followed these holdings of the BGH, which were approved, also, by the majority of the commentators. In the instant case, both the lower courts and the BGH itself based their decision on those previous holdings.

The defendants' constitutional complaint was based mainly on the following provisions of the German Federal Constitution:

Art. 5. . . . Freedom of the press and freedom of reporting by broadcast and film are guaranteed. . . .

These rights are limited by the provisions of general [written] laws,[40] by statutory measures for the protection of juveniles, and by the right of personal honour. . . .

Art. 20. . . . All of the State's power originates with the People. Such power can be exercised by the People through elections and ballots, and by special organs of the legislative, executive and judicial branches of the government.

The legislature is bound by the constitutional order. The executive and the judiciary are bound by statute and law.[41]

In particular, the defendants argued that the substantive rule pursuant to which the lower courts ordered them to pay money damages to the plaintiff had been created by the courts in violation of the principle of separation of powers laid down in Art. 20 of the Constitution. The BGH, they argued, had acted contra legem when it developed the right to money damages for violation of an individual's "personality right." This, it was contended, was a usurpation by the courts of legislative power.

The defendants did not question the constitutionality of the view that the personality right of a person is one of the "other rights" mentioned in the first paragraph of § 823 of the Civil Code. Their attack was directed only against the decisional rule which—contrary to the language of § 253 of the Civil Code—permits a plaintiff whose personality right has been gravely injured to recover a money judgment for non-monetary damages.

[40] The German term is "*allgemeine Gesetz.*"

[41] The German term is "*Gesetz and Recht.*" The words "*Gesetz*" and "*Recht*" are not synonymous. See *supra*. Literally, this provision of the Constitution means that the executive and judiciary are bound by written law and by other law.

The defendants did not deny that the recognition of plaintiff's personality right as one of the "other rights" protected by § 823 of the Civil Code was in part dictated by Arts. 1 and 2 of the Constitution. But they argued that the rights derived from Arts. 1 and 2, like other human rights protected by the Constitution, are essentially defensive in nature. For this reason, the defendants contended, it is not possible to treat those constitutional provisions as the direct foundation of a cause of action for money damages.

In addition, the defendants argued, the money judgment rendered by the courts below violated the constitutional principle of freedom of the press. In the defendants' view, the money damage rule developed by the courts and applied in this case did not constitute the kind of "general [written] law" which pursuant to Art. 5 of the Constitution may be used by the law-giver to limit the freedom of the press.

In holding that the constitutional complaint was unfounded and that the (ordinary) judges were entitled to (re-interpret) § 253 the way they did in the Professor of Canon Law decision the Constitutional Court included in its judgment the following crucial paragraph.

"*Occasionally, the law can be found outside the positive legal rules erected by the state; this is law which emanates from the entire constitutional order and which has as its purpose the 'correction' of written law. It is for the judge to 'discover' this law and through his opinions give it concrete effect. The Constitution does not restrict judges to apply statutes in their literary sense when deciding cases put before them. Such an approach assumes a basic completeness of statutory rules which is not attainable in practice . . . The insight of the judge may bring to light certain values of society . . . which are implicitly accepted by the constitutional order but which have received an insufficient expression in statutory texts. The judge's decision can help realize such ideas and give effect to such values.*"

Case Seven
Federal Supreme Court,
Sixth Civil Senate
19 December 1978,
BGHZ 73, 120

On the 3rd of October 1974, the first claimant, the chairman of the CDU [the Christian Democratic Union], had had a telephone conversation with the then general secretary of that party, the second claimant, which without the knowledge of either of them was "bugged" by an unknown person and recorded or taken down in shorthand. A written record of the conversation was received, with an anonymous letter posted in Kaiserlautern on the 2nd June 1975, at the editorial office of "Stern" Illustrated produced in the publishing house of the first defendants, whose editor-in-chief is the second defendant. The second claimant was told about this at an interview with two editors of "Stern". As the editor-in-chief (who was the second defendant) would not give to the claimants the confirmation they requested that publication would not take place, they obtained an interim injunction prohibiting the printing of the telephone conversation. But in the meantime an article about the "bugging affair" had already been printed (with the co-operation of an editor who was the third defendant) with the full content of the conversation and almost completely delivered, so that the claimants could no longer prevent its appearance.

In their claim they ask for the defendants to be prevented from publishing the telephone conversation between them, the claimants, in whole or in part, or otherwise passing it on to third parties.

The Landgericht and the Oberlandesgericht allowed the claim. The defendants' appeal in law, which is admissible, was unsuccessful.

Reasons

1. By publishing the telephone conversation, for which the first defendant as publisher and the second and third defendants as editors are indisputably responsible, the claimants' personalities have been affected in two overlapping protected areas.

a) Firstly, the publication interferes with the interest of the claimants in not allowing the content *of their conversation to reach the public.*

Their interest in keeping it secret arose simply because the subject matter of the conversation made it part of their personal sphere. Two friends in the party [the CDU], both in prominent positions within it, were discussing the emergence of the first claimant as a candidate for chancellorship in the face of attacks against him in this context, in particular by "stern" Illustrated. Their critical concern was the attitude of the leadership and the grass roots of the party to this candidature. They were talking about indiscretions which had resulted in internal party matters reaching the press, and about measures to combat these. Quite personal things were spoken about, even though they referred to the claimants' work in the public sphere. In the conversation, thoughts and feelings were expressed, which a person would only make so frankly to a confidant whose discretion can be trusted, and which he would not let the public hear in that form, even if he had no adverse consequences to fear for himself on this account.

The claimants have also left the defendants in no doubt about their wish for the maintenance of secrecy.

b) The extent of the interference which the claimants have suffered to their personalities by the publication is not, however, limited to their interest in keeping the content of their conversation secret. Their personalities were adversely affected more strongly than by an indiscretion, because of the area of the personality exposed by the publication of the transcript of the telephone conversation. The individual is especially reliant on this area being protected from the public in order to safeguard and develop his individuality.

Everyone, even a politician appearing in the public arena and seeking publicity, has in principle a claim protected by Articles 1 and 2 of the Basic Law to the safeguarding of his private sphere, to which others only have access insofar as he allows them to see it. In this private sphere he must be safe from control and censorship by the public, otherwise the basis on which his personality can be realized and develop would be endangered. All the events and expressions of life of this personal sphere are in principle protected by the right of the personality to self-determination in this way. This is above all true of a private conversation like the telephone call between the claimants, which did not lose its private character through the political aspect of the conversation. This is because what is said and how it is said depends a great deal on who is taking part in the conversation; a person can only participate uninhibitedly if he has control over the participants or at any rate knows them. This protection is removed if such a confidential conversation is secretly recorded and embodied in a transcript which is made available to the public. In a publication of this kind, therefore, the personality of the person affected is more strongly assailed than if merely something about the content of the conversation gets out; the reason is that it brings the personal sphere in all its complexity into the public eye. The recording does not only fix the content of the statements but also the expressions which the persons themselves have used in the conversation. Moreover, expressions acquire an importance of their own through a recording. All that was associated with the transitory nature of words in conversation and its own "dynamics" is, by being fixed in the transcript, transposed into a "static" condition, which can be accessed and repeated at any time for a completely different circle and a different situation, with a claim to authenticity. It is obvious that the personality in its intrinsic value is, even for that reason, considerably more strongly affected by such objectification, than by a mere indiscretion about a confidential conversation.

In order to protect the personality from such exposure and objectification of its sphere, everyone has the right guaranteed by virtue of the Constitution [and now actually extensively protected in criminal law (§ 201 of the StGB)] *that in particular private conversations cannot in principle be recorded on a sound recording system nor played from this and transmitted by third parties without his consent [references omitted]. It is also recognized on the same ground that recordings of a confidential character may in principle be published only with the agreement of the author and only in a manner approved by him [references omitted]. The case law on the protection of the personality from publication of pictures without approval rests in the end on this basis as well [references omitted].*

In the case in dispute it is admittedly not a question of a secret tape recording or the use of it; however, the personality must be protected to the same extent against publication of a written record of a telephone conversation. This is because the personal nature of such a record is scarcely less significant than for a tape recording. It makes the same claim to authentic recording of the individual sphere of the persons participating in the conversation, even though it does not reproduce the sound of the voice. At the same time, the fact that the reader is limited to what he sees carries with it the danger that the transcript acquires an importance of its own which is alien to the personality, and in which sharpening and weakening effects which are only expressed through speech are lost. Therefore, because of this special personal connection, the person affected must in principle keep control over who obtains insight by means of the transcript into his individual sphere and thereby the power of disposition over it.

2. *Admittedly the personality is not* absolutely *protected either against indiscretions about confidential private conversations nor from exposure of its private sphere by an unauthorized record of a conversation, insofar as it is not a question of the inviolable area of the intimate sphere, which is not affected here. In particular, in relation to a press publication, the right of personality guaranteed by the Constitution comes into tension with freedom of the press, which is guaranteed with equal status by the Basic Law [Article 5 para. 1 sentence 2 of the Basic Law]. The scope of protection of the personality is therefore to be determined as against that freedom on the basis of a balancing of rights and interests. This has to be orientated to the personal interests of the claimants which are affected and those interests of the press in publishing of the conversation which are worthy of protection, and it must take into account all the circumstances of the actual case [references omitted].*

In the end result, the Appeal Court correctly gave priority to the claimants here over the interest of the defendants in publication. Its statements need clarification, however, in order to avoid misunderstandings.

a) An absolute ban on use which prevented the press publishing any information from their conversation without regard to its value for the public, because of the claimants' interest in keeping their conversation secret, was not imposed on the defendants. This was not even to be the case if their informant himself had obtained the recording by a sound recording system or a bugging device in a criminal manner. Indisputably, the defendants did not participate in this invasion of the sphere of confidentiality, even though they reaped the benefits of the breach of confidentiality. As the appeal court correctly recognized, their action was therefore not even open to a criminal law conviction; the criminal law protection of § 201 of the StGB did not cover their conduct [references omitted]. It is admittedly beyond question that the claimants do not have to accept it simply on that account. Yet the gap which the criminal law creates here indicates that the interest in keeping secret the content *of the conversation is not to be simply equated with the interest in the preservation of the confidentiality of the spoken word, as the appeal court possibly thought. The right of personality cannot give absolute protection from indiscretions by the press either. It is true that such limitation may not be required by the mere fact that protection of this kind would scarcely be realizable because the diverse secret areas are of very different structure and the varied ways in which secrets get out can frequently not be investigated. But the need for such limitation follows from the fact that inalienable free communication would be burdened more heavily than in case of indiscretions if it were to be subject to a comprehensive legal control. In this respect the appeal in law refers pertinently to the fact that the constitutional guarantee of a free press would be limited to a questionable extent if publication of information which originates from invasion of the sphere of confidentiality was simply forbidden. It must, especially in questions which must interest the general public, also be allowed to report on events worthy of publicity which are not released for publication by the persons affected, even if they come from private areas which are not automatically accessible to the public.*

Even for information which, like the telephone transcript sent to the "Stern", has been obtained by invasion of the sphere of confidentiality which is especially protected in constitutional law by the secrecy of telecommunications [Article 10, para. 1 of the Basic Law], there can in principle be no difference, insofar as the press does not itself participate in this invasion. It can be left undecided here in what way and to what extent the special value which the Basic Law attributes to the inviolability of this area of secrecy has an effect on the legal relationships between private individuals [reference omitted]. At any rate, assessment of the question of whether such information is barred from the press because of the constitutional law guarantee of the secrecy of telecommunications must take into consideration the tension with the constitutional guarantee of press freedom. Communication takes place largely in areas which are protected by secrecy of letters, post and telecommunications. To exclude in a quite general or absolute way news from such occurrences from publication in the press would be to reduce the contribution of the press to the formation of opinion (which freedom of the press is to guarantee) to an extent which would not correspond to the status of this basic right. The constitutional law guarantee for the citizen "to inform himself unrestrictedly from generally accessible sources" [Article 5 para. 1 sentence 1] likewise does not put such limits on the press [references omitted]. The citizen's freedom of information does not, of course, coincide in subject matter and content with the right to information guaranteed by press freedom (references omitted). It is intended to protect the formation of the citizen's opinion from state limitations, but not to limit the sources of information of the press to "generally accessible" ones. The obtaining of information from not generally accessible sources as well—even if it is by exploiting a breach of confidence by its informant in which it did not itself take part—is not simply "unsuitable" for the press [reference omitted] so long as it keeps itself in this connection within the limits which are drawn for it under Article 2 of the Basic Law.

b) On the other hand, the knowledge that the information published by the press has been obtained, even if without its help, by invasion of the sphere of confidentiality requires a special degree of consideration towards the person affected.

aa) As has already been stated, the sphere of confidentiality not only underlines the private character which the statement has according to its content, but this is also to be respected by the public as a part of the personal sphere. The press must take also into account the interest which exists in being able to withdraw oneself from the public eye and which is worthy of protection. The fact that it did not force its way into the sphere of confidentiality itself does not free it from this responsibility. Publications from this area document and deepen the invasion; they also put the person's individual sphere in question. And not least the press must keep in mind that by taking up such information it can encourage third parties to invade that individual sphere.

In balancing the competing interests it is therefore in such cases not only necessary to look at the content of the information [references omitted]. The way in which their informant has obtained the information can also limit the right and duty of the press to publish. That does not, however, mean that information obtained illegally may only be published if the general public has a fundamental interest in being informed, as the appeal court seems to assume [references omitted]. There is likewise no room for parallels which can be drawn in this connection from the relationship of state power *to the citizen, for instance on the limitations on the secrecy of telecommunications by the statute of the 13th August 1968 based on Article 10 of the Basic Law [reference omitted], because here it is a question of the tension between the basic freedoms of the personality and the* press, *which assumes a different form. As already explained, the press cannot simply be barred from taking up information illegally obtained if it would thereby contribute to formation of opinion in a question which interests the public. Respect for the area of confidentiality from which the information comes, however, requires a limitation of the publication interest to information with a "publicity value" which exceeds the interests worthy of protection in the personal sphere, the preservation of which must matter not only for the person affected but also all citizens. This is especially so if a third party has made an unauthorized invasion of this area and the publication must therefore inevitably strengthen the effects of this illegal invasion. The stronger the private character of the information, the closer the link to it of personal interests in maintaining secrecy and the greater the disadvantages which the person affected has to fear from a publication, the more permanent must its "publicity value" be, if the press wants to disregard his wish not to let it reach the public.*

The judge must admittedly take into account the right of the press, likewise guaranteed with press freedom, not to expose its informant insofar as he, in this balancing operation which the judge has to undertake, is required, in favour of the person affected, to investigate the ways in which the information from his sphere of confidentiality reached the press. If the claimant refers to an invasion of his sphere of confidentiality, the proof which he has to provide of this cannot be made easier or even waived just because the defendant is not prepared to substantiate his opposition to such a claim [§ 138 of the Civil Procedure Code]. Nor can the judge lay the press open in some other way to the necessity of exposing its information source, in order to protect itself from disadvantages. Otherwise the work of the press, which enjoys the protection of Article 5 para. 1 of the Basic Law in the procuring of information, would be exposed to burdens which come into conflict with the freedom of the press guaranteed by virtue of the Constitution.

bb) In the case in dispute, the personal interests of the claimants are, as in particular the Landgericht has correctly emphasized, primarily affected by the fact that their personal sphere has been exposed to the public with special intensity by the printing of the record of the conversation. Such exposure is as a rule not offset by the desire of the press to report about the statements of leading politicians as comprehensively as possible. Consideration of the special value which the Constitution attributes to the non-disposability of the personality, requires, as has been explained, that only a very serious need for information on the part of the public can justify assailing a person in this way. But the defendants have not demonstrated such an interest in the publication of the telephone transcript.

They themselves say that the telephone call was even rather boring for an outsider from the point of view of its content. They wanted to publish it in order to show what language the first claimant, as a candidate for the chancellorship, used when he was not standing in front of a microphone; next, to reduce speculation about the "bugging affair" to a factual basis; and finally because of passages in which the other party to the conversation had criticized "Stern" Illustrated. These are not however prevailing grounds justifying the exposure of the individual sphere in this way. The actual personality of a leading politician in the centre of the public interest is affected by throwing open his private conversation for discussion, against his will, by means of a transcript of the conversation, to such an extent that it needs more to justify such an action than a certainly widely held interest in getting to know him in his private surroundings as well. Also the fact that politicians are discussing political and social questions in their private sphere does not of itself give the public access to this area; otherwise there would be no protected private sphere for politician and this should be undeniable for them also [reference omitted]. The same applies for the claimants' criticism of "Stern". Such private opinions are quite common. Thus here also they were not so capable of making an impact in characterizing political views and intentions of the critic which were of possible interest to the public that they therefore deserved the status, in public debate, of defining his position. There is also the fact that the defendants could get a public discussion going about the claimants' statements regarding "Stern" (if it had to be recognized that they had interests worthy of protection in the matter in this respect) even without printing the telephone transcript, especially as this issue only formed a proportionately small part of the conversation. Their objection, that they could by means of the transcript describe the facts in the greatest detail, is not acceptable; that does not justify them in exposing the personalities of the claimants in their private dealings with each other to such a wide extent. The fact that the telephone conversation in this respect revealed personal relationships and necessarily gave insights into the claimants' personalities could not be overlooked by the defendants; they have themselves admitted that this had been one of the grounds for their decision to publish the conversation.

The fact that the confidentiality of the conversation has since been removed, after it was published, does not prevent a ban on publication or other transmission of the telephone transcript. This is because it emerges from the above considerations that the defendants do not have to enforce the interests of the claimants in keeping the *content* of the telephone conversation secret but their right that the individual sphere of their personality embodied in the telephone transcript should only be dealt with with their agreement. Every unauthorized further use of the recording by the defendants violates this right. The finding of the Appeal Court that there is in this respect a danger of repetition is likewise not open to objection under the law to be applied in the appeal in law.

Case Eight
Federal Supreme Court,
Sixth Civil Senate
19 December 1995
NJW 1996, 1128

Facts

In these proceedings the plaintiff, Caroline of Monaco, is objecting to the publication of certain photographs distributed in Germany and France by the defendant, the publishers of the magazines F and B. In issue no. 30 of the F magazine, dated 22 July 1993, the defendant published a total of five so-called "paparazzi" photographs which show the plaintiff with the actor Vincent Lindon in a garden restaurant in S. (France). On the front page, next to a large photograph of the plaintiff (the use of which is not impugned in these proceedings) is a photograph of her, accompanied by reference to an article entitled "The most tender photographs of her romance with Vincent". The series of four photographs on pages 4 and 5 is entitled "These photos are proof of the most tender romance of our time". In issue no. 32, dated 5 August 1993 of the illustrated magazine B, the defendant published on page 88 a photograph of the plaintiff on horseback and on page 89 a photograph of the plaintiff with her children P. and A.; these photographs belong to an article entitled "Caroline: I don't think I am the ideal wife". In issue no 34 of the B magazine, dated 19 August 1993, the defendant published an article with several photographs entitled "Simple happiness", showing the plaintiff with her daughter in a paddling boat, going for a walk alone, carrying a wicker basket, riding a bicycle, together with Vincent Lindon in a pub, with Lindon and her son P., and, finally, with another woman in the market. After a lengthy dispute over the admissibility of these publications, the defendant brought an action against the claimant before the Landgericht of Munich requesting that the Court make a declaratory judgment to the effect that the defendant need not in future abstain from publishing these photographs. By these proceedings the plaintiff, who claims that the publication of these photographs infringes her right to personal privacy, requests under German and French law that the defendant in future abstain from any further publication of the photographs. The plaintiff claims that even as an 'absolute person of contemporary history' she does not have to put up with the publication of photographs of herself. All of these photographs had been taken from a great distance, without her knowledge, and are said to belong to her private life. The plaintiff is constantly followed by photographers leaving her in no peace outside of her home. Even for her, there must be a protected private area outside of her own home.

The Landgericht found in favour of the plaintiff as far as the distribution within France is concerned but otherwise rejected the claim. The plaintiff appealed against this decision, and the defendant cross-appealed. The Oberlandesgericht has rejected the claim. The further appeal, in so far as it was accepted, is partially successful.

Reasons

III. The reasoning of the Appeal Court is, in legal terms, partly flawed. The further appeal rightly claims that the photographs which show the plaintiff in an outdoor restaurant with Vincent Lindon fall into the sphere of her private life. Their publication infringes her right to personal privacy and is thus prohibited. The other photographs are legally unobjectionable.

A. 1. As far as the distribution of the magazines in Germany is concerned, the Appeal Court has rightly based its decision on German law. According to the principles of international private law, for claims based on tort and therefore, as here, claims to desist from certain actions [Unterlassungsanspruch] said to violate the right to one's own personality [references omitted], the law of the place where the tort was committed applies. For products of the newspaper industry, the place of commission is the place where the product was published and every other place where it was distributed [Senate, NJW 1977, 1590 with further references]. As regards the magazines distributed in Germany, the place of commission and the place where the effects of the tort were felt are both in Germany, so that German law applies at least for the German area of distribution. . . .

2. According to German law, the distribution of the photographs referred to above is illegal. In particular, it is not covered by the guarantee of press freedom set out in §§ 22, 23 of the Artistic Creations Act [KUG] or Article 5 I, Constitution.

(a) In principle, pictures of a person may only be distributed with the permission of the person depicted [§ 22 KUG]. The right to one's own image forms a particular aspect of the general right to one's own personality. It follows that basically only the person depicted is entitled to decide whether and in what way his picture will be shown to the public [references]. There is no doubt that the plaintiff has not given such permission.

(b) Pictures belonging to the sphere of contemporary history may, however, be distributed or shown without permission of the person involved, unless legally protected interests of the person depicted are thereby infringed [§ 23 I, No. 1, II KUG]. Pictures of persons regarded as "absolute contemporary persons" form part of contemporary history. The plaintiff belongs to this group of persons. The further appeal wrongly disputes this fact. Decisive for the classification of a person as an absolute person of contemporary history is the fact that the public regards his pictures as important and worthy of note just because of the particular person shown. The public has a justified interest, based on a real need for information, in seeing pictures of these persons [BGHZ 20, 345, 349 et seq.; Senate, NJW 1996, 985]. In particular Monarchs, Heads of State, and eminent politicians belong to this group [see KG JW 1928, 363—*Kaiser Wilhelm II*; AG Ahrensboeck DJZ 1920, 596—*Reichspräsident Ebert and Reichswehrminister Noske*; Senate NJW 1996, 593—*Bundeskanzler*; OLG München UFITA 41 [1964] 322—*Kanzlerkandidat*]. *As the eldest daughter of the reigning Prince of Monaco, the plaintiff belongs to this circle of persons as she, herself, has acknowledged. The Senate's decision of 12 December 1995 [NJW 1996, 985] is based on this view.*

(c) There are, however, limits to the publication without permission of pictures of persons who form part of contemporary history. According to § 23 II KUG publication is prohibited where the justified interests of the person shown outweigh the other interests at stake. Whether or not this is the case here, must be decided through a process of weighing up the various rights and interests involved so that in each individual case it is established whether the public interest in information protected by the freedom of the press [Art 5 of the Constitution], which the defendant can cite as justification, has precedence over the plaintiff's right to her personality [Art 2 GG] to which she refers. [BVerfGE 34, 269, 282; BVerfGE 35, 202, 221; Senate, NJW 1994, 124; BGHZ 128, 1, 10.]

(aa) The protection of a person's private sphere of life is of special importance when the two legal interests are weighed against each other. The right to respect one's own private sphere of life is an emanation of the general right to one's own personality, which grants every person an autonomous area of personal life within which he can develop and experience his own individuality, free from the interferences of others. The right to be left alone and "to belong to oneself" forms part of this area (BVerfGE 34, 238, 245 et seq.; BVerfGE 35, 202, 220; for the right to be left alone as part of the right to privacy under American law see *Katz* v. *United States* 389 Supreme Court (1967), 347, 350 et seq.; Warren/Brandeis, 4 Harvard Law Review [1980] 193 et seq.; Götting *Persönlichkeitsrechte als Vermögensrechte*, 1995, 168 et seq., 174). *As a result, since 1954, the German courts have, especially in the area of civil law consistently given particular weight to the right to respect one's own private sphere of life, i.e. treated it as a basic right, guaranteed by the constitution, which includes the right to one's own image* (BVerfGE 27, 1, 6; BVerfGE 34, 269, 282 et seq.; BVerfGE 35, 202; BVerfGE 44, 353, 372; BGHZ 24, 200, 208 et seq.; BGHZ 27, 284, 285 et seq.; BGHZ 73, 120, 122 et seq.; Senate JZ 1965, 411, 413—*Gretna Green*; OLG Hamburg UFITA 78 [1977] 252, 257; OLG Hamburg UFITA 81 [1978] 278, 285; OLG Hamburg, NJW 1970, 1325—*Haus Hohenzollern*).

(bb) The right to respect one's own sphere of private life can be claimed by anyone, and can therefore be claimed by the plaintiff, even if she is a person of contemporary history. For even such persons need not tolerate pictures which depict central aspects of their private life, for instance their domestic surroundings, being taken for later publication without their permission (BGHZ 24, 200, 208; BGH GRUR 1962, 211, 212—*Hochzeitsbild*; BGH NJW 1965, 2148—*Spielgefährtin*). *Only in exceptional circumstances, can the distribution of pictures from this area be permissible, i.e. where an overriding public interest justifies such an intrusion* (see Senate JZ 1965, 411, 413—*Gretna Green*; OLG Hamburg UFITA 78 [1977] 252, 257—*Grace Kelly*; OLG Hamburg UFITA 81 [1978], 278, 285; OLG Hamburg NJW 1970, 1325; OLG München UFITA 41 [1964] 322, 324).

(d) The Appeal Court applied these principles. But it was of the opinion that the public's justified interest in information ends "at the doorstep" of the person depicted and, therefore, extends to places open to anyone, e.g. as here, "in front of" a garden restaurant which is open to public view. The Appeal Court, therefore, restricted the private sphere of life to places inside people's

homes from which the public is excluded. This view has been widely adopted by the courts and is shared by the legal literature. (KG in, Schulze UrhRspr. KGZ 14; Schricker/Gerstenberg, UrheberR, 1987, § 23 KUG, n. 35; Wenzel *Das Recht der Wort- und Bildberichterstattung*, 4. edn. [1994], n. 5.46 and 5.60; Evers, *Privatsphäre und Ämter für Verfassungsschutz*, p. 44.)

This Division cannot share this view. A spatial restriction of the private sphere of life to the domestic area cannot have been intended under the KUG, since the explanatory notes to that Act state that the safeguards of the justified interests of the person depicted, set out in § 23 II KUG, were intended "especially to prevent events being shown to the public which pertain to the personal and domestic life" of that person [reference]. This formulation in no way limits the protection of the private sphere of life to the domestic area but, rather, leaves room for a wider interpretation. The necessity of protecting the private sphere of life outside the domestic area is also partially recognised by legal writers, though for different reasons and with varying intentions (Allfeld DJZ 1920, 702; Evers *Privatsphäre und Ämter für Verfassungsschutz*, 44; Hubmann *Das Persönlichkeitsrecht*, 2d edn., (1967), p. 322; Helle *Besondere Persönlichkeitsrechte im Privatrecht*, 1991, 180; Paeffgen JZ 1978, 738, 740; Prinz NJW 1995, 817, 820; Siegert DB 1958, 419, 421; Siegert NJW 1963, 1953, 1955. Likewise LG Köln AfP 1994, 166, 168; see also BGHSt 18, 182, 186—*Callgirlaffäre*). *This Division shares the view that there is a private area worthy of protection outside that of the purely domestic area. This is the case, where a person has retreated to a place of seclusion where he wishes to be left alone, as can be ascertained by objective criteria, and in a specific situation, where he, relying on the fact of seclusion, acts in a way in which he would not have done so in public. An unjustified intrusion into this protected area takes place where pictures of that person are published if taken secretly or by stealth.*[42]

(aa) Like anyone else, persons who are part of contemporary history have the right which must be respected by all third persons to retreat to places outside their own home where they wish to be alone or, at least, left secluded from the general public. This can even occur in places which are open to the public, i.e. in public places. But this presupposes that in the place and at the point in question the person "shut himself off" somewhat from the public at large; and this seclusion from the public must have been objectively obvious to third persons. This can, for instance, be the case in separate rooms of a restaurant or in hotels, sports grounds, telephone booths, under certain cir-

[42] Compare the above statement with the following opinion expressed by the Supreme Court of Iowa in *Stressman* v. *American Black Hawk Broadcasting Co.*, 416 N.W. 2d 685, 687 (Iowa 1987): "It is not inconceivable that Stressman was seated in the sort of private dining room offered by many restaurants. To film a person in a private dining room might conceivably be a highly offensive intrusion upon that person's seclusion . . . the mere fact a person can be seen by others does not mean that that person cannot legally be 'secluded' . . . Futher, plaintiff's visibility to some people does not strip him of the right to remain secluded from others." These are not isolated dicta and strongly suggest that the German reasoning should not be dismissed by any English lawyer as Germanic or untransplantable. There is no room for prejudice in comparative law; only opportunity to consider (and if necessary reject) new ideas by others.

cumstances even in the open, as long as the person does not appear more than just another member of the public.

(bb) Moreover, the right to demand that other persons respect one's privacy presupposes that the situation in which the person [observed] finds himself is one of a typically private nature. This is the case where a person, relying on the seclusion of the specific place where he finds himself in, behaves in a manner which he would not normally adopt in full view of the public. This may be the case whenever [the observed person] expresses personal emotions which are clearly not intended for the eyes of third persons or is acting in an "unrestrained" manner. Only in such situations can it be assumed and objectively verified that the person did not intend to allow other persons sharing the moment. In such circumstance he is entitled to have the chosen seclusion respected.

(cc) It is an unjustified infringement of the sphere of privacy which is worthy of protection if, for reasons of personal gain, pictures are taken/published which exploit the innocence of the person depicted who believes himself unobserved. This is always the case where the person is observed almost as if through a keyhole, or is surprised by the surreptitious taking of the pictures. The same applies where the picture is taken openly but so suddenly that the person photographed has no time to prepare himself. A restriction of the prohibition to these particular circumstances is justified because protection of the private sphere of life is here extended to places which are in theory open to everyone. In these cases the person's privacy is only unjustly infringed where the intrusion happened surreptitiously or by surprise. The courts have always held that the surreptitious taking of photographs by secret means is illegal (BGHZ 24, 200, 208; Senate NJW 1966, 2353, 2355—*Vor unserer eigenen Tür*; OLG Frankfurt NJW 1987, 1087; see also BGHZ 27. 284—*Tonbandaufnahme*; BGHZ 73, 120—*Telefonabhören*; BAG JZ 1988, 108). *Up to now, this only applied to the private domain within one's home, where the depicted person's consent was always required for the taking of photographs. But the same protection can legitimately be demanded in circumstances where persons, so to speak, transfer their private sphere of life to a place outside of their home. For the same reasons, photographs may then and there be taken, and later published, only if prior consent was given.*

3. In the light of these principles, the weighing up of the rights and interests involved in this case leads to the conclusion that the plaintiff's protected sphere of privacy was violated by photographs taken in a garden restaurant and published in issue no. 30 of the magazine F. under the headline "These photos are the proof of the most tender romance of our time". The plaintiff can prohibit any future publication of these pictures. . . .

(b) When weighing up the various interests involved, the information value of the events depicted plays a significant role. The greater the interest of the public in being informed, the more the protected interests of the person of contemporary history must recede in favour of the public's need for information. Conversely, the need to protect the depicted person's privacy gains in weight as the value of the information which the public obtains from the photographs decreases. In this case, the photographs which show the plaintiff

with Vincent Lindon in a garden restaurant contain little, if anything of value. Here, according to the Appeal Court, mere prying and sensationalism, and the public's wish to be entertained, outweighed all other considerations. Such motives, especially the mere wish of the public to be entertained, which is to be satisfied by pictures of totally private events of the plaintiff's life, cannot be recognised as worthy of protection. Our courts have repeatedly acknowledged this. [BVerGE 34, 269, 283; BGHZ 24, 200, 208; BGHZ 128, 1, 12; BGH NJW 1965, 2148, 2149; BGH JZ 1965, 411; OLG Hamburg AfP 1992, 376, 377].

4. However, the further appeal is unsuccessful in respect of the photographs in the other magazines since these are not concerned with the plaintiff's protected private sphere of life.

(a) . . . The plaintiff cannot prohibit the publication of such pictures. As a person of contemporary history, she must accept that the general public has a justifiable interest in knowing where she goes and how she behaves herself in public, be it during shopping trips in the market square, in a cafe or during sporting or other activities of daily life. This includes the picture reproduced in the issue no. 34 of the magazine B, taken in a restaurant and showing the plaintiff sitting at a table with other persons. This picture differs from the ones taken in the garden restaurant because here the characteristics which made the other ones an unjustifiable intrusion are missing. For here, the plaintiff had not retreated to a place secluded from the general public, and secondly the situation in which she was photographed was not of a somewhat private nature in the sense outlined above. The fact that the plaintiff was not aware of being photographed does not, in itself, provide a reason for demanding that the photo remain unpublished, since persons of contemporary history must normally tolerate unnoticed or even clandestine photographs of themselves if they appear in public [Frank *Persönlichkeitsschutz heute*, 1985, p. 118, n. 280].

(b) However, what all these pictures have in common is the fact that they do not show the plaintiff performing a public function. They are, instead, concerned with her private life in the wider sense of the term. The plaintiff wishes to prohibit generally the publication of these photographs in Germany and France. But this is not possible under German law. In France under Article 9 of the Code Civil, which is intended to protect private life (vie privée), the publication of a picture requires in principle the consent of the person shown. This can even apply to monarchs and other public figures, unless they are shown performing a public duty [see Cour de Cassation, Bulletin des arrêts Chambres civiles, No 98, p. 67—*Farah Diba*; Tribunal de grande instance de Paris Recueil Dalloz Sirey 1977, Jur. p. 364 et seq.—*Caroline de Monaco*; see also Hauser, GRUR Int. 1988, 839, 840; Ehlers/Baumann ZvglRWiss 1978, 421 et seq; Codes Dalloz, Code civil, 92. ed., [1992–1993], Art 9, n. 9].

Under German law (§ 23 KUG), this result is not possible. As this Division stated in its judgment of 14 November 1996 (NJW 1996, 539), under German law the public can have an undisputed interest in seeing photographs of an 'absolute person of contemporary history'. There is no further require-

ment that that person be performing a public function. As a consequence, within the scope of § 23 I No. 1 KUG, the public's interest in information which is worthy of protection can be assumed even where the photograph merely shows how a well-known person acts in normal public surroundings, i.e. when not performing public functions. This interest in being informed only needs to give way where, in quite specific situations, the justified interests of the person shown take precedence (s. 23 II KUG). This does not, however, apply to the photographs shown in issues nos. 32 and 34 of the magazine which are in fact quite flattering.

B. As far as distribution of the magazines in France is concerned, contrary to the plaintiff's contentions in this further appeal, the Court need not decide whether or not the plaintiff's claim would succeed if French law were applied.

1. As the Appeal Court rightly held, to apply French law in deciding in favour of a claim for an order to abstain from an action is barred by Art 38 EGBGB. According to this provision, claims based on tortious acts committed abroad against a German citizen are limited to the remedies available under German law. This principle also applies in favour of the defendant, a legal person domiciled within Germany (RGZ 129, 385, 388; OLG Hamburg IPRspr. 1930, No. 155; see also BGHZ 86, 234, 237). A comparison of the results under German and French law is thus superfluous when it is clear, as here, that German law provides no basis for a claim (BGHZ 71, 175, 177; BGHZ 86, 234, 237; BAG NJW 1964, 990, 991; *Prof.* v. *Bar* JZ 1985, 961, 963).

Case Nine
Federal Constitutional Court
(First Division)
15th December 1999
1 BvR 653/96

Summary

1. The private sphere protected by the general right of personality in Art 2 para 1 in combination with Art 1 para 1 of the Basic Law is not limited to the home. The individual must in principle have the opportunity of moving around in other places which are obviously secluded without being pestered by press photographers.

2. The general right of personality is not guaranteed in the interest of commercialization of that personality. The protection of the private sphere from the taking of pictures takes second place insofar as someone shows himself to be in agreement with certain material usually regarded as private being made public.

3. The protective content of the general right of personality of parents or a parent is strengthened by Art 6 paras 1 and 2 of the Basic Law, insofar as it concerns publication of pictures which have as their object specific parental attention to children.

4. The guarantee of press freedom contained in Art 5 para 1 sentence 2 of the Basic Law includes publications and contributions in the nature of entertainment as well as their illustrations. This also applies in principle to the publication of pictures which show people in public life in everyday or private contexts.

Judgment

The judgments of the Bundesgerichtshof of the 19th December 1995—VI ZR 15/95—of the Hanseatic Oberlandesgericht of Hamburg of the 8th December 1994—3 U 64/94—and of the Landgericht of Hamburg of the 4th February 1994—324 O 537/93—infringe the complainant's basic right under Article 2 paragraph 1 in combination with Article 1 paragraph 1 of the Basic Law insofar as her claim in relation to three pictures published in the Illustrated "Bunte" no. 32 of the 5th August 1993 and no. 34 of the 19th August 1993 which show the complainant with her children was refused. In this respect and in relation to the decision about costs the judgment of the Bundesgerichtshof is quashed and the case referred back to it.

In other respects the constitutional complaint is rejected.

The German Federal Republic must reimburse the complainant for a third of the necessary expenses.

Reasons

A.

The constitutional complaint concerns the publication of photographs from the everyday and private lives of prominent figures.

I.

1. The defendant in the original proceedings, Burda GmbH, publishes the magazines "Freizeit Revue" and "Bunte". In these magazines, photographs of the complainant Princess Caroline of Monaco were published in various articles. She claimed an injunction to prevent publication of these.

The subject of the original proceedings included at first five photos which were printed in the "Freizeit Revue" no. 30 of the 22nd July 1993. The complainant could be seen in them together with the actor Vincent Lindon at a table in a garden café in Saint-Rémy (France) in the evening. The photos are advertised on the title page as "The tenderest photos of her romance with Vincent" and show Vincent Lindon kissing the complainant's hand. As the complainant was successful in obtaining from the Bundesgerichtshof an injunction to prevent future publication of these photos, they are not the subject of the constitutional complaint.

The defendant then published in the Illustrated "Bunte" no. 32 of the 5th August 1993 the article "Caroline: I don't believe that I can be the ideal wife for a man", in which parts (mostly in indirect speech) of a book about the complainant which appeared in Spain are reproduced. Several photos illustrated the article. A photo on p.88 shows the complainant riding a horse in a paddock. No other people can be seen in the picture. It has the caption: "Caroline and melancholy. Her life is a novel with countless misfortunes, says the author, Roig". P.89 contains a photo of the complainant with her children Pierre and Andrea with the caption "Caroline with Pierre and Andrea, her children". In the photo, three people are visible in the foreground; in the background there are vehicles. The complainant is wearing sunglasses.

In no.34 of the Illustrated "Bunte" of the 19th August 1993, an article under the title "Simple Happiness" appeared on pp. 44 to 52 with several photos. On the first page of the article, the complainant can be seen together with her daughter in a canoe, in a close up. The accompanying text to the side states: "It is a hot day this summer. Princess Caroline paddles with her daughter on the Sorgues. This is a small river not far from St-Rémy, the village in Provence where Caroline lives. From New York to London, the rich and beautiful whisper about the Caroline style. A canoe instead of a yacht. A sandwich instead of caviar".

A further photo shows her with a basket slung round her on her way to the market. It includes an accompanying text in small print. "Housewife Caroline Casiraghi. She loves doing the shopping herself". The accompanying text at the side in large print states: "On Wednesday, it's market day. The Caroline style is copied world-wide. Her strap sandals which she wears to the flower market, her pareo which she wears as a skirt". In other photos—not the subject of challenge—within this frame, there are two shops in which the complainant allegedly make purchases, the bistro in which she usually drinks coffee and her country house.

The next photo objected to shows the complainant and the actor Vincent Lindon sitting side by side in a guest house, with other guests around them. The text in small print in the right hand lower corner says: "Every Saturday evening table no.3 here on the right of the entrance is reserved for Caroline". The accompanying text in large print states: "In the evenings, people sit in the "Sous les Micocouliers" and drink the light red summer wine. Caroline and Vincent Lindon are guests like the baker, the olive farmer or Father Philippe of the Church of St Martin".

A photo also shows the complainant cycling alone on a track across the fields. The text in small print for this photo says: "Caroline cycles home. Her mas (house or farm in southern France) lies at the end of the bumpy track, the 'Chemin du Pilou'". It is supplemented by the larger accompanying text: "The end of loneliness approaches. The Caroline style attracts the beautiful and the rich. Lady Di should have instructed an estate agent to find a property for her. Julio Iglesias is also looking".

The photo on p.51 shows the complainant together with Vincent Lindon, her son Pierre and another child. It is a close up and shows these persons from behind or from the side as they turn to the child. The text in small print says: "Caroline's youngest, Pierre, 6, has bumped himself. Vincent and Caroline comfort him".

The last photo shows the complainant wearing sunglasses with a female companion in the market by a flower stall. The text accompanying the photo states: "Caroline's bodyguard is a woman. She even looks like the princess. They mostly go to the market together".

2. The determining factor for the assessment of these photos by the civil courts was §§ 22 and 23 of the Statute as to Copyright in Works of Art and Photography of the 9th January 1907 [reference omitted]; (from now called the Kunsturhebergesetz—KUG). These provisions state as follows:

§ 22

Pictures of people can only be disseminated or displayed publicly with the consent of the persons portrayed. In cases of doubt, consent is to taken as having been given if the person portrayed received a payment for letting himself be portrayed. After the death of the person portrayed, the consent of the relatives of the person portrayed is needed until 10 years have elapsed . . .

§ 23

(1) The following may be disseminated and displayed without the consent necessary in accordance with § 22:

1. *Pictures of people from the realm of contemporary history;*
2. *Pictures in which the persons only appear as accessories near a landscape or other locality;*
3. *Pictures of meetings, processions and similar events in which the persons depicted have taken part;*
4. *Pictures of people which are not made to order insofar as the dissemination or display serves a higher interest of Art.*

(2) The authorization does not however extend to dissemination or display which violates a justified interest of the person portrayed or, if he has died, his relatives.

a) The Landgericht allowed the claim insofar as it concerned the publication of the photos in magazines sold in France. In other respects it rejected the claim.

. . .

b) The Oberlandesgericht rejected the appeal of the complainant, revised the judgment at first instance on the cross appeal of the defendant and rejected the claim insofar as the Landgericht had allowed it (reference omitted).

3. The Bundesgerichtshof quashed the judgment of the Oberlandesgericht in part, and revised the judgment of the Landgericht in part, so that the defendant in the original proceedings was ordered to refrain from fresh publication of the photographs printed in the magazine "Freizeit Revue" with the picture of the complainant. The remainder of the appeal in law was rejected.

...

II

The complainant contests all the civil court decisions, insofar as future dissemination of the photos was not forbidden, on the ground that they are violations of Art 2 para 1 in combination with Art 1 para 1 of the Basic Law, in particular of the right to pictures of oneself and the right to respect for the private sphere.

...

B.

The constitutional complaint is in part well founded.

I.

The judgments under challenge affect the complainant's general right of personality under Art 2 para 1 in combination with Art 1 para 1 of the Basic Law.

1. The protection of the general right of personality extends to pictures of a person by third parties.

a) The basic right has the task of guaranteeing elements of the personality which are not the object of the special guarantees of freedom in the Basic Law but which are just as important as these in their constitutive significance for the personality [references omitted]. There is a need for such a guarantee to close up the gaps, particularly in view of new types of danger to the development of the personality which mostly arise with scientific and technical progress [references omitted]. The assignment of an actual desire for legal protection to the different aspects of the right of personality must therefore be made with the danger to the personality to be deduced from the actual circumstances of the case primarily in mind.

b) Authority to publish photographs showing persons in private or every day contexts is to be measured by the right to pictures of oneself and the guarantee of the private sphere which are concrete forms of the general right of personality.

aa) Contrary to the view of the complainant, Art 2 para 1 in combination with Art 1 para 1 of the Basic Law does not contain a general and comprehensive right of control over pictures of oneself. Insofar as she seeks to deduce such a right from earlier decisions of the Federal Constitutional Court [references omitted], this is an incorrect generalization of the protective content of the basic right guarantee which is formulated in the light of the actual cases. As the Federal Constitutional Court has already emphasized many times, the general right of personality does not give the individual a claim only to be portrayed by others in the way in which he sees himself or wants to be seen [references omitted]. A wide protection of this kind would not only exceed the objective of avoiding endangering the development of the personality, but would also make deep inroads into the area of freedom of third parties.

The complainant also does not find any fault with the way she is portrayed in the disputed photos, which the civil courts have regarded as in every respect favourable. She is much more concerned with whether photographs of her ought to be taken and published at all, when she was not acting in an official function but in a private capacity or every day context in public. The answer to this question is to be deduced from those expressions of the general right of personality which protect the right to pictures of oneself and the private sphere.

bb) The right to pictures of oneself [references omitted] guarantees to the individual the opportunity to influence and make decisions about the making and use of photographs or drawings of himself by others. Whether these show the individual in a private or public context does not in principle play any role here. The need for protection arises instead principally from the possibility of removing the image of a person in a certain situation from this situation, recording it as data, and reproducing it at any time before an enormous number of people. (This is similar to the "right to one's own words", and the right to pictures of oneself entered into the constitutional case law following on from that right.) This possibility has grown even further through progress in photographic technology, which permits the taking of pictures from a great distance (recently even from satellite) and in bad light.

With the help of reproduction technology, the kind of public before which the individual appears can be changed. In particular, the visible public in which one moves in normal public appearances can be replaced by the media public. Thus for instance the public in court, ie the audience present in the court room, differs from the media public produced by television, because the audience experiences events itself and can itself be seen and assessed by the parties to the proceedings [reference omitted]. Besides this, the message conveyed by pictorial statements can change, or even be intentionally changed, with the change of the context in which a picture is reproduced.

Out of the different protective aspects of the right to pictures of oneself, though, the only one which is significant here is the one which concerns the production of certain photos and conveying them to a larger public. It is not a question of manipulated photos or falsifications by a change of context, which is the primary object of the protection. On the contrary, the complainant takes as a basis the fact that the photos which are the subject of the dispute (and the accompanying article, which is likewise relevant to their content) reproduce situations from her life accurately and in a manner in which observers who were present could have seen them. She merely does not wish these situations to be recorded in pictorial form and presented to a wider public, because in her opinion they belong to her private sphere.

cc) In contrast to the right to pictures of oneself, the protection of the private sphere (which is also rooted in the general personality right) does not refer specially to pictures but is determined thematically and spatially. It includes on the one hand matters which are typically classified as "private" because of their information content, because public discussion or display of them is regarded as improper, or because revelation of them is felt to be embarrassing or produces adverse reactions from the surrounding world, as is for instance the case with soliloquies in diaries [reference omitted], confidential communications between married couples [reference omitted], the realm of sexuality [reference omitted], socially deviant behaviour [reference omitted] or illnesses [reference omitted]. If there is no protection from the desire of others for knowledge here, soliloquies, uninhibited communications between close relations, sexual development or the obtaining of medical help would be interfered with or made impossible even though conduct protected by a basic right was involved.

On the other hand the protection extends to a spatial area in which the individual can sort himself out, unwind or even let go [reference omitted]. It is true that this area also gives the opportunity to behave in a manner which is not intended for the public and for it to be seen or portrayed by outsiders would be embarrassing or disadvantageous for the person concerned. But in essence it is a question of a space in which the individual can be free from public observation and therefore from the self control which this imposes, but without him necessarily behaving differently there than in public. If such areas of retreat no longer existed, the individual could be psychologically overtaxed, because he would always have to be paying attention to the effect he has on others and whether he is behaving correctly. He would lack periods for being alone and adjusting which are necessary for the development of the personality and without which it would suffer lasting damage.

Such a need for protection also exists for people who are subject to special public attention because of their rank or reputation, their office or influence, or their capabilities or actions. A person who, whether willingly or unwillingly, has become a figure in public life does not thereby lose the right to a private sphere which remains concealed from the eyes of the public. This also applies for democratically elected office holders, who admittedly are publicly accountable for the conduct of their office (and must put up with public attention in this area), but not for their private lives in so far as these do not affect the conduct of their office.

The home is generally recognized as constituting such a protected sphere. But because of the reference to the development of the personality, the area of retreat cannot from the outset be limited to it. This is so because the functions which it serves are only fulfilled if it does not end at the walls of the house or the boundaries of the garden. The free development of the personality would be substantially hindered if the individual could only escape from public curiosity in his own house. Necessary relaxation from a public which is marked by the pressure of functions and the presence of the media is to be obtained in many cases only in the seclusion of a natural environment, perhaps in a holiday resort. The individual must therefore in principle be able also to move in open but secluded countryside or in places which are clearly secluded from the general public in a manner free from public observation. That applies in relation to photographic techniques which surmount the spatial seclusion without the person affected being able to notice this.

It cannot be determined in a general and abstract manner where the boundaries of the protected private sphere run outside the house. They can only be determined on the basis of the nature of the place to which the person affected goes. The decisive factor is whether the individual finds or creates a situation in which he may reasonably (and therefore in a manner recognizable to third parties) proceed on the basis that he is not exposed to the eyes of the public.

Whether the prerequisites for seclusion are fulfilled can only be assessed in the situation in question. The individual can in one and the same place justifiably feel himself to be unobserved at times and not at other times. Being in an enclosed area also definitely does not always equate with seclusion. As the question is whether the individual may reasonably expect to be unobserved or whether he has gone to places where he will be in the public eye, seclusion, which is the prerequisite for protection of the private sphere outside one's own home, may also be lacking in enclosed areas.

Places in which the individual finds himself amongst many people lack from the outset the prerequisites for private sphere protection in the sense of Art 2 para 1 in combination with Art 1 para 1 of the Basic Law. They cannot fulfill the need for retreat and therefore do not warrant the basic right protection which this need serves on the grounds of development of the personality. The individual also cannot define such places as part of his private sphere by, for instance, conduct which would typically not be exhibited publicly. It is not his conduct, either alone or with others, which constitutes the private sphere, but the objective facts about the locality at the time in question. If he therefore behaves as if he was not being observed, in places which do not have the characteristics of seclusion, he will himself remove the need for protection for types of behaviour which do not in themselves concern the public.

The protection of the private sphere from public attention also does not apply when the individual himself indicates his agreement with certain matters, which usually count as private, being made public, for instance by concluding exclusive contracts about reporting on his private sphere. The protection of the private sphere in constitutional law under Art 2 para 1 in combination with Art 1 para 1 of the Basic Law is not guaranteed in the interests of a commercialization of the personality. Certainly no-one is prevented from such exploiting of private areas. But he cannot simultaneously appeal for the protection of the private sphere which is concealed from the public. The expectation that the outside world will not, or will only to a limited extent, take note of matters or types of behaviour in an area which has the function of a retreat must therefore be expressed in a manner which is consistent and covers situations comprehensively. That also applies for the case where the decision to allow or to accept the reporting of certain events relating to one's own private sphere is made retrospective.

dd) The Federal Constitutional Court has not yet decided what the protection of the private sphere means for family relationships between parents and children. But it is recognized that children need special protection because they must first develop into autonomous persons [references omitted]. This need for protection also exists in view of the dangers resulting from the interest of the media and users of the media in portrayal of children. This can disturb the development of their personalities more severely than those of adults. The area in which children feel themselves free from public observation and may develop must therefore be more comprehensively protected than that of adult persons.

Parents are primarily responsible for the development of the personalities of children. Insofar as upbringing depends on undisturbed relationships with children, the special basic right protection of children does not merely have a reflexive effect in favour of the father and the mother [references omitted]. Instead specifically parental turning attention to the children falls in principle within the protective area of Art 2 para 1 in combination with Art 1 para 1 of the Basic Law. The protective content of the general right of personality is then strengthened by Art 6 paras 1 and 2 of the Basic Law which puts the state under a duty to secure those conditions of life for children which are necessary for their healthy development, and to which, in particular, parental care belongs [references omitted].

How the strengthening of protection of the personality by Art 6 of the Basic Law should take effect in detail cannot be generally and abstractly determined. Certainly there will as a rule be no need for protection if parents deliberately enter the public arena with their children, for instance by participating together in public events or even taking a position in the centre of such events. In this respect they lay themselves open to the conditions of public appearances. In other respects the protection of the general right of personality can also however apply in principle in favour of specific parent-child relationships where the prerequisites for local seclusion are absent.

2. The decisions under challenge interfere with the complainant's general right of personality. As the pictures enjoy the protection of this basic right, the judicial finding that they may be published against her will curtails the protection which she can claim the courts should respect even in private law disputes (see BVerfGE 7, 198 [207]).

II.

The judgments under challenge do not completely fulfill the requirements of Art 2 para 1 in combination with Art 1 para 1 of the Basic Law.

1. The provisions of §§ 22 and 23 of the KUG on which the civil courts have based their decisions are certainly reconcilable with the Basic Law.

According to Art 2 para 1 of the Basic Law, the general right of personality is only guaranteed within the framework of the constitutional order. The provisions about the publication of photographs of persons in §§ 22 and 23 of the KUG are included in this. The regime goes back to a scandal (photographs of Bismarck on his deathbed [reference omitted]) and the ensuing legal and political debate [reference omitted] and seeks to establish an appropriate balance between regard for the personality and the interests of the general public in information [reference omitted].

According to § 22 sentence 1 of the KUG, pictures may only be disseminated or publicly displayed with the consent of the person portrayed. § 23 (1) of the KUG exempts, amongst other things, pictures from the realm of contemporary history (no. 1) from this principle. However, according to § 23 (2) of the KUG, this does not apply for a dissemination by which a justified interest of the person portrayed is violated. By this graduated concept of protection, the regime takes sufficient account of the need for protection of the person portrayed as well as of the public's wishes for information and the interests of the media who satisfy these wishes. That has already been established by the Federal Constitutional Court [reference omitted].

The view of the defendant that the regime contravenes the freedom of the press, because it amounts to a ban with a proviso for permission, gives no cause to assess the matter differently. There is no such ban, simply because the norms merely balance different legally protected interests of private persons. The regime here does not give a one-sided preference to protection of the personality. Admittedly it takes account primarily of the need for protection of the person portrayed at the first and third stages [§ 22 sentence 1 and § 23 (2) of the KUG]. But the interests of press freedom (and the freedom to form opinions which lies behind this) come into play sufficiently at the second stage [§ 23 (1) of the KUG]. Likewise it offers with its open formulations sufficient room for an interpretation and application which is in accordance with the basic rights.

2. The interpretation and application of the provisions do not however satisfy the requirements of the basic requirements in every respect.

a) The interpretation and application of provisions of the civil law which are in accordance with the constitution is a matter for the civil courts. They must however, in this connection, have regard to the meaning and scope of the basic rights affected by their decisions, in order that the significance of those rights in prescribing values is preserved even at the level of application of the law (see BVerfGE 7, 198; constant case law). For this purpose a balancing is necessary between the conflicting protective interests under the basic rights. This is to be undertaken within the framework of the features of the civil law provisions which are capable of being interpreted and has to take into consideration the special circumstances of the case [references omitted]. But as the legal dispute remains, in spite of the basic right influence, a private law one, and finds its solution in private law (interpreted as guided by the basic rights) the Federal Constitutional Court is limited to examining whether the civil courts have had sufficient regard to the basic right influence [reference omitted]. On the other hand, it is not the business of the Federal Constitutional Court to dictate to the civil courts how they have to decide the case in question in its outcome [reference omitted].

A violation of the basic rights will only lead to objection to the decisions under challenge if the fact that basic rights were to be complied with in interpreting and applying provisions of private law which were in conformity with the Constitution has been overlooked; or if the protected area of the basic rights to be complied with has been determined incorrectly or imperfectly or their weight has been incorrectly assessed so that the balancing of the legal positions on both sides within the framework of the private law regime suffers as a result [references omitted] and the decision is based on this mistake.

b) In the present case, not only is the general right of personality but also the freedom of the press guaranteed in Art 5 para 1 sentence 2 of the Basic

Law (which is likewise affected by these provisions) to be taken into consideration in interpreting and applying §§ 22 and 23 of the KUG.

In the centre of the basic right guarantee of freedom of the press is the right freely to determine the type, orientation, content and form of a publication [references omitted]. Included in this is the decision whether and how a publication is to be illustrated. The protection is not limited to certain subjects for illustration. It also includes the portrayal of persons. The protection does not depend on the particular nature or the level of the publication or of the report in detail [references omitted]. Every difference of this kind would amount in the end to assessment and control by state authorities which would contradict the essence of this basic right (reference omitted).

Press freedom serves the free, individual and public formation of opinion [reference omitted]. This can only succeed under conditions of free reporting for which certain objects or methods of presentation are neither prescribed nor excluded. In particular, formation of opinion is not limited to the political realm. It is true that it is of special importance there in the interest of a functioning democracy. Yet the political formation of opinion is embedded in a comprehensive multiply interlinked communication process which cannot be split into relevant or irrelevant zones either from the point of view of personal development or from that of democratic government [reference omitted]. The press must be able to decide according to journalistic criteria what it considers to be worthy of the public interest and what it does not.

The fact that the press has to fulfill a function of forming opinion does not exclude entertainment from the constitutional functional guarantee. Formation of opinion and entertainment are not antitheses. Even contributions of an entertaining kind can form opinions. They can in certain circumstances stimulate or influence the formation of opinion even more permanently than exclusively factual information. In addition a growing tendency can be observed in the media of removing the division between information and entertainment in relation to a publication as a whole as well as in the individual contributions and to disseminate information in an entertaining form or to mix it with entertainment ["infotainment"]. Many readers consequently obtain the information which appears to them to be important or interesting from entertaining contributions [reference omitted].

But the reference to freedom of formation of opinion cannot be denied from the outset even to mere entertainment. It would be unbalanced to assume that entertainment merely satisfies the wish for diversion, relaxation, flight from reality and distraction. It can also convey images of reality and makes available subjects for conversation. Ongoing discussions and unifying events which refer to attitudes to life, stances about values and behaviour patterns can be linked into this. Entertainment in this respect fulfills important social functions [references omitted]. Entertainment in the press, measured by the protective purpose of freedom of the press, is therefore not insignificant or even worthless and is also included in the basic right protection (reference omitted).

This also applies to news reports about people. Personalization forms an important journalistic means for arousing attention. It awakens interest in problems in many cases for the first time, and creates the wish for factual information. Participation in events and situations is also mostly communi-

cated by personalization. Besides this, prominent people stand for certain value concepts and stances about life. They therefore provide many people with a means of orientation in relation to their plans for their own lives. They become crystallization points for agreement or disapproval and fulfill the functions of a model or a contrast. The public interest in the most varied aspects of such persons' lives is based on this.

For persons in political life, such an interest on the part of the public has always been recognized as legitimate from the point of view of democratic transparency and control. It cannot however in principle be disputed for other people in public life. In this respect, description of people which is not confined to certain functions or events is in line with the tasks of the press and therefore likewise falls within the protected area of press freedom. Balancing against the conflicting rights of personality is needed to determine whether there is a serious and relevant discussion of questions which substantially concern the public or merely dissemination of private matters which only satisfy curiosity [reference omitted].

c) The judgment of the Bundesgerichtshof overwhelmingly satisfies constitutional law examination in the end result.

aa) There is no objection in constitutional law to the fact that the Bundesgerichtshof has determined the prerequisites of the definition in § 23 (1) no. 1 of the KUG according to the standard of the general public's interest in information; and on this basis has regarded publication of pictures of the complainant even outside her representative function in the principality of Monaco as permissible.

§ 23 (1) no. 1 of the KUG exempts the publication of pictures of people from the area of contemporary history from the requirement of consent in § 22 of the KUG. The provision according to its legislative intention [reference omitted] and according to the sense and purpose of its regime takes into consideration the general public's interest in information and the freedom of press. The interests of the public are therefore to be observed in the interpretation of the features of this definition. This is because pictures of people who are not important in terms of contemporary history may only be made freely available to the public, with the consent of the persons affected. The further feature contained in the definition in § 23 (2) of the KUG of the "justified interest", which is open to the influence of the basic right, only refers from the outset to persons of importance in terms of contemporary history and cannot consequently sufficiently uphold the interests of press freedom if these interests have been left out of consideration previously by the delimitation of that group of persons.

The concept of contemporary history in § 23 (1) no. 1 of the KUG does not, according to the standard of a judicial determination as to its content, only encompass for instance events of historical or political importance, but is determined by the interest of the public in information (reference omitted). This takes account of the meaning and scope of freedom of the press without cutting down disproportionately on protection of the personality. It is part of the core of freedom of the press and free formation of opinion that the press possesses sufficient leeway within the statutory boundaries within which to decide, according to its journalistic criteria, what the public interest claims; and that it will emerge in the process of formation of opinion what a matter of public interest is. Contributions in the form of entertainment are not, as has been explained, excepted from this.

There are further no grounds for objection to the fact that the Bundesgerichtshof also allocates to the "area of contemporary history" in accordance with § 23 (1) no. 1 of the KUG pictures of persons who have not attracted the public interest to themselves by a certain isolated event of contemporary history but who attract general public attention on the basis of their status and importance, independently of individual events. In this connection, the increased importance which applies to photographic reporting today, in comparison to the time when the Artistic Copyright Act was enacted, is significant. The concept of an "absolute person of contemporary history", which is usually regarded as related in this connection by the case law and the literature, admittedly does not necessarily arise either from statute law or from the Constitution. It is understood by the Oberlandesgericht and the Bundesgerichtshof as shorthand for persons whose image the public finds worthy of attention because of the person portrayed. The concept is not however open to objection from the point of view of constitutional law as long as there is a balancing related to the individual case between the public's interest in information and the justified interests of the person portrayed.

The general right of personality does not require limitation of publications not needing consent to pictures which show persons of importance in the context of contemporary history exercising the function which they fulfill in society. A frequent characteristic of the public interest which such persons claim is that it does not only hold good for the exercise of the function in the narrower sense. Instead it can, because of the distinctive function and the effect which this has, extend to information about how these persons generally behave in public, and therefore outside their respective functions. The public has a justified interest in learning if such persons, who are often regarded as idols or examples, bring their functional and personal behaviour convincingly into line.

A limitation of publication of images to the function of a person of importance in contemporary history would on the other hand not take sufficient account of the public interest which such people justifiably arouse. It would also encourage a selective presentation which would prevent the public from making assessments which are necessary in respect of persons of socio-political life because of their role function as models and their influence. This does not open up to the press unlimited access to pictures of persons of contemporary history. Instead § 23 (2) of the KUG gives the courts sufficient opportunity to put into effect the protective requirements of Art 2 para 1 in combination with Art 1 para 1 of the Basic Law [reference omitted].

bb) In principle, the criteria which the Bundesgerichtshof has developed in interpretation of the feature of "justified interest" in the definition in § 23 (2) of the KUG are not open to objection in constitutional law.

According to the judgment under challenge, the private sphere which deserves protection (which the so-called absolute person of contemporary history is also entitled to) presupposes a secluded space into which someone has withdrawn in order to be on his own there in a manner recognizable to others; and in which, trusting in this seclusion, he behaves in a way in which he would not when in the public eye. The Bundesgerichtshof assumes a violation of §§ 22 and 23 of the KUG if pictures are published which have been taken of the person affected in such a situation secretly or by using surprise tactics.

The criterion of spatial seclusion takes account on the one hand of the purpose of the general right of personality of securing for the individual a sphere outside his own home in which he knows he will not to be under continual public observation. He does not therefore have to control his behaviour in view of this observation, but has the opportunity to relax and come to himself. On the other hand it does not restrict the freedom of the press excessively, because it does not completely remove the everyday and private life of persons of contemporary history from photographic reporting, but only makes it accessible for portrayal where it takes place in public. In a case of paramount public interest in receiving information, freedom of the press can even take precedence over the protection of the private sphere, according to this case law [references omitted].

The Bundesgerichtshof might also regard the behaviour of the individual in a certain situation as having the indicative effect that he obviously finds himself in a sphere of seclusion. It is true that protection from portrayal in this sphere does not only start when the person affected behaves in a way in which he would not when in the public eye. The spatial seclusion only fulfills its protective function for the development of the personality when it secures for the individual a place for relaxation regardless of his behaviour at the time, in which he does not have continually to expect the presence of photographers and cameramen. But it does not matter in the present case because according to the findings on which the Bundesgerichtshof based its decision, the first condition for protection of the private sphere is absent.

Finally there are no grounds for objection in constitutional law to the fact that, in the balancing exercise between the public interest in information and protection of the private sphere, importance is attached to the method of obtaining information [reference omitted]. There are doubts however about whether the private sphere outside the home can only be violated by photography by secrecy or surprise. In the light of the function which this sphere should fulfill from a constitutional point of view and in the light of the fact that it often cannot be seen from a picture whether it has been taken secretly or by surprise, an impermissible invasion of the private sphere can be found even when these characteristics are not present. As the Bundesgerichtshof has however already denied that there was a sphere of seclusion for the disputed photographs, these doubts do not affect the outcome of its decision in this respect.

cc) The constitutional law requirements are not however fulfilled insofar as the decisions challenged have paid no attention to the fact that the complainant's protected position in relation to her right of personality is strengthened by Art 6 of the Basic Law in the case of family contact with her children.

dd) The following details result from this for the different photographs:

The decision of the Bundesgerichtshof in relation to those photographs which show the complainant on her way to the market, with a bodyguard at the market and with a companion in a well patronized café gives no cause for objection by the Constitutional Court. In the first two cases it is a question of places visited by the general public, which are not secluded. In the third case it is admittedly a question of an area which is spatially enclosed; but it is one in which the complainant is under the eyes of the members of the public who are present. For this reason the Bundesgerichtshof did not dispute the prohibition on dissemination of photos from the garden café which are admittedly a subject of the decisions challenged, but not of the constitutional complaint. The place which the complainant took there with her companion showed all the characteristics of seclusion. The fact that the photographs have obviously been taken from a great distance additionally points to the fact that the complainant might assume she was not exposed to the eyes of the public.

The decision is also not open to objection insofar as it concerns the photos in which the complainant is shown alone when riding and cycling. The Bundesgerichtshof on the basis of its view of the matter likewise attributed them not to the sphere of local seclusion but to the public sphere. That is not open to objection in constitutional law. The complainant herself counts the photographs as belonging to the secluded private sphere only because she let her wish be known to be alone. But according to the criteria which have been explained, it does not merely depend on her will.

On the other hand, the three photos in which the complainant is shown together with her children call for a renewed scrutiny from the constitutional law viewpoints which have been set out above. It cannot be ruled out that scrutiny on the basis of these standards will lead to another result in relation to individual photos or all of them. In this respect the judgment of the Bundesgerichtshof is to be quashed and the case referred back to it for a new decision.

d) As to the judgments of the Landgericht and the Oberlandesgericht which have been challenged, a violation of the basic right follows from the fact that they have limited the private sphere protected by Art 2 para 1 in combination with Art 1 para 1 of the Basic Law—admittedly in harmony with the case law at the time—to the area of the home. But it is not necessary to quash the decisions because the violation has been cured in this respect by the Bundesgerichtshof and the matter is in other respects been referred back to it.

Case Ten
Federal Constitutional Court
Decision of 24. 3. 1998—1 BvR 131/96

Facts

The complainant, who is now 41, is no longer capable of earning, and still bears her maiden name. She alleged first to friends in 1973, and later in 1986 to doctors who were treating her for, amongst other things, compulsive gambling, that her father had sexually abused her. She first wrote to her father about this in March 1987, claiming he had driven her to addiction. She also told the Youth Welfare Department, in order to protect her niece who was sometimes looked after by him. In 1990 she wrote to her father to say she forgave him. But she spoke about the abuse in a television broadcast in January 1991 and in a later programme. She also offered to a magazine an article about claims for compensation for psychological harm consequent on sexual abuse. Her father demanded that she should stop accusing him to others of sexual abuse, but she refused to comply. He then started a claim for an injunction alleging he had never sexually abused her; and that the real reason for the accusations was his refusal to pay for her gambling debts. The Landgericht found that he had sexually abused her regularly from the age of eight onwards; and perhaps from the age of twelve onwards by having sexual intercourse with her. It rejected his claim, on the basis that injunctions could only be used to prevent statements injurious to honour if they were untrue. When he appealed, the Oberlandesgericht ordered her not to make statements, using his name or her name, to the effect that he had sexually abused her. It held that regardless of the truth of the statements, such an order could be made under §§ 1004 and 823 para 1 BGB because of the violation of his right of personality. He could not prevent her allegations to state or judicial authorities that he had sexually abused her where she had a justified interest in making these allegations. But he did not have to put up with being denounced by name in public.

The constitutional complaint by the complainant against this judgment was successful.

Reasons

B. The constitutional complaint is well founded. The judgment of the Oberlandesgericht violates Art 5 (1) and Art 2 (1) in combination with Art 1 (1) GG.

I. These basic rights are affected by the decision which is being challenged.

1. The use of one's own name in connection with a statement comes within the protection of freedom of opinion.

The basic right of freedom of opinion protects statements of opinion of all kinds and assertions of fact as well as other forms of statement, at any rate if they are a prerequisite for the formation of opinions [references omitted].

The use of one's own name in connection with a statement is neither a form of independent statement nor a component of the statement in the narrow sense. Its content stands alone. But this does not mean that the giving of a name falls outside the protective area of the basic right. It is of substantial importance for the statement itself as well as for the individual and public process of opinion formation to which it contributes.

Freedom to state opinions is "the most direct expression of the human personality in society" (BVerfGE 7, 198 [208]). The name of the originator gives the connection between the person and the statement is made in a recognisable way. If the person making the statement adds his own name [to his statement], he shows that he wants to make the statement known as his personal opinion or description and is ready to vouch for it; and in the case of an assertion of facts, to be answerable personally for its truth. It is precisely in relation to those statements with which the speaker very fully identifies himself or which present his own story that the use of a name is one of the prerequisites of the communication of the sense of the statement.

Besides this the name of the person making the statement can contain messages which go beyond the simple content of the statement. Thus it is possible, for instance, that the personal description of oppressive experiences will encourage others affected to break their silence. Such a message could not be communicated in the same way without the use of one's own name and the associated disclosure of personal involvement. That applies especially if communication of certain events is subject to a taboo. Personal confession to the public can help in this case to break through the attribution of guilt often associated with social taboos.

However, the purpose of a statement is not fulfilled in making known personal views or communications. Statements are directed at others and as a rule are destined to have an effect on them in forming opinions or motivating to action. Art 5 (1) sentence 1 GG therefore does not only protect statements in the dimension of their dissemination but also in the dimension of their effect (see BVerfGE 7, 198 [210]). Freedom of opinion includes the right of the person making the statement to choose for his statement those forms and circumstances which ensure the greatest possible effect for it [reference omitted]. But the effect of a statement on third parties depends substantially on whether its originator is identifiable or not. Anonymous statements frequently lack that degree of authenticity and credibility that gives them the desired influence or causes a reaction.

Finally the effect of a statement is not limited to its reception and assimilation by third parties. Just as the statement will usually be connected with preceding communications, so it will in turn trigger further communications. In striving to guarantee free formation of opinions by the individual and the public Art 5 (1) GG is therefore not limited to protecting the individual statement. It also ensures the preconditions for the establishment and maintenance of the communication process in which every statement is embedded [reference omitted]. The use of a name is important for this likewise because it is only such use that makes it possible for participants in the communication process to refer to one another or make contact with each other.

2. The use of one's own name also falls into the protective area of the general right of personality arising from Art 2 (1) in combination with Art 1 (1) GG.

The name of a human being does not only have the function of creating order and differentiation. It is also the expression of identity and individuality. Therefore the individual can require the legal order to respect and protect his name. This protection has so far only become relevant in constitutional case law in relation to change of name on marriage as prescribed by the state [references omitted]. But it is also related to the wish not to use a name (which is not as such in dispute) in certain circumstances or to replace it by a pseudonym. As a name is an expression of identity and individuality it cannot be changed at will. It accompanies the life history of the person who bears it. This is recognisable as connected with [the concept of] a name. To give up the use of one's name does not therefore leave one's personality unaffected.

This also applies to the use of a name in connection with a statement. Statements do not fulfil their purpose in the passing on of a certain communication content. They are at the same time the expression of the personality of the person making the statement. By his statements he presents himself to third parties as a person. Other people identify him with them. On the basis of the use of a name third parties can not only attribute statements to their originator but also categorise him by the type of personality that they make him out to be. At the same time they get the opportunity to assess the person who stands behind the statement alongside its contents. If someone is obliged to refrain from using his name in connection with statements which he sees as personal and which he thinks it important to attribute to himself, such an obligation is to be measured against Art 2 (1) in combination with Art 1 (1) GG.

3. On the other hand, freedom of the press is not relevant. The question of the permissibility of a particular statement is to be judged in accordance with Art 5 (1) GG, independently of whether it is made or is to be made through a medium which enjoys the protection of press freedom. This will only come into play where it is something more than individual statements of opinion—where the press is important for the formation of individual and public opinion [references omitted]. That is lacking here.

4. Freedom of opinion and the right of personality have been limited by the complainant's obligation not to use her name when she speaks in public about sexual abuse by her father. The fact that the statement may incidentally be disseminated further in public does not change anything in view of the inclusion of the use of the name in the protective area of both basic rights.

II. The decision under challenge is not reconcilable with the basic right of freedom of opinion and the general right of personality.

1. Both basic rights are certainly subject to statutory limits. Freedom of opinion is, according to Art 5 (2) GG only guaranteed within the framework of the general laws, the statutory provisions for the protection of the young and the right to personal honour. Development of the personality is according to Art 2 (1) GG confined within the boundaries of the constitutional order.

This is to be understood as including all legal norms that are formally and materially in harmony with the Basic Law [reference omitted]. That is the case with the provisions of §§ 823 and 1004 of the BGB on which the Oberlandesgericht based the judgment under challenge.

2. But their application does not comply with the requirements of the basic rights.

a) The interpretation and application of the civil law provisions are just as much a matter for the civil courts as the establishment of the facts and the assessment of the evidence. But if, during the course of the application of norms of civil law which are unobjectionable in constitutional law, positions protected by the basic rights are affected, the civil courts must take account of the importance and scope of the basic rights. This is to guarantee their importance in setting values at the level of application of the law as well (see BVerfGE 7, 198 [205 ff]; constant case law). That requires as a rule a balancing operation, to be undertaken within the framework of the features of the statutory definition, between [two aspects of the matter]. On the one hand there is the significance in the actual case of the basic right which has been limited for the person entitled to it as well as the extent of the interference with it to which he has to submit. On the other hand there is the significance of the legal interest protected by the statute which is being applied and the severity of the interference with it by the exercise of the basic right. In this connection, the courts must have sufficient regard to both positions and bring them into a relationship that takes appropriate account of them. There will, in particular, be a violation of a basic right which the Federal Constitutional Court has to correct if the civil court has not considered the influence of the basic right at all or has evaluated it inappropriately and the decision is based on a misunderstanding of the influence of the basic right [reference omitted].

b) In this connection, on the complainant's side it must above all be taken into account, from the point of view of freedom of opinion and the right of personality, that the statement in dispute has an accentuated relationship with the personality. The prohibition on giving of [the complainant's] name would to a large extent cause it to lose the effect hoped for in the process of communication.

This statement, which the complainant is only allowed to make in public if she does not use her name, does not relate to some subject with which she only has a distant connection, but concerns her highly personal life story. On the basis of the facts as established by the civil courts, from which the Federal Constitutional Court has to proceed, it relates to an extremely serious experience that had a decisive influence on her physical and emotional development. Every person has the freedom to decide whether he turns to others or to the public with experiences of this kind. If he decides to do so, the prohibition on describing a story of the most personal kind in a personalised form contains as a rule a drastic interference with opportunities for communication and with development of the personality.

Nothing is changed by the circumstance that the judgment under challenge does not prevent the complainant from speaking about the abuse under her own name in the context of private contacts or therapeutic treatment. This is because she is still prevented from widening the radius of those with whom she can communicate beyond the circle of her personal acquaintances or persons professionally concerned with the development of her personality. The complainant can no longer appear before the public as an identifiable person, vouch for her story with her own name and meet directly any reactions of third parties to it.

The effect of her story on persons in a similar situation or a public disturbed by the problem of sexual abuse of children is also reduced because there is a danger of the story failing to acquire the credibility and authenticity generally associated with the use of a name. The encouragement which public analysis of one's own story can have for people in a similar situation is also reduced. Likewise feedback to the complainant who wants a response is made more difficult by the prohibition on the use of her name. Furthermore she loses the opportunity to get over her past experiences with the help of third persons who have only become aware of her through the statement.

It is clear that this experience which has had a decisive effect on the complainant and which she wants to speak about publicly is indissolubly linked with the person of her father. This has to be considered; but it has to be borne in mind that the complainant is reporting about the plaintiff in the initial proceedings from the perspective of the victim of his actions. The statement cannot therefore be understood just as an exposure of the father. It must also be seen in context of overcoming her status of a victim. This victim status (which the courts have found to be a necessary starting point) would be further reinforced if the victim were to be prevented from giving an account in a personalised form. In this respect her interest in making a statement is to be rated more highly than that of third persons or of the media who want to name the persons involved when they make statements about these kinds of events.

c) On the side of the plaintiff in the initial proceedings weight must be given to his right of personality protected under the basic rights. §§ 823 and 1004 of the BGB give expression to this in civil law. It certainly does not give to the person entitled to it a claim only to be represented to the public in a manner which corresponds to his self-image or which is pleasant for him. It does however protect him against representations which distort or falsify as well as against representations which can substantially interfere with the development of his personality [reference omitted]. Personality interests must as a rule take second place to freedom of opinion if the disputed statement has as its subject facts which are to be regarded as true.

But this principle is not without exceptions. In particular true stories can injure the right of personality of the person affected if the consequences of the representation are serious for the development of the personality and the need for protection outweighs the interest in the [making the] statement. Thus the Federal Constitutional Court in the Lebach judgment (BVerfGE 35, 202 = NJW 1973, 1226) granted personality interests priority over broadcasting freedom, because the transmission of a docudrama about a sensational crime was at a point very close in time to the release of one of the perpetrators from imprisonment. The widespread impact and suggestive power of television would also have made the reintegration of the person affected into society substantially more difficult, if it did not entirely prevent it.

It is true that things are different here to the extent that it is a question not of a report by the media but by the victim. There is therefore no need to decide what the position would be if when the victim tells her story, the media expand this by their own reports from the perpetrator's background. Unlike the Lebach case, no independent danger for the plaintiff in the initial proceedings arises here from the point in time of the statement. Nor is it a question of documentation about his conduct identifying him, but merely of the possibility of a conclusion being drawn because he has the same name as the complainant.

Nevertheless, the consequences for the plaintiff in the initial proceedings are serious. This is associated with the accusation of sexual abuse of his own child, which is regarded as an especially abhorrent crime. Reports of conduct of this kind mostly lead to stigmatisation of the perpetrator. Stigmatisations [of this kind] can lead to withdrawal of social recognition and social isolation of and fundamental loss of assurance and self-devaluation by the person affected in numerous areas of his life. This is based on assessment and behaviour mechanisms which are social and therefore not solely attributable to the responsibility of the person affected. The free development of the personality is thereby permanently impeded; and this cannot be treated as due to the usual limits to development opportunities or the unfavourable reactions of others which one has to accept as the consequence of one's own decisions or forms of behaviour.

The protection which Art 2 (1) in combination with Art 1 (1) GG gives in this respect is not dependent on the statements about a person being untrue. It also applies if the statements are true and for this reason become a cause of a social exclusion and isolation. As the protection of the personality has as its goal the maintenance of the basic conditions of social relationships between the person entitled to the basic right and his environment [reference omitted] it is also independent of whether it is the victim himself or third persons who speak about the facts.

The protective effects of the general right of personality are not ruled out simply because the use of the complainant's name cannot from the outset, in her view, affect her father's rights. The protection of the personality does not only apply to the content of an assertion, but also to the consequences which the assertion has as information for others. Therefore it is a question of the information and the chances of identification which the addressees of the statement receive. The possibility that an assertion can be related to a certain person and that this person will be exposed to consequences from which the constitutional law right of personality grants protection does not therefore only exist if his name is mentioned but also if other details facilitate his identification.

On the other hand, the weight of the infringement of the basic right depends upon the breadth of the impact of the discriminatory consequences. This can work out differently according to the extent to which the person affected is known. It must further be considered whether the effects of the statement are limited because of the commonness of the name. If it is a widely used name, the effects of the statement only occur with those persons who know the speaker and his family and therefore can deduce the identity of the perpetrator from his public appearance under his own name. With a television appearance, the interference with the personality by the mention of the name decreases further, because in this case the conclusion is possible even without the mention of the name.

d) These points of view which are to be taken into account in the context of the basic rights did not sufficiently influence consideration of the matter in the Oberlandesgericht.

The Oberlandesgericht has, in harmony with the civil law case law, considered the complainant's statement to have the effect of "pillorying" the plaintiff in the initial proceedings. This would have serious consequences for the development of his personality and therefore must only be accepted if weighty reasons on the opposite side argue for the publication of the assertion in a form which permitted his identification. There is no objection to this from a constitutional point of view.

However, the Oberlandesgericht did not have sufficient regard to the reasons which argue in favour of publication using the complainant's name. Its decision raises doubt as to whether it was conscious of the fact that the use of the complainant's name in connection with her statement falls under the protection of freedom of opinion and the general right of personality. In any case the complainant's interests protected by these basic rights have not entered sufficiently into the balancing operation. The court merely touched on the subject with the comment that a denunciation of the plaintiff in the initial proceedings could not be justified by the argument that the complainant as a victim was looking after supposed general information interests about the abuse of children in society because the use of a name was not as a rule necessary for this.

In particular there is here no consideration (taking account of the requirements of Art 5 (1) GG) of the functions which use of one's name for one's statements can have and which mean that the name cannot simply be left out or replaced. Thus the court has not considered the question—which is relevant also from the point of view of the right of personality—of whether and to what extent the complainant wants to overcome the experiences of abuse by presenting them to the public as her own experiences and under her own name.

Further, it did not discuss to what extent the adding of a name is needed for statements about the abuse to acquire the character of an authentic communication for the complainant as well as for the recipient of the statement. It did not consider whether the use of a name is needed in the given situation to communicate the contents of the statement to the recipients in the desired fashion and so that they obtain the opportunity of establishing contact with the complainant. The point of view, relevant in the context of formation of public opinion, that personifying the experience of sexual abuse can help to counteract a social taboo and encourage others affected to speak and act themselves, was also left out of consideration.

The Oberlandesgericht did not carry out the necessary evaluation because it did not adequately concretise those interests which are important from the point of view of freedom of opinion and the right of personality. The court did not address the fact that the using of one's own name for one's own statements is the part of freedom of expression of opinion which is close to the personality and an obligation to refrain from doing so therefore represents an especially intensive interference. It also did not take into account that sexual abuse of children is a question substantially affecting the public so that the interest of society in being informed from the perspective of the victim about such acts and their consequences increases the weight to be given to freedom of opinion.

On the other hand the court did not address the question of how great the danger of identification was on the basis of the name in the actual case, to what extent the consequences of an identification would affect him and whether he would have any opportunity to avoid these. This is relevant to the severity of the interference with those interests of the plaintiff in the initial proceedings which are protected by the basic rights.

e) The judgment under challenge is founded on these defects. The Oberlandesgericht gave priority to protecting the plaintiff in the initial proceedings from social stigmatisation because it did not make a sufficient determination of the protected interests of the complainant and therefore did not adequately consider her basic right position. It cannot therefore be excluded that the court, if it had considered the requirements of the basic rights, would have made a decision which was more in the complainant's favour.

Case Eleven
Federal Supreme Court,
6th Civil Senate,
29th June 1999, VI ZR 264/98

Facts

The claimant, a representative of the House of Hanover and prince of Great Britain and Ireland, asks the defendant, a German publishing company, to refrain from publishing certain parts of a report about his divorce.

The marriage of the claimant was dissolved on the 10th September 1997 in public proceedings before the High Court of Justice in London. From the divorce papers which, according to English law, are usually available to the public and press, it appears that the claimant had admitted to having committed adultery with an unnamed woman. The English news agency Reuters reported on the divorce on the same day, giving the ground for the divorce. This news was published on the 11th September 1997 by the "Daily Mail" newspaper. On the 13th September 1997 a report about the divorce appeared in issue no 39/97 of the magazine "Das Neue" published by the defendant. The article, in which several meetings by the claimant with Princess Caroline of Monaco were mentioned and which included two photographs of these, stated (making reference to a press agency) that family judge A had given as a ground for the divorce that the German prince had committed adultery with an unnamed woman.

The claimant feels that his right of personality has been violated by the publication by the defendant of the ground for the divorce. He has applied for an order that the defendant refrain from disseminating the statement, making reference to a press agency, that he has committed adultery with an unnamed woman.

The Landgericht allowed the claim. The Oberlandesgericht rejected the defendant's appeal. In the appeal in law (which is admissible) the defendant seeks the rejection of the claim.

Grounds

I.

The appeal court, applying the [German] law of the place of commission of the act, adjudges the part of the publication objected to by the claim to be unlawful and therefore, on appropriate application of §§ 823 para. 1 and 1004 of the BGB, an interference by the defendant in the claimant's general right of personality from which the defendant must refrain. The mention of adultery as the ground for divorce would give the impression to the average reader that such adultery had actually taken place. This statement was highly prejudicial to the claimant. In the required balancing of the claimant's right of personality with the public's justified interest in information, the claimant's interest in the protection of his private sphere prevailed. The public's interest in the claimant, which arose in view of the fact that he was the great-grandson of the last German Kaiser (and in substance from the significance and position of his ancestors and relations) could not justify the giving of the ground for the divorce. The position did not have to be assessed differently either because of the association of the claimant with Princess Caroline of Monaco nor because the dissolution of the claimant's marriage took place at a public hearing, adultery was expressly named then as a ground for divorce, and the divorce papers could be seen by third parties under English law. (The latter point is inconsistent with the standards applying to German courts) ...

II.

The judgment of the appeal court does not stand up to legal scrutiny.

1. The considerations which the appeal court uses with reference to the fundamentals of its decision are admittedly not open to objection.

a) ...

b) ...

c) The appeal court further thought it necessary to decide on the claim on the basis of balancing the claimant's general right of personality (protected in constitutional law in accordance with Article 2 para. 1 in combination with Article 1 para. 1 of the Basic Law) against the defendant's right to freedom of speech and freedom of the press (which likewise enjoys constitutional rank in accordance with Article 5 para. 1 of the Basic Law) (on the requirement for such a balancing, see [references omitted]). There are no legal objections to this approach. Such a balancing cannot be dispensed with here on the ground that an interference by the defendant with the claimant's right of personality is lacking. It is true that, as stated above, a report had already lawfully been made by an English news agency and an English newspaper about the ground for the claimant's divorce. But this circumstance cannot remove from the publication of it by the defendant for the first time in Germany the character of an interference. A balancing of interests is therefore correctly considered by both parties to be required.

d) The approach of the appeal court is also to be taken as a starting point in relation to the circumstances to be included in the balancing exercise.

aa) First, the content of the statement in the defendant's news report as interpreted by the appeal court is not open to objection. Assessing the announcement that the English judge had given the claimant's adultery as the ground for the divorce as meaning that such adultery had in fact taken place, should therefore also be a basis for the appeal in law proceedings. But it is not necessary to examine the additional claim of the reply to the appeal in law that the photo accompanying the news report with the caption "Ernst August and Caroline kiss each other" had also amounted to an innuendo by the defendant that the claimant had committed adultery with Princess Caroline of Monaco. This is because the claimant does not ask the defendant to refrain from a statement to this effect.

bb) The appeal court, without any error of law, further proceeds on the basis that the claimant is affected in his private sphere by the defendant's publication. This categorization which means that the claimant's intimate sphere (which as such would enjoy absolute protection) is not affected [references omitted] has its legal basis in the fact that the defendant's news report only announced the fact of the adultery but not details about it [references omitted].

2. However, the appeal court cannot be followed in how it weights the circumstances to be included in the balancing exercise and in the priority it derives from this for the claimant's right of personality.

a) It was argued (to the defendant's disadvantage) that the announcement about the claimant's adultery had no actual interest for the public, even though he belonged to the German and British nobility and was the great-grandson of the last Kaiser. This is based on a legally incorrect view.

aa) In the context of this qualification, the appeal court failed to pay sufficient attention to the fact that it is not only "valuable" items of information given by the press which fall within the freedom of the press in Article 5 para. 1 sentence 2 of the Basic Law. This freedom in principle also exists in favour of the tabloid and sensational press and thereby also for news which primarily satisfies the need of a more or less broad readership for superficial entertainment [references omitted].

bb) In the case in question, there is the additional fact that the claimant attracts the attention of a broad readership not only because of his ancestry but also as companion of Princess Caroline of Monaco, who is continually in the glare of publicity [reference omitted]. Even if the interest of this readership may not be described as particularly valuable, contrary to the view of the appeal court the need for its satisfaction cannot be excluded from the protected area of press freedom (which is simply constitutive for the free democratic order [reference omitted]) as unjustified. Instead, it is precisely in the case of the press that the need for limiting the freedom of news reporting must be convincingly proved [reference omitted].

b) Further, much too little weight has, to the defendant's disadvantage, been given by the appeal court to the fact that the announcement about the claimant's adultery, even with the content which the court of appeal ascribes to it, involved the assertion of a true fact. Nor does the reply to the appeal in law question this. It is true that a balancing of the basic rights positions on both sides is still required in principle for a true statement [reference omitted]; such a statement however must, even if it is disadvantageous for the person affected, be more readily accepted [references omitted]. This is particularly the case when it does not represent an especially intensive interference with the right of personality, like the mere general announcement of a formal ground for divorce in the case in question.

c) Finally the appeal court did not sufficiently consider the fact that the news about the dissolution of the claimant's marriage, with the giving of adultery as the ground for the divorce, had been published already by the news agency Reuters and the "Daily Mail" newspaper before publication by the defendant. It had thereby become known already to a large number of persons, who could then pass it on to others. This further reduces the gravity of the defendant's interference with the claimant's private sphere to a considerable extent [reference omitted].

3. Following all this, the result of the balancing of the basic rights positions of the parties by the appeal court cannot be left to stand. As the facts to be assessed are established, a further elucidation of the matter is therefore not necessary and the senate can finally decide itself on the basis of its own balancing exercise. In this connection it reaches the conclusion, in the light of the lesser weight of the interference with the claimant's right of personality stated under no. 2, as against the freedom of speech and freedom of the press claimed by the defendant, that the announcement by the defendant about the claimant's adultery as a ground for divorce does not appear to be unlawful and therefore must be accepted by the claimant. His claim must therefore be rejected.

Case Twelve
Marlene Dietrich
Translated by Mr Raymond Youngs, Southampton Institute of Further Education

a) The general right of personality and its special manifestations, like the right to one's own picture and the right to one's name, protect not only non-material but also commercial personality interests. If these components of the right of personality which are of financial value are culpably infringed by an unauthorised use of a picture, name or other characteristic feature of the personality, the holder of the right of personality is entitled to a claim to compensation for harm, independently of the severity of the interference.

b) The components of the right of personality which are of financial value remain after the death of the holder of the right of personality, at any rate as long as the non-material interests are still protected. The corresponding powers pass to the heir of the holder of the personality right and can be exercised by him in accordance with the express or presumed will of the deceased.

BGH, judgment of 1st December 1999—1 ZR 49/97—Kammergericht
LG Berlin

. . .

Facts

The claimant is the only child and sole heir of the actress Marlene Dietrich, who died on the 6th May 1992. She is also the executrix of her mother's estate.

The first defendant ("the defendant") produced a musical on the life of Marlene Dietrich in 1993. It had its première at the beginning of April 1993 in Berlin and was performed to start with until the end of May 1993 under the title "Tell me where the flowers are" and then until the end of June 1993 under the title "Marlene". There were no further performances of the musical, which was not very successful. The defendant was the sole manager of the Lighthouse Musical Production Company Ltd ("Lighthouse Musical"), which no longer exists. He is the owner of trade mark no. 2022193 "Marlene" which, following an application in June 1992 was registered in the same year for, amongst other things, the development, production and performance of literary and/or musical entertainments for stage and film. The claimant has already withdrawn at first instance an application to extinguish this trade mark.

Lighthouse Musical granted to FIAT Automobil AG—in accordance with a confirmatory letter by the defendant of the 23rd June 1993—rights to the production and marketing of two hundred models of the special Lancia type Y 10 "Marlene" and allowed it in particular to use the signature "Marlene", a picture of Marlene Dietrich from the year 1930 and the registered trade mark "Marlene". In return, FIAT advertised for the musical in accordance with the agreement when displaying the vehicle. It offered the Lancia special model "Marlene" with considerable advertising expenditure and sold a hundred of the vehicles.

In the programme for the performance of the musical "Tell me where the flowers are", a double-sided advertisement for the Ellen Betrix enterprise was printed, advertising cosmetics under the heading "the Marlene Look" and using a drawing of Marlene Dietrich. In return for this, the enterprise made available all the make-up materials for the performance of the musical to a value of 2,000 to 3,000 DM.

Lighthouse Musical also arranged for numerous so-called promotion articles (telephone cards, mugs, T-shirts, watches and badges) and postcards to be produced, which were provided with a picture of Marlene Dietrich and—with the exception of the badges—with the original title of the musical "Tell me where the flowers are". These objects were offered for sale in June 1993 at a stand in front of the theatre.

The claimant is claiming from the defendant injunctive relief, a declaration of his duty to compensate for harm and provision of information in respect of the use of the picture, name and signature of Marlene Dietrich, on the basis of her own rights and her legal status as executrix for the estate of her mother. She considers that the claims she is making arise from infringement of the posthumous personality rights of her mother. She has also based the claims she is making on the rights of the American law enterprises Marlene Inc and M Dietrich Inc which have been transferred to her.

The claimant in the end applied—insofar as it is still of importance for the decision on the appeal in law—

1. *for the defendant to be ordered under threat of punitive measures [*Ordnungsmitteln*] to refrain from*

a) using the name Marlene for the purpose of the advertising and/or labelling of goods by way of business and/or letting the name be used in connection with the person, life and work of Marlene Dietrich;

b) producing, and/or offering and/or disseminating objects of a commercial kind by way of business which are provided with pictures of Marlene Dietrich and/or letting them be produced and/or offered and/or disseminated;

c) producing, and/or offering and/or disseminating objects of a commercial kind by way of business which are provided with a handwritten signature of Marlene Dietrich by her first name and/or letting them be produced and/or offered and/or disseminated;

if these actions at a) to c) do not in each case occur within the framework of an artistic analysis of Marlene Dietrich or the interests of the general public in information about Marlene Dietrich as an absolute person of contemporary history;

alternatively:

*for the defendant to be ordered to refrain, in order to avoid punitive measures [*Ordnungsmitteln*] being taken, from*

a) allowing third parties to use pictures of Marlene Dietrich and/or to use pictures of Marlene Dietrich together with her handwritten signature and/or the name "Marlene" for the labelling of goods or commercial services and in advertising for goods or commercial services;

b) disseminating written material which contains advertisements by enterprises in which goods and commercial services are advertised by use of the name "Marlene" and a pictorial representation of Marlene Dietrich;

c) offering goods for sale, letting them be offered, disseminating them or letting them be disseminated, on which there is a picture of Marlene Dietrich, if the goods contain no additional verbal or symbolic information about the person, life or impact of Marlene Dietrich;

2. for a declaration that the defendant must compensate her for all harm which she has suffered so far from the actions from which he is to refrain and which she will in future suffer or that the defendant must hand over the enrichment he has obtained;

3. further that the defendant be ordered to give information to her about the extent of the actions causing harm which correspond to the requirements of the injunctions

a) by submission of a list of all sales which he has made by giving licences in the trade mark no. 2,022,193 "Marlene" or by other exploitation agreements about using the designation Marlene, arranged by calendar quarter years, giving the names and the complete addresses of the licensees, the content of the exploitation agreements, their length and the sales made by the individual licensees;

b) by submission of a list of the goods and services made and/or brought into circulation by Lighthouse Musical and/or by him insofar as they are provided with the designation or the name Marlene or Marlene Dietrich, with a picture of Marlene Dietrich and/or with her handwritten signature Marlene, giving

aa) an exact description of the goods and/or services concerned;

bb) the number of items manufactured and sold;

cc) the name and address for service of the manufacturer;

dd) the sales made by the marketing or the carrying out of the service arranged by calendar quarter years;

c) by submission of a list of sales which Lighthouse Musical and/or he himself have made by giving licences in the name or the designation Marlene or Marlene Dietrich, in pictures of Marlene Dietrich and in her hand-written signature Marlene, giving the names and complete addresses of the licensees, the content of the exploitation agreements and their length, and the sales made by the individual licensees.

The defendant has defended the claim. He is of the opinion that any possible invasion of the general right of personality of Marlene Dietrich by advertising measures for the musical is covered by artistic freedom. Besides this, an infringement of posthumous personality rights could not be the basis of any claims to compensation for harm, because these rights only protected non-material interests.

The Landgericht granted the application for injunctive relief in the form of the main application, and rejected the claim in other respects. In response to the appeal against this decision lodged by both sides, the Kammergericht—

*rejecting the appeal in other respects—allowed the application for injunctive relief in the form of the alternative application with limitations [reference omitted], and ordered the defendant, under threat of punitive measures (*Ordnungsmitteln*), to refrain from:*

a) Allowing third parties to use pictures of Marlene Dietrich and/or to use pictures of Marlene Dietrich together with her written signature and/or the name "Marlene" for labelling goods or commercial services or in advertising goods or commercial services, if this occurs as in the agreement between Lighthouse Musical and FIAT Automobil AG in accordance with the defendant's letter of the 23rd June 1993;

b) Disseminating written material which contains advertisements of enterprises in which goods or commercial services are advertised using the name "Marlene" and a pictorial representation of Marlene Dietrich, if this occurs as with the advertising of cosmetics by the "Ellen Betrix" enterprise in the programme for the performance of the musical "Tell me where the flowers are".

c) Offering goods for sale, or letting them to be offered, disseminating them or letting them be disseminated, on which there is a picture of Marlene Dietrich, if the goods contain no additional verbal or symbolic information about the person, life or impact of Marlene Dietrich or advertise for works of art which concern Marlene Dietrich.

The Senate has accepted for decision the claimant's appeal in law against this decision only insofar as the claimant is not suing on the basis of a transferred right. Within the scope of this acceptance, the claimant is pursuing the applications ultimately lodged by her. The defendant applies for the appeal in law to be rejected.

Reasons

The appeal in law is unsuccessful insofar as it objects to the appeal court only allowing the claim for injunctive relief in the limited form of the alternative application. It is however successful insofar as it is directed against rejection of the claim for a declaration and information. Within this scope the appeal in law leads to quashing of the judgment on appeal and to an order being made against the defendant.

I. The application for injunctive relief:

The appeal in law unsuccessfully objects to the appeal court dismissing the application for injunctive relief in the form of the principal application because of lack of certainty, and only allowing the application for injunctive relief in the form of the alternative application with limiting additional words.

1. The appeal court held the application for injunctive relief in the form of the principal application as granted by the Landgericht to be too uncertain, because the limiting subordinate clause "if these actions at a) to c) do not in each case occur within the framework of an artistic analysis of Marlene Dietrich or the general public's interests in information about Marlene Dietrich as an absolute person of contemporary history"

shifts the dispute about the scope of the prohibition to the enforcement proceedings in an impermissible manner. Contrary to the view of the appeal in law, this assessment shows no error in law.

*The use of concepts which need interpretation in a head of claim and in the wording of a judgment is certainly not simply impermissible. It can be accepted if no doubt exists about the meaning of the concepts or expressions used, so that the scope of the application and judgment is certain. But the position will be different if dispute exists between the parties on whether the conduct objected to falls within a concept which needs interpretation. In this situation the questionable concept cannot be used in the formal judgment, because otherwise the dispute to be settled in the proceedings for resolving it [*Erkenntnisverfahren*] would be shifted to the enforcement proceedings [constant case law; references omitted]. This is the situation present here. The parties are disputing about the conditions under which actions described generally in the principal application under a) to c) could take place in the context of an artistic analysis of the person of Marlene Dietrich. It is precisely the question of when consideration of Marlene Dietrich's personality is governed by artistic interests and when it is governed by business interests which is in dispute between the parties. Whilst the claimant thinks that the behaviour objected to is exclusively for the pur-suit of gain, the defendant takes the view that the actions which are being challenged are only to advertise the musical and are therefore indirectly artistic analysis of Marlene Dietrich's character.*

A fact-based decision on the principal application could in these circumstances merely explain by reference to the party's case and the grounds of the judgment [references omitted] how the actual behaviour objected to is to be assessed. But in her principal application the claimant pursues a more extensive concern: she wants a statement which is capable of generalisation on how other types of conduct are to be assessed. This could not, however, be deduced from the judgment, even by reference to the grounds of the decision.

2. The appeal court has only allowed the application for injunctive relief in the form of the alternative application with limiting additional words; the subsidiary applications at a) and b) were too widely formulated. The defendant could not be prevented from advertising with the name and picture of Marlene Dietrich for goods or commercial services in the area protected by Article 5 of the Basic Law of freedom of information, knowledge and art. In particular there could be no objection for instance to a biography, musical or a film about Marlene Dietrich being advertised with the first name of Marlene and a picture of Marlene Dietrich. Therefore the formal content of the prohibition was to be limited to the actual form of the infringement in each case.

These explanations stand up to examination in the appeal in law. The alternative applications are not impermissibly changed by the limitations imposed by the appeal court (§ 308 of the Civil Procedure Code). They are neither deprived of their certainty nor does the limited award of injunctive relief miss the core of the prohibition sought. It should be borne in mind here that in the present appeal in law proceedings, the only question which arises is whether the rejection of the more extensive claim which is inherent in the limiting words mentioned above should have occurred. The consequent judgment against the defendant is on the other hand not open to scrutiny (§ 559(1) of the Civil Procedure Code).

Contrary to the view of the appeal in law, the formal judgment is not made uncertain by the concretizing additions ("if this occurs as . . ."). The appeal court has limited the award of injunctive relief at a) and b) to the actual form of infringement in such a way that reference is made to the agreement (described in the definition of the tort in the judgment under challenge) between Lighthouse Musical and FIAT as well as to the advertisement (likewise described in the definition of the tort) for cosmetics by the Ellen Betrix enterprise. The range and scope of the formal judgment are thereby sufficiently determined.

The limited content of the formal judgment also expresses the core of the accusation of infringement correctly and does not curtail the claimant's desire for legal protection in an impermissible way. A prohibition which—as here—refers to the actual act of infringement is not limited to identical cases of infringement, but also includes variations which leave the core of the act of infringement untouched. It also extends to those actions which correspond to the prohibited behaviour in its characteristic features [constant case law; references omitted]. Insofar as the appeal in law objects here that on the basis of the limitation the sale of promotion articles, for example, would not be prohibited, it fails to consider the fact that behaviour of this kind, though admittedly not covered by a) and b), is covered by c) of the formal content of the prohibition.

Also, in so far as the appeal court has limited the prohibition applied for in c) by leaving out advertisement for works of art concerning Marlene Dietrich from the prohibition, the judgment is still sufficiently certain. It is clear from the grounds for the decision in the appeal court judgment, which are to be called on to interpret the formal part of it, that such an exception exists if the advertisement itself refers directly to a work of art concerning Marlene Dietrich—whether it is a musical, or whether it is films, books or plays.

II. The application for a declaration and the giving of information:

The objection by the appeal in law to the rejection by the appeal court of the applications for a declaration and the giving of information is successful. The appeal court was admittedly correct here in proceeding on the basis that a claim to enrichment against the defendant does not fall to be considered, because the person obliged to compensate for the enrichment would not have been the defendant personally but Lighthouse Musical. However, the appeal court's assumption that the claimant has no right to compensation for harm from any legal standpoint proves to be legally incorrect. Contrary to this view, the claimant can demand from the defendant compensation for harm under § 823(1) of the BGB. The general personality right protected by § 823(1) of the BGB and its special forms of manifestation, like the right to one's own picture and the right to one's name, do not only serve the protection of non-material personality interests, but also ones which are of financial value (see 1.). The corresponding components—protecting the interests which are of financial value—of the Marlene Dietrich's right of personality passed on her death to the claimant (see 2.). The defendant infringed these rights unlawfully and culpably, and therefore has to pay compensation for harm and give information to the claimant (see 3.). Under these circumstances, no decision is needed on whether such a claim could also arise under § 1 of the UWG (see 4.).

1. The general right of personality has been recognised in the case law of the Bundesgerichtshof since 1954 as a basic right constitutionally guaranteed by Articles 1 and 2 of the Basic Law and at the same time as an "other right" protected in civil law under § 823(1) of the BGB [constant case law since BGHZ 13, 334, 338—Readers' Letters]. It guarantees as against all the world the protection of human dignity and the right to free development of the personality. Special forms of manifestation of the general right of personality are the right to one's own picture (§§ 22 ff. *of the KUG) and the right to one's name (§ 12 of the BGB). They guarantee protection of the personality for the sphere regulated by them [reference omitted].*

The general right of personality and its special forms of manifestation primarily serve the protection of non-material interests, in particular the protection of the claim of the personality to worth and respect. This protection is realised by the fact that on an infringement of these rights, besides defensive claims, claims to compensation for harm come into consideration which aim at compensating not only material but also—when it is a question of a serious intrusion and the harm cannot be satisfactorily compensated in another way—non-material harm. This compensation is admittedly not based on a claim to compensation for pain and suffering under § 847 of the BGB, but on a legal remedy which originates directly from the protective mandate in Articles 1 and 2 para. 1 of the Basic Law [see BVerfGE 34, 269, 282 and 292 = GRUR 1974, 44, 46, 48 and 50—*Soraya*]. *The granting of monetary compensation in cases of this kind rests on the concept that without such a claim, violations of the dignity and honour of human beings frequently remain without sanction, with the consequence that legal protection of the personality would atrophy [references omitted].*

But besides this, the general right of personality and its special forms also protect those interests of the person which are of financial value. A considerable economic value can attach to the image, name and other features of the personality, like for example the voice. This value is generally based on the person's fame and reputation in the public eye—mostly as a result of special achievements in, for example, the areas of sport or the arts. A well known personality can exploit this popularity and the image connected with it economically by allowing third parties to use his picture or his name and also other features of his personality which facilitate recognition in advertising for goods or services in return for money. Frequently therefore fewer non-material than commercial interests of the person affected are harmed by an unauthorised use of the features of his personality for the purpose for instance of advertising, because he will feel himself harmed less in his honour and his reputation than he will see himself as disadvantaged financially [references omitted].

The Bundesgerichtshof has always included the commercial interests in the personality within the protection guaranteed by the personality rights. The personality rights should accordingly protect the right of free decision, belonging only to the person entitled, on the question of whether and under what conditions his picture or his name—and the same applies for other characteristic features of the personality—is used for the business interests of third parties [references omitted]. In relation to economic interests in the personality, the Bundesgerichtshof has recognised that the right of personality also shows elements which are of financial value [BGHZ 50, 133, 137—Mephisto]. It has accordingly described the right to one's own picture as an exclusive right of financial value and generally regarded claims for compensation as possible on violation of the right of personality [references omitted].

2. The elements of financial value in the right of Marlene Dietrich to her own picture and name have passed to the claimant as sole heir. This is because, regardless of their transferability between living persons, these elements are—in contrast to the highly personal elements which protect non-material interests—inheritable.

a) Insofar as the rights of personality protect non-material interests, they are indissolubly bound to the person of the holder of them and, as highly personal rights, are not renounceable and are inalienable, and are therefore not transferable and not inheritable [see BGHZ 50, 133, 137—Mephisto; other references omitted]. No-one can relinquish his right to his own picture, his right to his name or another personality right completely and conclusively. This would contradict the guarantee of human dignity [Article 1 of the Basic Law] and of the right to self-determination [Article 2 of the Basic Law; other references omitted].

b) The question of whether the elements of the right of personality which are of financial value and which protect commercial interests in the personality are transferable and inheritable has not yet been expressly decided by the Bundesgerichtshof. But in some decisions it has already been intimated that the principle of non-transferability and non-inheritability does not necessarily apply for all elements of the personality right. Thus it has stated in the Mephisto decision "that the right of personality—apart from its elements which are of financial value—is, as a highly personal right, not transferable and not inheritable" (BGHZ 50, 133, 137). In the "NENA" decision, it left open whether the transfer of the right to one's own picture is ruled out because of its legal character as a general personality right [reference omitted]. A considerable part of the academic literature argues for transferability and inheritability of the property law powers which are connected with the rights of personality [references omitted]. Others consider these powers to be simply non-transferable because of their personality right character [references omitted].

c) A number of considerations argue for the elements of the right of personality which are of financial value not being indissolubly bound to the person of the holder of the right in the same manner as the part of the right of personality which protects non-material interests. There is also the special need for protection which can only be taken into account by regarding the elements of the personality right which are of financial value as inheritable. Whether this part of the right of personality can be transferred between living persons or whether rights to the use of it can be granted does not, however, need to be decided in the present case.

aa) First the examples of other rights show that the character of a right can change in the estimation of the legal order.

Thus the Reichsgericht has regarded the right to the name of a firm as still being the right to a name and therefore as a right of personality [references omitted]. The Bundesgerichtshof has not maintained this case law. It has classified the material right to a firm's name as a property right, and based this on the fact that the name in this area has largely become separated from a particular person and becomes associated with an object—an enterprise or an association of persons. Considerable property law interests would thereby come into play which could outweigh the non-material interests in the name and completely displace them [reference omitted]. Even the firm which contains the name of a person can therefore—together with the trading enterprise [see §§ 22 and 23 of the Commercial Code]—in principle be transferred and inherited without limitations.

Trade mark law was likewise categorised by the Reichsgericht as still being a personality right [references omitted]. The trade mark has since become completely detached from its relationship to a business and the personality of an entrepreneur. It can be acquired without a business (§ 7 of the Trade Marks Act) and it can be transferred and inherited (§ 27 (1) of the Trade Marks Act). Even a mark which consists of a person's name or picture is today a non-material property right capable of being freely dealt with.

bb) The picture, name and other characterising features of the personality have always been capable—as a reflection of the defensive rights granted by the legal order against an unauthorised use—of being exploited commercially and in particular of being used for advertising purposes [reference omitted]. Protection of interests of financial value was also always connected with this, but it did not necessarily have to be regarded as an independent element of the right of personality. However in past decades technical, economic and business conditions have changed [reference omitted]. Features of the personality can with improved technical opportunities be recorded in sound and vision, and copied and disseminated. They have become economically exploitable to an extent not previously known, because of the continuing development of the mass media. So-called image transfer has a large role to play in advertising. It involves diverting the positive associations, which consumers connect with a well known personality, to the product to be advertised. In this respect well-known personalities contribute to creation of value to a considerable extent. The possibility of marketing the personality of, for instance, well-known figures in sport or the arts has—without passing judgement on this occurrence—become an important factor in product development which can no longer be imagined as not existing.

cc) Recognition of the inheritability of the elements of the right of personality which are of financial value is required to guarantee protection from commercial exploitation of a name, a picture and other features of the personality of a deceased person by those who are not entitled to do so. An effective posthumous protection of the elements of the right of personality which are of financial value is only guaranteed if the heir can step into the role of the holder of the right of personality and can, in defending the presumed interests of the deceased, proceed in the same way as that person could have done against an unauthorised exploitation.

*It is true that, according to constant case law, the continuing image of the personality is also protected after death against serious distortions [BGHZ 50, 133, 136*ff.*—Mephisto; other references omitted]. Likewise at any rate the right to one's own picture (§ 22 sentence 3 of the KUG) and possibly also the right to a name [reference omitted] continue to have an effect beyond death. But, on a posthumous violation of these rights, only defensive claims are granted to the person entitled to exercise them, and not claims to compensation for harm, because a deceased person could not suffer harm which is compensatable by a money payment [references omitted]. In these cases it is only a question of the infringement of non-material interests, for the protection of which the highly personal claim to respect continues to have an effect. This admittedly is not transferable and not inheritable, but it can be exercised after death for defensive purposes by a person authorised to do so [BGHZ 50, 133, 137*ff.*—Mephisto]. The defensive claims granted are of little use, however, if the violation of the right—as is frequently the case—has already ended, before the person entitled to the claim obtains knowledge of it. Besides this, it seems unfair to surrender the financial value created by the achievements of the deceased and embodied in his picture, his name or his other personality features after his death to the clutches of just any third party, instead of giving this financial value to his heirs or relations or other persons who were close to him when he was alive [references omitted].*

Doubts are certainly raised in part in the academic literature about promoting the increasing commercialisation of the personality. It is said that this is a possible unsatisfactory development in society, against which the legal order must take a stand, because the creation of a marketable non-material property right is in the end result directed against the individual and makes his personality available for third parties [references omitted]. These doubts should certainly not be simply dismissed, but in the end they do not prevail. For one thing, the protection of the personality is strengthened rather than weakened by the recognition of an independent inheritable element of the right of personality which has financial value, and on the violation of which the person entitled can acquire his own defensive rights and rights to compensation for harm. This applies not least in cases in which the name, picture or other personality features of a deceased person are used by a third party for commercial purposes contrary to the wishes of the heir and/or relatives and contrary to the presumed wishes of the deceased holder of the right of personality. This is because the right of personality in this situation will not be effectively protected with the help of defensive claims alone, as sanctions are only available in the case of repetition. A claim to enrichment can also fail in these cases, if—as here—the violator himself has not been enriched. Besides this, a claim for enrichment [reference omitted] also assumes a corresponding legal assignment of assets [reference omitted].

For another thing, it has to be borne in mind that the legal order in relation to marketing of legally protected positions does not form a rigid system to which reality would have to orientate itself. Instead, besides the indisputable task of setting predetermined boundaries by value judgements, the law also has an assisting function in that it must also offer a regulatory framework for new forms of marketing which are in the interest of the marketer as well as of the person who might permit such marketing of his personality. It is true that the legal order must confront the demands which arise from the growing commercialisation of the right of personality where legal or ethical principles of higher rank demand this [references omitted]. But an ineffective protection of the right of personality, limited to defensive powers, does not constitute a remedy against undesired exploitation of the personality. The interest which exists in not harming the image of a deceased person by unrestricted commercial exploitation of features of his personality can best be served by the heir being able to resist unauthorised exploitation, as holder of the elements of the right of personality which are of financial value. In this connection he has in principle at his disposal the same claims as the living holder of the right of personality—despite the differences which can arise after the death in respect of the scope of the content of the right [see BGHZ 50, 133, 140 ff.*—Mephisto].*

Finally, it should be pointed out that the powers of the heir derive from the holder of the right of personality and cannot be used in a manner contrary to his presumed wishes. The power of the heir to exploit the elements of the right of personality which are of financial value by taking action against an unauthorised use of the picture or name of a deceased person is therefore not linked to an unlimited positive right of use which could be exploited even against the express or presumed interests of the deceased holder of the personality right. The heir is only allowed to use the opportunities for marketing which exist or continue after the death on taking the deceased's will into account. In the present case, which concerns compensation for an unauthorised use, it is beyond doubt that the measures taken by the claimant are in the interest of her deceased mother.

d) Whilst the defensive claims which protect the deceased's non-material interests are to be made by the relatives [§ 22 sentences 3 and 4 of the KUG] or by a person entitled to exploit them appointed for this purpose [see BGHZ 50, 133, 139 ff.*—Mephisto], only the heirs are to be considered as holders of the powers which are of financial value [reference omitted] and they are not necessarily identical with the persons just mentioned. It is not however an argument against the inheritability of the elements of the right of personality which are of financial value that different persons can become entitled to the non-material and the financial interests.*

If the elements of the right of personality which are of financial value are inherited, they still remain, for the preservation of the non-material interests of the holder of the right, inseparably linked with the inalienable highly personal elements of the right of personality. This is because commercial exploitation frequently also affects the powers which belong to the relatives [§ 22 sentence 2 of the KUG] and other persons entitled to exploit them. In this respect the position is no different from that applying in copyright law. Here the powers in copyright personality law which are likewise aimed at protecting non-material interests (§§ 11 ff. *of the Copyright Act) are frequently not in the same hands as the rights of use [references omitted]. This means that uses which also interfere with powers in copyright personality law need not only the consent of the person entitled to the use but also of the owner of the copyright personality right. The situation is no different if, for example, the picture of the deceased is to be used for commercial purposes. Here the consent of the heirs as well as of the owner of the elements of the right of personality which are of financial value and also of the relatives is necessary (§ 22 sentence 3 of the KUG). Likewise the non-material interests of the deceased protected by the general right of personality can be affected by a commercial use of features of the personality, with the result that the person with the right of exploitation could take action against such a use in spite of agreement by the heirs. In the present case, such rights are however in one person's hands, because the claimant is the sole heir, as well as the only relative of Marlene Dietrich [see § 22 sentence 4 of the KUG].*

e) Nor *can the objection of lack of legal certainty be successfully raised against the inheritability of the elements of the right of personality which are of financial value. The possibility of commercial exploitation of the features of the personality has developed—as explained above [under II.2. c) aa)]—from the protection under the personality right of non-material interests. Therefore it seems reasonable to assume that the protection of commercial interests cannot extend in time beyond the protection of non-material interests in the personality. The ten year period of § 22 sentence 2 of the KUG offers a clue in this respect. But it can remain open whether longer protection of the commercial interests should be considered if and insofar as longer protection of non-material interests arises exceptionally from the general right of personality [see BGHZ 50, 133, 140* ff.*—Mephisto]. This is because in the present case it is a question of the use of the name and picture of Marlene Dietrich in the period shortly after her death.*

3. The defendant has unlawfully and culpably violated the elements of financial value of the right of Marlene Dietrich to her own picture and name which have passed to the claimant and he is therefore obliged to provide compensation for harm as well as to supply information.

Contrary to the view of the reply to the appeal in law, the application which has been made for a declaration that there is a duty to provide compensation does not require a special intensity of interference on violation of the right. It is true that, for violations of non-material interests, claims for monetary compensation only come into consideration in the lifetime of the holder of the right of personality [see above under II.1.] and only in relation to serious encroachments. But this does not apply on a violation of material interests of the kind under discussion here. A person who culpably violates the elements of the right of personality which are of financial value is liable for the harm which occurs, just as for a violation of other exclusive rights which are of financial value, regardless of how serious the interference was.

a) The right of Marlene Dietrich to her own picture [§ 22 of the KUG] has—as the appeal court has correctly accepted—been violated by her picture having been used without the necessary consent for the special model Lancia Y 10 "Marlene", for the cosmetics advertisement by the Ellen Betrix enterprise and for promotion articles.

aa) The photographs and drawings used are pictures in the sense of § 22 sentence 1 of the KUG. A picture in the sense of this provision is a portrayal of a person which reproduces their outward appearance in a manner recognisable to a third party [references omitted]. It does not matter in this connection how the picture has been produced, so the protection of pictures does not only include photographs but also other forms of portrayal as for example drawings [reference omitted].

bb) These pictures have been disseminated without the consent of the claimant as the owner of the elements of the right of personality which are of financial value and—which admittedly does not matter as the basis of an obligation to provide compensation for harm—as the person entitled under § 22 sentence 3 of the KUG.

cc) The consent of the claimant was also not dispensable. It is true that pictures from the realm of contemporary history may be disseminated under § 23 (1) no. 1 of the KUG without the consent necessary under § 22 of the KUG. Marlene Dietrich was—and the reply to the appeal in law also does not question this—a so-called absolute person of contemporary history [references omitted]. But a person who by publication is not fulfilling any interest of the general public in information which is worthy of protection, but is only using the picture of another for advertisement purposes to satisfy his business interest cannot refer to the exception provision of § 23 (1) no. 1 of the KUG [references omitted]. That is the position here. The use of the picture was not to give information about the life or work of Marlene Dietrich, but exclusively to advertise cars, cosmetics and promotion articles.

The defendant can also not successfully claim that these were advertising measures for the musical which are covered by artistic freedom. Admittedly advertising for a work of art falls within the protection of Article 5 para. 3 sentence 1 of the Basic Law. This is because artistic freedom does not only protect the actual artistic activity, the "work area" ["Werkbereich"] *of the artistic work, but also the "effect area"* ["Wirkbereich"] *in which access to the work of art is provided to the public. Advertisement for the work of art is also included in this [references omitted]. But the picture and name of Marlene Dietrich were not used to advertise for the musical, but exclusively to promote the sales of the products provided with it. According to the findings of the appeal court, which are free of legal error, there is no connection which is recognisable for third parties between these products and the musical. No reference is made to the musical on these products; even the words "Tell me where the flowers are" on the telephone cards, the wrist watches and the mugs were not only the former title of the musical, but also the title of a song which contributed in a special way to Marlene Dietrich's fame. No different assessment is required just because for instance the FIAT and Ellen Betrix enterprises have each provided consideration for the use of the picture and name of Marlene Dietrich, which was to benefit the musical. This does not change the fact that the picture of Marlene Dietrich was not directly used as a means to draw the public's attention to the musical.*

b) The right to determine whether one's own name may be used for advertising purposes, to which the claimant is entitled as heir of Marlene Dietrich, has further been infringed by the mention of the name "Marlene" in the advertising [references omitted]. This power likewise constitutes an inheritable element of the right of personality which is of financial value insofar as it protects commercial interests of the bearer of the name. It is not a question here of violation of the powers under the law on names (§ 12 of the BGB), which can possibly come into consideration even with a use which is not related to the name if the impression would arise in the ordinary affairs of life that the bearer of the name has granted to the user a right to appropriate use of the name [references omitted].

The appeal court has correctly assumed that the use to which objection has been made of the signature "Marlene" is to be seen as an unauthorised utilisation of the name of Marlene Dietrich. It is true that first names on their own are mostly not understood as a reference to a certain person. This may be different in the case of Marlene Dietrich in view of her outstanding fame and the comparatively strong identification power of her first name (reference omitted). But this can be left open here because in the actual form of the violation which the appeal court has alone made the subject of the judgment, the first name has not been used on its own, but has on each occasion been used with a picture of Marlene Dietrich.

c) The defendant must assume liability for the violation of the elements of the right of personality of Marlene Dietrich which are of financial value. He has as the sole manager of Lighthouse Musical allowed FIAT Automobil AG the use of the picture and of the first name of Marlene Dietrich and has thereby participated in the consequent violation of the law, at least as an assistant. He was further responsible for the publication and the content of the programme booklet in which cosmetics were advertised with the picture and first name of Marlene Dietrich. And finally the production company represented by him had the promotion articles manufactured with the picture of Marlene Dietrich and offered for sale. Under these circumstances it is not necessary to fall back on the possibility of liability for disturbance, because the conduct objected to is to be directly attributed to the defendant as manager.

Finally the defendant has acted not only unlawfully but also culpably. He could not assume, applying the care necessary in the affairs of life, that the picture and name of Marlene Dietrich, who had only recently died, could be used for advertising purposes without the consent of the sole heir and only relative [reference omitted].

d) The defendant must therefore compensate the claimant for the harm to her which has already arisen and will yet arise in the future through violations of the right of personality. The claimant can calculate the harm which has arisen for her either actually or by analogy with a licence, or demand the violator's profits [reference omitted]. In order to be able to choose the form of calculation of harm which is most favourable for her and in order to calculate the harm, the claimant has a claim to the supply of the information for which she has applied.

4. Under the given circumstances it does not need to be clarified whether the claimant is also entitled to claims under § 1 of the UWG. Competition law would anyway offer no possibility of resolving the present case without recourse to the right of personality. Even if a competition relationship existed between the parties, classification of the marketing opportunities is not to be founded on competition law but only on the right of personality.

III. The decision on costs is based on §§ 91, 97 (1) and 92 (1) of the Civil Procedure Code.

Case Thirteen
Federal Constitutional Court (*Lüth*)
(First Division)
15 January 1957
BVerfGE 7, 198

1. Basic rights are primarily to protect the citizen against the state, but as enacted in the Constitution (GG) they also incorporate an objective scale of values which applies, as a matter of constitutional law, throughout the entire legal system.

2. The substance of the basic rights is expressed indirectly in the rules of private law, most evidently in its mandatory provisions, and is best effectuated by the judges' use of the general clauses.

3. Basic rights may be infringed by a judicial decision which ignores the effect of basic rights on private law (§ 90 Act on Constitutional Court Procedure (BVerfGG)). Judicial decisions on private law are subject to review by the Constitutional Court, only in respect of such infringements of basic rights, not for errors of law in general.

4. Rules of private law may count as "general laws" which may restrict the basic right of freedom of expression under Article 5 II GG.

5. Such "general laws" must be interpreted in the light of the especial significance in a free democratic state of the basic right to freedom of expression.

6. The basic right in Article 5 GG protects not only the utterance of an opinion as such, but also the effect it has on others.

7. The expression of an opinion favouring a boycott does not necessarily infringe proper conduct (boni mores) under § 826 BGB; depending on all the circumstances such an expression may be justified as a matter of constitutional law.

Disposition

The decision of the Landgericht Hamburg of 22 November 1951 infringes the complainant's basic right under Article 5 I, 1 GG and is therefore vacated. The matter is remitted to the Landgericht Hamburg.

Reasons

At the opening of "German Film Week" on 20 September 1950 the complainant, then a Senator of the Free and Hanseatic City of Hamburg and Head of the State Press Office, gave an address, in his capacity as President of the Hamburg Press Club, to an audience of film distributors and directors. He said, inter alia*:*

The person least likely to restore the claim to morality which the German film forfeited during the Third Reich is the man who directed "Jud Süss" and wrote the script for it. If this very man is chosen to represent the German film industry, who can tell what harm we may suffer throughout the world? True he was acquitted in a formal sense in Hamburg, but substantially the judgment was a condemnation. We must call on the distributors and cinema owners to show character—not cheap, but worth the price. And I want the German film to show character as well. If it shows character in its imagination, visual daring and sterling craftsmanship, it will merit every assistance and achieve what it needs in order to survive: success with the public here in Germany and abroad.

Domnick-Film-Produktion GmbH immediately challenged the complainant to justify these charges against Veit Harlan, under whose direction and with whose screen-play they were making "Unsterbliche Geliebte".

On 27 October 1950 the complainant released an "open letter" to the Press by way of reply which contained the following:

The court did not gainsay the fact that for much of the Hitler régime Veit Harlan was the "Nazi film-director no. 1" or that his film "Jud Süss" showed him to be a committed exponent of the Nazis' murderous purge of the Jews. Some businessmen here and abroad may not be opposed to Veit Harlan's re-emergence, but the moral integrity of Germany must not be destroyed by hard-faced money-makers. Harlan's return can only reopen wounds barely healed, and resuscitate diminishing distrust fatal to German reconstruction. For all these reasons it is not only the right but the duty of all decent Germans to protest against, and even to boycott, this ignominious representative of the German film industry.

Domnick-Film-Produktion GmbH and Herzog-Film GmbH (the distributor of "Unsterbliche Geliebte" in the Federal Republic), obtained an interlocutory injunction from the Landgericht Hamburg . . . and the Oberlandesgericht dismissed the complainant's appeal. At the complainant's request the two film companies were required to bring suit within a certain time. They did so, and on 22 November 1951 the Landgericht Hamburg issued the following judgment:

The defendant is ordered, on pain of fine or imprisonment as determined by the court, to refrain (1) from calling on theatre managers and film distributors not to programme the film "Unsterbliche Geliebte" and (2) from calling on the German public not to go to see the film . . .

B. I.

The complaint is admissible since the preconditions for the application of § 90 II, 2 BVerfGG are satisfied [decision before exhaustion of legal remedies].

II.

The complainant alleges that the Landgericht's judgment infringes his basic right to free expression of opinion as laid down in Article 5 I, 1 GG.

The judgment of the Landgericht, an act of the public power of judicature, could infringe the complainant's basic right by its content only if the court was bound to take account of the complainant's basic right.

By enjoining the complainant from making statements apt to lead others to endorse his views about Harlan's re-emergence and to follow him in dis-

criminating against Harlan's films, the judgment clearly restricts the complainant's freedom of expression of opinion. The Landgericht granted the injunction as a matter of private law order on the basis that the complainant's statements were tortious under § 826 BGB. Thus the public power has restricted the complainant's freedom of expression on the basis of the plaintiff's private law claim. This can constitute an infringement of the complainant's basic right under Article 5 I, 1 GG only if the applicable rules of private law are so substantially affected that they can no longer support the judgment.

The question whether basic rights affect private law, and if so in what manner, is much debated [references]. The extreme positions are, on the one hand, that basic rights constrain only the state, and, on the other, that basic rights (or at any rate the most important of them) prevail against everyone in private legal relations. Previous decisions of this Court support neither of these extreme positions, the conclusions drawn by the Federal Labour court in its decision of 10 May 1957 [NJW 1957, 1688] from our decisions of 17 and 23 January 1957 [BVerfGE 6, 55 and 6, 84] being unwarranted. Nor is it necessary today to deal with all aspects of the debated question of the "effect on third parties" [Drittwirkung] of basic rights. The matter can be properly resolved by the following considerations:

1. There is no doubt that the main purpose of basic rights is to protect the individual's sphere of freedom against encroachment by public power: they are the citizen's bulwark against the state. This emerges from both their development as a matter of intellectual history and their adoption into the constitutions of the various states as a matter of political history: it is true also of the basic rights in the Basic Law, which emphasizes the priority of human dignity against the power of the state by placing the section on basic rights at its head and by providing that the constitutional complaint [Verfassungsbeschwerde], the special legal device for vindicating these rights, lies only in respect of acts of the public power.

But far from being a value-free system [references] the Constitution erects an objective system of values in its section on basic rights, and thus expresses and reinforces the validity of the basic rights [references]. This system of values, centring on the freedom of the human being to develop in society, must apply as a constitutional axiom throughout the whole legal system: it must direct and inform legislation, administration, and judicial decision. It naturally influences private law as well; no rule of private law may conflict with it, and all such rules must be construed in accordance with its spirit.

The legal content of basic rights as objective norms informs private law by means of the rules which directly control this area of law. Just as new rules must conform to the value-system of the basic rights, so existing and older rules receive from it a definite constitutional content which thereafter determines their construction. From the point of view of substantive and procedural law a dispute between private citizens on the rights and duties that arise from rules of conduct thus influenced by the basic rights remains a dispute of private law. It is private law which is interpreted and applied even if its interpreters must follow the public law of the constitution.

The influence of the value-system of the basic rights is clearest in those rules of private law which are mandatory [zwingendes Recht] and form part of ordre public in the wide sense, i.e. those rules which in the public interest apply to private legal relations whether the parties so choose or not. Such provisions, being functionally related and complementary to public law, are especially exposed to the influence of constitutional law. "General clauses", such as § 826 BGB, by which human conduct is measured against extralegal standards such as "proper conduct" [gute Sitten], allow the courts to respond to this influence since in deciding what is required in a particular case by such social commands, they must start from the value-system adopted by the society in its constitution at that stage of its cultural and spiritual development. The general clauses have thus been rightly described as "points of entry" for basic rights into private law [references].

The judge is constitutionally bound to ascertain whether the applicable rules of substantive private law have been influenced by basic rights in the manner described; if so, he must construe and apply the rules as so modified. This is what is meant by saying that the civil judge is bound by the basic rights (Article 1 III GG). If he issues a judgment which ignores this constitutional influence on the rules of private law, he contravenes not only objective constitutional law by misconceiving the content of the objective norm underlying the basic law, but also, by his judgment, in his capacity as a public official, contravenes the Constitution itself, which the citizen is constitutionally entitled to have respected by the judiciary. Quite apart from any remedies he may have to correct this error in the courts of private law, the citizen can invoke the Federal Constitutional Court by means of a Verfassungsbeschwerde.

The Constitutional Court must determine whether the reach and effect of the basic rights in private law has been correctly ascertained by the regular courts. But this is also the limit of its investigation: it is not for the Constitutional Court to check judgments of civil courts for errors of law in general; the Constitutional Court simply judges of the "radiant effect" of the basic rights on private law and implements the values inherent in the precept of constitutional law. The function of the Verfassungsbeschwerde is to test all acts, whether of the legislature, the executive or the judiciary, for "compatibility with the Constitution" (§ 90 BVerfGG). The Federal Constitutional Court is certainly not to act as a court of review, much less over-review, for the civil courts, but neither may it abjure consideration of such judgments entirely or leave uncorrected any instance which comes to its notice of the misapplication of the rules of basic rights.

2. The basic right to freedom of expression of opinion (Article 5 GG) seems to pose special problems with regard to the relationship between basic rights and private law. As in the Weimar Constitution (Article 118), this right is constitutionally guaranteed only within the limits of "general laws" (Article 5 II GG). Before inquiring what laws are "general laws" in this sense, one might suppose that the constitution's reference to such laws must be to such laws as judicially construed, with the result that no judicial construction of such a law which limited the basic right could be regarded as a "breach" of the basic right.

This is not, however, the sense of the reference to "general laws". The basic right to freedom of expression, the most immediate aspect of the human personality in society, is one of the most precious rights of man (Declaration of the Rights of Man and Citizen (1789) Article 11). It is absolutely essential to a free and democratic state, for it alone permits that constant spiritual interaction, the conflict of opinion, which is its vital element (BVerfGE 5, 85 (205)). In a certain sense it is the basis of freedom itself, "the matrix, the indispensable condition of nearly every other form of freedom" (Cardozo).

Given this fundamental importance for the free democratic state of freedom of expression of opinion, it would be illogical for a constitution to make its actual scope contingent on mere statute (and thus necessarily on the holdings of courts construing it). What was said earlier about the relationship between basic rights and private law applies here also: general laws which have the effect of limiting a basic right must be read in the light of its significance and always be construed so as to preserve the special value of this right, with, in a free democracy, a presumption in favour of freedom of speech in all areas, and especially in public life. We must not see the relationship between basic right and "general laws" as one in which "general laws" by their terms set limits to the basic right, but rather that relationship must be construed in the light of the special significance of this basic right in a free democratic state, so that the limiting effect of "general laws" on the basic right is itself limited.

In its function as ultimate guardian of the basic rights through the medium of the Verfassungsbeschwerde, the Federal Constitutional Court must therefore have the power to supervise the decisions of courts whose application of a general law in this area may unduly restrict the scope of the basic right in the individual case. This Court must be competent to uphold as against all organs of public power, including the civil courts, the special value it represents for a free democracy, and thus to reconcile, as required by constitutional law, the conflicting restrictive tendencies of the basic right and the "general laws".

3. The concept of "general" law has always been controversial. Leaving on one side the question whether the concept may not be due to an error in the drafting of Article 118 of the 1919 Constitution [reference], we may note that it was then construed to include all which "do not forbid an opinion as such and do not envisage the expression of opinion as such", but rather "serve to protect a legal interest which deserves protection without regard to any particular opinion", and protect "a community value superior to the activity of freedom of opinion" [reference]. Exponents of the Grundgesetz agree with this [reference: "laws which do not inhibit the purely intellectual effect of a mere expression of opinion"].

If the term "general laws" is so understood, we may state the protection of the basic right as follows:

It is unacceptable to hold that the Constitution protects only the expression of opinion, and not its inherent or intended effect on others, for the whole point of an expression of opinion is to have "an effect on the environment of ideas" [reference]. Thus value-judgments, which always have an intellectual aim, namely to persuade others, are protected by Article 5 I, 1 GG; indeed it is the stance of the speaker as expressed in the value-judgment by which he hopes to affect others which is principally protected by this basic right. To protect the expression and not to protect its effect would be a nonsense.

In this sense the expression of opinion is free in so far as its effect on the mind is concerned; but that does not mean that one is entitled, just because one is expressing an opinion, to prejudice interests of another which deserve protection against freedom of opinion. There has to be a "balance of interests"; the right to express an opinion must yield if its exercise infringes interests of another which have a superior claim to protection. Whether such an interest exists in a particular case depends on all the circumstances.

4. From this point of view the rules of private law may perfectly well be ranked as "general laws" in the sense of Article 5 II GG. If this has not been done by commentators hitherto [reference], that is simply because basic rights have been considered good only as against the state, so it was natural to consider as "general laws" having limiting effect only those laws which regulated state activity vis-à-vis the individual, that is, laws of a public law nature. But if the basic right to free expression of opinion affects relations of private law as well and favours free expression of opinion against the fellow-citizen also, then rules of private law which operate to protect superior legal interests must also be taken into account as possibly limiting the basic right. After all, if provisions of criminal law designed to protect honour or other essential aspects of human personality can set limits to the exercise of the fundamental right to freedom of expression, it is not obvious why similar provisions of private law should not equally do so.

Index

Please note that references to footnotes have a page number followed by "n" and the number of the note. Major references to topics are indicated by the page numbers being in bold print.